EU CRIMINAL LAW

EU Criminal Law is perhaps the fastest-growing area of EU law. It is also one of the most contested fields of EU action, covering measures which have a significant impact on the protection of fundamental rights and the relationship between the individual and the State, while at the same time presenting a challenge to State sovereignty in the field and potentially reconfiguring significantly the relationship between Member States and the EU. The book will examine in detail the main aspects of EU criminal law, in the light of these constitutional challenges. These include: the history and institutions of EU criminal law (including the evolution of the third pillar and its relationship with EC law); harmonisation in criminal law and procedure (with emphasis on competence questions); mutual recognition in criminal matters (including the operation of the European Arrest Warrant) and accompanying measures; action by EU bodies facilitating police and judicial co-operation in criminal matters (such as Europol, Eurojust and OLAF); the collection and exchange of personal data, in particular via EU databases and co-operation between law enforcement authorities; and the external dimension of EU action in criminal matters, including EU–US counter-terrorism co-operation. The analysis is forward-looking, taking into account the potential impact of the Lisbon Treaty on EU criminal law.

Volume 17 in the series Modern Studies in European Law

Modern Studies in European Law

_To Jo,_
with all best wishes
Valsamis

EU Criminal Law

Valsamis Mitsilegas

·HART·
PUBLISHING
OXFORD AND PORTLAND, OREGON
2009

Published in North America (US and Canada) by
Hart Publishing
c/o International Specialized Book Services
920 NE 58th Avenue, Suite 300
Portland, OR 97213-3786
USA
Tel: +1 503 287 3093 or toll-free: (1) 800 944 6190
Fax: +1 503 280 8832
E-mail: orders@isbs.com
Website: www.isbs.com

Hart Publishing Ltd, 16C Worcester Place, Oxford, OX1 2JW
Telephone: +44 (0)1865 517530 Fax: +44 (0)1865 510710
E-mail: mail@hartpub.co.uk
Website: http://www.hartpub.co.uk

British Library Cataloguing in Publication Data
Data Available

ISBN: 978-1-84113-585-4

Typeset by Hope Services, Abingdon
Printed and bound in Great Britain by
TJ International Ltd, Padstow, Cornwall

Foreword

One of the most striking developments in European Union law has been the growth of EU measures in the field of criminal law. The increasingly assertive presence of the Union in this field raises profound questions about national sovereignty, the relationship between the individual and the state and the role of the European Union. As an expression of the coercive powers of the State, criminal law is perceived to fall *par excellence* within the province of national sovereignty. There is no historical precedent of building a supra-national system of criminal law. Since the coming into force of the Treaty of Maastricht and, especially, the Treaty of Amsterdam, the EU has been increasingly active in penal matters. Its presence in this field may be seen as marking a new stage in the mutation of the European project. It appears to be at odds with the classic integration model of the Community. Traditionally, Community law has led to the erosion of national sovereignty through granting rights to citizens. Integration through law has always been rights-focused. This paradigm appears to be reversed in the field of criminal law where the emphasis lies firmly in facilitating the exercise of state powers rather than in bestowing rights. The European Union's intervention is mostly indirect. The model of integration in criminal law is based on the principle of mutual recognition rather that substantive harmonization. As this book potently reveals, however, mutual recognition and emphasis on procedure may have deep and wide repercussions on the national systems of criminal justice.

EU action in criminal law gives rise to new tensions in the relationship between the Union and the Member States. On the one hand, Member States provide the impetus for the adoption of Community measures. On the other hand, they seek to protect their sovereign powers through the exclusion of harmonisation legislation in this area. The adoption of EU measures occurs often through a tortuous process of negotiation and is the result of a careful, fine balance between functional needs and nation state prerogatives.

This book provides a thorough, skilful and intelligent analysis of EU criminal law. Its coverage is comprehensive. It examines the relationship between Community law and criminal law before Maastricht, the road to the Amsterdam Treaty, and the Union powers in the criminal field post-Amsterdam. It also assesses in detail the impact of the Lisbon Treaty. This tormented Treaty affects criminal law perhaps more than any other area. The book examines mutual recognition in criminal matters, EU agencies in the criminal sphere and the growth of measures on personal data. Its treatment of mutual recognition, as the favourable model of integration in Union matters, is particularly instructive and welcome. The book further explores the external dimension of EU criminal action with particular focus on international agreements concluded by the EU, anti-terrorism initiatives and the relationship between the EU and the United Nations. As the recent judgment of the European Court of Justice in *Kadi* reveals, these are not areas which lack controversy.

A further aspect of this book worth highlighting is its detailed discussion of Union agencies in the field of criminal law. One of the distinct features of EU law in recent years has been the growth of administrative agencies at Community and Union levels. Although in its early judgment in *Meroni* the ECJ imposed stringent limitations on the power of the Community institutions to establish agencies, the Union seems to have entered an agencies era. The themes of competent and efficient governance, democracy, accountability, transparency and legitimacy provide the parameters within which such agencies should be assessed.

Although criminal law is an emerging area of Union activity, the European Court of Justice has already influenced it substantially in a number of ways. First, as shown in the *European Arrest Warrant case*, it has condoned key Union initiatives. Secondly, it has contributed to establishing the overarching constitutional framework of the third pillar and the area of freedom, security and justice. In doing so, it has favoured the expansive interpretation of the first pillar at the expense of the third and their fusion through the exportation of Community law disciplines. The judgment in *Pupino* provides a striking example of *acquis communautaire* imperialism. Thirdly, the ECJ has began to articulate general principles, as illustrated in developing case law on *ne bis in idem* and the concept of mutual recognition. As the present book ably demonstrates, it is somewhat paradoxical that the ECJ is developing general principles of criminal law within the confines of the mutual recognition model and in the absence of substantive harmonisation. Finally, and most importantly, the Court's established body of case law on fundamental rights remains the strongest counterbalancing factor to the EU's emerging presence in criminal law.

This book is topical, informative, thorough, and analytical. It comes at a time when criminal law accounts for a substantial part of the Union's legislative activity and finds increasing presence in the Court's docket. It is a most welcome and valuable addition to the bibliography.

Takis Tridimas
January 2009

Preface and Acknowledgements

Writing a book on EU criminal law in the late 2000s is a moving target, in the light of the rapid growth of legislative and judicial developments in the field. One has therefore inevitably to draw a line on the legal framework to be covered and analysed. For this book this line is the end of July 2008. The book builds to some extent upon earlier work, with some parts being based on the following articles: 'The Constitutional Implications of Mutual Recognition in Criminal Matters in the EU', (2006) *Common Market Law Review* 43, 1277–1311; (2006) 'Constitutional Principles of the European Community and European Criminal Law', *European Journal of Law Reform* 8, 301–324; (2007) 'The External Dimension of EU Action in Criminal Matters', *European Foreign Affairs Review* 12, 457–497; and 'The Transformation of Criminal Law in the 'Area of Freedom, Security and Justice', *Yearbook of European Law 2007* 26, 1–32. A number of colleagues enriched the writing process by taking the time to read draft chapters. I am grateful to Peter Alldridge, Eileen Denza, Florian Geyer, Elspeth Guild, Jörg Monar and Takis Tridimas for their invaluable comments and suggestions on these drafts, as well as to José Gutierrez-Fons for his help. I am also grateful to Richard Hart for his patience, encouragement and faith in this project. Last, but not least, I would like to thank the students of my EU Justice and Home Affairs course at Queen Mary for their enthusiasm, commitment and insightful comments over the years. This book is dedicated to them.

Contents

Table of Cases

Introduction

EU CRIMINAL LAW is one of the fastest growing areas of Union law, both in terms of legislative production and increasingly in terms of case-law. The issues that it covers are central to the relationship between the individual and the State (and its reconfiguration at the Union level), and lie at the heart of State sovereignty (and the relationship and balance of powers between Member States and the EU). Taking into account these two aspects, this book will examine all major aspects of EU action in criminal matters. It will follow a thematic approach by examining the main ways in which EU action in criminal matters has developed in recent years. The analysis will focus on both content and context and will place particular emphasis on EU criminal law as a contested field reflecting the tension between the preservation of State sovereignty on the one hand and calls for enhancing co-operation in criminal matters at EU level on the other. The impact of this contested nature on current and future legislative and institutional arrangements on EU criminal law will be highlighted and the consequences of these compromise arrangements for the position of the individual and the protection of fundamental rights assessed.

Issues arising from the contested nature of EU criminal law are particularly relevant in chapter one, on the history, principles and institutional framework of EU criminal law. The chapter will begin with an overview of the relationship between the Community and criminal law before Maastricht. It will then examine the evolution and content of the third pillar, from Maastricht to Amsterdam and beyond, focusing in particular on the way in which Member States' sovereignty concerns have been translated into the Treaty provisions on the role of the institutions and their differences from the relevant Community pillar provisions. The chapter will then look at the extent to which the differences between the first and the third pillar have been bridged by the Court of Justice, which has increasingly been applying constitutional principles of the Community to third pillar law. The examination of the institutions will be completed by giving particular emphasis to the role of Member States in providing political *impetus* for the development of 'securitised' EU criminal law both within and outside the EU framework. The analysis of the institutional framework would not be complete without an examination of the significant changes that will be brought about if the Treaty of Lisbon enters into force. EU criminal law is perhaps the area most affected by Lisbon. Therefore, and notwithstanding the current uncertainty as to its entry into force (the book is being finalised after the Irish 2008 'no' vote), all chapters will include a specific part on the impact of Lisbon on the field covered therein.

The impact of EU criminal law on State sovereignty is also central in chapter two, which examines the closely linked issues of the harmonisation of criminal law in the EU and the existence and extent of Union (and Community) competence in criminal matters. The chapter will begin by looking at competence, and examine the relationship between criminal law and Community (first pillar) law. Particular emphasis will be placed on the two recent ECJ judgments on the environmental crime and ship-source pollution cases, where the Court confirmed the existence of Community competence in criminal law. Moving on from the first pillar, the chapter will examine the extent of Union competence and EU criminal law harmonisation under the third pillar. The harmonisation of criminal law will be examined in the light of its impact on domestic legal cultures, but also in the context of its relationship with other methods of European integration in criminal matters, such as mutual recognition.

Mutual recognition in criminal matters is the focus of chapter three. The chapter will begin by examining the principle of mutual recognition and its applicability in EU criminal law. Having analysed the main EU instruments in the field (with particular emphasis being placed on the European Arrest Warrant Framework Decision), the chapter will look at the constitutional concerns raised by the application of the principle of mutual recognition in the criminal law field. In this context, the chapter will examine the ways in which these concerns have been addressed by EU legislation, but also by courts both at the national and at the EU level. The examination of legislative instruments on mutual recognition will be coupled by an overview of another aspect of mutual recognition, namely the operation of the principle of *ne bis in idem* and its interpretation by the ECJ in the absence of legislative harmonisation of the principle at EU level. The chapter will examine the implications of mutual recognition for the reconfiguration of sovereignty and territoriality in a largely borderless 'area' of freedom, security and justice.

Chapter four will examine European integration in criminal matters via the establishment of bodies, offices and agencies of the Union. The chapter will examine in detail the legal framework and powers of the two major EU criminal law bodies established under the third pillar, Europol and Eurojust, as well as the role and powers of the EU anti-fraud office, OLAF. The examination of the work of these bodies will focus in particular on the extent to which Member States have transferred sovereignty to the EU in the context of their powers and accountability, as well as on the extent to which these bodies operate on the basis of synergy or competition. The underlying issue of proliferation of EU bodies will also be examined in the context of the analysis of the work of other EU bodies with a criminal law related remit (in particular SitCen and the EU Counter-terrorism Coordinator), along with the issues of cross-pillarisation, informality and transparency/scrutiny that arise from their work. The chapter will further examine the issue of the proliferation of bodies by focusing on the establishment of bodies and agencies as means of ensuring the accountability of the existing EU criminal law bodies. The choice of furthering European integration in criminal matters by establishing specific bodies will be examined in the light of the challenges it poses for scrutiny and democratic debate in the field and the potential depoliticisation of EU criminal law.

Similar issues arise in chapter five, which deals with the development of European integration in criminal matters through the establishment of databases and the emphasis on the collection, exchange and analysis of personal data. EU action in the field will be analysed as falling broadly under three categories: the establishment of EU databases (the Europol, Schengen and Customs Information Systems) and increasing calls towards maximum access and interoperability; efforts to boost the exchange of information between national law enforcement authorities (in particular by applying aspects of the principle of availability); and the increasing privatisation of the collection of personal data for criminal law purposes, as evidenced in particular by the debate on the role of airlines in transferring passenger (PNR) data to border and security authorities. The impact of the intensification of the collection, exchange and analysis of personal data at EU level on privacy and the protection of such data will be examined and the adequacy of the current and future EU legal framework in the field will be assessed.

The last chapter will focus on the external dimension of EU action in criminal matters. Its main focus is the assessment of the compatibility and coherence between EU internal and external action in the field. The chapter flags up the many different levels of EU external action in criminal law, and highlights their characteristic features. The chapter begins by examining EU action in the context of enlargement and the relations of the Union with its neighbours. It then goes on to provide a detailed analysis of international agreements in criminal matters between the Union (and its bodies) and third States and highlights both the institutional limits and human rights challenges surrounding these agreements, in particular those concluded between the Union and the United States in the name of the so-called 'war on terror'. The following part examines EU action in international organisations, focusing on the Union's role on both negotiating and implementing international standards. The relationship of the EU with international organisations such as the United Nations (in particular in the context of counter-terrorism sanctions) and the Council of Europe—but also bodies such as the Financial Action Task Force—is examined here. The chapter concludes by flagging up the inconsistencies between internal and external action in criminal matters and their potential impact on the protection of fundamental rights and the identity and values of the Union.

These chapters are followed by a conclusion aiming to highlight and systematise the major themes arising from the book as a whole. The discussion of these themes will cast light on the state of play of EU criminal law today, but also act as a starting point for a debate on the future of EU criminal law and its impact on the future of the European Union itself.

1

History, Principles and Institutions

I. INTRODUCTION

THE EVOLUTION OF the institutional framework of EU criminal law has
been a gradual process. Although the majority of legislative developments
in the field have occurred largely in the last decade and ECJ case law has
began to proliferate even more recently, steps for enhancing co-operation between
Member States in criminal matters outside the EU framework have appeared as
early as the 1970s. The fact that it took so long to achieve a phase of sustained legislative action in the field within the EU is indicative of the contested nature of EU
criminal law, a field which has significant consequences for State sovereignty.
Another indication of the contested nature of EU criminal law is the fact that it is
still, at the time of writing, a field of Union law largely confined to a separate pillar of the EU Treaty (the so-called 'third pillar'), which distinguishes it from
Community law and the first pillar 'Community' method and renders applicable
more 'intergovernmental' methods of law-making and scrutiny and a more limited involvement of EU institutions in the field. Focusing on the third pillar, this
chapter will examine this gradual, contested evolution of EU criminal law by looking at: the history and context of the development of EU action in the field; the
institutional framework governing action in the field as it has evolved from the
Maastricht Treaty to the Amsterdam Treaty and beyond; the extent to which
Community law principles apply to the third pillar; and the significant changes
that would be brought about should the Lisbon Treaty enters into force. In all
these steps, the focal point will be the extent to which competence is transferred
from the Member States to the Union level.

II. BACKGROUND: THE COMMUNITY AND CRIMINAL LAW
BEFORE MAASTRICHT

Over the years, there have been a number of factors influencing common action
in criminal matters among EU Member States. One of these factors has traditionally been the emergence of areas of criminality which were of common concern to Member States and which were perceived to necessitate co-operation.
Outside the EU framework, such co-operation has been longstanding within the

5

intergovernmental framework of the Council of Europe.[1] This has led to the adoption of a series of hard and soft law instruments in the criminal justice field, a number of which are still influential in the development of internal EU law.[2] It was the preference for intergovernmental co-operation within the Council of Europe that has reportedly blocked French plans in the late 1970s–early 1980s to establish an ambitiously named 'European judicial area in criminal matters' covering primarily judicial co-operation in criminal matters in the fields of terrorism.[3] However, the 1970s did witness efforts by Member States to explore the establishment of channels of co-operation between their law enforcement authorities in areas of common concern such as terrorism. A prime example has been the establishment of TREVI, a network of law enforcement officials meeting on an informal basis to discuss action on counter-terrorism issues.[4] The remit of TREVI (and its organisational chart)—which, however, remained an informal structure with no clear legal framework or standing under Community law—expanded in the 1980s, especially in the light of the emergence of new areas of criminality such as drugs and organised crime as areas of common interest of Member States.[5] The focus on drug trafficking as a threat in the 1980s also led to efforts for action within the Community law framework, in particular in the field of external action—as demonstrated by the involvement of the Community in the negotiation and signature of the 1988 United Nations Vienna Convention.[6]

Another factor leading to the emergence of EU criminal law has been the development of EU internal market law. Already in the 1980s, it had become evident in cases brought before the Court in Luxembourg that the focus of the Community on economic matters did not stop Community action having criminal law implications or being associated with the criminal law choices in Member States.[7] Moreover, calls for the abolition of internal frontiers in the single market—a central objective of the Commission and subsequently of the Community in the 1980s and early 1990s—and steps taken to achieve these objectives created a 'spill-over effect' of law and policy to broader issues to the economy/market, including criminal law.[8] A key to this process of spill-over has been the abolition of internal frontiers and the goal of free movement. The achievement of free movement brought about the realisation of the need to look at the implications of this free-

---

[1] See V Mitsilegas, J Monar and W Rees, *The European Union and Internal Security*, Basingstoke, Palgrave Macmillan, 2003, pp 19–22.

[2] See in particular in the field of data protection—see ch 5. On the relationship between EU and Council of Europe instruments covering similar topics, see ch 6.

[3] 'Espace judiciaire pénal européen': see A Weyembergh, *L'harmonisation des législations: Condition de l'espace pénal européen et révélateur de ses tensions*, Brussels, Éditions de l'Université de Bruxelles, 2004, pp 13–15.

[4] See Mitsilegas, Monar and Rees, above n 1, pp 22–24. For more on TREVI including bibliographical references, see ch 4.

[5] ibid, p 25.

[6] See V. Mitsilegas, *Money Laundering Counter-measures in the European Union. A New Paradigm of Security Governance versus Fundamental Legal Principles*, The Hague, London, Kluwer Law International, 2003, pp 52–54.

[7] For further information, see ch 2.

[8] See Mitsilegas, Monar and Rees, above n 1, pp 27–31.

dom and of the abolition of borders for issues such as immigration and crime. This link was already made to some extent by the Commission in its 1985 White Paper on the completion of the internal market.[9] It was put forward more forcefully in the Palma document,[10] whose conclusions were endorsed by the Madrid European Council in 1989[11]: the document asserted that the achievement of an area without internal frontiers could involve, as necessary, the approximation of laws, adding that the abolition of internal borders affects a whole range of matters including combating terrorism, drug trafficking and other illicit trafficking; improved law enforcement co-operation; and judicial co-operation. In the latter context it was noted that judicial co-operation in criminal matters should be intensified in order to combat terrorism, drug trafficking, crime and other illicit trafficking and that harmonisation of certain provisions should be studied.[12]

Another significant development involving the abolition of borders in the 1980s, this time outside the Community legal framework, has been the 1985 Schengen Agreement between the Benelux countries, France and Germany leading to the adoption of the 1990 Schengen Implementing Convention, which included a wide range of provisions on immigration, asylum, border controls and police co-operation, including the establishment of the Schengen Information System.[13] Schengen can be viewed as a compensation for freedom: the abolition of internal frontiers (including physical frontiers) among the participating states would be combined with further integration between these states in the fields of immigration and criminal law, leading thus to a strong external border compensating for the lack of internal borders. This model of closer integration between a number of Member States outside the Community framework at the time has been a pioneering step at the time and resulted into a momentum towards extending such closer integration into the EU. As will be seen below, the Schengen *acquis* has now been integrated into Community/Union law, a fact indicative of the influence of the Schengen logic on the development of the European Union as an 'area of freedom, security and justice'. The influence of the Schengen logic is dominant in the development of EU immigration and borders law, but it is also visible in the development of EU criminal law principles, in particular by the Court of Justice: when interpreting the operation of EU criminal law, the Court has repeatedly

[9] COM (85) 310, 14 June 1985. The Commission considered that matters such as the co-ordination of rules concerning extradition were essential for the removal of internal frontier controls. See P A Weber-Panariello, *The Integration of Matters of Justice and Home Affairs into Title VI of the Treaty on European Union. A Step Towards More Democracy?*, EUI Working Paper RSC No. 95/32, Florence, European University Institute, 1995, p 5.

[10] The Palma document was prepared by a Co-ordinators' Group set up by the European Council and composed of twelve high-ranking officials, a chairman and the vice-president of the Commission to co-ordinate Member States' actions with regard to free movement. See Weber-Panariello, n 9 above, pp 8–9.

[11] Council doc. 89/1, 27 June 1989, www.europa.eu/rapid/pressReleasesAction.do?reference=DOC/89/1&format=HTML.

[12] The Palma document is reproduced in E Guild and J Niessen, *The Developing Immigration and Asylum Policies in the EU*, The Hague and London, Martinus Nijhoff, 1996, pp 443–448.

[13] On the Schengen Information System, see ch 5.

examined criminal law in conjunction with free movement within the framework of an 'area' of freedom, security and justice.[14]

Calls for further integration in criminal matters were also linked with political events external to the Community at the close of the 1980s, namely the fall of the Berlin Wall. The collapse of the Soviet Bloc led to a number of concerns in Western Europe. These were linked most notably to fears that political instability in Eastern Europe and the lack of a stable legal and constitutional framework in countries in transition would lead to the increase of criminogenic factors therein and the export of criminality from the East to the West. These concerns resulted in calls—in particular by Member States such as Germany fearing they would be most affected by these developments—towards greater EU co-operation and integration in criminal matters. In this context, countries like Germany attempted to render domestic concerns into EU issues[15]—creating at the same time considerable impetus towards the development of European integration in the field. Lack of trust towards Eastern European countries—which subsequently became candidate countries and now many of them full EU Member States—continued in the 1990s and the 2000s during the enlargement process and has led to the Schengen logic increasing in political capital in accession negotiations and beyond, with compliance with the Schengen *acquis* becoming a central requirement for EU entry.[16]

The end of the Cold War also had broader implications for the reconfiguration of security threats globally. The shift from the emphasis on military threats to the securitisation of broader phenomena has been well documented early on by international relations scholars.[17] In the EU and beyond, one element of this securitisation shift has been the elevation of forms of criminality as threats which require urgent and concerted response by governments.[18] Security threats in this context have assumed a chameleon nature over the years—from drug trafficking in the '80s to organised crime in the 1990s and terrorism in the 2000s.[19] At EU level, such

---

[14] This is in particular with regard to the Court's case law on the European Arrest Warrant and *ne bis in idem*—see ch 3.

[15] On Germany's influence on developing police co-operation (and immigration and asylum law co-operation) as a response to developments in Eastern Europe, see J Monar, 'Justice and Home Affairs: Europeanization as a Government-Controlled Process', *Proceedings of the British Academy*, vol 119, 2003, pp 309–323 at pp 320–322.

[16] On EU criminal law and enlargement see ch 6.

[17] See in particular B Buzan, *People, States and Fear. An Agenda for International Security Studies in the Post-Cold War Era*, Brighton, Harvester Wheatsheaf, 1991; B Buzan, 'New Patterns of Global Security in the Twenty-First Century', *International Affairs*, vol 67, no 3, 1999, pp 431–451. In the context of securitisation and crime, see D Bigo, *Polices en réseaux: l'experiénce européenne*, Paris, Presses de Sciences Po, 1996.

[18] On the securitisation process, see B Buzan, O Waever and J de Wilde, *Security. A New Framework for Analysis*, Boulder and London, Lynne Rienner, 1998; and O Waever, 'Securitization and De-securitization', in R D Lipschutz (ed), *On Security*, New York, Columbia University Press, 1995, pp 46–86.

[19] On this changing focus in the context of the development of money laundering counter-measures, see V Mitsilegas, 'Countering the Chameleon Threat of Dirty Money: "Hard"and "Soft" Law in the Emergence of a Global Regime against Money Laundering and Terrorist Finance' in A Edwards and P Gill (eds), *Transnational Organised Crime: Perspectives on Global Security*, London, Routledge, 2003, pp 195–211

securitisation of crime—has largely acted as a factor justifying further EU integration in criminal matters and led to the adoption of a plethora of legal and policy initiatives at EU level. In this context, particular focus has been placed on the transnational elements of the perceived threats, which are deemed to require a common EU approach with Member States not being able to address these challenges solely at the national level.[20] The securitisation of crime and the focus on the transnational are also increasingly acting as a motor for the emergence of the Union as a global security actor speaking with 'one voice' and influencing the development of global standards in the field.[21] In this process, as will be seen in a number of instances in this book, the emergence of both internal and external EU criminal law is marked by a strong emphasis on security objectives.

III. THE THIRD PILLAR—THE INSTITUTIONAL FRAMEWORK

The factors discusses above became increasingly relevant in negotiations to amend the EC Treaty as a follow-up to the Single European Act. In these negotiations, the issue of whether the Community competence should extend to criminal law—and justice and home affairs more generally—proved extremely contested. The final compromise came with the adoption of the Maastricht Treaty, which introduced a three pillar structure for the European Union. The primary function of this structure was on the one hand to include within the Union's remit controversial areas such as foreign and security policy and justice and home affairs, but to ensure on the other that Union action in these sovereignty sensitive fields would not be under the supranational elements of the first pillar, but would be subject to a more intergovernmental legal framework.[22] This pillar structure has been retained until today, with Union action in criminal matters largely confined (but increasingly not limited to) the third pillar. This part will provide with an overview and analysis of the evolution of the third pillar from Maastricht to the Treaty of Amsterdam—the provisions of which largely provide the legal framework currently in force for the third pillar. The specificities of the third pillar will be examined from three perspectives: institutions, instruments and principles.

A. Maastricht

In Maastricht, provisions related to EU criminal law were included in Title VI of the EU Treaty entitled 'provisions on cooperation in the fields of justice and home

---

[20] On the concept and role of transnational crime, see Mitsilegas, n 6 above, pp 19–21.

[21] See ch 6.

[22] For a critique of the Maastricht Treaty, see inter alia D Curtin, 'The Constitutional Structure of the Union: A Europe of Bits and Pieces', *Common Market Law Review*, vol 30, 1993, pp 17–69; see also R Dehousse, 'From Community to Union', in R Dehousse (ed), *Europe After Maastricht. An Ever Closer Union?*, Law Books in Europe, Munich, Law Books in Europe, 1994, pp 5–15.

affairs' (or as it is better known, 'the third pillar').[23] For the first time the Treaty established a Union competence in the field of Justice and Home Affairs, including judicial co-operation in criminal matters, customs co-operation and police co-operation for the purposes of preventing and combating terrorism, unlawful drug trafficking and other serious forms of international crime, including the establishment of a European Police Office (Europol).[24] Moreover, the Treaty contained a legal basis for establishing a Co-ordinating Committee consisting of senior officials and contributing to the preparation of the Council's 'discussions' as well as giving opinions for the attention of the Council.[25] It has been argued that in this manner the Maastricht third pillar consolidated and formalised earlier law enforcement initiatives.[26] These initiatives, along with extra-EU mechanisms of co-operation such as the Council of Europe and Schengen have thus been accurately characterised as 'laboratories' of European integration in the field of Justice and Home Affairs.[27]

However, the provisions on the form of EU action in criminal matters remained extremely weak. The opening provision of the Maastricht third pillar, Article K, referred to 'cooperation in the fields of Justice and Home Affairs', and not to a common policy on justice and home affairs (as has been the case with both first pillar policies (such as the common agricultural policy) and second pillar initiatives (see the common foreign and security policy). As it has been noted, this approach and contrast 'suggested the much less ambitious objective of cooperation in making effective national policies which would remain unchanged'.[28] Moreover, Article K.1 merely declared that Member States must regard a number of areas in Justice and Home Affairs as 'matters of common interest'. The emphasis is here not on integration, but on 'matters of common interest'. Moreover, the emphasis is on Member States, with no explicit reference to the Union as an actor

[23] For an overview of the Maastricht third pillar see: P-C Müller-Graff, 'The Legal Bases of the Third Pillar and Its Position in the Framework of the Union Treaty', *Common Market Law Review*, vol 31, 1994, pp 493–510; D O'Keeffe, 'Recasting the Third Pillar', *Common Market Law Review*, vol 32, 1995, pp 893–920; G Barrett, 'Cooperation in Justice and Home Affairs in the European Union—An Overview and a Critique', in G Barrett (ed), *Justice Cooperation in the European Union*, Dublin, Institute of European Affairs, 1997, pp 3–48; M Anderson *et al*, *Policing the European Union*, Oxford, Clarendon Press, 1995, in particular pp 200–217; and the contributions in J Monar and R Morgan (eds), *The Third Pillar of the European Union. Cooperation in the Fields of Justice and Home Affairs*, Brussels, European Interuniversity Press, 1994.
[24] Art K.1, in particular paras (7) to (9).
[25] Art K.4.
[26] M den Boer, 'Europe and the Art of International Police Co-operation: Free Fall or Measured Scenario?', in D O'Keeffe and P Twomey (eds), *Legal Issues of the Maastricht Treaty*, London, Wiley Chancery, 1994, pp 279–294 at p 281.
[27] See J Monar, 'The Dynamics of Justice and Home Affairs: Laboratories, Driving Factors and Costs', *Journal of Common Market Studies*, vol 39, no 4, 2001, pp 747–764.
[28] E Denza, *The Intergovernmental Pillars of the European Union*, Oxford, Oxford University Press, 2002, p 194. Note also Art K.2(2) which stated that Title VI would not affect the exercise of the responsibilities incumbent upon Member States with regard to the maintenance of law and order and the safeguarding of internal security.

in the third pillar.[29] The extent to which the Union could take legally binding action in these areas of 'common interest' was further both limited and unclear. The main legally binding instrument provided for by the Maastricht third pillar was the instrument of Conventions which clearly mirrored intergovernmental co-operation under international law fora such as the United Nations and the Council of Europe.[30] The Council could also adopt the seemingly non-legally binding 'joint positions', and 'joint actions', the legally binding character of which is unclear and has been contested.[31] While thus in principle the Maastricht third pillar established a degree of competence for the Union in the field of Justice and Home Affairs, including criminal matters, the powers given to the Union to exercise such competence remained significantly limited and unclear.

The reluctance of—at least certain—Member States to communitarise Justice and Home Affairs was also reflected in the extremely limited role given to EU institutions in the third pillar, most notably in the area of criminal law. The Commission was not granted a right of initiative with regard to measures on the main areas related to criminal matters, with initiative granted only to Member States.[32] The European Parliament also was granted an extremely limited role: it was to be 'regularly informed of discussions' in third pillar areas; the Presidency would merely 'consult' the Parliament 'on the principal aspects of activities' in the third pillar; and it could 'ask questions or make recommendations'.[33] The only provision on the ECJ did not grant jurisdiction via the Treaty but mentioned that third pillar conventions adopted under the third pillar may provide for such jurisdiction to interpret their provisions and to rule on any disputes regarding their application.[34] Unsurprisingly, given the extent of the limits to the Community method, decision-making in the Council would—with limited exceptions—take place by unanimity.[35]

B. Amsterdam and beyond

i. General

The operation of the third pillar demonstrated the weaknesses and limits of the compromise reached in Maastricht. Legislative production was not abundant, and took mainly the form of Conventions, which proved extremely cumbersome to

---

[29] See in this context the observation of Müller-Graf (n.23 above, p.507) noting that the provisions of the third pillar do not even mention the Union as a separately acting agent in the relevant fields of policy.

[30] Art K.3(2)(c).

[31] For the view that Joint Actions are not legally binding, see Müller-Graf, n 23 above, p 509; for the contrary view under certain circumstances, see O'Keeffe, n 23 above, p 914.

[32] These are the areas referred to in Art K1 (7) to (9)–Art K.3(2).

[33] Art K.6.

[34] Art K.3(2)(c).

[35] Art K.4(3).

ratify.[36] A number of Joint Actions were adopted, some of them providing definitions of key concepts for EU criminal law such as organised crime, but their legal status was unclear and their implementation prospects questionable.[37] Enforcement and judicial control of third pillar law were minimal following the very limited Treaty provisions. The same applied to democratic control and transparency, with the European Parliament essentially marginalised. An assessment of the Maastricht third pillar in 1995 pointed out the inactivity in the field and noted that:

> Many of the reasons for this inactivity or lack of concrete progress are to be found in the structure of the Third Pillar itself. Other failures to achieve consensus seem to derive from an unwillingness to change the patterns of intergovernmental co-operation existing prior to the entry into force of the Third Pillar. A further disturbing trend is that the Third Pillar structure seems to have in no way assisted in making intergovernmental cooperation [sic] in this area more transparent, precisely at a time when transparency has become one of the major concerns at Union and Community level.[38]

The deficiencies of the Maastricht third pillar were discussed in the intergovernmental conference leading to the adoption of the Amsterdam Treaty.[39] Central to the debate have been again issues of competence, institutional framework and the question whether to transfer matters falling under the third pillar to the Community pillar.[40] The different national approaches on these matters did not stop the adoption of significant changes to the third pillar in Amsterdam: Maastricht third pillar areas of immigration, asylum, borders and civil law were 'communitarised', forming part of Title IV of the EC Treaty;[41] and the third pillar itself, now entitled 'provisions on police and judicial cooperation in criminal matters', was revamped and strengthened.[42] The Amsterdam provisions, subject to

---

[36] See, eg, the Europol Convention, signed in 1995 and entering into force in 1999: see ch 4.

[37] For an analysis of the Joint Action on organised crime see V Mitsilegas, 'Defining Organised Crime in the European Union: The Limits of European Criminal Law in an Area of Freedom, Security and Justice', *European Law Review*, vol 56, 2001, pp 565–581.

[38] O'Keeffe, n 23 above, p 894.

[39] For a diplomat's view of the Treaty of Amsterdam negotiations, including the provisions on Justice and Home Affairs, see B McDonagh, *Original Sin in a Brave New World. An Account of the Negotiation of the Treaty of Amsterdam*, Dublin, Institute of European Affairs, 1998; for a similar account of the UK position, see S Wall, *A Stranger in Europe. Britain and the EU from Thatcher to Blair*, Oxford, OUP, 2008 on the Amsterdam Intergovernmental Conference and Justice and Home Affairs see H Labayle, 'La coopération européenne en matière de justice et d'affaires intérieures et la Conférence intergouvernementale', *Revue trimestrielle du droit européen*, vol 33, no 1, 1997, pp 1–35; on the IGC see further J Grünhage, 'The 1996/97 Intergovernmental Conference: A Survey of the Process', in J Monar and W Wessels (eds), *The European Union After the Treaty of Amsterdam*, London and New York, Continuum, 2001, pp 9–30.

[40] See in this context the Progress Report on the IGC of June 1996—doc. CONF 360/1/96 REV 1, Brussels, 17 June 1996, at www.consilium.europa.eu/uedocs/cms_data/docs/cig1996/03860-r1en6.pdf

[41] And customs co-operation moving to a separate EC Treaty provision, Art 135—on Art 135 and criminal law see ch 2.

[42] On the evolution of Justice and Home Affairs matters in the Amsterdam Treaty see: S Peers, *EU Justice and Home Affairs Law*, 2nd edn, Oxford, Oxford University Press, 2006; Denza, n 28 above; J Monar, 'Justice and Home Affairs in the Treaty of Amsterdam: Reform at the Price of Fragmentation', *European Law Review*, vol 23, 1998, pp 320–335; H Labayle, 'Un espace de liberté, de

some limited amendments by the Treaty of Nice in particular regarding the role of Eurojust and enhanced co-operation, form the basis of the institutional framework currently in force for the third pillar. The latter now includes detailed provisions on competence and the types of common action in the fields of police co-operation, judicial co-operation in criminal maters, and criminal law approximation.[43] Significantly, these forms of common action are required to achieve a general Union objective

> to provide citizens with a high level of safety within an area of freedom, security and justice by developing common action among the Member States in the fields of police and judicial cooperation in criminal matters and by preventing and combating racism and xenophobia.[44]

ii. The Area of Freedom, Security and Justice and the incorporation of the Schengen acquis

The institutional developments in the third pillar brought about in Amsterdam must be viewed in the context of the express reference to the development of the Union as an 'area of freedom, security and justice' as a Union objective. According to Article 2 TEU, the Union aims

> to maintain and develop the Union as an area of freedom, security and justice, *in which the free movement of persons is assured* in conjunction with appropriate measures with respect to external border controls, asylum, immigration and *the prevention and combating of crime.* (emphasis added)

The inclusion of this objective, which is also visible in both Title IV of the EC Treaty (the 'communitarised' Maastricht third pillar[45]) and Title VI of the EU Treaty (the remaining third pillar dealing with criminal matters[46]) is significant in that it forms the framework within which EU action on Justice andHome Affairs, including criminal law, will be interpreted. While the concept of the 'area' is not clear, and the relationship between the three elements of 'freedom, security and justice' contested,[47] it

---

sécurité et de justice', *Revue trimestrielle du droit européen*, vol.34, 1998, pp.813–881; P. J. Kuijper, 'The Evolution of the Third Pillar from Maastricht to the European Constitution: Institutional Aspects', *Common Market Law Review* vol.41, 2004, pp.609–626; D. Kostakopoulou, 'The Area of Freedom, Security and Justice and the European Union's Constitutional Dialogue', in C. Barnard (ed), *The Fundamentals of EU Law Revisited. Assessing the Impact of the Constitutional Debate*, Oxford, OUP, 2007, pp.153–192; and M. den Boer, 'An Area of Freedom, Security and Justice: Bogged Down by Compromise', in D. O'Keeffe and P. Twomey (eds), *Legal Issues of the Amsterdam Treaty*, Oxford, Hart Publishing, 1999, pp.303–322. For a historical overview of the evolution of EU Justice and Home Affairs, see W. de Lobkowicz, *L'Europe et la sécurité intérieure. Une élaboration par étapes*, Paris, La documentation française, 2002.

[43] Arts 29–31 TEU.
[44] Art 29(1)TEU. On specific areas of criminal law competence under Art 29 see ch 2.
[45] Art 61 TEC.
[46] Art 29 TEU.
[47] On different takes on the concept of the 'area of freedom, security and justice' see H Lindahl, 'Finding a Place for Freedom, Security and Justice: The European Union's Claim to Territorial Unity', *European Law Review*, vol 29, 2004, pp 461–484; and P Twomey, 'Constructing a Secure Space: The Area of Freedom, Security and Justice', in O'Keeffe and Twomey, n 42 above, pp 351–374.

is important to note that the conception of the Union as an 'area' (or *espace* in French) is reminiscent of earlier initiatives, in particular the Schengen area (*espace Schengen*).[48] In this context it is noteworthy that the introduction of the development of the Union as an 'area of freedom, security and justice' has been accompanied in Amsterdam by the incorporation of the Schengen *acquis* into Community/Union law.[49] The latter was a complex process generating a raft of issues such as what constitutes the *acquis,* how to allocate this and subsequent Schengen-building measures between pillars, and of course issues related to variable geometry, ie non-participating Member States and participating non-EU Member States.[50] However, it also signified the affirmation of the Schengen logic within the Union framework.[51] Linked to the Schengen logic, the Union as an 'area' of freedom, security and justice is based on the objective of free movement in an area without internal frontiers, entailing thus a reconfiguration of territoriality at both the national and the Union level. While this reconfiguration of territoriality is particularly relevant in the field of EU immigration and borders law most notably with regard to practices of inclusion and exclusion,[52] it will be seen that it also has implications for the development of EU criminal law, both by the legislator and by the Court of Justice—in particular when the latter has had to approach the relationship between national legal orders under mutual recognition in criminal matters, and Schengen-related matters such as *ne bis in idem.*[53]

iii. The Institutional Framework

a. Decision-making

Intergovernmental elements in the third pillar remained in Amsterdam, although the role of the Union institutions was in general enhanced in comparison with

[48] See Labayle, n 42 above, p 824. See also the discussion in Mitsilegas, Monar and Rees, n 1 above, pp 84–86.

[49] See the Protocol Integrating the Schengen *Acquis* into the Framework of the European Union; for the subsequent definition of the Schengen *acquis,* see the Decision 1999/435 (OJ L176, 10 July 1999, p 1) corrected by Decision 2000/645, OJ L9, 13 January 2001, p 24.

[50] On the incorporation of Schengen into EC/EU law, see Peers, *EU Justice,* n 42 above, pp 44–46 and 55–64 (on the position of Member States with the option not to opt into Schengen measures and participating non-EU Member States); see also S Peers, '*Caveat Emptor?* Integrating the Schengen *Acquis* into the European Union Legal Order' *Cambridge Yearbook of European Legal Studies,* vol 2, 1999, pp 87–124; M den Boer, 'The Incorporation of Schengen into the TEU: A Bridge Too Far?' in Monar and Wessels, n 39 above, pp 296–320; and D Thym, 'The Schengen Law: A Challenge for Legal Accountability in the European Union' *European Law Journal,* vol 8, no 2, 2002, pp 218–245.

[51] Unsurprisingly, the incorporation of the Schengen *acquis* into the EC/EU framework was strongly supported by the Benelux countries—see Benelux Memorandum on the Intergovernmental Conference, doc CONF 3844/96, Brussels, 5 May 1996, p 10. At www.consilium.europa.eu/uedocs/cms_data/docs/cig1996/03844en6.pdf.

[52] In this context see E Guild, *Moving the Borders of Europe,* Inaugural Lecture, University of Nijmegen, www.cmr.jur.ru.nl/cmr/docs/oratie.eg_pdf; K Groenendijk, E Guild and P Minderhoud (eds), *In Search of Europe's Borders,* The Hague and London, Kluwer Law International, 2003; D Bigo and E Guild (eds), *Controlling Frontiers. Free Movement Into and Within Europe,* Aldershot, Ashgate, 2005; see also D Kostakopoulou, 'Is There an Alternative to "Schengenland"?', *Political Studies,* vol 46, 1998, pp 886–902.

[53] For an analysis of this case law, see ch 3.

Maastricht.[54] As far as *decision-making* is concerned, unanimity in the Council remains for the vast majority of third pillar law.[55] The European Parliament, while in an enhanced position in comparison with Maastricht, continues to have an extremely limited role: it is merely consulted in the adoption of Framework Decisions, Decisions and Conventions.[56] Thus, law-making in the third pillar remains firmly with Member States, which obtained a further reassurance on checking the Union's reach in criminal matters by retaining the Maastricht provision that the third pillar will 'not affect the exercise of responsibilities incumbent upon Member States with regard to the maintenance of law and order and the safeguarding of internal security'.[57] However, as an opening to Member States which supported further integration in criminal matters, the Treaty—as amended in Nice-includes provisions expressly allowing enhanced co-operation in the third pillar.[58] Moreover, Amsterdam also included a passerelle provision,[59] reformulated to state that the Council may decide unanimously after consulting the European Parliament to transfer action in areas mentioned in Article 29 TEU to Title IV of the EC Treaty.[60] The Commission—which has also embarked on a series of Court challenges contesting the legality of the choice of third pillar legal bases for EU criminal law harmonisation instruments[61]—proposed the use of this provision after the rejection of the Constitutional Treaty (which largely 'communitarised' decision-making in criminal matters by abolishing the third pillar) but the proposal was not taken on board by Member States.[62] It is not unlikely that similar proposals may resurface in case of delays in the entry into force of the Lisbon Treaty.

---

[54] For a comparison of a number of institutional aspects, see A Dashwood, 'Issues of Decision-making in the European Union after Nice', in A Arnull and D Wincott (eds), *Accountability and Legitimacy in the European Union*, Oxford, OUP, 2002, pp 13–40.

[55] Art 34(2) TEU. The exception is measures necessary to implement third pillar Decisions which are adopted by qualified majority: Art 34(2)(c).

[56] Art 39(1) TEU. Parliament also must be regularly informed of discussions on the third pillar by the Presidency and the Commission, and may ask questions of the Council and make recommendations (Art 39(2) and (3)). The role of the European Parliament is even more limited in the negotiation and conclusion of third pillar international agreements, under Arts 24 and 38 TEU—for details, see ch 6.

[57] Art 33. See Also Art 64(1) TEC in Title IV. See Art K.2(2) of the Maastricht Treaty.

[58] Arts 40, 40a and 40b TEU.

[59] See the passerelle in Art K.9 of the Maastricht Treaty, which, however, did not apply to judicial co-operation in criminal matters, customs and police co-operation.

[60] Art 42 TEU. Member States will adopt that decision in accordance with their constitutional requirements.

[61] See ch 2.

[62] On the Commission passerelle proposals and the evolution of Member States' reactions, see House of Commons Home Affairs Committee, *Justice and Home Affairs Issues at European Union Level*, 3rd Report, session 2006–07, HC 76-I, paras 328–333; and V Mitsilegas, 'Constitutional Principles of the European Community and European Criminal Law', *European Journal of Law Reform*, vol 8, 2006, pp 301–324 at pp 308–309.

b. Instruments

Although the decision-making arrangements remain in essence intergovernmental, the Amsterdam Treaty strengthened significantly the *legal instruments* under the third pillar. Conventions, which were introduced in Maastricht, remain in the Treaty[63], although their use post-Amsterdam has been minimal. Amsterdam introduced a series of new instruments for the third pillar. A new instrument is the *common position* 'defining the approach of the Union to a particular matter'.[64] Common positions are particularly relevant in the context of EU external action, with the Treaty stating that Member States must defend them within international organisations and at international conferences.[65] The Court has applied the duty of loyal co-operation to common positions, holding this to mean in particular that 'Member States are to take all appropriate measures, whether general or particular, to ensure fulfilment of their obligations under European Union law'.[66] The Court has not excluded the possibility for common positions to have legal effects vis-a-vis third parties.[67]

Third pillar measures which the Treaty introduces expressly as legally binding are *Decisions*—which exclude legal approximation and do not entail direct effect[68] and *Framework Decisions* for the purposes of legal approximation[69]. The introduction of Framework Decisions—which constituted the main form of third pillar law-making post-Amsterdam—has strengthened considerably third pillar law. Framework Decisions are very similar to first pillar Directives—according to the Treaty, they are binding upon the Member States as to the result to be achieved but leave to the national authorities the choice of form and methods.[70] The main difference with Directives is that Framework Decisions do not entail direct effect.[71] However, as will be seen below, this has not stopped the Court from stressing the legally binding character of third pillar law and boosting efforts to implement it in Member States.[72] Moreover, the Court has confirmed the discretion of the Council to choose which third pillar legal instrument to adopt: in a case involving the Framework Decision on the European Arrest Warrant, the Court upheld the legislative choice of a Framework Decision as a form of third pillar law-making against arguments that this was the wrong choice of instrument and that the Council should have adopted a Convention.[73]

[63] Art 34(2)(d).
[64] Art 34(2)(a).
[65] Art 37 TEU.
[66] Case C-354/04 P, *Gestoras Pro Amnistia et al v Council*, ECR [2007] I-5179, para 52; and Case C-355/04 P, *Segi et al v Council*, ECR [2007] I-6157, para 52. The Court applied here its earlier *Pupino* ruling analysed below.
[67] *Gestoras* and *Segi*, see the analysis below.
[68] Art 34(2)(c).
[69] Art 34(2)(b).
[70] ibid.
[71] ibid.
[72] See the analysis on the *Pupino* judgment.
[73] Case C-303/05, *Advocaten voor de Wereld VZW v Leden van de Ministerraad*, ECR [2007] I-3633. For an analysis, see ch 3.

The strengthening of the third pillar legal instruments is also confirmed by the elements of Maastricht which have *not* been included in the Treaty, namely joint positions, and in particular joint actions. The disappearance of joint actions from the Treaty resulted in a number of complex questions, in particular regarding the status of joint actions adopted under the Maastricht procedures post-Amsterdam, their effects and their judicial scrutiny by the ECJ.[74] While a number of proposals to replace joint actions by Framework Decisions were tabled by the Commission, these proposals—covering important aspects of criminal law harmonisation such as organised crime and racism and xenophobia—have not been formally adopted yet.[75] This exacerbates legal uncertainly, especially in the light of the unclear legal status of joint actions.

c. Initiative

Intergovernmental elements were also retained in the Amsterdam Treaty with regard to the *right of initiative*. While the Commission now has a right of initiative in the third pillar, this right is shared with Member States, with any Member State having the right to table a proposal for a third pillar instrument.[76] While the majority of third pillar proposals post-Amsterdam were tabled by the Commission, initiatives by Member States did not cease to exist. One form of Member State initiatives involved a number of Member States (at times consecutive EU presidencies) acting together to table proposals on matters perceived quite close to State sovereignty and thus rather 'intergovernmental'—examples in this context include a series of Member States' sole or joint initiatives promoting mutual recognition in criminal matters,[77] as well as initiatives than can be seen at times as a response or pre-emption to more integrationist proposals by the Commission.[78] Another form of intervention involved initiatives by one Member State, usually at the time of their holding of the EU Presidency. From a Union law and policy perspective, Member States initiatives present a number of challenges: being prepared at times by civil servants in domestic interior or justice ministries

---

[74] On the uncertainty on whether a measure of secondary law survive the repeal of its legal basis, see N Fennelly, 'The Area of "Freedom, Security and Justice" and the European Court of Justice— A Personal View', *International and Comparative Law Quarterly*, vol 49, 2000, pp 10–14 at p 12.

[75] For details see ch 2.

[76] Art 34 (2).

[77] These include proposals for the adopted Framework Decisions on the mutual recognition of: financial penalties (France, Sweden and the UK, Council doc 19710/01, Brussels, 12 July 2001, and accompanying Explanatory Memorandum (EM) ADD 1, Brussels, 16 July 2001); confiscation orders (Denmark, Council doc 9955/02, Brussels, 14 June 2002, and EM in ADD 1, Brussels, 2 July 2002); and freezing orders (France, Sweden and Belgium, Council doc 13986/00, Brussels, 30 November 200 and EM in ADD 1, Brussels, 22 December 2000). They also include more recent proposals such as the proposal on the recognition and supervision of suspended sentences and alternative sanctions (Germany and France, Council doc 5325/07, Brussels, 15 January 2007 and EM in ADD 1, Brussels, 1 February 2007); and the proposal on a common approach on judgments *in absentia* for mutual recognition purposes (Slovenia, France, the Czech Republic, Sweden, Slovakia, the UK and Germany, Council doc 5213/08, Brussels, 14 January 2008 and EM in ADD 1, Brussels, 30 January 2008). On mutual recognition, see ch 3.

[78] The example of the evolution of Eurojust is characteristic in this context; see ch 4.

whose job is to table draft domestic law, their structure and drafting leaves much to be desired in comparison to proposals prepared by expert EU law staff in the Commission; there is minimal consultation; their tabling may clash with the Commission's timetable as outlined in its annual work programmes; and they may reflect a very narrow agenda, or attempts to export a matter of purely domestic interest at EU level.[79] On some of these grounds, a number of Member State initiatives over the years have failed to be adopted.[80]

d. The Role of the ECJ

The Treaty Framework   Another significant limitation to the Commission's powers under the third pillar is that it does not have a right to institute infringement proceedings against Member States—particularly relevant in cases of mis- or non-implementation of third pillar law. This limitation of the Commission's role as 'guardian of the Treaties' presents considerable challenges in ensuring the timely and appropriate implementation of third pillar instruments by Member States, with Member States' implementation records in the third pillar consistently criticised by the Commission.[81] The absence of infringement proceedings is not the only limit to *judicial control* in the third pillar.[82] The role of the ECJ has been strengthened in comparison with Amsterdam, but remains subject to significant limitations. The Court's third pillar jurisdiction is delineated by Articles 46(b) and 35 TEU.[83] The Court does have jurisdiction to give preliminary rulings on the validity and interpretation of framework decisions and decisions, on the interpretation of conven-

[79] On this point, see H Nilsson, *Decision-Making in EU Justice and Home Affairs: Current Shortcomings and Reform Possibilities*, Sussex European Institute Working Paper No 57, November 2002, p 4.

[80] Examples of aborted presidency initiatives include a Spanish initiative for a Convention on the suppression by customs administrations of illicit drug trafficking on the high seas (Council doc 5382/02, Brussels, 4 February 2002); a Greek initiative for a Framework Decision on the prevention and control of trafficking in human organs (Council doc 6290/03, Brussels, 13 February 2003); and, more controversially, a Greek initiative for a Framework Decision on the application of the *ne bis in idem* principle (Council doc 6356/03, Brussels, 13 February 2003—on the issues resulting from the non-harmonisation of *ne bis in idem* across the EU see ch 3). An example of a 'watered down' proposal is the Spanish initiative on the setting up of a network of contact points of national authorities responsible for private security (Council doc 5135/02, Brussels, 29 January 2002), which ended up as a Council Recommendation (OJ C153, 27 June 2002, p 1).

[81] For recent criticism of Member States' implementation of third pillar measures, see European Commission, 'Report on Implementation of the Hague Programme for 2007' COM (2008) 373 final, Brussels, 2 July 2008; and for further detail see the accompanying Commission Staff Working Document SEC (2008) 2048, Brussels, 2 July 2008.

[82] On the role of the ECJ in the third pillar, see A Arnull, 'Taming the Beast? The Treaty of Amsterdam and the Court of Justice', in O'Keeffe and Twomey, n 42 above, pp 109–122; Dashwood, n 54 above; S Peers, 'Salvation Outside the Church: Judicial Protection in the Third Pillar After the *Pupino* and *Segi* Judgments', *Common Market Law Review*, vol 44, 2007, pp 883–929; Peers, *EU Justice*, n 42 above; Denza, n 28 above; Fennelly, n 74 above; A Albors-Llorens, 'Changes in the Jurisdiction of the European Court of Justice under the Treaty of Amsterdam', *Common Market Law Review*, vol 35, 1998, pp 1273–1294.

[83] See also Art 2(1) of the Protocol on the Schengen *acquis*. For further details, see Peers, 'Salvation', previous n.

tions and on the validity and interpretation of the measures implementing them.[84] However, such jurisdiction is subject to acceptance by Member States[85]—and not all Member States have declared acceptance thus far.[86] This limitation of the preliminary ruling jurisdiction—introduced largely at the insistence of the United Kingdom which, unsurprisingly, has not accepted such jurisdiction thus far[87]—is extremely detrimental in that it limits the avenues of co-operation between Luxembourg and national courts and it deprives national courts from influencing the development of Union law by sending to Luxembourg questions that have been shaped in their domestic legal system.[88] There may also be an impact on the consistency of the interpretation of Union law by national courts, although, as has been demonstrated by the interpretation of the European Arrest Warrant by the House of Lords, denying the right to send references to Luxembourg has not stopped domestic courts from taking into account Luxembourg interpretation of third pillar law and apply it in their domestic context.[89]

The Court also has jurisdiction to review the legality of framework decisions and decisions on grounds of lack of competence, infringement of an essential procedural requirement, infringement of the Treaty or of any rule of law relating to its application, or misuse of powers—standing is however limited to Member States and the Commission and is not extended to individuals.[90] The Court also has jurisdiction to rule under certain conditions on any dispute between Member States regarding the interpretation or application of third pillar instruments, and on similar disputes between Member States and the Commission regarding the interpretation of conventions only.[91] However, mirroring Member States'

---

[84] Art 35(1). Note the strengthening of the provision with regard to the pre-existing instrument of Conventions in comparison to Maastricht, which left the determination of ECJ jurisdiction to the specific Conventions and did not include a general, Treaty provision establishing such jurisdiction.

[85] Via a declaration—Art 35(2). Even if they accept jurisdiction, Member States can allow references only by courts and tribunals against whose decisions there is no judicial remedy under national law—this is similar to the limitation of the Court's jurisdiction in Title IV—see Art 68 TEC.

[86] Member States which have not made a Declaration under Art 35(2) TEU include Denmark, Ireland and the United Kingdom. According to the Court of Justice, no official information was available in March 2008 with regard to Declarations by Bulgaria, Cyprus, Estonia,, Malta, Poland, Romania and Slovakia. The remaining 17 Member States have made such Declarations with varying content. For details (including the relevant OJ references), see note by the ECJ Research and Documentation Service, *Jurisdiction of the Court of Justice to Give Preliminary Rulings on Police and Judicial Cooperation in Criminal Matters*, March 2008, at www.curia.europa/eu/en/instit/txtdocfr/txtsenvigueur/art35.pdf.

[87] On the UK resistance, see Denza, n 28 above, p 317.

[88] On this point, see also Arnull, n 82 above, p 118.

[89] See in particular the case of *Dabas v High Court of Justice, Madrid* [2007] UKHL 6, where the House of Lords referred to *Pupino* to interpret the domestic Extradition Act 2003 in the light of the Framework Decision on the European Arrest Warrant. For details, see V Mitsilegas, 'Drafting to Implement EU Law: the European Arrest Warrant in the United Kingdom', in H Xanthaki (ed), *Legislative Drafting: A Modern Approach. Essays in Honour of Sir William Dale*, Aldershot, Ashgate, forthcoming. For accurate predictions on the effect of ECJ third pillar preliminary rulings on UK courts, see Denza, n 28 above, p 317 and Arnull, n 82 above, p 118. On the *erga omnes* effects of preliminary rulings, see K Lenaerts, 'The Rule of Law and the Coherence of the Judicial System of the European Union', *Common Market Law Review*, vol 44, 2007, pp 1625–1659 at pp 1641–1645.

[90] Art 35(6). Arnull has criticised the failure to grant to individuals standing with regard Decisions: n 82 above, p 119.

[91] Art 35(7).

willingness to keep domestic operational action in criminal matters out of bounds, the Court does not have jurisdiction

> to review the validity or proportionality of operations carried out by the police or other law enforcement services of a Member State or the exercise of the responsibilities incumbent upon Member States with regard to the maintenance of law and order and the safeguarding of internal security.[92]

This may represent a considerable limitation of judicial control on operational action under the third pillar.[93]

Judicial Protection The limits to the Court's jurisdiction have raised a number of concerns regarding the capacity of the third pillar framework to provide effective judicial protection for affected individuals. The issue of judicial protection has arisen most prominently in the context of Union counter-terrorism measures: along with their significant human rights implications, these measures present considerable legal complexity as they may transcend one pillar and represent cross-pillar initiatives, while also representing a merging of internal with external EU criminal law and involve the incorporation into Union law of international commitments. In this context, a distinction can be made between two categories of situations: instances where the Union legislator did not have any discretion in implementing UN measures; and instances where the EU legislator has some degree of discretion in implementation, by specifying individually the persons, groups and entities affected.[94] The first category of cases will be examined in the chapter on EU external action.[95] In the second category, two important cases concerning judicial protection have arisen, involving the adoption of a cross-pillar Common Position which implemented Resolution 1373 (2001) of the UN Security Council on terrorist finance.[96] Individuals and organisations affected by this Common Position sought recourse to the Court of First Instance,[97] and on appeal to the Court of Justice.[98] Central to these cases has been the question of

---

[92] Art 35(5).

[93] It has been argued that the practical effect of Art 35(5) may be limited as the provision is concerned with national, and not Union, measures: A Arnull, *The European Union and its Court of Justice*, 2nd edn, Oxford, OUP, 2006, p 134. However, it remains to be seen whether this provision will be used to shield operational activities in Member States when national authorities co-operate on the basis of Union law (for instance when exchanging personal data or in the framework of joint investigation teams), or whether they operate in the context of the framework of Union bodies (such as Europol) or databases (such as the SIS).

[94] On this distinction, see Court of First Instance, Case T-47/03, *Sison v Council* ECR [2007] I-1233, paras 147–150.

[95] For an analysis of the issues raised by the relationship between international law and Union law for judicial protection, see ch 6.

[96] Council Common Position 2001/931 adopted under Arts 15 TEU 34 TEU 'on the application of specific measures to combat terrorism', OJ L344, 28 December 2001, p 93. This Common Position has been amended a number of times since to update the lists of individuals and organisations affected by it—for the latest version at the time of writing see Council Common Position 2008/586/CFSP, OJ L188, 16 July 2008, p 71.

[97] Cases T-338/02 ECR [2004] II-1647 (*Segi*) and T-333/02 (*Gestoras*).

[98] *Gestoras Pro Amnistia* and *Segi*, previous n.

effective judicial protection and remedies to challenge the inclusion of those concerned into the scope of Union restrictive measures.

The Court of Justice upheld the Court of First Instance ruling with regard to the applicant's action for damages: based on Articles 46 and 35 TEU (with the Court stating that the latter 'confers no jurisdiction on the Court of Justice to entertain any action for damages whatsoever'[99]), as well as Article 41(1) TEU (on compensation for damages caused by EU institutions[100]), the Court confirmed that no action for damages is provided for in the third pillar. However, the Court did go one step further when examining the issue of effective judicial protection in the context of preliminary rulings. In a striking judgment, the Court applied its first pillar case law on the right to make a reference for a preliminary ruling to the third pillar,[101] stating that this right exists 'in respect of all measures adopted by the Council, whatever their nature or form, which are intended to have legal effects in relation to third parties'.[102] On the basis of this substantive test, and notwithstanding the fact that Article 35 does not confer ECJ jurisdiction in this regard, the Court held that 'it has to be possible to make subject to review by the Court a common position which, because of its content, has a scope going beyond that assigned by the EU Treaty to that kind of act'.[103] The Court would have jurisdiction to find 'that the common position is intended to produce legal effects in relation to third parties, to accord it its true classification and to give it a preliminary ruling'.[104] The Court would also have jurisdiction to review the lawfulness of common positions under the conditions set out in Article 35(6) TEU.[105]

The Court's judgments in *Gestoras Pro Amnistia* and *Segi* represent a clear effort to address the criticism that the Court is reluctant to go beyond the Treaty constraints and provide effective judicial protection to individuals affected by far-reaching restrictive measures, adopted with little scrutiny[106]—such as their

---

[99] Para 46 *Gestoras* and *Segi*, n 97 above.

[100] Para 47 *Gestoras* and *Segi*, n 97 above. The Court referred to its judgment in the case *Spain v Eurojust*: see ch 4.

[101] The Court has also applied on a number of occasions the admissibility rules of Art 234 TEC to third pillar cases—see Peers, 'Salvation', n 82 above, pp 887–888.

[102] Para 53.

[103] Para 54.

[104] ibid.

[105] Para 55.

[106] A degree of willingness to provide some avenues for judicial review had been demonstrated a few months earlier by the Court of First Instance in case T-228/02 *OMPI v Council* ECR [2006] II-4665. The Court dismissed the applicant organisation's action for annulment of the Common Position as inadmissible, ruling that neither the second nor the third pillars contain provisions for action for annulment (paras 45–54, with the Court stressing in para 54 that these pillars provide a 'limited system of judicial review'). However, the Court did accept jurisdiction to hear an action for annulment directed against a Common Position adopted on the basis of Arts 15 and 34 EU 'only strictly to the extent that, in support of such an action, the applicant alleges an infringement of the Community's competences' (para 56)—in this context, the Court found the application to be unfounded. The Court then went on to examine issues of judicial protection with regard to first pillar measures implementing the Common Position. For commentaries on *OMPI* see E Guild, 'The Uses and Abuses of Counter-Terrorism Policies in Europe: The Case of the 'Terrorist Lists', *Journal of Common Market Studies*, vol 46, no 1, pp 173–193 and C Eckes, Case-note, *Common Market Law Review*, vol 44, 2007, pp 1117–1129.

inclusion in terrorist lists.[107] The substantive test adopted is welcome in that it may address the practice of Member States in the Council choosing to adopt restrictive measures with human rights implications by choosing a form of instrument, such as common positions, whose legal status is unclear and which are subject to minimal judicial scrutiny on the basis of the letter of the EU Treaty—this may be the case in particular also in cases of a combined second and third pillar legal basis.[108] The Court indicated its willingness to look behind the formal classification of a measure and to provide a mechanism for review for measures affecting the rights of individuals irrespective of such classification—albeit in a decentralised manner, via the preliminary rulings route.[109] According to the Court, this avenue constitutes a remedy—and ironically for the applicants, their claim that there is no effective judicial protection at EU level was rejected.[110]

Another source of judicial protection concerns has been not the letter of Title VI (and Title IV for that matter), but the implementation of these provisions in practice. It was thought that the conduct of preliminary ruling proceedings in Luxembourg, in particular their lengthy duration, were not appropriate for cases involving Justice and Home Affairs matters, which involve situations such as individuals in custody and are in need of speedy resolution.[111] The President of the Court subsequently presented to the Council a request by the Court to amend its Statute with a view to instituting an emergency preliminary ruling procedure.[112] Negotiations resulted in a Council Decision amending the Protocol on the Statute of the Court of Justice,[113] followed by amendments to the Court's Rules of Procedure.[114] The new framework allows, in particular with regard to preliminary rulings in Justice and Home Affairs matters, an urgent procedure at the request of the national court or, exceptionally, following the ECJ own motion.[115] Rulings will be given by a designated court Chamber, after hearing the Advocate General.[116]

[107] For a critical overview of the development of EU terrorist lists, see Guild, previous n.

[108] The impact of the judgment on Member States' discretion to choose the form of legislative action in the third pillar remains to be seen. It must be reminded in this context that the Court has accepted a wide range of discretion in the European Arrest Warrant case. However, there is a significant difference as that case involved the choice between two legally binding measures (a Convention and a Framework Decision). The solution may be different if the legal classification of a measure has a substantial impact on judicial protection.

[109] On this point, see also Peers, 'Salvation', n 82 above, p 898.

[110] Para 57. Commentators called the Court's rulings a 'Pyrrhic victory' for the applicants; see A Johnston, 'The European Union, the Ongoing Search for Terrorists' Assets and a Satisfactory Legal Framework: Getting Warmer or Colder?', *Cambridge Law Journal*, 2007, pp 523–525 at p 525.

[111] This issue was highlighted inter alia in a discussion paper presented by the Court in 2006 where it was noted that the average duration of preliminary ruling procedures has been reduced from 25.5 months in 2003 to 20.4 months in 2005—Mr V Skouris, President of the Court of Justice, Treatment of questions referred for a preliminary ruling concerning the area of freedom, security and justice, Council doc 13272/06, Brussels, 28 September 2006, p 2.

[112] Justice and Home Affairs Council Conclusions of 18 September 2007, p 15 (Council doc. 12604/07, Presse 194).

[113] OJ L24, 29 January 2008, p 42.

[114] OJ L24, 29 January 2008, p 39.

[115] For details see Rules of Procedure, new Art 104b inserted by the 2008 amendments.

[116] Art 104b(5). In cases of extreme urgency, the Chamber may decide to omit the written part of the procedure altogether—Art 104b(4).

According to an Information Note published by the Court, the urgent procedure should be requested 'only when it is absolutely necessary for the Court to give its ruling on the reference as quickly as possible', including cases where a person is detained or deprived of his liberty and where the answer to the question raised is decisive as to the assessment of the person's legal situation.[117] This new procedure may thus contribute significantly towards expediting procedures and achieving legal certainty in cases with significant impact on fundamental rights.[118]

IV. THE THIRD PILLAR AND THE CONSTITUTIONAL PRINCIPLES OF THE COMMUNITY: THE CONTRIBUTION OF THE COURT OF JUSTICE

Recent years have witnessed the proliferation of judgments from Luxembourg related to the third pillar. These judgments—which must be viewed in conjunction with case law by national courts, including constitutional courts—have played a major part in the development of the principles of EU criminal law. A central feature in this context has been the interpretation of the reach of the third pillar provisions (which, as explained above, form a more limited, less supranational framework than the Community law first pillar), and the determination of the applicability of first pillar, Community law principles to the third pillar.[119] The influence of the Court of Justice (and, where appropriate, national courts in the development of legal principles for the third pillar and EU criminal law more broadly will be examined in the relevant sections throughout this book. This section aims to provide a general overview of the development by the Court of such principles, by focusing in particular on the application of constitutional principles of (first pillar) Community law to the third pillar.[120] In this context, the development of the relationship between both the first and third pillars, but also between Union and national law are becoming increasingly significant.

A. Primacy

A question that would inevitably emerge in the context of the evolution of third pillar law is whether the latter has primacy over national law, in particular national constitutional law. This issue is particularly thorny in the light of the nature of the

---

[117] Information Note on References from National Courts fro a Preliminary Ruling. Supplement Following the Implementation of the Urgent Preliminary Ruling Procedure Applicable to References Concerning the Area of Freedom, Security and Justice, www.curia.europa.eu/instit/txtdocfr/txtsenvigueur/noteppu.pdf

[118] The Court has already applied the expedited procedure in a case involving the European Arrest Warrant—see the judgment of 17 July 2008 in Case C-66/08, *Kozlowski*.

[119] For details, see Mitsilegas, 'Constitutional Principles', n 62 above.

[120] The term 'constitutional principles of EC law' is understood to include 'systemic principles which underlie the constitutional structure of the Community and define the Community legal edifice'—T Tridimas, *The General Principles of EU Law*, 2nd edn, Oxford, Oxford University Press, 2006, p 4. Tridimas includes these principles as a sub-category of the general principles of Community law.

matters covered by the third pillar—being at the heart of State sovereignty and having considerable implications for both fundamental rights and national constitutional principles. Not surprisingly, it has been national constitutional and supreme courts that had to deal with primacy implications when examining the implementation of a flagship third pillar measure, the European Arrest Warrant Framework Decision, in their domestic legal orders. Different courts gave different solutions in the light of the domestic constitutional and legal framework—but no firm views on primacy have been offered. These courts began in varying degrees a constitutional dialogue with the Court of Justice with regard to the development of EU criminal law. However, as will be seen in chapter three, the Court's response to this dialogue in its own take on the European Arrest Warrant has been limited.[121] The Court has been more proactive in ruling on a different aspect of primacy, namely primacy of first pillar law over third pillar law. In a number of cases, dealing primarily with competence issues and legal basis disputes, the Court confirmed the primacy of the first pillar based on Article 47 TEU.[122]

B. Conferral in the Light of Effectiveness

The Court has had to rule in a number of high-profile cases on issues of conferral of competence in criminal matters. With the choice of pillars having significant repercussions for the powers of Union institutions, unsurprisingly these cases were prompted by efforts by EU institutions to boost their institutional prerogatives. In all these cases, the Court used first pillar principles and methods in order to allocate the appropriate legal basis. One line of case law concerned challenges by the Commission with regard to the choice of a third pillar legal basis for the adoption of legislation on the definition of criminal offences and the imposition of criminal sanctions—with the Court confirming first pillar competence in certain criminal matters twice, in the environmental crime and the ship-source pollution cases.[123] In both cases, effectiveness was central in the Court's reasoning. Rather than treating criminal law as a special case confined to the third pillar, the Court viewed it in the same way as any other field of law—*as a means to an end* towards the effectiveness of Community law.[124] Another case concerned an intervention by the European Parliament challenging the legal basis of an international agreement on PNR records concluded between the Community and the US under the first pillar. In this case, the Court applied the first pillar criteria in looking at the appropriate legal basis of an instrument, centred at the counter-terrorism

---

[121] For details, see ch 3.

[122] For details, see ch 2.

[123] For details, see ch 2.

[124] For further details, see ch 2. effectiveness also played a part in the Court's application of the first pillar principle of indirect effect to the third pillar. As will be seen below, in *Pupino* the Court linked effectiveness with the duty of loyal co-operation enshrined in Art 10 EC and justified the application of loyal co-operation in the third pillar—and subsequently indirect effect—on the grounds of the effective achievement of this time a Union objective—an ever closer Union as enshrined in Art 1 TEU.

focus of the agreement and went the opposite way to the previous cases ruling that the agreement should have been concluded under a third pillar legal basis.[125] These cases have had considerable implications for subsequent legislative action in criminal matters.

C. Fundamental Rights

Third pillar law is inextricably linked with issues related to the protection of fundamental rights. Such issues have arisen explicitly or implicitly in all cases involving EU criminal law. As seen above, one category of cases involves issues of fundamental rights as in judicial protection at EU level—concerning in particular access to the Luxembourg court and remedies. The Court has increasingly been trying to broaden avenues of judicial protection, with the issue of effective judicial protection becoming increasingly central. Another line of cases involves the implications of third pillar law on the rights of the defendant at *national* level. Major cases thus have involved the application of the European Arrest Warrant,[126] the rights of the defendant against the rights of the victim,[127] and the rights of the defendant in cases involving double jeopardy.[128] Two main—and not entirely consistent—trends can be discerned in this context. The first is the Court's assertions of the centrality of fundamental rights in EU law, including third pillar law (with the Court referring repeatedly to the ECHR, but also explicitly to the Charter of Fundamental Rights in the European Arrest Warrant case) and the obligations of national courts to take into account and uphold such rights. However, the second tendency of the Court is paradoxically to *limit* the applicability of these rights by ruling that aspects of third pillar law do not involve substantive criminal law, but *procedure*—therefore the special human rights safeguards reserved for criminal law do not apply.[129] This is a worrying trend, as it transforms criminal law to a field where maximum EU-led enforcement capacity is matched with a shrinking field of applicability of human rights safeguards.[130]

---

[125] For further details, see ch 6.

[126] See ch 3.

[127] See in particular *Pupino*, below.

[128] See ch 3.

[129] Note also the case law of the Court of First Instance regarding freezing orders: the Court has repeatedly held that as a precautionary measure, these measures do not constitute criminal sanctions and do not imply any accusation of a criminal nature (*Sison*, para 101; see also Case T-315/01, *Kadi v Council* [2005] II-3649, para 248 and Case T-306/01, *Yusuf and Al Barakaat International Foundation v Council* [2005] II-3533 para 299—the Court distinguished there between asset freezing and confiscation). The Court however has referred to the criminal procedure standards developed by the Strasbourg Court as a standard by which to interpret the extent of the obligation for a fair hearing in freezing decisions—Sison, para 182.

[130] On this point see V. Mitsilegas, 'The Transformation of Criminal Law in the 'Area of Freedom, Security and Justice', *Yearbook of European Law 2007*, vol 26, pp 1–32.

D. Loyal Co-operation and (in)Direct Effect—The Impact of Pupino

As said above, one of the fundamental differences between first and third pillar law is that, as is stated explicitly in the Treaty, Framework Decisions—the main legislative instrument in the third pillar and equivalent as to the form to Directives—do not have direct effect.[131] This limitation reflects Member States' sensitivity with regard to the potential effects of third pillar law. The limitation is significant as it restricts considerably the potential for enforcement of third pillar law by blocking avenues for individuals to challenge their legal position, resulting from EU criminal law, before domestic courts. With the Treaty referring only to direct effect and excluding it in the context of Framework Decisions, the question arises, however, of whether other principles of Community law ensuring the enforcement of EC law in national courts—such as indirect effect—apply to the third pillar.

The Luxembourg Court dealt with this issue in the *Pupino* judgment.[132] The case arose after a reference by an Italian court asking to what extent the Italian Code of Criminal Procedure could be interpreted, in the light of a Framework Decision on the standing of victims in criminal proceedings,[133] as allowing children allegedly having suffered a number of forms of abuse by their teacher to testify under a special procedure, and not in normal court proceedings, against the teacher. The Italian Code of Criminal Procedure allowed for this possibility for children (under 16) only in cases of sexual offences or offences with a sexual background. The Luxembourg Court was thus asked to decide whether, and in which terms, Framework Decisions entail indirect effect.

After asserting jurisdiction,[134] the Court accepted that the 'interpretative obligation' of national courts under Community law also extends to third pillar Framework Decision. The Court based its approach to a great extent on the binding character of Framework Decisions. It stressed that the wording of Article 34(2)(b) EU on Framework Decisions is very closely inspired by that of the third paragraph of Article 249 EC on Directives with Article 34(2)(b) EU conferring a binding character on Framework Decisions in the sense that they 'bind' the

[131] Art 34(2)(b) TEU. It is interesting that, while the judge-made principle of direct effect makes its appearance in the EU Treaty in this 'negative' manner.

[132] Case C-105/03, *Maria Pupino*, ECR [2005] I-5285. For commentaries on the case, see inter alia: S Prechal, 'Direct Effect, Indirect Effect, Supremacy and the Evolving Constitution of the European Union', in Barnard, (ed), *The Fundamentals of EU Law Revisited. Assessing the Impact of the Constitutional Debate*, Oxford, OUP, 2007, pp 35–70; Peers, 'Salvation', n 82 above; J R Spencer, 'Child Witnesses in the European Union', *Cambridge Law Journal*, 2005, 569–572; M Fletcher, 'Extending "Indirect Effect" to The Third Pillar: the Significance of *Pupino*?', *European Law Review*, vol 30, 2005, 862–877; *European Law Review* editorial, 'The Court of Justice and the third pillar', vol 30, 2005, 773–774; C Hillgruber, Anmerkung, *Juristenzeitung*, no 17, 2005, 841–844; D. Sarmiento, 'Un paso más en la constitucionalización del tercer pilar de la Union europea. La sentencia *Maria Pupino* y el efecto directo de las decisiones marco', *Revista electronica de estudios internacionales*, vol 10, 2005; and, more generally, H. Labayle, 'Architecte ou spectatrice? La Cour de justice de l'Union dans l'espace de liberté, sécurité et justice', *Revue trimestrielle du droit européen*, vol 42, 2006, pp 1–46.

[133] OJ L82, 22 March 2001, p 1.

[134] See paras 19–30 of the judgment—in particular on the applicability of the Art 234 TEC to the third pillar.

Member States 'as to the result to be achieved but shall leave to the national authorities the choice of form and methods'.[135] The Court then asserted that '*the binding character of framework decisions, formulated in terms identical to those of the third paragraph of Article 249 EC, places on national authorities, and particularly national courts, an obligation to interpret national law in conformity*' (emphasis added).[136] The limits placed on the jurisdiction of the Court do nothing to invalidate that conclusion.[137]

The Court backed up its conclusion with a further line of argumentation focusing on the need to achieve the objectives of the Union effectively, which is linked to the principle of loyal co-operation. According to the Court, *irrespective of the degree of integration envisaged by the Treaty of Amsterdam*, it is perfectly comprehensible that the authors of TEU should have considered it useful to make provision, in the context of Title VI of that Treaty, for recourse to legal instruments with effects *similar to those provided for by the EC Treaty, in order to contribute effectively to the Union's objectives.*[138] As with its case law on *ne bis in idem*, the Court seems to have adopted a rather ahistorical approach to European integration, effectively arguing that the degree of integration envisaged by Member States when signing the Amsterdam Treaty is irrelevant.[139] In this context, the Court stated that it would be difficult for the Union to carry out the task of creating an ever closer Union (enshrined in Article 1TEU) effectively if the principle of loyal co-operation—which is enshrined in Article 10 of the EC Treaty—were not also binding in the area of police and judicial co-operation in criminal matters.[140] On the basis of these arguments, the Court asserted that the principle of conforming interpretation is binding in relation to framework decisions.[141]

Having applied the Community law principle of interpretative obligation to the third pillar, the Court referred to first pillar case law to set out, in a manner similar to the first pillar, the limits and contours of indirect effect.[142] The Court reiterated that the interpretative obligation of national courts is limited by general principles of law, such as legal certainty and non-retroactivity, adding that in particular, those principles prevent that obligation from leading to the criminal liability of persons who contravene the provisions of a Framework Decision from being determined or aggravated on the basis of such decision alone, independently of an implementing law.[143] However, the Court, following the Opinion of AG Kokott,[144] noted that in the context of the present case *do not concern the extent*

---

[135] Para 33.
[136] Para 34.
[137] Para 35.
[138] Para 36.
[139] On the *ne bis in idem* case law, see ch 3.
[140] Paras 41 and 42.
[141] Para 43.
[142] For an analysis see inter alia G Betlem, 'The Doctrine of Consistent Interpretation—Managing Legal Uncertainty', *Oxford Journal of Legal Studies*, vol 22, 2002, 397–418.
[143] Paras 44 and 45, including references to the Court's case law.
[144] Opinion delivered on 11 November 2005, ECR [2005] I-5285, para 42.

of criminal liability of the person concerned but the conduct of the proceedings and the means of taking evidence.[145] Further in the judgment, the Court stated that the principle of conforming interpretation *cannot serve as the basis for an interpretation of national law contra legem.* Following its recent judgment in *Pfeiffer,*[146] the Court qualified this limitation however by adding that indirect effect does require that, where necessary, *the national court consider the whole of national law* in order to assess how far it can be applied in such a way as not to produce a result contrary to that envisaged by the framework decision.[147]

Having established the principle and its limits, the Court went on to examine the specific case.[148] It confirmed that the achievement of the aims of the Framework Decision on the rights of victims in criminal proceedings require that a national court should be able, in respect of particularly vulnerable victims, to use a special procedure, such as the one provided for already in Italian law.[149] However, in the light of the concerns raised regarding the potential impact of such interpretation on the rights of the defendant, the Court added two caveats: that, in the light of the Framework Decision, the adopted conditions for giving evidence must be compatible with the basic legal principles of the Member State;[150] and that the national court must ensure that the application of those measures is not likely to 'make the criminal proceedings against Mrs Pupino, considered as a whole, unfair within the meaning of Article 6 of the [ECHR], as interpreted by the European Court of Human Rights'.[151]

This is a landmark ruling from Luxembourg. The Court did not hesitate to transplant Community law to the third pillar, by stating that Framework Decisions entail indirect effect. This is notwithstanding the fact that the third pillar itself excludes the application of direct effect—the basic Community law principle whose limits are inextricably linked with the development of the indirect effect concept by the ECJ. It is also irrespective of the degree of integration the States signatory to the Amsterdam Treaty wished to achieve in criminal matters— the Court disassociates the envisaged degree of integration in Amsterdam from the need to ensure the effective achievement of Union objectives. The reasoning of the Court is noteworthy, especially the emphasis on the principle of loyal co-operation. The principle is enshrined in Article 10 of the EC Treaty, but not in the third pillar—the Court seems to apply loyal co-operation by analogy to the third pillar, based not on the specific objective of developing the Union as an 'area of freedom, security and justice', but rather on the very general provision of Article 1

---

[145] Para 46.

[146] Cases C-397/01 to C-403/01, *Pfeiffer et al v Deutsches Rotes Kreuz,* ECR [2004] I-8835, in particular para 115. For a commentary see the case-note of Sacha Prechal, *Common Market Law Review,* vol 42, 2005, 1445–1463.

[147] Para 47 (emphasis added). See also Fletcher, n 132 above, p 873.

[148] Paras 50–61.

[149] Para 56.

[150] Para 57. The Court referred to Art 8(4) of the Framework Decision.

[151] Para 60. In the preceding paras the Court stressed the fact that according to Art 6(2) TEU the Union respects fundamental rights and that the Framework Decision must be interpreted in a way that fundamental rights are respected (paras 58 and 59).

TEU calling for the establishment of an 'ever closer Union'.[152] By focusing on the principle of loyal co-operation, the Court not only emphasises the importance of the effective achievement of Treaty objectives (only this time these involve the *Union* and not the Community);[153] similarly to the *Pfeiffer* ruling,[154] the Court also avoids linking indirect effect with the primacy of Union law over national law.[155] The Court's silence in this regard may indicate that, as with the issue of the application of State liability in the third pillar,[156] the primacy issue remains open.[157]

The impact of the application of the interpretative obligation of the *national* judge in this case is striking. The Luxembourg Court has in reality re-written the Italian Code of Criminal Procedure. Following the Court's guidance the domestic judge has little choice but allow minors in this case to take advantage of the Code's protective provisions, although they were not covered by the legislation. This has led to the criticism that in fact the Court confers not indirect, but direct effect to the Framework Decision—in stark breach of the wording of Article 34 TEU.[158] The Court seems to overcome potential obstacles caused by the argument that adding a category of privileged witnesses to the Italian Code of Criminal

[152] See K Lenaerts and T Corthaut, 'Of Birds and Hedges: The Role of Primacy in Invoking Norms of EU Law', *European Law Review*, vol 31, 2006, 287–315. This reasoning has been heavily criticised by the *European Law Review* editorial (n 132 above), where it is stated that Art 1 TEU is not subject to the Court's jurisdiction (Art 46 TEU). Fletcher (n 132 above, p 71) also criticises the emphasis on loyal co-operation, by arguing that the third pillar covers co-operation *between* Member States. However, this seems to be an extremely 'intergovernmental' view of the third pillar, whose system indeed shares a number of common features with the first pillar and laws stemming from it represent a further degree of integration from international law instruments.

[153] For an interesting use of the duty of loyal co-operation in the context of first pillar measures with a criminal law dimension, see inter alia the judgments of the Court of First Instance in *OMPI* (n 106 above, para 122 f) and *Sison* (above n 94, para 17 f). Referring to *Pupino*, the Court held that on the basis of loyal co-operation it is in principle for the national courts to ensure the observance of fair hearing rights in the context of EU counter-terrorism listing measures—however, Luxembourg will be involved in cases where the Council bases its initial decision or a subsequent decision to freeze funds on information or evidence communicated to it by representatives of the Member States without it having been assessed by the competent national authority.

[154] See Prechal, case note, n 146 above.

[155] See Labayle, n 42 above, p 31. See also Lenaerts and Corthaut, n 152 above. The authors argue that

the Court could have avoided this frantic search for a ground for an equivalent provision, if it had recognised that the duty of consistent interpretation is inherent in any hierarchy of norms and thus a simple corollary of the principle of primacy in that it is the easiest way to ensure that no inconsistent national laws are applied over EU law (p 293).

[156] Prechal takes the view that the application of loyalty can form the basis of State liability: Prechal, 'Direct Effect, Indirect Effect', n 132 above, p 61.

[157] Peers ('Salvation' n 82 above, p 920) argues that primacy or the connected obligation to set aside national law in order to apply Community law does not apply to the third pillar. He makes the valid point that if these principles (and direct effect) applied to the third pillar, the essential distinctions between the first and third pillars would be lost and the intentions of the Treaty authors would clearly be ignored. A diametrically opposite view with regard to supremacy is put forward by Prechal, who also seems in favour of disapplication unless fundamental rights or general principles oppose such a disapplication or where the solution of the case would require the application of a Framework Decision—and not national law—to the facts of the case: Prechal, 'Direct Effect, Indirect Effect', n 132 above, pp 62–63.

[158] Sarmiento, n 132 above.

Procedure in the face of the silence of the Code in this regard would in fact be *contra legem*, by using the *Pfeiffer* formula that the national judge must consider national law 'as a whole'. However, this raises important questions regarding the impact of such consideration on the internal coherence of national criminal justice systems, whose balance may be disturbed by piecemeal attempts of national judges to accommodate Union law demands in specific cases. Judges themselves may be faced with difficult balancing exercises, especially in cases where Union law itself—as in the case of the Framework Decision in question—is drafted in broad terms, having to take into account all complex parameters and interests involved in a criminal trial.

In this balancing of competing interests, *Pupino* raises a number of questions regarding safeguarding the rights of the defendant in the development of the European Union as an 'area of freedom, security and justice'. In *Pupino*, it appears that the interpretation would emphasise the rights of the alleged victims at the expense of the rights of the defendant. The position of the defendant may become even worse if the legislative output of the third pillar continues to focus predominantly on enforcement/security aspects, rather than instruments protective of rights.[159] Moreover, in the light of the current focus on security, indirect effect may serve to stress the emphasis on enforcement. For instance, national courts may be asked to use indirect effect to supersede national implementing legislation on the European Arrest Warrant which may contain further safeguards for the individual than the actual EU Framework Decision. The Commission has already criticised a number of Member States for adding further safeguards in implementing laws (such as human rights protection as a ground for refusal of the execution of a European Arrest Warrant) as incompatible with the principle of mutual recognition.[160]

These concerns are accentuated by the limits posed by the Court in existing case law safeguards regarding indirect effect and criminal law. In *Pupino*, the Court seemed to transpose all the first pillar safeguards limiting indirect effect in criminal law cases, but then substantially qualified its position by stating that the present case *does not involve criminal law per se*, but the gathering of evidence, ie criminal procedure.[161] This narrow framing of protection in the criminal justice

---

[159] Indeed, the fact that negotiations on the Commission proposal on the rights of the defendant in criminal proceedings have stalled may be attributed partly (along with the weak legal basis) to Member States' reluctance to agree on an instrument that may have far-reaching consequences for their domestic legal system, especially post-Pupino. See V Mitsilegas, 'Trust-building Measures in the European Judicial Area in Criminal Matters: Issues of Competence, Legitimacy and Inter-institutional Balance', in S Carrera and T Balzacq, *Security versus Freedom? A Challenge for Europe's Future*, Aldershot, Ashgate, 2006, at pp 287–288.

[160] See 'Report from the Commission based on Art 34 of the Council Framework Decision of 13 June 2002 on the European Arrest Warrant and the surrender procedures between Member States' COM (2005) 63 final, Brussels, 23 February 2005 and SEC (2005) 267; and the subsequent 'Report from the Commission on the implementation since 2005 of the Council Framework Decision of 13 June 2002 on the European Arrest Warrant and the surrender procedures between Member States' COM (2007) 407 final, Brussels, 11 July 2007 and SEC (2007) 979.

[161] The question arises here of how the Court's approach in the first pillar cases setting limits to indirect effect to protect the individual, in particular *Berlusconi* (Cases C-387/02, C-391/02 and C-403/02, ECR [2005] I-3565) will apply to first pillar criminal law after the environmental crime case (for an

process raises particular concerns: not only is it at times difficult to disassociate aspects of criminal law from criminal procedure, but, more importantly, it is questionable to exclude the application of principles such as legal certainty, non-retroactivity and aggravation of a person's criminal liability from the criminal process and limit them, as the Court does, to 'the extent of the criminal liability of the person concerned' in the light of the significant consequences that the criminal process may have for the individual. This approach may be the source of serious clashes between national protective provisions—potentially constitutionally enshrined—and third pillar law, especially in the light of the increased focus on enforcement.

V. THE POLITICS OF THE THIRD PILLAR: MEMBER STATES' SECURITY AMBITION VERSUS INSTITUTIONAL CHECKS AND LIMITS

The gradual and contested institutional developments in EU criminal law as reflected in the evolution of the third pillar have been combined with increasing activity at the level of politics and strategy by Member States' governments. This activity has been prominent both within and outside the EU framework. Within the EU framework, governments have been proactive in defining strategy and policy targets within the framework of the European Council—which has determined the two major political blueprints for the development of EU Justice and Home Affairs, the five-year plans of action adopted in Tampere in 1999 and The Hague in 2004. Moreover, governments have developed a number of Action Plans as a response to events such as 9/11 and the need to provide an imminent reaction to them. Outside the EU framework, the Schengen example has been followed by similar concerted action by a number of Member States in the field of police co-operation recently. Moreover, large Member States meet regularly outside the EU framework and discuss priorities in the field. This section will focus on the impact of government initiative both within and outside the EU legal framework, and examine the implications of such action in the light of the current EU institutional framework in criminal matters.

A. Action Inside the EU Framework

A major actor influencing the direction of legislation and policy in EU Justice and Home Affairs in general and EU criminal law in particular has been the European Council.[162] Central to the development of EU action in Justice and Home Affairs

---

analysis, see ch 2). Lenaerts and Corthaut (n 152 above, p 312) are of the view that the limits posed by the Court will be applicable in these cases, assuming that first pillar criminal law will be limited to the determination of criminal liability.

[162] On the role of the European Council in EU Justice and Home Affairs, see J Monar, 'Decision-making in the Area of Freedom, Security and Justice', in Arnull and Wincott, n 54 above, pp 63–80.

has been the adoption by the European Council of two detailed, five-year legislative and policy programmes outlined in the Tampere European Council Conclusions in 1999[163] and in the successor to Tampere, the 2004 Hague Programme.[164] The strategy adopted by the European Council has thus been to provide political impetus for the development of the objective to develop the Union as an 'area of freedom, security and justice' via the adoption of target-setting mechanisms outlining long-term, detailed directives for law and policy development.[165] The agenda put forward in Tampere, but also to a lesser extent in the Hague, has been markedly ambitious, with the Programmes calling for the adoption of a plethora of EU legislative measures. However, this ambitious agenda did not sit comfortably with the considerable institutional limitations described earlier in this chapter. What the Member States' governments proclaimed in the European Council did not necessarily coincide with the powers they were prepared to grant to the EU in the third pillar—nor has it always led to the political will to translate the European Council mandate to third pillar law. This has been particularly the case with measures giving rights to individuals.[166]

Along with these all-encompassing Programmes, the European Council has provided further political impetus for developing EU criminal law by the adoption of detailed Action Plans promulgated as a response to phenomena framed as threats in a particular moment. In the 1990s, a major example has been the adoption, in 1997, of an Action Plan to fight organised crime.[167] In the 2000s, when terrorism replaced

[163] For the text of the Conclusions, see www.europarl.europa.eu/summits/tam_en.htm On the background, see House of Lords European Union Committee (then Select Committee on the European Communities), *Prospects for the Tampere Special European Council*, 19th Report, session 1998–99, HL Paper 101; see also Mitsilegas, Monar, Rees, n 1 above, pp 91–95.

[164] OJ C53, 3 March 2005, p 1. For details, see House of Lords European Union Committee, *The Hague Programme: A Five Year Agenda for EU Justice and Home Affairs*, 10th Report, session 2004–05, HL Paper 84. On different aspects of the Hague Programme, see also J W de Zwaan and F A N J Goudappel (eds), *Freedom, Security and Justice in the European Union*, The Hague, TCM Asser Press, 2006; T Balzacq and S Carrera, 'The Hague Programme: The Long Road to Freedom, Security and Justice', in Balzacq and Carrera, n 159 above, pp 1–34; D Bigo, 'Liberty, whose Liberty? The Hague Programme and the Conception of Freedom', in Balzacq and Carrera, n 159 above, pp 35–44; and V Mitsilegas, 'Operational Co-operation and Counter-terrorism in the EU', in F Pastore (ed), *Supranational Counter-Terrorism. A Test under Duress For EU Principles and Institutions*, CeSPI Working Paper 22/2005, Rome, Centro Studi di Political Internazionale (CeSPI), pp 10–20, at www.cespi.it.

[165] On the target setting function of Action Plans and Programmes in EU Justice and Home Affairs, see J Monar, *Specific Factors, Typology and Development Trends of Modes of Governance in the EU Justice and Home Affairs Domain*, NEWGOV Deliverable 01/17, May 2006, at www.eu-newgov.org/database/DELIV/D01D17_Emergence_NMG_in_JHA.pdf.http://www.eu-newgov.org/database/DELIV/D01D17_Emergence_NMG_in_JHA.pdf

[166] See in particular in this context the failure to adopt the Framework Decision on the rights of the defendant in criminal proceedings—which according to the Hague Programme should be adopted by the end of 2005. For details on the proposal, see ch 2.

[167] OJ C251, 15 August 1997, p 1. This was followed by the so-called 'Millennium' Action Plan on the Prevention and Control of Organised Crime, OJ C124, 3 May 2000, p 1. On the Action Plan, see Mitsilegas, Monar and Rees, n 1 above, pp 88–91; see also W C Gilmore, 'The EU Action Plan to Combat Organised Crime: The Scope and Implementation of Legal Instruments', in E Bort and R Keat (eds), *The Boundaries of Understanding. Essays in Honour of Malcolm Anderson*, The University of Edinburgh Social Sciences Institute, 1999, pp 97–106.

organised crime as the major threat in the political vocabulary, the European Council adopted an Action Plan to combat terrorism.[168] Both Action Plans were detailed and contained calls for a wide range of EU legislative action. The terrorism Action Plan was also followed by detailed implementation 'Roadmaps' and was regularly updated.[169] Each major attack in this decade—in New York, Madrid, London—was followed by a swift intervention by the European Council and calls for the adoption of further measures at EU level.[170] It is noteworthy in this context that, in both the cases of organised crime and terrorism, the European Council followed the strategy of framing a wide range of issues—not all of which were closely linked with fighting organised crime or terrorism specifically—as necessary EU responses, with the Action Plans thus calling for—and at times facilitating—the adoption of measures having a much broader scope and which have been justified as essential to fight organised crime or terrorism. As will be seen in a number of occasions in this book, the fight against terrorism rationale has justified and led to the swift adoption of measures as disparate as the Framework Decision on the European Arrest Warrant,[171] the Decision establishing Eurojust,[172] and a series of measures boosting police co-operation between the authorities of Member States.[173] Moreover, the terrorism Action Plans have included measures transcending the third pillar and covering the other two pillars as well, blurring the boundaries between criminal law and the market, but also between criminal law and foreign policy.[174] Framing a wide range of measures as essential to fight terrorism, responding to terrorist attacks with further calls for EU legislation, and revising the relevant Action Plans regularly all have contributed towards the adoption of a wide range of EU criminal law measures in the recent past.

In examining the outcome of this strategy, two major issues arise: the issue of securitisation[175] and the issue of scrutiny and transparency in the shaping of law

---

[168] Conclusions and Plan of Action of the Extraordinary Meeting on September 21, 2001, at http://www.consilium.europa.eu/ueDocs/cms_data/docs/pressData/en/ec/140.en.pdf www.consilium.europa.eu/ueDocs/cms_data/docs/pressData/en/ec/140.en.pdf.

[169] See R Bossong, 'The Action Plan on Combating Terrorism: A Flawed Instrument of EU Security Governance', *Journal of Common Market Studies*, vol 46, no1, 2008, pp 27–48.

[170] On the EU's reaction post-9/11 see B Gilmore, *The Twin Towers and the Third Pillar: Some Security Agenda Developments*, EUI Working Paper Law no.2003/7, Florence, European University Institute, 2003; and S Douglas-Scott, 'The Rule of Law in the European Union—Putting the Security into the 'Area of Freedom, Security and Justice'', *European Law Review*, vol 29, 2004, pp 219–242. On the EU response to the Madrid bombings see House of Lords European Union Committee, *After Madrid: the EU's Response to Terrorism*, 5th Report, session 2004–05, HL Paper 53.

[171] See ch 3.

[172] See ch 4.

[173] See ch 5.

[174] On the nexus between criminal law and the market in EU counter-terrorism efforts, in particular in the context of the fight against terrorist finance, see V Mitsilegas and B Gilmore, 'The EU Legislative Framework Against Money Laundering and Terrorist Finance: A Critical Analysis in the Light of Evolving Global Standards' *International and Comparative Law Quarterly*, vol 56, 2007, pp 119–141; on the nexus between the second and third pillars, see J Monar, 'Common Threat and Common Response? The European Union's Counter-Terrorism Strategy and its Problems', *Government and Opposition*, vol 42, no3, 2007, pp 292–313.

[175] On the securitisation process, see section II above.

and policy. On the first issue, an examination not only of the sectoral Action Plans on organised crime and terrorism, but also of the general five-year programmes, in particular the Hague Programme, reveals that the primary emphasis of the development of EU action is on security.[176] In terms of the sectoral Action Plans, such emphasis is perhaps unsurprising given the fact that, at least in terms of political discourse, these initiatives are the outcome of a securitisation process constituting blueprints for urgent responses to threats perceived to be in need of imminent combat. In terms of action to combat terrorism, the increasing blurring of boundaries between pillars—in particular the second and the third pillar— leads to important issues of accountability and judicial control.[177] Moreover, this process of securitisation has seeped through the formulation of the general EU strategy on criminal law. A prime example of such spill-over has been the Hague Programme: much less coherent than Tampere, large sectors of the Programme are devoted to specific issues such as boosting of operational action and co-operation, the exchange of personal data for police purposes and the development of inter-agency co-operation for security purposes.[178] On the contrary, the Hague Programme includes notably much less with regard to the protection of fundamental rights in this context.

The other matter of concern in the development of the EU policy—and subsequently legislative—agenda in criminal matters, especially in the light of the increasing securitisation in the field, is the lack of detailed scrutiny and transparency of the action of the European Council. While there has been—at least with regard to general Programmes such as the Hague Programme, some intervention by the EU institutions (and national parliaments) prior to the final adoption of the final documents,[179] the development of avenues of meaningful, detailed and open debate on the direction of EU criminal law leaves much to be desired. In this context, the process of formulating the new five-year Justice and Home Affairs Programme to follow the Hague Programme in 2009 is noteworthy: the process is driven by Interior Ministers of a number of Member States, who constituted a 'Future Group' to prepare recommendations to influence the formulation of the new programme.[180] The dominance of the interior ministries agenda in this con-

---

[176] On Tampere, see the warnings in a *Common Market Law Review* editorial entitled 'The Tampere Summit: The Ties that Bind *or* The Policemen's Ball', vol 36, 1999, pp 1119–1126; on security and the Hague Programme see in particular Bigo, 'Liberty, Whose Liberty', n 164 and Mitsilegas, 'Operational Co-operation', n 164 above.

[177] On judicial control with regard to cross-pillar measures involving the second and third pillar, see B III d (the role of the ECJ). On the cross-pillar aspect of inter-agency co-operation, see ch 4.

[178] On these aspects, see chs 4 and 5.

[179] See for instance the pre-Hague Commission Communication entitled 'Area of Freedom, Security and Justice: Assessment of the Tampere Programme and Future Orientations' COM (2004) 401 final, Brussels, 2 June 2004. For examples of national parliamentary scrutiny, see the House of Lords EU Committee Reports on Tampere and Hague.

[180] The Future Group—created in 2007 after the proposal of the German government and the Commission—was co chaired by the Vice President of the Commission responsible for Justice and Home Affairs and the Minister of the Interior of the acting EU Presidency. It brought together the Ministers of the Interior of the two current trios of Presidencies (Germany, Portugal, Slovenia; France, the Czech Republic, Sweden) and a representative of the future Presidency trio—it is thus evident that

text is evident, with the absence of Justice Ministers being striking.[181] More broadly of course it is clear that the development of key guidelines for future law and policy is largely taking place behind closed doors, mostly by experts and government officials.

B. Action Outside the EU Framework

Issues of transparency and democratic control have also arisen in instances where the primary impetus for the development of EU law and policy in criminal matters has come from *outside* the EU framework. A prime example of this process has been Schengen. As was mentioned earlier in this chapter, the Schengen Agreement and Convention and their implementing measures were adopted by certain EU Member States outside the Community—and then the Union—law framework. In Amsterdam, the Schengen *acquis* was effectively imported into the Community/Union legal order—which had to accommodate as a fait accompli a complex legal framework—and a potent logic of compensatory measures—which had been agreed and developed with a minimum of transparency and outside the EU scrutiny mechanisms.[182] Even post EU incorporation, fundamental aspects of the Schengen mechanism—in particular judging whether a country meets the criteria for becoming a full Schengen member—remain essentially intergovernmental, with membership being subject to the agreement of the existing Schengen full members.[183] A similar example of action à la Schengen has been the recent efforts to introduce in Union law the Prüm Convention, which was concluded by a number of EU Member States, again outside the Union framework.[184] As with Schengen, far-reaching standards agreed outside the EU framework are now being

not all Member States took part. Further participants were a common law observer (the UK), the President of the European Parliament Civil Liberties Committee and a representative of the Council General Secretariat. On the setting up of the Future Group, see M Niemeier, *La sécurité intérieure dans l'union européenne: après la présidence allemande et avant la présidence française*, Université Robert Schuman, Strasbourg, Collection Securint, Working Paper No.6, 2008.

[181] A parallel 'Future Group' on Justice was also established in 2007, at the initiative of the Portuguese EU Presidency—the membership logic was similar to the 'police' future group. Issues arising from interior and justice ministries were thus seemingly not integrated into a single discussion forum, but discussed separately. Both Reports were discussed at the Justice and Home Affairs Council of 24–25 July 2008 (Council doc 11653/08 Presse 205), pp 18 and 24. However, it is noteworthy that the Reports were still not publicly available on the Council documents website by the end of July 2008.

[182] With the decision on the integration of the Schengen *acquis* into the Community/Union framework being taken at the 1996 IGC. It is noteworthy that the Schengen Protocol containing rules on the allocation of the *acquis* in the respective pillars did not provide any role for the European Parliament—see in this context—and more generally on the implications of Schengen and Prüm for the EU democratic deficit, A Weyembergh and V Santamaria, 'Le contrôle démocratique dans l'espace pénal européen', in M Doni and L S Rossi, *Démocratie, cohérence et transparence: vers une constitutionnalisation de l'Union européenne?*, Brussels, Institut d'Études européennes, 2008, pp 73–92.

[183] On the basis of peer reviews conducted by Member States—on these reviews in the context of the increased centrality of evaluation mechanisms in EU criminal law, see the part on the Lisbon Treaty below.

[184] On Prüm, see ch 5.

introduced in the EU with minimal scrutiny and consultation—this time by the Council as third pillar legislator, rather than by Member States in the Intergovernmental Confernce (IGC). Prüm is perhaps more striking, in that it comes in a period where European integration in criminal matters has somewhat matured and the need for greater transparency and democratic control has been ascertained repeatedly in the context of the EU constitutional debate.[185] Even at this stage of European integration, it seems that the big countries are happy to lead the way outside the EU framework, subject to minimal scrutiny. This happens in particular in the context of the meetings of the G6, namely the United Kingdom, France, Germany, Italy, Spain and Poland. At regular meetings, the Interior Ministers of these countries discuss matters of common interest and reach agreement in principle on fundamental home affairs choices which can subsequently be imported—on the basis of the political strength of the G6 *inside* the EU legal framework. A prime example of such strategy has been the consensus on the need to maximise the exchange of personal data at a meeting at the German Baltic resort of Heiligendamm—a meeting, which as the House of Lords European Union Committee has noted, took place 'behind closed doors'.[186]

VI. THE FUTURE IN THE LIGHT OF LISBON

One of the central issues in the recent debate over the constitutional future of the European Union has been the future of the institutional framework underpinning EU Justice and Home Affairs, in particular with regard to the third pillar. These issues were discussed in detail within the framework of the Convention on the Future of Europe, which resulted into a 'blueprint' Treaty which formed the basis for the negotiations of the Constitutional Treaty.[187] Convention proceedings included the establishment of a specific Working Party on Justice and Home Affairs. Its final report recommended sweeping changes to the current legal and institutional framework, including the 'communitarisation' of decision-making and judicial control and the alignment of the third pillar legislative instruments with those proposed for the first pillar.[188] The Report also advocated inter alia an increased focus on the implementation of EU criminal law, including via the establishment of peer review mechanisms, and the enhancement of the role of national parliaments in scrutinising the development of legislation in the field.[189]

---

[185] On calls for further 'communautarisation' of the third pillar, see the part on the Lisbon Treaty below.

[186] House of Lords European Union Committee, *Behind Closed Doors: The Meeting of the G6 Interior Ministers at Heiligendamm*, 40th Report, session 2005–06, HL Paper 221.

[187] On the Convention on the Future of Europe, see in particular J Shaw, P Magnette, L Hoffmann and A Vergés Bausili, *The Convention on the Future of Europe. Working Towards an EU Constitution*, London The Federal Trust, 2003.

[188] Final Report of Working Group X 'Freedom, Security and Justice', CONV 426/02, WG X 14, Brussels, 2 December 2002.

[189] ibid.

The Convention's recommendations on Justice and Home Affairs were reflected to a great extent in the text of the Constitutional Treaty, which is now dead.[190] However, the provisions of the Constitutional Treaty are largely reflected in the Lisbon Treaty which, if it enters into force, will bring about major changes in the field.[191] The new legal framework consists mainly of two Treaties:[192] one on the European Union (TEU), containing general constitutional provisions and specific provisions on foreign policy, and another on the Functioning of the European Union (TFEU), containing mainly provisions on the different EU policies and areas of action.[193] A major change introduced by the new Treaty framework is the abolition of the current pillar structure.[194] This change has major implications for third pillar law: with the third pillar abolished, rules on police and judicial co-operation in criminal matters are—in principle at least—aligned with the 'ordinary' first pillar framework—with EU criminal law thus becoming 'communitarised'. A closer look at the Treaty reveals however that the undoubtedly significant 'communautarisation' of the third pillar is far from unqualified, with a number of 'intergovernmental' elements remaining. It is in this context that this part will examine the major changes brought about by the Lisbon Treaty to the third pillar: an examination of the elements 'communitarising' the third pillar will be followed by an overview of the number of instances where such 'communautarisation' is met with resistance in the Treaty. Prior to doing so however, it is essential to examine the general provisions of Lisbon with regard to the development of the Union as an 'area of freedom, security and justice'.

A. The 'Area of Freedom, Security and Justice'

The development of the Union as an 'area of freedom, security and justice' not only continues to feature in the Lisbon Treaty, but it can be said that it has assumed a rather prominent position therein. The 'area of freedom, security and

---

[190] On the Area of Freedom, Security and Justice in the Constitutional Treaty, see J Monar, 'Justice and Home Affairs in the EU Constitutional Treaty. What Added Value for the 'Area of Freedom, Security and Justice'?', *European Constitutional Law Review*, vol 1, 2005, pp 226–246. More specifically on EU criminal law, see M Kaiafa-Gbandi, 'The Treaty Establishing a Constitution for Europe and Challenges for Criminal Law at the Commencement of 21st Century', *European Journal of Crime, Criminal Law and Criminal Justice*, vol 13, no 4, 2005, pp 483–514. On the Constitutional Treaty in the broader context of the evolution of the Area of Freedom, Security and Justice see N Walker, 'In Search of the Area of Freedom, Security and Justice: A Constitutional Odyssey', in N Walker (ed), *Europe's Area of Freedom, Security and Justice*, Oxford, OUP, 2004, pp 3–40.

[191] For the consolidated version of the Lisbon Treaty, see OJ C115, 9 May 2008, p 1.

[192] And, of course, of a series of Protocols and Declarations annexed therein. For the purposes of this book the term Lisbon Treaty will encompass both the TEU and the TFEU.

[193] For commentaries on the Lisbon Treaty, see P Craig, 'The Treaty of Lisbon: Process, Architecture and Substance', *European Law Review*, vol 33, 2008, pp 137–166; M Dougan, 'The Treaty of Lisbon 2007: Winning Minds, Not Hearts', *Common Market Law Review*, vol 45, 2008, pp 617–703; House of Lords European Union Committee, *The Treaty of Lisbon: An Impact Assessment*, Volume 1, 10th Report, session 2007–08, HL Paper 62-I.

[194] Although special rules largely apply for matters of Common Foreign and Security Policy (CFSP).

justice' appears early on in the new EU Treaty, high on the list of the Union's stated objectives: according to Article 3(2) TEU, the Union will

> *offer its citizens* an area of freedom, security and justice without internal frontiers, in which *the free movement of persons is ensured* in conjunction with appropriate measures with respect to external border controls, asylum, immigration and *the prevention and combating of crime*.[195]

The 'Area of Freedom, Security and Justice' also constitutes the heading of Title V TFEU, which contains the provisions on Justice and Home Affairs (including areas currently under the third pillar).[196] The opening Article states that the Union will

> constitute an area of freedom, security and justice with respect for fundamental rights and the different legal systems and traditions of the Member States.[197]

It also contains three more paragraphs aiming to provide a categorisation of the areas covered by the field: borders, immigration and asylum;[198] criminal law, placed under the logic of ensuring a' high level of security';[199] and civil law, under the banner of the facilitation of 'access to justice'.[200] This rather superficial categorisation is striking in that it seems to link 'freedom' (which is however not expressly mentioned in the relevant paragraph) with internal frontiers, immigration and asylum; 'security' with criminal law; and 'justice' with civil law.

What, if any, conclusions can be drawn with regard to the future direction of EU action in Justice and Home Affairs—whose prominence in the EU agenda Lisbon seems to confirm—and the relationship between freedom, security and justice from the general provisions of the Lisbon Treaty? First of all, the emphasis in Article 3(2) TEU on the Union 'offering' an area of freedom, security and justice to its citizens is noteworthy: it implies a positive duty for the EU, but also a duty geared only to EU citizens (and not necessarily to third country nationals). Moreover, the Treaty retains the emphasis on the concept of an 'area', with Article 3(2) TEU again linking Union Justice and Home Affairs law—including criminal law—with free movement. However, this link is less explicit in the actual Title V TFEU, in particular Article 67: there, freedom is strikingly absent from the specific provision on criminal law (it is even absent from the provision on immigration); justice is also absent; criminal law is specifically, and exclusively, linked with security in Article 67(3) TFEU. However, this overtly 'securitised' discourse is tempered

---

[195] Emphasis added.

[196] According to Art 4(2)(j) TFEU, the area of freedom, security and justice is an area of shared competence between the Union and Member States. However, Declaration 36 annexed to the Treaty confirms that Member States, may negotiate and conclude agreements with third countries or international organisations in the field of police and judicial co-operation in criminal matters in so far as these agreements comply with Union law. Moreover, Title V itself also contains an area of supporting action in criminal matters, crime prevention—Art 84 TFEU. However, crime prevention is not listed ain the areas of supporting action outlined in Art 6 TFEU. On the legal issues arising from the provisions on shared competence in the Lisbon Treaty, see Craig, n 193 above, pp 145–147.

[197] Art 67(1).

[198] Art 67(2).

[199] Art 67(3).

[200] Art 67(4).

by two broader Treaty provisions: the provision on the values of the Union, which include human dignity, freedom, the rule of law and respect for fundamental rights (but notably not security);[201] and the provision incorporating the Charter of Fundamental Rights into Union law and providing a legal basis for the accession of the Union to the ECHR.[202] While the precise impact of these provisions to the reconfiguration of the relationship between freedom, security and justice in the EU remains to be seen, they provide useful tools for taking into account fundamental rights in the development and interpretation of the EU 'Area of Freedom, Security and Justice' provisions. The role of the Court of Justice will be central in this context.

B. The 'Communautarisation' of the Third Pillar

The Lisbon Treaty introduces a number of major changes in the role of EU institutions in criminal matters, 'comunautarising' to a great extent the third pillar. The first major change concerns *decision-making*, which, for the vast majority of Title V measures will take place under the 'ordinary' legislative procedure, ie co-decision between the Council (which will decide by majority voting) and the European Parliament.[203] This represents a considerable strengthening of the role of the European Parliament, which effectively is granted a right of veto. The ordinary legislative procedure largely applies to law-making in the fields of mutual recognition[204] and harmonisation in criminal matters[205], framework legislation on restrictive measures regarding terrorism[206], crime prevention,[207] the development of Europol[208] and Eurojust[209], and police co-operation between national authorities.[210] The strengthening of the role of the European Parliament in this context may help address concerns regarding the democratic deficit in the third pillar. However, both the recent conduct of the European Parliament in negotiation concerning recently fully 'communitarised' Title IV matters,[211] and the

---

[201] Art 2 TEU.

[202] Art 6 TEU.

[203] On the 'ordinary' legislative procedure see Art 289(1) and 294 TFEU.

[204] Art 82(1) and (2) TFEU.

[205] Art 83(1) and (2) TFEU.

[206] Art 75(1) TFEU.

[207] Art 84 TFEU.

[208] Art 88(2) TFEU.

[209] Art 85(2) TFEU.

[210] Art 87(2) TFEU. See the relevant chapters for details on these specific areas.

[211] It has been noted that the European Parliament's strategy has been to act as the '28th' Member State in negotiations with the Council, with the aim of reaching 'first reading' agreements. This conduct has been criticised in that it has made effectively decision-making *less* transparent, as it resulted in negotiations behind closed doors and fewer drafts being made publicly available for scrutiny. On 'first reading deals', see House of Lords European Union Committee, *The Treaty of Lisbon*, HL Paper 62-I, n 193 above, para 4.130. See also the Memorandum to the Committee by Steve Peers, reproduced in House of Lords European Union Committee, *The Treaty of Lisbon: An Impact Assessment*, Volume II: Evidence, 10th Report, session 2007–08, HL Paper 62-II, p S153 and oral evidence by Steve Peers and Tony Bunyan, same Report, QQ 82–87 (pp E15–E17).

choice of methods of EU criminal law integration such as mutual recognition and the establishment of criminal law bodies[212] demonstrate that the Lisbon provisions per se may not prove to be sufficient to address fully issues of transparency, democratic control and legitimacy of EU criminal law.

Another major institutional change involves the role of the Court of Justice, and the 'communautarisation' of *judicial control*. The Court has now full jurisdiction to rule on infringement proceedings in criminal matters[213]—a move that strengthens the Commission's role as 'guardian of the Treaties' to monitor the implementation of EU criminal law by Member States. Moreover, the full jurisdiction of the Court in the field of preliminary rulings now applies—with the limitations currently applying in the third pillar abolished.[214] The Court also assumes full jurisdiction to actions for compensation for damages[215] and the review of legality, with the general jurisdiction being expanded to: remove the 'individual concern' standing requirement for natural or legal persons challenging regulatory acts not entailing implementing measures[216]; review the compliance of legislative acts with the principle of subsidiarity;[217] and review the legality of acts of the European Council and bodies, offices or agencies of the Union intended to produce legal effects vis-a-vis third parties[218]—reflecting thus the increasing role that these institutions and bodies play in policy and law-making in EU criminal law.[219] All these changes will contribute significantly to the achievement of effective judicial protection in the field of criminal law.[220] Extending the Court's jurisdiction on preliminary rulings in particular will open new avenues enabling a dialogue between national courts and the ECJ on matters of constitutional significance such as the relationship between EU criminal law and domestic constitutional law.[221]

Another major move towards 'communautarisation' has been the change in the legal instruments adopted for criminal law. According to the Treaty, the legal acts of the Union are Regulations, Directives, Decisions, Recommendations and Opinions.[222] This means that under Lisbon, legislation under the 'Area of Freedom, Security and Justice', including criminal law, must take the form of one of the instruments mentioned above. The major change that this introduces is the

[212] On issues of democracy, legitimacy and transparency in this context, see ch 3 (mutual recognition) and ch 4 (EU criminal law bodies).

[213] Arts 258–260 TFEU.

[214] On the preliminary ruling jurisdiction under Lisbon, see Art 267 TEU. The last paragraph states that such rulings must be given with a minimum of delay in cases involving individuals in custody.

[215] Art 268 TFEU.

[216] Art 263(4) TFEU.

[217] Art 8, Protocol No 2 on the Application of the Principles of Subsidiarity and Proportionality. For further analysis, see below.

[218] Art 263(1) TFEU—see also Art 277 TFEU. For further details on the judicial control of EU bodies, see ch 4.

[219] On the role of EU bodies in criminal law, see ch 4.

[220] Note also Art 19(1) TEU which states that Member States must provide remedies sufficient to ensure effective legal protection in the fields covered by Union law. The impact of the Charter may be considerable in this context—see K Lenaerts, 'The Rule of Law', n 89 above at pp 1629–1630.

[221] On these questions in the context of the European Arrest Warrant, see ch 3.

[222] Art 288(1) TFEU.

possibility for EU criminal law—which is highly likely to take mostly the form of Directives post-Lisbon—to have direct effect (something that is expressly excluded in the current third pillar). More broadly, the abolition of the third pillar will mean that Community law principles will apply to areas currently under the third pillar. What is also noteworthy is that current third pillar legal instruments—including Framework Decisions, Conventions and Common Positions—are not included in the Lisbon Treaty. According to the Protocol on Transitional Provisions annexed to the Treaty, the legal effects of EU Acts will be preserved until those Acts are repealed, annulled or amended in implementation of the Treaties.[223] The current third pillar institutional framework (ECJ jurisdiction, Commission powers) will remain with respect of third pillar measures.[224] The amendment of an Act will trigger the applicability of the Lisbon institutional framework.[225] In any case, the legal effects of Union law adopted before the entry into force of Lisbon will cease five years after such entry into force.[226] It is highly likely that this provision will create an impetus for the tabling of a number of proposals post-Lisbon, replacing existing third pillar law with new legislation in the form of Regulations, Directives or Decisions, giving thus a fresh momentum to EU criminal law making.

C. Resistance to communautarisation

The changes proposed in the negotiations for the Constitutional and the Lisbon Treaties with regard to the third pillar have raised a number of sovereignty concerns in a number of Member States. The accommodation of these concerns has been reflected in a number of instances in the Lisbon Treaty. A closer look at its provisions—in particular Title V on the 'Area of Freedom, Security and Justice'—reveals that the 'communautarisation' of the third pillar is far from absolute, with a number of 'intergovernmental' elements being either retained or newly introduced by the Treaty. This part aims to categorise and examine these intergovernmental elements, which reveal to a lesser or greater extent a certain resistance to the 'communautarisation' of criminal law. Such resistance is expressed by exceptions to the 'Community' rules on decision-making, initiative and judicial control; it is also expressed by placing Member States at centre stage in the development and scrutiny of EU criminal law.

---

[223] Art 9.

[224] Art 10(1).

[225] Art 10(2). In this context, the question has been raised on whether, in cases where only part of the legislation is amended, the 'Community' effects will apply to the parts of the current third pillar law which have not been amended—see House of Lords European Union Committee *The Treaty of Lisbon*, HL Paper 62-I, n 193 above, paras 6.326–6.334. Contrary to the Commission's view, the Committee concluded that the amendment will affect the measure as a whole (para 6.331). This view is shared by the UK Government—see Foreign and Commonwealth Office, *Government Response to the European Union Select Committee on The Treaty of Lisbon: An Impact Assessment*, Cm 7389, June 2008, p 38.

[226] Art 10(4).

i. Diversity of national legal systems

The first element revealing resistance to communautarisation—coupled with resistance to the top–down uniformity of EU criminal law—is the sustained emphasis of the Lisbon Treaty to the respect for the diversity of national legal systems. Respect for national diversity already occupies a central place in the very opening Article of Title V TFEU, Article 67(1), which states that the Union will constitute an area of freedom, security and justice 'with respect for fundamental rights *and the different legal systems and traditions of Member States*' (emphasis added). The obligation to take into account the differences between national legal traditions and systems also appears in the provision establishing a legal basis for the adoption of certain minimum EU standards in criminal procedure, reflecting again the willingness of Member States not to provide the Union with an open-ended competence in the field.[227]

Two further points are noteworthy in this context. The first is that competence for the harmonisation of criminal procedure is only conferred on the EU to the extent necessary to facilitate mutual recognition.[228] The Lisbon Treaty places great emphasis on mutual recognition as a method of European integration in criminal matters, and in this instance effectively subordinates harmonisation to mutual recognition[229]—this choice is significant as mutual recognition does not involve in principle the adoption of harmonised EU standards and is perceived, at least prima facie, by governments as less threatening to State sovereignty as they would not have to change their law.[230] The second point involves the form of EU legislative action concerning harmonisation of substantive criminal law and criminal procedure: in both cases, harmonisation will take place by means of Directives.[231] This choice is significant as Directives leave Member States a considerable margin of manoeuvre as to how to implement EU law, being binding as to the result to be achieved but leaving to the national authorities the choice of form and methods.[232] This discretion left to Member States may serve to take into account the particularities of their domestic criminal justice systems when called to implement EU measures on matters such as rules on the admissibility of evidence or the rights of the defendant in criminal proceedings.[233] It is clear that Member States opted for such discretion rather than for top–down uniform standards across the EU.

Concerns with regard to the respect of national diversity and the challenges to State sovereignty posed by the communautarisation of decision-making in EU criminal law have been articulated perhaps in the clearest manner in the intro-

---

[227] Art 82(2) TFEU. For further details, see ch 2.
[228] ibid.
[229] On the subordination of harmonisation to mutual recognition in this context, see ch 2.
[230] On mutual recognition, see ch 3.
[231] Arts 82(2), 83(1) and (2) respectively.
[232] Art 288(3) TFEU.
[233] For legal bases for such measures see Art 82(2)(a) and (b) TFEU respectively.

duction of provisions establishing a so-called 'emergency brake' in the adoption of Directives in the fields of criminal procedure and substantive criminal law. Under the 'emergency brake' procedure, where a Member State considers that a draft directive in the field 'would affect fundamental aspects of its criminal justice system', it may request that the draft directive be referred to the European Council—leading to the suspension of the ordinary legislative procedure. After discussions in the European Council, in case of consensus, within four months of this suspension the proposal is sent back to the Council of Ministers for the resumption of negotiations. In case of disagreement, within the same timeframe, authorisation for Member States who wish to proceed with the proposal under enhanced co-operation referred to in Articles 20(2) TEU and 329(1) TFEU is deemed to be granted.[234] In this manner, reluctant Member States which may be in the minority may ensure that they do not take part in the measure, while allowing those in favour of the measure to proceed with its adoption. As witnessed by the inclusion of the European Council in the legislative process, the emergency brake is a primarily political mechanism. It remains to be seen whether and how often it will be used in practice should the Lisbon Treaty enters into force.[235]

ii. Security, Counter-Terrorism and Judicial Control

a. Internal and National Security

On a number of occasions, the Lisbon Treaty contains provisions aiming to safeguard State sovereignty in the field of security. Early on in the Treaty on the European Union, in the paragraph following the one on the principle of conferral, it is stated that the Union will respect the essential State functions of Member States, 'including ensuring the territorial integrity of the State, maintaining law and order and safeguarding national security' and that in particular, 'national security remains the sole responsibility of each Member State'.[236] Title V TFEU on the 'Area of Freedom, Security and Justice' (AFSJ) contains a provision—reminiscent to the current Treaty—stating that the Title will 'not affect the exercise of the responsibilities incumbent upon Member States with regard to the maintenance of law and order and the safeguarding of internal security'.[237] Moreover, the

[234] Art 82(3) TFEU on criminal procedure; Art 83(3) TFEU on substantive criminal law.
[235] For a discussion of the 'emergency brake' provisions, see House of Lords European Union Committee *The Treaty of Lisbon*, HL Paper 62-I, n 193 above, paras 6.44–6.66. Note in this context in particular the oral evidence of the UK Justice Secretary, Jack Straw (reproduced in House of Lords European Union Committee, *The Treaty of Lisbon*, HL Paper 62-II, n.211 above, Evidence to the Lisbon Treaty Report, QQ 502–507, E115–116). Mr Straw demonstrated the ways in which the emergency brake may be used to strengthen a Member State's negotiating position. Mr Straw noted in particular that 'in the areas where the emergency brake applies if we support the principle of an instrument which is being put forward we can opt into it and in extremis, having opted into it but then some unforeseen difficulty arises from the way in which it is being negotiated which does affect "some fundamental aspects of our criminal justice system", then we can pull the emergency brake'—Q502.
[236] Art 4(2) TEU.
[237] Art 72 TFEU.

Treaty continues to limit the jurisdiction of the Court in exercising its powers with regard to judicial co-operation in criminal matters and police co-operation under Title V: the Court will have no jurisdiction to review the validity or proportionality of operations carried out by the police or other law enforcement services of a Member State or the exercise of the responsibilities incumbent upon Member States with regard to the maintenance of law and order and the safeguarding of internal security.[238]

The degree to which these provisions will limit legislative action in EU criminal law and the Court's involvement in the review of operations with a national dimension but following obligations under Union law is questionable and remains to be seen.[239] In examining the impact of these provisions, the terminology used is, however, noteworthy: there is no reference to the 'Area of Freedom, Security and Justice'—at the domestic level, this is replaced by 'internal security', or 'national security'. As with 'security' in the AFSJ, these terms are not defined and their content is unclear.[240] It is further not clear whether 'national security' coincides or overlaps with 'internal security', or whether 'internal security' should be seen as covering primarily police co-operation, while 'national security' should be seen as covering military and/or intelligence action. If this is the case, the implications of including references to 'national security' in the chapter on the 'Area of Freedom, Security and Justice' may need to be further explored should the Treaty enter into force.[241]

b. Counter-terrorism

Limits to the Court's jurisdiction still remain with regard to EU restrictive measures imposed on individuals in the framework of EU counter-terrorism policy. The Lisbon Treaty provides with a legal basis for the adoption under Title V (Area of Freedom, Security and Justice), of 'a framework for administrative measures

---

[238] Art 276 TFEU. Note also Art 88(3) TFEU on Europol, which states that the application of coercive measures will be the exclusive responsibility of the competent national authorities. For further details, see ch 4.

[239] For a discussion on the current limitation, see above section III.

[240] For a discussion on the relationship between the terms 'national security' and 'internal security', see House of Lords European Union Committee, *The Treaty of Lisbon*, HL Paper 62-I, n 193 above, paras 6.235–6.243. See also C. Ladenburger, 'Police and Criminal Law in the Treaty of Lisbon. A New Dimension for the Community Model', *European Constitutional Law Review*, vol 4, 2008, pp 20–40 at p 36. Both comments stress the uncertainty of the terms. Ladenburger also notes that the 'national security' exception has been repeatedly requested (and finally accepted) by the UK Government (p 28). In this context, the approach of the latter is noteworthy: in its response to the House of Lords Report, the Government notes that 'the concept of "internal security" is distinct from that of "national security"', adding that it applies specifically in the context of Justice and Home Affairs activity including aspects f law enforcement and illegal migration and it would cover in particular matters relating to public order within a Member State and in particular matters falling within the responsibility of the police authorities—FCO, n 225 above, p 32.

[241] Art 73 TFEU states that it will be open to Member States 'to organise between themselves and under their responsibility such forms of cooperation and coordination as they deem appropriate between the competent departments of their administrations responsible for safeguarding *national security*' (emphasis added).

with regard to capital movements and payments, such as the freezing of funds, financial assets or economic gains belonging to, or owned or held by, natural or legal persons, groups or non-State entities'.[242] However, the Treaty also retains a more intergovernmental, Common Foreign and Security Policy (CFSP) element: according to Article 215 TFEU, where a decision adopted under Title V TEU (on CFSP) provides for the interruption or reduction, in part or completely, of economic and financial relations with one or more third countries, the Council, acting by a qualified majority on a joint proposal from the High Representative of the Union for Foreign Affairs and Security Policy and the Commission will adopt the necessary measures.[243] Where such decision is adopted, the Council may adopt restrictive measures under the above procedure against natural or legal persons and groups or non-State entities.[244]

This intergovernmental approach is reflected in the formulation of a specific provision on the Court's jurisdiction: this applies only in the context on proceedings brought by natural or legal persons in the terms provided by Article 263(4) TFEU reviewing the legality of restrictive measures adopted under Title V TEU.[245] While the express granting of jurisdiction to natural or legal persons in these cases is welcome in recognising the need and providing a clear avenue for judicial protection,[246] the jurisdiction of the Court under Article 275(2) TFEU is limited to the review of the legality of 'decisions providing for restrictive measures against natural or legal persons'. This seems to exclude from the Court's jurisdiction the *implementing* measures adopted by the Council under Article 215(2) TFEU—however, these measures that may affect significantly the position of individuals.[247] Moreover, the wording of Article 275(2) TFEU seems to limit the Court's jurisdiction to the review of legality, excluding thus other levels of jurisdiction such as preliminary references.[248] It remains to be seen how this provision will relate with the Court's increasing efforts to broaden avenues of judicial protection for natural and legal persons in this context.[249]

---

[242] Art 75(1) TFEU. Art 75(2) provides for the adoption of implementing measures.

[243] Art 215(1) TFEU.

[244] Art 215(2) TFEU.

[245] Art 275(2) TFEU.

[246] Note also Arts 75(3) and 215(3) TFEU explicitly referring to the inclusion of provisions on legal safeguards.

[247] Note that the conditions of standing for individuals with regard to implementing measures—to the extent that these are regulatory acts not entailing further implementing measures have been relaxed in Lisbon under Art 263(4) TFEU. On the standing issue with regard to Art 275 TFEU in general, see the Memorandum submitted by T Tridimas to the House of Lords Constitution Committee for their inquiry on the European Union (Amendment) Bill: see House of Lords Constitution Committee, *European Union (Amendment) Bill and the Lisbon Treaty: Implications for the UK Constitution*, 6th Report, session 2007–08, HL Paper 84 (p 78).

[248] On this point, see also Tridimas ibid.

[249] In this context, the question arises on how the Court will formulate its jurisdiction with regard to future measures adopted under a dual legal basis (à la *Segi*), ie under Arts 75 and 215 TFEU (AFSJ and CFSP respectively). The jurisdiction of the Court is significantly more extensive with regard to measures adopted under Art 75 TFEU. It remains to be seen whether the Court will apply such jurisdiction to these measures.

iii. Initiative

An important institutional development in the Lisbon Treaty is the express recognition of the European Council as one of the EU institutions.[250] According to the Treaty, the European Council will provide the Union with the necessary impetus for its development and define the general political directions and priorities thereof—but will not exercise legislative functions.[251] This is an example of what has been characterised as the 'high politics' nature of the European Council decisions.[252] This role of the European Council is further confirmed in the specific context of EU Justice and Home Affairs, with Title V TFEU stating that the European Council will define 'the strategic guidelines for legislative and operational planning within the Area of Freedom, Security and Justice'.[253] It is thus Member States' leaders who will continue to provide (as in the cases of Tampere and the Hague) with the general guidelines for the development of EU Justice and Home Affairs law—with little involvement (at least according to the Treaty) from other EU institutions or civil society. Initiative remains with governments not only at the stage of the initiation of policy and strategy, but also at the stage of the initiation of legislation: Member States retain the right of initiative, shared between them and the Commission—proposals for EU legislation on police co-operation and judicial co-operation in criminal matters can be tabled either by the Commission or on the initiative of a quarter of the Member States.[254]

Along with its role as a policy and strategy *initiator*, the European Council also assumes under Lisbon the role of a *broker* in cases where Member States express concerns with the development of EU criminal law. As mentioned above, the European Council plays a central part in the 'emergency brake' procedure, with Member States concerned that a proposal on the harmonisation of criminal law or procedure would affect fundamental aspects of their domestic criminal justice system referring the proposal to the European Council. It is discussions in the European Council which will determine the future handling of the proposal, and may trigger enhanced co-operation in the field. A similar procedure is envisaged in case of disagreement on legislation establishing a European Public Prosecutor, and legislation establishing operational co-operation between national law enforcement authorities (in both cases, however, unanimity is in principle required in the Council).[255] Moreover, the European Council assumes a central role in determining the consequences of non-participation of the UK and Ireland

---

[250] See Art 13(1) TEU. Under Lisbon, the European Council will consist of the Heads of State or Government of the Member States, together with its President and the President of the Commission—with the High Representative of the Union for Foreign Affairs and Security Policy also taking part in its work—Art 15(2) TEU.

[251] Art 15(1) TEU. Note though that the Treaty does not preclude acts of the European Council from having effects on third parties and thus establishing ECJ jurisdiction—see Art 263(1) TFEU. On the role of and procedures in the European Council see Art 15 TEU and Arts 235 and 236 TFEU.

[252] See Dougan, above n 193, p 627.

[253] Art 68 TFEU.

[254] Art 76 TFEU.

[255] Arts 86(1) TFEU and 87(3) TFEU respectively.

in future Schengen-building measures, which build upon legislation to which these Member States have currently opted in. If the UK and Ireland decide not to participate in such a measure, they must bear the direct financial consequences as a result of the cessation of their participation.[256] These financial consequences will be determined by the Council, on the basis of the criteria of retaining 'the widest possible measure of participation of the Member State concerned without seriously affecting the practical operability of the various parts of the Schengen *acquis*, while respecting their coherence'.[257] If the Council fails to adopt a decision on the basis of these criteria, a Member State may request that the matter be referred to the European Council, which must take a decision at its next meeting.[258]

iv. Decision-making

Notwithstanding the general move of the Lisbon Treaty towards the 'communitarisation' of decision-making in matters currently falling under the third pillar, there remains a number of exceptions to the rule (of majority voting in the Council and co-decision with the European Parliament). The first category of exceptions involves *legislation which would expand Union competence in criminal matters*. In these cases, given the sensitivity of the issues, the 'Community method' weakens with regard to the Council but is strengthened with regard to the European Parliament. Thus unanimity is required in the Council (along with a much stronger role for the European Parliament, which must give its consent), for legislation identifying further areas of criminal procedure (in addition to those exhaustively enumerated in the Treaty) where the Union can adopt minimum rules.[259] The same procedure applies for the adoption of legislation expanding the Union's competence in harmonisation of substantive criminal law for crimes other than those enumerated in the Treaty;[260] and for the adoption—and further development—of legislation establishing a European Public Prosecutor's Office.[261] The second category of exceptions involves *operational co-operation*, where the more traditional 'intergovernmental' method of decision-making applies: unanimity in the Council and the mere consultation of the European Parliament is required for the adoption of legislation establishing measures concerning operational co-operation between national competent (in particular law enforcement) authorities;[262] legislation laying down the conditions under which

---

[256] Declaration 47 on Art 5(3), (4) and (5) of the Protocol on the Schengen *acquis* integrated into the framework of the European Union.

[257] Art 5(3) of Protocol No 19 on the Schengen *Acquis* integrated into the Framework of the European Union.

[258] Art 5(4). Note that, as in the Council, decision-making in the European Council in this case will be by majority voting.

[259] Art 82(2) TFEU.

[260] Art 83(1) TFEU.

[261] Art 86(1) and (4) TFEU respectively. In the absence of unanimity, the provision establishes a procedure that may lead to enhanced co-operation.

[262] Art 87(3) TFEU. Again, in the absence of unanimity, the provision establishes a procedure that may lead to enhanced co-operation.

police and judicial authorities may operate in the territory of another Member State;[263] and measures to ensure administrative co-operation between the relevant departments of Member States.[264] The third category of exceptions involves *measures implementing restrictive counter-terrorism law*—where the European Parliament is completely sidelined: according to the Treaty, it is the Council only which will adopt such implementing measures.[265] The limited role of the European Parliament in the two latter categories of cases reflects strongly the political sensitivity of the issues for Member States.[266]

v. Subsidiarity

A central theme in the discussions on the reform of the current EU Treaties, underpinning both the Constitutional and the Lisbon Treaty, has been the issue of 'bringing Europe closer to its citizens'—with the principle of subsidiarity, used to best allocate the level of desired action in Europe, playing a central part in this context.[267] The focus on subsidiarity in the EU constitutional debate is evidenced by the establishment of two related Working Groups in the Convention on the Future of Europe: one on subsidiarity,[268] and one on the role of national parliaments.[269] Indeed, the push towards a greater focus on subsidiarity in the EU—as a means of better justifying action at EU level and of connecting citizens with the EU—has been inextricably linked with calls to provide *national* parliaments with a greater role in the development of EU legislation.[270] The view that national parliaments can address the democratic deficit in the EU by providing a useful intermediate link between the Union and citizens in the various Member States, and can provide extra checks to proposed EU action in particular by monitoring subsidiarity,

---

[263] Art 89 TFEU.

[264] Art 74 TFEU.

[265] Arts 75(2) TFEU and 215(2) TFEU.

[266] Note also the exclusion of the European Parliament from the adoption of legislation setting out arrangements for the evaluation of the implementation of EU Justice and Home Affairs law—Art 70 TFEU. On the role of evaluation as an element of resistance to 'communautarisation', see below.

[267] From the voluminous literature on subsidiarity in the EU, see P Craig, *EU Administrative Law*, Oxford, OUP, 2006, pp 419–427 and references therein; Tridimas, *General Principles of EU Law*, n 120 above, ch 4.

[268] See in particular the Conclusions of Working Group I on the Principle of Subsidiarity, CONV 286/02, WGI 15, Brussels, 23 September 2002.

[269] See in particular the Final Report of Working Group IV on the Role of National Parliaments, CONV 353/02, WG IV 17, Brussels, 22 October 2002.

[270] On the link between national parliaments, subsidiarity and monitoring EU powers, see A Vergés Bausili, *Rethinking the Methods of Dividing and Exercising Powers in the EU: Reforming Subsidiarity and National Parliaments*, Jean Monnet Working Paper 9/02, NYU School of Law, www.jeanmonnetprogram. org; on national parliaments and subsidiarity in the specific context of the Convention on the Future of Europe, see I Cooper, 'The Watchdogs of Subsidiarity: National Parliaments and the Logic of Arguing in the EU', *Journal of Common Market Studies*, vol 44, no 2, 2006, pp 281–304; see also House of Lords European Union Committee (then Select Committee on the European Union), *The Future of Europe: National Parliaments and Subsidiarity—The Proposed Protocols*, 11th Report, session 2002–03, HL Paper 70.

justifies and underpins the expansion of the relevant provisions in the Lisbon Treaty.[271]

The Lisbon Treaty brings national parliaments more prominently into the Union legal framework. According to Article 12 TEU, national parliaments contribute actively to the good functioning of the Union in a number of ways, including being informed by EU institutions of draft legislation[272] and seeing that the principle of subsidiarity is respected[273]—with more detailed provisions on both roles included in separate Protocols annexed in the Treaty.[274] A specific provision on national parliaments and subsidiarity is also included in Title V TFEU, stating that national parliaments ensure that proposals and legislative initiatives in the field of police co-operation and judicial co-operation in criminal matters comply with the principle of subsidiarity in accordance with the relevant Protocol.[275] The subsidiarity Protocol establishes a so-called 'early warning mechanism' leading to a 'yellow card': any national parliament or any chamber of a national parliament can send to EU institutions,[276] within eight weeks from the transmission of draft legislative acts (and their amended drafts), a reasoned opinion stating why it considers that the draft in question does not comply with the principle of subsidiarity;[277] where such reasoned opinions for EU criminal law proposals represent at least a quarter of the votes allocated to national parliaments, the draft must be reviewed.[278] The Protocol contains a further, 'orange card' mechanism: under the ordinary legislative procedure, where reasoned opinions represent at least a simple majority of the votes allocated to national parliaments, the proposal must be reviewed, and if the Commission chooses to maintain the proposal, a special procedure is triggered in the Council and the European Parliament examining whether negotiations should go ahead.[279] The Protocol also contains a provision on the ex post control of subsidiarity, granting jurisdiction to the Court of Justice in actions against adopted legislation on grounds of infringement of the principle of subsidiarity under Article 263 TFEU.[280]

There are many questions regarding the application of these provisions in practice, in particular as regards the operation of the 'yellow' and 'orange' cards: would the reasoned opinions contain the same content/grounds on the breach of subsidiarity in order for them to achieve the votes threshold required by the Protocol, or are diverse subsidiarity objections allowed in this context? Will

[271] For a general analysis of the role of national parliaments in the EU, see House of Commons European Scrutiny Committee, *Democracy and Accountability in the EU and the Role of National Parliaments*, 33rd Report, session 2001–02, HC 152.
[272] Art 12(a) TEU.
[273] Art 12(b) TEU. See also Art 5(1) and (3) TEU on the principle of subsidiarity.
[274] Protocol No 1 on the Role of National Parliaments in the European Union and Protocol No 2 on the Application of the Principles of Subsidiarity and Proportionality respectively.
[275] Art 69 TFEU.
[276] And Member States if they have tabled the proposal.
[277] Arts 4 and 6 of the Protocol.
[278] Art 7(2). For all other proposals the threshold is one third of the votes.
[279] Art 7(3).
[280] Art 8.

national parliaments—along with the issues of practical co-ordination they face[281]—focus solely on subsidiarity, or will subsidiarity objections be fused or confused with objections on proportionality and competence?[282] Moreover, there is an issue regarding the application of the Court's legality review: standing is granted in this context to Member States 'on behalf of their national parliament or a chamber thereof'.[283] The formulation of this provision reflects the difficulties in inserting national parliaments in the EU legislative framework, as the latter do not constitute an EU institution in the terms of the Treaties. In order not to destabilise the inter institutional balance in the EU, standing is granted to Member States on behalf of their parliaments—however, given the general wording of Article 7, the question of how binding a request from a parliament to its Government to bring an action before the ECJ is remains open. It is submitted that *Union* law imposes on national Governments the obligation to bring an action before the ECJ if the national parliament makes such a request, but it is *national* law which covers the precise procedural details in this context.[284] Notwithstanding these difficulties, the provisions on subsidiarity represent a clear trend towards devolving scrutiny of EU legislation *at the national level,* in particular by obliging EU institutions to justify in detail *why* it is necessary to proceed to action at the Union level each time legislation is being put forward.[285]

vi. Evaluation

Another element of the Lisbon Treaty demonstrating the increased emphasis on the need to justify and prove the so-called 'added value' of EU law, in particular in Justice and Home Affairs, is the legal basis established in Title V TFEU enabling the launch of mechanisms for the 'objective and impartial evaluation' of the implementation of the Union policies referred to in this Title by national author-

---

[281] For a discussion of these issues in the context of the—very similar—provisions included in the Constitutional Treaty, see House of Lords European Union Committee, *Strengthening National Parliamentary Scrutiny of the EU—The Constitution's Subsidiarity Early Warning Mechanism,* 14th Report, session 2004–05, HL Paper 101.

[282] National parliaments have already started to organise subsidiarity monitoring exercises within the framework of COSAC (the Conference of Community and European Affairs Committees). For details of the results of these monitoring exercises (which have included one in the field of EU criminal law, involving the proposal to amend the Framework Decision on terrorism) can be found at www.cosac.eu/en/info/earlywarning.

[283] Art 8(1). See also Art 8(2) which also grants standing under certain conditions to the Committee of the Regions.

[284] For the view that the Protocol grants national parliaments a right of action see also the Memoranda submitted by T Tridimas and J Usher to the House of Lords Constitution Committee for their inquiry on the European Union (Amendment) Bill: see House of Lords Constitution Committee, n 247 above (pp 76 and 81 respectively). For a detailed discussion on the legal and practical issues arising from this provision, see House of Lords European Union Committee, *Strengthening National Parliamentary Scrutiny,* n 281 above, paras 228–240.

[285] According to the subsidiarity Protocol, draft legislative acts must be justified via a detailed statement with regard to the principles of subsidiarity and proportionality (Art 5). Moreover, the initiator institutions deciding to maintain, amend or withdraw a draft legislative act after the yellow card procedure must give reasons for this decision (Art 7(2)). The Commission must also give reasons if it decided to maintain the proposal under the 'orange card' mechanism—Art 7(3).

ities in particular in order to facilitate full application of the principle of mutual recognition.[286] Evaluation is thus an ex post scrutiny mechanism, containing strong intergovernmental elements: it will be conducted by Member States (in collaboration with the Commission)—with the European Parliament *and* national parliaments being 'informed' of its content and results.[287] A joint interparliamentary involvement (of the European Parliament and national parliaments) is also envisaged with regard to the evaluation of the activities of Eurojust.[288]

The Lisbon Treaty reflects growing calls for the establishment of mechanisms for the evaluation of the implementation of EU criminal law by Member States.[289] In particular regarding the application of the principle of mutual recognition in criminal matters, it has been put forward that evaluation would enhance the trust in Member States' criminal justice systems.[290] Evaluation mechanisms in criminal matters are not new for Member States: the latter have been participating in peer review mechanisms in international fora.[291] Moreover, a number of evaluation mechanisms are already in place in the third pillar context:[292] at present they exist in the form of peer reviews of Schengen preparedness (which have played a prominent role in enlargement and the evaluation of applications for full Schengen membership)[293] and in the form of evaluation mechanisms of the implementation of specific third pillar legislation on organised crime and terrorism.[294]

---

[286] Art 70 TFEU.

[287] ibid.

[288] Art 85(1) TFEU and 12(c) TEU. See also Art 88(2) TFEU and 12(c) TEU with regard to arrangements for the scrutiny of Europol's activities by the European Parliament and national parliaments. For further details on the scrutiny of EU bodies, see ch 4.

[289] This is the case in particular regarding the third pillar, where the Commission currently does not have the power to institute infringement proceedings for mis—or non-implementation of Union law by Member States. For recent proposals see Commission Communication on the 'evaluation of EU policies on freedom, security and justice', COM (2006) 332 final, 28 June 2006.

[290] The Commission defence rights proposal contained an evaluation clause, but this was deleted by Member States in negotiations—on the proposal, see ch 2.

[291] EU Member States have been participating in peer review exercised within the framework of their membership in bodies such as the OECD, and the Financial Action Task Force. On this form of evaluation in the context of compliance with money laundering measures, see M Levi and B Gilmore, 'Terrorist Finance, Money Laundering and the Rise and Rise of Mutual Evaluation: A New Paradigm of Crime Control?', *European Journal of Law Reform*, vol 4, 2002, pp 341–368.

[292] For a discussion of the various evaluation methods and proposals at EU level, see the contributions in A Weyembergh and S de Biolley (eds), *Comment évaluer le droit pénal européen?*, Brussels, Institut d'études européennes, 2006. On existing methods of Justice and Home Affairs evaluation, see also O de Schutter, 'The Role of Fundamental Rights Evaluation in the Establishment of the Area of Freedom, Security and Justice', in M Martin (ed), *Crime, Rights and the EU. The Future of Police and Judicial Cooperation*, London, JUSTICE, 2008, pp 44–88.

[293] See for instance the evaluation mechanism for implementation by candidate countries of the EU JHA *acquis* (Joint Action 98/429/JHA, OJ L191, 7 July 1998, p.8). On the Schengen evaluations, see R Genson and W van de Rijt, 'L'évaluation de Schengen dans le cadre de l'élargissement', in Weyembergh and de Biolley, n 292 above, pp 219–234.

[294] See the evaluation mechanism for implementation of international undertakings in the field of organised crime (Joint Action 97/827/JHA, OJ L344, 15 December 1997, p 7), and the evaluation of Member States' legal systems and their implementation in the fight against terrorism (Decision 2002/996/JHA, OJ L349, 24 December 2002, p 1). For an assessment of evaluation in practice, see H Nilsson, 'Eight Years of Experiences of Mutual Evaluation within the EU', in Weyembergh and de Biolley, n 292 above, pp 115–124.

The objective and impartial evaluation of the implementation of EU Justice and Home Affairs legislation, especially in areas related to the rights of the individual, is unobjectionable in principle. However, its exact parameters are still highly contested, given the legal and constitutional limits of the current state of EU law.[295] It is not clear *who will evaluate* under the Lisbon Treaty: Article 70 TFEU refers to evaluation by Member States with the involvement of the Commission—however the role of the latter—and the relationship between the Commission and Member States—are not clear. Moreover, it is not clear whether EU bodies such as the Fundamental Rights Agency (FRA) will be involved in such evaluation exercises, and if not, what would the relationship be between 'Article 70' evaluations and FRA evaluations.[296] The *method of evaluation* is also unclear—along with the question of who will evaluate, questions of the criteria of evaluation and the management of its results are relevant in this context—for instance, will the results be made public, and is the goal a 'naming and shaming' exercise?[297] The same can be said about the *impact of the evaluation*. The type of sanctions involved for non-compliance needs to be further discussed. Similarly, the relationship between the Commission's power to institute infringement proceedings with the evaluation mechanism established under Lisbon is unclear: the Treaty states that this mechanism is 'without prejudice' to Articles 258–260 TFEU dealing with the infringement procedure: however, it is not clear whether a positive evaluation under Article 70 TFEU will actually *preclude* infringement action by the Commission—in the latter case, the Commission's role as 'guardian of the Treaties' will be weakened considerably, with Member States themselves assuming the central role in assessing their own compliance with EU criminal law. On the other hand, the impact of a negative evaluation needs also to be considered: will such negative evaluation trigger the mechanism of Article 7 TEU?[298] Finally, the issue of *what will be the object of the evaluation exercise* is not clear. It may be difficult to distinguish between the evaluation of the implementation of a specific EU criminal law measure (such as the defence rights proposal) and the evaluation of a Member State's criminal justice/human rights protection system as a whole. The existence of EU competence to embark on such a far-reaching evaluation is questionable. The Commission's recent Communications however seem to envisage a broader evaluation.[299]

[295] For details, see Mitsilegas, 'Trust-building Measures', n 159 above; and V Mitsilegas, 'The Constitutional Implications of Mutual Recognition in Criminal Matters in the EU', *Common Market Law Review*, vol 43, 2006, pp 1277–1311.

[296] On the role of the Fundamental Rights Agency, see ch 4.

[297] A number of the evaluations currently conducted under the third pillar remain confidential—see Commission Communication, 'On the Creation of a Forum for Discussing EU Justice Policies and Practice' COM (2008) 38 final, Brussels, 4 February 2008, p 4.

[298] The EU Network of Independent Experts on Fundamental Rights proposed to combine the evaluation mechanism of Art III-260 of the Constitutional Treaty with improving the mechanism of Art 7 TEU—*Report on the Situation of Fundamental Rights in the EU in 2004*, p 31.

[299] The Commission stated that 'a more general evaluation of the conditions in which judgments are produced in order to ensure that they meet high quality standards enabling mutual trust between judicial systems to be reinforced' providing 'a fully comprehensive view of national systems' COM (2005) 195 final, pp 8, 9. Similarly, the 2008 Communication on the Justice Forum advocates looking at how judicial co-operation operates 'as a whole'—n 297 above, p 7.

vii. Non-participation ('opt-outs')

Concerns with regard to the impact of the 'communitarisation' of criminal law in the Lisbon Treaty on national sovereignty have led—in addition to the numerous instances of resistance to comunautarisation analysed above—to the proliferation of arrangements whereby Member States were offered the ultimate 'opt-out': the possibility not to participate in EU criminal law adopted under the Treaty. Following the pattern emerging in the Maastricht and Amsterdam Treaties, a key Member State among the sceptics has been the United Kingdom: indeed, the deepening of integration in criminal matters has been a so-called 'red line' in the UK negotiating position on the Constitutional Treaty, but even more so in the Lisbon Treaty.[300] Focusing primarily on the UK, this part will examine the various mechanisms introduced in the Lisbon Treaty to enable non-participation by Member States in EU legislation related to criminal matters.

The first mechanism which may lead potentially to non-participation is the *emergency brake* procedure analysed earlier in the chapter.[301] This procedure is open to any Member State in the field of harmonisation of substantive criminal law and criminal procedure—concerns lead to the referral of the draft measure to the European Council and, in case of disagreement, Member States wishing to proceed may proceed under enhanced co-operation. The second mechanism of non-participation, as with Amsterdam, involves the *non-participation of the UK and Ireland in Schengen-building measures.*[302] As mentioned earlier in the chapter, the main change in this context is that the Treaty now makes explicit that these countries may choose not to opt in to legislation building upon parts of Schengen in which they already participate—in this case, these States may be called to bear the direct financial consequences of such non-participation.[303] The third mechanism of non-participation extends *the right of the UK and Ireland not to participate in measures falling currently under Title IV TEC to include non-participation in the whole of Title V TFEU on the 'Area of Freedom, Security and Justice'*, including thus non-participation in EU criminal law measures.[304] The

---

[300] See the UK Government's Explanatory Memorandum to the Lisbon Treaty submitted to the House of Lords Constitution Committee, n 248 above, where it is stated that 'the Government was clear that protecting our common law system and police and judicial processes is a UK red line'—p 26, para 28). Another area of difficulty for the UK has been the incorporation of the Charter of Fundamental Rights into EU law—with protection of UK labour and social law also being a 'red line' (Constitution Committee, n 247 above, p 27) The concession for the UK (and Poland) in this context has been Protocol No 30 to the Treaty, attempting to limit the application of the Charter in the domestic legal orders of these Member States. For a discussion of the Protocol, see House of Lords European Union Committee, *The Treaty of Lisbon*, HL Paper 62-I, n 193 above, paras 5.84–5.111.

[301] Arts 82(3) and 83(3) TFEU—see also sub-section VI C ii a above.

[302] See Protocol No 19 Art 5.

[303] See Art 5(3) of the Schengen Protocol and Declaration 47 annexed to the Final Act of the Lisbon IGC.

[304] See Protocol No 21 on the position of the United Kingdom and Ireland in respect of the Area of Freedom, Security and Justice. Note that Ireland has declared its 'firm intention' to exercise its right to participate to Title V measures, in particular to participate 'to the maximum possible extent' in measures in the field of police co-operation (Declaration 56 annexed to the Final Act of the Lisbon Treaty). The UK has declared its intention to participate in restrictive counter-terrorism measures under Art 75 TFEU (Declaration 65 annexed to the Final Act of the Lisbon Treaty).

right not to participate[305] also extends to legislation amending existing measures which are binding upon the UK and Ireland.[306] In such cases, the period in which the UK and Ireland must notify their participation is extended if the Council determines that their non-participation makes the measure inoperable in other Member States.[307] Similarly to the Schengen Protocol, non-participation of these countries in legislation amending an existing measure by which they are bound may lead to them bearing the direct financial consequences resulting from such non-participation.[308] The fourth—and ultimate—mechanism of non-participation can be found in the Protocol on Transitional Provisions, which as mentioned earlier in the chapter delays the application of the 'full' Community effect to measures adopted under the current third pillar for a period up to five years after the entry into force of the Lisbon Treaty.[309] This Protocol grants *the UK the right not to accept the 'Community' powers of the institutions in third pillar law,*[310] *in which case such legislation will cease to apply to the UK.*[311] This (and the similar amendment to the Schengen Protocol) is an unprecedented move, allowing a Member State to withdraw from measures which are already legally binding upon it.[312]

These 'opt-outs', in particular the drastic solution to allow Member States to effectively withdraw from EU legislation which is already binding upon them, may have been deemed necessary to ensure the smooth ratification of the Lisbon Treaty in particular in Westminster. However, along with the broader issue of variable geometry that they raise, they may also have significant political consequences

---

[305] See also Protocol No 22 on the position of Denmark, stating that Denmark will not take part in the adoption of all Title V measures (Art 1(1)) and that no Title V measure will be binding upon or applicable to it (Art 2). Denmark may decide to opt into Schengen building measures, and in such cases the measures will create an obligation under international law between Denmark and the other Member States bound by the measure (Art 4(1)). At any time Denmark may decide not to avail itself of all or part of the Protocol, in which case Denmark will apply in full all relevant measures then in force taken within the framework of the EU (Art 7). Moreover, at any time Denmark may notify the other Member States of the replacement of Part I of the Protocol with provisions attached in its annex, introducing inter alia an 'opt-in' mechanism similar to the arrangements on the UK and Ireland (Art 8 and annex). Denmark has also declared that it will not block measures which contain both provisions applicable to it and provisions not applicable to it (Declaration 48 annexed to the Final Act of the Lisbon Treaty).

[306] Art 4a(1).

[307] Art 4a(2). See also Declaration 26 annexed to the Final Act of the Lisbon Treaty stating that, where a Member State opts not to participate in a Title V measure the Council will hold a 'full discussion' on the possible implications and effects of such non-participation. For a discussion on the threshold required for a measure to be deemed 'inoperable', see House of Lords European Union Committee (*Lisbon Treaty Report*), n 193 above, paras 6.262–6.269.

[308] Art 4a(3).

[309] Protocol No 36, Art 10(3).

[310] Which has not been amended after the entry into force of the Lisbon Treaty—in which case the UK would have the right to choose whether to participate in the new legislation (to which the full Lisbon provisions would apply) under the AFSJ Protocol.

[311] Art 10(4)—which also states that the Council may adopt a decision determining that the UK may bear the direct financial consequences incurred because of the cessation of its participation. The UK may, at any time afterwards, notify the Council of its wish to participate in acts which have ceased to apply to it (Art 10(5)).

[312] See also in this context Dougan, n 193 above p 683.

with regard to the development of EU action in criminal matters. The application of the emergency brake procedure may lead to speedier action by willing Member States under enhanced co-operation. Moreover, the way in which the transitional arrangement Protocol is drafted may actually have the effect of boosting the EU legislative production in criminal matters post-Lisbon. The emphasis on the possibility of amending existing third pillar law (which accompanies the transitional provisions)[313] may create a significant momentum towards the adoption of *more* EU criminal law, and prompting a series of amendments to important third pillar instruments, such as the European Arrest Warrant.[314] The Protocol states that the full 'Community' powers of the EU institutions will apply to post-Lisbon measures which amend current third pillar measures.[315] This may create an incentive for the Commission to table a series of proposals amending (and in this context potentially expanding) third pillar law soon after the entry into force of the Lisbon Treaty: in this manner, both the legal form of these instruments would be streamlined (for example Framework Decisions would be replaced by Directives) and the full 'Community' effect would apply.[316]

The 'pick-and-choose' approach of Member States, in particular the UK, in combination with the contested provisions defining Union competence in criminal matters, may also lead to a high degree of legal complexity with regard to the application of EU criminal law to Member States with 'opt-outs'. This is in particular the case in the light of the subordination of EU criminal procedure measures under the logic of mutual recognition. To take the example of EU standards on defence rights: currently the UK Government is opposed to the adoption of a legally binding third pillar measure in the field, and has tabled as an alternative a non-legally-binding resolution.[317] At the same time, the UK has been an enthusiastic supporter of the European Arrest Warrant, a prime example of mutual recognition which the defence rights proposal aims partly to complement. As said above, the United Kingdom has under Lisbon the option of not opting into Title V measures, including measures on criminal procedure. The position is not clear, however, in situations where the UK has participated or wishes to take part in future mutual recognition measures (such as the European Arrest Warrant and its amending legislation post-Lisbon) but does not wish to participate in criminal

---

[313] See also the Declaration concerning Art 10 of the Protocol on transitional provisions, where EU institutions are invited to adopt, in appropriate cases and as far as possible within the five year period set out in the Protocol, legal acts amending or replacing existing measures.

[314] On this point, see Memorandum submitted by V Mitsilegas to the House of Lords European Union Committee for the inquiry on the Lisbon Treaty (House of Lords European Union Committee, HL Paper 62-II, n 211 above—Evidence to the Lisbon Treaty Report, E166–E169, para 11).

[315] Art 10(2).

[316] See in this context also Declaration No 50 concerning Art 10 of the transitional provisions Protocol, whereby EU institutions are invited to seek to adopt, 'in appropriate cases' and as far as possible within the five-year period referred to in Art 10(3) of the Protocol legal acts amending or replacing existing third pillar law.

[317] On the UK position, see House of Lords European Union Committee, *Breaking the Deadlock: What Future for EU procedural Rights?*, 2nd Report, session 2006–07, HL Paper 20. For more on the defence rights proposal see ch 2.

procedure measures (such as the rights of the defendant) which are deemed necessary to facilitate such mutual recognition. While the letter of the law indicates that the UK has the option not to participate if the Government so wishes, the political and practical repercussions of such a decision may be significant. In the case where the EU has adopted minimum standards on the rights of the defendant and the UK has not opted into this measure, the viability of the operation of the European Arrest Warrant in the UK may be seriously questioned.[318] The extent to which the UK will wish to stay out of important developments in EU criminal law in the light of these complexities remains to be seen. In an increasingly integrated 'area of freedom, security and justice', the UK 'pick and choose' approach on EU home affairs may prove much harder to sustain.

VII. CONCLUSION

The development of the institutional framework on the third pillar demonstrates the strong tension between the development of EU-wide action in criminal matters on the one hand and the maintenance of State sovereignty in the criminal law field on the other. In this light, the development of the third pillar has been a gradual process, and the outcome of a series of hard-fought compromises reached in the Maastricht and Amsterdam Intergovernmental Conferences. These compromises are translated into a very complex legal framework, granting Union competence in criminal matters but on the other hand comprising a number of very strong intergovernmental elements: along with the maintenance of a separate pillar for EU action in criminal matters, these elements are in particular the effective maintenance of the right to veto by Member States (ensured by unanimity in the Council); the considerable limits to the jurisdiction of the Court of Justice; the weak (although strengthened in Amsterdam) third pillar legal instruments; and the acute democratic deficit in the third pillar, highlighted in particular by the limited role (consultation) of the European Parliament.

As will be seen in detail further in this book, these are not the only limits to democratic scrutiny, judicial control and accountability in the third pillar. A closer look at the *form* of EU action in third pillar matters indicates a move from harmonisation, and the negotiation of EU-wide standards, to the development of European integration in the field increasingly by mutual recognition, the establishment of EU bodies such as Europol and Eurojust and the emphasis on operational co-operation and EU databases. These forms of EU action retain a number of strong intergovernmental elements and raise a number of issues with regard to democratic control, legitimacy and accountability as they are largely shielded from the scrutiny arrangements that accompany the standard adoption of a Union harmonisation measure.[319]

---

[318] See V Mitsilegas, Memorandum to House of Lords Constitution Committee, n 314 above, pp 63–64 (paras 14–15).

[319] On these issues, see V Mitsilegas, 'Legitimacy, Accountability and Fundamental Rights in the Area of Freedom, Security and Justice', in M Martin, n 292 above, pp 34–43.

The limits to the third pillar institutional framework stand in sharp contrast with two features in the development of EU criminal law post-Amsterdam. The first feature has been the political *impetus* by Member States, as expressed in particular by action in the European Council, to promote EU action in criminal matters in order to boost security. This has led to the adoption of a series of ambitious long-term plans (such as the Tampere Conclusions and the Hague Programme), which have, however, remained partially implemented. The paradoxical symbiosis between the institutional limits to the third pillar on the hand, and the ambitious security agenda of Member States on the other, has led to unfulfilled political promises in particular with regard to the adoption of third pillar law protecting human rights. The second noteworthy feature is the treatment of the third pillar by the Court of Justice. The Court delivered a series of seminal rulings of great constitutional significance for the EU in an era of stagnation of constitutional reform in the EU, most notably after the rejection of the Constitutional Treaty. The Court attempted on a number of occasions to 'streamline' the third pillar in particular by exporting a series of principles from the first pillar to the third. The Court has also not hesitated to 'protect' the first pillar in competence terms, by ruling—as will be seen in greater detail in the next chapter—that criminal law can also by adopted by the Community in the first pillar.

The Lisbon Treaty, if and when it enters into force, will change the institutional framework drastically. The third pillar will be abolished and EU action in criminal matters will be largely 'communitarised'. This move has the potential to enhance greatly the scrutiny of EU criminal law by both the European Parliament and the Court of Justice. However, a closer look at the Lisbon constitutional arrangements reveals that a number of intergovernmental elements remain in the field of EU criminal law. Of particular relevance in this context is the central position of Member States in EU criminal law: the diversity of national legal systems must be respected; Member State governments retain largely the initiative on EU criminal law in the European Council and the Council of Ministers; fundamental changes to EU competence in criminal matters require unanimity in the Council; operational action is designed to remain largely out of bounds for the European Parliament and the Court; and EU action in criminal matters is intensely scrutinised at the national level both ex ante (in particular via the subsidiarity checks by national parliaments) and ex post (by the evaluation of the implementation of EU criminal law by Member States). It remains to be seen whether this emphasis on the Member States will have an impact on the production of EU criminal law post-Lisbon, as well as on legitimacy, transparency and accountability. In this context, it is also noteworthy that European integration in criminal matters in forms other than harmonisation—in particular mutual recognition and EU criminal law bodies—feature prominently in the Lisbon Treaty.

2

Harmonisation and Competence

I. INTRODUCTION

ARMONISATION OF CRIMINAL law in the European Community/ Union has been for a number of years now a topic of constant contro- versy.[1] Prior to the establishment of the third pillar by the Maastricht Treaty, which introduced an express Union competence to act in criminal matters, the debate had been focusing on the extent to which Community law had an impact on criminal law. The establishment of the third pillar did not put a halt on this debate, which has resurfaced strongly in the recent past. On the other hand, EU action in the third pillar produced some degree of criminal law harmonisation, but the extent and precise contours of EU competence on the matter remain con- tested. Two questions are central when one looks at criminal law harmonisation in the Community/Union: the extent of Community/Union *competence* and *powers* to legislate in criminal matters; and the impact of such action on the *substance* of criminal law. This chapter will address both these questions. It will begin by look- ing at the transformation of Community and Union competence in criminal law (covering both substantive criminal law and criminal procedure), focusing in particular on the relationship between Community law and criminal law and the

---

[1] The term 'harmonisation' is a commonly used term regarding Community action in the first pil- lar, in particular with regard to the development of the internal market but also expanding into other areas of Community competence—for an overview, see S. Weatherill, 'Harmonisation: How Much, How Little?', *European Business Law Review*, 2005, pp 533–545; and same author, 'Why Harmonise?', in T Tridimas and P Nebbia (eds), *European Law for the Twenty-First Century. Rethinking the New Legal Order*, vol 2, Oxford, Hart Publishing, 2004, pp 11–32. For a discussion on the applicability of the con- cept in EU criminal law, see the contributions in A Klip and H van der Wilt, *Harmonisation and Harmonising Measures in Criminal Law*, Amsterdam, Royal Netherlands Academy of Arts and Sciences, 2002. Harmonisation in the context of EU criminal law has also been examined in comparison to the term of 'approximation', which is also used in the EU Treaty. It has been argued that, with the differ- ence between the two concepts being unclear, they can be deemed to be in effect synonymous— A Weyembergh, *L'harmonisation des législations: condition de l'espace pénal européen et révélateur de ses tensions*, Éditions de l'Université de Bruxelles, 2004, p 33. 'Approximation may be seen as a process of "bringing things closer to each other"' (see F M Tadic, 'How Harmonious Can Harmonisation Be? A Theoretical Approach towards Harmonisation of (Criminal) Law' in Klip and van der Wilt, above, p 9), and as such can certainly apply to EC/EU criminal law. However, the difference of this process to harmonisation may indeed be a matter of degree and is not always clear. While both approximation and harmonisation are different from uniformity and from the development of a 'one-size-fits-all' criminal law, harmonisation can be seen to imply—along with the approximation of *national* criminal laws—the creation of common standards aiming at ensuring 'harmony' in the *Community/Union* system of criminal law. It is in this context that the term 'harmonisation' will be used in this chapter.

debate on the existence of Community competence in criminal matters. It will then examine the degree and substance of criminal law harmonisation under the third pillar and look at the challenges surrounding the production of harmonised criminal law standards at EU level in the light of substantial differences among Member States' legal and constitutional traditions. The analysis will be complemented by the examination of the reconfiguration of the competence question by the provisions of the Lisbon Treaty, which will introduce a number of significant changes in Union powers to harmonise criminal law, and potentially on the substance of such criminal law.

II. COMMUNITY LAW AND CRIMINAL LAW

A. The Symbiotical Relationship Between Community Law and (National) Criminal Law

i. General

The debate on the existence and extent of a role for the Community in the field of criminal law has been long-standing.[2] A key factor leading to ambiguity and conflicting views on the existence of competence of the European Community in criminal matters has been the silence of the Community Treaty on the matter, from 1957 to today. At first sight, the primary focus of Community law on the market and free movement could be seen –at least on the surface—to preclude any interaction between the European (economic) Community and criminal law. However, there have been a number of occasions where Community law and criminal law have had to interact in the enactment or implementation of Community law. Such interaction has led to a substantial body of case law by the Court of Justice, which demonstrates that shielding criminal law from the objectives and legislation of the Community has not always been possible. There are three main lines of cases in which the Court has affirmed the interrelationship

---

[2] From the plethora of academic writing in the field, see in particular M Delmas-Marty, 'The European Union and Penal Law', *European Law Journal* vol 4/1, 1998, 87–115; H Labayle, 'L'ouverture de la jarre de Pandore: réflexions sur la compétence de la Communauté en matière pénale', *Cahiers de droit européen*, 2006, pp 382–428 (in particular pp 379–388); C Harding, 'Exploring the Intersection of European Law and National Criminal Law' *European Law Review*, vol 25, 2000, pp 374–390; U Sieber, 'Union européenne et droit pénal européen', *Revue de science criminelle et du droit pénal comparé*, 1993, 249–264; J Dine, 'European Community Criminal Law?', *Criminal Law Review*, 1993, pp 246–254; H G Sevenster, 'Criminal Law and EC Law', *Common Market Law Review*, vol 29, 1992, 29–70; M Wasmeier and N Thwaites, 'The "Battle of the Pillars": Does the European Community have the Power to Approximate National Criminal Laws?', *European Law Review*, vol 29, 2004, 613–635; A Klip, 'European Integration and Harmonisation and Criminal Law', in D. Curtin et al, *European Integration and Law*, Antwerp and Oxford: Intersentia, 2006, 109–150; S Peers, *EU Justice and Home Affairs Law*, 2nd edn, Oxford, Oxford University Press, 2006, ch 8; and G Giudicelli-Delage and S Manacorda (eds), *L'intégration pénale indirecte*, Paris, Société de législation comparée, 2005. For an early analysis, see J W Bridge, 'The European Communities and the Criminal Law', *Criminal Law Review*, 1976, pp 88–97.

between criminal law and Community law—the first two confirm the impact of Community law on national criminal law, while the third demonstrates the impact that domestic criminal law principles may have on Community law.

ii. The Impact of Community Law on National Criminal Law—Proportionality and the Limits to National Criminal Law

In a number of cases, the Court of Justice has confirmed that Community law places limits on the application of national criminal law, if the latter would have as its effect to limit disproportionately rights established by Community law, in particular rights related to free movement. As early as 1981, the Court stated in *Casati* that

> In principle, criminal legislation and the rules of criminal procedure are matters for which the Member States are still responsible. However, it is clear from a consistent line of cases decided by the Court, that Community law also sets *certain limits* in that area as regards the control measures which it permits the Member States to maintain in connection with the free movement of goods and persons. The administrative measures or penalties must not go beyond what is strictly necessary, the control procedures must not be concerned in such a way as to restrict the freedom required by the Treaty and they must not be accompanied by a penalty which is so disproportionate to the gravity of the infringement that it becomes an obstacle to the exercise of that freedom. (emphasis added).[3]

The Court justified this approach, notwithstanding the objections of a number of Member States,[4] on the grounds of the necessity to prevent the erosion of Community law freedoms by national measures.[5] The Court's approach is based on the principle of proportionality. As Tridimas has noted, the Court followed in *Casati* a strict proportionality test, and confirmed this approach in a series of cases concerning obstacles posed by national criminal law to the exercise of Community free movement rights.[6] In order to ensure the exercise of Community rights, the Court has not hesitated to check the compatibility with Community law of domestic criminal laws penalising conduct as diverse as driving without a licence in the host Member State (resulting from failure to exchange within the time limits prescribed by the law of the host State the home state driving licence with the host state licence),[7] and pursuing the organised activity of collecting bets without a

---

[3] Case 203/80, [1981] ECR 2595, para 27.

[4] See in particular the views of Ireland and Denmark, both arguing that in principle penalties are a matter for Member States to determine. Casati, previous n, para 2606.

[5] Para 28.

[6] T Tridimas, *The General Principles of EU Law*, 2nd edn, Oxford, Oxford University Press, 2006, p 234. See also pp 234–238 for an overview of the Court's application of proportionality to a series of cases concerning the free movement of persons and goods—see in particular cases concerning residence conditions of EU nationals in other Member States. For a similar overview, see also Peers, *EU Justice*, n 2 above, pp 397–399.

[7] Case C-193/94 *Skanavi and Chryssanthakopoulos* [1996] ECR I-929. For an overview see Tridimas, previous n, pp 235–236.

licence or a police authorisation.[8] In addition to limits to the imposition of criminal sanctions by Member States, the Court has held that State sovereignty in choosing the language of criminal proceedings may be limited in order to ensure non-discrimination against persons to whom Community law grants equal treatment rights, as well as free movement.[9]

iii. The Impact of Community Law on National Criminal Law—Effectiveness and Assimilation

The Court's intervention in criminal matters has not been confined to cases limiting the application of national criminal law. On the contrary, in a number of cases the Court has developed mechanisms whereby the use of criminal law at national level might be encouraged, and thus increased. This increase in the application of national criminal law concerns primarily cases where the latter is deemed necessary to ensure the effectiveness of Community law. Already in the '70s, the Court more than hinted at the use of national criminal law for that purpose, stating that

> [a]lthough Article 5 of the EEC Treaty places Member States under a duty to take all appropriate measures, whether general or particular, to ensure fulfilment of the obligations resulting from action taken by the institutions of the Community, it allows the various Member States to choose the measures which they consider appropriate, including sanctions *which may even be criminal in nature.* (emphasis added)[10]

Amsterdam Bulb is a clear reflection of the view that criminal law may be used as a means to an end, with the end being the achievement of the effectiveness of Community law.[11] This view applies here in the context of criminal law *at the national level,* while, as will be seen below, it has also played a central role in the development of *Community* competence to legislate in criminal matters. The

---

[8] Joint Cases C-338/04, C-359/04 and C-360/04, *Placanica, Palazzese and Sorricchio*, ECR [2007] I-1891. The Court referred therein to the case of *Calfa*, Case 48/96 [1999] ECR I-11, where it was held that the penalty of expulsion of a Community national found guilty of drug possession for personal use was precluded by Arts 48, 52 and 59 of the EC Treaty and Art 3 of Directive 64/221/EC. Being a tourist, Calfa was deemed by the Court to be a recipient of services following the earlier *Cowan* ruling (Case 186/87 *Cowan v Trésor Public* [1989] ECR 195).

[9] Case C-274/96 *Bickel and Franz*, ECR [1998] I-7637.

[10] Case 50/76 *Amsterdam Bulb* [1977] ECR 137, para 32. The Court continued by stating that in the absence of any provision in the Community rules providing for specific sanctions to be imposed on individuals for a failure to observe those rules, the Member States are competent to adopt such sanctions as appear to them to be appropriate (para 33).

[11] See also the Commission's submission in the case, stating that:

> It is clear that, as regards Community law, the validity of a national provision imposing penal sanctions depends on that of the provisions whose observance it is intended to ensure. A provision which imposes penal sanctions is compatible with Community law to the extent to which the rule of substance in relation to which it was adopted is itself compatible with that law. As regards rules of substance which are compatible with Community law, it is certain that *Member States are not only empowered but also, with Art 5 of the EEC Treaty, obliged to take all appropriate measures, whether general or particular, to ensure the proper implementation of Community rules.* (ibid, at p 144, emphasis added).

Court maintained effectiveness at the heart of its case law on the impact of Community law on national criminal law, and in the late '80s took its reasoning a step further in a landmark judgment concerning the possibility of imposition of national criminal sanctions for the protection of the financial interests of the Community. In *Commission v Greece*,[12] the Court stated that:

> where Community legislation does not specifically provide any penalty for an infringement or refers for that purpose to national laws, regulations and administrative provisions, Article 5 of the Treaty requires the Member States to take all measures necessary to guarantee the application and effectiveness of Community law.
>
> For that purpose, whilst the choice of penalties remains within their discretion, they must ensure in particular that infringements of Community law are penalised under conditions, both procedural and substantive, which are analogous to those applicable to infringements of national law of a similar nature and importance and which, in any event, make the penalty effective, proportionate and dissuasive.
>
> Moreover, the national authorities must proceed, with respect to infringements of Community law, with the same diligence as that which they bring to bear in implementing corresponding national laws.[13]

Based on effectiveness, the Court thus introduced the principle of assimilation: community law must be 'assimilated' in national legal systems, and infringements of community law must be treated in a manner analogous to the manner that breaches of similar domestic law are treated. In the present case (also referred to as the Greek maize case), this would effectively mean that Greek authorities would have to treat fraud against the community budget in an analogous way to the treatment of fraud against the national budget—if the latter is punishable by criminal sanctions at the national level, the former must be punishable by criminal sanctions too. The assimilation principle has been developed further by the Court, which stated that effective national measures 'may include criminal penalties even where the community legislation only provides for civil sanctions'.[14] The principle has also been reflected, as will be seen below, in primary and secondary community law in the context of fraud. Moreover, the requirement for 'effective, dissuasive and proportionate' sanctions has now appeared in a plethora of community law instruments.[15]

iv. The Impact of National Criminal Law on Community Law—Criminal Law Principles as General Principles of Community Law

The potential impact of Community law on national criminal law (especially when this results in an increase of criminalisation) has brought into the fore a number of issues related to the need to accommodate, by both the Community and national legal systems, safeguards for the individual in the application of criminal

---

[12] Case C-68/88 [1989] ECR 2965.
[13] Paras 23–25.
[14] Case C-186/98 *Nunes de Matos*, ECR [1999] 4883 para 14.
[15] For an overview, see Labayle, 'L'ouverture', n 2 above, p 387.

law—in particular safeguards related to the principles of legal certainty and non-retroactivity in criminal proceedings. To address this issue, the Court has developed extensive case law, confirmed by the *Pupino* judgment,[16] on the limits imposed to the obligation of national courts to interpret national law to the extent possible in conformity with Community/Union law to take into account the particular position of the individual in the criminal process.[17] However, along with the limits to indirect effect, considerations related to the potential severe consequences of criminal law to the individual and the need to protect fundamental rights in the context of the criminal justice process have also led to the *export* of national law safeguards related to legal certainty and non-retroactivity to the Community legal order.

A prime example of such exported norm is the principle of the retroactive application of the more lenient penalty, which, according to the Court in *Berlusconi,*[18] forms part of the constitutional traditions common to the Member States and thus must be regarded as forming part of the general principles of Community law which the courts must respect when applying national legislation implementing Community law.[19] The Court appears to use this principle as a counter-weight to the assimilation principle which it reiterates earlier in the judgment.[20] It also places the application of the principle in the present case in the particular context of the fact that the Community legislation in question was a Directive—the Court reiterated its earlier case law that a Directive cannot, of itself and independently of a national law for its implementation, have the effect of determining or aggravating the liability in criminal law of persons who act in contravention of the provisions of that directive.[21] Given the focus of the judgment on the *form* of the legal instrument concerned, the question arises whether this general principle of Community law would also apply if the requirement to impose penalties was included in a Regulation (and not in a Directive). It has been suggested that the national court might be under an obligation to set aside national law in such cases.[22] As seen in chapter 1, post-Lisbon EU criminal law will primarily take the form of Directives.[23] However, this may not necessarily be the case with measures on mutual recognition or substantive criminal Law measures adopted on a legal basis outside the AFSJ Title.

---

[16] Case C-105/03, *Maria Pupino*, ECR [2005] I-5285.

[17] For further analysis, see ch 1.

[18] Joint Cases C-387/02, C-391/02, C-403/02, *Berlusconi, Adelchi, Dell'Utri and Others,* ECR [2005] I-3585. See comments by H van der Wilt, 'Case Note', *European Constitutional Law Review,* vol 2, 2006, pp 303–309 and by A Biondi and R Mastroianni, 'Case Note', *Common Market Law Review,* vol 43, 2006, pp 553–569.

[19] Paras 68 and 69.

[20] Para 65.

[21] Para 74, referring to the Case 80/86 *Kolpinghuis Nijmegen* [1987] ECR 3969 and Case C-60/02 *X* [2004] ECR [2004] I-651.

[22] Tridimas, n 6 above, pp 264–265.

[23] See in particular Art 82(2) TFEU on measures on criminal procedure and Art 83(1) and (2) TFEU with regard to substantive criminal law.

B. The Community Competence to Define Criminal Offences and Impose Criminal Sanctions

i. Background

Notwithstanding its extensive case law affirming the interaction between Community law and national criminal law, at least until recently, the Court of Justice has not conferred to the Community explicitly the competence to define *criminal* offences and impose *criminal* sanctions.[24] This stance, coupled with the silence of the EC Treaty on the matter (and thus the lack of express provisions therein attributing to the Community competence to define criminal offences and impose criminal sanctions), has fuelled the debate on the existence and extent of Community competence in the field. As I have noted elsewhere, in extremis this silence could lead to two diametrically opposed views regarding Community competence in the field, views which are affected by the attitude that one has towards criminal law—in particular whether one considers that criminal law is a special case and should be treated differently from economic law. Those in favour of Community competence to define criminal offences and impose criminal sanctions argue that criminal law should not be distinguished from other fields of law and that the Community should have powers to interfere in one way or another in Member States' decisions in criminal matters in order to safeguard the integrity of the Community legal order. Those more sceptical argue that the criminal law is a special case. It is inextricably linked with State sovereignty and deals with sensitive areas such as the relationship between the individual and the State. They argue that any conferral of competence in criminal matters by Member States to the Community must be express in the Treaties and that intervention in criminal matters does not sit well with the character of the Community as a primarily economic space.[25]

The debate regarding the existence and extent of Community competence in the field of criminal offences and sanctions took the form of inter-institutional battles in the proposal and negotiation of Community legislation touching upon criminal law—with the European Commission arguing on a number of occasions that the Community does have competence in the field in order to ensure the effective application of Community law. A prime example of such stance before

---

[24] This is to distinguish criminal offences and sanctions (the object of this analysis) from Community administrative offences or sanctions (which may, as it has been argued, be in fact criminal sanctions on occasions). The latter will not be examined here. For commentary on administrative offences and sanctions and their potential relationship with EC/EU criminal law, see inter alia Harding above.; P -A Albrecht and S Braum, 'Deficiencies in the Development of European Criminal Law', *European Law Journal*, vol 5, 1999, pp 293–310.

[25] See V Mitsilegas, 'Constitutional Principles of the European Community and European Criminal Law', *European Journal of Law Reform*, vol 8, 2006, pp 301–324 at p 302; see also Wasmeier and Thwaites, n 2 above The authors argue in this context that criminal law should not be viewed as a separate Community policy (like the internal market, the environment etc), but as a field of law which can horizontally advance the Community objectives.

the entry into force of the Maastricht Treaty (which via the third pillar introduced an express Union—but not a Community—competence to adopt legislation in criminal matters) has been the negotiation of the first Money Laundering Directive, which was eventually adopted in 1991.[26] The Community institutions, bound by commitments undertaken under the 1988 UN Convention on drug trafficking and the 1990 Financial Action Task Force (FATF) Recommendations, initiated a process of negotiation of a Community instrument aimed at fighting money laundering—an instrument which should involve, in accordance with the preceding international standards, some degree of criminalisation of money laundering. Given both its aim to fight crime and the need to criminalise money laundering, the proposal for an EC Directive in the field raised the two-fold issue of whether the EC Treaty contained an appropriate legal basis for such an instrument; and whether, even if such legal basis was found (in the event, internal market and free movement legal bases were used),[27] the Community had competence to criminalise money laundering and impose criminal sanctions for such offence(s).[28] In its original proposal, the Commission proposed the criminalisation of money laundering arguing that the use of criminal law would ensure the effectiveness of Community law.[29] The Council, however, was not ready for the conferral of such competence to the Community and the compromise reached in the final text was that money laundering would be 'prohibited' in Member States. This wording—which was repeated in the second and third Money Laundering Directives adopted in 2001 and 2005 respectively, long after the third pillar was introduced (which would have allowed the adoption of Union legislation

---

[26] Council Directive 91/308/EEC of 10 June 1991 on prevention of the use of the financial system for the purpose of money laundering, OJ L 166, 28 June 1991, p 77.

[27] Money laundering has been an example where the need for custodial penalties was accepted by the Commission in order to ensure the smooth functioning of the internal market. On this aspect and the broader debate on the use of penalties in the internal market context, see European Commission, 'Communication on the Role of Penalties in Implementing Community Internal Market Legislation' COM (95) 162 final, Brussels, 3 May 1995.

[28] For a detailed discussion of both aspects, see V Mitsilegas, *Money Laundering Counter-measures in the European Union*, The Hague, London, Kluwer Law International, 2003, ch 3.

[29] OJ C106, 28 April 1990, p 6. According to the Preamble of the proposal,

> making money laundering a criminal offence in the Member States, although it goes beyond the scope of the financial system, constitutes a necessary condition for any action to combat this phenomenon and in particular to permit cooperation between financial institutions or banking supervisors and judicial authorities (recital 10).

In evidence to the House of Lords (then) Select Committee on the European Communities, the Commission justified the choice for criminalisation stating that

> the Community was competent to impose obligations on Member States to carry out penal action, if it deemed that this was necessary to obtain the full effect of the measures which it adopted.

House of Lords Select Committee on the European Communities, *Money Laundering*, session 1990–91, HL Paper 6, p 29. For further analysis, see Mitsilegas, *Money Laundering Counter-measures*, n 28 above, pp 58–63.

criminalising money laundering)—has led to a de facto criminalisation of money laundering in all EU Member States.[30]

The introduction of a Union competence in criminal matters in Maastricht in the third pillar did not change the legal framework regarding criminal law and Community law, with the EC Treaty remaining silent regarding action in criminal matters. If anything, the introduction of the third pillar could strengthen the argument that the Community has no competence to define criminal offences and impose criminal sanctions, as such competence is expressly attributed (and thus limited to) the Union in the third pillar. However, the European Commission continued to press for the adoption of first pillar criminal law measures, which it deemed necessary to achieve the effectiveness of Community law. A key focus of the Commission's effort has been the fight against fraud relating to the Community budget, which was perceived as a quintessential 'Community' interest necessitating criminal law harmonisation in the first pillar. In the second half of the 1990s, the Commission funded an academic study which proposed a so-called *Corpus Juris* to fight fraud against the Community financial interests. The *Corpus Juris* was essentially a mini criminal code, including definitions of a series of criminal offences (for instance fraud, corruption and money laundering), as well as provisions on criminal procedure (including the controversial proposal for the establishment of a European Public Prosecutor).[31] It could thus be seen as an attempt to 'unify' rather than harmonise Community criminal law on the subject.[32] The idea was floated to adopt part or all of the *Corpus Juris* under a first pillar legal basis—in particular Article 280(4) TEC which envisages the adoption of Community measures to prevent and fight fraud, and notwithstanding the fact that according to the same provision these measures 'shall not concern the application of national criminal law or the national administration of justice'.[33]

---

[30] The Directive definitions were eventually linked with provisions contained in parallel EU third pillar measures on confiscation—see the 2001 Framework Decision on money laundering and confiscation (2001/500/JHA OJ L182, 5 July 2001, p 1). On the situation after the adoption of the third Money Laundering Directive, see V Mitsilegas and B Gilmore, 'The EU Legislative Framework Against Money Laundering and Terrorist Finance: A Critical Analysis in the Light of Evolving Global Standards', *International and Comparative Law Quarterly*, vol 56, 2007, pp 119–141.

[31] On the *Corpus Juris* see inter alia: M Delmas-Marty and J Vervaele, *The Implementation of the Corpus Juris in the Member States*, vol 1, Antwerp, Intersentia, 2000; M Delmas-Marty, 'Guest Editorial: Combating Fraud—Necessity, Legitimacy and Feasibility of the *Corpus Juris*', *Common Market Law Review*, vol 37, 2000, pp 247–256; M Delmas-Marty, 'Towards an Integrated European Criminal Law', *Cambridge Yearbook of European Legal Studies*, vol 7, 2004–05, pp.17–31; J R Spencer, 'The Corpus Juris Project and the Fight Against Budgetary Fraud', *Cambridge Yearbook of European Legal Studies*, vol 1, 1998, pp 77–106; J R Spencer, 'The Corpus Juris Project—Has it a Future?', *Cambridge Yearbook of European Legal Studies*, vol 2, 1999, pp 87–124 . For a critical commentary, see M Kaiafa-Gbandi, 'Das Corpus Juris und die Typiesierung des Strafphänomens im Bereich der Europäischen Union', *KritV*, vol 82, 1999, pp 162–180; and I Manoledakis, 'Das Corpus Juris als falsche Grundlage eines gesamteuropäischen Strafjustizsystems', *KritV*, vol 82, 1999, pp 181–190.

[32] On the unification of criminal law in Europe in the context of fraud, see Delmas-Marty, 'Combating Fraud', previous n.

[33] A similar exception can be found in Art 135 TEC concerning customs co-operation. Members of the Group drafting the *Corpus Juris* held a variety of different views on whether the Community had competence to adopt the instrument via a 280(4) legal basis—for an overview, see Delmas-Marty and Vervaele, n 31 above, pp 369–394.

The *Corpus Juris* was not integrated as such in the Community legal order, although some harmonisation of substantive criminal law has taken place in the third (and, in the case of money laundering as stated above in the first) pillar and the idea for the establishment of a European Public Prosecutor is still alive and included in the Lisbon Treaty.[34] Criminal law measures on fraud were adopted in the form of a third pillar Convention and subsequent Protocols.[35] This did not stop the Commission putting forward, in 2001, a proposal for first pillar legislation aimed at harmonising Member States' criminal law in order to tackle fraud against the Community's financial interests.[36] According to the Commission, the third pillar anti-fraud legislation in place had not achieved satisfactory criminal law harmonisation, not least because it was in the form of a Convention which results in delays in ratification. According to the Commission, Community law would help achieve appropriate harmonisation, and the EC Treaty contained a suitable legal basis for aligning substantive criminal law in the Member States as regards the definition of fraud, corruption and money laundering affecting Community financial interests as well as the applicable criminal penalties—Article 280 TEC. The Commission brushed aside the exceptions in Article 280(4) TEC, by stating that:

> the exception does not refer to the whole of criminal law in general but specifically to two aspects of it, namely 'the application of national criminal law' and 'the national administration of justice'. Since, in principle, Article 280(4) covers all measures in the area of preventing and curbing fraud, it is in this context that the second sentence specifies exceptions to this, so given the general purpose of the article, the second sentence can but be interpreted narrowly. The wording and the legal context of the article do not preclude the adoption of measures setting certain harmonisation objectives of a criminal type, provided that they do not 'concern the application of national criminal law or the national administration of justice'.[37]

This reasoning, which attempted somewhat artificially to distinguish between 'national' and 'Community' criminal law [38] did not convince Member States and the Directive proposal was not taken forward by the Council.[39] A similar (but not

---

[34] See ch 4.

[35] See the 1995 Fraud Convention OJ C316, 27 November 1995, p 49) and its Protocols of 1996 (First Protocol, OJ C151, 20 May 1997, p 1) and 1997 (Second Protocol, OJ C221, 19 July 1997, p 12). For an analysis, see S White, *Protection of the Financial Interests of the European Communities: The Fight against Fraud and Corruption*, The Hague, London, Kluwer Law International, 1998.

[36] 'Proposal for a Directive of the European Parliament and of the Council on the criminal-law protection of the Community's financial interests' COM (2001) 272 final, Brussels 23 May 2001.

[37] ibid, pp 5–6. See the analysis in G J M Corstens, 'Criminal Law in the First Pillar?', *European Journal of Crime, Criminal Law and Criminal Justice*, vol 11, 2003, pp 131–144.

[38] In this sense, the Commission seems to reflect the view of K Tiedemann that Art 280(4) guarantees the application of national criminal law, 'without excluding a complementary Community criminal competence going further than the legislation of a Member State' (in Delmas-Marty and Vervaele, n 31 above, p 386; see also on this point the comments of a number of other contributors, in particular Delmas-Marty, Grasso and Spencer—the latter two are particularly sceptical of the appropriateness of Art 280 to act as a legal basis for the *Corpus Juris*).

[39] Although the European Parliament commented on the proposal at first reading leading to an amended Commission proposal—COM (2002) 577 final, Brussels, 16 October 2002.

identical) feat awaited another proposal put forward by the Commission in 2001 aiming at harmonising criminal law by a first pillar measure—a Directive on the protection of the environment through criminal law.[40] The Commission justified the adoption of criminal law via the first pillar as necessary to provide for sufficiently dissuasive and effective penalties ensuring the full compliance of Member States with Community law protecting the environment.[41] Criminal law was thus used in order to ensure the effectiveness of Community law, with the Community having competence to legislate since the objective was environmental protection—with the proposed legal basis being Article 175 EC on environmental protection. As in the Fraud Draft Directive, Member States did not take up the proposal for a first pillar criminal law measure in the Council. However, unlike the fraud case (where some form of criminalisation existed in the third pillar), Member States in this case opted to legislate on environmental crime, but in the third (and not the first) pillar—two years later, the Council adopted a Framework Decision on environmental crime.[42]

We have examined thus far three different outcomes to Commission proposals for Community law harmonising criminal law: cases where criminal law harmonisation was dictated by Community law de facto but not de jure (with Community law referring to prohibition and not expressly to criminalisation: the Money Laundering Directives); cases where the Commission proposal effectively fell in the Council (the Fraud Draft Directive); and cases where the Council opted to legislate in the third—and not the first—pillar (the Environmental Crime Framework Decision). In a fourth scenario, first pillar legislation has been combined with parallel third pillar legislation, with the criminal law aspects moved to the third pillar, but defined by reference to the first pillar. The situation has arisen in particular post-Amsterdam, when asylum and immigration matters were transferred from the third to the first pillar and the issue of the correct legal basis and the existence of competence in criminal matters has arisen in the context of negotiations of measures in the field of irregular migration. A legal basis for the adoption of such measures could be found in the first pillar (in Title IV), but it was unclear whether such first pillar law could include criminal offences and sanctions.[43] The compromise reached in this instance (concerning legislative action on human smuggling), in the light of Member States' reluctance to confer to the Community competence in criminal matters, was to adopt two parallel and interlinked measures: a first pillar Directive describing the regulated conduct, and a third pillar Framework Decision stipulating that the conduct described in the first pillar would be treated as a criminal offence and determining criminal

---

[40] COM (2001) 139 final, Brussels 13 November 2001.

[41] ibid, p 1. For a detailed analysis of the proposal, see Corstens, n 37 above, pp 137–139.

[42] OJ L29, 5 February 2003, p 55.

[43] The umbrella provision of Title IV, Art 61, states that the Council shall adopt inter alia 'measures in the field of police and judicial co-operation in criminal matters aimed at a high level of security by preventing and combating crime within the Union in accordance with the provisions of the Treaty on European Union'. Moreover, as Peers points out, Art 63(3)(b) does not contain an exception along the lines of the wording in Arts 280(4) and 135 TEC (Peers, *EU Justice*, n 2 above, p 390).

sanctions.[44] This strategy[45] was repeated subsequently in legislation relating to other first pillar policies: a Directive and accompanying Framework Decision were adopted regarding the criminalisation of ship-source pollution.[46] However, the legality of the adoption of third pillar legislation in both the ship-source pollution and the environmental crime cases was challenged by the Commission, leading to the Court of Justice to intervene in two cases with substantial constitutional implications.

ii. The Environmental Crime Case

The European Commission decided to react to the Council's choice to adopt criminal legislation in matters deemed to be related to the achievement of Community objectives by challenging the legality of the adoption of the relevant third pillar law. This led initially to the intervention by the Court of Justice which was called to rule on the legality of the adoption of the Framework Decision on environmental crime and gave a ruling with major implications for EU criminal and constitutional law.[47] The Commission, supported by the European Parliament, instituted an action for annulment of the Framework Decision, arguing that the third pillar measure was adopted under the wrong legal basis. It should have been adopted according to the Commission under the first pillar, as the protection of the environment is a first pillar objective. The Commission argued that while the Community does not have a general competence in criminal matters, it has competence to prescribe criminal penalties for infringements of Community environmental protection legislation if it takes the view that that is a *necessary means* of ensuring that the *legislation is effective*—adding that the harmonisation of national criminal law is *designed to be an aid* to the Community policy in question.[48] Along with this argument—based on the view that criminal law is merely an auxiliary, 'horizontal' means of achieving Community objectives—the Commission evoked

---

[44] Council Directive 2002/90/EC of 8 November 2002 defining the facilitation of unauthorised entry, transit and residence, OJ L328, 5 December 2002, p 4, and corresponding Framework Decision, same OJ, p 1. For an analysis, see V Mitsilegas, J Monar and W Rees, *The European Union and Internal Security,* Basingstoke, Palgrave Macmillan, 2003, ch 4.

[45] Vervaele calls this a 'cohabitation forcée'—see 'The European Community and Harmonization of the Criminal Law Enforcement of Community Policy', *European Criminal Law Associations' Forum,* vols 3–4, 2006, p 88. Vervaele also refers to the 'warding off' of Commission first pillar legislative proposals by Member States, and 'hijacking' of proposals such as the environmental crime Directive by Member States and their adoption in the third pillar.

[46] OJ L255, 30 September 2005, p 11 and 164.

[47] Case C-176/03, *Commission v Council,* ECR [2005] I-7879. For case commentaries, see C Tobler, Case-note, *Common Market Law Review,* vol 43, 2006, 835–854; S. White, 'Harmonisation of Criminal Law under the First Pillar', *European Law Review,* vol 31, 2006, 81–92; M Böse, 'Die Zustaendigkeit der Europäischen Gemeinschaft fuer das Strafrecht Zugleich Besprechung von EuGH, Urteil vom 13.9.2005', *Goldtammer's Archiv,* 2006, pp 211–224; and E Herlin-Karnell, '*Commission v. Council:* Some Reflections on Criminal Law in the First Pillar', *European Public Law,* vol 13, 2007, pp 69–84. See also Labayle, 'L'ouverture', n 2 above, pp 379–428.

[48] Para 19 of the judgment.

Member States' duty of loyal co-operation and the general principles of effectiveness and equivalence, constantly present in the Court's case law.[49]

The Council, supported by no less than 11 Member States,[50] opposed this view. The Council and the vast majority of the Member States[51] argued that as the law currently stands, the Community does not have power to require Member States to impose criminal penalties in respect of the conduct covered by the Framework Decision.[52] Not only is there *no express conferral of power in that regard*, but, given the considerable *significance of criminal law for the sovereignty of Member States*, there are no grounds for accepting that this power can have been implicitly transferred to the Community at the time where substantive competences, such as those exercised under Article 175 EC, were conferred on it.[53] Moreover, Articles 135 EC and 280 EC, which expressly reserve to the Member States the application of national criminal law and the administration of justice, confirm that interpretation. It is also borne out by the fact that the Treaty on the European Union devotes a specific title to judicial co-operation in criminal matters, which *expressly confers on the European Union competence in criminal matters*.[54] Finally, the Council argued, the Court has never obliged Member States to adopt criminal penalties and legislative practice is in keeping with that interpretation.[55]

The Court found for the Commission and annulled the Framework Decision. The Court used Articles 47 and 29 TEU, according to which nothing in the TEU is to affect the EC Treaty.[56] The Court then focused on the environment as a Community objective. It confirmed that the environment constitutes one of the *essential objectives* of the Community; reminded that, according to settled case law, the choice of legal basis must rest on objective factors that are amenable to judicial review, including in particular the aim and the content of the measure; and stated that the aim is the protection of the environment and the content particularly serious environmental offences.[57] The essential character of environmental protection as a Community objective is crucial for determining whether criminal law can be used to achieve this objective in the Community pillar. According to the Court, while *as a general rule, neither criminal law nor the rules of criminal procedure fall*

---

[49] Para 20. A similar argument was advanced in 2003 by the European Parliament Legal Affairs Committee in its Report on legal bases and compliance with Community law (A5–0180/2003, 22 May 2003, *rapporteur.* I Koukiadis). The Committee used Art 10 EC on loyal co-operation to argue in favour of the existence of EC competence in criminal matters in certain circumstances. However, the Committee took a seemingly more limited view to that of the Commission, arguing that EC competence to require the Member States to make provision for criminal penalties must be limited to cases in which the Community legislator considers that compliance with Community law can *only* be safeguarded by such means (point 5, emphasis added).

[50] Denmark, Germany, Greece, Spain, France, Ireland, the Netherlands, Portugal, Finland, Sweden and the United Kingdom.

[51] With the exception of the Netherlands who supported the Council but via a different reasoning.

[52] Para 26.

[53] Para 27.

[54] Paras 28 and 29.

[55] Paras 31 and 32.

[56] Para 38.

[57] Paras 41 and 45–47.

71

within EC competence, this does not prevent the EC legislature, *when the application of effective, proportionate and dissuasive criminal penalties* by the competent national authorities is an *essential measure* for combating serious environmental offences, from taking measures which relate to the criminal law of the Member States which it considers *necessary* in order to ensure that the rules which it lays down on environmental protection *are fully effective.*[58] The Court found that Articles 1 to 7 of the Framework Decision (which relate to the environmental crime offences) have as their main purpose the protection of the environment and they could have been properly adopted on the basis of Article 175 EC.[59] That finding is not called into question by the existence of Articles 135 EC and 280 (4) EC.[60] However, the Court added that although Articles 1–7 of the Framework Decision determine that certain conduct which is particularly detrimental to the environment is to be criminal, they leave to the Member States the choice of the criminal penalties to apply (although these must be effective, proportionate and dissuasive).[61]

This is a seminal ruling, reminiscent of the Court's landmark judgments in the 1960s on primacy and direct effect. In the face of a significant number of Member States, and the wording of the Treaties which confer express powers to the Union to act on criminal matters, while being silent on the role of the Community, the Court decided to interpret the Treaties creatively in order to expressly establish a Community competence to act in criminal matters. The timing of the judgment is noteworthy, as it came at a time when the Constitutional Treaty—which would put an end to the pillar structure and in effect would (with some exceptions) fully 'communitarise' the third pillar was 'frozen', having been rejected in France and the Netherlands. This would effectively mean that criminal law harmonisation—if confined to the third pillar only—would necessitate unanimity of the then 25 (and, from 1 January 2007, 27) Member States, and require mere consultation of the European Parliament—thus potentially leading to legislative paralysis and the exacerbation of the democratic deficit in criminal matters. In the light of this timing, a further parallel could be drawn here with the '60s, where the Court pushed European integration in the face of legislative stagnation.

The starting point in the Court's reasoning in ascertaining the conferral of criminal law competence to the Community is the focus on the effect of Articles 29 and 47 TEU, which state respectively that third pillar action must be 'without

---

[58] Paras 47–48.

[59] Para 51.

[60] Para 52. The Court added that it is not possible to infer from those provisions that, for the purposes of the implementation of environmental policy, any harmonisation of criminal law, even as limited as that resulting from the Framework Decision, must be ruled out even where it is necessary in order to ensure the effectiveness of Community law.

[61] Para 49. In this context the Court seems to follow the distinction made between criminalisation and the choice of the appropriate penalty in the Opinion of AG Ruiz-Jarabo Colomer, who stated that

> it seems clear that the response to conduct which seriously harms the environment must be a criminal one but, in terms of punishment, the choice of the penalty to admonish that conduct and to ensure the effectiveness of Community law is the province of the Member States (para 84). ECR 2005, I-7879.

prejudice to the powers of the European Community and that nothing in the EU Treaty will affect the Treaties establishing the European Communities. The Court used these provisions to strengthen the Community pillar and to address its centrality and primacy over the intergovernmental pillars. It sent thus a strong signal that third pillar action must not jeopardise Community action.[62] Having asserted the primacy and the need to ensure the integrity of the Community pillar, the Court did not take up the Commission's reference to the principle of loyal co-operation, and did not take up the Advocate General's extensive analysis of the specific need for a high level protection of the environment.[63] It rather chose to focus specifically and extensively on an analysis justifying the conferral to the Community of a criminal law competence on the basis of the need to ensure the effective achievement of Community objectives. In this respect, the fact that the case involved the protection of the environment—an 'essential' Community objective according to the Court—may have been of particular relevance, notwithstanding the fact that the Court did not focus on environmental protection to such a great length as had the Advocate General.[64] What is significant in this context is that the Court did not hesitate to apply its reasoning on the effective achievement of Community objectives in the field of criminal law, viewing criminal law as a means to an end, rather as a special field of law where special rules must apply. Criminal law will fall within Community competence, like any other field of law, if Community objectives are at stake. This conclusion may appear striking bearing in mind the express exclusion of the application of national criminal law in matters relating to customs co-operation and fraud by the EC Treaty (Articles 135 and 280(4)) and the express conferral of competence in criminal matters on the Union (and not the Community).[65]

However, it is not clear whether the judgment has established in principle that the Community may, under certain circumstances, have competence in the field

---

[62] Manacorda has called this a censure by the Court of 'prohibited intergovernmentalisation' (*intergouverementalisation prohibée*). S Manacorda, '*Judicial Activism* dans le cadre de l'espace de liberté, de justice et de sécurité de l'Union européenne', *Revue de science criminelle et du droit pénal comparé*, 2005, p 956.

[63] On this point, see H Labayle, 'Architecte ou spectatrice? La Cour de justice de l'Union dans l'espace de liberté, sécurité et justice', *Revue trimestrielle du droit européen*, vol 42, 2006, pp 1–46 at pp 10–11.

[64] On the significance of environmental protection in the development of the Court's case law, see F Jacobs, 'The Role of the European Court of Justice in the Protection of the Environment', *Journal of Environmental Law*, vol 18, 2006, 185–205.

[65] For a critical view, see the evidence of Richard Plender to the House of Lords European Union Committee. Plender, who was counsel for the United Kingdom in the case, wonders whether the conferral of an implied Community power in criminal law was legitimate in the face of the absence of a subjective intention by Member States to confer such power and the existence of an express EU power in the third pillar. See House of Lords European Union Committee, *The Criminal Law Competence of the European Community*, 42nd Report, session 2005–06, HL Paper 227, Q1. For the opposite view, see C Tobler (n 47 above, p 851), who argues that the Council seems to forget that the EC Treaty does not confer a catalogue of negative competences. For a view advocating Community action in criminal matters—very much along the lines put forward by the Court—see also Wasmeier and Thwaites, n 2 above.

of criminal law in general, or that it is limited to environmental crime only.[66] While the second case is highly unlikely, questions regarding the extent and scope of Community competence in criminal matters still remain.[67] The Court did not specify whether Community competence in criminal law is limited to the definition of criminal offences or extends also to the imposition and precise definition of criminal sanctions.[68] The Court mentions that, while the annulled Framework Decision criminalises conduct that is particularly detrimental to the environment, it leaves to the Member States the choice of the criminal penalties to apply.[69] It is not clear, however, if this means that the Community is granted powers to criminalise only or also to impose criminal sanctions, at least in the environmental crime field.[70] It seems paradoxical—and potentially incoherent—to confer competence to define criminal offences and impose the criminalisation of certain types of conduct but leave the choice of the sanctions to Member States. Moreover, the imposition of a criminalisation requirement to Member States in the first place (which, under the qualified majority voting arrangements of the first pillar may be outvoted in such a measure) arguably constitutes at least as great a challenge to State sovereignty and the exercise of power in the criminal law sphere as the dictation of the imposition of specific criminal sanctions.

A related issue involves the objectives for the achievement of which the Community has a criminal law competence.[71] The case involved environmental crime, which, according to the Court, is one of the 'essential' objectives of the Community.[72] It is not clear, however, whether Community competence in criminal matters concerning environmental protection played a part in the Court's ruling and therefore the Court's approach regarding the delimitation of EC competence in criminal matters in the future.[73] Is the environment a special case? Is Community competence in criminal matters limited when necessary to achieve

[66] A very narrow view in this context has been put forward by ECJ Judge Puissochet, who stated before the French Senate that the Court has only said in this case that the Community has competence to oblige Member States to impose criminal sanctions *to protect the environment*. It has not recognised a Community competence to harmonise criminal law. Sénat, Réunion de la délégation pour l'Union européenne du mercredi 22 février 2006.

[67] See also Labayle, 'Architecte', n 63 above, p 14 and evidence by Steve Peers to the House of Lords European Union Committee, n 65 above, Q52.

[68] Some authors seem to suggest that Community competence is limited to criminalisation only. See C Haguenau-Moizard, 'Vers une harmonisation communautaire du droit pénal?', *Revue trimestrielle du droit européen*, vol 42, 2006, pp 377–389 at p 384.

[69] Para 49.

[70] Wasmeier and Thwaites (n 2 above, p 634) argue that if a measure specifically aims at a concrete Community objective, particularly at the enforcement of related Community provisions through dissuasive (criminal) sanctions, it may fall into Community competence—however, detailed rules on the type and scale of sanctions would go beyond such an 'implied power'. In case of such a situation one could still have a cross-pillar split.

[71] And of course whether EC competence in criminal matters could be viewed outside the framework of the achievement of Community objectives.

[72] Para 41.

[73] The Court did not hesitate to annul the 'PNR' international agreement between the Community and the US, on the grounds that the main objective of the agreement (to fight terrorism) was really a third pillar issue. Cases C-317/04 and C-318/04—for an analysis see ch 6.

an 'essential' Community objective, and if yes, what constitutes such an objective?[74] Or, at the other extreme, does EC competence in criminal matters extend to the achievement of any Community objective? Does Community competence extend beyond the effective achievement of Community *objectives* to the effective achievement of Community *policies*? Varied interpretations have been put forward by Union institutions in their reactions to the judgment.

iii. Reactions to the Court's Judgment on Environmental Crime

Shortly after the environmental crime judgment, the Commission published a Communication arguing for a recasting of a number of existing EU measures and proposals, while also stating that it would apply the Court's test in future legislative proposals it would table.[75] The Commission interpreted the Court's ruling broadly, arguing that

> from the point of view of subject matter, in addition to environmental protection the Court's reasoning can therefore be applied to all Community policies and freedoms which involve binding legislation with which criminal penalties should be associated in order to ensure their effectiveness.[76]

According to the Commission, the Court's ruling clarified that criminal law provisions required for the effective implementation of Community law are a matter for the first pillar, bringing measures adopted under a dual legal basis in both first/third pillars to an end—with the Commission proposing a quick procedure of recasting existing texts it deems affected by the environmental crime judgment;[77] third pillar legislation would only cover measures related to police and judicial co-operation in criminal matters more broadly.[78] However, the reaction by Member States to the Commission Communication has been rather lukewarm,

---

[74] The latter question has been posed by Plender, n 65 above, Q10, and Labayle, n 63 above, 14. In its Report on the judgment, the French Assembly seems to understand the judgment as limited to the achievement of 'essential' objectives. In their view, it is not enough that an objective is listed as such in the EC Treaty, but it must be essential and transversal. Assemblée Nationale, *Rapport d'information sur les consequences de l'arret de la Cour de Justice du 13 Septembre 2005*, 25 January 2006, Rapport No 2829, p 10.

[75] 'Communication on the implications of the Court's judgment of 13 September 2005' COM (2005) 583 final/2, Brussels, 24.11.2005. The European Parliament supported the Commission's view that a number of EU instruments need to be recast in the light of the Court's judgment, but called for a review on a case-by-case basis and urged the Commission not to automatically extend the conclusions of the Court to every other field falling within the scope of the first pillar—Resolution on the consequences of the judgment of the Court of 13 September 2005 (C-176/03 *Commission v Council*) (2006/2007(INI)), 14 June 2006.

[76] ibid, para 8.

[77] For a list of measures needing to be recast, see the annex to the Communication. These include dual instruments such as those on the facilitation of unauthorised entry, transit and residence mentioned above, but also the adoption in the first pillar of measures thus far adopted under the third pillar (such as the Framework Decision on corruption in the private sector—OJ L192, 31 July 2003, p 54), and the adoption in the first pillar of proposals which had failed in the Council (such as the Proposal for a Directive on the criminal law protection of the Community's financial interests, also mentioned at n 36 above).

[78] ibid, para 11.

with a number of Governments taking the view that future Commission proposals should be considered on a case by case basis.[79] This cautious approach was confirmed at the February 2006 Justice and Home Affairs Council, which agreed merely on a procedure for the examination of future Commission legislative proposals containing provisions on criminal law.[80]

The Commission sought to enhance further the Community's competence in criminal matters by putting forward in 2006—and against the backdrop of the 'freezing' of the ratification process of the Constitutional Treaty (which would abolish the pillars)—a proposal for moving third pillar matters to the first pillar by using the so-called 'passerelle' provision of Article 42 TEU.[81] The Commission called for the use of Article 42 TEU (and the move towards the 'Community method' of decision-making in Title IV) on both democracy and efficiency grounds. It stated that

> Action and accountability in some areas of policy making are hindered by the current decision making arrangements which lead to deadlock and lack of proper democratic scrutiny. Existing Treaty provisions (Articles 42 of the Treaty on the European Union and 67(2) of the Treaty establishing the European Community) allow for changes to these arrangements, which would improve decision taking in the Council and allow proper democratic scrutiny by the European Parliament; and the enhancement of the role of the Court of Justice.[82]

The use of the passerelle provision of the TEU was also strongly backed by Commission President Barroso, who placed more emphasis on security, stating that the latter 'is increasingly becoming a concern of people in Europe' and that 'the most effective response in the field of security is a European response', 'with or without a Constitution'.[83] However, Member States again appeared rather

---

[79] See, eg, the reaction of the UK Government: in the Explanatory Memorandum to the Westminster European Union Committees regarding the Commission Communication, it was noted that the Commission's proposal to simply repeal the offending third pillar provision and re-enact it in new first pillar instruments was not favoured by the Government 'because we consider that any new provisions relating to the criminal law introduced under the First Pillar should be considered on a case by case basis'. Explanatory Memorandum by Ms Fiona MacTaggart (then Parliamentary Under Secretary of State, Home Office) of 16 January 2006, para 17.

[80] According to the Council conclusions, in these cases, the Presidency will draw the attention of COREPER II and, following the latter's guidance, will refer the proposal to an 'appropriate' working party for examination, taking into account all relevant factors, such as its content, aim and required expertise. The opportunity for Justice and Home Affairs experts to given an input to the negotiations of criminal law proposals should be ensured. Doc 6077/06 (Presse 38), p 10.

[81] This states that

> the Council, acting unanimously on the initiative of the Commission or a Member State, and after consulting the European Parliament, may decide that action in areas referred to in Art 29 [the umbrella provision for the third pillar] shall fall under Title IV of the Treaty establishing the European Community, and at the same time determine the relevant voting conditions relating to it. It shall recommend the Member States to adopt that decision in accordance with their respective constitutional requirements.

[82] Communication from the Commission to the European Council, 'A Citizens' Agenda: Delivering Results for Europe' COM (2006) 211 final, Brussels, 10 May 2006 p 6.

[83] Speech of Mr Barroso, *Strengthening a Citizens' Europe*, 9 May Celebrations, Bélem Cultural Centre, 8 May 2006 (speech/06/283) from www.europa.eu.

sceptical of the Commission's initiative. In the Tampere Council of September 2006 no less than 14 Member States rejected the proposals to use the 'passerelle' provision [84] and by the end of 2006 the debate was deemed to be concluded against the use of Article 42 TEU.[85]

Following its Communication reacting to the Court's environmental crime ruling, and notwithstanding the cautious reaction by the Council and the passerelle setback, the Commission tabled three major first pillar proposals involving Community action on the definition of criminal offences and the imposition of criminal sanctions—all of which are currently under negotiation. The first Commission initiative of this kind was a proposal for a Directive on criminal measures aimed at the enforcement of intellectual property rights.[86] The proposal replaced earlier Commission proposals following the 'dual' model of a first pillar Directive and a parallel third pillar Framework Decision on the enforcement of intellectual property rights, both of which were tabled prior to the Court's ruling.[87] The legal basis of the proposal is Article 95 TEC (on the internal market) and contains not only detailed provisions on criminal sanctions, but also provisions on confiscation, joint investigation teams and the initiation of criminal proceedings[88]—something that constitutes a very broad interpretation of the scope of Community competence and which arguably falls outside Community criminal law competence as defined by the Court.

The second proposal, as expected, was a proposal for a Directive on the protection of the environment through criminal law.[89] The proposal addresses specifically the Court's ruling on environmental crime, with the Commission aiming at recasting the proposal in the light of its interpretation of the judgment. The legal basis of the proposal is Article 175(1) on environmental protection. The proposal includes detailed definitions of offences and detailed provisions on criminal sanctions, both for natural and legal persons (but, unlike the intellectual property rights proposal, no provisions on criminal procedure). Negotiations are ongoing, with the Justice and Home Affairs Council accepting that the Directive 'will probably be one of the first sets of legal instruments by means of which criminal law arrangements can be made in the context of the first pillar, and as such will to some extent serve as an example'.[90] The Council notes that fundamental issues need to be clarified regarding both the scope of the criminal offences and the rule on criminal sanctions—with discussions on the latter having being postponed until the

---

[84] 'EU Plan to Fight Terror in Tatters', *Financial Times* (23–24 September 2006).

[85] See House of Lords European Union Committee, *The Criminal Law Competence of the EC: follow-up Report*, 11th Report, session 2006–07, HL Paper 63. See also ch 1. According to the then UK Minister for Europe, Geoff Hoon, the situation with regard to the use of Art 42 was 'a matter of intellectual inquiry only'—para 4.

[86] COM (2006) 168 final, Brussels, 26 April 2006.

[87] COM (2005) 276 final. The recasting of the proposals was mentioned in the Commission's post-environmental crime case Communication.

[88] Arts 6–8 of the Commission Proposal.

[89] COM (2007) 51 final, Brussels 9 February 2007.

[90] Conclusions of the Justice and Home Affairs Council of 12–13 June 2007, Council doc 10267/07 (Presse 125), p 41.

Court rules on the second major case concerning the extent of Community criminal law competence, on ship-source pollution.[91] In the meantime, concerns have been expressed that the broad list of proposed criminal offences exceeds the scope of Community competence after the environmental crime case.[92] Similar concerns have been expressed regarding the provisions criminalising participation in the offences set out in the draft Directive and setting penalty levels. [93]

Another first pillar proposal containing criminal law provisions is the draft Directive on sanctions against employers of illegally staying third-country nationals.[94] The proposed legal basis is Article 63(3)(b) TEC (measures on illegal immigration and illegal residence). The main avenue of enforcement of employers' duties under the Directive appear to be administrative sanctions. However, the draft Directive also provides for the criminalisation of serious cases of non-compliance with its provisions and introduces criminal sanctions for such cases.[95] The introduction of criminal offences and sanctions (which, unlike the earlier examples, is not the sole focus of the Commission proposal) is justified by the Commission on the grounds that administrative fines may not have a sufficiently dissuasive effect in certain cases.[96]

Given the uncertainty as to the precise extent of Community criminal law competence following the Court's judgment on the environmental crime case, all three proposals mentioned above have been subject to rigorous scrutiny. The debate has already been focusing on the *content* of some of these proposals, in particular the extent of criminalisation and the levels of proposed criminal sanctions. It is also interesting to look at the *legal bases* of the proposals—the protection of the internal market and the environment, and action against illegal immigration—and link them with the relevant *objectives* of the Community in order to address the question on whether these objectives constitute 'essential' objectives justifying the employment of Community criminal law for their achievement. These questions of competence, however, cannot be disassociated with questions of the necessity of criminalisation and severity of the criminal sanction envisaged. On both the intellectual property rights[97] and the employers' sanctions proposals,[98] concerns have been raised regarding the suitability of the criminal law to regulate the

---

[91] Conclusions of the Justice and Home Affairs Council of 12–13 June 2007, Council doc 10267/07 (Presse 125), p 42. On the case, see the following section of this chapter.

[92] See House of Commons European Scrutiny Committee, 14th Report, session 2006–07, pp 20–21.

[93] European Parliament Committee on Legal Affairs, 'Working Document on Protection of the Environment through Criminal Law', Rapporteur: H Nassauer, 12 June 2007, PE 390.607v02–00.

[94] COM (2007) 249 final, Brussels, 16 May 2007.

[95] ibid. Arts 10–11. See also the specific provisions on the liability of legal persons in Arts 12–13.

[96] ibid, p 10.

[97] See the comments by the Law Society of England and Wales, August 2006, where concern is expressed that the introduction of broad criminal sanctions may upset the balance that exists between the use of civil and criminal proceedings (para 19). The Justice and Home Affairs Council of 5–6 October 2006 noted in this context that criminal law is considered as a means of last resort, and that further scrutiny is needed regarding the need for criminal measures on the EU level in order to protect intellectual property rights. Council doc. 13068/06 (Presse 258), p 22.

[98] See S Carrera and E Guild, *An EU Framework on Sanctions against Employers of Irregular Immigrants*, CEPS Policy Brief No.140, Brussels, CEPS, August 2007, avilable at www.ceps.eu.

matter. At the time of writing, it is clear that concerns related to both legality and overcriminalisation have led to difficulties in the negotiations of both the illegal work and intellectual property proposals.[99] In the negotiations of these proposals, one must not lose sight of the fact that criminalisation may not always be necessary, and that it must not be used in the competence game in order to establish precedents for Community competence in criminal law.

iv. The Ship-Source Pollution Case[100]

Further clarification on the scope of Community criminal law competence has been expected from the Court of Justice on the ship-source pollution case. The subject matter is very similar to the environmental crime case. The Commission has challenged the legality of the adoption of a Framework Decision on ship-source pollution, arguing that parts of the measure should have been adopted under the first pillar.[101] In this case, the Framework Decision has been accompanied by a parallel first pillar Directive, defining the conduct that was criminalised by the Framework Decision. Given the timing and constitutional significance of the case, no less than 20 Member States intervened in support of the Council, and against the Commission's challenge.

The main arguments of the parties are described in detail in the Opinion of Advocate General Mazák.[102] The Commission argued that Articles 1 to 10 of the Framework Decision could have been adopted on the basis of Article 80(2) TEC relating to the Community common transport policy and that consequently, the entire Framework Decision (due to its indivisibility) infringes Article 47 TEU.[103] In a broad interpretation of the environmental crime judgment, and stressing again the need to ensure the effectiveness of Community law, the Commission was of the view that principles that the Court laid down in its environmental crime judgment apply 'in their entirety to other Community policies' such as the transport policy, arguing that the importance of environmental protection in the Community and its particular characteristics (such as its 'transversal' nature) had

---

[99] See inter alia: 'Member States Split over Commission Powers', *European Voice*, 28 February 2008, and 'France Seeks Quick Deal to Penalise Employment of Illegal Immigrants', *European Voice*, 17 July 2008 (both by Jim Brunsden); and 'EU States Clash over Penalties for Hiring Illegal Immigrants', www.euobserver.com, 24 July 2008 (by Renata Goldirova). See also the rather generally worded conclusions of the July 2008 Justice and Home Affairs Council: Council doc. 11653/08 (Presse 205), p 13.

[100] For an earlier version, focusing on the Opinion of the Advocate General, see V Mitsilegas, 'The Competence Question: The European Community and Criminal Law', in E Guild and F Geyer (eds), *Security versus Justice. Police and Judicial Co-operation in the European Union*, Aldershot, Ashgate, 2008, pp 153–170.

[101] Case C-440/05, *Commission v. Council* ECR [2007] I-9097. For a commentary, see S Peers, 'The European Community's Criminal Law Competence: The Plot Thickens', *European Law Review*, vol 33, no 3, 2008, pp 399–410.

[102] Opinion delivered on 28 June 2007.

[103] Para 27. A similar view was put forward by the European Parliament, which stressed the similarities with the environmental crime case and argued that the Framework Decision in question is also concerned with environmental protection (paras 32–35).

in fact no decisive bearing on the environmental crime decision in principle.[104] According to the Commission, the Community legislature may provide for criminal measures in so far as necessary to ensure the *full effectiveness* of Community rules and regulations. Such action may be based only on implied Community powers which are determined by the need to guarantee compliance with Community measures, *but are not confined to criminal law measures in a certain area of law or of a certain nature*.[105] The Community is therefore according to the Commission competent to define the type and level of penalties *if and in so far as it is established that this is necessary to ensure the full effectiveness of a Community policy*.[106]

The Council on the other hand defended the choice of the third pillar instrument (supported by all intervening Member States) and denied that criminal law measures should have been adopted in the first pillar under Article 80(2) TEC. The Council's strategy was primarily to attempt to differentiate between the ship-source pollution and the environmental crime cases. According to the Council, it is undisputed Article 80(2) TEC (on transport) is the correct legal basis for the adoption of the first pillar Directive, even if it also pursues objectives related to the environmental protection.[107] The common transport policy lacks the specific characteristics and importance of environmental protection; moreover, the Community powers to act on transport matters depends on the decision of the Council.[108] In the alternative, the Council argued that the provisions of the Ship-source Pollution Framework Decision differed from those of the third pillar measure on environmental crime in that they were more detailed in particular with regard to the level and type of penalties to be imposed. Given the leeway provided by the environmental crime judgment to Member States regarding the imposition of criminal sanctions when the first pillar is involved, the Council argued that a number of provisions in the present Framework Decision could not have been adopted under the first pillar—adding that, if the environmental crime case were to be interpreted along the lines advocated by the Commission, Title VI of TEU would largely be deprived of practical effect.[109] According to the Council, it cannot be concluded from the adoption of the Ship-source Pollution Framework Decision that the criminal law measures provided for must be regarded as 'necessary' within the meaning of the environmental crime case.[110]

A similarly narrow interpretation of the environmental crime case was provided by the Member States which intervened in favour of the Council. In their view, the implied Community competence to legislate on criminal law matters is confined to measures which are 'necessary' or (absolutely) 'essential' for combating serious

---

[104] Para 28.
[105] Para 29.
[106] ibid.
[107] Para 36.
[108] Para 38.
[109] Para 39.
[110] Para 40.

environmental offences—adding that such competence does not extend beyond the field of environmental protection to another common policy such as the transport policy at issue, and in any event excludes harmonisation of the type and level of penalties as laid down in the Framework Decision.[111] In support of this minimalist interpretation, Member States put forward a number of arguments linked with their broader concern of loss of sovereignty in criminal matters—related to

> the principles of subsidiarity, attributed powers and proportionality; the particular nature and necessary coherence of criminal law; the margin of appreciation to be left for the Member States; and the system set up by the Treaty on the European Union which would be undermined if the arguments of the Commission were upheld.[112]

Member States also argued that Article 47 TEU is intended to lay down a clear delimitation of competences between the first and the third pillars but not to establish that the former has primacy over the latter.[113]

It is with the interpretation of Article 47 TEU that the Advocate General (AG) began his Opinion.[114] The AG interpreted the provision broadly, stating that Article 47 TEU is not designed merely to ensure that nothing under the EU Treaty affected or run counter to existing substantive provisions of Community law—it was intended rather also *to preserve the powers conferred on the Community as such.*[115] In order to determine whether Article 47 TEU has been infringed, the question to be asked is whether the provisions in question could have been adopted potentially on the basis of the EC Treaty.[116] The Opinion of the AG differs substantially from the submissions of Member States in this context. He categorically stated that:

> Contrary to the view expressed by certain Governments, Article 47 EU thus establishes the 'primacy' of Community law or, more particularly, the primacy of Community action under the EC Treaty over activities undertaken on the basis of Title V or Title VI of the EU Treaty, in that the Council and, as the case may be, the other institutions of the Union *must* act on the basis of the EC Treaty if and in so far as it provides an appropriate legal basis for the purposes of the action envisaged.[117]

The AG thus established in a clear-cut manner a hierarchy between the pillars, granting 'primacy' to the first pillar and a presumption for Community action. This approach was also based on a Community-friendly reading of Article 1 TEU, whereby the supplementary character of the Union provisions to the foundational Community pillar is stressed.[118] On the basis of this reasoning, the AG went on to

---

[111] Para 41.

[112] Para 42.

[113] Para 43.

[114] Art 47 TEU states that 'nothing in this Treaty [on the European Union] shall affect the Treaties establishing the European Communities or the subsequent Treaties and Acts modifying or supplementing them'.

[115] Para 50. According to the AG, that is confirmed by Art 29(1) TEU which expressly provides that third pillar provisions are 'without prejudice to the powers of the European Community' (para 51).

[116] Para 52.

[117] Para 53.

[118] Para 54.

look at whether the Community pillar contains a legal basis which would mean that the adoption of criminal law legislation on ship-source pollution in the third pillar would infringe the horizontal distribution of competence described above. According to the AG, a first pillar legal basis could include—but is not limited to—Article 80(2) TEC on transport—in principle, if it were found that the provisions of the Framework Decision could have been adopted using a legal basis provided for elsewhere in the EC Treaty (such as in the part on the environment) that would mean that the Framework Decision infringes Article 47 TEU.[119] He took the view that Article 80(2) TEC could provide the correct legal basis for ship-source pollution measures, even if these measures pursue also the aim of environmental protection. [120] What did fall within the first pillar—and could have been adopted under Article 80(2) TEC, are the Framework Decision provisions on the constituent elements of criminal offences, as well as the requirement that these are punishable by effective, proportionate and dissuasive penalties.[121] Since this is the case and the Framework Decision is to be regarded as indivisible, the AG recommended that the entire Framework Decision be annulled as it was adopted in infringement of Article 47 TEU.[122]

Like the Advocate General, and similarly to the environmental crime judgment, the Court used Article 47 TEU as a starting point in affirming that it is its task to ensure that acts which, according to the Council, fall within the scope of Title VI do not encroach upon the powers conferred by the EC Treaty on the Community.[123] The Court would thus have to look at whether the Framework Decision affected the Community's competence on transport under Article 80(2) TEC.[124] In doing so, the Court followed a twofold approach: it examined the nature of Community competence on transport in the general Treaty framework; and it linked Community transport policy with the objective of environmental protection. The Court noted first that the common transport policy is one of the foundations of the Community, with the latter having broad legislative powers under Article 80(2) EC including powers in the field of maritime transport.[125] The existence of the legislative competence conferred to the Community by Article 80(2) TEC is not dependent on a decision by the legislature to actually exercise this competence.[126] Secondly, the Court linked Community transport policy with the

---

[119] Para 65. The AG noted that the need for a prior Council decision for the Community to act on transport was not a decisive factor with regard to the application of Art 47 TEU (para 62).

[120] Paras 128 and 130.

[121] Para 132 and 138.

[122] Para 139.

[123] The Court used the same approach—and referred expressly to both the environmental crime and the ship-source pollution judgments—in the 'small arms' case where it determined, on the basis of Art 47 TEU, the relationship between the first and the second pillars—see Case C-91/05, *Commission v Council* (delivered on 20 May 2008). For a critical comment see P Koutrakos, 'Development and Foreign Policy: Where to Draw the Line between the Pillars', *European Law Review*, vol 33, no 3, pp 289–290 (editorial).

[124] Judgment of 23 October 2007, paras 53 and 54 respectively.

[125] Paras 55 and 58 respectively.

[126] Para 59.

objective of environmental protection. The latter is, according to the Court, one of the essential objectives of the Community which must, according to Article 6 TEC 'be integrated into the definition and implementation of . . . Community policies and activities' including transport policy.[127]

Having highlighted the environmental dimension of the legislation in question, the Court reiterated its findings in the environmental crime case, namely that although as a general rule neither criminal law nor the rules of criminal procedure fall within the Community's competence, the fact remains that when the application of effective, proportionate and dissuasive criminal penalties by the competent national authorities is an essential measure for combating serious environmental offences, the Community legislature may require the Member States to introduce such penalties in order to ensure that the rules which it lays down in that field are fully effective.[128]

The Court then examined the Framework Decision in this light, asserting that the latter's provisions relate to conduct which 'is likely to cause particularly serious environmental damage as a result, in this case, of the infringement of the Community rules on maritime safety'.[129] According to the Court, it is also clear that the Council took the view that criminal penalties were necessary to ensure compliance with Community rules on maritime safety.[130] In the light of these two considerations and the Court's earlier ruling on the environmental crime case,[131] the Court took the view that Articles 2, 3 and 5 of the Framework Decision on ship-source pollution, which 'are designed to ensure the efficacy of the rules adopted in the field of maritime safety, non-compliance with which may have serious environmental consequences, by requiring Member States to apply criminal penalties to certain forms of conduct' are essentially aimed at improving maritime safety *as well as environmental protection* and could have been validly adopted on the basis of Article 80(2) TEC.[132] However, the Court noted that Community competence in the field does not extend to the determination of the type and level of criminal penalties—therefore it does not extend to provisions such as Articles 4 and 6 of the Framework Decision determining specific levels of criminal sanctions.[133] However, these sets of provisions being inextricably linked to each other, the Court annulled the Framework Decision as a whole.

The Court's ruling offers a degree of clarification regarding the delimitation of Community criminal law competence. For supporters of first pillar criminal law, the judgment will be seen as a further affirmation of the existence of Community

---

[127] Para 60.

[128] Para 66.

[129] Para 67. The Court also noted that the purpose of the Framework Decision, according to its Preamble, was to enhance maritime safety and improve protection of the marine environment against ship-source pollution (para 62).

[130] Para 68.

[131] See also para 66 of the judgment.

[132] Para 69.

[133] Paras 70–71. Similarly, the Court noted that provisions on jurisdiction and information exchange are third pillar matters (para 73).

competence in criminal matters and as an expansion of such competence in the field of ship-source pollution. Moreover, the Court reiterated its emphasis on effectiveness, reaffirming the view of criminal law as a means to an end.[134] However, the Court has by no means given *carte blanche* to the adoption of a wide range of first pillar criminal law measures. First of all, the relative vagueness of the environmental crime ruling on the extent of first pillar criminal law competence has been remedied to some extent in this case, with the Court stating that while *criminalisation* in this case would fall within the first pillar, the imposition of precise sanctions (such as levels of custodial sentences) still falls within the third pillar.[135] Moreover, the Court embarked on a delicate balancing act regarding the question of whether Community criminal law competence is limited to the achievement of 'essential' Community objectives, or whether it extends to all Community objectives and/or policies. The Court certainly refrained from doing the latter.[136] While it accepted that a first pillar measure with a transport legal basis may include criminal law provisions, this appears to be justified on the grounds of the strong link between the measure in question with the protection of the environment—an essential Community objective whose protection may necessitate criminal law. The extent of Community criminal law competence in this context remains thus still contested; it appears, however, that the Court has left the door open to Member States sceptical to further 'communitarisation' of criminal law at this stage (before the Treaty of Lisbon enters into force) to argue that such 'communitarisation' does not extend beyond measures having an environmental protection objective.

---

[134] Note that the Advocate General devoted a substantial part of his Opinion to discuss the special nature of criminal law and the relationship between criminal law and Community law and the *potential subordination of criminal law to the effectiveness of Community law*. The AG accepts that effectiveness is an imprecise criterion on the basis of which to establish criminal law competence and does not encapsulate entirely the essence of criminal law. Having broadened Community competence in criminal matters by extending it potentially to any Community policy, he now tries to place some limits by stating that the necessity of Community criminal law does not stem only from the objective criterion of the existence of a legal basis in the EC Treaty, but also from a degree of judgment by the institutions involved. Moreover, the AG accepts that it is not ideal for Community criminal law to be considered a mere accessory to the specific Community competences and only a single aspect of the policies involved. Finally, the AG hints at the necessity of a uniform Community legislative procedure to accommodate Community criminal law (paras 114–121).

[135] These issues may well arise in the negotiations of the recent 'Commission Proposal for an amendment to the Ship-source Pollution Directive including penalties for infringements' COM (2008) 134 final, Brussels, 11 March 2008. Negotiations on the proposal are under way (see Conclusions of the Justice and Home Affairs Council of 5–6 June 2008, Council doc. 9956/08 (Presse 146), p 18). The Council and the European Parliament have already reached a first reading agreement on the environmental crime Directive—ibid, p 16.

[136] See the significantly broader approach of the AG—see in particular paras. 94–97 of Opinion.

III. CRIMINAL LAW IN THE THIRD PILLAR

A. The Extent of Union Competence to Adopt Criminal Law

Express reference to the competence of the Union to legislate in criminal matters is currently made in the 'third pillar' of the EU Treaty, Title VI entitled 'provisions on police and judicial co-operation in criminal matters'. Article 29 TEU, the opening provision of Title VI, states that

> [w]ithout prejudice to the powers of the European Community, the Union's objective shall be to provide citizens with a high level of safety within an area of freedom, security and justice by developing common action among the Member States in the field of police and judicial cooperation in criminal matters and by preventing and combating racism and xenophobia.
>
> That objective shall be achieved by preventing and combating crime, organised or otherwise, in particular terrorism, trafficking in persons and offences against children, illicit drug trafficking and illicit arms trafficking, corruption and fraud through . . . approximation, where necessary, of rules on criminal matters in the Member States, in accordance with the provisions of Article 31(e).

Article 31(1)(e) in turn states that common action on judicial co-operation in criminal matters shall include 'progressively adopting measures establishing minimum rules relating to the constituent elements of criminal acts and to penalties in the fields of organised crime, terrorism and illicit drug trafficking'.

The wording is broad and not specific with regard to the extent of Union competence to legislate in criminal matters. It leaves open the question of whether the Union has the power to adopt legislation in matters other than those relating to the constituent acts of offences and to penalties—for instance, measures related to criminal procedure. It is in particular contested whether the power to legislate on criminal acts and penalties refers exclusively to the areas of criminality mentioned in Article 31(1)(e)—namely organised crime, terrorism and illicit drug trafficking. It is not clear in both contexts whether the phrase 'shall include' indicates an exhaustive enumeration of areas of Union competence or whether it indicates that further areas may be added. Moreover, with regard to the areas of criminality on which competence to legislate has been conferred to the Union, it must be noted that the wording in Article 31(1)(e) does not coincide with the wording of the broader provision of Article 29, which refers to additional offences (such as fraud and corruption) and seems, with the use of the phrase 'in particular' not to delimit exhaustively the scope of Union action in criminal law (Article 29 also refers to preventing and combating racism and xenophobia, but not in the subparagraph referring specifically to criminal law approximation). Finally, it is contested whether Union competence is limited to the areas mentioned in Article 31(1)(e) or whether Article 29 should be used as a starting point to determine competence.[137] This lack of clarity in the Treaty wording has resulted in a number of competence discussions in the negotiations of draft third pillar instruments.

B. EU Criminal Law Measures Adopted under the Third Pillar

i. *Substantive Criminal Law*

The decisive push towards the harmonisation of substantive criminal law under the third pillar happened after the entry into force of the Amsterdam Treaty. This was a result of the stronger Treaty legal basis, the more effective legal instruments provided for in the third pillar (in particular Framework Decisions) and the policy impetus provided in Tampere and the various EU action plans to combat organised crime and terrorism.[138] In the field of harmonisation of criminal offences and sanctions, we have already seen that action has taken the form of: first pillar measures defining and 'prohibiting' certain conduct while calling at Member States to establish effective sanctions (the Money Laundering Directive); dual first and third pillar measures (in areas linked to Community policies), with the conduct defined in the first pillar and criminalisation occurring in the third (facilitation of unauthorised entry; ship-source pollution); third pillar measures related to Community policies (environmental crime); and pre-Amsterdam third pillar measures, mainly in the form of Conventions (in particular on fraud affecting the Community's financial interests). Post-Amsterdam, harmonisation has occurred primarily via Framework Decisions. Such Framework Decisions harmonising criminal offences and sanctions involve issues such as terrorism,[139] trafficking in human beings,[140] sexual exploitation of children and child pornography,[141] drug trafficking,[142] corruption in the private sector,[143] attacks against information systems,[144] counterfeiting of the Euro[145] and non-cash means of

---

[137] See also the discussion in Peers, *EU Justice*, n 2 above, p 387. He argues that in the present state of the law the EU is not limited to harmonising national law concerning a fixed list of crimes.

[138] For a background see ch 1.

[139] Council Framework Decision 2002/475/JHA, OJ L164, 22 June 2002, p 3. For an analysis of the Framework Decision see A Weyembergh and V Santamaria, 'Lutte contre le terrorisme et droits fondamentaux dans le cadre du troisième pilier. La décision-cadre du 13 juin 2002 relative à la lutte contre le terrorisme et le principe de la légalité', typescript with author; see also E Symeonidou-Kastanidou, 'Defining Terrorism', *European Journal of Crime, Criminal Law and Criminal Justice*, vol 12, 2004, pp 14–35.

[140] Council Framework Decision 2002/629/JHA, OJ L203, 1 August 2003, p.1. For an analysis see T Obokata, 'EU Council Framework Decision on Combating Trafficking in Human Beings: a Critical Appraisal' *Common Market Law Review*, vol 40, 2003, pp 917–936.

[141] Council Framework Decision 2004/68/JHA, OJ L13, 20 January 2004, p 44.

[142] Council Framework Decision 2004/757/JHA, OJ L335, 11 November 2004, p 8.

[143] Council Framework Decision 2003/568/JHA, OJ L192, 31 July 2003, p 54.

[144] Council Framework Decision 2005/222/JHA, OJ L69, 16 March 2003, p 67.

[145] Council Framework Decision 2000/383/JHA, OJ L140, 14 June 2000, p 1 (amended in 2001, OJ L329, 14 December 2001, p 3).

payment.[146] Two further Framework Decisions, on racism and xenophobia and organised crime, both replacing earlier Joint Actions in the respective fields, have been 'agreed' in the Council but not yet formally adopted at the time of writing.[147]

EU harmonisation on substantive criminal law thus touches upon a wide range of areas of criminality. Some of these involve the protection of Community specific interests (such as the protection of the Euro and fraud against the Community budget). Other measures focus in major areas of transnational criminality, such as organised crime, money laundering and drug trafficking. A number of Union initiatives are linked with parallel instruments of international law (the FATF anti-money-laundering standards and the United Nations Convention on transnational organised crime (the Palermo Convention) and its Protocols covering offences such as organised crime, trafficking in human beings and facilitation of unauthorised entry)—with the Community, the Union or institutions such as the Commission playing an active role in the formulation of such instruments.[148] Other measures (such as the criminalisation of racism and xenophobia, and again human trafficking and smuggling) focus on issues that are linked with the achievement of Community policies such as immigration and anti-discrimination. In terms of timing, the proposal and negotiation/adoption of instruments has at times been very closely linked with specific events—with the 9/11 attacks resulting in swift negotiations and adoption of the Framework Decision on terrorism, and the paedophilia incidents in Belgium resulting in EU harmonised action in the field of sexual exploitation of children. In some instances, the timing of measures adopted reflects the shift in EU and global priorities against crime, with the 1990s focusing primarily on money laundering and organised crime (and, in the EU context, on fraud and corruption), and this decade focusing primarily on terrorism.[149]

In terms of structure, a common feature in third pillar Framework Decisions is obviously provisions defining criminal offences. In terms of *what* has been criminalised, a number of EU harmonisation measures (in particular those concerning terrorism and organised crime) have been criticised for lack of clarity and for introducing sweeping criminalisation of a wide range of conduct, not necessarily related to a specific act.[150] In particular in the context of terrorism, it has been

---

[146] Council Framework Decision 2001/413/JHA, OJ L149, 2 June 2001, p 1.

[147] For details on these instruments see the following part of this chapter.

[148] For further details, see ch 6.

[149] This shift is reflected very clearly in the evolution of the EU money laundering counter-measures (closely linked to global initiatives in the field) since the early '90s. While the main focus initially was the criminalisation of the laundering of the proceeds from drug trafficking, this gradually shifted to the laundering of the proceeds of organised crime and all serious crime, and has mutated, post-9/11, into the application of the anti-money laundering framework on terrorist finance. For an overview, see V Mitsilegas, 'Countering the Chameleon Threat of Dirty Money: "Hard" and "Soft" Law in the Emergence of a Global Regime against Money Laundering and Terrorist Finance' in A Edwards and P Gill (eds), *Transnational Organised Crime: Perspectives on Global Security*, London, Routledge, 2003, pp 195–211.

[150] On the Terrorism Framework Decision, see Weyembergh and Santamaria, n 139 above; and Symeonidou-Kastanidou, n 139 above. On organised crime, see V Mitsilegas, 'Defining Organised Crime in the European Union: The Limits of European Criminal Law in an Area of Freedom, Security and Justice' *European Law Review*, vol 26, 2001, pp 565–581; see also the following section of this chapter.

noted that EU action has served not only to harmonise national laws, but also to create new offences which did not exist at the national level, extending thus the scope of criminal law.[151] This has also been the case where Community/Union instruments served to import in the EU new offences developed in international fora.[152] Moreover, in the light of the current unanimity requirement for the adoption of third pillar law, negotiations on harmonised definitions of criminal offences have not always been easy especially in areas such as drug trafficking where Member States hold very different views on what conduct should be criminalised.[153] Last, but not least, the foray of the Union (and in some instances the Community) into harmonising criminal offences raises questions of interpretation related to the 'general part' of criminal law, in particular when it comes to determining *mens rea* requirements. It will be increasingly for the Court of Justice to interpret these principles when it comes to Union criminal law. The recent case concerning the interpretation of 'negligence' in the EC/EU ship-source pollution measures is a prime example where the Court has had to grapple with general principles of criminal law.[154] Further such instances may arise in the future in the light of the inclusion, in a number of Framework Decisions, of a requirement for Member States to criminalise incitement, aiding and betting, and attempt.[155]

Provisions on offences are inevitably coupled with provisions on criminal penalties. In the light of differences between Member States regarding severity of punishment for certain offences, similar controversies have arisen in the context of agreeing common penalties, with the Framework Decision on human trafficking being a prime example.[156] National differences on penalties are recognised by the Commission, which in its Green Paper on the issue has stated that

> The differences between the Member States' legislation on penalties are still quite sharp. There are historical, cultural and legal reasons for this, deeply-rooted in their legal systems, which have evolved over time and the expression of the way in which Member States have faced and answered fundamental questions about criminal law. These systems have their own internal coherence, and amending individual rules without regard to the overall picture would risk generating distortions.[157]

---

[151] See M L Cesoni, 'Droit pénal européen: Une harmonisation périlleuse' in G de Kerchove and A Weyembergh (eds), *L'Espace pénal européen: Enjeux et perspectives*, Éditions de l'Université de Bruxelles, 2002, pp 153–168 (in particular pp 154–155).

[152] This is in particular the case with the criminalisation of money laundering. See Mitsilegas, *Money Laundering*, n 28 above.

[153] For a background to the negotiations of the drug trafficking Framework Decision, see Mitsilegas, Monar and Rees, n 44 above, pp 102–104.

[154] Case C-308/06 *The International Association of Independent Tanker Owners and Others*, judgment delivered on 3 June 2008. The Court has also had to grapple with the scope of fundamental rights such as the legality principle (in particular in the context of the European Arrest Warrant) and *ne bis in idem*—for an analysis see ch 3.

[155] See inter alia Art 3 of the Drug Trafficking and Corruption Framework Decisions; and Art 2 of the Framework Decision on trafficking in human beings.

[156] Mitsilegas, Monar and Rees, n 44 above, p 106.

[157] 'The approximation, mutual recognition and enforcement of criminal sanctions in the EU' (Green Paper) COM (2004) 334 final, Brussels, 30 April 2004, p 8. The Green Paper launched a consultation regarding the desirability of a more coherent approach and greater harmonisation in the field

The strategy followed regarding penalties is for Framework Decisions to prescribe a series of penalty levels, indicating only the minimum *maximum* penalty that Member States are obliged to adopt. There is thus considerable flexibility left to the Member States.[158] In spite of the existence of considerable differences between Member States on the issue,[159] Framework Decisions also include as a rule provisions establishing the liability of legal persons,[160] followed by a standard provision on sanctions for legal persons.[161] The liability of legal persons provisions (and the debate regarding the requisite *mens rea*) may present the Court of Justice with further challenges related to the interpretation of general principles of criminal law. Similar issues may arise by the inclusion, in a number of Framework Decisions, of provisions on aggravating[162] and mitigating circumstances.[163] These provisions are on occasion more loosely related to Article 31(1)(e) TEU which refers to 'the constituent elements of criminal acts' and related 'penalties' as they may extend to *create* new offences in domestic law by reference to the EU Framework Decisions.[164]

of penalties in the EU. It contains an overview of the penalty levels in the various third pillar instruments, and of the main issues arising in the implementation in Member States, given the diverse features of the domestic criminal justice systems.

[158] The Justice and Home Affairs Council on 25–26 April 2002 put forward a list of ranges determining various levels of 'minimum maximum' penalty: level 1 concerns minimum maximum penalties of between 1–3 years of imprisonment; level 2 is between 2–5 years; level 3 between 5–10 years; and level 4 with a minimum maximum penalty of at least 10 years of imprisonment.

[159] See Commission above, pp 31–32.

[160] Liability extends to offences committed for their benefit by any person, acting either individually or as a part of an organ of the legal person, who has a leading position within the legal person, based on one of the following: (a) a power of representation of the legal person; (b) an authority to take decisions on behalf of the legal person; (c) an authority to exercise control within the legal person—see inter alia Art 7(1) of the terrorism Framework Decision; Art 6(1) of the drug trafficking Framework Decision; Art 5(1) of the Framework Decision on corruption in the private sector; and Art 4(1) of the human trafficking Framework Decision. For a background to the development of these criteria, see Peers, *EU Justice*, n 2 above, pp 411–412.

[161] Member States must ensure that effective, proportionate and dissuasive penalties are imposed, including criminal and non-criminal fines and may include other penalties, such as: (a) exclusion from entitlement to public benefits or aid; (b) temporary or permanent disqualification from the practice of commercial activities; (c) placing under judicial supervision; (d) a judicial winding-up order; (e) temporary or permanent closure of establishments which have been used for committing the offence. See inter alia Art 8(1) of the Terrorism Framework Decision; Art 7(1) of the Drug Trafficking Framework Decision; Art 6(1) of the Framework Decision on corruption in the private sector; and Art 5(1) of the Human Trafficking Framework Decision.

[162] Provisions on aggravating circumstances are either included in the general provisions on penalties (see for instance Art 3 of the Human Trafficking Framework Decision), or appear in a separate provision (see for instance Art 7 of the Framework Decision on attacks against information systems).

[163] On mitigating circumstances, see Art 6 of the Terrorism Framework Decision, and Art 5 of the Drug Trafficking Framework Decision, both entitled 'particular circumstances'. These include instances where the offender renounces terrorism or drug trafficking or provides information to the authorities.

[164] See for instance Art 3(a) of the Terrorism Framework Decision, which calls on Member States to take the necessary measures to ensure that terrorist-linked offences include 'aggravated theft' with a view to committing one of the acts listed in Art 1(1) of the Framework Decision.

A common provision in Framework Decisions, related to judicial co-operation, involves rules on jurisdiction.[165] What is more striking in terms of the legal basis used, is that a number of Framework Decisions aiming to harmonise offences and sanctions, due to their subject matter include also provisions related to criminal procedure. The Framework Decisions on terrorism, trafficking in human beings and the sexual exploitation of children all include a specific provision on victims.[166] The victims provisions in all three Framework Decisions call on Member States to establish that investigations into or prosecution of the offences involved are not dependent on the report or accusation made by a person subjected to the offence, at least when such offences have been committed in their territory.[167] All three instruments call for assistance to be granted to the victims families.[168] The trafficking and sexual exploitation measures also contain provisions calling on Member States to treat individuals involved (in the case of trafficking this is limited to children) as particularly vulnerable victims.[169] The determination of a 'particularly vulnerable' victim and the assistance to the families involved is linked with a specific EU Framework Decision on the rights of victims in criminal proceedings[170]—a noteworthy instance where a 'self-standing' measure on criminal procedure has been adopted under the third pillar. The implications of this measure for EU criminal—but also constitutional—law will be examined below.

ii. Criminal Procedure

The existence and extent of Union competence to harmonise rules on criminal procedure is contested. Unlike the case of criminal offences and sanctions, Title VI of the EU Treaty does not contain an express legal basis for the adoption of measures on criminal procedure. However, this has not stopped the negotiation, and at times the adoption, of third pillar measures related to criminal procedure. One strand of these measures involves legislation deemed necessary for the facilitation of mutual recognition, which will be discussed in section V below. However, the

---

[165] See for instance Art 9(1) of the Terrorism Framework Decision and Art 7 of the Framework Decision on corruption in the private sector. The wording of the jurisdiction provisions in the various Framework Decisions is similar (for instance: Art 7(1) of the Corruption Framework Decision calls on Member States to establish jurisdiction where the offence has been committed (a) in whole or in part within their territory; (b) by one of their nationals; or (c) for the benefit of a legal person that has its head office in their territory. Art 7(2) then gives the option to Member States not to apply extraterritorial jurisdiction). However, in a number of instances it is tailor-made to the specific subject-matter (in particular cases potentially involving extraterritorial elements—see Art 10 of the Framework Decision on attacks against information systems). Some Framework Decisions also include rules on the allocation of prosecutions in cases of concurrent jurisdictions (see for instance Art 9(2) of the Terrorism Framework Decision).

[166] Arts 10, 7 and 9 respectively.

[167] Arts 10(1), 7(1) and 9(1) respectively.

[168] Arts 10(2), 7(3) (when the victim of trafficking is a child) and 9(3) respectively.

[169] Arts 7(2) and 9(2) respectively. Note that in the field of trafficking, the Council has also adopted a first pillar Directive on residence permits for victims of trafficking who co-operate with police, prosecution or judicial authorities in Member States (Directive 2004/81/EC, OJ L261, 6 August 2004, p 19).

[170] Council Framework Decision 2001/220/JHA, OJ L82, 22 March 2001, p 1.

Council has also adopted a 'self-standing' piece of legislation related to criminal procedure, in the form of a Framework Decision on the standing of victims in criminal proceedings.[171] The Framework Decision is accompanied by a first pillar Directive 'relating to compensation to crime victims', which mainly concerns the procedure for application for compensation and payment.[172]

The issue of how to fit in legislation on crime victims within the Community and the Union legal framework has been rather complex, as no legal basis covering expressly these issues can be found in the Treaties. The only legal basis that could be found for the compensation Directive was Article 308 TEC. As far as the Framework Decision is concerned, the legal bases used have been Article 34(2)(b) TEU (on Framework Decisions as a form of third pillar law) and Article 31 TEU. It is noteworthy that none of the specific sections of Article 31 (concerning judicial co-operation in criminal matters), which flesh out its exact scope, have been used in this context. As was mentioned above, this provision contains an express legal basis for the adoption of measures on offences and penalties (Article 31(1)(e)). However, no such legal basis exists for criminal procedure in general and the rights of crime victims in particular. It could further be argued that the link between judicial co-operation in criminal matters in the EU and common rules on the standing of victims in criminal proceedings is not readily apparent.

However, it is on the vague legal basis of Article 31 TEU that the Framework Decision has been adopted. The content of the measure is also vague.[173] The Framework Decision includes provisions aimed at ensuring 'respect and recognition' for victims (respect for their dignity and recognition of their rights and legitimate interests) and an 'appropriate role' for them in the national criminal legal systems;[174] a 'right to protection' for victims and where appropriate their families, in particular regarding privacy and including criminal proceedings;[175] and a wide range of provisions aiming at providing assistance of various forms to the victim, including provisions on legal aid and compensation.[176] The impact of such provisions on national criminal justice systems may be far-reaching and uncertain in the light of the vague wording of most of the Framework Decision provisions. It is thus perhaps unsurprising that the Framework Decision has been subject to litigation in the Court of Justice.

---

[171] 2001/220/JHA, OJ L82, 22 March 2001, p 1.

[172] 2004/80/EC, OJ L261, 6 August 2004, p 15.

[173] See in this context: S de Biolley and A Weyembergh, 'L'espace pénal européen et les droits des victimes', *Revue de la Faculté de droit université libre de Bruxelles*, vol 31, 2005, pp 93–122 (in particular pp.101–102); E Herlin-Karnell, 'In the Wake of *Pupino: Advocaten voor der Wereld* and *Dell'Orto*', *German Law Journal*, vol 8, 2007, pp 1147–1160 (in particular pp 1156–1157); and Peers, *EU Justice*, n 2 above, p 451.

[174] Art 2.

[175] Art 8.

[176] Inter alia Art 3—hearings and provision of evidence by the victim; Art 4—right to receive information; Art 5—communication safeguards for the victim; Art 6—access to free of charge advice and legal aid where appropriate; Art 7—reimbursement of expenses with respect to criminal proceedings; Art 9—right to compensation.

The first major case to arise regarding the interpretation of the Framework Decision on victims was *Pupino*.[177] The implications of this landmark constitutional ruling which extended indirect effect to the third pillar are analysed in chapter 1. Here it suffices to reiterate the potentially far-reaching consequences that the combination of indirect effect and vague provisions of Framework Decisions (such as Articles 2 and 8 of the victims Framework Decision) may have on both the internal coherence of national criminal justice systems, as well as on the rights of the defendant. This is in particular the case in the light of the minimalistic interpretation of the Court regarding what constitutes 'criminal law' (and thus carries an enhanced level of protection). The Court was further asked to interpret the Framework Decision in *Dell' Orto*.[178] In a reference again by an Italian Court, the Luxembourg Court was asked if it would be possible to interpret the Framework Decision in the light of the parallel Directive on crime victims as including within its scope victims who are not only natural, but also legal persons. Along with the interesting constitutional points that the question raises,[179] the question gave the opportunity to the Court to interpret the precise *ratione personae* scope of the Framework Decision—according to the Court, this only applies (consistently with its Article 1(a)) to natural persons.[180]

IV. DOMESTIC LEGAL CULTURES AND CRIMINAL LAW HARMONISATION

A. General

As indicated above, the task of harmonising criminal law at Union level has not always been straightforward. There have been a number of instances where proposed measures were perceived to clash with Member States' interests or domestic legal cultures—with Member States not wishing to change their domestic criminal law as a result of EU harmonisation. With decision-making in the third pillar requiring unanimity, this has resulted in lengthy negotiations on a number of instruments, resulting on occasions in either very limited harmonisation or even in negotiations being slowed down or even aborted. Focusing in particular on

---

[177] See n 16 above.

[178] Case C-467/05 *Giovanni Dell' Orto* ECR [2007] I-5557.

[179] In particular to what extent can a third pillar measure be interpreted in the light of a first pillar related measure. In this case the Court remained vague on the answer in principle, but stated that in the concrete case the Directive and the Framework Decision 'are not linked in a manner which would call for a uniform interpretation of the concept in question'—para 59. For commentary, see Herlin-Karnell, n 173 above, p 1157.

[180] See paras 54–55. For another example of the impact of the Court's interpretation of the broadly drafted victims of crime Framework Decision on the internal coherence of national criminal justice system see also the recent case of *Katz* where the Court will have to ascertain whether the Framework Decision can be interpreted as allowing a victim who can assume the prosecutorial function under national law (in this case the law of Hungary) to also be granted the status of a witness in the same trial—Case C-404/07, and see the Opinion by AG Kokott delivered on 10 July 2008. In this context, the Court will also have to inevitably look at the determination of the rights of the defendant in such a case.

the UK position in negotiations, this section will examine instances where national objections and the unanimity requirement have led to either very limited harmonisation or to negotiations being ultimately discontinued. The next part, which focuses on attempts to harmonise criminal law and procedure with the aim of facilitating mutual recognition, will also look at how Member States' perceptions regarding the threat posed by EU harmonisation have influenced negotiations.

B. Organised Crime

The need to fight organised crime has been one of the main motors for the advancement of European integration in the field of criminal law. It justified to a great extent the expansion of Union competence in criminal matters in Maastricht and beyond, and was elevated to a top Union priority by a number of political declarations in the 1990s, including (with eastward enlargement looming) two Action Plans to combat organised crime in 1997 and 2000.[181] With organised crime forming a central part of EU action in the third pillar, and being included in the mandate of Europol, calls surfaced in the 1990s regarding the need for a harmonised definition of the term across the EU.[182] These calls resulted in the adoption in 1998, under a Maastricht legal basis, of a Joint Action on making it a criminal offence to participate in a criminal organisation in the Member States of the European Union.[183]

A central term to be agreed in this context has been the concept of a 'criminal organisation'. This has by no means been an easy task, given the lack of clarity as to the required degree of organisation and the differences in views within the criminological and law enforcement community (is organised crime understood as involving hierarchically structured criminal groups? Or are we talking about more loosely constructed networks?) and the different national priorities and paradigms in fighting organised crime (for instance, is the Mafia model applicable across Europe?).[184] The solution reached in the Joint Action has been to define a criminal organisation as

> a structured association, established over a period of time, of more than two persons, acting in concert with a view to committing offences which are punishable by deprivation of liberty or a detention order of a maximum of at least four years or a more serious penalty, whether such offences are an end in themselves or a means of obtaining material benefits and, where appropriate, of improperly influencing the operation of public authorities.[185]

---

[181] For the background see Mitsilegas, Monar and Rees, n 44 above, chs 1 and 3.

[182] See Mitsilegas, 'Defining Organised Crime', n 150 above, pp 565–568.

[183] 98/733/JHA, L351, 29 December 1998, p 1.

[184] For an analysis, see V Mitsilegas, 'From National to Global, from Empirical to Legal: The Ambivalent Concept of Transnational Organised Crime', in M Beare (ed), *Critical Reflections on Transnational Organized Crime, Money Laundering and Corruption*, University of Toronto Press, 2003, pp 55–87.

[185] Art 1, sub-para 1. These offences include those mentioned in Art 2 of the Europol Convention and its Annex and carrying an equivalent sentence to that mentioned above (Art 1 sub-para 2).

This definition is far from clear, as terms such as 'structured association' and a 'period of time' remain unspecified.[186] However, it proved to be influential towards the development of a definition of organised crime in the subsequent United Nations Convention on Transnational Organised Crime, signed in Palermo in 2000.[187] The definition of an organised criminal group therein is very similar to the one in the Joint Action,[188] with the Convention in addition containing a definition of what constitutes a 'structured group'.[189] The latter definition is also far from clear and seems at odds with the very requirement of 'structure' in an organised crime group.

A further issue of complexity in the negotiations of the Joint Action was the criminalisation and legal definition of participation in an organised crime group. The latter conduct had been a criminal offence only in a number of EU Member States, and even in those cases there had been significant differences with regard to the concepts used in domestic law.[190] Moreover, in countries such as the United Kingdom, participation in organised crime was a concept used by law enforcement agencies, but not a legal term, with the law criminalising more broadly conspiracy.[191] In the light of these different legal approaches, the compromise reached in the Joint Action has been to offer Member States a choice between two options of criminalisation: Member States are called to punish by 'effective, proportionate and dissuasive penalties' one or both of the following types of conduct:

(a) conduct by any person who, with intent and with knowledge of either the aim and general criminal activity of the organisation or the intention of the organisation to commit the offences in question, actively takes part in:

—the organisation's criminal activities falling within Article 1, even where that person does not take part in the actual execution of the offences concerned and, subject to the general principles of the criminal law of the Member State concerned, even where the offences concerned are not committed,

—the organisation's other activities in the further knowledge that his participation will contribute to the achievement of the organisation's criminal activities falling within Article 1;

(b) conduct by any person consisting in an agreement with one or more persons that an activity should be pursued which, if carried out, would amount to the commission

---

[186] See Mitsilegas, 'Defining Organised Crime', n 150 above.

[187] For a commentary see D McClean, *Transnational Organized Crime. A Commentary on the UN Convention and its Protocols*, Oxford, Oxford University Press, 2007.

[188] Art 2(a) of the Convention defines an organised crime group as

a structured group of three or more persons, existing for a period of time and acting in concert with the aim of committing one or more serious crimes or offences established in accordance with this Convention, in order to obtain, directly or indirectly, a financial or other material benefit.

[189] Art 2(c) defines a structured group as 'a group that is not randomly formed for the immediate commission of an offence and that does not need to have formally defined roles for its members, continuity of its membership or a developed structure'.

[190] For a comparison between Italy and Germany, see Mitsilegas, 'From National to Global', n 184 above. For an overview of national approaches to organised crime in Europe, see C Fijnaut and L Paoli (eds), *Organised Crime in Europe. Concepts, Patterns and Control Policies in the European Union and Beyond*, Dordrecht, Springer, 2004.

[191] Mitsilegas, 'From National to Global', n 184 above.

of offences falling within Article 1, even if that person does not take part in the actual execution of the activity.[192]

This result effectively meant that the United Kingdom would not have to change its law to create a specific offence on participation in a criminal organisation, but continue to prosecute on the basis of conspiracy elements of which are clearly reflected in the second option cited above. For those seeking a harmonised legal definition of participation in a criminal organisation, the result may be far from satisfactory as the two options used do not converge on the central element of participation.[193] However, this 'dual' model has also been adopted by the Palermo Convention presumably to take into account specificities in common law jurisdictions.[194] The wording of the options used in the Palermo Convention is similar to the wording of the Joint Action,[195] with the Convention adding the criminalisation of 'organising, directing, aiding, abetting, facilitating or counselling the commission of serious crime involving an organised crime group'.[196]

In 2005, the Commission tabled a proposal for a Framework Decision 'on the fight against organised crime' aiming at replacing the 1998 Joint Action.[197] According to the Commission, the new proposal took into account developments since 1998, including the introduction of Framework Decisions as a form of third pillar law in Amsterdam and the need to take into account of legislative developments such as the Palermo Convention and the EU Framework Decision on terrorism.[198] The Commission proposal harmonised further the crime of participation in a criminal organisation (by deleting the conspiracy variant),[199] aligned EU law with the Palermo Convention by the criminalisation of directing a criminal organisation[200] and the definition of an organised crime group (including what constitutes a 'structured' group),[201] added provisions on mitigating circumstances[202] as well as specific provisions on penalty levels[203] and introduced specific provisions on the position of victims, along the lines of the Framework Decision on terrorism.[204]

---

[192] Art 2(1).

[193] For a discussion, see Mitsilegas, 'Defining Organised Crime', n 150 above, pp 571–572.

[194] See also McClean, n 187 above, p 67. Commenting on the implementation of Art 5, he notes that

> the statute books of the common law countries which have ratified the Convention will be searched in vain for crimes defined as set out in this Article. As has been clear from the beginning, the offences of conspiracy, soliciting, and other forms of participation in criminal conduct more than adequately cover the field described in the text of the Article.

[195] Art 5(1)(a).

[196] Art 5(1)(b).

[197] COM (2005) final, Brussels 19 January 2005.

[198] ibid, pp 3,4.

[199] Art 2 of the proposal.

[200] Art 2(b).

[201] Art 1.

[202] Art 4.

[203] Art 3.

[204] Art 8.

Following complex negotiations, the Justice and Home Affairs Council reached in April 2006 a 'consensus' on the Framework Decision[205]—but the latter had not been formally adopted at the time of writing.[206] The 'agreed' text retains the Commission's draft as regards the definition of a criminal organisation.[207] It introduces a series of penalty levels on the basis of the 'minimum maximum' model described above,[208] as well as granting Member States the discretion to introduce in their domestic law certain aggravating circumstances.[209] Provisions on mitigating circumstances and (albeit slightly watered down) the position of victims have also been retained in the 'agreed' draft.[210] However, there have also been major changes to the Commission's proposal: the criminalisation of directing an organised crime group has been deleted from the text; and, strikingly, the Framework Decision re-introduces the approach adopted by the Joint Action of offering Member States the option of criminalising either participation in a criminal organisation, or conspiracy.[211]

The re-introduction of options to allow Member States to choose between the criminalisation of participation in a criminal organisation and conspiracy can been seen as a victory for the United Kingdom. While introducing specific legislation covering membership of an organised crime group in the UK has been recently under consideration,[212] this has not been translated into changes in domestic law. The 'agreed' draft of the Framework Decision thus allows the UK to continue with the current position, without having to change the domestic law in order to implement Union criminal law.[213] This has caused the reaction of the Commission which issued (joined by France and Italy) a strongly worded statement which is annexed to the Framework Decision. It states that:

---

[205] Justice and Home Affairs Council of 27–28 April 2006, doc 8402/06 (Presse 106).

[206] For the text, see Council doc 9067/06, Brussels, 10 May 2006.

[207] Art 1.

[208] Art 3(1)—minimum maximum penalty of 2 to 5 years. For the common law variant the punishment may be the same maximum term of imprisonment as the offence at which the agreement is aimed. On the background regarding the penalty for the 'common law' variant, see Council doc. 5468/2/06, Brussels 20 March 2006

[209] Art 3(2). The insertion of aggravating circumstances in the text has not been uncontroversial, in the light of the very different approaches on aggravating circumstances between Member States. A number of Member States objected to mandatory aggravating circumstances arguing that this should be left to the judiciary—see Council doc 5468/2/06.

[210] Arts 4 and 8 respectively—the provision for assistance to victims' families has been deleted.

[211] Art 2.

[212] See the Home Office, 'One Step Ahead. A 21st Century Strategy to Defeat Organised Crime' (White Paper, Cm 6167, 2004), pp 40–41; see also C Harding, 'The Offence of Belonging: Capturing Participation in Organised Crime', *Criminal Law Review*, 2005, pp 690–698.

[213] On the implications of the Commission's initial proposal on UK law and the outcome of negotiations, see also the correspondence between the House of Lords European Union Committee and the Home Office, in particular: Letter of 7 April 2005 from Lord Grenfell, Chairman of the EU Committee, to Caroline Flint, then Parliamentary Under Secretary of State, Home Office (reproduced in House of Lords European Union Committee, *Correspondence with Ministers. March 2005 to January 2006*, 45th Report, session 2005–06, HL Paper 243, pp 427–428); and letter of 24 April 2006 from Paul Goggins, then Parliamentary Under Secretary of State, Home Office, to Lord Grenfell (reproduced in House of Lords European Union Committee, *Correspondence with Ministers. January 2006 to September 2006*, 40th Report, session 2006–07, HL Paper 187, p 350).

The Commission considers that the Framework Decision on the fight against organised crime *fails* to achieve the objective sought by the Commission in relation to Joint Action 98/733/JHA on making it a criminal offence to participate in a criminal organisation in the Member States of the European Union, and in relation to the United Nations Convention Against Transnational Organised Crime ... to which the Community has been a party since 29 April 2004. The Framework Decision *does not* achieve the minimum degree of approximation of acts of directing and participating in a criminal organisation on the basis of a single concept of such an organisation, as proposed by the Commission and as already adopted in Framework Decision 2002/475/JHA on the fight against terrorism. Furthermore, the Framework Decision enables Member States *not* to introduce the concept of criminal organisation *but to continue to apply existing national criminal law* by having recourse to general rules on participation in and preparation of specific offences.

The Commission is therefore obliged to note that the Framework Decision does not achieve the objective of approximation of legislation on the fight against organised crime as provided for in the Hague Programme. (emphasis added)

It appears thus that—at least as far as criminalisation in concerned—the concept of organised crime is far from harmonised at EU level. This is striking in the light of the fact that organised crime has a substantial transnational dimension and forms the basis of co-operation between national judicial and police authorities across the EU. The lack of a common definition seems also at odds with the fact that the fight against organised crime justifies to a great extent the existence—and is central to the mandate—of Union criminal justice bodies such as Europol and Eurojust. Both forms of EU stimulated action may be seen as requiring harmonisation.[214] In assessing the situation it is important to look at what has been the ultimate aim of harmonisation of substantive criminal law in this context. The Commission talks about harmonisation across the EU, but Council documents refer to 'prosecutorial benefits' at national level.[215] If one looks at the Framework Decision strictly as necessary to ensure prosecutorial efficiency at the *national* level, then the lack of clarity and the absence of a high level of harmonisation is perhaps not as crucial. However, if one considers the *transnational* dimension of the fight against criminality in the EU, things become much more complicated. Classifying conduct as 'organised crime' justifies judicial co-operation in criminal matters (with organised crime being one of the offences for which dual criminality has been abolished in the European Arrest

---

[214] On the necessity of harmonisation (or 'approximation') in order to ensure the proper functioning of the relevant EU organs, see Weyembergh, *L'harmonisation*, n 1 above, pp 166–171. Weyembergh has developed a typology of approximation functions of criminal law in the EU: see more specifically 'The Functions of Approximation of Penal Legislation within the European Union', *Maastricht Journal of European and Comparative Law*, vol 12, 2005, pp 149–172; see also Weyembergh, 'Approximation of Criminal Laws, the Constitutional Treaty and the Hague Programme', *Common Market Law Review*, vol 42, 2005, pp 1567–1597.

[215] See Council document 5468/2/06, where the penalty levels for organised crime (which were considered low by a number of delegations and the Commission) were justified on the grounds that 'the main prosecutorial benefit of having the offences referred to in Art 2 is that they can be used in cases where a suspect was not involved in the perpetration of another offence' as in the latter cases the suspect ' is likely to incur a much higher sentence (as determined by the national law of the Member State concerned)—p 2.

Warrant and other mutual recognition instruments), police co-operation between national authorities and the role of Europol and Eurojust. In the light of its potentially broad scope the less harmonised the concept of organised crime is, the less clear the scope of enforcement at Union level may become.

C. Racism and Xenophobia

EU criminal law harmonisation in the field of racism and xenophobia has been a matter of great controversy, notwithstanding the fact that combating racism and xenophobia is expressly mentioned within the mandate of the EU action in the third pillar. Attempts to reach a harmonised approach in criminalising racist and xenophobic conduct have stumbled upon the great divergence in national attitudes to the extent to which such conduct should be criminalised. The first step towards using EU criminal law in the field occurred in the Maastricht era, with Member States adopting in 1996 a Joint Action 'concerning action to combat racism and xenophobia'.[216] The Joint Action defined racism and xenophobia as:

(a) public incitement to discrimination, violence or racial hatred in respect of a group of persons or a member of such a group defined by reference to colour, race, religion or national or ethnic origin;
(b) public condoning, for racist or xenophobic purposes, of crimes against humanity and human rights violations;
(c) public denial of the crimes defined in Article 6 of the Charter of the International Military Tribunal appended to the London Agreement of 8 April 1945 insofar as it includes behaviour which is contemptuous of, or degrading to, a group of persons defined by reference to colour, race, religion or national or ethnic origin;
(d) public dissemination or distribution of tracts, pictures or other material containing expressions of racism and xenophobia;
(e) participation in the activities of groups, organisations or associations, which involve discrimination, violence, or racial, ethnic or religious hatred.[217]

The Joint Action required Member States to ensure 'effective judicial cooperation' with regard to offences based on the above types of behaviour. Effective judicial co-operation would be achieved either by criminalising such behaviour, or, failing that, and pending the adoption of any necessary provisions, by derogating from the principle of dual criminality for such behaviour.[218] The Joint Action did not thus introduce a strong obligation for Member States to criminalise racism and xenophobia as defined therein. However, this relative 'weakness' of the text (along with the weakness of its form, it being merely a Joint Action), did not stop Member States—concerned with the potential impact of the measure on their domestic criminal justice systems—from inserting declarations aiming at preserving the domestic status quo. Hence, the United Kingdom stated that it would only apply the above obligations 'where the relevant behaviour is threatening, abusive or

---

[216] 96/443/JHA, OJ L185, 24 July 1996, p 5.
[217] Title I, (A).
[218] ibid.

insulting and is carried out with the intention of stirring up racial hatred or is likely to do so'[219]—a wording which reflected UK domestic law in the field.

Post-Amsterdam, in 2001, the Commission tabled a proposal for a Framework Decision aimed at replacing the 1996 Joint Action.[220] The purpose of the Commission proposal was to ensure that the same racist and xenophobic conduct would be punishable in all Member States under a common criminal law approach and thus achieve effective judicial co-operation. The list of offences in the 1996 Joint Action was thus expanded, and common definitions and penalties were introduced. The proposal caused concern in a number of Member States and was subject to lengthy negotiations, reflecting the differences in approaches in the various Member States.[221]. In the United Kingdom, one of the main concerns was that domestic law would have to be amended to include the criminalisation of incitement to religious hatred—an issue which has been controversial in recent years.[222] However, incitement to religious hatred eventually entered the criminal law statute book in the UK, before the adoption of the Framework Decision.[223] A criminalisation in similar terms in the EU instrument would thus seem to be acceptable to the UK, but again only if the EU instrument would reflect domestic law—or at least if it did not require a change in the domestic law. The Council reached in April 2007 a 'general approach' on the text of the Framework Decision,[224] which had not been formally adopted at the time of writing.[225] The Framework Decision does criminalise inter alia incitement to religious hatred, as well as, under certain conditions, 'publicly condoning, denying or grossly trivialising' crimes of inter alia genocide, war crimes and the holocaust.[226] However, there are exceptions aiming at addressing national sensitivities. With regard to criminalisation at national level, a UK-inspired exception states that Member States

> may choose to punish only conduct which is either carried out in a manner likely to disturb public order or which is threatening, abusive or insulting' as well as that the reference to religion is intended to cover at least 'conduct which is a pretext for directing acts against a group of persons or a member of such a group defined by reference to race, colour, descent, or national or ethnic origin'.[227]

---

[219] See annex, Declaration 3. See also the Danish Declaration (Declaration 4), indicating that Denmark would apply the above obligations only where the relevant behaviour is threatening, abusive or insulting.

[220] COM (2001) 664 final, Brussels, 28 November 2001.

[221] See M Bell, *Race, Equality and the European Union*, Oxford, OUP, forthcoming.

[222] See the UK Government's Explanatory Memorandum accompanying the Commission's original proposal, para 13, reproduced in House of Lords European Union Committee, *Combating Racism and Xenophobia—Defining Criminal Offences in the EU*, 29th Report, session 2001–02, HL Paper 162.

[223] Via the Racial and Religious Hatred Act 2006: for an analysis see K Goodall, 'Incitement to Religious Hatred: All Talk and No Substance?', *Modern Law Review*, vol 70, 2007, pp 89–113.

[224] Doc. 8665/07 (Presse 84).

[225] Latest draft Council doc. 8704/07, Brussels 25 April 2007.

[226] Art 1(1).

[227] Arts 1a and 1b respectively.

These provisions are aimed at ensuring that the UK will not have to change its— controversial and subject to lengthy negotiations—domestic criminal law.[228]

This is not the only limitation to the EU-wide criminalisation of racism and xenophobia. Member States' concerns regarding the impact of such criminalisation on their domestic constitutions and fundamental rights, in particular freedom of expression, have led to the introduction in the body of the Framework Decision of a provision stating that the latter will not have the effect of modifying the obligation to respect fundamental rights and fundamental legal principles, including freedom of expression and association.[229] The provision becomes more specific by stating that the Framework Decision

> shall not have the effect of requiring Member States to take measures in contradiction to fundamental principles relating to freedom of association and freedom of expression, in particular freedom of the press and the freedom of expression in other media as they result from constitutional traditions or rules governing the rights and responsibilities of, and the procedural guarantees for, the press or other media where these rules relate to the determination or limitation of liability.[230]

The impact of this clause on the implementation of the Framework Decision remains to be seen. It may lead to quite divergent implementing laws as it may be seen as an invitation for Member States not to obstruct the balance between free speech and the criminalisation of racism which already exists in their domestic legal and constitutional systems. From a harmonisation point of view, however, this may not lead to optimal solutions, in particular for those hoping that the Framework Decision would create a level of legal certainty and common understanding regarding racism and xenophobia.[231] According to the Commission, the clause may even be interpreted as giving precedence to national law in relation to Union law.[232] However, this compromise clause has perhaps proven to be crucial in reaching (unanimous) agreement in such a controversial proposal where the need to send a strong EU message against racism and xenophobia eventually clashed with concerns regarding over-criminalisation and breach of fundamental rights. A view of the glass as 'half-full' may also indicate that this is a Framework Decision (repealing the weaker earlier Joint Action and expanding its content) containing some degree of criminal law harmonisation in the field of both offences

---

[228] See the Explanatory Memorandum of the UK Government accompanying an earlier draft of the Framework Decision, doc 5118/07 (EM of 14 February 2007, para 20).

[229] Art 7(1).

[230] Art 7(2).

[231] This is in particular in the light of the fact that racism and xenophobia is one of the offences for which the dual criminality requirement has been abolished in the European Arrest Warrant. However, Art 3 of the Framework Decision introduces minimum maximum sanctions of at least 1 to 3 years of imprisonment—this may mean in practice that in the implementation of the Framework Decision the three-year threshold required for the abolition of dual criminality in the Warrant may not be met. See also Bell, n 221 above.

[232] See attached declaration by the Commission to the Framework Decision. The Commission also refers to primacy of 'Union' law.

and sanctions.[233] From a substantive criminal law point of view, it is noteworthy that the export of domestic criminalisation approaches (for instance on Holocaust denial) have led to calls for an even greater criminalisation of denial of other historical events or periods such as totalitarianism in Europe or of offences committed by totalitarian regimes. While this has not happened at present,[234] this is an example of the potential of national diversity when exported across the EU. While the export of national criminal law models may result in the extension of criminalisation across the EU regarding racism and xenophobia, the respect for national constitutional diversity may actually temper such criminalisation.

V. HARMONISATION FOR MUTUAL RECOGNITION

A. General

As will be seen in the next chapter, mutual recognition has emerged as a central avenue of European integration in criminal matters. Mutual recognition entails the acceptance of judgments issued by *national* criminal courts, reflecting their domestic criminal justice systems. A court in the executing Member State is under the obligation to recognise and execute the judgment from its counterpart in the issuing Member State with the minimum of formality and with limited grounds for refusal. Moreover, for an extensive list of offences, dual criminality is abolished subject to a penalty threshold. This emphasis on the facilitation of the movement of national criminal law judgments across the EU on the basis of quasi-automaticity, has led to a number of calls for further harmonisation of criminal law and procedure to accompany mutual recognition. Harmonisation has been deemed necessary at three levels: harmonisation of offences in order to address the abolition of dual criminality; harmonisation of the very area of law giving rise to judgments whose mutual recognition is required; and harmonisation of procedural standards governing the legal situation primarily once a judgment has been recognised and executed.

B. Harmonisation Addressing the Abolition of Dual Criminality

The contribution of substantive criminal law approximation towards the enhancement of mutual trust has been accepted by the Commission in its approximation Green Paper.[235] In the Council, the issue has arise prominently in the context of the abolition of dual criminality in the negotiations of the European

---

[233] In this context, it is noteworthy that the Framework Decision contains a general provision on racist and xenophobic motivation as aggravating factor for any offence other than those criminalised therein (Art 4).

[234] See the Council Declaration attached to the Framework Decision.

[235] Council Declaration attached to the Framework Decision, previous n, p 10.

Evidence Warrant, which have resulted in Germany accepting the measure only if it could exceptionally reapply dual criminality in relation to a series of offences on the list.[236] At the meeting where a 'general approach' was reached on the Evidence Warrant, the Justice and Home Affairs Council instructed its preparatory bodies to give further consideration to the broader issue of the categories of offence, with a view to the adoption by the Council of a horizontal approach by the end of 2007 in relation to terrorism, computer-related crime, racism and xenophobia, sabotage, racketeering and extortion, and swindling.[237] This exercise reflected the wishes of Germany, which argued that a common understanding regarding these offences would facilitate mutual recognition. A questionnaire was sent to Member States and various options discussed, but no concrete measures will be taken regarding a horizontal approach before the implementation of the Evidence Warrant is completed in Member States.[238] At present, Member States' authorities will have to operate mutual recognition on the basis of the abolition of dual criminality for a wide range of offences, some of which are not subject to EU harmonisation at all, while others (as seen above in the examples of organised crime and racism and xenophobia) may still diverge considerably among Member States.

C. Harmonisation Addressing Differences in National Legal Systems which Produce the Judgments to be Recognised

The need to address such differences appeared prominently in the case of mutual recognition of confiscation orders. Although international anti-money-laundering standards do call for some degree of harmonisation regarding the confiscation of the proceeds of crime, creating a harmonised regime in the European Union has been extremely complicated. This is due to the fact that, for a number of EU Member States, attempts to extend the confiscation regime beyond specific crimes or beyond proof that proceeds emanate from a specific offence appeared to challenge domestic criminal and constitutional law. Extended confiscation provisions along the lines of the UK Proceeds of Crime Act 2002 (introducing the so-called 'criminal lifestyle' provisions enabling extended confiscation) may be unconstitutional in a number of other Member States.[239] In the light of these differences, introducing mutual recognition without some degree of harmonisation in the field could create serious constitutional issues in Member States.

The response has thus been to accompany negotiations on an instrument on mutual recognition of confiscation orders[240] with parallel talks on a harmonisation instrument. This has resulted in a Framework Decision on 'confiscation of crime-related proceeds, instrumentalities and property'.[241] Article 3(1) of the

---

[236] See ch 3.
[237] See JHA Council Conclusions of 12–13 June 2007, doc. 10267/07 (Presse 125), p 38.
[238] ibid, p 40.
[239] On the UK system, see P Alldridge, *Money Laundering Law,* Oxford, Hart Publishing, 2003, ch 7.
[240] See further ch 3.
[241] 2005/212/JHA, OJ L68, 15 March 2005, p 49.

Framework Decision established a list of offences conviction for which must lead to confiscation.[242] Article 3(2) represents a more ambitious attempt to harmonise confiscation *systems* in Member States. Given the discrepancies across the EU, the provision introduces *alternative* confiscation systems. Member States must enable confiscation at least:

(a) where a national court based on specific facts is fully convinced that eh property in question has been derived from criminal activities of the convicted person during a period prior to conviction for the offence referred to in paragraph 1 which is deemed reasonable by the court in the circumstances of the particular case, or, alternatively,

(b) where a national court based on specific facts is fully convinced that the property in question has been derived from similar criminal activities of the convicted person during a period prior to conviction for the offence referred to in paragraph 1 which is deemed reasonable by the court in the circumstances of the particular case, or alternatively,

(c) where it is established that the value of the property is disproportionate to the lawful income of the convicted person and a national court based on specific facts is fully convinced that the property in question has been derived from the criminal activity of that convicted person.

The extent to which this effort will lead to effective implementation and contribute to national courts setting aside doubts regarding the execution of confiscation orders from their counterparts in Member States with very different domestic confiscation regimes remains to be seen.[243]

D. Harmonisation Accompanying the Recognition and Execution of Judgments—Defence Rights

i. Background and Content

The adoption of the European Arrest Warrant and the related human rights and constitutional concerns led to calls for measures enhancing the protection of the defendant after he or she has been surrendered to the issuing Member State. Rather than creating a level playing-field by minimum harmonisation ex ante—of the systems leading to decisions subject to mutual recognition, the aim here is to provide safeguards by harmonising standards ex post. This 'ex post' harmonisation is expressed by the adoption of minimum standards governing the treatment of persons once mutual recognition has occurred, the main focus being the rights of the defendant once (s)he has been surrendered to the Member State issuing a European Arrest Warrant. The Commission started work on such proposals in

---

[242] These include a series of offences when committed within the framework of a criminal organisation or within a terrorist framework.

[243] It is indicative in this context that the Commission has recently criticised Member States for their slow progress to implement the Framework Decision—'Report from the Commission pursuant to Art 6 of the Council Framework Decision of 24 February 2005 on Confiscation of Crime-Related Proceeds, Instrumentalities and Property' COM (92007) 805 final, Brussels, 17 December 2007.

2002, with its consultation continuing to mid-2003.[244] With noticeable delay, the Commission finally tabled at the end of April 2004 a draft Framework Decision 'on certain procedural rights in criminal proceedings throughout the European Union'.[245] The proposal aims at minimum standards and contains provisions on the right to legal advice, the right to translation and interpretation, the right to communication and specific attention and the duty to inform a suspect of his rights in writing through a common EU 'Letter of Rights'.

Although modest in its scope and aiming at minimum standards, the proposal has been quite controversial. A number of Member States fear that the proposal has potentially far-reaching implications for the integrity of their domestic criminal justice systems. This is also linked with a reluctance to accept that the European Union has competence in this matter and to bring issues of defence rights within the framework of Union law. Member States have voiced concerns regarding both the existence and extent of EU competence in the field, and in the negotiations of each individual article.[246] In the light of decision-making by unanimity, the result has been a very slow pace of negotiations. In fact, although the adoption of the proposal was a priority under the Hague Programme, negotiations nearly stalled during the UK Presidency (in the second half of 2005), which led the Austrian Presidency to relaunch a consultation with Member States addressing fundamental issues such as the scope of the proposal (would it apply to terrorist offences?), its relationship with the ECHR and the contested issue of the legal basis.[247] It appears that in this case it has been easier for Member States to agree on a political declaration on the necessity of measures (in the Hague Programme) than reaching agreement on the substance of a number of complicated issues that have arisen in negotiations to a proposal on which the Commission has—at least in the early stages—invested considerably.

This view has been confirmed by subsequent developments, and notwithstanding the very dynamic relaunch of the proposal by the German EU Presidency in 2007. This proposal followed attempts to reach agreement by the Austrian Presidency, which were, however, undermined by the tabling of a parallel text for a non-binding Resolution by the UK, the Czech Republic, Ireland, Malta, Cyprus and Slovakia.[248] The German Presidency devoted a number of Council Working Group meetings in the proposal, and attempted to make it as consistent as possible with the European Convention on Human Rights asking in this process the opinion of the Council of Europe.[249] With the German Presidency aiming to reach

---

[244] See C Morgan, 'Proposal for a Framework Decision on Procedural Safeguards for Suspects and Defendants in Criminal Proceedings throughout the European Union', 4 *ERA-Forum* (2003), 91.

[245] COM (2004) 328 final.

[246] See Council doc 12353/05.

[247] Council doc 7527/06, Brussels 27 March 2006.

[248] See House of Lords European Union Committee, *Breaking the Deadlock: What Future for EU Procedural Rights?*, 2nd Report, session 2006–07, HL Paper 20. See also Council doc 7349/07, Brussels, 13 March 2007.

[249] For background, see Council doc 10287/07, Brussels, 5 June 2007. For the Council of Europe comments see Council doc 5431/07, Brussels, 18 January 2007.

agreement in the proposal, its text has been watered down (in particular the 'Letter of Rights' provisions were dropped) and concessions appeared to have been made to Member States wishing to exclude from the scope of the measure proceedings against suspected terrorists.[250] However, agreement on the proposal has not proven to be possible. One reason for this is the uncertainty regarding the existence of Union competence to adopt measures in the field of criminal procedure (see the part on 'legal basis' below). However, even if the issue of the legal basis were resolved, it is clear that the attempt to reach harmonisation on the rights of the defendant in criminal proceedings at EU level—in particular at the level of common definitions—is far from a straightforward task. It requires agreement on definitions of concepts as fundamental as the very concept of 'criminal proceedings'[251] and concepts such as who is 'arrested' and 'charged' with a criminal offence.[252] Such an exercise may not always be productive, with Member States wary of agreeing definitions in Brussels which may not reflect the balance of their internal criminal justice systems. At the same time, by entering the EU vocabulary these concepts (and the rights of the defendant) become subject to interpretation and enforcement by Luxembourg, and may become autonomous Union concepts of criminal law. This may appear a challenge to both state sovereignty and the relevant interpretation by the Strasbourg court, notwithstanding attempts to align the EU instrument with the Strasbourg jurisprudence.

ii. The Question of the Existence of EU Competence

The issue of the appropriateness of the legal basis is inextricably linked with the constitutional question of whether, at this stage of European integration, Member States have conferred to the EU competence to legislate in the field of rights of the defence and criminal procedure.[253] The proposed legal basis is Article 31(1)(c) TEU, which enables common action to be taken on judicial co-operation in criminal matters 'ensuring compatibility in rules applicable in the Member States, as may be necessary to improve such co-operation'. The Commission defends this choice by stating that the proposal constitutes the 'necessary complement' to the mutual recognition measures that are designed to increase efficiency of prosecution.[254] It has argued that the proposal is necessary to ensure compatibility between the

---

[250] See Preamble, indent 5, of doc 10287/07, stating:

> Without prejudice to Art 7 [a non-regression clause] the provisions of the Framework Decision are not intended to affect special measures based on national legal provisions to combat crime which is aimed at destroying the foundations of the rule of law. Prosecution of these serious and complex forms of crime, in particular terrorism, may justify restrictions on procedural standards, provided that such restrictions are strictly necessary and proportionate and that the procedural rights are not drained of their substance.

[251] The general definition used in Art 1 of doc 10287/07 is 'any proceedings which could lad to a criminal penalty ordered by a criminal court' (Art 1(1))—but see exceptions in Art 1(5).

[252] Art 1(2) states that these terms will be interpreted in accordance with the Strasbourg case law.

[253] On this debate, see the views expressed in House of Lords European Union Committee, *Procedural Rights in Criminal Proceedings*, 1st Report, session 2004–05, paras 29–41.

[254] Commission COM (2004) 328 final, n 245 above, para 51.

criminal justice systems of Member States and to build trust and promote mutual confidence across the EU whereby :'not only the judicial authorities, but all actors in the criminal process see decisions of the judicial authorities of other Member States as equivalent to their own and do not call in question their judicial capacity and respect for fair trial rights'.[255]

The proposal may indeed contribute towards enhancing compatibility between some aspects of the criminal justice systems of Member States, potentially leading to improvements in the situation of defendants in Member States. However, serious objections can be raised against the view advocating the existence of EU competence to adopt this measure in its present form.[256] The main constitutional objection is that *the Treaty contains at present no express legal basis for the adoption of criminal procedure measures.* An express legal basis would seem necessary to enable the EU to act in an area so inextricably linked with national sovereignty. No current Treaty provision can be interpreted as reflecting Member States' will to confer to the EU competence to legislate on criminal procedure when agreeing the Nice Treaty. The existence of an express—but limited—legal basis for EU criminal procedure measures regarding the rights of the individual exists in the Lisbon Treaty strengthens this view:[257] The need for such a provision in the Lisbon Treaty (and earlier in the Constitutional Treaty) results from the lack of an express provision conferring clear-cut competence to the EU in this field at present.[258]

A further argument that can be added is that *the achievement of 'mutual trust' is too indirect and subjective a legitimating link.*[259] The Commission justifies the proposal as necessary to introduce rules which will lead to compatibility *which lead to trust* which in turn leads to the improvement of judicial co-operation. So it is not compatibility *as such* that will improve co-operation, but the trust it may create. However, the concept of trust is inherently subjective and it is questionable whether such a subjective frame of mind should be set as a goal of a legal measure. How will 'trust' be achieved and measured? Is the existence of legal rules *per se* in foreign countries sufficient to increase public trust, especially in the face of hostile press coverage and the many times ingrained belief in the superiority of one's domestic criminal justice system? These are open questions, which may point to the fact that the concept of 'mutual trust' is too subjective in this context, and thus not necessarily amenable to judicial review. This would, however, run counter to

---

[255] Commission COM (2004) 328 final, n 245 above, para 28.

[256] For details, see V Mitsilegas, 'Trust-building Measures in the European Judicial Area in Criminal Matters: Issues of Competence, Legitimacy and Inter-institutional Balance' in S Carrera and T Balzacq, *Security versus Freedom? A Challenge for Europe's Future*, Aldershot, Ashgate, 2006, pp 279–289; and V Mitsilegas, 'The Constitutional Implications of Mutual Recognition in Criminal Matters in the European Union', *Common Market Law Review*, vol 43, 2006, pp 1277–1311.

[257] See Art 82(2) TFEU and analysis in part VI below.

[258] This view was also echoed by the Convention on the Future of Europe: in its final Report, Working Group X on 'Freedom, Security and Justice' highlighted the need for clearer identification of Union competence in the fields of substantive and procedural criminal law and noted that, in the field of procedural approximation, 'at present, Art 31 TEU does not reflect sufficiently this point and is too vague on concrete possibilities for such approximation' pp 8 and 11 respectively.

[259] See also ch 3.

settled ECJ case law on the first pillar, according to which the choice of legal basis for a measure may not depend simply on an institution's conviction as to the object pursued, but must be based on objective factors which are amenable to judicial review.[260] It may also contradict the ECJ assertion in the ne bis in idem cases that mutual trust in Member States' criminal justice systems already exists.[261]

VI. THE FUTURE IN THE LIGHT OF LISBON[262]

A. Substantive Criminal Law

As has been mentioned in the first chapter, the Lisbon Treaty introduces far-reaching changes EU criminal law. The collapse of the third pillar it entails would mean that criminal law would be adopted in principle under the legislative procedure (ie the current 'Community method' of decision-making) and would take the form of 'Community' instruments (such as Directives) with EU institutions playing a full role. It would seem thus that the current debate over the extent of Community criminal law competence would be settled. However, a number of questions related to the extent of the Union criminal law competence remain.[263] These arise in particular from the wording of the Lisbon Treaty when combined with the Court's case law on environmental crime. According to the Lisbon Treaty, the Union (succeeding the Community as a single pillar organisation with legal personality) will have competence to establish *minimum rules* concerning *the definition of criminal offences and sanctions* in the areas of *particularly serious crime with a cross-border dimension* resulting from the nature or impact of such offences or from a special need to combat them on a common basis.[264] According to the Treaty, these areas of crime are the following:

> Terrorism, trafficking in human beings and sexual exploitation of women and children, illicit drug trafficking, illicit arms trafficking, money laundering, corruption, counterfeiting of means of payment, computer crime and organised crime.[265]
>
> The list of these offences may be expanded 'on the basis of developments in crime' by the Council acting unanimously after obtaining the consent of the European Parliament.[266]

It appears thus that the Lisbon Treaty expands criminal law competence (for what is now the Community) in granting the Union powers to adopt (albeit *minimum*) rules on criminal sanctions (and not merely to require Member States to adopt

[260] See inter alia Case C-300/89, *Commission v Council* [1991], ECR I-2867 (the Titanium Dioxide case).
[261] See ch 3.
[262] This section is based on V Mitsilegas, Memorandum submitted to the House of Lords European Union Committee for their inquiry into the Lisbon Treaty, reproduced in House of Lords European Union Committee, *The Treaty of Lisbon: An Impact Assessment*, Volume II: Evidence, 10th Report, session 2007–08, HL Paper 62-II, at E166–169; and Mitsilegas, 'Trust-building Measures', n 256 above.
[263] See also the discussion in House of Lords European Union Committee, *The Treaty of Lisbon: An Impact Assessment*, Volume 1, 10th Report, session 2007–08, HL Paper 62-I, paras 6.162–6.189.
[264] Art 83(1) TFEU.
[265] ibid.
[266] ibid.

proportionate, effective and dissuasive penalties). However, the scope of competence regarding criminal offences and sanctions appears to be narrower than the current law and practice in the third pillar. The Treaty delimits competence on the basis of an exhaustive list of offences, which must also fulfil a number of conditions set out in Article 83(1) TFEU (seriousness, cross-border dimensions, impact or the need to combat on a common basis). The list of these areas of crime can only be extended by a unanimous decision by the Council.

The scope of the Union's competence to act in criminal matters is expanded by Article 83(2) TFEU, which grants the Union competence to approximate (with 'approximation' being the term used in the Treaty) criminal laws *and regulations* if such approximation *proves essential* to ensure the effective implementation of a Union policy in an area which has been subject to harmonisation measures. It is important to note that the provision refers specifically to *approximation* of criminal laws, and the adoption of *minimum standards with regard to the definition of criminal offences and sanctions*—implying thus a limited degree of integration. However, such approximation is not limited to laws, but also extends to regulations—the precise meaning of the reference to regulations in this context remains to be seen.

However, perhaps the central issue to be resolved with regard to Article 83(2) is its relationship with the existing Court case law regarding the extent of Community competence in criminal matters in the environmental crime and ship-source pollution. Like the Court, the Treaty uses effectiveness as a justification for Union competence in criminal matters. The scope of such action appears to be broader in the Treaty, which refers to the effectiveness of Union *policies* (and not only objectives), on the condition that these policies are in an area which has been subject to harmonisation measures. There are, however, a number of elements that are unclear in Article 83(2). First of all, uncertainty surrounds the precise meaning of the term 'essential' to ensure *effet utile*. The concept is not clear and is highly likely to be the subject of ECJ litigation. Secondly, it is not clear which institution will 'prove' that a criminal law measure is essential in this context. Will for instance the case law of the Court be taken into account in this context? Again, the wording is a prime candidate for litigation, as it is highly likely that there will be disagreement between the Council on the one hand and the Commission and the Parliament on the other on what will 'prove essential' in this context. It is also contested whether Article 83(2) is a sufficient, self-standing legal basis for the adoption of criminal law or whether a dual legal basis (in conjunction with the specific EU sectoral provision) will be necessary in this context. The answer may have implications for the future development of enhanced co-operation in the field.[267]

---

[267] The issue is of particular significance with regard to Member States such as the UK which have been offered the possibility not to opt-in to EU criminal law in the future. If a dual legal basis is required, it appears that a Member State which has participated in and is bound by the underlying Union policy is also bound by measures adopted under Art 83(2). Otherwise the effectiveness of Union law may be seriously jeopardised. This view is supported by the wording of 83(2) and the link between criminal law action under this legal basis and a Union policy already subject to harmonisation. See also the discussion of whether Art 83(2) TFEU is *lex specialis* in this context in House of Lords EU Committee, n 262 above, paras 6.179–6.189.

Another issue which causes uncertainty regarding the exact scope of EU competence on substantive criminal law stems from different parts of the Lisbon Treaty. A development that may imply that the Union's criminal law competence may extend beyond the offences enumerated in Article 83 TFEU is the deletion of the last sentence in current Article 280(4) TEC (Article 325 TFEU post-Lisbon). This sentence states that measures to combat fraud (an area which is not expressly listed in Article 83(1) TFEU but may be included in 83(2)) will not concern the application of national criminal law and the national administration of justice.[268] With the deletion of this sentence, the Union will now have competence under Article 280(4) to adopt 'the necessary measures in the fields of the prevention and fight against fraud affecting the financial interests of the [Union] with a view to affording effective and equivalent protection in the Member States'. It is not clear whether the wording here (in an area dealing with issues closely related to criminal law) signifies that the Union has competence under Article 325 TFEU to adopt criminal laws on fraud without the need to have recourse to Article 83(2).

B. Criminal Procedure

The Lisbon Treaty also introduces significant changes with regard Union competence on criminal procedure. As seen above, there is currently a controversy regarding the existence and extent of such competence in the third pillar, vividly demonstrated by the ongoing negotiations for a Framework Decision on the rights of the defendant in criminal proceedings. Article 82(2) of the Lisbon Treaty expressly confers to the Union the competence to adopt, under the legislative procedure, *minimum* rules concerning mutual admissibility of evidence between Member States (which may follow the adoption of the European Evidence Warrant), the rights of individuals in criminal procedure and the rights of the victims of crime—with further areas potentially added after a unanimous decision by the Council and the consent of the European Parliament. However, Union competence in the field of criminal procedure applies only to the extent necessary to facilitate mutual recognition of judgments and police and judicial co-operation in criminal matters.[269] Criminal procedure measures—and the human rights implications which they may have—are thus subordinated to the efficiency logic of mutual recognition, which is according to the Lisbon Treaty, the basis for judicial co-operation in criminal matters in the EU. Moreover, the need to demonstrate that a measure of criminal procedure is necessary for the facilitation of mutual recognition may not always lead to straightforward results—as demonstrated earlier in the chapter in the context of the discussion on the proposal on the rights

---

[268] A similar clause was deleted from Art 135 EC concerning customs co-operation (this is Art 33 in the TFEU).

[269] Note also the requirement for these matters to have a cross-border dimension. This limits the scope of EU competence and may be seen as an attempt to limit the applicability of EU criminal procedure law to cross-border cases.

of the defendant. While the Lisbon Treaty contains an express legal basis for the adoption of such an instrument, the details of its adoption remain contested as its impact on the facilitation of mutual recognition needs to be demonstrated and may be contested. The facilitation requirement in Article 82(2) TFEU may lead not only to lengthy negotiations in the Council and the European Parliament, but also to litigation.[270]

C. Crime Prevention

Another new area of Union action post-Lisbon is crime prevention. Article 84 TFEU which provides the legal basis for crime prevention measures specifies that action in the field is merely supporting—the European Parliament and the Council may co-decide to establish 'measures to promote and support the action of Member States in the field of crime prevention'.[271] Moreover, according to Article 84 EU action on crime prevention will exclude any harmonisation of the laws and regulations of Member States. In the light of the limits set out by this provision, the adoption of legislation in the field is likely to be very limited—however, Article 84 may provide the basis for more concerted action in the field by means of the open method of co-ordination.

VII. CONCLUSION. CRIMINAL LAW HARMONISATION AS A MEANS TO WHICH END?

The debate on criminal law harmonisation has recently been conducted within a Community/Union constitutional context, with the question of criminal law harmonisation being presented primarily as a competence question: does the Community have competence to adopt criminal offences and sanctions under the first pillar, or is criminal law solely a Union, third pillar matter? The answers given by the Court of Justice (accepting under certain conditions first pillar criminal law competence) are of undoubted constitutional significance. They are also, however, significant for shaping the treatment of criminal law in the Union legal order. It is clear that the Court, following largely the reasoning of the European Commission, treats criminal law *as a means to an end* by accepting Community competence to legislate in the field in order to achieve the effectiveness of Community law. Criminal law is thus treated *not* as a separate Community policy or objective, but rather merely as yet another field of law (along with civil law, administrative law etc) which is there to serve the achievement of Community policies. This approach towards criminal law may be of concern to the extent that it disregards the special place of criminal law in domestic legal systems and the extensive safeguards

---

[270] On the impact that this requirement may have for Member States which have ensured the possibility not to participate in EU criminal law instruments post-Lisbon, see ch 1.

[271] Note also that, as noted in ch 1, crime prevention is not expressly included in the list of areas of EU supporting action under Art 6 TFEU.

surrounding criminal law at the national level. Moreover, it leads to uncertainty regarding the exact *scope* of EU criminal law. It is not clear from the Court's case law whether EU criminal law is necessary to achieve *any* Community policy, or *any* Community *objective*. A maximalist view may lead to an overproduction of criminal law in the EU. This danger is exacerbated by the placement of EU criminal law at the heart of interinstitutional constitutional battles in the EU. The Commission's recent proposals for Directives using criminal law in fields such as intellectual property and illegal employment demonstrate the danger that criminal law may be used in areas where it may not be necessary in order to help push forward the constitutional point that the Community has an extensive competence to legislate in criminal matters. In this constitutional game, the question of 'why criminal law', or whether criminal law is actually necessary in specific EC instruments appears to be sidelined.

However, it is not only in the first pillar that the answer to the question of 'why criminal law' appears to be unclear. A similar situation arises on occasions in the criminal law Treaty part *par excellence,* the third pillar. The third pillar legal basis for the adoption of harmonised EU criminal law is quite extensive and perhaps deliberately unclear to ensure flexibility. The harmonisation outcome thus far does not always reflect coherent, long-term policy strategy.[272] Yes, major areas of transnational or serious crime have been harmonised, with harmonisation following on a number of occasions concrete political commitments in various European Council and Council Conclusions and Action Plans. Although not always stated expressly, such harmonisation may be beneficial in giving greater legal certainty in the functioning of Union criminal law bodies such as Europol and Eurojust, whose mandate is based on such offences. However, the third pillar legal basis has also been used to adopt measures such as the victims of crime Framework Decision, whose legality under the Treaty and quality in terms of legal certainty can both be questioned. The limits of current Union competence are also evident in attempts to adopt criminal law to accompany mutual recognition—an aim that is increasingly becoming central in EU criminal law harmonisation attempts. The justification and legality of criminal law measures under the third pillar is thus not always clear.[273] This trend for 'more' criminal law is also confirmed when one goes to look at 'what kind of criminal law' has been adopted under the third pillar: the harmonisation that has actually taken place has resulted

---

[272] For this point in the context of the EU normative response post-9/11, see S de Biolley, 'Liberté et sécurité dans la constitution de l'espace européen de justice pénale: cristallisation de la tension sous présidence belge', in de Kerchove and Weyembergh, n 151 above, pp 169–198.

[273] It has also been argued that criminalisation is increased or taken for granted by the very fact that Union law focuses on the severest of all criminality—making the use of imprisonment look natural: see K Nuotio, 'Harmonization of Criminal Sanctions in the European Union—Criminal Law Science Fiction' in J Husabo and A. Strandbakken (eds), *Harmonisation of Criminal Law in Europe,* Antwerp, Oxford, Intersentia, 2005, pp 79–102 (p 100). On Depenalisation in the European Union, see also R Hefendehl, 'European Criminal Law: How Far and No Further?', in B Schünemann (ed), *A Programme for European Criminal Justice,* Cologne, Berlin, Munich, Carl Heymanns Verlag, 2006, pp 450–466.

on occasions (such as organised crime and terrorism, but also, under the influence of global standards, money laundering) in the adoption of heavily securitised, very broad EU criminal legislation.[274]

The Lisbon Treaty introduces the major change of abolishing the pillars and perhaps by doing so moving the debate on EU criminal law harmonisation from the inter-pillar constitutional debate to the questions of 'why criminal law' and 'what kind of criminal law' for the EU. The delimitation of EU competence in the field is of central importance in this context. As far as substantive criminal law is concerned, the Treaty contains a clear legal basis for EU action on specific offences, which must be cross-border and serious. However, this clarity is undermined by the reproduction of the effectiveness logic in the Treaty, whereby EU criminal offences and sanctions may be adopted if they are essential for the implementation of Union policies which have been subject to harmonisation. Criminal law is thus treated again as a means to an end and is evoked to protect a potentially wide range of interests. In this context, it may be argued that the categories of interests protected by criminal law in the legal systems of Member States may be significantly expanded, if to these categories one adds the achievement of any number of Community policies whose implementation is sought via criminal law.[275] This may lead to an expansion of criminal law in the EU and Member States, along of course with the express expansion of Union competence to allow for the adoption of EU measures in criminal procedure. However, such competence only exists to facilitate the achievement of mutual recognition in criminal matters, although it is not clear whether mutual recognition has the status of a separate Union policy in the Lisbon Treaty. Like in the field of offences and sanctions, criminal law is also used here as a means to an end.

The impact of the Lisbon Treaty changes on criminal law harmonisation may be substantial. On the one hand, the move to the 'Community method' of decision-making may lead to increased quantity (if not quality) of harmonisation measures. On the other, the expansion of EU action in criminal matters into criminal procedure and the increased production of substantive criminal law may necessitate increased interpretative intervention by the Court of Justice. The Court may be asked to look increasingly at the content of EU measures in the light of domestic criminal law and justice principles reflecting an internal balance between the individual and the State. The Court has already faced such dilemmas in cases such as *Pupino* and *Dell' Orto* but the challenges will multiply, in particular if further

---

[274] For an analysis of the impact of the securitisation process on the development of EU criminal law, see ch 1. For the latest example of securitised, broad criminal law see the Framework Decision amending the 2002 terrorism Framework Decision to include three new offences: public provocation to commit terrorist offences; recruitment for terrorism; and training for terrorism (see doc 8807/08, Brussels 18 July 2008). The Justice and Home Affairs Council reached a 'general approach' on the instrument in April 2008 (Council doc 8397/08, Presse 96, p 15).

[275] On an attempt to put forward a theory of 'European legal interests', see N Bitzilekis, M Kaiafa-Gbandi and E Symeonidou-Kastanidou, 'Theory of the Genuine European Legal Interests', in Schünemann, n 273 above, pp 467–476.

EU measures on criminal procedure are adopted. Both legislation and judicial interpretation may bring about autonomous Union definitions and principles of criminal law. How these will be accommodated in the domestic and Union legal orders remains to be seen.

3

Mutual Recognition

Prosecution, Jurisdiction and Trust in an 'Area' of Freedom, Security and Justice

I. INTRODUCTION

APPLYING THE PRINCIPLE of mutual recognition has been the motor of European integration in criminal matters in the recent past. The adoption in 2002 of the Framework Decision on the European Arrest Warrant—a prime example of mutual recognition in criminal matters—constituted a spectacular development for European Union criminal law, and was subsequently followed by the adoption of a series of further mutual recognition measures. However, the application of the principle in practice has not been devoid of controversy. As demonstrated by the negotiations and implementation of the European Arrest Warrant Framework Decision, the application of the mutual recognition principle in criminal law raises significant challenges for the constitutional and criminal justice traditions of Member States and the protection of fundamental rights and has caused the debate on primacy to resurface—the focus being this time on primacy of third pillar (Union) law over national law. At the same time, the application of mutual recognition in criminal matters may also have significant constitutional implications for the European Union, bringing into the fore issues of competence and legitimacy, and the reframing of the relationship between the Union and Member States in the field of criminal law. This chapter will examine the application of the principle of mutual recognition in criminal matters in the European Union in the light of these challenges. It will begin by an analysis of mutual recognition and of its application in EU criminal law and continue by an overview of the constitutional implications of mutual recognition and how they have been addressed by legislation and courts. The chapter will continue with a more specific examination of the relationship between mutual recognition and issues of prosecution and jurisdiction in the EU by looking at the development of *ne bis in idem* as a fundamental principle of Union law and at the evolution of mechanisms to manage State sovereignty on the issue of which Member State should prosecute in the case of concurrent jurisdictions. In this context, the chapter will cast light on the reconfiguration of territoriality, sovereignty and the relationship between the individual and the State in EU criminal law.

II. THE PRINCIPLE OF MUTUAL RECOGNITION IN EU CRIMINAL LAW

Proposals to introduce the principle of mutual recognition in EU criminal law can be seen as a balancing act between on the one hand the need to address concerns with regard to the slow pace of improvement of judicial co-operation in criminal matters in the EU post-Maastricht, and on the other hand the need to reassure Member States sceptical of further EU harmonisation in criminal matters, in particular at a time (the late 1990s) when ambitious proposals for criminal law uniformity in the EU such as the *Corpus Juris* had emerged.[1] In this light, the UK Government put forward during its EU Presidency in 1998 the idea of applying the mutual recognition principle in the field of criminal law, leading to the recognition by the European Council at Cardiff of 'the need to enhance the ability of national legal systems to work closely together' and a request to the Council 'to identify the scope for greater mutual recognition of decisions of each others' courts'.[2] The emphasis on mutual recognition was justified by the UK on the grounds that the differences between Member States' legal systems limit the progress which is possible by other means and render harmonisation of criminal law time consuming, difficult to negotiate and (if full scale) unrealistic.[3] According to Jack Straw, then UK Home Secretary, one could be inspired from the way in which the internal market was 'unblocked' in the 1980s and, instead of opting for total harmonisation, conceive a situation 'where each Member State recognises the validity of decisions of courts from other Member States in criminal matters with a minimum of procedure and formality'.[4]

The momentum for enhancing co-operation in criminal matters in the EU via mutual recognition was maintained in the following years.[5] In its 1999 Tampere Conclusions, setting up a five year agenda for EU Justice and Home Affairs, the European Council endorsed the principle of mutual recognition, which in its view,

---

[1] On the background to EU legislative production in criminal matters post-Maastricht and the *Corpus Juris* proposals see ch 2.

[2] Para 39, doc SN 150/1/98 REV 1.

[3] See document submitted by the UK delegation to the (then) K.4 Committee, doc 7090/99, Brussels, 29 March 1999, paras 7 and 8.

[4] In La documentation française, Ministère de la Justice, *L'espace judiciaire européen. Actes du Colloque d'Avignon*, Paris, 1999, p 89 (my translation).

[5] For a detailed look at negotiations at the time see H Nilsson, "Mutual Trust or Mutual Mistrust?', in G de Kerchove and A Weyembergh (eds), *La confiance mutuelle dans l'espace pénal européen=Mutual Trust in the European Criminal Area*, Brussels, Éditions de l'Université de Bruxelles, 2005, pp 29–33. For an overview of the development of the internal market principle in criminal matters, see also S Peers, 'Mutual Recognition and Criminal Law in the European Union: Has the Council Got it Wrong?', *Common Market Law Review*, vol 41, 2004, pp 5–36; and S Lavenex, 'Mutual Recognition and the Monopoly of Force: Limits of the Single Market Analogy', *Journal of European Public Policy*, vol 14, no 5, 2007, pp 762–779.

'should become the cornerstone of judicial co-operation' in criminal matters.[6] This led in 2001 to the adoption by Member States of a very detailed Programme of measures to implement the principle of mutual recognition of decisions in criminal matters, which called on the Council to adopt no less than 24 measures in the field.[7] The previous year, the Commission published a Communication presenting the institution's thoughts on mutual recognition.[8] The Commission expressed the view that the traditional system of co-operation is slow, cumbersome and uncertain, and provided its own understanding of how mutual recognition might work:

> Thus, borrowing from concepts that have worked very well in the creation of the Single Market, the idea was born that judicial co-operation might also benefit from the concept of mutual recognition which, simply stated, means that once a certain measure, such as a decision taken by a judge in exercising his or her official powers in one Member State, has been taken, that measure—in so far as it has extranational implications—would *automatically* be accepted in all other Member States, and have the same or at least similar effects there. (emphasis added)[9]

Thus, the turn of the century saw a consensus on the desirability of the application of the mutual recognition principle in the criminal law sphere in the EU. For those opposing harmonisation in criminal matters, mutual recognition comes handy as it can provide results for judges and prosecutors when co-operating across borders, while *prima facie* Member States do not have to change their domestic criminal law to implement EU standards. For supporters of integration on the other hand, mutual recognition is also welcome. It helps avoid EU legislative stagnation in criminal matters, by pushing forward a detailed legislative agenda to achieve mutual recognition and promoting co-operation. On the other hand, as evidenced in the Commission's 2000 Communication,[10] supporters of integration also view mutual recognition as a motor for harmonisation, as—like in the internal market—the smooth functioning of mutual recognition would require minimum harmonisation of standards among Member States and thus lead to a 'spill-over' of further measures in the field.[11]

However, the extent to which one can successfully 'borrow' the mutual recognition principle from its internal market framework and transplant it to the criminal law sphere is a contested issue. The main objection that could be voiced to such transplant is one of principle, namely that criminal law and justice is an area

---

[6] Para 33. The reference to mutual recognition as the 'cornerstone' of judicial co-operation in criminal matters in the EU was reiterated five years later, in the Hague Programme extending the EU JHA agenda to 2009—para 3.3.1.

[7] OJ C12, 15 January 2001, p 10.

[8] Communication from the Commission to the Council and the European Parliament, Mutual Recognition of Final Decisions in Criminal Matters, COM (2000) 495 final, Brussels, 26 July 2000.

[9] ibid, p 2.

[10] ibid, p 4.

[11] See V Mitsilegas, 'Trust-building Measures in the European Judicial Area in Criminal Matters: Issues of Competence, Legitimacy and Inter-institutional Balance', in S Carrera and T Balzacq (eds), *Security versus Freedom: A Challenge for Europe's Future*, Aldershot, Ashgate, 2006, pp 279–290.

of law and regulation which is qualitatively different from the regulation of trade and markets. Criminal law regulates the relationship between the individual and the State, and guarantees not only State interests but also individual freedoms and rights in limiting State intervention. Court orders and judgments in the criminal sphere may have a substantial impact on fundamental rights, and any inroads to such rights caused by criminal law must be extensively debated and justified. Using mutual recognition to achieve regulatory competition (as has been the case in the internal market) cannot be repeated in the criminal law sphere, as the logic of criminal law is different and market considerations cannot give a solution.[12] While market efficiency requires a degree of flexibility and aims at profit maximisation, clear and predictable criminal law principles are essential to provide legal certainty in a society based on the rule of law. The existence of these—publicly negotiated—rules is a condition of public trust to the national legal order. For these reasons, EU intervention in criminal matters must not be equated with intervention regarding the internal market.

This fundamental objection is coupled with a further pivotal difference between market and crime mutual recognition: this concerns the mode and effect of recognition. Mutual recognition in the internal market involves the recognition of national regulatory standards and controls,[13] is geared to national administrators and legislators.[14] And results in facilitating the free movement of products and persons, thus enabling the enjoyment of fundamental Community law rights. Mutual recognition in criminal matters on the other hand involves the recognition and execution of court decisions by judges, in order to primarily facilitate the movement of enforcement rulings. Moreover, the intensity of intervention of the requested authority is greater in criminal matters, as further action may be needed in order to execute the judgment/order (such as arrest and surrender to the requesting State). While the logic behind recognition in the internal market and criminal law may be similar (there should be no obstacles to movement in a borderless EU)—which, in criminal matters leads to calls for compensatory measures (criminals should not benefit from the abolition of borders in the EU)—there is a different rationale between facilitating the exercise of a right to free movement of an individual and facilitating a decision that may ultimately limit this and other rights.

These differences notwithstanding, the founding principle of mutual recognition in both internal market and criminal law is similar: the recognition of national standards by other EU Member States. In that sense, as Nicolaidis and Shaffer have noted, 'recognition creates extraterritoriality'.[15] National standards

---

[12] On mutual recognition and regulatory competition see G Majone, *Dilemmas of European Integration. The Ambiguities and Pitfalls of Integration by Stealth,* Oxford, OUP, 2005, p 71. On the incompatibility of the two fields see A Weyembergh and S Khabipour, 'Quelle confiance mutuelle ailleurs?', in de Kerchove and Weyembergh, *La confiance mutuelle,* n 5 above, p 265.

[13] K Armstrong, 'Mutual Recognition', in C Barnard and J Scott, *The Law of the Single European Market: Unpacking the Premises,* Oxford, Hart Publishing, 2002, pp 225–267 at pp 230–231.

[14] C Barnard, *The Substantive Law of the EU. The Four Freedoms,* Oxford, OUP, 2004, p 507.

[15] K Nicolaidis and G Shaffer, 'Transnational Mutual Recognition Regimes: Governance without Global Government', *Law and Contemporary Problems,* vol 68, 2005, pp 263–317 at p 267.

must be recognised 'extraterritorially', in the sense that they must be applied and/or enforced by another Member State. The central element of the mechanism is that it is an individual *national* standard, judgment or order that must be recognised by other Member States—and not an EU-wide negotiated standard.[16] In recognising these standards in specific cases, national authorities implicitly accept as legitimate the national regulatory/legal/justice system which has produced them in the first place.[17] In that sense, mutual recognition represents a *'journey into the unknown'*, where national authorities are in principle obliged to recognise standards emanating from the national system of any EU Member State on the basis of mutual trust, with a minimum of formality.[18]

It is this potential 'journey into the unknown' which has led to mechanisms of checks in order to avoid total automaticity when it comes to mutual recognition in the internal market. These checks may take the form of leaving to national authorities a leeway to assess whether there is a level of functional equivalence between the systems of the home and host country prior to accepting to recognise the home country's standards;[19] and the possibility for Member States to refuse mutual recognition when evoking mandatory requirements.[20] As will be seen below, similar mechanisms and safeguards have been introduced in the context of mutual recognition in criminal matters, in order to avoid the automatic recognition and execution of judgments in the field. However, these efforts—along with the very application of the mutual recognition principle in the criminal law field— are being contested. Mutual recognition challenges traditional concepts of territoriality and sovereignty. Viewing the European Union as a single 'area' where national enforcement tools circulate freely, even if no EU-wide standards are created, may lead to a renegotiation of fundamental constitutional principles both at

---

[16] Guild seems to find this at odds with the abolition of borders in the EU. She notes that 'there is an inversion of an area without borders into an area that respects without question borders (ie mutual recognition)'. E Guild, 'Crime and the EU's Constitutional Future in an Area of Freedom, Security and Justice', *European Law Journal*, vol 10, no 2, 2004, pp 218–234 at p 219.

[17] On the need to look at the specific regulatory history of a product for standards to be recognised in the context of the internal market, see Armstrong, n 13 above, p 231.

[18] See V Mitsilegas, 'The Constitutional Implications of Mutual above Recognition in Criminal Matters in the European Union', *Common Market Law Review*, vol 43, 2006, pp 1277–1311, at pp 1281–1282. Maduro calls this 'systems recognition'—see M. Poiares Maduro, 'So Close and Yet So Far: The Paradoxes of Mutual Recognition', *Journal of European Public Policy*, vol 14, no 5, 2007, pp 814–825 at p 823.

[19] Armstrong calls this 'active' mutual recognition—n 13 above, p 241. Peers (n 5 above, pp 19–23) refers to 'comparability' between systems. He argues that such comparability does not exist in criminal matters, due to the abolition of the dual criminality requirement regarding a number of offences when recognising court decisions in criminal matters. However, comparability refers to the system that produces the specific standard. In the internal market an example (which Peers uses) would be comparability of training requirements to enter a profession. In criminal law, this would translate to comparability of national judicial systems and procedures leading to the judgement to be recognised and executed (and not whether a behaviour is an offence in both the requesting and requested State).

[20] The concept was introduced by the Cassis de Dijon ruling (Case 120/78, *Rewe-Zentralfinanz v Bundesmonopolverwaltung fuer Branntwein* [1979] ECR 649). On the evolution of mandatory requirements see inter alia Barnard, n 14 above, pp 108–112; P Craig and G de Búrca, *EU Law. Text, Cases and Materials*, 4th edn., Oxford, OUP, 2008, pp 705–714.

national and EU level.[21] This renegotiation is under way as the first examples of mutual recognition in criminal matters have emerged.

III. INSTRUMENTS OF MUTUAL RECOGNITION IN CRIMINAL MATTERS AND RESULTING CONSTITUTIONAL CONCERNS

A. The Mutual Recognition Instruments

The first, and most analysed, example of mutual recognition in criminal matters in the European Union has been the European Arrest Warrant.[22] Its adoption was prioritised after the 9/11 events, and political agreement on the relevant Framework Decision was reached in the Council in December 2001, after very limited debate in the European Parliament and national parliaments.[23] Pushed through as 'emergency legislation', the European Arrest Warrant has changed radically existing arrangements of co-operation on extradition and constitutes a strong precedent for the application of mutual recognition in criminal matters in the European Union.[24] This is recognised in the Preamble of the Framework Decision which states that the warrant 'is the first concrete measure in the field of criminal law implementing the principle of mutual recognition which the European Council referred to as the 'cornerstone' of judicial co-operation'.[25]

The European Arrest Warrant is a judicial decision issued by a Member State with a view to the arrest and surrender by another Member State of an individual for the purposes of conducting a criminal prosecution or executing a custodial sentence or detention order.[26] The Warrant is thus a national judicial decision

---

[21] Françoise Tulkens spoke as early as 2001 of 'reinvention' of paradigms. F Tulkens, 'La reconnaissance mutuelle des décisions sentencielles. Enjeux et perspectives' in G de Kerchove and A Weyembergh (eds), *La reconnaissance mutuelle des décisions judiciaires pénales dans l'Union europeenne*, Brussels, Éditions de l'Université de Bruxelles, 2001, p 166.

[22] Council Framework Decision of 13 June 2002 on the European Arrest Warrant and the surrender procedures between Member States (2002/584/JHA), OJ L190, 18 July 2002, p 1.

[23] For a background to the negotiations of the European Arrest warrant see M Plachta and W van Ballegooij, 'The Framework Decision on the European Arrest Warrant and Surrender Procedures between Member States of the European Union' in R Blekxtoon (ed), *Handbook on the European Arrest Warrant*, The Hague, TMC Asser Press, 2005, pp 32–36. On scrutiny by national parliaments and the limited time available see House of Lords European Union Committee, *The European Arrest Warrant*, 16th Report, session 2001–02, HL Paper 89.

[24] For an analysis of various aspects of the European Arrest Warrant see inter alia: S Alegre and M Leaf, 'Mutual Recognition in European Judicial Co-operation: A Step Too Far Too Soon? Case Study—The European Arrest Warrant', *European Law Journal*, vol 10, no 2, 2004, pp 200–217; N Venemann, 'The European Arrest Warrant and its Human Rights Implications', *Zeitschrift für Ausländisches Öffentliches Recht und Völkerrecht*, vol 63, 2003, pp 103–121; J Wouters and F Naert, 'Of Arrest Warrants, Terrorist Offences and Extradition Deals: An Appraisal of the EU's Main Criminal Law Measures against Terrorism after "11 September"', *Common Market Law Review*, vol.41, 2004, pp 911–926; B Gilmore, *The Twin Towers and the Third Pillar: Some Security Agenda Developments*, EUI Working Paper LAW No 2003/7; J R Spencer, 'The European Arrest Warrant', *Cambridge Yearbook of European Legal Studies* 2003–04, pp 201–217; Blekxtoon, n 23 above.

[25] Recital 6.

[26] Art 1(1) of Framework Decision.

which must be recognised and executed by the requested State. Co-operation is formalised, as the Warrant takes the form of a Certificate—a pro-forma form which is attached to the Framework Decision and contains a series of information on the requested person and the offence committed.[27] The Warrant must be dealt with as a matter of urgency and the final decision on its execution must be taken within a period of 60 days—or exceptionally 90 days—from the arrest of the requested person.[28] The requested authority is provided with very limited grounds for refusal to recognise and execute a Warrant.[29] With some exceptions, the arrested person must be surrendered no later than 10 days after the final decision on the execution of the Warrant.[30] The European Arrest Warrant introduces thus a procedure marked by automatisation and speed. A judicial authority of an EU Member State must give effect to a decision by a similar authority in another Member State with a minimum of formality: suspects or convicted persons must be surrendered as soon as possible, on the basis of completed forms, and ideally without the executing authorities looking behind the form.

Given its adoption as a response to the 9/11 events, a striking feature of the European Arrest Warrant is that its scope is not limited to terrorist offences. A Warrant may in fact be issued for acts punishable by the law of the issuing Member State by a custodial sentence or detention order of a maximum period of at least 12 months or, where a sentence has been passed or a detention order made, for sentences of at least four months.[31] So a wide range of conduct and offences may fall within the scope of the Framework Decision. Moreover, a wide range of offences give rise to surrender without verification of the dual criminality of the act. This is the case for a list of 32 offences expressly enumerated in the Framework Decision, provided that they are punishable in the Member State issuing the European Arrest Warrant by a custodial sentence or a detention order for a maximum period of at least three years.[32] The list includes offences at the same time very common and diverse, both national and transnational. Some of these have been subject to harmonisation at EU level (such as drug trafficking, human trafficking and organised crime), whereas others remain defined strictly by national law (such as murder, grievous bodily injury, rape).[33] For offences other than the 32 on the list, Member States may require that dual criminality is verified prior to the execution of a Warrant.[34]

The European Arrest Warrant is not the only example of mutual recognition in criminal matters. It was followed by the adoption of a series of measures applying the mutual recognition principle to primarily the financial side of criminal law

---

[27] See also Art 8(1).
[28] Art 17(1), (3) and (4).
[29] For further details, see ch 4.
[30] Art 23(2)–(4).
[31] Art 2(1).
[32] Art 2(2).
[33] For an analysis see N Keijzer, 'The Double Criminality Requirement', in Blekxtoon, n 23 above, pp 137–163.
[34] Art 2(4).

enforcement. In 2003, the Council adopted a Framework Decision on the execution of orders freezing property and evidence.[35] Freezing orders from the issuing State must be recognised 'without any further formality' by the executing State, which must 'forthwith' take the necessary measures for their 'immediate execution' in the same way as for a freezing order made by the executing State.[36] This was followed by the adoption of a Framework Decision applying mutual recognition to financial penalties.[37] In a similar wording to the freezing orders instrument, decisions imposing financial penalties must be recognised without formality and executed 'forthwith'.[38] Finally, the Council adopted a Framework Decision on the application of the principle of mutual recognition to confiscation orders.[39] Recognition and execution of confiscation orders must take place in similar terms to the other Framework Decisions.[40] But in the light of the very different constitutional traditions of Member States, this measure was accompanied by a Framework Decision aiming to bring about a minimum harmonisation of confiscation procedures in Member States.[41] As in the European Arrest Warrant, in all three instruments co-operation takes place on the basis of a Certificate that has to be completed by the issuing State, and a standard form is attached in each of the Framework Decisions. Similarly to the European Arrest warrant, the three Framework Decisions apply to a wide range of offences, for many of which the verification of the dual criminality requirement is abolished.[42]

---

[35] OJ L196, 2 August 2003, p 45.

[36] Art 5(1). For background to the proposal for the Framework Decision see G. Stessens, 'The Joint Initiative of France, Sweden and Belgium for the Adoption of a Council Framework Decision on the Execution in the European Union of Orders Freezing Assets and Evidence', in de Kerchove and Weyembergh, *La reconnaissance mutuelle*, n 21 above, pp 91–100.

[37] OJ L76, 22 March 2005, p 16.

[38] Art 6. For background to the proposal for the Framework Decision see R Bradley, 'The Joint Initiative of the UK, France and Sweden for the Adoption of a Council Framework Decision on the Application of the Principle of Mutual Recognition to Financial Penalties', in de Kerchove and Weyembergh, *La reconnaissance mutuelle*, n 21 above, pp 125–132. See also R Genson, 'Observations Personelles à propos des initiatives récentes relatives aux sanctions pécuniaires', ibid., pp 141–146.

[39] OJ L328, 24 November 2006, p 59. It is interesting to note that all three Framework Decisions were tabled on the initiative of Member States, within the framework of their powers under the third pillar.

[40] Art 7(1).

[41] OJ L68, 15 March 2005, p 49. As Peers (n 5 above, p 31) notes, the relationship of these two measures follows the classic internal market pattern. For an analysis of the relationship between the two instruments with regard to the grounds for refusal, see section 4 below).

[42] All three Framework Decisions apply to orders stemming from acts constituting any offence under the laws of the executing State (Arts 3(3), 5(3) and 2(d)/6(3) respectively—unlike the European Arrest Warrant, there is no penalty threshold for these offences in these instruments). Verification of dual criminality is abolished in similar terms to the European Arrest Warrant on the Framework Decisions on freezing orders and confiscation (3 year maximum penalty threshold and list of 32 offences—Arts 3(2) and 6(1) respectively). The scope of the financial penalties Framework Decision is broader: verification of dual criminality is abolished for a list of 39 offences, without any penalty threshold being required (Art 5(1)).

B. Constitutional Concerns

The application of the mutual recognition principle in criminal matters on the terms described above, has raised a number of constitutional concerns. A major objection has centred on the abolition of the dual criminality requirement, which is seen to constitute a breach of the legality principle. While proponents of mutual recognition have argued that maintaining dual criminality is contrary to the very principle of mutual recognition,[43] those expressing concerns note that the abolition of dual criminality is contrary to the—constitutionally enshrined in a number of Member States—principle of legality (or *nullum crimen sine lege*). As it has been noted, constitutionally it is not acceptable to execute an enforcement decision related to an act that is not an offence under the law of the executing State.[44] The executing State should not be asked to employ its criminal enforcement mechanism to help prosecuting/punishing behaviour which is not a criminal offence in its national legal order.[45] Concerns in this context involve in particular offences such as murder which have not been harmonised at EU level—although harmonisation does not always provide the answer.[46]

A related, but broader concern involves the link between legality and legitimacy of criminal law at the national—and EU—level.[47] As noted above, criminal law is fundamental in a society governed by the rule of law, as it contains rules delineating the relationship between the individual and the State and thus providing guarantees and safeguards for the individual regarding the extent and limits of acceptable behaviour and reach of State power and force.[48] Criminal law and the limits that it sets must be openly negotiated and agreed via a democratic process, and citizens must be aware of exactly what the rules are. However, mutual recognition challenges

---

[43] Nilsson, n 5 above, p 158.

[44] See in particular M. Kaiafa-Gbandi, *To poiniko dikaio stin Europaiki Enossi (Criminal Law in the European Union)*, Athens-Thessaloniki, Sakkoulas, 2003, p.328 (in Greek, my translation).

[45] These concerns are exacerbated when the enforcement measures used in the executing State are themselves invasive. In the first major challenge to the abolition of dual criminality in mutual recognition, Germany, playing the unanimity card, recently insisted that inroads to the list of the 32 offences were made regarding another major mutual recognition proposal, the European Evidence Warrant (EEW). On the EEW see part C of this section below.

[46] For instance, offences such as participation in a criminal organisation, although 'harmonised', still leave great discretion to Member States as to implementation—this may lead to considerable discrepancies in the treatment of the offence in national criminal laws—see V Mitsilegas, 'Defining Organised Crime in the European Union: the Limits of European Criminal Law in an Area of Freedom, Security and Justice', *European Law Review*, vol 26, 2001, pp 565–581.

[47] On the link between legality and legitimacy in EU criminal law in general see C van den Wyngaert, 'Eurojust and the European Public Prosecutor in the *Corpus Juris* Model: Water and Fire?', in N Walker (ed), *Europe's Area of Freedom, Security and Justice*, Oxford, Oxford University Press, 2004, pp 201–240 at p 232. The article draws upon the analysis of legitimacy in K Lenaerts and M Desomer, 'New Models of Constitution-Making in Europe: The Quest for Legitimacy', *Common Market Law Review* vol 39, 2002, pp 1217–1253, especially at pp 1223–1228.

[48] Kaiafa-Gbandi calls criminal law 'a measure of the citizen's freedom'. M Kaiafa-Gbandi, 'The Development towards Harmonization within Criminal Law in the European Union—A Citizen's Perspective', *European Journal of Crime, Criminal Law and Criminal Justice*, vol 9, 2001, pp 239–263 at p 242.

this framework. Contrary to harmonisation, which would involve—even with the current prominent democratic deficit in the third pillar—a set of concrete EU-wide standards which would be negotiated and agreed by the EU institutions, mutual recognition does not involve a commonly negotiated standard.[49] On the contrary, EU Member States must recognise decisions stemming from the national law of other Member States. Aspects of the legal systems of each Member State must thus be recognised—however, as mentioned above, this constitutes a 'journey into the unknown', as citizens in the other Member States are not in the position to know how other national systems have developed. Agreeing on the *procedure* to recognise *national* decisions, rather than *substantive rules* in the field of criminal law reflects a legitimacy and democracy deficit. Indeed, it has been said that one is led towards a 'government-led', as opposed to parliamentary, production of criminal law norms.[50] At the same time, mutual recognition without any level of open, democratic debate contributes towards a lack of clarity as to the objectives, content and direction of EU criminal law—what, if any, are the interests to be protected by it?[51]

The 'extraterritorial' reach of national criminal law decisions in these terms poses significant challenges to the position of the individual in the national legal order. By recognising and executing a decision by another Member State, the guarantees of the criminal law of the executing Member State are challenged, as the limits of the criminal law become uncertain. This may lead to the worsening of the position of the individual, by enhancing prosecutorial efficiency. It may lead to cases where applying mutual recognition would result in compromising well established constitutional protections in the executing State and thus challenge the relationship between the individual and the State created on the basis of citizenship and territoriality (such as, in the case of the European Arrest Warrant, the constitutional bar to extraditing own nationals).[52] By requiring authorities in EU Member States to recognise and execute enforcement decisions from any other Member State, citizens and residents in the EU are subject to an area where, in order to address the abolition of borders and the movement it entails, the individual is subject to a proliferation of enforcement action taken to protect interests

---

[49] This has led to calls for a level of approximation/harmonisation to accompany mutual recognition in criminal matters. See Peers, n 5 above; A Weyembergh, 'Approximation of Criminal Laws, the Constitutional Treaty and the Hague Programme', *Common Market Law Review*, vol 42, 2005, pp 1574–1577; Weyembergh, 'The Functions of Approximation of Penal Legislation within the European Union', *Maastricht Journal of European and Comparative Law*, vol 12, 2005, pp 155–163.

[50] See B Schünemann, 'Fortschritte und Fehltritte in der Strafrechtspflege der EU', in *Goldtammer's Archiv für Strafrecht*, 2004, pp 193–209 at p 203. See also the discussion in S. Braum, 'Das Prinzip der gegenseitigen Anerkennung', *Goldtammer's Archiv für Strafrecht*, 2005, pp 688–692.

[51] On this question, also in the context of the Constitutional Treaty, see W Hassemer, 'Strafrecht in einem europäischen Verfassungsvertrag', *Zeitschrift für die gesamte Strafrechtswissenschaft*, vol 116, 2004, pp 304–319 at pp 312–313.

[52] On this issue, see section IV below. Another constitutional concern arises from the very different national constitutional traditions regarding confiscation. What is acceptable in some countries (such as the 'criminal lifestyle' provisions in the UK Proceeds of Crime Act) may be unconstitutional in other Member States, where confiscation powers are much narrower. These differences are reflected in the Framework Decision on confiscation, which—as a minimum harmonisation—contains three different options for confiscation for Member States to choose from.

defined at national level. This leads to the over-extension of the punitive sphere in the 'area of freedom, security and justice'.[53]

A related concern, voiced primarily with regard to the application of the European Arrest Warrant in practice, is the concern that the recognition of Warrants with the minimum of formality along with the abolition of the dual criminality requirement will lead to the breach of the suspect's rights.[54] Concerns have been focusing in particular on whether the suspect will enjoy ECHR rights in the issuing State, in particular the right to a fair trial and the protection from torture. The issue of human rights protection was very prominent in the debate on the European Arrest Warrant in national parliaments, and is inextricably linked with perceptions of the existence—or not—of mutual trust in Member States' criminal justice systems. The mutual recognition measures themselves assume that a high level of confidence between Member States exists, and this has been reiterated by the ECJ.[55] However, debates in national parliaments and the press have shown that this is not necessarily the case.[56] The legal profession, in particular defence lawyers, have also shown a particular scepticism as to the capacity of the criminal justice systems across the enlarged EU to protect human rights in the light of the intensification of prosecutorial co-operation with the European Arrest Warrant.[57] Human rights (and, to some extent, broader constitutional) concerns, along with the implicit lack of trust in the legal systems of Member States, have led to the introduction of a series of safeguards in the mutual recognition instruments and elsewhere.

C. Renewed Concerns: The European Evidence Warrant

The debate regarding the legality and legitimacy of mutual recognition in criminal matters has also been extended to the negotiation of the latest—and one of the most prominent—mutual recognition instruments, the European Evidence Warrant.[58]

---

[53] See also Schünemann, n 50 above, p 313.

[54] See in particular Alegre and Leaf, n 24 above; Venemann, above; P Garlick, 'The European Arrest Warrant and the ECHR', in Blekxtoon, n 23 above, pp 167–182.

[55] See for instance recital 10 of the European Arrest Warrant and recital 4 of the freezing orders Framework Decision and the Court's ruling in *Gözütok*—for an analysis see part VI below.

[56] The debate on the 2003 Extradition Act—which implemented the European Arrest Warrant in the UK—is illuminating. David Cameron, then only an MP for the Conservative Party, opposed the abolition of dual criminality and said:

> To put the matter in tabloid form, the Minister is not telling us to trust the current Greek, Portuguese or Spanish criminal justice systems. Instead, he is saying that we must trust any criminal justice system of any present or future EU country not as it is today but as it may be decades in the future. (*Hansard*, 25 March 2003, col 197).

[57] See the debate on defence rights, section IV below. Spencer is very critical of what he calls 'a smug sense of cultural superiority' in this context—see n 24 above, p 217.

[58] The Justice and Home Affairs Council reached a general approach on the relevant Framework Decision in June 2006. The latest publicly available draft at the time of writing was doc 16870/1/06 REV 1 COPEN 133, 15 January 2007.

The European Evidence Warrant will perhaps be the most far-reaching mutual recognition instrument, as it is the first step towards achieving the 'free movement of evidence' across the EU, on the basis of the quasi-automatic recognition and execution of evidence warrants. Given the central place of the gathering and use of evidence in any national criminal justice system, and the significant differences on these issues in the laws of EU Member States (linked with the absence of harmonisation of rules on admissibility of evidence in the EU), concerns regarding the operation of the European Evidence Warrant were expressed throughout the negotiations and accentuated by the parallel constitutional debate on the European Arrest Warrant. Two main issues have been at stake: whether the issuing State can obtain evidence which is admissible and/or can be obtained lawfully in the executing State, when this is not necessarily the case under the law of the issuing State (a kind of a 'fishing expedition'); and whether the issuing State can oblige the executing State to use coercive measures to obtain evidence which may be unlawful under the laws of the latter.[59] These concerns have led to the insertion of a number of safeguards in the agreed text, which aim to limit the powers of the issuing State and grant procedural safeguards with regard to the execution of the warrant.[60] Moreover, they have led to calls for harmonisation, namely for the adoption of a 'horizontal' approach with regard to certain categories of offences falling within the scope of the European Evidence Warrant.[61]

It remains to be seen how these safeguards—which demonstrate the reluctance of Member States to accept the principle of mutual recognition on the basis of total automaticity—will operate in practice and be interpreted by courts. The outcome of lengthy negotiations, these safeguards were also coupled by a Declaration by Germany that it will reserve its right to make execution of the Evidence warrant subject to verification of dual criminality for a number of offences included in those for which this test has been abolished.[62] This backtracking from the concept of mutual recognition on the basis of the abolition of dual criminality may be explained if connected to the internal debate in Germany over the legitimacy and

---

[59] For these and other concerns see J R Spencer, 'An Academic Critique of the EU Acquis in Relation to Trans-Border Evidence Gathering', *ERA-Forum*, 2005 (special issue on European Evidence in Criminal Proceedings), pp 28–40; and S. Gless, 'Mutual Recognition, Judicial Inquiries, Due Process and Fundamental Rights', in J A E Vervaele (ed), *European Evidence Warrant. Transnational Judicial Inquiries in the EU*, Antwerp/Oxford, Intersentia, 2005, pp 121–130.

[60] Art 6 includes as a condition of issuing the Evidence Warrant that objects can be obtained by the issuing State 'in a comparable case'—however these conditions are to be assessed only in the issuing State, and this does not constitute a ground for refusal. Arts 11 and 13 refer to the execution of the warrant, and appear to provide a safeguard to the extent that the executing State is not obliged to use coercive measures—however, as Art 13 states, the executing authority must in principle comply with instructions by the issuing authority provided that they are not contrary to the fundamental principles of law in the executing State.

[61] For details, see ch 2.

[62] See Art 25(2)b of the Framework Decision. These offences are terrorism, computer-related crime, racism and xenophobia, sabotage, racketeering and extortion or swindling—dual criminality will be examined if it is necessary to carry out a search or seizure for the execution of the European Evidence Warrant.

legality of the European Arrest Warrant.[63] Yet this development is still spectacular and demonstrates legislation fatigue and that perhaps mutual recognition in criminal matters has reached its limits.[64]

IV. ADDRESSING CONSTITUTIONAL CONCERNS IN LEGISLATION

A. The Mutual Recognition Instruments

Concerns on the operation of the mutual recognition principle have been addressed mainly by stopping short from making the recognition and execution of decisions automatic, and giving to the executing judge the power to refuse to execute such decision on the basis of limited and expressly enumerated grounds. The European Arrest Warrant contains grounds of mandatory non-execution, including the granting of amnesty in the executing Member State, the existence of a final judgment in a Member State for the same acts, and the suspect being a minor.[65] The text also contains in Article 4 a longer list of optional grounds of non-execution of a Warrant. The provision includes the existence of aspects of *ne bis in idem* as a ground for refusal, and addresses the territoriality/dual criminality concern by granting discretion to national authorities to refuse execution if an offence is regarded by the law of the executing State as having been committed in whole or in part in its territory, or if an offence has been committed outside the territory of the issuing Member State and the law of the executing State does not allow prosecution for the same offences when committed outside its territory.[66] This provision aims to alleviate concerns regarding the abolition of dual criminality by preventing the execution of a warrant if there is some sort of connection with the territory of the executing Member State, or if there is no connection with the territory of the issuing State (which exercises extraterritorial jurisdiction).[67] Finally, beyond the specifically enumerated grounds for refusal, the Framework Decision grants discretion to the executing Member State to make the execution of a Warrant conditional upon the existence of a series of safeguards and assurances by the issuing State.[68]

---

[63] The minutes of the June Justice and Home Affairs Council of June 2006 include a statement explaining that Art 25(2)(b) was a compromise in order to proceed to the agreement of the text while taking into account Germany's concerns—see statement 7 in doc 16870/1/06.

[64] The same can be said about proposals put forward to 'compensate' for mutual recognition, such as the Commission proposal for a Framework Decision on the rights of the defendant—for details see ch 2.

[65] Art 3.

[66] Art 4(7).

[67] However, as it has been noted, for the safeguard of this provision to be more clear-cut, Art 4(7) should refer to 'acts', and not 'offences'. Blekxtoon, 'Commentary on an Art by Art Basis', in Blekxtoon, n 23 above, p 236.

[68] Art 5—these include cases where a person is being surrendered to execute a sentence imposes by an in absentia decision; surrender for an offence punishable by custodial life sentence or life-time detention order; and cases involving nationals of residents of the executing State.

The other mutual recognition instruments contain less extensive grounds for refusal. In all three instruments, grounds for non-recognition and execution (of a freezing or confiscation order or a financial penalty) are optional.[69] All three instruments contain a ground for refusal specifically linked to the Certificate—they can refuse if the latter has not been produced, is incomplete or manifestly does not correspond to the order made.[70] Similarly, they all in some form or other make reference to refusal to execute on *ne bis in idem* grounds.[71] Other grounds for refusal appear in some of the instruments, but not all: for instance, a similar 'territoriality' clause to the European Arrest Warrant appears in the financial penalties instrument[72] and the confiscation Framework Decision.[73] Finally, given the considerable differences between the confiscation systems of Member States, the Framework Decision on the execution of confiscation orders provides that, if the executing Member State has not adopted the same confiscation option (from those listed in the parallel Framework Decision on confiscation) to the issuing Member State, the executing Member State must execute the confiscation order 'at least to the extent provided for in similar domestic cases under national law'.[74]

Another way to alleviate constitutional concerns arising from mutual recognition instruments has been to add references to human rights protection in their text. However, adequate protection of human rights was not added as a specific ground for refusal. This reflects the tension in the debate on the European Arrest Warrant—and subsequent instruments—between those of the view that the protection of human rights must be paramount and must be taken into account by the judge when dealing with European Arrest Warrants and similar decisions and those believing that a reference to human rights protection is superfluous. Proponents of the first view advocated an examination of the substance of decisions to be executed, looking behind the form, while opponents noted that this was contrary to mutual trust and the almost automatic character of mutual recognition leading to speed and efficiency. Proponents of the importance of human rights noted that mutual trust is not always justified, as all EU Member States have been and are potentially in breach of international human rights instruments—such as the ECHR, while opponents noted that all Member States are ECHR signatories in the first place, and their human rights credentials are good enough to

---

[69] Art 7(1), freezing orders and financial penalties; Art 8(1) confiscation orders.
[70] Art 7(1)(a) freezing orders; Art 7(1) financial penalties; Art 8(1) confiscation orders.
[71] Freezing orders 7(1)(c), confiscation orders 8(2)(a) specifically refer to '*ne bis in idem*'. Art 7(2)(a) of the financial penalties instrument on the other hand provides a ground for refusal

if it is established that decision against the sentenced person in respect of the same acts has been delivered in the executing State or in any State other than the issuing or the executing State, and in the latter case, the decision has been executed.

[72] Art 7(2)(d).
[73] Art 8(2)(f).
[74] Art 8(3).

grant them membership of the European Union, which is founded upon human rights and the rule of law and where respect for human rights is a condition of entry and disrespect may bring sanctions (Articles 6 and 7 TEU).[75]

In the case of the European Arrest Warrant, the compromise reached was Article 1(3), stating that 'this Framework Decision shall not have the effect of modifying the obligation to respect fundamental rights and fundamental legal principles as enshrined in Article 6 of the TEU'.[76] Moreover, recital 12 in the Preamble, using a slightly different wording, confirms that 'this Framework Decision respects fundamental rights' and observes the principles recognised in Article 6 TEU and the Charter of Fundamental Rights and adds that nothing in the Framework Decision may be interpreted as prohibiting refusal to surrender when there are objective reasons to believe that the Warrant has been issued 'for the purpose of prosecuting or punishing a person on the grounds of his or her sex, race, religion, ethnic origin, nationality, language, political opinions or sexual orientation, or that that person's position may be prejudiced for any of these reasons'. The recital continues by affirming that the Framework Decision does not prevent a Member State from applying its constitutional rules relating to due process, freedom of association, freedom of the press and freedom of expression in other media.[77] The exact effect of these preambular clauses is not clear, especially given the debate regarding the binding force and influence of Preambles. However, the wording of recital 12 has been repeated verbatim in the three other adopted mutual recognition instruments.[78] However, neither of these contains in its text a clause similar to Article 1(3). It is this clause—and its potential to justify refusals of execution—that has caused considerable debate in the implementation of the European Arrest Warrant Framework Decision.[79]

---

[75] See Alegre and Leaf, n 24 above; for a vivid illustration of the concerns raised, see the evidence produced in House of Lords EU Committee, *The European Arrest Warrant*, 16th Report, session 2001–02, HL Paper 89.

[76] But this provision is not under Art 3—grounds for mandatory execution, but Art 1, headed 'Definition of the European arrest warrant and obligation to execute it'.

[77] Recital 13 on the other hand contains extradition-specific safeguards.

[78] Recital 6, freezing orders (recital 5 also states that 'rights granted to the parties or bona fide interested third parties should be preserved'). Recitals 5 and 6, financial penalties instrument. Recitals 13 and 14, confiscation instrument.

[79] A number of Member States have included non-compliance with fundamental rights as a ground for refusal in their implementing legislation. This tendency has been criticised by the Commission in its report on the implementation of the European Arrest Warrant Framework Decision. See 'Report from the Commission based on Art 34 of the Council Framework Decision of 13 June 2002 on the European Arrest Warrant and the surrender procedures between Member States' COM (2005) 63 final, Brussels, 23 February 2005 and SEC (2005) 267. For a more recent overview of implementation status see 'Report from the Commission on the implementation since 2005 of the Council Framework Decision of 13 June 2002 on the European Arrest Warrant and the surrender procedures between Member States' COM (2007) final, Brussels, 11 July 2007 and SEC (2007) 979.

B. Harmonisation of the Grounds for Refusal to Recognise and Execute

As seen above, one of the ways to address concerns with regard to the constitutional implications of mutual recognition in criminal matters has been to insert in the mutual recognition instruments themselves a series of grounds for refusal of requests for recognition and execution of judgments by the authorities in the executing Member State. However, these grounds for refusal—which are predominantly related to fundamental concepts of domestic criminal justice systems—are not harmonised across the EU. This has been perceived at creating problems of both legal certainty and trust, and a number of attempts have now surfaced to harmonise—or at least adopt a common approach towards—these concepts. The first major attempt in this context—which as will be seen later in this chapter—failed spectacularly, has been a proposal by the 2003 EU Greek Presidency for a Framework Decision on the principle of *ne bis in idem*. Although the principle *does* exist in various international human rights instruments, as well as in the Schengen Implementing Convention, differences in Member States' approaches and the strong link of *ne bis in idem* with the administration of justice at the national level did not permit agreement on the text. A second attempt, which appears to be more successful at the time of writing, has been to harmonise, or create a common understanding of, what constitutes a trial *in absentia* for the purposes of mutual recognition instruments.

The proposal for a Framework Decision on judgments *in absentia* was a Member State initiative, tabled jointly by Slovenia, France, the Czech Republic, Sweden, Slovakia, the UK and Germany.[80] Its Explanatory Memorandum pointed out that *in absentia* judgments are a common ground for refusal in mutual recognition instruments, but under different conditions in each instrument. In this light, the initiative aimed at addressing the legal uncertainty caused for the individual and at the same time enhancing mutual recognition by clarifying and rendering more compatible the criteria applying for non-recognition related to decisions rendered *in absentia*.[81] Such 'common approach' would introduce an exception to the *in absentia* ground for refusal related to the existence of a right of retrial within a defined minimum timeframe. According to the Explanatory Memorandum, a retrial can be defined as new proceedings on the same subject-matter as the proceedings which took place *in absentia* and which are characterised by three elements: the person concerned has the right to be present; merits of the case will be (re)examined; and the proceedings can lead to reversing the original decision *in absentia*.[82]

The proposal adopted a 'horizontal' approach, by amending four mutual recognition Framework Decisions to amend the provisions related to *in absentia*

---

[80] Council doc 5213/08, Brussels, 14 January 2008.
[81] Council doc 5213/08 ADD 1, Brussels, 30 January 2008, pp 3–4.
[82] ibid, p.4.

judgments contained therein.[83] It contained a definition of what constitutes a decision rendered *in absentia*[84] and a detailed description of conditions under which the *in absentia* ground for refusal would not apply.[85] The attempt to provide an EU definition of what constitutes an *in absentia* judgment was a bold attempt to introduce common EU standards for a central aspect of domestic criminal justice systems (albeit somewhat from 'the back door', by adopting the definition for the purposes of amending mutual recognition instruments). It is exactly due to the closeness of the concept to national criminal justice particularities and variations that this definition had eventually to be dropped from the text.[86] However, negotiations proceeded relatively swiftly, with the Justice and Home Affairs Council reaching a 'general approach' to the text in June 2008.[87] The text follows a similar approach to the initial proposal, with a greater emphasis on national law requirements of the issuing State.[88] It remains to be seen whether the text, when formally adopted and implemented, will contribute towards the elimination of diversity among Member States and the protection of fundamental rights. The emphasis of the measure on the *exceptions* to the *in absentia* safeguards do not send very positive signals in the latter direction.

C. Adoption of Accompanying Trust-Building Measures

i. Defence Rights

One of the ways of addressing constitutional concerns arising from mutual recognition—and the European Arrest Warrant in particular—has been the proposal by the Commission of a Framework Decision on minimum standards on defence rights in the European Union. The Commission's proposal proved to be controversial, with Member States' concerns regarding both its content and legality leading to negotiations stalling in the Council. These aspects have been

---

[83] These are three Framework Decisions already formally adopted (on the European Arrest Warrant, financial penalties and confiscation orders), but also the Framework Decision on the application of the principle of mutual recognition to judgments in criminal matters imposing custodial sentences or measures involving deprivation of liberty for the purpose of their enforcement in the EU, which has not been formally adopted at the time of writing (see Council doc 164754/07, Brussels, 20 December 2007).

[84] 'A custodial sentence or a detention order, when the person did not personally appear in the proceedings resulting in this decision'—see Art 2 of the draft concerning the amendment to the European Arrest Warrant Framework Decision.

[85] See Art 3 of the draft concerning the amendment to the European Arrest Warrant Framework Decision. This would also amend the Framework Decision to include *in absentia* judgments as an optional ground for refusal.

[86] See House of Commons European Scrutiny Committee, *Recognition and Enforcement of Judgments Given in Absentia*, 20th Report, session 2007–08, pp 83–86.

[87] Justice and Home Affairs Council of 5–6 June 2008, Council doc. 9956/08 (Presse 146), p 19.

[88] For the 'general approach' text see Council doc 10435/08, Brussels, 6 June 2008. Art 2 introduces inter alia new Art 4a to the European Arrest Warrant Framework Decision. This confirms *in absentia* judgments as an optional ground for refusal, but also introduces an exception if certain conditions apply *in accordance with further procedural requirements defined in the national law of the issuing State*.

examined in detail in chapter two. For the purposes of this chapter, it suffices to reiterate the justification of the proposal by the Commission, and its framing as a 'trust-building' measure for the purposes of mutual recognition. According to the Commission, the proposal constituted the 'necessary complement' to the mutual recognition measures that are designed to increase efficiency of prosecution.[89] The Commission further argued that the proposal is necessary to ensure compatibility between the criminal justice systems of Member States and to build trust and promote mutual confidence across the EU whereby:

> not only the judicial authorities, but all actors in the criminal process see decisions of the judicial authorities of other Member States as equivalent to their own and do not call in question their judicial capacity and respect for fair trial rights.[90]

However, it must be reiterated in this context that *the achievement of 'mutual trust' is too indirect and subjective as a legitimating link* for EU legislation of this kind. The Commission justifies the proposal as necessary to introduce rules which will lead to compatibility *which lead to trust* which in turn leads to the improvement of judicial co-operation. So it is not compatibility *as such* that will improve co-operation, but the trust it may create. However, the concept of trust is inherently subjective and thus not necessarily amenable to judicial review.[91]

ii. Evaluation

Another way of addressing concerns emanating from mutual recognition, in particular the lack of mutual trust, has been to promote the idea of evaluating the implementation of third pillar law—with the Commission's proposal on defence rights including a provision on evaluation. However, as has been demonstrated in chapter one, the evaluation of the implementation of criminal law—which is also central in the Lisbon Treaty—raises a number of constitutional issues at national and EU level, in particular issues of competence and inter-institutional balance.[92] For the purposes of this chapter, it is significant to note that one of the unresolved issues, should the evaluation become the norm, is which elements of domestic criminal justice systems will be reviewed for the evaluation exercise to be meaningful. In the light of the fact that mutual recognition involves the recognition of judgments emanating from a particular domestic criminal justice system as a whole, and that applying it could have significant repercussions for the internal coherence of domestic criminal justice systems, it may prove impossible to evaluate the implementation of EU criminal law without actually evaluating domestic criminal justice systems as a whole. As noted in chapter one, the existence of EU competence to embark on such a far-reaching evaluation is however questionable.

[89] COM (2004) 328 final, para 51.
[90] ibid, para 28.
[91] For further details see ch 2.
[92] See also in detail Mitsilegas, 'Trust-building Measures', n 11 above.

V. CONSTITUTIONAL CONCERNS IN THE COURTS

A. National Courts

In the light of the challenges posed by the application of the mutual recognition principle in criminal matters to national constitutional provisions, intervention by national courts addressing these issues was only a matter of time. Recent years witnessed the first major decisions by national constitutional courts on the compatibility of legislation implementing the European Arrest Warrant with the national constitution. These cases cast light on the different tensions caused by mutual recognition when applied in the national constitutional framework and signify the resurfacing of the debate regarding primacy of European law (this time European Union, and not European Community law) over national constitutions.[93]

An important case in this context has been the examination by the *Bundesverfassungsgericht* of the compatibility of the law implementing the European Arrest Warrant with the German Basic Law.[94] The case involved a European Arrest Warrant issued by Spain and requesting the surrender of Mamoun Darkazanli. Darkazanli, who had both German and Syrian citizenship, was prosecuted in Spain for being actively involved in the activities of Al-Qaeda. His extradition to Spain was approved by the lower German court. The defendant launched a constitutional complaint before the German constitutional court challenging these decisions on a wide range of constitutional grounds. These included claims inter alia that the European Arrest Warrant and the implementing legislation lacked democratic legitimacy, that the abolition of dual criminality would result in the application of foreign law within the domestic legal order, and that the defendant's right to judicial review was breached.[95]

---

[93] On attempts to synthesise the case law of a number of national constitutional courts, see D Leczykiewicz, 'Constitutional Conflicts and the Third Pillar', *European Law Review*, vol 33, 2008, pp 230–242; and Z Deen-Racsmány, 'The European Arrest Warrant and the Surrender of Nationals Revisited: The Lessons of Constitutional Challenges', *European Journal of Crime, Criminal Law and Criminal Justice*, vol 14, no 3, 2006, pp 271–306.

[94] Judgment of 18 July 2005, 2 BvR 2236/04. The text of the judgment, (and a press release in English—press release no 64/2005) can be found at www.bundesverfassungsgericht.de. For the English version see [2006] 1 CMLR 16.

[95] On commentaries to the judgment see inter alia: F Geyer, 'The European Arrest Warrant in Germany. Constitutional Mistrust towards the Concept of Mutual Trust', in E Guild (ed) *Constitutional Challenges to the European Arrest Warrant*, Nijmegen, Wolf Legal Publishers, 2006, pp 101–124; J Komarek, *European Constitutionalism and the European Arrest Warrant: Contrapunctual Principles in Democracy*, Jean Monnet Working Paper 10/05, www.jeanmonnetprogram.org; S Mölders, 'European Arrest Warrant is Void—The Decision of the Federal Constitutional Court of 18 July 2005', *German Law Journal*, vol 7, 2005, pp 45–57, www.germanlawjournal.com; J Vogel, 'Europäischer Haftbefehl und deutsches Verfassungsrecht', *Juristenzeitung*, vol.60, 2005, pp 801–809; S. Wolf, 'Demokratische Legitimation in der EU aus Sicht des Bundesverfassungsgerichts nach dem Urteil zum Europäischen Haftbefehlsgesetz', *Kritische Justiz*, vol 38, 2005, pp 350–358; case-note by A Hinajeros Parga, *Common Market Law Review*, vol 43, 2006, pp 583–595; C. Tomuschat, 'Inconsistencies—The German Federal Constitutional Court on the European Arrest Warrant', *European Constitutional Law Review*, vol 2,

The Court accepted the complaint. However, rather than declaring that the Framework Decision itself was in breach of the German Constitution (which could take us back straight to the *Solange* debate and explicitly apply this to third pillar—EU—law), the Court took the view that it was the German implementing law that was at fault, as it did not transpose all the safeguards included in the European Arrest Warrant Framework Decision into national law. The implementing legislation was declared void and the complainant not surrendered.

In reaching this decision, the Court focused predominantly on concepts of legitimacy, territory and citizenship and the protection of fundamental rights. A central concept was the special bond between the citizen and the State, and the legitimate expectations of citizens to be protected within the framework of their State of belonging. The Court examined in detail the issue of extradition of German citizens. Article 16(2) of the German Basic Law was amended in 2000 to provide with the possibility of an exception to the principle of non-extradition of German nationals 'to a Member State of the European Union or to an international court of justice as long as (*soweit*) constitutional provisions are upheld'.[96] In examining this provision, the Court stressed the specific link between German citizens and the German legal order. Citizens must be protected, if they remain within the German territory, from uncertainty, and their trust to the German legal system has a high value. In implementing the European Arrest Warrant, the German Parliament did not take into account this special link between citizen and State, by not transposing in the national legislation the 'territoriality' grounds for refusal enshrined in Article 4(7) of the Framework Decision. The implementing law constituted thus a breach of Article 16(2) of the Basic Law.

This emphasis of the Court on the nation-State must be viewed in conjunction with its comments on mutual recognition in EU law. The Court stressed that co-operation in the third pillar is based on limited mutual recognition, which does not presuppose harmonisation and can be seen as a means to preserve national identity and statehood.[97] Article 6(1) TEU, which emphasises the respect by all EU Member States of fundamental rights, provides the foundation for mutual trust in this context. However, the national legislator continues to have a duty to react if the trust is breached. The Basic Law requires that in every individual case a concrete review of whether the rights of the defendant are respected should be made. The Court concluded that Articles 6 and 7 TEU (which proclaim respect for human rights by all EU Member States) do not justify the assumption that State

2006, pp 209–226; H Satzger and T Pohl, 'The German Constitutional Court and the European Arrest Warrant. "Cryptic Signals" from Karlsruhe', *Journal of International Criminal Justice,* vol 4, 2006, pp 686–701; and C Lebeck, 'National Constitutional Control and the Limits of European Integration— The European Arrest Warrant in the German Federal Constitutional Court', *Public Law,* 2007, pp 23–33.

[96] My translation. See also Geyer, 'European Arrest Warrant', n 95 above; Komarek, n 95 above. The influence of the 'Solange' reasoning of the Court with regard to the relationship between German Constitutional law and EU law is evident in the wording.

[97] Komarek places emphasis on the use of the word 'limited', and contrasts this to the ECJ ruling in *Gözütok* (n 95 above, p 17).

law structures in EU Member States are materially synchronised and that review of individual cases is nugatory, adding that the effect of the strict principle of mutual recognition and the wide mutual trust connected thereto cannot limit the constitutional guarantee of fundamental rights.[98]

The Court thus rejected the automaticity introduced by mutual recognition with a minimum of formality on the basis of mutual trust. It did not take the existence of mutual trust for granted, but stressed the paramount importance of upholding national constitutional values and fundamental rights. The emphasis of the German Court in upholding national constitutional guarantees even in fields where the country has undertaken obligations under EU law is in sharp contrast with the ECJ approach in *Pupino*, where the Luxembourg court stressed the application of the principle of loyal co-operation in the third pillar.[99] The *Bundesfervassungsgericht* does not seem to exclude a clash with EU law in cases where the national constitutional framework concerning human rights and the rule of law is deemed to be threatened.[100]

The relationship between the European Arrest Warrant and national legislation implementing it on the one hand and constitutional bars to extradition of nationals on the other was also examined in judgments by the Polish Constitutional Tribunal[101] and the Supreme Court of Cyprus[102]. Unlike the *Bundesverfassungsgericht*, which examined the European Arrest Warrant in the light of the general framework of respect of national constitutional guarantees, the Polish and Cypriot courts adopted a somewhat narrower approach, by focusing primarily on the compatibility of the obligations their Governments undertook under EU law with the specific constitutional provisions prohibiting the extradition of their nationals.[103] Both courts found that the surrender of citizens of their countries on the basis of legislation implementing the European Arrest Warrant clashed with their national Constitution, but the reasoning ascertaining to this clash and the solutions offered are slightly different.

---

[98] See in particular para 118 of the judgment. See also Komarek, n 95 above, and Geyer, 'European Arrest Warrant', n 95 above.

[99] Case C-105/03, *Maria Pupino*, ECR [2005] I-5285. For an analysis see ch 1.

[100] This point has been raised by a number of dissenting judges, in particular Judges Lubbe-Wolff and Gerhardt. The majority opinion has been criticised for being too ready to infringe EU law, and for disregarding developments in the ECJ.

[101] *Re Enforcement of a European Arrest Warrant*, Judgment of 27 April 2005, P 1/05. Reported in [2006] 1 CMLR 36. For comments, see Komarek, n 95 above; K Kowalik-Banczyk, 'Should We Polish It Up? The Polish Constitutional Tribunal and the Idea of Supremacy of EU Law', *German Law Journal*, vol 6, 2005, pp 1355–1366, www.germanlawjournal.com; D Leczykiewicz, Case Note, *Common Market Law Review*, vol 43, 2006, 1181–1191; and A Lazowski, 'Constitutional Tribunal on the Surrender of Polish Citizens under the European Arrest Warrant. Decision of 27 April 2005', *European Constitutional Law Review*, vol 1, 2005, pp 569–581.

[102] *Attorney General of the Republic v Konstantinou*, Decision of 7 November 2005, Council document 14281/05, Brussels, 11 November 2005. See also [2007] 3 CMLR 42.

[103] On this distinction regarding what he calls 'lines of national constitutional resistance' to EU law, see M Kumm, 'The Jurisprudence of Constitutional Conflict: Constitutional Supremacy in Europe before and after the Constitutional Treaty', *European Law Journal*, vol 11, 2005, pp 262–307 at p 264.

The Polish Court examined the compatibility between Article 607t(1) of the Polish Code of Criminal Procedure, implementing the European Arrest Warrant, with Article 55(1) of the Polish Constitution, which prohibits the extradition of Polish citizens. The Court viewed Article 55(1) as expressing a right for Polish citizens to be held criminally accountable before a Polish court. The provision is absolute and surrender to another EU Member State on the basis of executing a European Arrest Warrant would be an infringement of this right.[104] Article 607t(1) of the Criminal Procedure Code therefore does not conform to the Polish Constitution.[105] However, the Court did not declare the provision immediately void, but extended its validity for 18 months, until an appropriate solution was found by the legislature.[106]

The Court's approach was markedly different to the *Bundesverfassungsgericht* as to the relationship between EU law and the domestic Constitution. The Polish Court attempted to accommodate to a great extent the EU requirements. It placed great emphasis on the obligation of national courts to interpret domestic law in a manner compatible with EU law and discussed at length whether indirect effect applies in the third pillar. [107]However, the Court noted that this interpretative obligation has its limits, and cannot worsen an individual's situation, especially in criminal matters.[108]

The Court also stressed the constitutional obligation of Poland to observe international law, which binds it, and the importance of the European Arrest Warrant for improving security. Although the relevant provision of the Code of Criminal Procedure is unconstitutional, the prolongation of its application along the lines proposed by the Court is justified by the fact that Poland (along with the other EU Member States) are 'bound by the community of principles of the political system, assuring proper administration of justice and trial before an independent court of law'.[109] However, in principle the Court *did* examine the European Arrest Warrant and its implementation on the basis of the domestic Constitution and the EU-friendly elements of its reasoning were not sufficient to avoid the ruling of unconstitutionality.[110]

The Cypriot Supreme Court also ruled that the national legislation implementing the European Arrest Warrant was contrary to the national Constitution, which prohibits the extradition of own nationals (Article 11(2)).[111] The Court based its

---

[104] See part 4 of the judgment.

[105] See para 4.4.

[106] See part 5 of the judgment, in particular para 5.2.

[107] See in particular para 3.4.

[108] ibid. The Court noted in this context that the surrender of a person indicted on the basis of a European Arrest Warrant for an act which, according to Polish law is not a crime, could undoubtedly lead to the aggravation of the situation of the indicted person.

[109] Para 5.2 as translated in the CMLR English version of the judgment.

[110] On the balance between the Polish Court's EU-friendly discourse and its findings see also W Sadurski, 'Solange, Chapter 3: Constitutional Courts in Central Europe-Democracy-European Union', *European Law Journal*, vol 14, no 1, 2008, pp 1–35, at pp 22–23.

[111] For comments, see E A Stefanou and A Kapardis, 'The First Two Years of Fiddling around with the Implementation of the European Arrest Warrant in Cyprus', in Guild, *Constitutional Challenges*, n 95 above, pp 75–88; and A Tsadiras, Case Note, *Common Market Law Review*, vol 44, 2007, pp 1515–1528.

reasoning to a great extent on the legal nature of the European Arrest Warrant, it being a third pillar Framework Decision. Although Framework Decisions are binding, they do not have direct effect and are transposed in Member States only with the proper legal procedure. According to the Court, this had not happened in Cyprus, as the implementing legislation is contrary to the Constitution. The Court appears reluctant to explicitly state that the national Constitution has primacy over EU law, at least over Framework Decisions. The judgment implies that Framework Decisions are in a weaker constitutional position due to their lack of direct effect. Having said that, the Cypriot Court was at pains to stress its respect for the ECJ *Pupino* ruling[112] and referred in detail to judgments of other Supreme Courts, such as the Courts of Poland, Greece and Germany. However, again the national Court's EU-friendly tone—and in this case the express reference to *Pupino*—have not been enough to avoid the ruling of unconstitutionality.[113]

A similar case has arisen before the Czech Constitutional Court.[114] The Court had in particular to examine the compatibility of legislation implementing the European Arrest Warrant in the Czech Republic with the Czech Charter of Fundamental Rights and Basic Freedoms.[115] While the latter does not—as with the Polish and Cypriot Constitutions—include a provision explicitly prohibiting the extradition of own nationals, it includes a provision—Article 14(4) which provides that every citizen has the right to freely enter the Czech Republic and that no citizen might be forced to leave the country. The Czech Court held that the assertion that the adoption into domestic law of the European Arrest Warrant would disrupt the permanent relationship between citizen and the State is not tenable, as a citizen surrendered to an EU Member State for criminal prosecution remains, even for the duration of such a proceeding, under the protection of the Czech State.[116] The Court also expressly referred to *Pupino*, by stating that as follows from Art.1(2) of the Constitution in conjunction with the principle of co-operation in Article 10 TEC, there is a constitutional principle according to which national legal enactments, including the Constitution, should whenever possible be interpreted in conformity with the process of European integration.[117] However, this constitutional principle 'is limited by the possible significations of the constitutional text'.[118] It is noteworthy that here the Court seems to accept the obligations arising from the Framework Decision on the European Arrest Warrant, but to accommodate them in domestic constitutional terms: surrender is not unconstitutional as the special bond between the citizen and the Czech

---

[112] Stressing that the Court's case law could not have been different, since if EU Member States did not conform with their obligations stemming from the EU treaty, this would collapse.

[113] On this point, see in particular the analysis of Leczykiewicz, n 101 above, p 236.

[114] Re Constitutionality of Framework Decision on the European Arrest Warrant, [2007] 3 C.M.L.R. 24.

[115] For comments on the case see I Slosarcík, 'Czech Republic and the European Union Law in 2004–2006', *European Public Law*, vol 13, issue 3, 2007, pp 367–378; and Leczykiewicz, n 101 above.

[116] Para 86 (62).

[117] Para 105 (81).

[118] ibid.

Republic is not disrupted—citizens maintain this bond even when surrendered under the European Arrest Warrant; and loyal co-operation and indirect effect are accepted at least partly as *domestic* constitutional requirements, and under *domestic* constitutional limits.

These cases highlight the constitutional concerns raised by the application of mutual recognition in criminal matters, as evidenced by the implementation of the European Arrest Warrant. Of central importance for the courts in all the cases mentioned above has been the emphasis in and protection of the special bond between the citizen and the State. This may explain the readiness of national courts—in spite of their general willingness to comply to the extent possible with Union law—to rule that implementing Arrest Warrant legislation is unconstitutional in order to affirm the constitutional protection to their citizens.[119] In this context, the cases also bring back into the fore the debate over the primacy of—this time European Union—law over national constitutional law. When examined in detail, the approaches of the courts have been different, with the German Constitutional Court being the most reluctant to accept uncritically obligations imposed by the law of the European Union. However, all courts paid due attention to the provisions of their national constitutions and none of them ruled explicitly that EU law has primacy over national constitutional law. Whether this is ultimately due to the fact that the third pillar is viewed by these courts as a 'special case', its legislation lacking legitimacy, democratic debate and/or direct effect—or whether constitutional sensitivities are more acute in cases involving criminal law enforcement and the protection of fundamental rights—remains to be seen (especially if the Lisbon Treaty, which 'streamlines' the third pillar, comes into force).

B. The Court of Justice—Advocaten voor de Wereld

The first case where the Court of Justice was called to rule upon the Framework Decision on the European Arrest Warrant constituted a reference from a preliminary ruling from the Belgian Arbitragehof.[120] The reference involved the assessment of the validity of the European Arrest Warrant, and was submitted in the course of an action brought before the national court seeking the annulment of the Belgian implementing law of the relevant Framework Decision.[121] Annulment was

[119] It will be interesting to see how national courts will react in European Arrest Warrant cases involving non-citizens (nationals of other EU Member States or third country nationals) and whether they will be willing to offer the same level of protection as to the one afforded to their citizens. In this context, see the reference for a preliminary ruling by a German Court as regards a warrant issued for a Polish national present in Germany—Case C-66/08, *Kozlowski*, judgment of the Court of 17 July 2008 (the first case under the accelerated procedure mentioned in ch.1).

[120] Case C-303/05, *Advocaten voor de Wereld VZW v Leden van de Ministerraad*, ECR [2007] I-3633.

[121] For comments on the case, see: D Sarmiento, 'European Union: The European Arrest Warrant and the Quest for Constitutional Coherence', *International Journal of Constitutional Law*, vol 6, no 1, 2008, pp 171–183; F Geyer, 'Case Note: European Arrest Warrant. Court of Justice of the European Communities', *European Constitutional Law Review*, vol 4, 2008, pp 149–161; A Hinarejos, 'Recent

sought on three grounds: that EU third pillar legislation on the European Arrest Warrant ought to have been adopted by way of a Convention and not a Framework Decision since, under Article 34(2)(b) TEU Framework Decisions may be adopted only for the purpose of approximation of national laws; that the domestic provisions implementing Article 2(2) of the Framework Decision which abolishes dual criminality for a number of offences infringes the principle of equality and non-discrimination as they differentiate without objective and reasonable justification between offences for which dual criminality is abolished and offences for which dual criminality is retained; and that the implementing legislation fails to satisfy the conditions of the principle of legality in criminal matters as it lists vague categories of undesirable behaviour rather than offences having a sufficiently clear and precise legal content. This leads to a disparate application of the legislation and thus also infringes the principle of equality and non-discrimination.[122]

The Court dismissed all three arguments in a relatively short judgment. On the choice of legal instrument (a Framework Decision instead of a Convention), the Court stressed the discretion of the Council as to the adopted form of legal instrument and held that it is within this discretion to give preference to a Framework Decision if the conditions for the adoption of such a measure are satisfied.[123] In this context, the Court rejected the argument that the adoption of Framework Decisions under Article 34(2)(b) TEU must relate only to areas mentioned in Article 31(1)(e) TEU which provides a legal basis for criminal law approximation (and which do not include the European Arrest Warrant).[124] More generally, the Court confirmed that there is no distinction in the third pillar as to the type of measures which may be adopted on the basis of the subject-matter to which EU action relates,[125] and that Article 34(2) TEU does not establish any order of priority between the different instruments included therein.[126] The Court also dismissed the argument that the European Arrest Warrant should have been adopted by a Convention since it replaces earlier EU Conventions on extradition: the Court used effectiveness in this context, stating that any other interpretation to the one give in this case 'would risk depriving of its essential effectiveness the Council's recognised power to adopt framework decisions in fields previously governed by international conventions'.[127]

Human Rights Developments in the EU Courts: The Charter of Fundamental Rights, the European Arrest Warrant and Terror Lists', *Human Rights Law Review*, vol 7, no 4, 2007, pp 793–811; and Leczykiewicz, n 101 above.

[122] See paras 11–13 of the judgment.
[123] Para 41. On discretion, see also Sarmiento, n 121 above, pp 178–180.
[124] Para 38.
[125] Para 36.
[126] Para 37.
[127] Para 42. The judgment reflects here to some extent the emphasis of AG Ruiz-Jarabo Colomer on effectiveness. In his Opinion, delivered on 12 September 2006, the AG stated that Member States (and the institutions) are required to achieve the objectives of Art 2 TEU (which include the establishment of an 'area of freedom, security and justice') and are obliged to use the most appropriate tools to meet that requirement; Member States and the institutions are bound to ensure the effectiveness of Community law in general and of Union law in particular; it follows from this that the Council was 'not only entitled but, moreover, *obliged*, to establish a mechanism for the European Arrest Warrant' in a Framework Decision (para 67, emphasis added).

On the questions involving the substance of the implementing law and the Framework Decision, the Court began by stressing that the EU is founded on the principle of the rule of law and respects fundamental rights as general principles of Community law.[128] Referring explicitly to the Charter of Fundamental Rights, the Court added that it is 'common ground' that these general principles include both the principle of legality and the principle of equality and non-discrimination.[129] If the reference to the Charter is noteworthy (in that it is one of the first times the Court of Justice has done so, all more importantly on a subject-matter with fundamental human rights implications[130]), it is also noteworthy that the Court exports the review of EU institutions on the basis of the general principles of *Community* law (including the protection of fundamental rights) to review of action under *Union* law, in the third pillar. This is yet another example of the Court treating third pillar law as subject to the same constitutional principles applying to the first pillar.

The Court dismissed summarily the argument that the Framework Decision infringes the principle of equality and non-discrimination. The Court held first that the Council was able to form the view that the 32 categories of offences for which the verification of dual criminality has been abolished under Article 2(2) of the Framework Decision are serious enough in terms of adversely affecting public order and public safety for such abolition to be justified (implying thus that these offences are not comparable with the offences for which verification of dual criminality remains).[131] The Court added that *even if* one were to assume that the situation of persons suspected of having committed or convicted of having committed Article 2(2) offences is comparable to the situation of persons similarly related to other offences, '*the distinction is, in any event, objectively justified*' (emphasis added).[132] The Court also dismissed the argument that the lack of precision in the definition of the categories of offences in question leads to discrimination: employing a reasoning similar to the one applied in earlier *ne bis in idem* cases,[133] the Court the objective of the Framework Decision is not to harmonise the substantive criminal law of Member States and nothing in the third pillar makes the application of the European Arrest Warrant conditional on criminal law harmonisation.[134]

In examining the compatibility of the European Arrest Warrant with the principle of legality, the Court stressed the link between this principle and the protection of fundamental rights. The Court confirmed that the legality principle is

---

[128] Para 45.

[129] Para 46.

[130] The Court has evoked the charter for the first time in a case concerning the family reunion Directive—Case C-540/03, *Parliament v Council*, ECR [2006] I-5769, para 38. As Geyer notes, in the European Arrest Warrant case the Court went further by refraining from noting that the Charter is currently non-legally binding—Geyer, 'Case Note', n 121 above, p 158.

[131] Para 57.

[132] Para 58.

[133] See next section below.

[134] Para 59.

one of the general legal principles underlying the constitutional traditions common to the Member States, and also referred to the ECHR.[135] The Court further defined the principle by reference to the Strasbourg case law.[136] However, the Court dismissed the argument that the Framework Decision infringes the legality principle on the ground that the principle is ensured by the fact that legislation is defined in the *issuing* Member State. The Court noted that the Framework Decision does not seek to harmonise the criminal offences set out in Article 2(2) and that, even if Member States reproduce word for word the list of categories included in Article 2(2) for the purposes of implementation, the actual definition of those offences and the penalties applicable are those which follow from the law of the issuing Member State.[137] The definition of Article 2(2) offences and the applicable penalties continue to be matters determined by the law of the issuing Member State

> which, as is, moreover, stated in Article 1(3) of the Framework Decision, must respect fundamental rights and fundamental legal principles as enshrined in Article 6 EU, and consequently, the principle of the legality of criminal offences and penalties.[138]

The approach of the Court with regard to the assessment of the compatibility of the European Arrest Warrant Framework Decision with fundamental rights (in particular the principle of legality in the light of the abolition of dual criminality) is noteworthy, especially when compared with the approach of AG Ruiz-Jarabo Colomer and the case law of national constitutional courts. The Court did not follow the 'procedural' approach of the Advocate General, who argued that the enhanced safeguards of criminal law do not apply in this context as the European Arrest Warrant is not 'punitive in nature' but merely a mechanism facilitating judicial co-operation in criminal matters in the EU.[139] Moreover, the Court—while taking care to address national concerns in proclaiming that the Union (including in activities under the third pillar which contained the legal basis for the Framework Decision) does respect fundamental rights and the rule of law—did

---

[135] Para 49.

[136] 'This principle implies that legislation must define clearly offences and the penalties which they attract. That condition is met in the case where the individual concerned is in a position, on the basis of the wording of the relevant provision and with the help of the interpretative assistance given by the courts, to know which acts or omissions will make him criminally liable'—para 50. The Court referred to the definition of legality in *Advocaten* also in its recent judgment on the interpretation of the ship-source pollution Directive—see Case C-308/06 *Intertanko*, judgment delivered on 3 June 2008, paras 70–71.

[137] Para 52.

[138] Para 53.

[139] According to the AG, the legality principle 'comes into play during the exercise of the State's right to punish and during the application of acts which may be strictly construed as imposing a penalty'; the Framework Decision on the other hand 'does not provide for any punishments or even seek to harmonise the criminal laws of the Member States'—instead, it creates a mechanism of *assistance* between the courts of Member States (para 103, emphasis added) In this light, the arrest and surrender procedure entailed in the execution of a European Arrest Warrant 'is not punitive in nature' (para 105). For an analysis of the implications of this reasoning for the protection of fundamental rights in EU criminal law, see V Mitsilegas, 'The Transformation of Criminal Law in the 'Area of Freedom, Security and Justice', *Yearbook of European Law 2007*, vol 26, 2008, pp 1–32.

not follow or address the emphasis that a number of national constitutional courts have placed in the special bond between citizen and State. Rather, the Court chose to follow an approach based on the logic and structure of mutual recognition: on the basis of this approach, it held that the legality requirement is met by the existence of legislation in the *issuing* Member State. In addressing potential concerns emanating from lack of trust among Member States in this context, the Court added a second layer of human rights protection (along with protection at EU level): using the very broad human rights clause in the Framework Decision itself, the Court stated that the issuing Member State *must* respect fundamental rights and consequently the legality principle. The wording is significant, as it implies that the performance of *national* authorities when applying the Framework Decision is subject to a human rights review by Luxembourg.[140]

VI. PROSECUTION AND JURISDICTION IN THE 'AREA' OF FREEDOM, SECURITY AND JUSTICE

A. General

The interaction between national criminal justice systems in the borderless 'area of freedom, security and justice' has had a significant impact in recent years on issues regarding the maintenance of State sovereignty in assuming jurisdiction and initiating prosecutions for alleged criminal offences. EU criminal law may affect such claim and exercise of sovereignty in criminal matters in a twofold manner: in not allowing a Member State to initiate prosecutions for behaviour covered by the *ne bis in idem* principle; and, at an earlier stage of the criminal process, in requesting a Member State to exercise or limit its capacity to prosecute in cases of concurrent jurisdiction: in negative conflicts of jurisdiction, the question arises on whether a Member State may be asked to prosecute a certain behaviour; in positive conflicts of jurisdiction (of particular relevance in cases of transnational organised crime), where more than one Member State claims jurisdiction to prosecute, a similar question involves whether Member States should abstain from exercising their jurisdiction in favour of another Member State which is deemed to be 'better placed' to prosecute. As with the application of mutual recognition in criminal matters in the EU, answers to these questions have far-reaching implications both for the protection of fundamental rights, and for State sovereignty and the legitimacy of criminal law: choices on whether to prosecute may be linked with citizens' sense of justice in a country, society or community.

---

[140] See in this context Sarmiento, n 121 above, pp 176–177; Geyer, 'Case Note', n 121 above, p 160

B. *Ne bis in idem*

Ne bis in idem (expressed as the prohibition of double jeopardy in common law jurisdictions) is a fundamental principle at the national level in most, if not all, EU Member States. However, its application in transnational cases involving more than one jurisdictions has been contested, and the issue of the extent to which a national legal order should respect the termination of a prosecution in another country debated.[141] The principle of *ne bis in idem* in criminal matters can be found in EU law, as a consequence of the incorporation of the Schengen *acquis* in the EC and EU legal order by the Amsterdam Treaty.[142] Article 54 of the Schengen Convention sets out the principle as follows:

> A person whose trial has been finally disposed of in one Contracting Party may not be prosecuted in another Contracting Party for the same acts provided that, if a penalty has been imposed, it has been enforced, is actually in the process of being enforced or can no longer be enforced under the laws of the sentencing Contracting Party.

The incorporation of the *ne bis in idem* principle in the Schengen Convention, and subsequently in EU law, is inextricably linked with rethinking territoriality in the European Union—in particular as regards the Schengen area. A person who is exercising free movement rights in a borderless area may not be penalised doubly by being subject to multiple prosecutions for the same acts as a result of him/her crossing borders. EU Member States must respect the outcome of proceedings in other Member States in this context in the conditions set out by the Schengen Convention. This represents thus another side of mutual recognition in criminal matters, the recognition of decisions finally disposing trials. This form of mutual recognition differs from the European Arrest Warrant and the other measures described above as it does not require the active enforcement of an order in the executing Member State by coercive means, but rather action stopping prosecution. In this manner, it constitutes a safeguard for the individual concerned and may have protective, and not enforcement consequences.[143]

Notwithstanding this broad definition of the principle, the fact that the Schengen wording differs from international *ne bis in idem* provisions included in

---

[141] See inter alia A Weyembergh, 'Le Principe *ne bis in idem*: pierre d'achoppement de l'espace pénal européen?', *Cahiers de droit européen*, 2004, pp 337–375; C van den Wyngaert and G Stessens, 'The International *non bis in idem* Principle: Resolving Some of the Unanswered Questions', *International and Comparative Law Quarterly*, vol 48, 1999, pp 779–804; J Vervaele, 'European Criminal Law and General Principles of Union Law', in Vervaele (ed), *European Evidence Warrant. Transnational Judicial Inquiries in the EU*, Antwerp, Oxford, Intersentia, 2005, pp 131–156; Vervaele, 'The Transnational *ne bis in idem* Principle in the EU', *Utrecht Law Review*, vol 1, issue 2, 2005, pp 100–118; and H van der Wilt, 'The European Arrest Warrant and the Principle *ne bis in idem*', in Blekxtoon, n 23 above, pp 99–118.

[142] The *ne bis in idem* principle has also been developed in the context of EC competition law: see inter alia W Wils, 'The Principle of "*ne bis in idem*" in EC Antitrust Enforcement: A Legal and Economic Analysis', vol 26, no 2, 2003 *World Competition*, pp 131–148.

[143] As mentioned above, *ne bis in idem*, in one form or other, constitutes a ground for refusal to execute all the mutual recognition measures adopted by the Council thus far.

instruments such as the ECHR (but also the EU Charter of Fundamental Rights), and the inclusion of *ne bis in idem* as a ground for refusal in the mutual recognition instruments, there has been no further elaboration or clarification of the principle by EU legislation.[144] A number of questions have thus arisen regarding the precise definition of elements of *ne bis in idem*, such as the definition of *idem*[145], and the definition of *bis*—what is essentially meant by a trial being 'finally disposed of'.[146] In the light of this uncertainty regarding the reach of *ne bis in idem* in the Schengen area, it has not always been easy for national courts to grapple with the principle and define its parameters. This has led to a series of references by national courts to Luxembourg for preliminary rulings, which have resulted in the development of a quite substantial ECJ case law on *ne bis in idem*. The Luxembourg Court first dealt with the principle in 2003 in its landmark judgment on the *Gözütok and Brügge* case.[147] The cases involved the termination of prosecutions by the Public Prosecutor (in the Netherlands and Germany respectively) following out-of-court settlements with the defendants, with the Luxembourg court asked to determine whether such termination was capable to trigger the application of the Schengen *ne bis in idem* principle. The Court answered in the affirmative to apply the principle in such cases, which involve the discontinuation of prosecution by a Public Prosecutor—without the involvement of a court—once the accused has fulfilled certain obligations. The need to achieve Community/Union objectives and facilitate the exercise of rights under EC law were central to the Court's approach, which examined the purpose of the integration of the Schengen *acquis* into the Union legal order. The Court noted that such integration 'is aimed at enhancing European integration and, in particular, at enabling the Union to become more rapidly the area of freedom, security and justice which is its objective to maintain and develop'.[148] Examining specifically

---

[144] The Greek Government tabled during its 2003 EU Presidency a proposal for third pillar legislation harmonising the definition of *ne bis in idem*: see Initiative of the Hellenic Republic for the adoption of a Framework Decision of the Council on the application of the '*ne bis in idem*' principle, Council doc 6356/03, Brussels, 13 February 2003. Negotiations on the proposal were, however, suspended in 2004 (see Conclusions of Justice and Home Affairs Council of 19 December 2004, doc. 11161/04, p.15). The Commission has since tabled a Green Paper on conflicts of jurisdiction and *ne bis in idem* attempting to take the issue further. See COM (2005) 696 final, Brussels, 23 December 2005 and SEC (2005) 1767.

[145] Whether the principle applies to the 'same acts', or to the 'same offences', and what constitutes a 'same' act or offence.

[146] Whether the application of the principle is limited to judicial decisions determining a person's guilt or innocence, or whether it has a broader application to include cases where a prosecution is terminated on procedural grounds (eg if dropped by a Public Prosecutor in cases such as plea bargaining, or application of the statute of limitations).

[147] Joined cases C-187/01 and C-385/01, [2003] ECR I-1345. For comments on the case, see inter alia: Case-note by J Vervaele, *Common Market Law Review*, vol 42, 2004, pp 795–812; M Fletcher, 'Some Developments to the *ne bis in idem* Principle in the European Union: *Criminal Proceedings against Huseyn Gözütok and Klaus Brügge*', *Modern Law Review*, vol 66, 2003, pp 769–780; N Thwaites, 'Mutual Trust in Criminal Matters: The European Court of Justice Gives Its First Interpretation of a Provision of the Convention Implementing the Schengen Agreement', *German Law Journal*, vol 4, 2003, pp 253–262, www.germanlawjournal.com.

[148] Para 37.

Article 54 of the Schengen Convention, the Court emphasised its objective to ensure that no one is prosecuted on the same facts in several Member States on account of his having exercised his right to freedom of movement—Article 54 cannot play a useful role in bringing about the full attainment of that objective unless it applies to the decisions under examination in this case.[149] The purposive interpretation of the Court and its emphasis on the attainment of EU objectives is backed by an 'ahistorical' approach to European integration, with the Court rejecting Member States' arguments that the intentions of the Schengen Contracting Parties were not to adopt such a broad definition of Article 54, as, in particular, documents demonstrating such intentions 'predate' the integration of the Schengen *acquis* into the EU framework.[150]

In *Gözütok and Brügge* the Court interpreted criminal law principles in the light of the need to achieve Union objectives and uphold fundamental principles of EC law such as freedom of movement. This approach has led in this case in a broad interpretation of *ne bis in idem* as a protective criminal law principle. The Court followed consistently this reasoning in a number of subsequent cases, which led to the adoption of a similarly protective approach to *ne bis in idem*, by defining the scope of both *bis* and *idem* in a broad manner. In *Van Esbroek*, [151] the Court interpreted the *idem* aspect of Article 54 of the Schengen Convention as based on 'the identity of the material acts, understood as the existence of a set of facts which are linked together, irrespective of their legal classification given to them or the legal interest protected'.[152] This interpretation is much broader than the limitation of *ne bis in idem* as covering the same offences. The Court rejected an approach defining *idem* on the basis of its legal classification by viewing the issue from the perspective of achieving free movement—given that there is no harmonisation of national laws, a criterion based on the legal classification or the legal interest protected at national level 'might create as many barriers to freedom of movement within Schengen as there are legal systems'.[153] The Court reiterated its case law in *Gözütok and Brügge*[154] stating that the objective of Article 54 is that no one is prosecuted for the same acts on account of his having exercised his right to freedom of movement.[155] Making express reference to the Opinion of Advocate General Jarabo Colomer, the Court further noted that the right of free movement is guaranteed

---

[149] See paras 35–38.

[150] Para 46.

[151] Case C-436/04 ECR [2006] I-2333. For comments, see M Wasmeier and N Thwaites, 'The Development of *ne bis in idem* into a Transnational Fundamental Right in EU Law: Comments on Recent Developments', *European Law Review*, vol 31, 2006, pp 565–578; and case-note by H-H Kuhne, *Juristenzeitung*, vol 20, 2006, pp 1018–1021.

[152] Para 36.

[153] Para 35. See also the Opinion of AG Ruiz-Jarabo Colomer, of 20 October 2005, who rejected the legal classification criterion as inconsistent with the right of freedom of movement. He noted that, in a drug-trafficking case, it is ironic to speak of 'import' and 'export' (between different Schengen countries) in a territory which is subject to one legal order which has exactly as its aim by its nature the abolition of borders for goods as well as persons—para 52.

[154] And also in the case of *Miraglia*, [2005] ECR I-2009.

[155] Para 33.

only if the perpetrator of an act knows that, once he has been found guilty and served his sentence, or, where applicable, been acquitted by a final judgment, he may travel within the Schengen territory without fear of prosecution in another Member State.[156]

The Court examined further the definitions of *bis* and *idem* in two 2006 cases which were delivered on the same day: *Van Straaten*[157] and *Gasparini*.[158] The Court both confirmed and expanded its earlier case law. In *Van Straaten*, the Court had to deal with both *bis* and *idem*. On *idem* the Court—looking at the issue of the movement of drugs between two Schengen countries (which would constitute 'export' from one country and 'import' into the other)—reiterated the *Van Esbroek* reasoning, adding that exporting and importing are in principle the same acts.[159] On *bis*, the Court had to consider whether a final decision acquitting the accused for lack of evidence would fall within the scope of Article 54. It found that this is the case, as not applying Article 54 to such cases would have the effect of jeopardising the exercise of the right of freedom of movement.[160] Following AG Jarabo Colomer's strong emphasis on the rationale behind *ne bis in idem*,[161] the Court noted that in such a case—where the decision is based on the determination of the merits of the case[162]—the bringing of criminal proceedings in another Contracting State for the same acts would undermine the principles of legal certainty and legitimate expectations.[163]

Gasparini was a more challenging case for the Court, as it involved the question of whether time-barred prosecutions are final judgments for the purposes of Article 54, and as the Court had to deal with the Opinion of Advocate General Sharpston, which in many aspects departed from the approach of AG Colomer and the Court's earlier case law. Advocate General Sharpston took the view that time-barred prosecutions should not merit the protection of Article 54, as they do not involve an examination of the merits of a case. The AG based her conclusion mainly on the arguments that a time-barred prosecution does not settle society's account with the individual[164], that there must be a 'balance' between free movement and fighting crime[165] (as free movement 'is not an absolute principle and must not be distorted out of proportion'[166]), and that a broad interpretation of *bis* would lead to 'criminal jurisdiction shopping'.[167] This 'securitised' approach to the limits of protection in criminal law reflects to a great extent the 'war on terror'

---

[156] Para 34.

[157] Case C-150/05, *Van Straaten v the Netherlands and Italy* ECR [2006] I-9327.

[158] Case C-467/04 ECR [2006] I-9199.

[159] But the assessment is for the national courts to make. The quantities of the drugs involved are not required to be identical. Para 53.

[160] Para 58.

[161] Opinion, para 56. However, the Court did not go as far as the AG in using a fundamental rights vocabulary in the context of *ne bis in idem*.

[162] Para 60.

[163] Para 59. On legal certainty, see also *Gözütok* para 119.

[164] Paras 74–76.

[165] Para 81.

[166] Para 84.

[167] Para 104.

discourse justifying exceptional measures in the UK[168] and the approach to free movement is a striking departure from the Court's case law.[169] The Court, however, did not change its approach on *ne bis in idem*. It included time-barred prosecutions within the scope of Article 54, and reiterated the earlier case law and the importance to ensure the exercise of the right of free movement. Not to apply Article 54, when a court has made a decision acquitting the accused finally because prosecution of the offence is time-barred, 'would undermine the implementation of that objective'.[170]

The *ne bis in idem* case law is another example of the subordination of criminal law to Community/Union law. The principle has been interpreted by the Court in the light of the need to ensure that fundamental rights of the Community legal order, in the form of free movement—are exercised effectively. The emphasis on free movement is inextricably linked with a specific view of territoriality in the Schengen area. With the logic of Schengen resulting in the abolition of borders, the Schengen area is viewed as a borderless area, and thus effectively as one territory in which free movement must be ensured and enjoyed. Differences between national criminal justice systems should not pose an obstacle to free movement. This approach is not devoid of further questions. The Court has consistently emphasised freedom of movement, however this has been predominantly developed in the first pillar. Schengen on the other hand applies to both first and third pillars, and the *ne bis in idem* provisions would fall within the third pillar. Would it therefore be a more accurate reflection of the current state of European integration for the Court to use the development of the EU as an 'area of freedom, security and justice', as a central objective to be achieved rather than the (undoubtedly related, but not quite the same) freedom of movement? If this were the case, the approach to *ne bis in idem* might have been slightly different. As hinted by the Opinion of AG Sharpston in *Gasparini*, when one looks at the AFSJ one might have to examine the interrelationship between all three elements—freedom, security and justice. However, the Court has stressed freedom as a central element in the 'area of freedom, security and justice' and emphasised the link between EU third pillar law and the attainment of free movement. One must not disregard that freedom in the context of the protective provisions of *ne bis in idem* in the framework of the Schengen Convention has been included as a safeguard to the substantial security 'compensatory' measures introduced by the Schengen Implementing Convention in order to enhance border and police co-operation.

The transposition of the *ne bis in idem* principle from the national to the European Union level may have considerable implications for sovereignty and

---

[168] In particular the standard discourse on 'balancing' different interests.

[169] It is noteworthy that the AG also refers to the inconsistencies between the definition of *ne bis in idem* in criminal law and its narrower definition in EC competition law (arguing implicitly for the latter). However, the suggestion not to treat criminal law as a special case and to equate it with the different rationale and impact of competition law would appear to be hard to reconcile with the strong security-oriented approach of the AG in terms of fighting crime.

[170] Para 28. The Court also examined an aspect of *idem* in examining whether marketing and importing goods in respective states constitute the same act—paras 53–56.

legitimacy of the criminal law at the national level. The interpretation of *ne bis in idem* with the purpose of achieving Community objectives has thus far led to broad, protective definitions for the individual. At the same time, the Court is increasingly proceeding with treating *ne bis in idem* and related concepts as general principles of Community law. The Court in *Van Esbroek* expressly stated that *ne bis in idem* is a fundamental principle of Community law.[171] The application of the *ne bis in idem* principle in the Schengen context effectively prohibits a Member State in a wide range of cases from prosecuting conduct that could constitute a criminal offence. This constitutes a considerable limitation in the capacity of the State to administer criminal justice and may have considerable implications for citizens' acceptance of such action. The tensions surrounding this issue are evident from the examination of *ne bis in idem* in Luxembourg, where cases reveal that national courts are agonising over the extent to which they can define the principle and the Court of Justice and Advocates General have to grapple with what constitutes the examination of the merits of a case and with what conditions will prevent a prosecution in Schengen Member States.[172] Tensions are also evident by the fact that there is no common understanding by Member States of what should constitute *ne bis in idem* at the European Union level, as efforts to adopt third pillar law introducing a common EU definition of the principle have failed.[173] At present there are considerable differences in how Member States treat *ne bis in idem* at the national level, and how they envisage the principle to be applied at the transnational, EU level.

Absence of harmonisation of *ne bis in idem* across the EU has thus not been an obstacle for the Court in developing further the principle. The Court seems to have disregarded concerns voiced in the context of the application of the principle of mutual recognition in criminal matters in view of the absence of mutual trust among Member States. In the *ne bis in idem* cases, the Court assumes the existence of such trust, most notably of a 'high level' of trust between Member States. Whether such level of trust actually exists is an open question.[174] What is noteworthy is that, in assuming trust, and not viewing harmonisation as a necessary condition for interpreting the *ne bis in idem* in a broad manner, the *ne bis in idem* principle (which involves the movement of final national criminal law judgments in the Schengen area) is viewed in a manner analogous with the operation of the mutual recognition principle (where national judgments/orders also move across

---

[171] Para 40. In her recent Opinions, AG Sharpston also put forward the view that the principle of set-off is a general principle of EU, and even of EC law. (Case C-367/05 *Norma Kraajenbrink*, ECR [2007] I-619 paras 58–60; Case C-288/05 *Jürgen Kretzinger*, ECR [2007] I-6641 para 65). The AG argues that both *ne bis in idem* and the set-off principle are manifestations of the general requirement of natural justice and fairness in criminal proceedings, that the principle would apply whether or not *ne bis in idem* applies (*Kraajenbrink*, paras 61–63.) However, this approach was not adopted by the Court.

[172] The tension between *ne bis in idem* and the administration of justice is clearly demonstrated in AG Sharpston's Opinion in *Gasparini*.

[173] See Initiative of the Hellenic Republic, n 144 above.

[174] The assumption that a high level of trust in criminal justice systems across the EU exists would weaken the justification of proposals tabled by the European Commission in order to enhance trust in Member States criminal justice systems (most notably the defence rights proposal).

the EU). While the maximum mutual recognition of coercive measures such as the European Arrest Warrant leads to concerns regarding the extension of the State's punitive sphere, a broad application of *ne bis in idem* (viewed as a facilitator of free movement) has thus far led to the opposite results—an extension of the protective sphere for the individual in the 'area of freedom, security and justice'.

Differences in Member States' approaches to *ne bis in idem*, and their reluctance to agree common EU standards in the field, reflect the sensitivity surrounding the exercise of criminal law powers by Member States, as well as a phenomenon shared with the development of mutual recognition in criminal matters in the EU, the lack of mutual trust among legal systems in the EU.[175] The absence of harmonisation of national systems is a factor which has been brought by sceptical Member States to the attention of the Luxembourg Court which, in the absence of common EU rules beyond the Schengen Convention, has to interpret and develop *ne bis in idem* as an EU concept. In *Gözütok and Brügge*, the Court, stated that nowhere in the EU Treaty or the Schengen Convention 'is the application of Article 54 of the Convention made conditional upon harmonisation, or at least approximation, of the criminal laws of the Member States relating to procedures whereby further prosecution is barred'.[176] The Court added that in those circumstances, 'there is a necessary implication that the Member States have *mutual trust* in their criminal justice systems and that each of them recognises the criminal law in force in the other Member States even when the outcome would be different if its own national law were applied' (emphasis added).[177] The Court reiterated this statement in *Van Esbroek*,[178] where the Court added that because of the existence of mutual trust, the possibility of divergent legal classifications of the same acts in two different States or varying criteria protecting legal interests across Member States cannot stop the application of Article 54 of the Schengen Convention.[179] The Court further reiterated these points—by reference to *Van Esbroek*—in both *Van Straaten*[180] and (contrary to the AG Opinion, which stressed the differences between national legal systems) in *Gasparini*.[181]

This tension between the lack of mutual trust among EU Member States and the willingness by the Court to promote free movement in its interpretation of the *ne*

---

[175] In the context of *ne bis in idem*, see J L de la Cuesta, 'Concurrent National and International Jurisdiction and the Principle "*ne bis in idem*"—General Report', *International Review of Penal Law*, vol 73, 2004, p 717.

[176] Para 32.

[177] Para 33. See also the Opinion of AG Ruiz-Jarabo Colomer, delivered on 19 September 2002, paras 119–124, and para 55, where the AG states that

the construction of a Europe without borders, with its corollary of the approximation of the various national legal systems, including the criminal systems, presupposes that the States involved will be guided by the same values.

[178] Para 30.

[179] Paras 31 and 32. As mentioned in part 2 above, the Court noted that basing *idem* on different legal classifications or interests 'might create as many barriers to freedom of movement within the Schengen territory as there are penal systems in the Contracting States' (para 35).

[180] Para 43 and 47 (where the Court reiterates its point on the 'legal classification' interest in the context of *ne bis in idem*).

[181] Paras 29 and 30.

bis in idem principle surfaced very prominently in the *Kretzinger* case.[182] The case involved the transportation (without declaring this to any customs authority) by Mr Kretzinger of cigarettes from countries that were not members of the European Union, which had previously been smuggled into Greece by third parties, by lorry through Italy and Germany, bound for the United Kingdom. The Venice Court of Appeal imposed to Mr Kretzinger *in absentia* a suspended custodial sentence of one year and eight months, finding him guilty of offences of tobacco smuggling and failing to pay customs duty. The Tribunale di Ancona subsequently imposed again *in absentia* and under the same provisions a two-year custodial sentence (not suspended) for a second consignment of tobacco. Both sentences have become final. However, awareness of the Italian final judgments has not stopped a Court in another Member State, Germany (the Landsgericht Augsburg) from sentencing Mr Kretzinger to one year and ten months imprisonment in respect of the first consignment and one year imprisonment in respect of the second—finding the defendant guilty of evasion of the customs duties which had arisen on the importation of the smuggled goods into Greece in accordance with the German Tax Code. According to the Landsgericht Augsburg, Article 54 of the Schengen Implementing Convention did not apply in this case. On appeal, the Bundesgerichtshof decided to send a reference for a preliminary ruling to Luxembourg, asking in particular whether the case in question would involve the 'same acts' under Article 54 and whether in essence the Italian handling of the case constitutes 'enforcement' of a sentence under the same provision.[183]

The case is significant as it has been generated by an attempt by a lower national court to apply and enforce its domestic law notwithstanding the EU rules on *ne bis in idem*. This choice, and the related questions in the *Bundesgerichthof*'s reference, raise two questions which are central to the interpretation of *ne bis in idem*. The first question relates to the concept of the territory and its link with jurisdiction: here, it seems that the national court has attempted to circumvent EU law requirements by applying the domestic law whose reach extends beyond its national border and covers the EU external border (in Greece)—under this logic, tobacco smuggling on the Union external border is not the 'same acts' as tobacco smuggling from Italy to Germany. The second, and perhaps more significant, question, is a question of trust: throughout the description of the facts and in the *Bundesgerichthof*'s questions themselves, implicit but clear is the lack of trust towards the Italian authorities and the manner in which they have handled the *Kretzinger* cases post-conviction. What the German Court is asking effectively is the extent to which *ne bis in idem* rules are bent or limited when another Member State is deemed as not taking its enforcement obligations seriously: do final decisions in another Member State per se, if they are not properly enforced, bind the hands of activist courts in other Member States under the *ne bis in idem* principle?

---

[182] Case C-288/05, *Jürgen Kretzinger*, ECR [2007] I-6641.
[183] For the background and the questions of the national court see paras 14–26 of the judgment.

On the question of what constitutes the 'same acts', the Court followed and expanded upon its earlier case law. It reiterated the *Van Esbroek* test that the only relevant criterion is identity of the material acts, understood as the existence of a set of facts which are inextricably linked together, adding that that criterion applies irrespective of the legal classification given to those acts or the legal interest protected.[184] The Court rejected the position put forward by the German and Spanish Governments that the national court must also take into account the legal interest protected when assessing a set of concrete circumstances: the Court reiterated that legal interest considerations are not to be deemed relevant and repeated *Van Esbroek* in stating that 'because there is no harmonisation of national criminal law, considerations based on the legal interest protected might create as many barriers to freedom of movement within the Schengen area as there are penal systems in the Contracting States'.[185] According to the Court, while the final assessment is for the national courts to make, the transportation of contraband cigarettes involving successive crossings of internal Schengen area borders, is therefore capable of constituting a set of facts covered by the notion of the 'same acts'.[186] The Court thus remained focused on ensuring freedom of movement, and reinforced the centrality and broad definition of the concept of 'same acts' in the interpretation of *ne bis in idem*[187], by clarifying in this context that successive border crossings *within* the Schengen area may not change the fact that the 'same acts' apply.[188]

On the question of enforcement, the Court's response is somewhat more nuanced. From the outset, the Court clarifies that suspended custodial sentences constitute penalties within the meaning of Article 54 of the Schengen Convention, in so far as they penalise the unlawful conduct of a convicted person—with the penalty regarded as 'actually in the process of being enforced' as soon as the

---

[184] Para 29.

[185] Para 33.

[186] Para 36.

[187] Note also however the Court's ruling in Case C-367/05, *Norma Kraajenbrink*, delivered on the same day as *Kretzinger*—ECR [2007] I-619. The case involved transnational crime par excellence, ie money laundering. The case involved money laundering related convictions in Belgium and the Netherlands—while different acts giving rise to these convictions constitute 'the successive and continuous implementation of the same criminal intention' (para 18), it was not clear if they involved the same sums of money. In this context, the Court reiterated the earlier case law and stressed that the acts in question must make up 'an inseparable whole'—but the Court noted that if the acts do not make up an inseparable whole the fact that they were committed with the same criminal intention does not suffice to meet the test of what constitutes 'same acts' under Art 54 of the Schengen Convention (para 29). However, the Court also found that in cases where it has not been clearly established that the financial gain in question in the two Member States are identical, in principle the conduct involved can be covered by the notion of the 'same acts' if an objective link is established (para 31).

[188] This is a logical conclusion of the establishment of a single area with no internal frontiers and a common external border under Schengen. This approach, however, would seem to imply that the position of the Court might be different in cases involving Member States not fully participating into Schengen, such as the United Kingdom—although the latter does apply the criminal law part of Schengen. Should Mr Kretzinger manage to smuggle tobacco into the United Kingdom, the final destination of the journey, would UK courts be shielded from applying the EU *ne bis in idem* principle by virtue of the external crossing of the goods? this seems to follow from the emphasis of the Court on Schengen free movement.

sentence has become enforceable and during the probation period.[189] However, the Court found that periods spent in police custody and/or remand pending trial must not be regarded automatically as the enforcement of a penalty for the purposes of Article 54.[190] Moreover, the Court rejected Mr Kretzinger's argument that the fact that it is legally possible under the Framework Decision on the European Arrest Warrant for the sentencing State to issue a Warrant in order to enforce a judgment which has become final and binding means that the enforcement condition must be regarded as satisfied (and the German courts can no longer prosecute him).[191] The Court found that this factor cannot affect the interpretation of the notion of 'enforcement' under Article 54 of the Schengen Convention as the latter requires not only a conviction, but also the satisfaction of the enforcement condition.[192] The Court is thus prepared to extend *ne bis in idem* in cases of suspended sentences, implicitly accepting that this is a legitimate choice of penal enforcement by Member States which, if adopted at the domestic level, must be recognised as enforcement across the Schengen area for Article 54 purposes. However, it is noteworthy that the Court is not prepared to link *ne bis in idem* enforcement with the European Arrest Warrant, or rather with the *possibility* for a Member State to issue a European Arrest Warrant on a specific case. The Court seems to recognise that this would pose an undue burden on domestic criminal justice systems, as well as an inroad to prosecutorial or judicial discretion: if Mr Kretzinger's argument were accepted, the decision not to issue a European Arrest Warrant would effectively shield defendants from prosecutions as it would in essence constitute an act equivalent to a decision triggering the *ne bis in idem* principle.

The content and framing of the questions in the *ne bis in idem* cases, in particular in *Gasparini* and *Kretzinger*, demonstrate the difficulties in negotiating an acceptable definition of *ne bis in idem* across the EU. In the absence of the—ever elusive—EU legislative harmonisation in the field, and the close link of *ne bis in idem* with the legitimacy of domestic criminal justice systems, standards developed by the European Court of Justice may lead to challenges to the formulation and acceptance of these standards in Member States. At present, national definitions of *ne bis in idem* differ from the definition adopted by the Court.[193] Differences between the EU concept of *ne bis in idem* and national definitions may lead to double standards—and perhaps reverse discrimination—between those exercising free movement rights and those subject to a purely domestic legal framework. Court-made standards may also encounter resistance in a national context, and have a significant impact on national legal systems and cultures—for

---

[189] Para 42.

[190] Para 48 f.

[191] Para 57.

[192] Paras 59 and 63. The Court also based this conclusion on the fact that Member States bound by the Framework Decision on the European Arrest Warrant are not all bound by the Schengen Convention—and linking the two in this manner would create 'legal uncertainty'—para 62.

[193] See, eg, the UK Criminal Justice Act 2003, which permits re-opening of a trial in a number of cases, even against persons who have formerly been acquitted (s 75).

example in cases where the Court's approach in *Gözütok* and *Gasparini* type cases—clashes with national rules requiring a substantive determination of innocence or guilt for a case to be 'finally disposed of'. Moreover, they may prove inadequate to address the fact that a fundamental principle of EU law—and EU criminal law—such as *ne bis in idem* has a strong 'variable geometry' dimension, linked primarily with the full Schengen members. With or without harmonisation, the Court will continue to face important questions on the interpretation of *ne bis in idem*.[194] However, relaunching the effort to harmonise *ne bis in idem* at EU level (with binding legislation incorporating the elements of the Luxembourg case law) will be challenging, but may be the only way for these concerns to be addressed.

C. Concurrent Jurisdiction

A question that has been linked with, but is broader than, the definition of the *ne bis in idem* principle in a borderless 'area of freedom, security and justice' concerns the extent to which Member States should co-ordinate prior to initiating prosecutions for offences with a transnational element—extending thus co-operation at the stage *prior to* the initiation of criminal prosecutions and/or investigations. It has been argued that it is not coherent to allow the extraterritorial reach of national judicial decisions in criminal matters across the EU, without in parallel limiting the number of jurisdictions which can prosecute, and can prosecute effectively.[195] Some form of co-ordination on jurisdiction might complement the operation of mutual recognition and the determination of the fate of prosecutions in accordance to the *ne bis in idem* principle. In the absence of a uniform criminal law and procedure across the European Union, the question arises on whether any such co-ordination will result in the worsening of the position of the defendant, by aiming at allocating jurisdiction to investigate and prosecute to the Member State where it is easiest to obtain a conviction, and whether 'effectiveness' in this context is synonymous with the maximum information gathering possible and maximum convictions. Another issue is related to legitimacy, and to what extent it is acceptable for a Member State to be prevented from prosecuting an alleged offence where jurisdiction can be established solely on the grounds of 'effectiveness'.

There is currently no centralised binding mechanism of jurisdiction allocation in criminal matters in the European Union. The Decision establishing Eurojust

[194] For the latest example, see the Opinion of AG Ruiz-Jarabo Colomer in Case C-297/07 *Bourquain*, delivered on 8 April 2008. The case involves Mr Bourquain, a German national participating in the French Foreign Legion and on whom the death penalty was imposed by a military tribunal in 1960. He then fled to West Germany and the penalty was not executed. In 2002, a German Court in Regensburg re-opened the case. But on that date, the penalty could no longer be executed in France. AG Colomer argues that Art 54 of the Schengen Convention also applies to final judgments which, by reasons of procedural particularities of the domestic law (like in this case) could never be executed (paras 66–75).
[195] See D Flore and S de Biolley, 'Des organes jurisdictionnels en matière pénale pour l'Union européenne', *Cahiers de droit européen*, 2003, pp 597–637 at p 610.

states that the organisation—acting through its national members or as a College—may ask the competent authorities of Member States to co-ordinate.[196] Eurojust may also ask these authorities 'to accept that one of them may be in a better position to undertake an investigation or to prosecute specific acts'.[197] Respectful of Member States' wish to maintain sovereignty in the initiation of investigations and prosecutions, Eurojust may (as in the cases of investigating or prosecuting) only *ask*—but not oblige—national authorities to consider these issues. Eurojust has been conducting a number of co-ordination meetings with national officials, and in 2003, adopted a series of (non-binding) guidelines on 'which jurisdiction should prosecute'.[198] The Guidelines call for a 'preliminary presumption' that a prosecution should take place in the jurisdiction where the majority of criminality occurred or where the majority of the loss was sustained— in reaching the decision, prosecutors 'should balance carefully and fairly all the factors both for and against commencing a prosecution in each jurisdiction where it is possible to do so'.[199] The Guidelines contain a series of criteria to be taken into account including the location of the accused, capacity to extradite or surrender, centralising prosecutions of many suspects in one jurisdiction, the attendance and protection of witnesses and victims. According to the Guidelines, the relative sentencing powers of the courts must not be a 'primary' factor in deciding where to prosecute, but availability and use of evidence is a relevant factor.[200]

Mechanisms and criteria of allocating jurisdiction do exist in sectoral third pillar instruments. The Framework Decision on combating terrorism[201] stipulates that, when an offences falls within the jurisdiction of more than one Member State and when any of the States concerned can prosecute validly on the basis of the same facts, the Member States concerned must co-operate in order to decide where to prosecute, with the aim if possible of centralising proceedings in one Member State. Member States 'may have recourse to any body or mechanism established within the European Union in order to facilitate co-operation'[202] and in allocating jurisdiction, 'sequential account' must be taken of the following criteria: territory of the commission of the acts; nationality or residence of the perpetrator; 'origin' of the victims; and the place where the perpetrator 'was found'.[203] A similar list can be found in the latest draft of the Framework Decision on the fight against organised crime, with the difference that express reference to Eurojust is made therein and the text currently talks about 'special' and not

[196] OJ L63, 6 March 2002, p 1 Arts 6(a)(iii) and 7(a)(iii) respectively. For further details on Eurojust, see ch 4.
[197] Arts 6(a)(ii) and 7(a)(ii) respectively.
[198] Found in the Annex to Eurojust Annual Report 2003, pp 60 et seq.
[199] ibid, p.62.
[200] Eurojust has conducted a jurisdiction allocation exercise in the *Prestige* case. The College decided that Spain was better placed to prosecute than France on the grounds that a larger amount of evidence was gathered in Spain, and the number of injured parties was also much higher in Spain—see Eurojust press release of 23 November 2005, www.eurojust.eu.int/press_releases/2005/23–11–2005.htm
[201] OJ L164, 22 June 2002, p 3.
[202] Wording which may cover Eurojust.
[203] Art 9(2).

'sequential' account.[204] It is interesting to note that these criteria do not necessarily coincide with the Guidelines developed by Eurojust, with the former being more objective compared to Eurojust's more subjective, case-by-case, approach.

The Commission has recently relaunched the debate on whether there should be common rules on conflicts of jurisdiction by linking the issue with the question of the development of an EU definition of *ne bis in idem*. The Commission Green Paper on conflicts of jurisdiction, published in December 2005,[205] was the next step after the freezing of negotiations on the proposal by the Greek Presidency for a Framework Decision on *ne bis in idem*, which encountered substantial difficulties in the Council.[206] The *idem* principle with a system of allocating jurisdiction: in the background to the Green Paper, it is noted that Commission links the operation of the *ne bis in idem* with concurrent jurisdiction:

> without a system for allocating cases to an appropriate jurisdiction while proceedings are ongoing, *ne bis in idem* can lead to accidental or even arbitrary results: by giving preference to whichever jurisdiction can first take a final decision, its effects amount to a 'first come first served' principle. The choice of jurisdiction is currently left to chance, and this seems to be the reason why the principle of *ne bis in idem* is subject to several exceptions.[207]

Following the use of this—rather critical—language, the Commission floats the idea of creating an EU mechanism for the choice of jurisdiction, which, if applied, would do away with the exceptions to the *ne bis in idem* principle. The Commission calls for criteria on jurisdiction allocation to be listed in a future EU instrument. The Commission refers to criteria such as territoriality, criteria related to the suspect or defendant, victims' interests, criteria related to the State interests, and 'certain other criteria related to the efficiency and rapidity of the proceedings'[208] It also asserts that

> since new findings can often change the picture of what at first might seem the 'best place' to prosecute, it may not be wise to force the competent authorities to make a definitive choice of jurisdiction at an early stage.[209]

The need to give as much flexibility as possible to prosecutors has also been reflected in the response of Eurojust to the Green Paper, where it is noted that immediate centralisation of proceedings in a single Member State 'is not always the best solution' and that in complex cases, it might be more appropriate ' to carry

---

[204] Doc 12279/06, 28 September 2006, Art 7(2).This has been a change from the wording in the 1998 Joint Action on organised crime (OJ L351, 29 December 1998, p 1), which this Framework Decision will replace. A similar list (but excluding the criterion of the victims' origin) can be found in the Framework Decision on attacks against information systems (OJ L69, 16 March 2003, p 67, art 11). For a comparative table, see Annex to the Commission Green Paper on Conflicts of Jurisdiction and the Principle of *ne bis in idem* in Criminal Proceedings, SEC (2005) 1767, 23 December 2005. See also S Peers, *EU Justice and Home Affairs Law*, 2nd edn, Oxford, OUP, 2006, p 458.

[205] COM (2005) 696 final, 23 December 2005.

[206] See section VI B above.

[207] ibid p 3.

[208] ibid p 8.

[209] ibid p 7.

on well co-ordinated investigations and prosecutions in two or more jurisdictions instead of centralising them in a single Member State'.[210]

Where does all this leave us? The Commission appears to be advocating centralisation and EU binding legislation in determining jurisdiction allocation criteria. From the tone and the content of the Green Paper—ranging from the criteria of allocating jurisdiction to the dismissive tone regarding the application of the protective *ne bis in idem* principle—concerns are raised that such criteria would prioritise the goal of prosecutorial efficiency.[211] Eurojust's comments appear in the same spirit, with the organisation calling for the maximum prosecution possible until a very late stage—in a sense defeating thus the very purpose of centralising prosecutions at an early stage and creating thus legal certainty (which could then lead to the abolition of *ne bis in idem* exceptions). Concerns related to the proliferation of prosecutorial power at the expense of the defendant are coupled with issues of legitimacy. Should Member States be ordered not to prosecute behaviour which may lead to a criminal conviction in their jurisdiction? It is one thing for Member States to be bound by an EU body/instrument to initiate prosecutions, and quite another for these States to be prevented or prohibited from initiating prosecutions for conduct that may be a serious criminal offence under their law. The powers of Eurojust along with the extent of the jurisdiction of the Court of Justice in examining EU criteria and decisions on jurisdiction allocation are central issues in this debate.

VII. THE FUTURE IN THE LIGHT OF LISBON

Notwithstanding the increasing reluctance of Member States to agree new far-reaching secondary EU legislation on mutual recognition and the unsatisfactory state of implementation of the majority of mutual recognition measures adopted in the early years of this decade following the European Arrest Warrant momentum, mutual recognition appears to be the big winner in the Lisbon Treaty especially when compared with harmonisation of criminal law. The opening provision of Title V on the 'Area of Freedom, Security and Justice', states that the Union will endeavour to ensure a high level of security through mutual recognition in criminal matters and, *if necessary*, through the approximation of criminal laws.[212] Not only is mutual recognition explicitly linked with security in this context, but its dominant position in relation to the secondary role of harmonisation is evident. The dominance of mutual recognition is further confirmed in the specific Lisbon provision on judicial co-operation in criminal matters, stating that this will be

---

[210] p 3. Interestingly Eurojust also places emphasis on the so-called 'negative conflicts of jurisdiction', where no Member Sate wishes to prosecute (notably in the field of economic crime). The implications of this emphasis on the discussion on the potential increase in the powers of Eurojust may be considerable.

[211] Note the Commission's reference to 'certain other criteria related to the efficiency and rapidity of the proceedings' when citing criteria of allocation of prosecution.

[212] Art 67(3) TFEU.

based on mutual recognition and will include the approximation of national laws on substantive criminal law and criminal procedure.[213] Moreover, the conferral to the Union of competence to adopt measures in the field of criminal procedure *is subordinated to mutual recognition*: such a legal basis exists to adopt minimum rules on specific areas 'to the extent necessary to facilitate mutual recognition of judgments and judicial decisions'.[214] Therefore, the adoption of every measure on criminal procedure under this provision must be justified as facilitating mutual recognition, with legislation aiming to ensure the protection of fundamental rights in criminal procedure (such as the defence rights proposal discussed earlier in the chapter) subordinated thus to a logic of achieving the efficiency of mutual recognition. Lisbon provides an express legal basis for the adoption of such proposal in these terms, as well as for criminal procedure measures related to victims' rights and (in an attempt to address the multitude of issues arising from the European Evidence Warrant), rules on the mutual admissibility of evidence.[215] The link between the adoption of 'trust-building' procedural measures and the facilitation of mutual recognition may not always be straightforward and may lead to controversy during negotiations, and litigation after the adoption of such measures.[216]

As regards mutual recognition measures per se, Lisbon contains a legal basis for the adoption of a series of measures including measures on the recognition of *all forms of judgments and judicial decisions*.[217] The wording is significant as it implies the construction of a European criminal justice area on the basis of a series of measures enabling the mutual recognition of all aspects of criminal justice. This trend is gradually emerging at EU level with the plethora of 'enforcement' mutual recognition measures adopted thus far slowly being followed by proposals aiming at 'protective' mutual recognition.[218] Moreover, the combination of the various mutual recognition instruments leads to a framework for rules embracing all stages of the criminal justice process (from arrest to the execution of sentences). The extent to which Lisbon will provide a fresh *impetus* towards the adoption of further measures leading to a system of EU criminal justice operating on the basis of mutual recognition of all stages of the criminal justice process remains to be seen. The quest for coherence in the interaction of national legal systems is, however, evident in other Treaty provisions, in particular the legal basis for the

---

[213] Art 82(1) TFEU.

[214] Art 82(2) TFEU. For further details, see ch 2.

[215] ibid.

[216] On the implications of the link between criminal procedure and mutual recognition for negotiations and Member States' participation, see ch 1.

[217] Art 82(1)(a) TFEU.

[218] See in this context the proposals for mutual recognition of decisions on bail (Council doc. 16494/07, Brussels, 13 December 2007), and on the recognition of suspended sentences, alternative sanctions and conditional sentences (Council doc. 16573/07, Brussels, 21 December 2007). The Justice and Home Affairs Council reached a 'general approach' on the latter (Council of 6–7 December 2007, doc 15966/07, Presse 125, p 29), while negotiations on bail seem to be ongoing. On these proposals see also House of Lords European Union Committee, European Supervision Order, 31st Report, session 2006–07, HL Paper 145.

adoption of measures to prevent and settle conflicts of jurisdiction between Member States.[219] The adoption of such measures may prove to be challenging in the light of their impact on State sovereignty to prosecute. However, Lisbon may provide an opportunity for the adoption of clear, transparent rules, taking into account the rights of the defendant and avoiding prosecutorial 'forum shopping'.

VIII. CONCLUSION: SOVEREIGNTY, TERRITORIALITY AND RIGHTS IN AN 'AREA' OF FREEDOM, SECURITY AND JUSTICE

The application of the principle of mutual recognition in criminal matters in the European Union has led to a rethinking of national sovereignty, and national and EU constitutional principles. Mutual recognition in this context is based on a rethinking of territoriality: linked with the fundamental objective of the abolition of borders in the European Union, in particular within the Schengen area, the new territoriality views the Union as a single 'area', where facilitation of free movement must be the primary aim. However, in criminal matters, this aim has not been achieved by attempting to create common rules and standards underpinning free movement. Rather, the emphasis has been placed at the national level: equating people with court decisions, the logic of this system dictates that it is *national* judicial decisions, and consequently national legal and constitutional systems, that must move freely with the minimum of formality and be respected by other national jurisdictions in the EU. The latter is one 'area', but with no coherent 'system'—it is national systems that must be recognised. This 'extraterritoriality' of the national, based on mutual trust, has nevertheless been accompanied by very limited efforts to create a common understanding, and a level playing field, between these systems.

The operation of mutual recognition in this manner in the field of criminal law, closely linked with State sovereignty and legitimacy, the protection of fundamental rights and the rule of law, inevitably has significant constitutional implications both for national legal systems and for EU law as such. At the national level, courts and citizens are asked to embark on a 'journey into the unknown' and to recognise with the minimum of formality (and be subject to) decisions emanating from the system of any given Member State, even in cases where the behaviour at stake is not an offence in the legal system of the executing State. This raises serious concerns of legality and legitimacy—citizens must accept completely 'external' standards, standards that were not the product of an open, democratic debate which would delimit the fundamental rules regulating the relationship between the individual and the State in criminal matters. This way of proceeding does little to promote either trust between national systems or trust of citizens in their own national polity.

---

[219] Art 82(1)(b) TFEU. See also Art 85(1) TFEU envisaging new legislation on Eurojust, whose tasks may include the resolution of conflicts of jurisdiction.

Similar issues of legitimacy and democratic deficit arise at the level of the European Union. With mutual recognition, Member States in the Council (and with the given lack of any substantial influence by the European Parliament which is currently merely consulted in criminal matters), agree on *procedure* and not on the substance of EU criminal law. They agree to extend the enforcement of national decisions in criminal matters, reproducing thus to a great extent their national systems, but no debate has taken place on the direction and aims of EU criminal law—rendering EU action in the field far from coherent. This lack of coherence is visible when one tries to address the inevitable effects of mutual recognition in nationals and the EU legal order. Attempts to remedy short-comings, especially in the area of fundamental rights protection, and to enhance trust, stumble upon EU constitutional limitations. Attempts to circumvent such limitations, by law-making or by judicial activism, may also have the effect of alienating further citizens from the EU project.

The Lisbon Treaty, if ratified, will bring about some changes in this context. The democratic deficit at EU level will be addressed by granting the European Parliament co-decision powers, while agreement on controversial measures (such as the defence rights proposal) may be easier under qualified majority voting. The Lisbon Treaty would make the adoption of such measure less complicated, as it includes a new competence for the EU to adopt measures in the field of criminal procedure, including on the rights of the defendant. However, it must be stressed that this competence has been conferred specifically in order to promote mutual recognition—which, as a method of European integration, will not lead to a debate over the development of common EU criminal law standards or the direc-tion of EU criminal law. If further legislative action on mutual recognition is forth-coming, the combination of the various mutual recognition instruments may lead to a framework for rules embracing all stages of the criminal justice process (from arrest to the execution of sentences). However, such accumulation—especially if achieved without transparency—will not necessarily lead to legitimacy or coher-ence in EU criminal law and policy and is far from guaranteeing that no gaps as to the protection of fundamental rights arise in a borderless 'area of freedom, secu-rity and justice'. In this light, developing further mutual recognition and the smooth interaction of national criminal justice systems under this system is diffi-cult to envisage, if an open, transparent debate as to the direction, content and aims of EU criminal law does not take place and the emphasis on automaticity of mutual recognition is maintained.

4

Bodies, Offices and Agencies

I. INTRODUCTION

EUROPEAN INTEGRATION IN criminal matters has been promoted significantly in recent years by the establishment of a number of EU bodies and organs with responsibilities in the field of criminal law. Some of these bodies (like Europol and Eurojust) have been established by Union legislation under the third pillar. Others, like OLAF, have a hybrid status under Community law. And others, like SitCen and the EU Counter-terrorism co-ordinator, fall mainly under the second (CFSP) pillar but have a much shakier legal basis. This chapter will place the development of these bodies in context and look in detail at their legal framework and impact in the development of EU powers in criminal matters. In doing so, the chapter will focus extensively on the extent to which EU criminal law bodies challenge State sovereignty in criminal matters. In this context, the tensions between visions of these bodies as centralised EU agencies on the one hand and looser, intergovernmental forms of co-operation on the other are particularly relevant. An examination of the powers of these bodies will be coupled with an analysis of their various accountability mechanisms as well as of the complex picture of inter-agency co-operation in criminal matters in the EU.[1] In doing so, the chapter will assess the impact of EU bodies on the development of EU criminal law and the position of the individual in this framework.

II. EUROPOL

A. Background

The establishment of the European Police Office (Europol) is emblematic of the development of EU criminal law through the creation of Union structures in the

---

[1] There have been various attempts in pinning down the concept of 'accountability' in the EU—note in particular C Harlow, *Accountability in the European Union*, Oxford, OUP 2002; and D Curtin and A Nollkaemper, 'Conceptualizing Accountability in International and European Law', *Netherlands Yearbook of International Law*, 2005, pp 3–20. Various categorisations of accountability have been put forward, including legal accountability, political accountability, administrative accountability, parliamentary accountability, financial accountability. For the purposes of this chapter, legal accountability will be treated separately under 'judicial control' and the term accountability will encompass all the other aspects, including democratic control and scrutiny.

field. The ongoing debate surrounding its role, powers and future epitomises the tension between a centralising approach viewing Europol as a central, Union police force overseeing national police forces on the one hand, and a more 'inter-governmental' approach viewing Europol as a body responsible for the co-operation and co-ordination between national police forces, with little, if any, 'operational' or coercive powers. The first view, supportive of a centralised European police force replacing looser mechanisms of police co-operation in Europe (such as TREVI[2]), was strongly put forward in the late '80s and early '90s, with the then Chancellor Helmut Kohl who repeatedly argued in favour of the establishment of a 'European FBI'.[3] This view was put forward forcefully during the negotiations, which led to the adoption of the Maastricht Treaty: under the headline 'fight against international drug trafficking and organised crime', annex 1 to the Presidency Conclusions emanating from the Luxembourg European Council of 28 and 29 June 1991 called for:

> Treaty commitment to full establishment of a *Central European Criminal Investigation Office ('Europol')* for these areas by 31.12.1993 at the latest. Details to be laid down by unanimous decision of the Council. Gradual development of Europol functions: first of all relay station for exchange of information and experience (up to 31.12.1992), then in the second phase *powers to act also within the Member States would be granted.* Right of initiative for the Commission and also for individual Member States. (emphasis added)[4]

This centralising approach was met with resistance by a number of Member States, including the United Kingdom, Denmark, the Netherlands and France.[5] National differences on the nature of police co-operation in Europe, in particular with regard to the question of how many and what kind of powers should be given to a

---

[2] TREVI was formally established following to a resolution adopted by the EC Ministers of Justice and Home Affairs in 1976. It was not based on any formal Treaty provisions and operated outside the formal Community law framework. It consisted initially of two working groups (on terrorism and public order issues) but expanded in the 1980s to cover organised crime. TREVI—which ceased to exist following the entry into force of the Maastricht Treaty which envisaged more permanent forms of co-operation within the EU framework—has been instrumental in the groundwork for the establishment of Europol. See inter alia V Mitsilegas, J Monar and W Rees, *The European Union and Internal Security*, Basingstoke, Palgrave Macmillan, 2003, pp 23–25; see also J Benyon, 'The Politics of Police Co-opera-tion in the European Union', *International Journal of the Sociology of Law*, vol 24, 1996, pp 353–379 at pp 362–363. A degree of police co-operation was also achieved by the Schengen Agreement and Convention—On the Schengen framework on police co-operation, see C. Fijnaut, 'The Schengen Treaties and European Police Co-operation', *European Journal of Crime, Criminal Law and Criminal Justice*, vol 1, 1993, pp 37–56; and more recently, M Daman, 'Cross-Border Hot Pursuit in the EU', *European Journal of Crime, Criminal Law and Criminal Justice*, vol 6, 2008, pp 171–207.

[3] For the German proposals, set in the context of the overall German position towards EU policing, see C J F Fijnaut, 'The 'Communitization' of Police Cooperation in Western Europe', in H G Schermers (ed), *Free Movement of Persons in Europe. Legal Problems and Experiences*, (Dordrecht/Boston/London: Kluwer Academic Publishers, 1993), pp 75–92.

[4] Downloaded from www.europarl.europa.eu/summits/luxembourg/lu_1en.pdf.

[5] For various reactions, see D Bigo, *Polices en réseaux. l'expérience européenne*, Paris, Presses de Sciences Po, 1996, in particular pp 210–212; M Anderson et al, *Policing the European Union*, Oxford, Clarendon Press, 1995, pp 81–82; J D Occhipinti, *The Politics of EU Police Cooperation. Toward a European FBI?*, Boulder and London, Lynne Rienner, 2003, ch 3; and Fijnaut, 'The "Communitization" of Police Cooperation', n 3 above, pp 88–91.

new EU body in the field and the closely linked question of the degree of erosion of national sovereignty in the field, gave rise to extensive debate in the negotiations of both the Maastricht Treaty and the Europol Convention itself. The main issues of contention were: the *mandate* of Europol (which offences would fall within its remit, and in particular whether terrorism would fall within its remit); its *powers* (and whether it should have 'operational' or 'coercive' powers); and its account-ability and judicial control (in particular the role of the Court of Justice in this context).[6] The compromise reached in the Maastricht Treaty has been a reference in Article K1 of the then third pillar to 'the organisation of a Union-wide *system* of exchanging information within a *European Police Office* (Europol)' (emphasis added).[7]

The entry into force of the Maastricht Treaty provided a legal basis for the nego-tiations and eventual signature of the Europol Convention in 1995. However, EU mechanisms of police co-operation were already established prior to the signature of the Europol Convention: a European Drugs Unit (EDU) was set up by Ministerial Agreement in 1993 and further formalised by a 1995 Joint Action.[8] The Unit was envisaged as a 'non-operational' team where liaison officers sent by Member States would exchange and analyse information with regard to drug trafficking, trafficking in radioactive and nuclear substances, crimes involving 'clandestine migration networks' and illicit vehicle trafficking.[9] It acted as a precursor to Europol until the start of the latter's operations in 1999.[10]

B. The Europol Convention and its Protocols

i. General

The Europol Convention was signed in 1995.[11] However, its entry into force was delayed substantially—this was largely due to the fact that the form of the adopted

---

[6] See Anderson *et al*, n 5 above., in particular pp 64–67 and 207–209; Bigo, *Polices en réseaux*, n 5 above, pp 208–248; Occhipinti, n 5 above, pp 57–59.

[7] It has been argued that the name 'European Police Office' is both neutral and flexible in allowing further extension of Europol's remit (Anderson *et al.* above, p 64—they also point out that the Treaty was accompanied by a Political Declaration where Member States expressed their commitment towards exploring ways of inter alia coordinating national investigation and search operations, creat-ing new databases and providing a central analytical facility for the planning of criminal investiga-tions—p 63). On the flexibility of the 'Europol' name see also M den Boer and W Brüggeman, 'Shifting Gear: Europol in the Contemporary Policing Era', *Politique européenne*, no 23, 2007, pp 77–91, at p 79.

[8] Joint Action 95/73/JHA, OJ L62, 20 March 1995, p 1. For details on the EDU see F R Monaco, 'Europol: The Culmination of the European Union's International Police Cooperation Efforts', *Fordham International Law Journal*, vol 19, 1995–96, pp 247–308 at pp 277 f.

[9] Art 2 of Joint Action. Its competence was extended in 1996 to cover human trafficking—OJ L342, 31 December 1996, p 4.

[10] It has been noted that the EDU's first and only coordinator was Jürgen Storbeck, who has con-tinued to serve as Director of Europol—Occhipinti, n 5 above, p 51.

[11] OJ C316, 27 November 1995, p 2.

instrument was a third pillar Convention, requiring ratification by all the (then fifteen) Member States prior to its entry into force.[12] The Convention eventually entered into force in 1998 and Europol started operations in the Hague in 1999.[13] The Europol Convention has since its signature been amended by a series of legal acts—mostly in the form of Protocols—which have clarified and extended Europol's mandate and tasks. Such legislation includes a Protocol on the interpretation of the Europol Convention by way of preliminary rulings by the ECJ;[14] Protocols on privileges and immunities;[15] a Protocol,[16] and a number of Council Decisions[17] extending Europol's competence to deal with a number of offences; a Decision designating Europol as the Central Office for combating Euro counterfeiting;[18] a Protocol on joint investigation teams and the initiation of criminal investigations;[19] and a wide-ranging Protocol introducing a number of changes in Europol's operations.[20] These measures are supplemented by a series of acts implementing the Europol Convention[21] some of which refer specifically to Europol's external action.[22] All in all, this presents a mosaic of legal provisions, incrementally expanding Europol's mandate, and entering into force in different times over the recent years. With Protocols requiring the same ratification process as the 'mother' Convention, the last amending Protocols entered into force only in 2007.[23] The next paragraphs will aim to synthesise the various legal acts in providing an overview of Europol's organisation, mandate and tasks.

ii. Europol's Organisation and Structure

Europol has legal personality and enjoys legal and contractual capacity in each Member State.[24] Its organs are the Management Board, the Director, the Financial Controller and the Financial Committee.[25] A striking 'intergovernmental' feature

---

[12] On Conventions as a third pillar legislative instrument, see ch 1.

[13] See S Peers, *EU Justice and Home Affairs Law*, 2nd edn, Oxford, Oxford University Press, 2006, p 536; see also House of Lords Select Committee on the European Union, *Europol's Role in Fighting Crime*, 5th Report, session 2002–03, HL Paper 43.

[14] OJ C299, 9 October 1996, p 2.

[15] OJ C221, 19 July 1997, p 2; and amending Protocol of 28 November 2002, OJ C312, 16 December 2002, p 2.

[16] Protocol of 30 November 2000 amending Art 2 and the Annex to the Europol Convention—extending Europol's mandate to cover money laundering offences—OJ C358, 13 December 2000, p.1.

[17] Human Trafficking (OJ C26, 30 January 1999, p 21); Terrorism (OJ C26, 30 January 1999, p 22); Forgery of money and means of payment (OJ C149, 28 May 1999, p 16); and a Council Decision authorising Europol to deal with the forms of serious crime listed in the Annex of the Europol Convention (OJ C362, 18 December 2001, p 1).

[18] OJ L185, 16 July 2005, p 35.

[19] OJ C312, 16 December 2002, p 2 (the same as the amending immunities Protocol).

[20] OJ C2, 6 January 2004, p 3.

[21] Such as Rules of Procedure—see below for further references.

[22] For details, see ch 6.

[23] For a list indicating the entry into force of the various amending Acts, see www.europa.eu/scadplus/leg/en/lvb/114005b.htm.

[24] Art 26 of the Europol Convention (paras 1 and 2 respectively).

[25] Art 27. For further details in the context of accountability arrangements see the part on accountability below.

of Europol is that its Management Board is composed of one representative per Member State (each having one vote)—with the Commission being invited at the discretion of the Board to its meetings and having non-voting status.[26] The Director—who is appointed (for a once-renewable four-year term) by the Council unanimously after receiving the opinion of the Management Board[27]—is Europol's legal representative.[28] The Director is also in charge of Europol's Deputy Directors and employees.[29]

The relationship between Europol and Member States takes place in two ways: via the Europol national units and via the liaison officers posted in Europol. The role of national units was central in the Europol Convention, its opening Article specifying that Europol will liaise 'with a single national unit in each Member State'.[30] The centrality of the national unit was also stressed in Article 4 of the Convention, stating that the national unit is 'the *only* liaison body between Europol and the competent national authorities' (emphasis added).[31] This can be seen as a safeguard for national sovereignty, limiting Europol's involvement in domestic police systems. However, this centrality of the national unit has been seriously undermined by the 2003 Protocol amending the Europol Convention (the so-called 'Danish' Protocol).[32] The latter amended the Europol Convention, which now also states that Member States 'may allow direct contacts between designated competent authorities and Europol subject to conditions determined by the Member State in question, including prior involvement of the national unit'.[33]

This provision may alter significantly the relationship between Europol and the national law enforcement systems, as it may allow a system of decentralised co-operation between Europol and national authorities. Given the discretionary character of the provision, it may lead to considerable discrepancies in national approaches, and in the number and type of national authorities enjoying direct relations with Europol. The attempt to broaden Europol's interlocutors in Member States may have to do with calls to increase the flow of information from the national level to Europol and vice-versa.[34] Among the tasks of national units as outlined in the Convention are the supply to Europol on the units' own initiative with information and intelligence, and the supply to Europol of information

---

[26] Art 28(2) and (4) respectively.

[27] Art 29(1). Europol's Directors thus far have been Jürgen Storbeck and Max-Peter Ratzel, both from Germnay.

[28] Art 29(5).

[29] Art 30(2).

[30] Art 1(2).

[31] Art 4(2). The paragraph continues by stating that relationships between the national unit and the competent authorities will be governed by national law, and in particular the relevant national constitutional requirements.

[32] See n 20 above.

[33] Amended Art 4(2).

[34] The same Protocol added a fourth paragraph to Art 9 of the Europol Convention allowing competent authorities designated as such by Member States to also query the Europol information system. However, the result of the query will only indicate whether the requested data is available in the Europol information system—further information may then be obtained via the Europol national unit.

for storage in its computerised system.[35] This aspect of co-operation between national units and Europol is perceived to be central to the effectiveness of Europol, and the involvement of a greater number of national authorities may be deemed as a step towards maximising such co-operation. To this end, a further amendment brought forward in the Danish Protocol calls on the Heads of Europol national units (HENUs) to meet 'on a regular basis' to assist Europol 'at their own motion or on request', by giving advice.[36]

The other side of Europol's relationship with national authorities is the secondment of national liaison officers to Europol—each national unit must send at least one such officer to the Hague.[37] In a noteworthy provision, stressing—at least on paper—the centrality of Member States, the Convention states that liaison officers must be instructed by their national units '*to represent the interests of the latter* within Europol in accordance with the national law of the seconding Member State and in compliance with the provisions applicable to the administration of Europol'(emphasis added).[38] Liaison officers have the task of assisting in the exchange of information between national units and Europol, in particular by providing information from the national unit to Europol and vice-versa, and by providing analysis advice to Europol regarding information from their Member State.[39] In this context, liaison officers have the right to consult Europol information.[40] The presence of liaison officers in the Hague not only represents a socialisation process of police officers from the different Member States towards a framework of European policing, but may also constitute in practice a considerable pool of information exchange and analysis on the basis of informal relations.[41]

iii. Europol's Objectives and Mandate

It is noteworthy that, in the Europol Convention, Europol's objective is inextricably linked with its mandate (namely the offences for which it is competent to act). The determination of Europol's mandate has been a gradual process of extension, provided for by the Convention itself and, as seen above, a series of amending legislation. The determination of Europol's mandate has thus been the subject of ongoing debate, a debate which lies at the heart of the discussion on what Europol should really be about. The core provision on Europol's objective and mandate,

[35] Art 4(1) and (6) respectively.

[36] Amended Art 4(7). On the role of HENUs, see Europol's 2007 Annual Report which can be found at www.europol.europa.eu/publications/Annual_Reports/Annual%20Report%202007.pdf.

[37] Art 5(1). See also the Act of the Europol Management Board concerning the rights and obligations of liaison officers, OJ C26, 30 January 1999, p 86.

[38] Art 5(2).

[39] Art 5(3).

[40] Art 5(5).

[41] On informality in the work of Europol but also its relationship with other EU bodies, see D Bigo et al, *The Field of the EU Internal Security Agencies*, Paris, L'Harmatan/Centre d'études sur les conflits, 2007, in particular at p 29. For examples of informality involving the external aspect of Europol's work, see the Europol Annual Report for 2007 above, indicating that FBI officers are now located in The Hague.

Article 2 of the Europol Convention, has been amended by the 2003 'Danish Protocol' which in this context attempted to consolidate a number of previous amendments. The first part of Article 2(1) now reads as follows (the main changes to the original Europol Convention are indicated in italics):

> The objective of Europol shall be, within the framework of police cooperation between the Member States pursuant to the Treaty of the European Union, to improve, by means of the measures referred to in this Convention, the effectiveness and cooperation of the competent authorities in the Member States in preventing and combating *serious international crime* where there are factual indications *or reasonable grounds for believing that* an organised criminal structure is involved and two or more Member States are affected in such a way as to require a common approach by the Member States owing to the scale, significance and consequences of the offences concerned. (emphasis added)

Europol's mandate (and consequently objective) has thus been expanded to include serious international crime in general, including instances where there are merely 'reasonable grounds to believe' that serious, transnational, organised crime is involved—this test is broader than the original version of Article 2 which required the existence of factual indications for Europol's involvement. On the other hand, it is noteworthy that Europol's mandate remains limited to serious, transnational, organised crime (this is notwithstanding the fact that the legal definition of organised crime in EU law is not conductive to legal certainty)[42]. Amended Article 2(1) continues by stating which forms of crime will be considered as serious international crime: following earlier amendments to the Convention, these now include a wide range of offences including terrorism and money laundering. There is also reference to the annex of the Convention, which includes inter alia fraud offences. The inclusion of fraud in Europol's mandate has raised the issue of the reach of Europol into the domestic administrative systems—this has been addressed by a Declaration attached to the Danish Protocol limiting Europol's competence in the field.[43] It has also raised inevitably the issue of overlap between Europol and OLAF, the European Anti-Fraud Office, whose primary purpose is the investigation of fraud against the Community budget.[44] The issue of overlap, and a certain competition between the two bodies, could already be discerned when Europol was designated as the Central Office for Euro

---

[42] See ch.2.

[43] OJ C2, 6 January 2004, p 2. It is stated that fraud covers,

> as far as tax fraud and customs fraud is concerned, competences to Europol only in the field of improvement of the effectiveness and cooperation of the competent authorities of the Member States responsible for the functioning of the criminal law enforcement system and not their authorities responsible for ensuring the levying of taxes and customs duties.

This repeats a similar Declaration attached to the 2001 Council Decision extending Europol's mandate to deal with the crimes listed in the annex of the Europol Convention—OJ C362, 18 December 2001, p 2, para 1.

[44] On OLAF see part IV below. On the challenges surrounding the relationship between Europol and OLAF see C Fijnaut, 'Police Co-operation and the Area of Freedom, Security and Justice', in N Walker (ed), *Europe's Area of Freedom, Security and Justice*, Oxford, Oxford University Press, 2004, pp 241–282 at pp 264–265.

counterfeiting.[45] The 2001 Decision extending Europol's mandate to cover fraud (as one of the offences listed in the annex of the Europol Convention) contained a Declaration whereby the Council agreed that this extension 'must take into account of OLAF's competence for fraud and lead to the negotiation of an agreement between Europol and the Commission'.[46] However, this Declaration was not repeated in the subsequent Danish Protocol.[47]

iv. Europol's Tasks

a. General

The tasks of Europol are outlined in Article 3 of the Convention, which has also been subject to a number of amendments.[48] All of Europol's tasks take place within the framework of the objective defined in Article 2(1). Tasks are divided into 'principal', 'additional', and further supporting actions. According to Article 3(1), as amended, Europol's principal tasks are:

1. to facilitate the exchange of information between the Member States
2. to obtain, collate and analyse information and intelligence
3. to notify the competent authorities of the Member States without delay via the national units referred to in Article 4 of information concerning them and of any connections identified between criminal offences
4. to aid investigations in the Member States by forwarding all relevant information to the national units
5. to maintain a computerised system of collected information containing data
6. to participate in a support capacity in joint investigation teams[49]
7. to ask the competent authorities of the Member States concerned to conduct or co-ordinate investigations in specific cases[50]

Article 3(2) sets 'additional' tasks for Europol. These include developing specialist knowledge of the investigative procedures of the competent authorities in the

---

[45] See also new Art 3(4) of the Europol Convention as inserted by the 'Danish' Protocol. On the tensions between Europol and OLAF in this context, see House of Lords European Union Committee, *Europol's Role in Fighting Crime*, n 13 above, paras 27–29.

[46] OJ C362, 18 December 2001, p 2, para 2.

[47] An 'Administrative Arrangement' between Europol and OLAF was concluded in 2004, following a 2003 'Administrative Agreement' between Europol and the Commission (which included specific arrangements regarding Euro counterfeiting—for both texts see www.europol.eu). The Europol-OLAF document refers inter alia to the exchange of strategic and technical information between the two bodies, to intelligence co-operation and participation in joint investigation teams. However, it is not clear whether this document fully addresses the 2001 Council Declaration calling on Europol to take into account OLAF's fraud competence.

[48] See in particular the 2002 and 2003 Protocols—see above.

[49] Added by the 2002 Protocol.

[50] ibid. In his evidence to the House of Lords European Union Committee, the Europol Director Max-Peter Ratzel described Europol's role in relation to Member States as threefold: information facilitator; provider of strategic and operational analysis; and provider of operational support. Uncorrected oral evidence for the inquiry into Europol, 24 June 2008, Q167, at www.publications.parliament.uk/pa/ld/lduncorr/euf240608ev5.pdf.

Member States and providing advice on investigations; providing strategic intelligence; and preparing general situation reports. According to Article 3(3), Europol may have a number of additional tasks 'in accordance with the staffing and budgetary resources at its disposal and within the limits set by the Management Board'—these take the form of assisting Member States through advice and research in areas such as training, technical support and crime prevention. As mentioned above, new Article 3(4) confirms that Europol will act as an EU contact point for Euro counterfeiting.[51]

It is evident from the above that the collection, exchange and analysis of personal data are central to the existence of Europol. The role of Europol in this context will be examined in a separate section below, which will provide an analysis of the Europol databases, its powers in this context and the underlying data protection framework.[52] This section will focus on a number of other tasks, which are also important and represent to some extent the evolution of Europol over the years.

b. Initiation of Investigations

As mentioned above, one of Europol's new tasks is to ask the competent authorities of Member States to conduct or co-ordinate investigations. The framework for such requests is outlined in new Article 3b of the Convention (also inserted by the 2002 Protocol), according to which Member States 'should deal with' any request from Europol to initiate, conduct or co-ordinate investigations and should give such requests 'due consideration'.[53] Member States are not obliged to accept Europol's requests but they must inform Europol of whether the requested investigation will be initiated, and, if the answer is negative, they must in principle give reasons for their refusal.[54] This provision largely mirrors the provision in the Eurojust Decision granting Eurojust the power to ask national authorities to begin investigations.[55] National authorities can be requested to initiate investigations by both Europol and Eurojust. This duplication of tasks between the two EU bodies may lead to increased pressure for the initiation of investigations at national level. It also signifies that the boundaries between police and prosecutorial/judicial functions at EU level are blurred.

c. Joint Investigation Teams and Europol participation

Another amendment to the Europol Convention concerns its participation in joint investigation teams. The establishment of such teams was mandated by the

---

[51] For the wording of Arts 3(3) and 3(4) see the 'Danish' 2003 Protocol.
[52] Sub-section vi below.
[53] Art 3b(1) first indent.
[54] Art 3b (1) last indent and Art 3b (2) respectively.
[55] This is implicitly acknowledged in the Europol Convention, which requires Europol to inform Eurojust when making a request for the initiation of investigations—Art 3b(4).

2000 Convention on Mutual Legal Assistance (MLA Convention),[56] and later by a Framework Decision on Joint Investigation Teams (JIT Framework Decision).[57] These instruments enable Member States to set up Joint Investigation Teams 'for a specific purpose and a limited period, which may be extended by mutual consent, to carry out criminal investigations in one or more of the Member States setting up the team'.[58] The setting up of such teams would be by 'mutual agreement' between the participating Member States[59]—with the Council adopting subsequently a Recommendation on such a model agreement.[60] Joint investigation teams thus represent a significant inroad into State sovereignty in policing, by allowing officers from various Member States to operate in the territory of another Member State.[61] The establishment of joint investigation teams raises a number of practical and legal issues related to trust, liability and applicable law.[62]

Neither the MLA Convention nor the JIT Framework Decision contain detailed rules regarding the participation of Union bodies such as Europol in joint investigation teams.[63] Detailed rules concerning Europol were introduced in the Europol Convention by the 2002 Protocol. New Article 3a of the Europol Convention provides a legal basis for the participation of Europol officials in joint investigation teams. Such participation (whose administrative implementation will be laid down in an 'arrangement' between the Director of Europol and the authorities of the participating Member States[64]) must be *in a support capacity* and as far as these teams are investigating criminal offences for which Europol is competent.[65] Europol officials may *assist in all activities and exchange information* with all members of the joint investigation team but they cannot take part in the 'taking of any coercive measures'.[66] Europol officials may liaise directly with the members of the team and provide them with information from any of the components of its com-

---

[56] OJ C197, 12 July 2000, Art 13.

[57] OJ L162, 20 June 2002, p 1. The Framework Decision largely replicates the text of the Mutual Legal Assistance Convention and was deemed necessary at the time because of the delay in the entry into force of the latter (largely due, as with the Europol Convention, to the ratification requirements for this type of Union law instrument).

[58] Art 13(1) of the MLA Convention; Art 1(1) of the JIT Framework Decision.

[59] ibid.

[60] OJ C121, 23 May 2003, p 1.

[61] This goes further than the limited provisions of hot pursuit in the Schengen Convention—see in particular Art 40 of the Convention.

[62] On various aspects of joint investigation teams, see C Rijken and G Vermeulen (eds.), *Joint Investigation Teams in the European Union. From Theory to Practice*, The Hague, T M C Asser Press, 2006.

[63] Although the Preamble to the Framework Decision states that Member States should have the possibility to allow participation in joint investigation teams of representatives of bodies such as Europol and OLAF (recital 9). Similarly, the Model Agreement put forward by the Council includes a section on participation by officials from Europol/Eurojust/OLAF (s7).

[64] Art 3a(2) See also the—rather skeleton—Decision of the Europol Management Board laying down the rules governing such arrangements (OJ C72, 29 March 2007, p 35, in particular Arts 2 and 3).

[65] Art 3a(1) first indent.

[66] Art 3a(1) second indent.

puterised information system.[67] Information obtained by Europol officials may be included, under certain conditions, in the Europol databases.[68]

The above overview of both the establishment of EU joint investigation teams and the legal framework underlying Europol's participation therein demonstrate the potential for a significant expansion of police powers via two main features: extraterritoriality and informality. Police officers from Member States, and Europol officials, are allowed to operate 'extraterritorially', in the territory of another Member State. This arrangement leads to a spatial expansion of the reach of police powers in the EU. Such powers may increase, in particular in the light of the minimalist EU legal framework regulating joint investigation teams, a framework which leaves a wide range of issues to be determined by further implementing agreements or 'arrangements' between the authorities concerned.[69] Moreover, with regard to Europol, the wording of a number of the few legal provisions which were inserted in the Convention has been drafted in broad, unclear terms—in particular the provision stipulating that Europol may 'assist in all activities' of a joint investigation team.[70] While Europol officials are precluded from taking 'coercive' measures, it is not clear whether this will stop them in practice assuming operational tasks on the ground as members of a joint investigation team.

This lack of legal certainty is also linked with another major feature of common action under EU joint investigation teams—informality. As it has been noted, the informal exchange of information has been a major factor behind the establishment of joint investigation teams, in the light of the long delays in formal cooperation in criminal matters.[71] For Europol, this is significant because its participating officials may liaise and exchange information on the ground with officers from a number of EU Member States, with very little by way of legislation covering such interaction. Moreover, information gathered within the framework of a joint investigation team may be inserted in the Europol databases. This may serve as a major boost to Europol's work in its attempt to gather more information from Member States.

---

[67] Art 3a(4). The Decision of the Europol Management Board laying down arrangements for the participation of Europol officials in joint investigation teams states that such arrangements will specify that Europol officials will have access to the Europol computerised system for the duration of their membership in the joint investigation team (Art 5).

[68] Art 3a(5). There are also provisions on the applicable law in cases of the commission of offences by or against Europol officials in the context of joint investigation teams (Art 3a(6)) and provisions on liability (new Art 39a of the Europol Convention) and privileges and immunities (new Art 8(4) added to the Protocol on privileges and immunities of Europol officials).

[69] On this point, see also C Rijken, 'Joint Investigation Teams: Principles, Practice, and Problems. Lessons Learnt from the First Efforts to Establish a JIT', *Utrecht Law Review*, vol 2, issue 2, 2006, pp 99–118 at p 102.

[70] See B de Buck, 'Joint Investigation Teams: The Participation of Europol Officials', *ERA Forum* vol 8, 2007, pp 253–264 at p 259.

[71] Rijken, n 59 above, p 117.

d. Providing Intelligence

One of the 'additional' tasks set out in the Europol Convention, which has assumed increased importance over the years, is the task of providing strategic intelligence.[72] It has been argued that the logic of intelligence-led policing seems to be 'pervasive' in the case of Europol.[73] This argument is based on the increasing emphasis by Europol on the production of Threat Assessments 'to assess *future* threats and the groups of populations from which they are likely to emanate' (emphasis added).[74] This trend was prevalent in the Hague Programme, which called on Europol with effect from 1 January 2006 to replace its crime situation reports by yearly threat assessments.[75] A look at Europol's website seems to confirm this change: the publications page begins by the Europol 'EU Terrorism Situation and Trend Reports' and continues with the 'European Organised Crime Threat Assessments' (which have replaced, since 2006, Europol's Organised Crime Reports).[76] As it has been noted, the replacement of the traditional organised crime reports by threat assessments codifies a practice of making 'anticipatory analytical reports' on crime phenomena.[77] Europol itself claims that:

> the various threat assessments produced by the organisation, on the basis of information and intelligence sent by the Member States, constitute the cornerstone of a European intelligence-led policing system for the fight against organised crime. Europol's analytical input sets in motion the execution of the European Criminal Intelligence Model (ECIM). Based on the experience of the National Criminal Intelligence Model (NIM) currently used in the UK, the ECIM is a four-step cyclical process which starts by an assessment of the threat at European level from which political priorities in internal security are drawn. *By anticipating better* the criminal developments, the intelligence-led policing approach enables the political level to decide about the priorities while the operational level use resources more effectively. (emphasis added)[78]

v. Europol's Databases

Central to the work of Europol is the maintenance of a computerised information system. This system consists of the following components:

—an information system (the so-called Europol Information System);
—analysis work files (AWFs); and
—an index system[79]

---

[72] Art 3(2)(2).
[73] D Bigo *et al*, n 41 above, p 39.
[74] ibid
[75] OJ C53, 3 March 2005, p 1, point 2.3.
[76] www.europol.europa.eu/index.asp?page=publications&language=
[77] M den Boer, 'New Dimensions in EU Police Co-operation: the Hague Milestones for What They Are Worth', in J W de Zwaan and F A N J Goudappel (eds), *Freedom, Security and Justice in the European Union*, The Hague, T C M Asser Press, 2006, pp 221–232 at p 226.
[78] Europol, submission to the House of Lords Select Committee to the European Union, Inquiry into Europol, The Hague, 28 April 2008, File no 3100–174, para 1.1.
[79] Art 6(1) of the Europol Convention.

A central principle of the Europol Convention is that the Europol computerised information system 'must under no circumstances be linked to other automated processing systems, except for the automated processing systems of the national units'.[80]

The *Europol Information System* was only established in 2005.[81] According to Europol, it was technically ready to be used by Member States at national level in October 2005, but each Member State had to sign a bilateral agreement for the interconnection of the computer networks between Europol and the national competent services, a process which was completed for all Member States in February 2008.[82] The Information System contains information which is the direct input of the Europol national units and liaison officers, as well as data which Europol itself inserted directly (such data is supplied to Europol by third States and bodies or consists of analysis data).[83] It contains information on persons who have been convicted for one of the offences which fall within Europol's mandate; persons who are suspected of having committed or having taken part in one of these offences; and persons for whom there are serious grounds under national law for believing that they will commit such offences.[84] Personal data may include in principle *only* name, date and place of birth, nationality, sex and where necessary 'other characteristics likely to assist in identification'.[85] Data in the Europol Information System is directly accessible for consultation by national units, liaison officers, the Director, the Deputy Directors and 'duly empowered Europol officials'.[86] However, the 'Danish' Protocol allowed Member States to extend (albeit more limited) access to other designated competent authorities.[87]

Europol may also open *Analysis Work Files* (AWFs) for the purposes of analysis 'defined as the assembly, processing or utilisation of data with the aim of helping a criminal investigation'.[88] The information contained therein is more extensive than the limited categories of data included in its Information System: information in AWFs may also include a wide range of information on witnesses (actual or potential), victims, contacts and associates and informers.[89] Details on the information which may be contained in an AWF and its processing are included in the Rules applicable to such files.[90] These specify that AWFs are opened on the

---

[80] Art 6(2).

[81] See Peers, *EU Justice*, n 13 above, p 551; see also R Genson and P Zanders, 'Le développement de la coopération policiere dans l'Union européenne. Quel avenir pour Europol?', *Revue du Marché commun et de l'Union européenne*, 2007, pp 5–13 at p 8. The authors note that the first instances of work by the system were organised by the Belgian presidency in 2001, but that the final decision as to the technical components of the system was taken in 2005.

[82] Europol, submission to House of Lords, n 78 above, para 5.1.3 where further details can be found.

[83] Art 7(1).

[84] Art 8(1) of the Europol Convention.

[85] Art 8(2). But see a list of further information which can be included in Art 8(3).

[86] Arts 7(1) and 9(1).

[87] New Art 9(4).

[88] Art 7(2).

[89] Art 10(1).

[90] Council Act adopting rules applicable to Europol analysis files, OJ C26, 30 January 1999, p 1. These were amended in 2007 (OJ L277, 20 October 2007, p 23).

initiative of Europol or at the request of the Member States supplying the data[91] and classifies AWF as general or strategic, and operational.[92] According to the Rules, personal data in AWFs related to persons mentioned in Article 10(1)(1) of the Europol Convention (namely suspects) include data such as personal details, physical description, identification means (including forensic identification information such as fingerprints, DNA evaluation results, voice profile, blood group, dental information), occupation and skills, economic and financial information, behavioural data (including lifestyle, movements, places frequented, weapons, danger rating, specific risks, criminal-related traits and profiles, and drug abuse), contacts and associates, means of communication and transport, information related to criminal activities, references to other databases (including those of public and private bodies) and information on legal persons.[93] Analysis Work Files are closely linked with 'intelligence-led' policing.[94]

Access to Europol Analysis Files was originally limited to analysis groups consisting of analysts and other Europol officials designated by the Europol Directorate (only analysts are authorised to enter data into and retrieve data from an AWF) and the liaison officers and/or experts of the Member States supplying the information or concerned by the analysis.[95] However, the 2003 'Danish' Protocol amended the Europol Convention to significantly extend access to AWFs. A new paragraph was added to Article 10 of the Convention, stating that Europol may invite experts of third States or third bodies to be associated with the activities of an analysis group.[96] The association of such experts with Europol analysis groups will be subject to an 'arrangement' between Europol and a third State/body and the rules governing such arrangements will be determined by the Europol Management Board acting by a majority of two thirds of its members.[97] In this manner, the precise rules and safeguards underlying a significant extension of access to Europol analysis files containing a wide range of personal data is left to an executive decision subject to minimal scrutiny and transparency.[98]

---

[91] Art 12(1).

[92] Art 10. This distinction is also implicit in Art 10(6) of the Europol Convention.

[93] Art 6, where further details on data included in AWFs can be found.

[94] This link was explained by the Director of Europol to the House of Lords European Union Committee (n 78 above, Q172) as follows:

> Crime analysis can be done in various different ways. You can do crime scene analysis. You can analyse the *modus operandi*, you can analyse the dates of the events, you can analyse the places of the events, et cetera, and you can mix up the various approaches, so a close interaction is needed between the people who do the analysis and those people who are investigating the case. This is exactly one of the triggering points of intelligence-led policing.

[95] Art 10(2) of the Europol Convention.

[96] New Art 10(9).

[97] ibid.

[98] The move to majority voting is also noteworthy, suggesting a shift from an extreme intergovernmental approach. However, the shift concerns only decisions by Member States (which are members of the Management Board) and does not extend to other Union institutions in this context.

Europol databases also contain an *Index System* for data stored in Analysis Work Files.[99] The Director, Deputy Directors and 'duly empowered officials' of Europol and liaison officers have the right to consult the index system.[100] The index system is designed to help the liaison officers consulting it to ascertain that the files in question contain data concerning their seconding Member State (and whether specific items of information are stored therein)—however, it must not be possible to establish 'connections or further conclusions regarding the content of the files'.[101]

vi. Data Processing and Data Protection

The Europol legal framework contains a wide range of sources and provisions on the processing of data collected and analysed by Europol and data protection (with data protection provisions largely included systematically within broader provisions on processing). Provisions on data processing and data protection can be found in the Europol Convention itself, but also in implementing instruments such as the Rules on Analysis Work Files.[102] Provisions may be general, applying to all forms of data processing by Europol, but also specific to certain categories of Europol files, such as Analysis Work Files.[103] This part will deal primarily with the general rules on Europol data processing and protection, with references to other, more specific provisions included when necessary.

The main body of law related to data processing and protection by Europol can be found in Title IV of the Europol Convention entitled 'common provisions on information processing'.[104] These include specific rules on the use of data, [105] the reporting on and identification of retrievals of personal data by Europol,[106] of the right of access of individuals to their personal data,[107] correction and deletion of data,[108] time limits for the storage and deletion of data,[109] the transfer of data to

---

[99] Art 11(1).

[100] Art 11(2).

[101] ibid.

[102] See for instance Art 4 of the Rules.

[103] See for instance Art 10(1) of the Europol Convention.

[104] Arts 13–25. To this body of law, the 2003 'Danish' Protocol added a new provision, located in a different part of the Convention: new Art 6a entitled 'information processing by Europol'. This provision in effect extends Europol's powers of data processing by allowing it to also process data for the purpose of determining whether such data are relevant for its tasks and can be included in its databases. Art 6a does not contain specific rules on processing: rather, it leaves the adoption of such rules to the Council, which will determine (in another indication of a slight shift from an extreme 'intergovernmental' position) conditions related to the processing of such data by a two-thirds majority.

[105] Art 17.

[106] Art 16. See also the Decision of the Management Board of Europol on the control mechanisms for retrievals from the computerised system of collected information, OJ C72, 29 March 2007, p 30.

[107] Art 19.

[108] Art 20.

[109] Art 21. Its third para states that storage of personal data on suspects may not exceed a total of three years—but adding that each time limit will begin to run afresh on the date on which an event leading to the storage of data relating to the individual occurs. Art 22 concerns the correction and storage of data in paper files.

third states and bodies,[110] and data security.[111] The general standard of data protection is defined by reference not to European Union, but to Council of Europe instruments of varying legal force. The Europol data protection standard must at least correspond to the standard resulting from the implementation of the 1981 Council of Europe data protection Convention taking into account the Council of Europe Recommendation No R(87) 15 concerning the use of personal data in the police sector.[112]

Responsibility for data protection lies with the Member States for the information that they input into the Europol system, and with Europol in respect of data communicated to it by third parties or which result from analyses conducted by it.[113] Europol is also responsible for all data received and processed by it.[114] This two-fold system of data protection (shared between Europol and Member States) is also adopted in the design of data protection monitoring mechanisms. Each Member State must designate a national supervisory body, the task of which is to monitor independently, in accordance with its respective national law, the input to and retrieval from the Europol system of personal data by the Member State concerned, as well as to monitor the activities of the Europol national unit in that Member State.[115] In addition to national supervisory bodies, there is also a Europol Joint Supervisory Body (JSB), which has the task of ensuring that the rights of the individual are not violated and of monitoring the transmission of data originating by Europol.[116] In this context, the Europol JSB, which is composed of members of the national supervisory bodies,[117] has access to Europol documents and databases, as well as free access at any time to the Europol premises.[118] Individuals have the right to request the JSB to ensure the lawfulness and accuracy of the collection, storage, processing and use of their personal data by Europol.[119] The JSB is also an appellate body for cases involving access of individuals to Europol data and correction and deletion of personal data by Europol[120]— Europol must then 'carry out' the JSB decisions in such cases.[121] The JSB must also

---

[110] Art 18. For more on the transfer of data to third bodies see sub—part x below. For more on third states, see ch.6.

[111] Art 25.

[112] Art 14.

[113] Art 15(1).

[114] Art 15(2).

[115] Art 23(1). The Convention also grants, in accordance with national law, a right to individuals to request the national supervisory body to ensure that the entry or communication of data concerning them to Europol and the consultation of the data by the Member State concerned are lawful—Art 23(2).

[116] Art 24(1). The JSB is also competent for the examination of questions relating to the implementation and interpretation in connection with Europol's activities as regards the processing and use of personal data (Art 24(3)).

[117] ibid.

[118] Art 24(2) indents (1) and (2). For more details regarding the JSB's tasks and powers see the JSB Rules of Procedure, OJ C149, 28 May 1999, p 1.

[119] Art 24(4).

[120] Arts 19(7) and 20(4) respectively.

[121] Art 24(2) indent (3).

be consulted with regard to the transfer of personal data by Europol to third States or bodies—but its opinion is not binding.[122]

vii. Judicial Control

One of the thorniest issues in the negotiations of the Europol Convention has been the subjection of Europol to the judicial control of the Court of Justice (ECJ). With multiple changes in the drafts, and Member States such as the United Kingdom strongly opposed to ECJ involvement, the finally adopted text contains very little on the issue.[123] The Europol Convention merely included a provision on the 'settlement of disputes' providing that disputes between Member States on the interpretation or application of the Europol Convention will initially be discussed at the Council with the aim of finding a settlement and, if this is not possible within six months, parties to the dispute will decide among themselves on the modalities of settlement.[124] There followed however a Protocol amending the Europol Convention to allow the interpretation, by way of preliminary rulings, of the Convention by the ECJ.[125] The adoption of the Protocol did not mean however that the Court's jurisdiction extended automatically to all Member States: in a technique similar to the one followed with regard to the Court's jurisdiction in the third pillar in Amsterdam, Member States are asked to make a Declaration by which they accept ECJ jurisdiction to give preliminary rulings on the interpretation of the Europol Convention.[126] The already limited judicial control of Europol acts[127] is thus further limited, made subject to the political will of Member States.[128]

viii. Accountability and Transparency

As mentioned above, a body having a central role in the functioning of Europol is the Management Board, which consists of one representative per Member State. The Management Board is responsible for a wide range of aspects of the

---

[122] Art 18(2).

[123] On the background, see in particular Anderson *et al.* above, pp 207–209; Occhipinti, n 5 above, pp 57–58; E Denza, *The Intergovernmental Pillars of the European Union*, Oxford, OUP, 2002, pp 314–315.

[124] Art 40(1) and (2). By a Declaration attached to the Convention, a number of Member States agreed to submit such disputes to the Court of Justice.

[125] OJ C299, 9 October 1996, p 1.

[126] Art 2 of the Protocol.

[127] See also the extensive privileges and immunities enjoyed by the Europol Directors, members and employees—Art 41 of the Convention and the privileges and immunities Protocol (OJ C221, 19 July 1997, p 2), as amended (OJ C312, 16 December 2002, p 1).

[128] The former Europol Director, Jürgen Storbeck, is held to also advocating limited judicial control of Europol, on the basis of the argument that there is only place for judicial control of Europol in the European context if Europol is able to independently instigate investigations—quoted in T Schalken and M Pronk, 'On Joint Investigation Teams, Europol and Supervision of Their Joint Actions', *European Journal of Crime, Criminal Law and Criminal Justice*, vol 10, no 1, 2002, pp 70–82 at p 74.

implementation of the Europol Convention (including the adoption of a number of sets of implementing rules), has a role in budgetary matters, as well as the appointment and dismissal of Europol's Director.[129] The latter is accountable to the Management Board in respect of the performance of his/her duties.[130] The Management Board is vested thus with considerable powers, but there is very little in terms of its accountability, which is achieved primarily by adopting and submitting annual Reports to the Council.[131] It is thus the Council (which also appoints the Europol Director)[132] which is responsible for this form of 'soft' accountability for the Management Board—this mechanism, along with the appointment and composition of the Board confirm the largely intergovernmental character of Europol. Another striking intergovernmental feature of Europol (along with the framework applying to its Management Board and Director, and the issue of judicial control examined above), can be found in the budget arrangements, with Europol being funded by Member States' contributions and not by the EU budget.[133]

Another form of accountability of Europol comes via transparency, in particular access to documents.[134] While the Europol Convention did not say much in this respect, the 2003 'Danish' Protocol inserted new Article 32a on a right to access to Europol documents—this provision called upon the Management Board[135] to adopt rules for access to Europol documents taking into account the relevant Community law. The outcome of this amendment—which demonstrates a remarkable shift towards the application of first pillar principles to Europol— has been the adoption of specific Rules for Access to Europol documents, the Preamble of which stresses the need for openness and cross-refers again to Community law.[136]

ix. Parliamentary Scrutiny

With the Europol Convention and its Protocols being third pillar instruments, the European Parliament's role towards their adoption was extremely limited.[137] Moreover, as seen in various instances thus far, the European Parliament (but also

---

[129] See Art 28 of the Europol Convention.

[130] Art 29(5).

[131] A general report on Europol's activities during the previous year, and a report on Europol's future activities—Art 28(9).

[132] Art 29(1).

[133] Art 35(2).

[134] On access to documents provisions with regard to Community/Union agencies/bodies, as well as a comparison of Europol accountability provisions with Community agencies, see D Curtin, 'Delegation to EU Non-majoritarian Agencies and Emerging Practices of Public Accountability', in D Geradin, R Munoz and N Petit, *Regulation through Agencies in the EU. A New Paradigm of European Governance*, Cheltenham, Edward Elgar, 2005, pp 88–119.

[135] Again acting by two-thirds majority.

[136] OJ C72, 29 March 2007, p 37. See in particular recitals 3 and 5.

[137] However, the need for domestic ratification of this type of third pillar instrument does give an— albeit ex post—say to national parliaments.

the Council itself) has a minimal role in the development of implementing rules to the Europol Convention, the adoption of a number of which is delegated to the Management Board. In terms of informing the European Parliament of Europol's activities, the Europol Convention included a provision calling for the submission of an annual 'special report' by the Council Presidency to the Parliament.[138] However, even in dispensing with this very weak accountability duty, the Presidency should 'take into account the obligations of discretion and confidentiality'.[139] This provision has now been amended: instead of a written Report, the Presidency or its representative 'may appear' before the Parliament 'with a view to discuss general questions relating to Europol'.[140] The Presidency may be assisted by the Director of Europol and must again take into account discretion and confidentiality.[141] The obligation to submit a written Report has thus been replaced by a—rather weakly worded—possibility of appearance of the Presidency (and possibly, the word 'may' is repeated here, the Europol Director), before Parliament but seemingly only to discuss general questions—a clear sign of the intergovernmental emphasis in Europol and of the very limited role of the European Parliament.

x. Relations with Other Bodies

Articles 10(4) and 42 of the Europol Convention provide the legal basis for co-operation between Europol and third bodies (including EU bodies) and states for the purposes of information exchange.[142] In the light of these provisions,[143] and amendments to the Europol Convention,[144] Europol has entered into a number of co-operation agreements and arrangements with third bodies and states. As far as EU bodies are concerned, along with the Europol–OLAF co-operation arrangements mentioned earlier in this chapter, of note are the 2004 agreement on the exchange of information between Europol and Eurojust[145] and the recently signed 'strategic co-operation agreement' between Europol and Frontex.[146] The latter

---

[138] Art 34(1), which also stated that the Parliament would be consulted should the Europol Convention be amended in any way.

[139] Art 34(2).

[140] See 'Danish' Protocol, amended Art 34(2).

[141] ibid.

[142] See also the rules governing Europol's external relations with EU-related bodies (adopted by the Management Board, OJ C26, 30 January 1999, p 89) and those governing relations with third states and non-EU related bodies (drawn up by the Council, OJ C26, 30 January 1999, p 19). See also the Council Decision authorising the Director of Europol to enter into negotiations on agreements with third states and non-EU related bodies (OJ C106, 13 April 2000, p 1) and its subsequent amendments.

[143] And the specific conditions in relation to the transfer of Europol data to third states and bodies contained in Art 18 of the Europol Convention.

[144] See in particular the association of experts of third parties with Europol analysis files—see sub-section v above.

[145] The Agreement was mandated by the new Art 42(3) inserted in the Europol Convention by the Danish Protocol. For the text of the agreement itself, see www.europol.europa.eu; for further information see section III below on Eurojust.

[146] www.europol.europa.eu/index.asp?page=news&news=pr080402.htm

raises the issue of the extent of co-operation between bodies established for different purposes, including the exchange of data between these bodies.[147] Such co-operation blurs the boundaries both between the pillars, and between the functions and powers of the various bodies and agencies—a further example is the calls to boost co-operation between Europol and civilian ESDP Missions as regards the mutual exchange of information.[148] As far as third bodies and states are concerned, noteworthy are the agreements on exchange of information between Europol and Interpol, and Europol and the United States.[149] In all these agreements, the issue of whether privacy and data protection are safeguarded in the light of the extensive exchange of personal data envisaged is central.[150]

C. The Future of Europol—The Europol Decision

The completion of the amendments to the Europol Convention and the fact that the last of the Protocols entered into force only in 2007 has not stopped ongoing discussions on the future Europol (which was also prominent in the negotiations leading to the EU Constitutional Treaty).[151] Discussions, which continued notwithstanding the 'freezing' of the Constitutional Treaty, focused on two main issues: the change in the legal basis of Europol (with calls to replace the Europol Convention with a more flexible third pillar instrument such as a Decision), and the change in Europol's mandate and powers (in particular the question of whether Europol should become more 'operational'). The 2006 Austrian EU Presidency prioritised the debate, by organising a High Level Conference on the Future of Europol and by commissioning a 'Friends of the Presidency' Working Group to discuss the issue. Both initiatives proposed sweeping changes to the current Europol framework: The High Level Conference called for making Europol 'operational', and called for ways to be found 'to enable Europol to exchange information also with countries that do not have the same data protection standards as those that are applicable within the European Union'.[152] The 'Friends of the Presidency' Report went further, in particular as regards the issue of information collection and exchange. Introducing far-reaching proposals which would change both the mandate and the nature of Europol, the Report called for Europol to inter alia:

---

[147] See section VI below on interagency co-operation.

[148] Council Conclusions on possible cooperation mechanisms between civilian ESDP Missions and Europol as regards the mutual exchange of information, Justice and Home Affairs Council, 5–6 June 2008.

[149] For the texts, see www.europol.europa.eu.

[150] On the issue with regard to exchange of information between EU bodies see ch 5. On the issue regarding Europol and third bodies/states, see ch 6.

[151] See the Final Report of Working Group X on 'Freedom, Security and Justice', CONV 426/02, WG X 14, Brussels, 2 December 2002, p 18; see also Constitutional Treaty, Art III-276.

[152] Chairman's Summary of the High Level Conference on the Future of Europol (23 and 24 February 2006), Council doc 7868/06, Brussels, 29 March 2006, p 3.

—act as a service provider for EU information systems within the area of internal security but *outside* its current competence (for example a DNA or PNR database);

—be allowed to co-operate with *private* entities, such as universities and credit card companies; be given access to other EU databases (and access to be given to Europol national units to all information on the Europol database introduce an automated cross-check mechanism in various Europol systems);

—and be given access to *national* IT systems on the basis of the principle of availability. (emphasis added)[153]

Taking note of the 'Friends of the Presidency' Report, the Justice and Home Affairs Council at the end of the Austrian EU Presidency adopted a series of conclusions sketching a number of options on the future of Europol.[154] These were followed by further conclusions at the end of 2006, whereby the Council agreed that the Europol Convention should be replaced by a Council Decision.[155] A few days later, the Commission tabled such a draft Decision.[156] Along with the change in the legal instrument of Europol from a Convention to a Decision, which the Commission justified as 'relatively easy to adapt to changing circumstances because it does not require ratification',[157] the proposal introduced a number of changes in the organisation's mandate and powers. These included the partial 'communautarisation' of Europol by inter alia funding it from the Union budget (and not by Member States) and by establishing it as an 'agency of the Union', the broadening if its mandate to cover a wide range of forms of criminality, and the extension of Europol's powers with regard to data collection and processing. In this context, the Commission proposal followed to a great extent the 'Friends of the Presidency' proposals by extending the reach of Europol to information and intelligence forwarded by third countries or other public or private entities. It also envisaged the possibility of the establishment by Europol of a system for processing of personal data other than its current Information System and called upon Europol to ensure the interoperability of its data processing systems with the data processing systems in the Member States and in particular with the processing systems of EC or EU bodies.[158]

Negotiations on the Commission proposal[159] began under the German EU Presidency. These proceeded relatively fast for such a complex instrument, but the

---

[153] Austrian Presidency of the European Union, Future of Europol. Options Paper reflecting the outcome of the discussion on the future of Europol held during the Austrian Presidency, May 2006, (Council doc. 9184/1/06 REV 1, Brussels, 19 May 2006), pp 6, 8 and 9 respectively. See also V Mitsilegas, 'Databases in the Area of Freedom, Security and Justice', in C. Stefanou and H. Xanthaki (eds), *Towards a European Criminal Record*, Cambridge, Cambridge University Press, 2008, pp 311–335. On the principle of availability see ch 5.

[154] Justice and Home Affairs Council of 1–2 June 2006, doc 9409/06 (Presse 144), pp 22–23.

[155] Justice and Home Affairs Council of 4–5 December 2006, doc 15801/06 (Presse 341), pp 20–21.

[156] 'Proposal for a Council Decision establishing the European Police Office (EUROPOL)' COM (2006) 817 final, Brussels, 20 December 2006. See also Mitsilegas, 'Databases', n 153 above.

[157] COM (2006) 817 final, previous n, p 2.

[158] See Mitsilegas, 'Databases', n 153 above.

[159] Which, as the Commission admits, were not subject to detailed consultation from its part, with consultations taking place only by the Austrian Presidency which extended at the level of governments and technical experts—Commission, n 156 above, p 4.

'urgent' aim of reaching agreement by the end of the German Presidency was not achieved.[160] Member States reached gradually 'general approaches' on parts of the proposal on a chapter by chapter basis,[161] and proclaimed the aim to reach political agreement by June 2008 at the latest.[162] This deadline—which seems quite tight in the light of the scale of the task of replacing the whole Europol Convention as amended with a new piece of legislation—was of political significance at the time, as it would pre-empt the prospective entry into force of the Lisbon Treaty (then expected in January 2009 prior to the Irish 'no' vote), which would grant the European Parliament co-decision powers with regard to legislation related to Europol.[163] With this in mind, the European Parliament in its Opinion on the Commission Proposal under the consultation procedure amended the proposal to allow the revision of the Europol Decision within a period of six months following the entry into force of the Treaty of Lisbon.[164] However, this amendment was not taken up by Member States, which reached 'political agreement'—notwithstanding a number of difficult issues in negotiations[165]—on the Europol Decision at the Luxembourg April 2008 Justice and Home Affairs Council.[166] The text[167] is expected to be formally adopted in the autumn of 2008.[168] The main changes that the agreed Europol Decision will bring about are the following:

—the partial 'communautarisation' of Europol and the further move away from a purely 'intergovernmental' concept of this body: the Commission's proposals talked about establishing Europol as an 'agency of the Union'. This wording has not been replicated in the agreed text, with the body of the Decision referring merely to the establishment of a 'European Police Office',[169] and the Preamble referring to Europol as 'an entity of the European Union'.[170] However, significant 'communautarisation' developments relate to issues that proved to be very

---

[160] See also D Kietz and V Perthes (eds), *The Potential of the Council Presidency. An Analysis of Germany's Chairmanship of the EU, 2007*, SWP Research Paper 1, January 2008, Berlin, www.swp-berlin.org.

[161] See for instance the Conclusions of the Justice and Home Affairs Councils of 12–13 June 2007 (Council doc 10267/07, Presse 125, p 9), 8–9 November 2007 (Council doc 1461/07, Presse 253, p 10) and 6–7 December 2007 (Council doc 15966/07 (Presse 275, p 18).

[162] See the Conclusions of the Justice and Home Affairs Council of 12–13 June 2007, where it was stated that the Europol Decision would be finalised by 30 June 2008 the latest—previous n, p 10.

[163] See in this context also the letter of Tony McNulty, Minster of State for the Home Office, to Lord Grenfell, Chairman of the House of Lords European Union Committee, 7 November 2007, noting that 'provided it comes into force before the Reform Treaty, the Europol Decision will continue to have the same third pillar legal effects until such time as it is amended or repealed and replaced'.

[164] T6-0015-2008, new Art 62(2)(a).

[165] In this context, see the evidence of the Home Office Minister of State Tony McNulty to the House of Commons Select Committee on European Scrutiny, 16 January 2008, on www.publications.parliament.uk/pa/cm200708/cmselect/cmeuleg/247/8011602, Q8 in particular.

[166] Conclusions of Justice and Home Affairs Council of 18 April 2008, Council doc 8397/08 (Presse 96), p 13

[167] Council doc 8296/08, Brussels, 10 April 2008.

[168] See letter of Tony McNulty, Minister of State for the Home Office, to Lord Grenfell, Chairman of the House of Lords European Union Committee, 27 March 2008.

[169] Art 1(1).

[170] Recital 5.

controversial in negotiations,[171] including the funding of Europol by the EU budget (and no longer by Member States),[172] the application of EC staff regulations to (at least some categories of) Europol staff,[173] as well as the application of EC rules on privileges and immunities to Europol's Director, Deputy Directors and staff.[174] A trend towards 'communautarisation' is also reflected by the Commission's participation in the Europol Management Board,[175] and by rules on voting, in particular the following: the Management Board will in principle act by a two thirds majority of its members[176] and the Europol Director will now be appointed by the Council acting by qualified majority.[177]

—*The—somewhat—enhanced role of the European Parliament:* Along with its strengthened budgetary powers in relation to Europol, the European Parliament is granted more binding and broader information rights—now the Council Presidency, the Europol Director, but also the Chairperson of the Management Board *must* ('shall') appear before the European Parliament at its request with a view to discuss maters related to Europol.[178]

—*. . . and the limits to the role of the European Parliament due to delegation:* However, the level of democratic control over the development of Europol leaves much to be desired: although the Lisbon Treaty will bring in the Parliament as co-legislator in any amendments to the Europol Decision, the Decision itself contains a number of provisions which delegate further law-making powers under procedures where the role of the European Parliament is marginal. This is, in particular, the case in matters related to the protection of fundamental rights, such as the establishment of a new data-processing system by Europol by a Decision of the Management Board which must merely be approved by the Council;[179] and the adoption of implementing rules concerning Europol's relations with third states and bodies and EU bodies, which will be determined by the Council by qualified majority but merely with the consultation of the European Parliament.[180] The compatibility of this provision with

---

[171] See in this context inter alia House of Commons European Scrutiny Committee, 20th Report, session 2007–08, pp 75–78. See also Council doc 7008/08, Brussels, 27 February 2008, outlining the then outstanding issues on the draft Decision.

[172] Art 41 f. Already in 2002, the House of Lords European Union Committee predicted that funding Europol from the EU budget 'would be a major step towards transferring Europol from an essentially intergovernmental institution into a Community institution, responsible to the Commission and the European Parliament for its funding and in consequence—at least to some extent—for its operations—*Europol's Role in Fighting Crime*, n 13 above, para 42.

[173] Art 56

[174] Art 50.

[175] Art 36(1).

[176] Art 36(7).

[177] Art 37(1). The Council will also act by qualified majority to adopt the rules of procedure of the Europol Joint Supervisory Body—Art 33(8).

[178] Art 47, where the requirement to take into account 'the obligations of discretion and confidentiality' is however retained.

[179] Art 10(2).

[180] Art 25(1). The limits to democratic scrutiny are even more striking in Art 25(2), which allows the Management Board to determine a list of private parties with which Europol can co-operate.

Union law after the entry into force of the Lisbon Treaty (which grants the European Parliament co-decision in the field) is questionable.[181]

—*The changing role of national parliaments*: given the fact that the current form of legal instrument used for Europol is a Convention, national parliaments have played a considerable role in the adoption of the Convention and its amendments in the form of Protocols via the national ratification process.[182] With the change of the form of Europol legislation from a Convention to a Decision (which does not require ratification in Member States), the position of national parliaments seems to be weakened at least in the short term. However, national parliamentary scrutiny of Europol may be substantially enhanced following the entry into force of the Treaty of Lisbon.[183]

—*The restatement of the role of the ECJ:* The Preamble to the Decision now states that 'judicial control over Europol will be exercised in accordance with Article 35 of the Treaty on European Union'.[184] This reference seems not to introduce any major changes to the current status quo. However, the Court has now under Article 35(7) TEU an enhanced role in dispute settlement compared to the provisions on the matter in the Europol Convention, which have been deleted from the Decision.[185] With regard to preliminary rulings, Member States retain under Article 35 the option not to opt in to the ECJ jurisdiction on preliminary rulings. This is the case regarding the UK. However, the legal situation is unclear with Member States which have declared in favour of ECJ jurisdiction on preliminary rulings under the 1997 Protocol, but not under Article 35 TEU. If the Decision repeals this Protocol, then judicial control with regard to these two states seems—at least in the short term—to be weakened.

—*Scope—mandate*: the Commission proposal expanded Europol's mandate to cover serious crime in general and aligned the list of offences in the annex to the

---

[181] In this context, it is worth noting the ECJ recent judgment in case C-133/06 *European Parliament v Council*. The case involved a provision in the asylum procedures Directive (Art 29) stating that a minimum common list of safe countries of origin would be established by majority voting in the Council but by mere consultation by the European Parliament. This was notwithstanding the fact that Art 67(5) TEC stated that the 'Community method' of decision-making (including co-decision between the Council and the Parliament) would apply to the 'second generation' EC asylum measures. The Court found that the adoption procedure in Art 29 of the Procedures Directive was in conflict with the co-decision procedure and that, arguing otherwise 'effectively accords provisions of secondary legislation primacy over primary legislation' (para 58 of the judgment). The Court ruled that the co-decision procedure is applicable with regard to the future adoption of safe third country lists and annulled the relevant Directive Arts. While in the Europol case the delegating provision is inserted in secondary legislation *preceding* the entry into force of the Lisbon Treaty, it must be noted that the Governments of Member States negotiating the Europol Decision have also signed the Lisbon Treaty and agreed to the change in decision-making as regards Europol.

[182] As is noted by Peers, national parliaments have currently the essentially negative power to block any amendments to the Europol Convention—S Peers, 'Governance and the Third Pillar: the Accountability of Europol', in D M Curtin and R A Wessel (eds), *Good Governance and the European Union. Reflections on Concepts, Institutions and Substance*, Oxford, Intersentia, 2005, pp 253–276 at p 259.

[183] See section on the Lisbon Treaty below.

[184] Recital 22.

[185] On Art 35(7) TEU see Peers, *EU Justice*, n 13 above, pp 41–42.

Europol Decision with the list of offences for which dual criminality has been abolished under the European Arrest Warrant (which includes offences such as murder, rape and arson).[186] This extension (in particular the deletion of the reference to cross-border crime) caused concerns in Member States, seen as signifying a shift of focus for Europol from cross-border crime to purely domestic criminal investigations.[187] Such concerns resulted in the retention of the wording of the Europol Convention with regard to the requirement for offences to constitute cross-border serious crime in order to fall within Europol's mandate and in the retention of the list of offences for which Europol is currently competent to act.[188] The main significant change is the extension of Europol's competence from serious cross-border organised crime to serious cross-border crime (with organised crime indications no longer necessary to trigger Europol's competence).

—*The intensification of data collection, analysis and exchange*: the Europol Decision has the potential to substantially increase Europol's powers with regard to the collection, analysis and exchange of personal data. As mentioned above, it envisages the establishment (to be decided by the Management Board and approved by the Council) of a new system processing personal data, which will contain information on a wide range of individuals currently included in Europol's Analysis Work Files (AWF).[189] The Europol Information System may contain a wide range of data beyond those specifically enumerated in the Decision including DNA information.[190] Access to EIS data by national units is expanded.[191] The time limit for storage of personal data is being increased (to three plus three years).[192] Moreover, a significant extension of Europol's reach comes via the provisions on its relations with third countries and bodies and EU bodies. The Decision confirms the involvement of experts in Europol's AWFs.[193] It also contains legal bases for the development of Europol's relations and exchange of data with EU bodies and agencies (as diverse as Eurojust, OLAF, Frontex, CEPOL, the European Central Bank and the European Drug Addiction Centre),[194] and with

---

[186] Art 2(2) of the European Arrest Warrant Framework Decision—for more on this instrument, see ch 3.

[187] Tony McNulty, Minster of State for the Home Office, to Lord Grenfell, Chairman of the House of Lords European Union Committee, 7 November 2007, noting that the re-insertion of the criteria of cross-border crime requiring a common approach was introduced by the UK to 'prevent anty possibility of Europol becoming involved in purely national criminal investigations'.

[188] See Art 4(1) (but also Art 3 on Europol's objectives) and the annex to the Decision respectively.

[189] Art 10(2) and (3).

[190] Art 12(2)(g).

[191] Art 13(1). This expansion has been criticised by the Europol Joint Supervisory Body which notes that the restriction of direct access for national units to data relating to persons of whom it is believed that they will commit crimes in the future has been deleted (see Art 7(1) of the Europol Convention)—Opinion 07/07 with respect to the proposal for a Council Decision establishing the European Police Office, 5 March 2007.

[192] Art 20(1) and (2).

[193] Art 14(8), containing a specific reference to OLAF.

[194] Art 22(1). These provisions must also be viewed in the light of parallel proposals to grant Europol access to non-police databases such as the Visa Information System—see ch 5.

third states and bodies (such as Interpol).[195] Last, but not least, Europol's powers are expanded substantially by a provision allowing it to include in its databases and process information provided by private parties and persons, including private parties established in third states.[196]

—*Data protection*: the real and potential extension of Europol's powers to collect, exchange and analyse a wide range of personal data has not been accompanied by major amendments in its privacy framework. The Preamble to the Decision states that the draft Framework Decision on data protection in the third pillar, currently under negotiation, will be applicable only to the transfer of personal data by Member States to Europol.[197] The Europol Decision thus retains a series of data protection rules, which, as *lex specialis*, apply to the Europol databases and the work of Europol. In this context, not many changes have been introduced to the Europol Convention, with the general data protection framework still being prescribed by reference to Council of Europe measures.[198] The main innovation is a provision establishing the post of an 'independent' Data Protection Officer.[199] The specific data protection provisions, including the provisions on the role and powers of the Joint Supervisory Body (in particular on appeals) have been redrafted and restructured in clearer, more accessible manner.[200]

Notwithstanding the fact that the degree of desired influence of an EU police body such as Europol to national police and criminal justice systems remains contested, the legal framework governing Europol has been subject to constant amendment and revision since the signature of the Europol Convention in 1995. While the recently agreed Europol Decision is certainly a significant way forward, a number of very important changes were introduced earlier, via Protocols amending the Europol Convention, and expanding its tasks and powers to a considerable extent. On paper, Europol still does not have 'executive powers'.[201] However, it may increasingly be seen as 'operational'. It has powers to request national authorities to initiate or co-ordinate criminal investigations; it also has powers to participate in joint investigation teams, something that in practice may mean that Europol officers may operate in the territory of a Member State. In this context, the line between assisting and operating may become rather blurred.

---

[195] Art 23.
[196] Art 24. Co-operation between Europol and private parties is based in principle on a conclusion of a Memorandum of Understanding—Art 24(2).
[197] Preamble, Recital 11bis.
[198] Art 26.
[199] Who will, however, be appointed by the Europol Management Board—Art 27(1).
[200] See in particular Arts 28–31.
[201] See the Preamble of the Europol Decision, stating that

> further simplification and improvement of Europol's functioning can be achieved through measures aimed at widening the possibilities for Europol to assist and support the competent law enforcement authorities of the Member States, without providing for executive powers for Europol staff. (Recital 7).

But it is in the field of the collection, analysis and exchange of personal data that Europol's powers have been substantially increased. Ironically, the constant expansion of such powers comes in the light of sustained criticism of Europol's efficiency and added value, criticism that at times focuses on the very design of Europol, it being the outcome of a political compromise.[202] Calls to enhance Europol's efficiency, along with an increased emphasis in the EU on intelligence-led policing and inter-agency co-operation, have created a legal framework that allows Europol to substantially expand (many times via delegated powers) its analytical capacity and databases, in particular by establishing channels of co-operation with a wide range of public and private authorities both within and out-side the EU. This expansion of Europol's powers poses great challenges for the protection of fundamental rights in the EU, in particular privacy. In the light of these challenges, the adequacy of the current legislative framework governing Europol in terms of privacy protection, judicial control, transparency and accountability remains questionable.

III. EUROJUST

A. Background

The establishment of Europol was coupled with calls to apply this model of pro-moting European integration in the sphere of police co-operation in the EU via an agency to the field of judicial co-operation in criminal matters. In this context, ideas for the establishment of an EU 'judicial' body in criminal matters were put forward—its name, Eurojust, appears to be a clear analogy to the use of the term 'Europol' for the European Police Office.[203] A body like Eurojust was envisaged as a 'counterpart' to Europol, although views on the precise relationship between the two bodies were far from uniform: one view envisaged Eurojust's role as a judicial back-up to Europol's activities;[204] another perceived Eurojust action as necessary to legitimise police action at national and EU level;[205] and a third view went fur-ther, arguing that Eurojust should assume the judicial supervision of Europol.[206]

---

[202] See inter alia the recent criticism in B Müller-Witte, 'The Effect of International Terrorism on EU Intelligence Co-operation', *Journal of Common Market Studies*, vol 46, no 1, 2008, pp 49–73 at pp 54 f. The author asks whether Europol is 'flawed by design'—p 54.

[203] For a detailed analysis of the background to the establishment of Eurojust, with a specific focus on the role of the different EU institutions in its development, see M Mangenot, 'Jeux européens et innovation institutionnelle: Les logiques de création d'Eurojust', *Cultures et conflits*, vol 62, 2006, pp 43–62.

[204] European Commission, 'Communication on the Establishment of Eurojust' COM (2000) 746 final, Brussels, 22 November 2000, p 10.

[205] H Labayle (2000), 'Three Principles of Reflection' in Notre Europe, *Protecting European Citizens against International Crime*, pp 12–22 at p 20.

[206] See the written evidence of Joachim Vogel to House of Lords European Union Committee, *Judicial Cooperation in the EU: The Role of Eurojust*, 23rd Report, session 2003–04, HL Paper 138, pp 105–106.

In any case, the establishment of Europol provided an important precedent for the establishment of greater co-operation and co-ordination and the development of EU structures operating in the field of judicial co-operation in criminal matters.

The first major attempt to coordinate EU action in the field took place by the adoption in 1998 of a Joint Action establishing the European Judicial Network (EJN).[207] Far from being a centralised EU body, the network consists of national contact points which provide legal and practical information to local judicial authorities in other countries to prepare effective judicial co-operation requests. The network consists of national judicial authorities responsible for judicial co-operation in criminal matters—its aim being 'to identify and promote people in every Member State who play a fundamental role in practice in the area of judicial co-operation in criminal matters, with the purpose of creating a network of experts *to ensure the proper execution of mutual legal assistance requests*'(emphasis added)[208]—in this context, the EJN promotes direct contacts between its members.[209]

Notwithstanding the establishment of the European Judicial Network, the idea of the creation of an EU-wide body still remained. This is in view of various factors which were perceived as impeding effective judicial co-operation, such as the lack of trust between national authorities, problems in the implementation of the relevant Conventions and in language and translation, processing delays, lack of training and resources and problems in legal harmonisation regarding criminal offences, especially organised crime. These problems were already highlighted in 1997 within the framework of a meeting of the then K.4 Committee and led to the proposal for the establishment of a Judicial Co-operation Unit.[210] The role of the Council Secretariat in pushing for the development of such a unit (and eventually Eurojust) has been central—with Council officials reportedly promoting the creation of such a unit at various crucial stages of the formation of EU Justice and Home Affairs strategy by the European Council or the various EU Presidencies.[211]

The development of Eurojust in that period must be viewed in the context of the ongoing debate regarding the nature and extent European integration in criminal matters across the EU. We are in the second half of the 1990s, where the Commission on the one hand is advocating a largely harmonised, almost uniform, model of EU criminal justice by commissioning the *Corpus Juris* project and floating ideas about the establishment of a European Public Prosecutor on the one

---

[207] OJ L191, 7 July 1998, p 4. On the background to the European Judicial Network and, later, to Eurojust, see H Nilsson, 'EUROJUST: The Beginning or the End of the European Public Prosecutor?', paper presented to the third EUROJUSTICE conference in Santander, Spain, 24–27 October 2000 (typescript with author). See also G Vermeulen, 'A European Judicial Network linked to Europol? In Search of a Model for Structuring Trans-national Criminal Investigations in the EU' *Maastricht Journal of European and Comparative Law*, vol 4, 1997, pp 346–372.

[208] See the European Judicial Network website, at www.ejn-crimjust.europa.eu/about-ejn.aspx.

[209] ibid. According to the website (accessed on 21 February 2008), there exist almost 250 national contact points.

[210] For a detailed analysis, see Nilsson, 'EUROJUST', n 207 above.

[211] For a detailed background, and a fascinating name-dropping exercise, see Mangenot, n 203 above.

hand; and a number of Member States appearing reluctant to go that far, and on the contrary stressing the intergovernmental character of the third pillar and putting forward alternatives to harmonisation in criminal law, in particular mutual recognition.[212] The role of this tension in discussions on Eurojust has been demonstrated eloquently by Hans Nilsson, one of the Council Secretariat officials who have been instrumental in the establishment of this body. He states that:

> It is in the crossroads between these two 'ideologies'/tendencies that Eurojust is situated. In fact, it is highly likely that Eurojust would never had seen the day had it not been for the fact that its very idea has something that could satisfy both 'camps'—for one it is the beginning, for the other it is the end.[213]

Indeed, the tension between these two 'camps' has been a prevailing feature in both the negotiations and finally agreed content of the legislation establishing Eurojust. The debate on Eurojust involved both its eventual powers and role (where tensions between the intergovernmental and more supranational 'camps' could be discerned), but also its very existence and relationship with other proposals which were on the table in the 1990s—in particular proposals on the establishment of the European Public Prosecutor (with Eurojust being perceived by some and an intergovernmental 'Trojan Horse' aiming at annulling in practice more integrationist proposals such as the EPP). Eurojust seemed to have won this latter 'battle' at the EU constitutional level at the time—the Nice Treaty included a specific legal basis for Eurojust,[214] and nothing on the European Public Prosecutor.[215] However, as will be seen below, the EPP seems to be potentially resurfacing (ironically perhaps, 'from Eurojust') under the Lisbon Treaty.

The momentum towards the establishment of Eurojust in the late 1990s was reflected in the Tampere European Council Conclusions, which expressly stated that:

> To reinforce the fight against serious organised crime, the European Council has agreed that a unit (EUROJUST) should be set up composed of national prosecutors, magistrates, or police officers of equivalent competence, detached from each Member State according to its legal system. EUROJUST should have the task of facilitating the proper co-ordination of national prosecuting authorities and of supporting criminal investigations in organised crime cases, notably based on Europol's analysis, as well as of co-operating closely with the European Judicial Network, in particular in order to simplify the execution of letters rogatory. The European Council requests the Council to adopt the necessary legal instrument by the end of 2001.[216]

---

[212] On the evolution of mutual recognition in EU criminal matters, see ch 3.

[213] Nilsson, 'EUROJUST', n 207 above, para 3.

[214] See amended Art 31 TEU.

[215] On the background to the Commission reactions to the Nice developments, see Mangenot, n 203 above. He also cites an article in Les Échos asserting that Eurojust has been included in the Nice Treaty, as if it had 'slid in the bed prepared for the EPP' ('comme s'il c'était glissé dans le lit prepare pour le parquet européen')—p 57.

[216] Para 46.

This impetus by the Tampere European Council (which defined the mission of Eurojust in rather general terms[217]), along with different views on the nature of Eurojust and perhaps a desire by certain Member States to assume ownership of the idea[218] resulted in not one, but two legislative proposals for the establishment of Eurojust: one from Germany[219] and one from the four EU presidencies which would have to negotiate Eurojust until the final deadline of the end of 2001 (Portugal, France, Sweden and Belgium, or the 'four presidencies').[220] These initiatives were characterised by marked differences regarding the Unit's nature and powers, as well as data protection issues.[221] The 'four presidencies' proposal already contained a number of compromise provisions resulting from earlier consultations regarding the role of Eurojust.[222] In the course of negotiations, three major issues of controversy have arisen, all inextricably linked with the nature and powers of Eurojust, and all reflecting the various models put forward with regard to the unit's development.[223]

The first controversial issue concerned the *offences falling within the remit of Eurojust*. The Tampere conclusions referred to the role of Eurojust in reinforcing the fight against 'serious organised crime', without further specification. In negotiations, a number of views were put forward regarding the delimitation of Eurojust's mandate in this context. In its communication 'on the establishment of Eurojust', the Commission opted for the inclusion within its remit of 'all major criminal offences' in respect of which judicial legal assistance may be required. The Commission justified this approach in view of the general Tampere mandate and of the fact the establishment of a list of offences, rather than a general reference to serious crime, would require a new Council decision if it were to be amended.[224] A general mandate was also supported by Member States such as the United Kingdom, arguing that competence expressed in general terms would be in the interests of flexibility.[225] Different views advocated the adoption of a list of offences forming Eurojust's mandate, with some support for aligning Eurojust's mandate with the one of Europol (transplanting thus the offences mentioned in the Europol Convention into the eventual Eurojust instrument).[226] This view

[217] On this point, see S Brammertz, 'Eurojust: Parquet Européen de la Première Génération?', in G de Kerchove and A Weyembergh (eds), *Vers un espace judiciaire pénal européen = Towards a European Judicial Criminal Area*, Brussels, Éditions de l'Université de Bruxelles, 2000, pp. 105–118.

[218] Mangenot (n 203 above, p 51) argues that Germany has tabled its own proposal before the planned proposal by the four presidencies in order to claim 'paternity' of the proposal. Hans Nilsson ('EUROJUST', n 207 above, para 19) also refers to Germany, as claiming 'maternity rights'.

[219] OJ C 206, 19 July 2000, p 1.

[220] OJ C 243 24 August 2000, p 15.

[221] Nilsson, 'EUROJUST', n 207 above.

[222] Mangenot, n 203 above, p 52.

[223] See Mitsilegas, Monar and Rees, n 2 above, pp 119–121.

[224] Commission, n 204 above, pp 2–3.

[225] See letter from Bob Ainsworth, then Parliamentary Under Secretary of State, Home Office, to Lord Brabazon of Tara, then chairman of the House of Lords Select Committee on the European Union, 29 November 2001, in House of Lords Select Committee on the European Union, *Correspondence with Ministers*, 18th Report, session 2001–02, HL Paper 99, p 61.

[226] The Commission stated that, if a list were to be accepted, it should contain the offences in the Europol Convention and Annex, with particular emphasis on cross-border organised crime—n 204 above.

largely reflects the perception of Eurojust as a 'counterpart' to Europol. Another controversial issue regarding Eurojust's mandate concerned the inclusion within Eurojust's mandate of fraud against the Community budget.[227] Inclusion of fraud in Eurojust's mandate could have significant repercussions regarding its nature and relationship with other EU structures (in particular OLAF, the European anti-fraud office and—if established—the European Public Prosecutor).

A further issue of controversy involved the *status* and *powers* of Eurojust and its members. Regarding status, the prevailing view was to grant the unit a separate legal personality.[228] The situation was less clear-cut regarding the unit's powers. The Commission has noted that the existing consensus at the time of its communication centred on a common denominator that was so low, that the tasks in question could also be carried out by the European Judicial Network.[229] The exact delimitation of such tasks was however controversial, in view of the differences between Member States. A further issue of controversy concerned the status and position of Eurojust members. Certain Member States were not in favour of replicating the Europol model but emphasising the 'Union' character of Eurojust members. However, this approach would clash with more 'intergovernmentally minded' Member States wishing to retain a national dimension into Eurojust[230]—arguably in order to dispel the potential development of Eurojust from a more 'intergovernmental' co-ordinating body into a centralised Euro-unit reminiscent of the European Public Prosecutor. For that reason, the role, status and powers of national members have been central, existential issues to the development of Eurojust.

A further issue of controversy in negotiations was the *relationship of Eurojust with other EU institutions and bodies*. An overlap could arise with the activities of the *European Judicial Network*, as both bodies would have as their general task the enhancement of judicial co-operation in criminal matters. It was believed, however, that no major problems would arise as, while Eurojust was envisaged to operate on an independent, EU-wide basis, the Network would operate within a national context and was limited to bilateral co-operation.[231] Queries have also been raised regarding the extent of the involvement of the *Commission* (including OLAF) in the work of Eurojust. There has been pressure to associate the Commission with the latter's work in full,[232] but the precise involvement of the Commission in Eurojust has been the subject of lengthy negotiations.[233] Moreover, the potential involvement of Eurojust in fraud cases rasied the issue of

---

[227] Nilsson ('EUROJUST', n 207 above) argues in that respect that competence should not be restricted either to specific offences, or to serious crime, as in this manner offences as financial fraud would fall outside of the mandate of Eurojust.

[228] For arguments advocating a separate legal personality, see Commission, n 204 above, p 6; and Nilsson, 'EUROJUST', n 207 above.

[229] Commission, n 204 above, p 3.

[230] On this clash, see the remarks of Daniel Flore, a Belgian official involved in the Eurojust negotiations, in Mangenot, n 203 above, p 52.

[231] See Nilsson, 'EUROJUST', n 207 above.

[232] ibid.

[233] See House of Lords, *Correspondence with Ministers*, n 225 above, p 62.

its relationship and potential overlap with OLAF. Last, but not least, a number of issues have arisen with regard to the relationship between

Eurojust and *Europol*. A major issue in negotiations has been the ability of Europol to transfer analysed data to Eurojust (and vice-versa) and the ability of Eurojust to protect such data in an equivalent manner to that of Europol. Issues relating to the dissemination and use of data were also controversial.[234]

With negotiations ongoing, the momentum towards the establishment of Eurojust was sustained by the adoption by the Council of a Decision establishing a Provisional Judicial Cooperation Unit (or Pro-Eurojust),[235] aimed at being a precursor to Eurojust—located in Brussels and supported by the infrastructure of the Council.[236] According to the Pro-Eurojust Decision, the objectives of the Provisional Unit were to improve co-operation and stimulate co-ordination between national authorities with regard to the investigation and prosecution of serious crime[237]—however, there was little in terms of formal legal standards regarding its work (including standards on data protection) in the Pro-Eurojust Decision.[238] The establishment of this unit has been characterised as an example of 'institutional mimetism', as it is strongly reminiscent of the establishment of the European Drugs Unit (EDU) which preceded Europol.[239] The unit was competent for 'serious crime' in general and its tasks involved the improvement of co-operation between national authorities regarding investigations and prosecutions and the improvement of their co-ordination. It started work in March 2001 and consisted of a roundtable of 15 prosecutors based in the Council Secretariat.[240]

B. The Eurojust Decision

i. Background

9/11 accelerated negotiations, with agreement reached at the end of the Belgian Presidency in December of 2001 and the Eurojust Decision finally adopted in 2002.[241] The Decision establishes Eurojust as 'a body of the Union' with legal personality.[242] It is composed of one national member seconded by each Member

[234] On the relationship between Europol and Eurojust see Nilsson, 'EUROJUST', n 207 above and Commission, n 204 above, p 10.
[235] OJ L324, 21 December 2000, p 2.
[236] Art 1.
[237] Art 2(1).
[238] The lack of such standards has also been highlighted by the European Parliament Committee on Citizens' Freedoms and Rights, Justice and Home Affairs (Doc A5–0317/2000 final, 30 October 2000, rapporteur: E Gebhardt).
[239] Mangenot, n 203 above, p 59.
[240] Personal communication, DG JHA, Brussels, 5 December 2000. For further details, see Mangenot, n 203 above, p 60.
[241] OJ L63, 6.3.2002, p 1. For the Rules of Procedure of Eurojust, see OJ C286, 22 November 2002, p 1.
[242] Art 1.

State in accordance with its legal system, 'being a prosecutor, judge or police officer of equivalent competence'.[243] Each Member State may also appoint Eurojust national correspondents.[244] National members can act individually or as a College.[245] The College consists of all the national members, with each national member having one vote.[246] It is responsible for the organisation and operation of Eurojust.[247] It elects the President of Eurojust from among the national members, who exercises his/her duties on behalf of the College and under its authority.[248] The first President of Eurojust was Mike Kennedy from the UK, recently succeeded by José Luís Lopes da Mota from Portugal. Reflecting to some extent the vision of Eurojust as the 'judicial counterpart' of Europol, the seat of Eurojust is located in The Hague.[249]

It may be discerned from the brief introductory paragraph above that the finally adopted Decision reflects the tensions between the various visions for Eurojust's role and its relationship with other EU bodies and institutions and contains a number of compromise provisions aiming to reconcile competing views and the conflict between a largely 'intergovernmental' model on the one hand and a more centralised model on the other.[250] These tensions are evident throughout the Eurojust Decision, in a number of fundamental provisions addressing Eurojust's powers, accountability and position within the EU institutional framework.

ii. Eurojust's Mandate and Powers

As regards the *types of crime* which would fall within the mandate of Eurojust, the Decision largely mirrors the competence of Eurojust with that of Europol: Eurojust covers 'the types of crime and the offences in respect of which Europol is

---

[243] Art 2(1).

[244] Art 12. Council Decision 2005/671/JHA on the exchange of information and cooperation concerning terrorist offences (OJ L 253, 29 September 2005, p 22) made it mandatory for Member States to designate Eurojust national correspondents for terrorism matters (Art 2(2)). The Decision also called on Member States to ensure that information related to prosecutions and convictions for terrorist offences which affect or may affect two or more Member States are transmitted to Eurojust (Art 2(3)). The Decision contains similar provisions with regard to Europol.

[245] Art 5.

[246] Art 10(1).

[247] Art 28(1).

[248] Art 28(2) and (3). The term of office of the Eurojust President is 3 years renewable once (Art 28(4)).

[249] See Decision 2004/97/EC on the location of the seats of certain offices and agencies of the Union, OJ L29, 3 February 2004, p 15. According to its then President, 'Eurojust was sent to work in the Hague because Europol was already there'—Mike Kennedy, oral evidence to House of Commons Home Affairs Committee for their inquiry on EU Justice and Home Affairs, reproduced in *Justice and Home Affairs Issues at European Union Level*, 3rd Report, session 2006–07, vol 2, HC 76-II, Q210.

[250] On Eurojust in general, see House of Lords European Union Committee, *Judicial Cooperation in the EU*, n 206 above; N Thwaites, 'Eurojust. autre brique dans l'édifice de la coopération judiciaire en matière pénale ou solide mortier?', *Revue de science criminelle et de droit pénal comparé*, 2003, pp 45–61; H Xanthaki, 'Eurojust: Fulfilled or Empty Promises in EU Criminal Law?', *European Journal of Law Reform*, vol 8, 2006, pp 175–198; and C van den Wyngaert, 'Eurojust and the European Public Prosecutor in the *Corpus Juris* Model: Water and Fire?' in N Walker (ed), *Europe's Area of Freedom, Security and Justice*, Oxford, Oxford University Press, 2004, pp 201–240.

at all times competent to act pursuant to Article 2 of the Europol Convention'.[251] Eurojust's mandate extends further to cover expressly computer crime, fraud and corruption, money laundering, environmental crime and organised crime.[252] It may also assist 'in accordance with its objectives' in investigations and prosecutions of other, additional offences at the request of a competent authority of a Member State.[253] This provision appears to be a source of uncertainty regarding the determination of Eurojust's mandate, but it also demonstrates the centrality of Member States in the determination of further Eurojust powers. With regard to the offences specifically mentioned in the Eurojust Decision, of particular controversy has been the inclusion of fraud affecting the Community's financial interests: as in the case of the inclusion of fraud within the mandate of Europol,[254] the extension of Eurojust's mandate to cover fraud raises the issue of its relationship and potential overlap with OLAF, a body whose primary objective is the fight against fraud affecting the financial interests of the Community. While co-operation and/or competition between Eurojust and OLAF is very much a live issue,[255] at this point it is noteworthy that according to the 2007 Eurojust Annual Report, fraud-related offences form a great part of Eurojust's work.[256]

The Eurojust Decision contains a series of overlapping provisions on Eurojust's objectives and tasks. These provisions reflect clearly the delicate balancing exercise which took place in order to ensure the establishment of a Union body in the field, while at the same time reassuring Member States that their sovereignty in the field of criminal justice would remain intact to the extent possible. The Decision limits Eurojust's work in the context in principle of investigations and prosecutions concerning *two or more Member States*[257] of criminal behaviour as defined above *in relation to serious crime, particularly when it is organised*[258]—in this context, Eurojust's objectives are:

(a) to stimulate and improve the *co-ordination*, between the competent authorities of the Member States, of investigations and prosecutions in the Member States, taking into account any request emanating from a competent author-

---

[251] Art 4(1)(a). It is not clear whether this provision can be read as covering the replacement of the Europol Convention by a Decision, to the extent that the latter will change the scope of the offences covered by Europol. However, this uncertainty will be addressed if the Decision amending the Europol Convention is formally adopted before the instrument amending the Eurojust Decision (which can define Eurojusts' mandate on the basis of the amended Europol law)—on these proposals see below (sub-sections on the future of Europol and the future of Eurojust respectively).

[252] Art 4(1)(b). Note that Eurojust also has competence to act with regard to other offences committed together with the types of crime referred to in Art 491)(a) and (b) (Art 4(1)(a)(c)).

[253] Art 4(2).

[254] See sub-section II b iii above.

[255] See the following sub-section.

[256] 2007 Report found at www.eurojust.europa.eu/press_annual_report_2007.htm

[257] But note that Eurojust may also assist in investigations and prosecutions concerning a Member State and a non-Member State (Art 3(2)), or concerning only one Member State and the Community (Art 3(3)).

[258] It is not clear what is meant by the words 'in relation to' serious crime and how these are linked to the potentially broad definition of Eurojust's mandate in Art 4.

ity of a Member State and any information provided by any body competent by virtue of provisions adopted within the framework of the Treaties;

(b) to improve *cooperation* between the competent authorities of the Member States, in particular by facilitating the execution of international mutual legal assistance and the implementation of extradition requests;

(c) to *support* otherwise the competent authorities of the Member States in order to render their investigations and prosecutions more effective. (emphasis added)[259]

The Decision thus views Eurojust not merely as a body facilitating mutual legal assistance across the European Union,[260] but also as a body with more extensive, co-ordination functions. The extent and legal framework of Eurojust's co-ordination function are not always clear, and Eurojust's powers in this context are at the heart of the debate over what degree of EU centralisation should exist in judicial co-operation in criminal matters. Some answers are given by Articles 5–7 of the Eurojust Decision, laying out the *tasks* that Eurojust must fulfil 'in order to accomplish its objectives'.[261]. The technique followed by the Decision has been to distinguish between tasks of Eurojust *acting though its national members*, and tasks of Eurojust *acting as a College*—the latter will kick in inter alia when a case involves investigations or prosecutions 'which have repercussions at Union level or which might affect Member States other than those directly concerned'.[262] This can be seen as an attempt to distinguish between bilateral or simpler cases (involving a Eurojust national member and his/her Member State of origin) and multilateral or more complex cases (involving more than two Member States)— it is in particular in the latter scenario where the question of Eurojust's powers and the degree of its influence in domestic criminal justice systems comes into play.

The Eurojust Decision contains two separate provisions on the tasks of Eurojust acting through its national members and Eurojust acting as a College. However, to a great extent, the tasks are defined in a similar if not identical manner in both provisions.[263] In both cases, for instance, Eurojust may ask the competent authorities of the Member States concerned to consider:

---

[259] Art 3(1)

[260] On the role of Eurojust in the context of EU mutual legal assistance arrangements, in particular the 2000 EU Mutual Legal Assistance Convention, see Xanthaki, 'Eurojust Fulfilled', n 250 above. On the Convention itself, see E Denza, 'The 2000 Convention on Mutual Legal Assistance in Criminal Matters', *Common Market Law Review,* vol 40, 2003, pp 1047–1074.

[261] Art 5(1).

[262] Art 5(1)(b).

[263] The main differences concern the specificities of action as a national member or as the Eurojust College—for instance Eurojust acting through its national members may also forward mutual legal assistance requests (Art 6(g)); and Eurojust acting as a College may also assist Europol, in particular by providing it with opinions based on analyses carried out by Europol (Art 7(f)). Common tasks of Eurojust through its national members and Eurojust as a College include a variety of assistance functions to national authorities, as well as co-operation with the European Judicial Network.

(i)   undertaking an investigation or prosecution of specific acts;

(ii) accepting that one of them may be in a better position to undertake an investigation or to prosecute specific acts;

(iii) coordinating between the competent authorities of the Member States concerned;

(iv) setting up a joint investigation team in keeping with the relevant cooperation instruments;

(v)   providing it with any information that is necessary for it to carry out its tasks.[264]

These provisions are key in determining the extent of Eurojust's powers with regard to domestic criminal justice systems. It is noteworthy that Eurojust can *ask* Member States' authorities to consider undertaking an investigation or prosecution of specific acts—however, it cannot *compel* these authorities to do so (addressing thus—at least in the short term—concerns that Eurojust would have mandatory powers to initiate investigations and prosecutions in Member States following the model of the European Public Prosecutor).[265] However, when Eurojust acts as a College, if the competent authorities in Member States refuse to comply with a request by the College under Article 7(a) of the Eurojust Decision, they must in principle give reasons for their refusal.[266] According to Eurojust, this 'naming and shaming' provision, which enables the identification of non-cooperative authorities, has not been used very often but can yield results.[267] However, as will be seen below, recent proposals for the amendment of the Eurojust Decision call for mandatory powers for Eurojust in this context.

Another key provision in determining the relationship between Eurojust and domestic competent authorities—which also highlights the prosecutorial nature of Eurojust—concerns the issue of *concurrent jurisdictions*. An extensive analysis of the issue can be found in chapter three of this book. Here it suffices to say that Eurojust can ask national authorities to accept that one of them may be in a better position to undertake an investigation or to prosecute specific acts—again this is not a mandatory power. The issue of determining which jurisdiction should investigate or prosecute in cases where more than one Member States can establish jurisdiction has considerable implications for both State sovereignty (to what extent can a Member State be precluded from investigating or prosecuting an alleged offence if no *ne bis in idem* case arises?) and for fundamental rights (would Eurojust intervention lead to 'forum shopping' in favour of the prosecution, by choosing the jurisdiction where a conviction is easiest to secure?). Eurojust has published a series of (non-legally binding) criteria determining which jurisdiction

---

[264] Art 6(a) and 7(a) respectively.

[265] Note that when Eurojust acts as a College it must give reasons for these requests and it may act only in relation to the types of crime referred to in Art 4(1) of the Decision (the Europol crimes)—Art 7(a).

[266] Art 8.

[267] See the oral evidence of the then Eurojust president, Mike Kennedy, to the Commons Home Affairs Committee—n 249 above, Q206.

should prosecute.[268] However, in the light of the significant implications of action on concurrent jurisdictions, the adoption of clear legal rules regulating Eurojust action in the field, including oversight and potential judicial review of such action is a matter of urgency.

A co-ordination function in cases of concurrent jurisdictions is also envisaged for Eurojust in cases concerning European Arrest Warrants. The European Arrest Warrant Framework Decision allows the executing authorities in Member States to seek the advice of Eurojust when they have to make a decision in cases of multiple requests.[269] The Framework Decision also obliges national authorities to inform Eurojust of cases where they cannot observe the time limits for the execution of a European Arrest Warrant provided for therein, giving reasons for the delay.[270] Details of such notifications can be found in the Eurojust Annual Reports.[271]

Refraining from granting Eurojust a binding say over the initiation of investigations and prosecutions in Member States has been one way of addressing the willingness of Member States to keep their criminal justice systems 'immune' from mandatory EU intervention by Eurojust. Another way of preserving State sovereignty has been to define to a large extent the powers of Eurojust members on the basis of *national law*. One way of reliance on national law has been the distinction mentioned above between Eurojust acting as a College and Eurojust acting via its national members. It has been rightly argued that this 'hybrid' solution creates a certain flexibility towards the future development of Eurojust, while at the same time addressing concerns of reluctant Member States.[272] However, the emphasis on national law also contributes to both a lack of clarity and substantial discrepancies regarding the powers of Eurojust in Member States. This conclusion is affirmed by Article 9 of the Eurojust Decision, which states inter alia that:

> National members shall be subject to the national law of their Member State as regards their status. The length of a national member's term of office shall be determined by the Member State of origin. It shall be such as to allow Eurojust to operate properly;

and

> Each Member State shall define the nature and extent of the judicial powers it grants its national member within its own territory. It shall also define the right for a national member to act in relation to foreign judicial authorities, in accordance with its international commitments.[273]

The determination of the powers of Eurojust national members by reference to the domestic law of their State of origin has resulted in considerable discrepancies

---

[268] For further details, see ch 3.
[269] OJ L190, 18 July 2002, p 1 Art 16(2).
[270] Art 17(5).
[271] See n 256 above for the 2007 Report.
[272] See D Flore and S de Biolley, 'Des organes juridictionnels en matière pénale pour l'Union européenne', *Cahiers de droit européen*, 2003, pp 597–637 at p 623.
[273] Art 9(1) and (3) of the Eurojust Decision respectively.

with regard to the way in which Member States have actually defined these powers. It has been pointed out that a number of Member States have not implemented the Eurojust Decision in their domestic legal order.[274] To take the example of one of these States, the United Kingdom: implementation has not been deemed necessary. It has been stated some years ago that the powers of the UK national member (a Crown Prosecutor in the UK) were retained while at Eurojust—however, this would mean these powers vis-a-vis the domestic legal order may change in the future, if the UK chooses to appoint a national member from an agency other than the Crown Prosecution Service.[275] This approach raises two issues: the issue of legal certainty at both the domestic and EU level with regard to the extent of the powers of the national member; and the issue of whether in this example the UK member acts as a Crown Prosecutor under English domestic law, or as a Eurojust national member—and if the latter, at which stage—would Union law kick in. While it may be politically convenient—and pragmatically flexible—for Member States to send national members to Eurojust without detailed legal provisions covering their mandate, this may result in a lack of certainty with regard to Eurojust powers.

This lack of certainty is compounded by the substantial differences in Member States' conferral of powers to their national members—which is to some extent the outcome of the diversity of domestic criminal justice and constitutional systems. An issue which has arisen has been that the territorial mandate of prosecutors or magistrates could be limited on a prefectural or regional basis—raising the issue of how these limitations are going to be reconciled with Eurojust powers to cover the whole national territory.[276] A much-cited example has been the one of Germany, where tensions between the competence of the Länder in criminal justice and those of the federal level have appeared in the context of the powers of the German national member for Eurojust. As will be seen below, recent draft legislation aiming at amending the Eurojust Decision contains a number of provisions addressing the issue of discrepancies of the mandate and powers of national members.

iii. Eurojust's Relations with Other Bodies

a. The Eurojust Decision

The Eurojust Decision contains a number of provisions devoted to the relation between Eurojust and 'partners'. Eurojust will 'establish and maintain close cooperation with Europol'; 'maintain privileged relations with the European Judicial Network based on consultation and complementarity'; and 'establish and

---

[274] On the state of implementation of the Eurojust Decision, see European Commission, 'Communication on the Role of Eurojust and the European Judicial Network in the Fight Against Organised Crime and Terrorism in the European Union' COM (2007) 644 final, Brussels, 23 October 2007.

[275] House of Lords European Union Committee, *Judicial Cooperation in the EU*, n 206 above, para 37.

[276] Interview, DG JHA, Brussels, 5 December 2000—see Mitsilegas, Monar and Rees, n 2 above.

maintain close cooperation with OLAF'.[277] Eurojust may also exchange 'any information necessary for the performance of its tasks' with 'bodies competent by virtue of provisions adopted within the framework of the Treaties'.[278] Eurojust has since been in the process of developing relations with other EU bodies along these lines with varying degrees of success.[279]

b. Relations with OLAF

In its Report on Eurojust, the House of Lords European Union Committee noted that 'the picture on the relationship between OLAF and Eurojust is far from rosy',[280] concluding that (at least back in 2004), 'the current state of affairs in the relationship between OLAF and Eurojust is regrettable',[281] with co-operation being 'hampered by suspicion and antagonism, to the detriment of effective action against fraud'.[282] This rather bleak picture of the relationship between the two bodies can partly be explained if placed in the context of the inter-institutional competition within the European Union.[283] Eurojust—already perceived by some as a threat to centralised or unified models of prosecution in the EU, introduced to stave off calls for a European Public Prosecutor—may be seen to represent also a threat to *existing* EU anti-fraud structures such as OLAF. As will be seen below, OLAF is responsible for co-operating with national authorities towards the investigation and prosecution of fraud against the Community budget—however, this task appears to be also within the remit of Eurojust. Overlap (and the proliferation of bodies in the not unlimited EU criminal justice space) may generate competition instead of co-operation between the various bodies. These elements were reflected in evidence of both bodies to the House of Lords Committee, with the then President of Eurojust Mike Kennedy noting that initially Eurojust had been faced with 'quite a hostile situation', while OLAF acknowledging the potential overlap and pointing out that Eurojust was still in a start up phase.[284]

This climate of mistrust was prevalent notwithstanding the signature in 2003 of a 'Memorandum of Understanding' (MoU) between Eurojust and OLAF.[285] The MoU called on both parties to inform each other immediately and spontaneously

---

[277] Art 26(1),(2) and (3) respectively.
[278] Art 27(1)(a). The provision continues by extending the possibility of data exchange between Eurojust and third country authorities and/or international organisations and bodies—on such exchanges see ch 6.
[279] See also House of Lords European Union Committee, *Judicial Cooperation in the EU*, n 206 above.
[280] House of Lords European Union Committee, *Judicial Cooperation in the EU*, n 206 above, para 63.
[281] Para 68.
[282] ibid.
[283] For the position of Eurojust within the framework of such competition, see also A Mégie, 'L'institutionnalisation d'un pouvoir judiciaire européen incertain en quête de légitimité: l'unité de coopération Eurojust', *Politique européenne*, no 23, 2007, pp 57–75.
[284] Paras 64 and 65.
[285] Memorandum of Understanding between Eurojust and OLAF, www.ec.europa.eu/anti-fraud/press_room/pr/2003/memo_en.pdf.

of the existence of case of mutual interest, and exchange any necessary information and provide mutual assistance in this context.[286] This was followed up by a Heads of Agreement, signed in December 2005—this provided practical guidance and served as a declaration of intent towards a more formal agreement.[287] More recently, the Justice and Home Affairs Council approved a draft Practical Agreement on arrangements of co-operation between Eurojust and OLAF.[288] However, discussions regarding the relationship between the two bodies is likely to be ongoing, especially within the broader debate regarding their nature and direction which will emerge in the light of the entry into force of the Lisbon Treaty and the future developments it may trigger (in particular the establishment of a European Public Prosecutor 'from Eurojust').[289]

c. Relations with Europol

The relationship between Eurojust and Europol appears to be closer than that between Eurojust and OLAF. Following the relevant requirement of the Eurojust Decision, an agreement between the two bodies was signed in 2003.[290] While this agreement was not ambitious enough for Eurojust, it was seen by it as 'an important first step'.[291] One of the thorny issues of negotiations at the time was access by Eurojust to Europol's Analysis Work Files (AWFs)—with Europol noting that the interests of other 'stakeholders' had to be taken into account in this context.[292] However, recent developments—namely the entry into force of the Protocol of 27 November 2003 amending the Europol Convention, which allows Europol to invite experts of third states or bodies to be associated with the activities of an analysis group[293]—have addressed the issue of Eurojust's access to AWFs. According to the Eurojust 2007 Annual Report, Eurojust signed six Arrangements with Europol on 7 June 2007 and appointed national members and case analysts to be associated as experts from Eurojust on judicial co-operation.[294] This move—which is promoted by governments[295]—may represent a considerable strengthening of co-operation between the two bodies, but it may also have considerable implications both for data protection and for Eurojust's recommendations and

---

[286] It also contains inter alia provisions on participation in joint investigation teams, communication with other partners and information collection.

[287] Eurojust Annual Report 2006, p 18.

[288] Document 9346/08, Brussels, 14 May 2008, approved by the Justice and Home Affairs Council of 24–25 July 2008, doc. 11653/08 (Presse 205), p 28.

[289] See section VIII below.

[290] Agreement between Eurojust and Europol, www.eurojust.europa.eu/official_documents/Agreements/04%20Europol-EJ%20agreement.pdf.

[291] House of Lords European Union Committee, n 206 above, para 69.

[292] ibid, para 72.

[293] See section II B v above.

[294] p 55.

[295] See also the Conclusions of the Justice and Home Affairs Council of 5–6 June 2008, calling inter alia for the formalisation of Eurojust's participation in Analysis Work Files (Council doc 9956/08, Presse 46, p 20).

decisions on whether, and in which jurisdiction, particular conduct should be investigated or prosecuted. Moreover, it blurs the boundaries between Eurojust's perceived 'judicial' nature, and its involvement with police and intelligence work.

The current arrangements do not address a potential overlap between the two bodies. This issue has also largely been ignored in the discussion of recent instruments aimed at replacing the Europol Convention by a Decision on the one hand, and amending the Eurojust Decision on the other. While the membership, institutional arrangements and databases of the two bodies are distinct, there is an overlap regarding their tasks as both of them are dealing with aspects of the investigation of criminal offences. Diversity in domestic criminal justice systems may serve to retain the current complexity, with investigation falling within the realm of the judiciary in some Member States, and within the realm of the police in others. Intensified co-operation between Europol and Eurojust may serve to boost the chances for the investigation and prosecution of crime. At present, this efficiency logic, along with a logic of boosting the powers of both bodies seems to have prevailed. A more systematic examination of the relationship between the two bodies in the context of the development of an EU criminal justice system seems to be avoided.

d. Relations with the European Judicial Network

Questions of overlap appear very prominently as regards the relationship between Eurojust and the European Judicial Network (EJN)—in particular when Eurojust is asked to deal with bilateral or relatively straightforward cases which could also be dealt by the EJN. The question in particular has been whether there is added value in having two Union bodies dealing with the same type of judicial co-operation caseload.[296] Rather than dismantling the Network, or changing the mandate of Eurojust to focus on more complex cases, the political choice has been to make the EJN Secretariat form part of the Eurojust Secretariat[297]—leading to charges that Eurojust has effectively 'bought up' the EJN.[298] This seems to give a certain degree of EJN oversight to the President of Eurojust,[299] but the legal basis for such oversight is unclear. Parallel recent proposals for new legislation on both Eurojust and the EJN indicate the continuation of the current model.[300]

---

[296] The House of Lords European Union Committee (n 206 above, para 81) proposed that the EJN deals with bilateral cases, whereas Eurojust with complex, multilateral cases. On the EJN, see http://www.ejn-crimjust.europa/eu.

[297] Eurojust Annual Report 2007, n 256 above, p 55.

[298] See A Mégie, 'Mapping the Actors of European Judicial Cooperation' in D Bigo *et al*, n 41 above, pp 67–87 at p 85.

[299] See also oral evidence of the then Eurojust President, Mike Kennedy, to the House of Commons Home Affairs Committee, above n 249 at Q210.

[300] According to the 2007 Eurojust Annual Report (n 256 above), Eurojust has also developed links with: liaison magistrates; the EU Genocide network; the European Judicial Training Network; and the CARIN and Cybercrime Networks. Eurojust has recently signed a Memorandum of Understanding on co-operation with the European Judicial Training Network, envisaging in particular secondments of judges and prosecutors to Eurojust—www.eurojust.europa.eu/official_documents/Agreements/MOU_EJ-EJTN_7Feb08.pdf.

iv. Data Protection

The work of Eurojust involves the collection, processing and exchange of a wide range of personal data. As in the case of Europol, the relevant data protection framework is provided for in the Eurojust Decision itself.[301] A series of provisions contained therein regulate issues such as data processing,[302] access to personal data[303], the correction and deletion of personal data[304] and data storage.[305] The Eurojust Decision calls for the appointment of a Data Protection Officer, who is a member of Eurojust staff and is responsible for ensuring compliance with the data protection provisions of the Eurojust Decision.[306] As in the case of Europol, the Eurojust Decision also calls for the establishment of a Joint Supervisory Body whose task is to monitor collectively Eurojust's activities with regard to the processing of personal data.[307] Unlike Europol, where JSB members come from national data protection authorities, here JSB members are judges (taking into account the 'judicial' nature of Eurojust).[308]

v. Judicial Control

The Eurojust Decision contains no express provisions with regard to the judicial control or interpretation of Eurojust acts. This gap—which might be explained by Member States' sovereignty concerns as well as the framing of Eurojust as a 'judicial' body—has resulted in ECJ litigation. In the case of *Spain v Eurojust*,[309] the Spanish Government sought the annulment of various points in seven calls for applications for the recruitment of temporary staff issued by Eurojust, related to matters of linguistic competence (in particular the emphasis of the calls on knowledge of English and French). It challenged the calls on the grounds of infringement of rules on the condition of employment of Community servants and rules related to the linguistic arrangements applicable to Eurojust, as well as on the grounds of them being in breach of the EC anti-discrimination principle and the obligation to give reasons.[310] Spain brought the action under a first pillar legal basis—Article 230 of the EC Treaty.[311]

The Court dismissed the action as inadmissible. It stated that the acts contested therein are not included in the list of acts the legality of which the Court may

---

[301] Arts 14–25. See also the Rules of Procedure on the processing and protection of personal data at Eurojust, OJ C68, 19 March 2005, p 1.

[302] Arts 14 and 15.

[303] Arts 18, 19.

[304] Art 20.

[305] Art 21.

[306] Art 17.

[307] Art 23(1).

[308] Art 23 third indent. On the Rules of Procedure of the Eurojust JSB, see OJ C86, 6 April 2004, p 1.

[309] Case C-160/03, ECR [2005] I-2077.

[310] Paras 22–24.

[311] Para 35.

review under Article 230 EC—with ECJ jurisdiction on judicial co-operation in criminal matters defined in the third pillar, namely in Article 35 EU.[312] This is a marked departure from the position of AG Poiares Maduro, who was ready to extend 'the Community system of law and the guarantees deriving from it' to the European Union.[313] In a similar logic to the Court's reasoning in *Pupino*,[314] AG Maduro interpreted the EU Treaty (based in particular on Article 46 EU) as 'transferring' the application of Community law principles to the third pillar.

The AG then went on to examine admissibility of the action under the third pillar. He declared the action admissible. As was the case in his examination of admissibility under the first pillar, the AG conclusion was based on the fact that the Community is based on the rule of law.[315]In this context, the AG noted that the fact that Eurojust is not expressly mentioned in Article 35 EU does not mean that it is not included in its scope.[316] The difference between this position and the eventual Court judgment is striking. The Court stopped in the distinction between the first and the third pillar and did not even embark on the consideration of the possibility of admissibility of the action under the third pillar. The Court did address the issue of effective judicial protection and the rule of law, but did not find that its refusal to declare the action admissible created an obstacle in this context. The Court argued that the acts contested in the case are not exempt from judicial review, as Article 30 of the Eurojust Decision, interpreted in the light of ECJ case law, granted the candidates for the various positions in the contested calls for applications access to the Community courts.[317] While this may be the case, the refusal of the Court to examine the applicability of Article 35 TEU to Eurojust was a missed opportunity to clarify the issue of judicial control of EU bodies under the third pillar.[318]

vi. Accountability and Scrutiny

In order to address these issues, it is important to focus on the organisational structure of Eurojust. In this context, the centrality of the Eurojust College is noteworthy. As noted above, the College consists of the national Eurojust representatives. Unlike Europol, where the Management Board consisting of representatives of national governments, plays a central role in organisational matters and decision-making, Eurojust is run by its national expert members (mostly judges or prosecutors) who (perhaps as a reflection of their 'judicial' status) enjoy a large

---

[312] Paras 37 and 38.

[313] Opinion of 16 December 2004, para 17.

[314] Case C-105/03, *Pupino*, ECR [2005] I-5285. For further details see ch 1.

[315] Ser paras 15 and 20 of the Opinion, and the reference to the Court's judgment in *Les Verts* (case 294/83 *Les Verts v Parliament* [1986] ECR 1339).

[316] Para 20.

[317] Paras 41 and 42.

[318] See also in this context Craig, who argues that the Court was unwilling to apply the *Les Verts* reasoning to Eurojust primarily because it was an EU body—P Craig, *EU Administrative Law*, Oxford, OUP, 2006, p 167.

degree of independence.[319] According to the Eurojust Decision, the College is responsible for the organisation and operation of Eurojust.[320] As mentioned above, it elects the President of Eurojust from among the national members—the President exercises his/her duties 'on behalf of the College and under its authority'.[321] The College also appoints Eurojust's Administrative Director, who works 'under the authority of the College and its President'.[322] The Eurojust Data Protection Officer is also 'under the direct authority of the College'.[323] The rules and regulations applicable to EC officials also apply to Eurojust staff,[324] who must carry out their tasks 'under the authority of the College' and without seeking or accepting instructions from any government, authority, organisation or person extraneous to Eurojust.[325]

The College also has a role in drawing up the Eurojust budget—it must produce and forward to the Commission annually a budget estimate, and ultimately adopt the budget on the basis of the sums authorised by the EU budgetary authorities.[326] The Eurojust budget does not cover the salaries of national members, which, in another example of Eurojust's 'intergovernmental' features, are funded by Member States.[327] The finally adopted budget may not necessarily coincide with the initial College estimate.[328] The budgetary involvement is perhaps the strongest role of the EU institutions with regard to the control and accountability of Eurojust. The Commission is 'fully associated with the work of Eurojust'[329] and it may be invited to provide its expertise in investigations and prosecutions.[330] However, it does not have a formal role under the Decision and does not participate in the Eurojust College. The European Parliament on the other hand merely receives annually a report 'on the work carried out by Eurojust and on the activities of the Joint Supervisory Body'.[331] The information provisions with regard to the Council are stronger—the President of Eurojust, on behalf of the College, reports annually to the Council on the activities and management of Eurojust, including budgetary management—this includes an annual report.[332] Overall, the limited avenues for transparency and information regarding the work of Eurojust are evident, as are the strong intergovernmental elements in its organisational and accountability structures. However, these also demonstrate an increased indepen-

---

[319] Not many provisions regarding control of the College exist in the Eurojust Decision—an example is Art 10(2), which establishes that Eurojust's Rules of Procedure must be approved by the Council.
[320] Art 28(1).
[321] Art 28 (3).
[322] Art 29(4).
[323] Art 17(1).
[324] Art 30(1).
[325] Art 30(3).
[326] Art 35 as amended by Council Decision 2003/659/JHA, L245, 29 September 2004, p 44.
[327] Art 33(1).
[328] In the second year of Eurojust's operation, the draft budget was reduced by 20%—see House of Lords EU Committee, para 22.
[329] Art 11(1).
[330] Art 11(2).
[331] Art 32(2).
[332] Art 32(1).

dence of Eurojust as an organisation, based in particular on the fact that its members come primarily from the judiciary.

C. The Future of Eurojust

Its Annual Reports indicate that the workload of Eurojust has been growing steadily year after year—with the latest Report claiming 2007 as an important landmark, witnessing 'the historic crossing of the threshold of 1 000 cases handled by Eurojust in a single year'.[333] However, the *nature* of the cases referred to Eurojust may not have proven to be what was originally expected (namely, mainly multilateral cases for Eurojust, with the bilateral cases left primarily for the European Judicial Network). This reality may have resulted in a change of branding by Eurojust: its 2006 Annual Report claimed that the classification of cases by Eurojust as bilateral/multilateral, taking place since the beginning of its operations, 'did not reflect the reality of the work done by Eurojust'.[334] Interestingly, no data on the basis of the distinction between bilateral/multilateral cases appeared in that Report. Instead, it was noted that cases would be reclassified as 'standard or complex'.[335] According to the 2007 Annual Report, this distinction is based on an assessment of factors such as 'the number of countries involved and on the nature of Eurojust's involvement, e.g. whether a case requires co-operation and/or co-ordination'.[336] According to the Report, Eurojust dealt with 849 standard and 236 simple cases in 2007—with the ratio of bilateral/multilateral cases being 813: 272.[337] The difference does not seem significant—at least at this stage—and confirms that the vast majority of Eurojust's caseload is standard and/or bilateral cases, where the main contribution of Eurojust could be to act as a broker or contact facilitator between two jurisdictions.

Notwithstanding these indications, and the remaining potential overlap between Eurojust and the European Judicial Network, recent months have witnessed a momentum towards an increase of Eurojust's powers. Contributing to this momentum has been the organisation of two seminars, one by the Austrian EU Presidency in 2006[338] and another by the Portuguese EU Presidency in 2007,[339] where—in a process reminiscent of the method applied in the Convention of the future of Europe, aiming to give legitimacy to future action—the future of Eurojust has been extensively discussed by Eurojust members, representatives of governments and EU

---

[333] 2007 Annual Report, n 256 above, p 8.

[334] 2006 Annual Report, p 26.

[335] ibid, p 15.

[336] 2007 Annual Report, n 256 above, p 15.

[337] pp 15–16.

[338] See Report of the seminar: 'A Seminar with 2020 Vision: The Future of Eurojust and the European Judicial Network', Vienna, 25–26 September 2006, Council doc 14123/06, Brussels, 19 October 2006.

[339] See General Report on the seminar 'Eurojust: Navigating the Way Forward', Lisbon 29 and 30 October 2007, Council doc 15542/07, Brussels, 21 November 2007.

institutions, and practitioners and experts from Member States. The second seminar coincided with the publication of a Commission Communication 'on the role of Eurojust and the European Judicial Network in the fight against organised crime and terrorism in the European Union'.[340] These initiatives, all of which focused one way or another on the issue of Eurojust's powers,[341] maintained a momentum culminating into action by Member States' Governments.[342] The Justice and Home Affairs Council of 6–7 December 2007 adopted specific conclusions on Eurojust:[343] these note a number of features in Eurojust's current work, while cautiously open the door to future legislative reform. The Council inter alia:

—noted that Member States have implemented the Eurojust Decision taking into account their different legal traditions, thus contributing to an objective lack of balance among national members as regards the capacity to perform their tasks in an equivalent manner. Both for Eurojust and the national members, this situation and the actual use of available powers, including any problems encountered, should be thoroughly assessed when examining any needs for improvements

—invited Member States to examine the possibility of enabling national members to play a pro-active and effective role in facilitating co-operation and co-ordination of trans-national serious investigations, while respecting allocation of competences within national systems

—shared the Commission's view that the relationship between Eurojust, Europol, OLAF and other relevant counterparts acting in the area of judicial co-operation could be improved.[344]

The Council conclusions were followed shortly afterwards by a draft Council Decision tabled by no less than 14 Member States under their third pillar right of initiative, aimed at amending the Eurojust Decision.[345] It is noteworthy that the exercise of the right of initiative under the third pillar by Member States has pre-empted a proposal on Eurojust by the European Commission, which might have been more ambitious with regard to the powers of Eurojust and/or the establishment of a European Public Prosecutor.[346] According to the Explanatory Memorandum accompanying the proposal, its aim is to 'reinforce the role and

---

[340] See COM (2007) 644 final, n 274 above.

[341] This issue was also highlighted in Eurojust's initial contribution to the Commission's 2007 Communication—see Council doc 13079/07, Brussels 20 September 2007.

[342] See also the press Art by the Justice Ministers of France, Portugal Spain, Italy, Slovenia and Germany, published in September 2007 and calling inter alia for the strengthening of Eurojust, in particular in the context of transnational criminal investigations and the work of joint investigation teams: see 'Maintenant, il faut un vrai espace judiciaire européen', *Le Figaro* (15 September 2007).

[343] Council doc 15966/07 (Presse 275), pp 25–27.

[344] *Ibid*, points 5, 7 and 12 respectively.

[345] Council doc 5037/08, Brussels, 7 January 2008. This was accompanied by a parallel draft Decision on the European Judicial Network—Council doc 5039/08, Brussels, 7 January 2008.

[346] In this context see, 'EU States Muscle in on Bloc's Judicial Body' (6 May 2008), www.euobserver. com/9/26082/?print=1. According to the article, the Commission stated that it will no longer table a legislative proposal on Eurojust as the planning has been overtaken by the submission of the Member States' initiative.

capacities' of Eurojust in the light of what the EM deems as 'significant changes' since the beginning of Eurojust's operation—namely the enlargement of the European Union, the decentralisation of judicial co-operation in criminal matters in the EU (in particular via the 2000 Mutual Legal Assistance Convention), and the shift towards intelligence-led policing in the EU.[347] The proposal itself contains a number of changes, many of which are related to the powers of Eurojust. Principal changes include:

—the insertion of a new provision regarding the powers of Eurojust when acting as a College with regard to *conflicts of jurisdiction*—where national members are not in agreement on how to resolve such cases with regard to the undertaking of investigations or prosecutions, the College will issue 'a written non-binding opinion on how the case should be solved'[348]
—the clarification and strengthening of the provisions regarding the *powers* of Eurojust national members—the latter continue to be subject to the national law of their Member State as regards their status, but their term of office is a minimum of 4 years;[349] the draft Decision also expressly grants Eurojust national members full access to a wide range of personal data, including data contained in national criminal records, registers of arrested persons, investigation registers, DNA registers, and 'other' national registers containing information necessary for the fulfilment of the national members' tasks.[350] The modalities of such access will be 'at least in the same way as stipulated by national law in the case of a prosecutor, judge or police officer of equivalent competence'.[351]
—Moreover, as regards the *powers* of national members, in an important new provision, Member States are expressly obliged to define the nature and extent of the judicial powers conferred on national members. The proposal calls for a minimum of *equivalent* powers of national members including handling information on judicial co-operation requests, preparing the setting up of joint investigation teams, performing all tasks carried out by competent national authorities in relation to Europol's Analysis Work Files.[352] National members will also have, in their capacity as judicial authorities and in agreement with the competent national authority, powers of issuing judicial co-operation requests, ordering search and seizure measures and authorising and co-ordinating controlled deliveries.[353]
—The significant extension of Eurojust's powers with regard to the *processing of personal data*—amended Article 15 not only renders the list of personal data which Eurojust can process from exhaustive to indicative, but it also adds, in

[347] Council doc 5038/08, Brussels, 30 January 2008, pp 2–3.
[348] New Art 7(2).
[349] Amended Art 9(1).
[350] Amended Art 9(4).
[351] New Art 9(4)(a).
[352] New Art 9a(1).
[353] New Artcile 9a(2).

paragraph 1, to the categories of data to be processed a wide range of data, namely telephone numbers, vehicle registration data, e-mail accounts, phone and e-mail trafficked data, DNA records and photographs.

—The extension of and addition to the provisions concerning the *relations of Eurojust with other EU bodies*—in this context, Member States must ensure that the College may effectively be able to open a Europol Analysis Work File and participate in its functioning;[354] the administrative relationship between Eurojust and the European Judicial Network is further formalised;[355] the Eurojust secretariat will also encompass the secretariats of a variety of other EU networks (such as the Joint Investigation Teams network);[356] and Eurojust will establish close co-operation with bodies both inside (Frontex, SitCen) and outside (Interpol, the World Customs Organisation) the EU.[357]

—The extension of Eurojust's role in *external matters*—Eurojust may detach liaison officers to a third State (these will be magistrates 'for the benefit of Eurojust');[358] it will also co-ordinate the execution of requests for judicial co-operation issued by third States[359]—such requests may be received directly by Eurojust, reflecting thus the model of Eurojust as a 'one-stop shop' for judicial co-operation in criminal matters for the EU.[360]

It is noteworthy that the adoption of the new Eurojust Decision has been a political priority for Member States, perhaps in order to pre-empt the entry into force of the Lisbon Treaty which would change the decision-making process on this dossier.[361] Although a number of the elements of the proposal were particularly controversial, the Justice and Home Affairs Council reached a 'general approach' on the proposal in July 2008.[362] Although the new proposals refrain from introducing changes with regard to the mandatory character of Eurojust's requests to national authorities to initiate investigations and prosecutions, their potential impact on State sovereignty and the relationship between the EU and the national level in judicial co-operation in criminal matters should not be underestimated. The detailed provisions on the powers of national members of Eurojust under their national law may transform this relationship. The proposal would impose on Member States to confer to their Eurojust national members a series of powers—

---

[354] New Art 26(1)(a).

[355] Amended Art 26(2).

[356] New Art 26(2)9f).

[357] New Art 26(7)–(10).

[358] New Art 26a(1) and (2).

[359] New Art 27a(1).

[360] New Art 27a(2).

[361] The proposal has been one of the priorities of the Slovenian EU Presidency (first half of 2008)—see House of Lords European Union Committee, *Priorities of the European Union: Evidence from the Minister of Europe and the Ambassador of Slovenia*, 11th Report, session 2007–08, HL Paper 73, p 28.

[362] Justice and Home Affairs Council of 24–25 July 2008, doc 11653/08 (Presse 205), p 20. The Council also agree a 'general approach' on a draft Decision on the European Judicial Network. At the time of writing however, the Eurojust text upon which a 'general approach' was agreed was not available on the Council website. For indications of the controversial aspects of negotiations, see Council docs 9114/08, Brussels, 8 May 2008, and 9980/1/08 REV 1, Brussels, 30 May 2008.

while it is claimed in the EM that these powers 'must be understood as powers used by the national member acting as a national authority of its Member State of origin' and conferring such powers 'does not in any way make Eurojust a supra-national body',[363] the fact that it is *Union* law which imposes such powers is unde-niable. The impact of the Union law on domestic criminal justice systems is further recognised by the EM and the draft Decision itself, in a provision acknow-ledging the divergent constitutional rules regarding the division of powers between prosecutors and judges, but requiring even in these cases that a level of powers equivalent to the national competent authorities is granted to the national Eurojust member.[364] While the proposal continues—as the current Eurojust Decision—to pay lip service to national diversity and powers defined at national level, the new proposals may change the landscape drastically by introducing pow-ers for Eurojust national members by Union law—transforming the relationship between national law and Union law with regard to the functioning of Eurojust and the impact of Union law on domestic criminal justice systems.[365]

The proposal also triggers a number of important insights in relation to the *nature* of Eurojust. It is confirmed that the 'judicial' framing of the body, promi-nently expressed in its title and a number of the provisions with regard to its accountability, may be much narrower than Eurojust's actual tasks. Along with the tasks of a judicial authority, its members are also called upon to assume pro-secutorial tasks, but also tasks largely related to investigations and policing. The prosecutorial dimension is enhanced by the granting to Eurojsut national mem-bers powers to order search and seizure.[366] The investigative dimension is strongly emphasised in the new proposals, which stress again the participation of Eurojust in Europol's analysis work and stress Eurojust's participation in joint investigation teams, but also extend considerably the possibilities of Eurojust data processing, including the processing of sensitive personal data such as DNA data. These devel-opments demonstrate that the model of Eurojust as a 'judicial' authority oversee-ing the policemen of Europol has not been adopted.[367] On the contrary, there is an increasing synergy, if not convergence in the tasks of Europol and Eurojust—notwithstanding their different membership—leading to a considerable strength-ening of the investigatory branch in EU criminal law.

[363] p 14.
[364] New Art 9a(6). According to the EM, this derogation guarantees 'the coherence of national sys-tems by preserving the division between the roles of prosecutors and judges'—p 17.
[365] The proposals imply also instances whereby national rules—as mandated by the new proposal—may have an impact on Union law and practice—see in particular rules designing the setting up and participation of national members in joint investigation teams and performing tasks related to a Europol Analysis Work File.
[366] In this context, the European Scrutiny Committee of the House of Commons expressed con-cerns that these powers 'would be a first step towards the creation of a European Public Prosecutor's Office within Eurojust'. See 20th Report, session 2007–08, para 6.3.
[367] See also Bigo *et al*, n 41 above, p 40.

IV. OLAF

A. Background and Legislative Framework

An area of criminality which has drawn the attention of Community institutions early on has been fraud against the financial interests of the Community. The need to protect Community's finances resulted in calls for increased intervention of Community law into the sphere of domestic criminal law.[368] At the institutional level, the Commission decided to establish, already in 1987 an anti-fraud unit based within its auspices (UCLAF)[369]—UCLAF became operational in 1988,[370] one year prior to the ECJ *Greek Maize* judgment.[371] UCLAF operated in the 1990s, within the context of a growing emphasis at EU level on the adoption of criminal law against fraud, in an effort in particular to boost the *external* dimension of the fight against fraud, namely by providing an incentive for Member States to prosecute fraud against the Community's financial interests in their jurisdiction.[372] However, it was allegations with regard to the management of Community funds *internally* which led to the reform of the Community anti-fraud institutional framework. Such allegations led in the late '90s to a major political crisis in the EU, culminating in the fall of the Santer Commission in 1999.[373] One of the responses to this crisis has been internal institutional reform—with the Task Force for Coordination of Fraud Prevention (which had in the meantime succeeded UCLAF) being replaced by a new unit, OLAF[374]: as one author noted, the latter is thus 'the fruit of exceptional circumstances in the aftermath of a scandal' and 'reflects the necessity of restoring credibility'.[375]

---

[368] For such intervention in the field of criminal law harmonisation, see ch 2.

[369] UCLAF stands for Unité de coordination de la lutte anti-fraude.

[370] On the establishment and role of UCLAF see J A E Vervaele, 'Towards an Independent European Agency to Fight Fraud and Corruption in the EU?', *European Journal of Crime, Criminal Law and Criminal Justice*, vol 7, no 3, 1999, pp 331–346; V Pujas, 'Les difficultés de l'OLAF pour s' imposer en tant qu'acteur légitime de la protection des interets économiques et financiers européens', *Cultures et conflits*, no 62, 2006, pp 107–129 at pp 109–116; and V Pujas, 'The European Anti-Fraud Office (OLAF): A European Policy to Fight Against Economic and Financial Fraud?', *Journal of European Public Policy*, vol 10, no 5, 2003, pp 778–797 at pp 779–782.

[371] On the *Greek Maize* judgment, which introduced the principle of assimilation in a case involving alleged fraud against Community funds, see ch 2.

[372] See in particular the third pillar fraud Convention and its Protocols and the subsequent Commission *Corpus Juris* proposals—see ch.2.

[373] See P Craig, 'The Fall and Renewal of the Commission: Accountability, Contract and Administrative Organisation', *European Law Journal*, vol 6, no 2, 2000, pp 98–116; A Tomkins, 'Responsibility and Resignation in the European Commission', *Modern Law Review*, vol 62, no 5, 1999, pp 744–765; and D Georgakakis, 'La démission de la Commission européenne: Scandale et tournant institutionnel (octobre 1998—mars 1999)', *Cultures et conflits*, nos 38–39, 2000, at www.conflits.org.

[374] For a brief chronology, see the Report by the French National Assembly—Assemblée Nationale, Rapport d'information déposé par la Délégation de l' Assemblée Nationale pour l'Union européenne sur l'Office européen de lutte anti-fraude (OLAF), No 1533, 8 April 2004, pp.9–10.

[375] Pujas, 'European Anti-Fraud Office', above n 370, p 792.

OLAF (the European Anti-Fraud Office)[376] was established by a Commission Decision in April 1999.[377] The Decision confirms that OLAF's tasks would include the conduct of both external and internal administrative investigation[378]—with OLAF exercising the Commission's powers to carry out external investigations.[379] It also confirms the independence of OLAF's investigative function.[380] The Decision also calls for the establishment of a 'surveillance committee' responsible for monitoring such investigative function[381]—the latter will also have a role in the appointment of OLAF'S Director, who will be nominated by the Commission after consulting the European Parliament and the Council.[382] This rather short instrument was complemented by a Regulation fleshing out rules concerning OLAF investigations.[383] The Regulation contains the rules applicable to the conduct of OLAF's external (primarily by reference to pre-existing EC-law rules concerning Commission powers) and internal investigations.[384] The Regulation also includes specific rules on the opening[385] and the procedure of investigations,[386] and emphasises the need for confidentiality. [387]Central to the conduct of investigations are also the provision calling for forwarding of information by OLAF to the competent (including judicial) authorities of Member States,[388] and the provision stating that OLAF will draw up a report on completion of its investigations.[389] These provisions raise a number of questions concerning the relationship of OLAF's activities with the domestic criminal procedure systems of Member States, in particular as regards the impact of the use of information forwarded by OLAF on defence rights[390] and the use of the OLAF investigation report as evidence in domestic criminal proceedings.[391] The use of 'EU'-produced

[376] OLAF stands for Office lutte anti-fraude.

[377] OJ L136, 31 May 1999, p 20.

[378] The Court of Justice resisted attempts to limit the powers of OLAF with regard to Community bodies, by annulling Decisions of the European Central Bank and the Management Committee of the European Investment Bank aiming to exclude to a great extent these bodies from OLAF's remit. See Case C-11/00 *Commission v European Central Bank* ECR [2003] I-7417; and Case C-15/00 *Commission v European Investment Bank* ECR [2003] I-7281.

[379] Art 2(1). For such powers, see in particular Council Regulation (Euratom, EC) No 2185/96 concerning on-the-spot checks and inspections carried out by the Commission in order to protect the European Communities' financial interests against fraud and other irregularities, OJ L292, 15 November 1996, p 2.

[380] Art 3.

[381] Art 4.

[382] Art 5(1).

[383] Regulation (EC) No 1073/1999 concerning investigations conducted by OLAF, OJ L136, 31 May 1999, p 1.

[384] Arts 3 and 4 respectively.

[385] Art 5.

[386] Art 6.

[387] Art 8.

[388] Art 10.

[389] Art 9.

[390] On this issue, see the *Tillack* saga below.

[391] The OLAF Regulation states that the Reports 'constitute admissible evidence in administrative or judicial proceedings of the Member State in which their use proves necessary, in the same way and under the same conditions as administrative reports drawn up by national administrative inspectors'— Art 9(2).

evidence in domestic criminal proceedings is far from straightforward and has led to concerns regarding the maintenance of State sovereignty in criminal matters.[392] As far as accountability and judicial control are concerned, the Regulation contains a number of express provisions varying in detail. The Director of OLAF [393]— who directs the conduct of OLAF's investigations[394] and must neither seek nor take instructions from any government or institution in his/her investigative capacity[395]—must report regularly to the European Parliament, the Council, the Commission and the Court of Auditors on the findings of investigations carried out by OLAF.[396] Financing of OLAF is—although under a separate heading—part of the general Commission budget.[397] Judicial review is provided by the Regulation only for EC officials against OLAF acts forming part of internal investigations (but no provisions are included with regard to external investigations).[398] Moreover, no specific provisions on data protection are included, but the general EC data protection rules are assumed to apply to OLAF.[399] OLAF's investigative function is monitored by a Supervisory Committee, which will 'reinforce the Office's independence'.[400] The Committee is composed of five 'independent outside persons' appointed by common accord of the European Parliament,

---

[392] There have been reports of the reluctance of national courts accepting evidence collected by OLAF—see House of Lords European Union Committee, *Strengthening OLAF, the European Anti-Fraud Office*, 24th Report, session 2003–04, HL Paper 139, para 54. Issues related to the admissibility of evidence have led to the centralising proposals in the *Corpus Juris*—for a discussion see W Hetzer, 'National Criminal Prosecution and European Tendering of Evidence. Perspectives of the European Anti-Fraud Office (OLAF)', *European Journal of Crime, Criminal Law and Criminal Justice*, vol 12, no 2, 2004, pp 166–183.

[393] The Director of OLAF since 2000 has been Franz-Hermann Brüner from Germany. His term was renewed in 2006 (according to Art 12(1) of the OLAF Regulation, the OLAF Director is appointed for a term of five years, renewable once).

[394] Art 6(1).

[395] Art 12(3).

[396] ibid. OLAF is also accountable under a number of Treaty provisions aiming at ensuring the accountability of the Commission to other EU institutions, such as the European Parliament and the Court of Auditors—see for instance the Commission annual reports to the European Parliament and the Council on the fight against fraud, produced under Art 280 EC (for the latest Report, see COM (2007) 390, 6 July 2007). For a detailed analysis of OLAF's accountability in the context of general EC law provisions see H Xanthaki, 'Fraud in the EU: Review of OLAF's Regulatory Framework' in I Bantekas and G Keramidas (eds), *International and European Financial Criminal Law*, London, Buttterworths, 2006, pp 120–153. See in particular the section on the relationship between OLAF and the Parliament's Committee on Budgetary Control (COCOBU)—pp 141–149.

[397] Art 13.

[398] Art 14. The general Art 230 EC provides, under certain conditions, for an avenue for individuals to bring forward actions against the Commission in Luxembourg (however, this provision does obviously not cover actions by individuals before national courts)—see also European Commission, 'Evaluation of the Activities of the European Anti-Fraud Office (OLAF)' COM (2003) 154 final, Brussels, 2 April 2003, p 41. The Court has refused standing to MEPs seeking annulment of amendments to the EP Rules of Procedure following the adoption of an Inter-institutional Agreement between inter alia the Parliament and OLAF—however, it reiterated its case law that the rules relating to recourse to Community Courts must be interpreted in the light of the principle of effective judicial protection—Case C-167/02P, *Rothley and Others v European Parliament*, [2004] ECR I-3149, paras 46–54.

[399] See also the OLAF webpage on data protection, www.ec.europa.eu/dgs/olaf/data/index_en.html.

[400] Art 11(1).

the Council and the Commission for a mandate of 3 years renewable once.[401] Members have included judges, prosecutors, former MEPs, academics and civil servants.[402] In carrying out their duties, members must neither seek nor take instructions from any government or any institution, body, office or agency.[403] The Committee's main task is to deliver opinions to the Director concerning OLAF's activities, 'without however interfering with the conduct of the investigation process'.[404] Regularly informed by the OLAF Director,[405] the Committee also adopts at least one annual activity report, and may submit reports to the European Parliament, the Council, the Commission and the Court of Auditors on the results of OLAF's investigations.[406]

This legislative framework has led to the justified conclusion that OLAF's status is 'hybrid and ambiguous'.[407] OLAF was set up as a response to grave allegations of financial irregularities within the Commission, in order partly to investigate any such irregularities independently—yet it is not an independent Community agency, but it rather remains a department of the Commission itself, under the Commission's control. The paradox—and potential conflict of interest—with regard to OLAF's role in *internal* investigations is glaring: the office set out to 'clean up' the financial affairs of the Commission is basically—with some added safeguards of independence—in essence the Commission itself. This paradox may account for what is deemed as the 'increased politicisation' of OLAF investigations.[408] It has also led to difficult situations with regard to ensuring meaningful accountability of OLAF towards other EU institutions, in particular the European Parliament. These difficulties were recognised by the Commission itself in its 2003 evaluation of OLAF. Discussing the parliamentary oversight of OLAF, the Commission noted that:

> this situation is likely to generate expectations that will be tricky for the Office to solve as, particularly in the context of the discharge or parliamentary questions, it must both help the Commission to fulfil its obligations and satisfy Parliament's wish for facts allowing it to exert its financial management audit task, while complying with the legal framework for its investigations that place restrictions on its communication activities. For the Commission, the situation with regard to the current investigations can prove delicate, because of the Office's independence, as it must answer questions from Parliament even though the Office's independent status means that the Commission does not always have

---

[401] Arts 11(2) and (3).

[402] The Supervisory Committee is currently chaired by Luis Lopez Sanz-Aranguez, Public Prosecutor at Supreme Court in Spain. Its first chairperson was Professor Mireille Delmas-Marty, who led the *Corpus Juris* project.

[403] Art 11(5).

[404] Art 11(1).

[405] Art 11(7), which states that the Director must forward each year to the Supervisory Committee the Office's programme of activities and must keep the Committee regularly informed of the Office's activities, its investigations, the results thereof and the action taken on them.

[406] Art 11(8).

[407] '*Un statut hybride et ambigu*'—Assemblée nationale, n 374 above, p 10. On OLAF's hybrid status, see also House of Lords European Union Committee, *Strengthening OLAF*, n 392 above, para 29.

[408] '*Une politisation croissante*'—Assemblée nationale, n 374 above, p 21.

the requisite information, and at the same time it must abide by the principle of confidentiality of investigations.[409]

This ambiguous status of OLAF (which may lead to gaps in its accountability and judicial control), coupled with its considerable investigative powers have led to broader concerns regarding the impact of OLAF action on fundamental rights.[410] Such concerns were expressed strongly by the Court of Auditors in its special Report on OLAF, expressly stating that '*there is no independent guarantee of the legality of investigative procedures in progress or that the fundamental rights of persons under investigation are safeguarded*'(emphasis added) and adding that 'for want of a clear codification of investigative procedures the situation is prone to litigation'.[411] The lack of clear investigatory procedures and of structured supervision of OLAF investigations has also been highlighted by the OLAF Supervisory Committee.[412] The Commission attempted to address these criticisms by tabling a proposal for legislation amending the OLAF Regulation, which would introduce a specific provision on certain procedural guarantees and strengthen somewhat the role of the OLAF Supervisory Committee.[413] However, the proposal—whose potential contribution towards addressing fundamental rights concerns is not straightforward[414]—has not been adopted at the time of writing. The legal framework currently in force relies on the Supervisory Committee of OLAF to point out breaches of fundamental rights in OLAF investigations. However, the powers of the Committee are limited and its role within the ambiguous status of OLAF contested. As the Court of Auditors has noted:

> The discharge of the mandate of the Supervisory Committee is delicate on several counts. The Committee is required to be the guarantor of *both the Office's independence and the rights of persons under investigation*. The legislation gives it no decision-taking power to do this. By restricting its pronouncements to issues of principle, it is laying down a doctrine which *has no real effects on investigations*. Finally, as the Committee cannot

---

[409] Commission, n 398 above, p 41. In the same document, the Commission confirms that it had initially proposed the establishment of an external body, and notes that OLAF's current status can be explained by the circumstances surrounding its establishment, with the aim being ' to find a good way of increasing the effectiveness and credibility of the fight against fraud, corruption and other illegal activities *as quickly as possible*'(emphasis added)—*ibid*, p 31.

[410] In this context, see S Gless and H E Zeitler, 'Fair Trial Rights and the European Community's Fight Against Fraud', *European Law Journal*, vol 7, 2001, pp 219–237; and W Hetzer, 'Fight Against Fraud and Protection of Fundamental Rights in the European Union', *European Journal of Crime, Criminal Law and Criminal Justice*, vol 14, no 1, 2006, pp 20–45.

[411] Court of Auditors, Special Report No 1/2005 Concerning the Management of the European Anti-Fraud Office (OLAF), OJ C202, 18 August 2005, p 1, point IX at p 3.

[412] OLAF Supervisory Committee, Activity Report of OLAF Supervisory Committee December 2005-May 2007, 17 October 2007.

[413] 'Proposal for a Regulation of the European Parliament and of the Council amending Regulation (EC) No 1073/1999 concerning investigations conducted by the European Anti-Fraud Office (OLAF)' COM (2006) 244 final, Brussels, 24 May 2006.

[414] See the opinion of the OLAF Supervisory Committee, noting that 'the rights of the person under investigation require further protection *de lege ferenda* than provided in the draft'—n 412 above, p 21.

intervene during the course of investigations, it in no way constitutes a mechanism to monitor the legality of investigations while they are in progress. (emphasis added)[415]

B. The Judicial Control of OLAF—The *Tillack* Saga and Beyond

OLAF's hybrid status, along with its extensive investigative powers, may have significant implications for the position of individuals under investigation. This is in particular the case in the light of the inevitable politicisation of cases involving alleged irregularities within the European Commission, where OLAF's zeal to pursue the matter along with its extended avenues of communication with national investigative authorities may lead to unleashing a wide range of—largely unchecked—powers against individuals who happen to be involved in these cases. A prime example of such a situation has been the Tillack saga. OLAF's investigation concerned the publication in February and March of 2002 by Hans-Martin Tillack in *Stern* of two articles containing reports of alleged irregularities based on a report by an EU official (Paul van Buitenen) and on confidential OLAF documents. OLAF issued on 27 March 2002 a press release announcing an internal inquiry which would also include an investigation on bribery as 'it is not excluded that payment may have been made to somebody within OLAF (or possibly another EU institution) for these documents'.[416] Following a complaint by Mr Tillack, the European Ombudsman found that the publication of such allegations by OLAF without a factual basis was disproportionate and constituted an act of maladministration—and subsequently found, in a special report to the European Parliament, that OLAF made incorrect and misleading statements in its submissions to the Ombudsman in the context of this inquiry.[417] Allegations of maladministration did not stop OLAF from forwarding in February 2004 information concerning suspicions of breach of professional secrecy and bribery to the judicial authorities in Brussels and Hamburg.[418] Both authorities opened investigations, and the Belgian investigation led to the Belgian police carrying out a search of Mr Tillack's home and office and the seizure of professional documents and personal belongings.[419]

Following these developments, Mr Tillack brought an action for annulment of the measure by which OLAF forwarded certain information to the Hamburg and Brussels prosecuting authorities to the Court of First Instance. He also asked the CFI to take interim measures to order the suspension of any further action by the Belgian and German authorities and to order that OLAF refrain from obtaining,

---

[415] Court of Auditors above, para 67.

[416] Cited in the facts of the Court of First Instance judgment on the *Tillack* case (Case T-193/04, *Tillack v Commission*, [2006] ECR II-3995 para 14).

[417] European Ombudsman, Special Report to the European Parliament following the draft recommendation to the European Anti-Fraud Office in complaint 2485/2004/GG, Strasbourg, 12 May 2005, www.ombudsman.europa.eu/special/pdf/en/042485.pdf.

[418] ECJ para 27.

[419] ECJ para 29.

inspecting or examining the contents of any documents in possession of the Belgian authorities as a result of their search and seizure operation. Both the Court of First Instance and the Court of Justice on appeal rejected the application for interim measures.[420] Finally, in October 2006, the judgment of the Court of First Instance was published.[421] The Court dismissed both the applicant's action for damages and his action for annulment of the act by which OLAF, on the basis of Article 10(2) of Regulation 1073/1999, forwarded information to the German and Belgium judicial authorities. On the second point, the Court followed largely the interim measures orders by finding that in the present case 'the contested act does not bring about a distinct change in the applicant's legal position'.[422] While national authorities are under a duty to examine the information forwarded by OLAF carefully, this does not mean that the forwarded information has binding effect, 'in the sense that the national authorities are obliged to take specific measures, since such an interpretation would alter the division of tasks and responsibilities as prescribed for the implementation of Regulation No 1073/99'.[423]

In *Tillack*, the Court of First Instance thus has tried not to rock the boat regarding the role of OLAF in domestic criminal investigations—by emphasising the autonomy of national authorities in deciding on whether to act on the basis of OLAF reports. However, in stressing national autonomy, the Court at the same time refused to look at the substance of the document which triggered the domestic investigation and search and seizure measures, namely *OLAF's report in itself*. The reluctance of the Court to examine the substance and accuracy of a report *by a Community institution*, which has resulted—albeit in a domestic context—in the taking of coercive measures against an individual, is hardly indicative of meaningful judicial control of OLAF, or of effective judicial protection for the individuals concerned. By rejecting the action for damages, the Court appeared also not to be inclined to examine the general conduct of OLAF's campaign against Mr Tillack—notwithstanding the sustained criticism of such conduct by the European Ombudmsan.[424]

---

[420] Order of the President of the Court of First Instance of 15 October 2004 in case T-193/04R, [2004] ECR II-3575; and Order of the President of the Court of 19 April 2005 in case C-521/04 P(R) [2005] ECR I-3103. For a background and analysis of these judgments see J Wakefield, 'Good Governance and the European Anti-Fraud Office', *European Public Law*, vol 12, no 4, 2006, pp 549–575.

[421] Case T-193/04, *Hans-Martin Tillack v Commission*, n 410 above. For a commentary, see the note of J Wakefield in *Common Market Law Review*, vol 45, 2008, pp 199–221.

[422] Para 68.

[423] Para 72.

[424] The Court found that the applicant has failed to show the existence of a sufficiently serious breach of Community law attributable to OLAF capable of causing him harm (para 135). It found that the applicant has not established the existence of a sufficiently direct causal link between the forwarding of the information by OLAF to the Belgian judicial authorities and the damage claimed (para 124). According to the Court, the recommendations of the European Ombudsman in this context are not relevant, as 'the classification as an 'act of maladministration' by the Ombudsman does not mean, in itself, that OLAF's conduct constitutes a sufficiently serious breach of a rule of law', adding that the alternative non-judicial Ombudsman remedy 'meets specific criteria and does not necessarily have the same objective as judicial proceedings' (para 128).

The CFI refusal to look at the substance of OLAF's report (which was linked with an aggressive campaign against a journalist publicising allegations of internal mismanagement in the Commission) also comes in sharp contrast with the stance of the European Court of Human Rights in Strasbourg. In its examination of the case of Mr Tillack against Belgium, alleging breach of his fundamental rights by the measures taken by the Belgian authorities following the forwarding of the OLAF report to them, the Strasbourg Court found that these measures are disproportionate and thus have violated the applicant's right of freedom of expression under Article 10 ECHR.[425] In reaching this conclusion, the Court took into account the fact that the applicant was a journalist (triggering thus freedom of the press issues).[426] It also looked at the measures taken by the Belgian authorities *in the light of the information provided to them by OLAF*. The Court agreeing with the European Ombudsman that the corruption suspicions against the applicant were founded upon 'simple rumours'—there was thus no preponderant imperative of public interest which could justify the measures taken by the national authorities.[427] Judicial protection to Mr Tillack was thus provided in the context of the examination of measures taken by *national* authorities. This seems to be in line with the approach of the Court of First Instance. However, one cannot help but notice the following paradox: the examination of the substance of the OLAF Report was conducted in Strasbourg and not in Luxembourg—thus it was not a Community Court which examined the action of a Community institution, but the Strasbourg Court in the context of its investigation of national proceedings.[428] The differences in the outcome of the *Tillack* cases highlights the limits to effective judicial protection for the individuals affected and the detailed scrutiny of OLAF's activities before the Union courts.

The Court of First Instance (CFI) can be seen as addressing these concerns in its recent judgment in *Franchet and Byk v Commission*.[429] The case involved OLAF internal investigations against Mr Franchet and Mr Byk, former general director and director of Eurostat respectively, which resulted in the transmission of files and the opening of prosecutions in courts in France and Luxembourg. The Court began by differentiating between the eventual outcome of the cases at the national level and the need to examine the manner in which OLAF conducted its investigations.[430] The Court found that the transmission of the dossiers by OLAF to the national authorities involved an internal (and not an external) investigation.[431] In examining the conduct of the internal investigation, the Court found in no

---

[425] *Affaire Tillack c. Belgique*, Requete no 20477/05, 27 November 2007 (final version 27 February 2008), para 68.

[426] See in particular para 65.

[427] Para 63 (my translation).

[428] It has been reported that the Belgian police have now dropped the case against Mr Tillack—see 'Belgian Police Drop Case Against EU Journalist' at euobserver.com (30 January 2008) www.euobserver.com/9/25567/?print=1.

[429] Case T-48/05, delivered on 8 July 2008 and reported in French.

[430] Para 90.

[431] Para 124.

uncertain terms that OLAF violated not only Article 4 of Decision 1999/396 on the right to inform the interested party and the rights of the defendants in the context of the transmission of the dossiers to the national authorities,[432] but also Article 11 of Regulation 1073/1999 in not informing the OLAF Supervisory Committee of the transmission of the dossiers to national authorities.[433] Of equal significance are the findings of the Court with regard to the spreading of rumours by OLAF with regard to the defendants. In a departure from its outlook in *Tillack*, the Court found that OLAF was responsible for information leaks with regard to one of the dossiers[434] (para 206) and that, in doing so, it violated the principle of the presumption of innocence.[435] The Court also found that the principle of the presumption of innocence was violated by the Commission too, by the publication of a press release concerning the defendants[436] and ordered the Commission to pay the sum of 56,000 Euros to the applicants. The CFI judgment is extremely significant, not only in finding that there is a causal link between the conduct of OLAF and the European Commission and the worsening of the position of individuals under investigation, but also in signalling that the Court is ready to scrutinise in detail the activities of OLAF and their impact on the rights of individuals affected by OLAF's operations. It is particularly noteworthy that in this case, the Court looked in detail at the substance of OLAF's conduct and was not hindered by the formal distinction between what constitutes an 'internal' or an 'external' OLAF investigation. This step is welcome as it should stop cases where OLAF may hide behind the transmission of information to national authorities to shield its activities from scrutiny.[437] On the other hand, the Court's ruling against the Commission on the question of the presumption of innocence may also signify that the latter may not evade responsibility in evoking the fact that an OLAF investigation is taking place.

C. The Future of OLAF

The reform of the role of the Supervisory Committee discussed above must be viewed within the broader context of the discussion regarding the future status and powers of OLAF and its relationship with national investigative and judicial authorities. In this context, the examination of the relationship between OLAF and Union bodies such as Europol and Eurojust is central, in particular in the light of the potential future establishment of a European Public Prosecutor. As has been

---

[432] Para 152. The Decision concerns the terms and conditions of internal investigations in relation to the prevention of fraud, corruption and any other illegal activity detrimental to the Communities' interests—OJ L149, 16 June 1999, p 57.

[433] Paras 164 and 166.

[434] Para 206.

[435] Para 217.

[436] Para 313

[437] Unsurprisingly, the Court's ruling was criticised by the OLAF Director: 'Brüner: Court Paralyses EU's Anti-Crime Efforts', *European Voice* (17–23 July 2008), p 1 (reporting by Simon Taylor).

noted earlier in this chapter, there is great potential of overlap between the work of Europol, Eurojust and OLAF: the mandate of all three bodies includes in one form or another criminal investigations. This potential overlap, along with existential concerns regarding the role and future of OLAF and fears that it may be subsumed under, or merged with, one of the other EU criminal justice bodies may explain the fact that the relationship between OLAF on the one hand and Europol and in particular Eurojust on the other is marred by competition rather than co-operation.[438] Indeed, there have been calls for a merger (*'fusion'*) between OLAF and Europol under the control of the European Public Prosecutor.[439] Moreover, as will be seen below, the Lisbon Treaty calls for a European Public Prosecutor (EPP) to be established 'from Eurojust',[440] a provision which raises questions about the future of OLAF.[441] The discussion on the future of OLAF and its relationship with Europol, Eurojust and perhaps eventually the EPP will certainly be relaunched if and when the Lisbon Treaty enters into force—with issues related to the independence and status of OLAF, its relationship with national authorities and the protection of fundamental rights being particularly pressing.

V. OTHER BODIES: COUNTER-TERRORISM, INFORMALITY AND CROSS-PILLARISATION

Along with the above flagship bodies in EU action in criminal law, a number of other organisations have emerged in recent years at EU-level working on various aspects of police and judicial co-operation in criminal matters in the EU. The nature, legal basis and degree of centralisation of these bodies vary considerably. In the field of judicial co-operation in criminal maters, the main body complementing the work of Eurojust is the European Judicial Network.[442] In the field of police co-operation, EU initiatives other than Europol include the European Police College (CEPOL) and the Police Chiefs' Task Force. CEPOL was first established in 2000[443] and was relaunched in 2005 by a Decision granting it legal personality and outlining in greater detail the body's objectives and tasks.[444] CEPOL, which is based in Bramshill, UK,[445] is essentially a network bringing together the

---

[438] On the competitive relationship between OLAF and Eurojust in particular see part III above. See also House of Lords European Union Committee, *Strengthening OLAF*, n 392 above, paras 88 f.

[439] Assemblée nationale, n 374 above. See also evidence in House of Lords European Union Committee, *Strengthening OLAF*, n 392 above, para 90.

[440] Art 86(1) TFEU.

[441] The Commission has defended OLAF in the context of the potential establishment of the EPP (and its relationship with Europol and Eurojust), by noting that 'at this point the question will once again arise of hiving off an Office that might come to assume the role of a judicial officer in internal investigations as well as external investigations'—Commission Evaluation Report on OLAF, n 398 above, p 47.

[442] See section III above.

[443] Council Decision of 22 December 2000 establishing a European Police College (CEPOL), OJ L336, 30 December 2000, p 1.

[444] OJ L256, 1 October 2005, p 63.

[445] Art 4 of the 2005 Decision.

national police training institutes of Member States[446] and its main purpose is to train senior police officers and develop in this context 'a European approach' in the fight against crime.[447] The European Police Chiefs' Task Force (EPCTF) on the other hand does not have a formal legal basis. It was established, following the relevant mandate of the Tampere European Council, in 2000.[448] Given the absence of a legal basis and a clear mandate for the EPCTF (which would meet within the framework of Europol as regards its operational tasks and within the Council as regards its strategic tasks),[449] there is still a considerable lack of clarity and transparency as to what it actually does.[450] This opaqueness does not contribute to meaningful scrutiny and accountability with regard to its operations.

But it is the development of an EU response to terrorism which proved to be a catalyst for putting yet more bodies on the map of EU criminal law co-operation. Part of the EU's response to terrorism has been to strengthen its institutional capacity, either by expanding and focusing the mandate of *existing* structures on counter-terrorism, or by creating *new* structures to deal with the issue.[451] These structures transcended the third pillar, with counter-terrorism viewed both as a criminal law and foreign policy issue. A prime example of focusing existing EU structures on counter-terrorism has been the development of the work of the EU Joint Situation Centre (SitCen) in the field. SitCen does not have a formal legal basis, but it has been established under the second pillar to report to the EU Secretary General High Representative (SGHR—currently Javier Solana). According to SitCen's Director, William Shapcott, SitCen was given an intelli-

[446] Art 1(2).

[447] Art 5. On the work of CEPOL, see www.cepol.europa.eu.

[448] See M den Boer, C Hillebrand and A Noelke, 'Legitimacy under Pressure: The European Web of Counter-Terrorism Networks', *Journal of Common Market Studies*, vol 46, no 1, pp 101–124 at p 113; Peers, *EU Justice*, n 13 above, p 541.

[449] Conclusions of Justice and Home Affairs Council of 19 November 2004, Council doc 14615/04 (Presse 321), 19 November 2004. For further information, see Peers, ibid, p 542.

[450] In their evidence to the House of Lords European Union Committee in 2004, the European Commission described the desired role of the EPCTF within the EU framework as follows:

> Under the aegis of Europol, the Member States' Criminal Intelligence communities should assemble national strategic and operational assessments and present the resulting EU strategic assessment to Coreper and the JHA Council and the EU operational assessment to the EPCTF to be handed down to the national operational levels. Europol should contribute with all intelligence it has available. The intelligence could be collated to produce EU strategic assessments twice a year, and EU operational assessments every month. The EU strategic assessments would allow the Council to set law enforcement priorities. The EPCTF should then hand down the operational assessments to the operational levels within national law enforcement communities. This approach should lead to a situation where strategic assessments are readily available to the decision makers in order to revise law enforcement priorities as often as necessary. Operational assessments would be made available to the EPCTF providing the law enforcement community with the best available tactical knowledge to prevent or combat the threat of terrorism. (House of Lords European Union Committee, *After Madrid: The EU's Response to Terrorism*, 5th Report, session 2004–05, p.37 (evidence)).

[451] On the proliferation of these structures, see House of Lords, *After Madrid*, previous n. On the strengthening of the institutional aspect, see J. Monar, 'Common Threat and Common Response? The European Union's Counter-Terrorism Strategy and its Problems', *Government and Opposition*, vol 42, no 3, pp 292–313 at pp 307–308.

gence assessment function by Javier Solana in 2001.[452] It is located within the General Secretariat of the Council,[453] includes national intelligence analysts seconded by a number of Member States, and produces external intelligence disseminated mainly to second pillar structures.[454] However, SitCen is also increasingly involved in the production and exchange of 'internal' intelligence, mainly by developing links with Europol.[455] Given the absence of a concrete legal framework governing SitCen, and the very limited information concerning its work,[456] the limits of knowing what exactly SitCen does are evident, as are the limits to scrutiny, transparency, accountability and judicial control of this body. The challenges in this context may be considerable if there is a spill-over of second pillar, foreign policy secrecy into EU criminal law.

Another example of cross-pillarisation in EU counter-terrorism action, this time via the establishment of a new structure, has been the creation of the post of an EU Counter-terrorism Co-ordinator. Again there is no legislation establishing the post and setting out the Co-ordinator's powers. Rather, the post was established by the European Council in its Declaration on Combating Terrorism, adopted shortly after the Madrid bombings.[457] According to the European Council,

> the Co-ordinator, who will work within the Council Secretariat, will co-ordinate the work of the Council in combating terrorism and, with due regard to the responsibilities of the Commission maintain an overview of all the instruments at the Union's disposal with a view to regular reporting to the Council and effective follow-up of Council decisions.[458]

However, this job description is rather general, and the precise tasks of the Co-ordinator not entirely clear. This lack of clarity was also ascertained a few months after the creation of the post by the House of Lords European Union Committee,

---

[452] Oral evidence to House of Lords European Union Committee, *After Madrid*, n 450 above, Q152.

[453] SitCen is divided into three units: the Civilian Intelligence Cell (CIC), comprising civilian intelligence analysts working on political and counter-terrorism assessment; the General Operations Unit (GOU), providing 24-hour operational support, research and non-intelligence analysis; and the Communications Unit, handling communications security issues and running the council's communications centre (ComCen).—Written Answer of Charles Clarke (then UK Home Secretary), Hansard HC (27 June 2005), col 1249W.

[454] See B Müller-Witte, *For our Eyes Only? Shaping an Intelligence Community within the EU*, European Union Institute for Security Studies, Occasional Paper no.50, January 2004, p.29, www.iss-eu.org.

[455] See D Keohane, 'The Absent Friend: EU Foreign Policy and Counter-terrorism', *Journal of Common Market Studies*, vol 46, no 1, pp 125–146 at p 129. See also the Hague Programme stating that with effect from 1 January 2005, SitCen will provide the Council with strategic analysis of the terrorist threat based on intelligence from Member States' intelligence and security services and, where appropriate, on information provided by Europol (OJ C53, 3 March 2005, p 1, point 2.2). On the prioritisation of SitCen links with Europol, see Shapcott above, Q180.

[456] Some—but very limited—information is available in the EU SitCen work programmes.

[457] Declaration of 25 March 2004, para 14, at www.ue.eu.int/uedocs/cmsUpload/DECL-25.3.pdf.

[458] ibid. In this context, see the Report by the Counter-terrorism Coordinator on the 'Implementation of the EU Counter-Terrorism Strategy—Priorities for further action', Council doc 9417/08, Brussels, 19 May 2008, which was presented to the June 2008 Justice and Home Affairs Council. The Report contains a lengthy section on transmission of information to Europol and Eurojust.

which took evidence from the first EU Counter-terrorism Co-ordinator (Gijs de Vries), whose appointment (by Javier Solana) was confirmed by the European Council in the same Declaration.[459] The Committee also pointed out the lack of oversight with regard to the Co-ordinator's work. This lack of clarity and oversight has been seen by EU officials as granting the Co-ordinator flexibility to help the General Secretary wherever possible,[460] but does not provide (beyond his reporting to the HRGS) sufficient accountability mechanisms. Moreover, the broad reference to co-ordination and follow-up of Council Decisions by the Co-ordinator may create competition or overlap with EU institutions such as the European Commission, which is entrusted to monitor the implementation of legislation.[461] The situation has not changed following the appointment of Mr de Vries's successor, Gilles de Kerchove (formerly of the Council Secretariat)—while the replacement of a diplomat by a high-ranking Union civil servant for the post is noteworthy, the job description—as described in the Council press release confirming the appointment—has not really changed.[462] What is not clearly visible from this press release is the potential role of the Co-ordinator as the EU's representative, or 'voice' in external relations.[463]

VI. INTER-AGENCY CO-OPERATION

The proliferation of Union bodies and networks in the field of criminal law has been accompanied by increased calls to enhance co-operation between them, in particular as regards the exchange of strategic and personal data. Such calls for co-operation have been translated on a number of occasions, as seen above, into legally binding provisions in secondary legislation regulating EU bodies such as Europol and Eurojust, while also leading to the conclusion of bilateral agreements between EU bodies. Calls for co-operation are frequently made also by Ministers at the Justice and Home Affairs Council.[464] Calls for 'inter-agency' co-operation were also central to the Hague Programme, where Member States' leaders stressed both operational work and operational co-operation across the EU. In this context, the Hague Programme emphasised that 'coordination of operational

---

[459] *After Madrid,* n 450 above, paras 54–60.

[460] See M Wesseling, *Gijs de Vries: Vers la coordination des politiques antiterroristes européennes, efficacité ou symbolisme?*, Master Mémoire, Institut d'Etudes Politiques de Paris, 2005, p.49.

[461] On the reactions of the Commission to the creation of a Co-ordinator's post within the Council, see Wesseling, n 460 above, who also provides a very interesting picture of the inter-institutional battles behind the creation of the post—pp 41–43.

[462] Javier Solana, EU High Representative for the CFSP, appoints Mr Gilles de Kerchove as EU Counter-Terrorism Coordinator, Brussels, 19 September 2007, S256/07.

[463] Such a role was envisaged by the Presidency Conclusions of 17 and 18 June 2004, stating that the appointment of an EU Counter-terrorism Coordinator will help to improve coordination *and visibility* of the EU's actions in this field—para 13 (emphasis added).

[464] A good example is the recent Council of June 2008, which stressed not only the need to formalise co-operation between Europol and Eurojust, but also called—in the context of the Conclusions on the management of the external borders of EU Member States, for closer co-operation between FRONTEX (the European Border Agency) and Europol (point 4 of Conclusions).

activities by law enforcement agencies and other agencies in all parts of the area of freedom, security and justice, and monitoring of the strategic priorities set by the Council, must be ensured'.[465] It also called (in line with proposals in the then Constitutional Treaty) for preparations for the establishment of an EU Committee of Internal Security (COSI), adding that

> to gain practical experience with coordination in the meantime, the Council is invited to organise a joint meeting every six months between the chairpersons of the Strategic Committee on Immigration, Frontiers and Asylum (SCIFA) and the Article 36 Committee (CATS) and representatives of the Commission, Europol, Eurojust, the European Borders Agency, the Police Chiefs' Task Force, and the SitCen.[466]

This move towards greater interagency co-operation does not always sit at ease with the fact that the various EU bodies are vested with different powers, and have been established under different legal bases for different purposes. A well-documented example is the move to link the policy fields of immigration and crime under a strategy of creating an (in)security continuum, presenting co-operation between immigration and police authorities as necessary to achieve security.[467] This approach, which is particularly highlighted post-9/11 with the emergence of the concept of 'border security' in government discourse across the Atlantic, has led to calls at EU level for co-operation between Frontex on the one hand and enforcement authorities such as Europol on the other.[468] However, such co-operation, in particular as regards the exchange and transfer of personal data, may disregard the different nature and tasks of these bodies and the principle of purpose limitation which forms the backbone of data protection systems.[469] Similar issues arise with regard to calls for co-operation between EU police and defence/military bodies, as well as co-operation between police and intelligence bodies.[470]

In the current stage of constitutional development of the EU, calls for maximum interagency co-operation also raise a number of issues of legality and accountability. It has been demonstrated that EU bodies dealing with criminal matters exist in the first (OLAF), second (SitCen, Counter-terrorism Co-ordinator), and third (Europol, Eurojust) pillars. Moreover, while some of these bodies have been established under a clear legal basis and via secondary Union/Community law, others do not have a clear legal basis or tasks. In the light of this constitutional and functional fragmentation, it is difficult to establish

---

[465] OJ C53, 3 March 2005, p 1. Point 2.5

[466] ibid.

[467] On the (in)security continuum, see Bigo, *Polices en réseaux*, n 5 above.

[468] On border security see V Mitsilegas, 'Border Security in the European Union. Towards Centralised Controls and Maximum Surveillance', in E Guild, H Toner and A Baldaccini (eds), *Whose Freedom, Security and Justice? EU Immigration and Asylum Law and Policy*, Oxford, Hart Publishing, 2007, pp 359–394.

[469] On purpose limitation in the context of data protection and the exchange of personal data see ch 5.

[470] For different takes on cross-pillarisation and interagency co-operation in this context see Müller-Witte, 'The Effect of International Terrorism', n 202 above and Bigo *et al*, n 41 above.

mechanisms of meaningful scrutiny of such interagency co-operation. Moreover, the increased emphasis on operational co-operation raises further questions regarding transparency and accountability—in particular if the emphasis on operational co-operation may lead to the choice of action which will not take the form of publicly negotiated legislation.

However, calls for increased inter-agency co-operation may also reveal tensions between the various EU bodies and stress competition rather than co-operation and overlap rather than synergy. The prime example of such complexity is the relationship between Eurojust and OLAF, which continues to be fraught in the light of the ongoing debate regarding the establishment of a European Public Prosecutor. As was highlighted on a number of occasions in this chapter, tensions in inter-agency co-operation may be caused by both the lack of clarity with regard to the tasks of the various EU bodies and the potential overlap with regard to their tasks. Negotiations on the development of Europol and Eurojust—but also the debate over the future of OLAF—demonstrate clearly that effective and accountable interagency co-operation presupposes a clear answer to the existential questions with regard to the role, powers and tasks of the EU bodies.

VII. CONTROLLING BODIES BY OTHER BODIES AND AGENCIES

The proliferation of bodies in EU criminal law has been accompanied by the introduction of a number of forms of control and accountability. As mentioned in the analysis of the legal framework on Eurojust and Europol in particular, these bodies are accountable in one form or another to a number of EU institutions. However, there are also specific provisions inserted in the legislation establishing these bodies which provide for their control by other bodies. Prime examples of such control—in the specific field of data protection—are the Joint Supervisory Bodies (JSBs) of Europol and Eurojust.[471] Consisting of representatives of national data protection authorities in the first case and judicial authorities in the second, these bodies are designed as independent and are entrusted with a number of tasks related to the oversight of the bodies in question with regard to data protection—however, their powers are limited from the point of view of the binding nature of their actions.[472] A similar example is the Supervisory Committee of OLAF—it consists of independent experts, monitors compliance with fundamental rights more broadly, but its recommendations are not legally binding.

These bodies are *internal* to the EU criminal law bodies, and have *specific, sectoral tasks*, dealing primarily with the protection of personal data. At the same time, further bodies and organs have been established—at Community level—

---

[471] On the role of Joint Supervisory Bodies in relation to the monitoring of EU databases, see ch 5.

[472] On Joint Supervisory Bodies and data protection supervision more generally, see G González Fuster and P Paepe, 'Reflexive Governance and the EU Third Pillar: Analysis of Data Protection and Criminal Law Aspects', in E Guild and F Geyer (eds), *Security versus Justice? Police and Judicial Cooperation in the European Union*, Aldershot, Ashgate, 2008, pp 129–152.

with the aim of monitoring, at a more 'horizontal' level, the protection of a number of fundamental rights. A prime example is the European Data Protection Supervisor (EDPS), an independent authority established by Regulation No 45/2001 of the European Parliament and the Council[473] and providing with independent supervision of Community institutions and bodies.[474] However, and notwithstanding the activist role of the EDPS in practice, its powers are limited and its mandate does not currently extend to the third pillar. The story is similar with regard to the recently established Fundamental Rights Agency (FRA).[475] Its powers are limited and it currently covers Community law only.[476] Notwithstanding these limits, the move towards specialised bodies and agencies to monitor data protection and human rights raises the question of 'agency inflation', but also the broader question of whether it is desirable to focus predominantly on *sectoral agencies* as protectors of fundamental constitutional values and rights in the EU—rather than mainstreaming such rights in the work of EU institutions and agencies.[477]

VIII. THE FUTURE IN THE LIGHT OF LISBON

The Lisbon Treaty would go some way to address a number of the contested issues surrounding EU criminal law bodies. It contains both general provisions and provisions geared towards specific bodies such as Europol and Eurojust. Both at the general and the specific level, the Treaty would bring a number of changes with regard to accountability and judicial control of EU criminal law bodies, as well as a fresh impetus with regard to the discussion of their tasks and powers. The main developments brought about by Lisbon are outlined in this section.

---

[473] OJ L8, 12 January 2001, p 1.2001.

[474] On the EDPS see H Hijmans, 'The European Data Protection Supervisor: The Institutions of the EC Controlled by an Independent Authority', *Common Market Law Review*, vol 43, 2006, pp 1313–1342.

[475] Council Regulation (EC) No 168/2007 establishing a European Union Agency for Fundamental Rights, OJ L 53, 22 February 2007, p 1. For one of the first studies of the potential of the Agency, see P Alston and O. de Schutter (eds), *Monitoring Fundamental Rights in the EU: The Contribution of the Fundamental Rights Agency*, Oxford, Hart Publishing, 2005. See also G N Toggenburg, 'The Role of the New EU Fundamental Rights Agency: Debating the "Sex of Angels" or Improving Europe's Human Rights Performance', *European Law Review*, vol 33, no 3, 2008, pp 385–398.

[476] On the debate regarding extending the mandate of the Agency to the third pillar, see House of Lords European Union Committee, *Human Rights Protection in Europe: the Fundamental Rights Agency*, 29th Report, session 2005–06, HL Paper 155; see also G N Toggenburg, 'The EU Fundamental Rights Agency: Satellite or Guiding Star?', SWP Comments 5, March 2007, www.swp-berlin.org.

[477] Further proposals for the creation of EU bodies perceived as necessary to counter-balance the emphasis of EU criminal law on enforcement include the creation of a 'Eurodefensor', who would monitor the protection of the rights of the defendant in the EU—see the section on 'Eurodefensor' in B Schünemann (ed), *A Programme for European Criminal Justice*, Cologne, Berlin, Munich, Carl Heymanns Verlag, 2006.

A. Emphasis on Operational Co-Operation

The emphasis on operational co-operation which was central to the Hague Programme can also be discerned in the Lisbon Treaty. Following the recommendations of the Working Group on Freedom, Security and Justice at the Convention on the Future of Europe,[478] and mirroring the Constitutional Treaty, the Lisbon Treaty confirms the establishment of an 'internal security' committee within the Council (COSI): a standing committee to ensure that 'operational cooperation on internal security is promoted and strengthened within the Union'.[479] Representatives of the Union bodies, offices and agencies concerned may be involved in the proceedings of the Committee, which will facilitate coordination of the action of Member States' competent authorities.[480] The emphasis is thus placed quite heavily on both operational co-operation—which is not defined—and the creation of an *EU* steering body[481] co-ordinating action of *national* authorities.[482] However, the tasks and powers of this new Committee are not precisely defined, something that raises questions of both transparency and accountability,[483] but also of transfer of sovereignty by Member States to the EU in the field of operational action.[484]

B. Judicial Control

Calls for enhancing judicial control of EU bodies and agencies have already been made at the Convention on the Future of Europe and reflected in the Constitutional Treaty.[485] These provisions are largely reflected in the Lisbon Treaty, which contains a series of provisions focusing expressly on the judicial

---

[478] Final Report of Working Group X 'Freedom, Security and Justice', CONV 426/02, WG X 14, Brussels, 2 December 2002. The Report contained a specific part on 'strengthening operational collaboration'.

[479] Art 71 TFEU.

[480] ibid.

[481] The setting up of this Committee is based on the current 'Art 36 Committee', the Co-ordinating Committee consisting of senior officials by Member States, provided for in Art 36 TEU—but unlike the Art 36 Committee, COSI will not have legislative tasks—see C Ladenburger, 'Police and Criminal Law in the Treaty of Lisbon. A New Dimension for the Community Method', *European Constitutional Law Review*, vol 4, 2008, pp 20–40 at p 33.

[482] Boosting administrative cooperation between national authorities is also flagged up in Art 74 TFEU.

[483] In this context Art 71 TFEU states that the European Parliament and national parliaments will be informed of the proceedings.

[484] In this context, see Art 73 TFEU stating that it will be open to Member States to organise between themselves and under their responsibility such forms of cooperation and coordination as they deem appropriate between the competent departments of their administrations responsible for safeguarding internal security. This provision seems to have been included to confirm Member States' competence in the field.

[485] See E Nieto-Garrido and I Martín Delgado, *European Administrative Law in the Constitutional Treaty*, Oxford, Hart Publishing, 2007, pp 159–161.

review of action by EU bodies—which would include bodies such as Europol and Eurojust. Article 263(1) TFEU extends the Court of Justice review of legality to 'acts of bodies, offices or agencies of the Union intended to produce legal effects vis-à-vis third parties'.[486] Moreover, actions for failure to act will also apply to bodies, offices and agencies of the Union,[487] and the Court will have jurisdiction to give preliminary rulings concerning the validity and interpretation of acts of the institutions, bodies, offices or agencies of the Union.[488]

This is in principle a welcome extension of the Court's jurisdiction on EU bodies and agencies, and it may have important consequences towards the review of acts of Europol and Eurojust in particular.[489] However, two important caveats must be raised in this context. The first concerns the potential limitation of the Court's jurisdiction on the review of legality, with the Lisbon Treaty stating expressly that 'acts setting up bodies, offices and agencies of the Union may lay down specific conditions and arrangements concerning actions brought by natural or legal persons against acts of these bodies, offices or agencies intended to produce legal effects in relation to them'.[490] This provision may mean that, as *lex specialis,* provisions in secondary legislation on Eurojust and Europol may limit the Court's jurisdiction in this context. However, it is not clear whether *existing clauses* which may constitute such *lex specialis* in legislation currently in force will suffice to provide such limitation. It is submitted that the spirit and wording of the Treaty actually require the adoption of *future* legislation explicitly limiting the Court's jurisdiction in this context.

The second caveat is related to the lack of clarity regarding the nature, role and legal basis of a number of EU criminal law bodies. Would bodies which have not been established by secondary EU law, or which are not called 'bodies' as such (for example SitCen or the Counter-terrorism Co-ordinator) be considered as Union bodies or offices within the meaning of the Treaty and thus be subject to the Court's jurisdiction? Even in the affirmative, would the labelling of such bodies as 'second pillar'—'foreign affairs' bodies shield them from judicial control, which remains limited with regard to the CFSP post-Lisbon? The increased informality in the establishment of structures of co-operation raises important concerns as regards accountability and judicial control. Similarly, the provisions of the Lisbon Treaty do not address directly the issue that has arisen in the *Tillack* litigation, namely the extent to which Community/Union agencies or bodies may hide behind action by national authorities in order to claim that their action did not produce legal effects vis-a-vis third parties.

---

[486] See also Art 277 TFEU with regard to acts of general application adopted by bodies or agencies.

[487] Art 265(1) TFEU.

[488] Art 267(1)(b) TFEU. Art 234 TEC currently grants the ECJ jurisdiction to give preliminary rulings on the validity and interpretation of acts of the institutions and the European Central Bank, as well as the interpretation of the *statutes* of bodies established by an act of the Council, *where these statutes so provide.*

[489] See also in this context the powers of the European Ombudsman to conduct inquiries on alleged maladministration of EU institutions, bodies, offices or agencies—Art 228(1) TFEU.

[490] Art 263(5) TFEU.

C. Accountability and Scrutiny

In addition to the general changes with regard to the involvement of the European Parliament and national parliaments in the scrutiny of EU criminal law,[491] the Lisbon Treaty contains a number of provisions focusing on the democratic control of specific bodies in the field. Article 70 TFEU provides that the European Parliament and national parliaments will be kept 'informed' of the proceedings of the new Internal Security Committee (COSI). A joint system of scrutiny (perhaps reflecting the view that the work of EU criminal law bodies is closely linked to State sovereignty and that delegation is made by the Council and not the Commission[492]) involving both the European Parliament and national parliaments is also envisaged for Eurojust[493] and Europol.[494] While the details of such involvement will be determined in the future, the nuances in the wording of the Treaty provides a number of insights regarding its nature: the European Parliament *and* national parliaments will be involved *in the evaluation* of Eurojust's work—implying thus perhaps an ex post, and not necessarily joined-up, scrutiny. On the other hand, the European Parliament *together with* national parliaments will be involved in the *scrutiny of Europol's activities*: the wording here implies a more joined-up control of Europol between the European Parliament and national parliaments, and a more day to day scrutiny of Europol's activities.[495]

D. Role and Powers

In addition to the legal basis for the establishment of the Internal Security Committee, the Lisbon Treaty contains specific provisions which provide the legal basis for future legislation on Europol and Eurojust. Both provisions may result in the expansion of the role and powers of these bodies, and it remains to be seen whether (if and when the Lisbon Treaty enters into force) the Commission will table new proposals (to be adopted by co-decision) given the fact that new proposals for Decisions bringing changes to Europol and Eurojust are currently being negotiated under the third pillar procedure (perhaps as an effort to pre-empt Lisbon) by Member States. As regards Europol, Article 88(1) TFEU extends its mandate to include also forms of crime which 'affect a common interest covered by a Union policy'. Future legislation will determine Europol's structure and tasks,

---

[491] See ch 1.

[492] On delegation by the Council, see Curtin, 'Delegation', n 134 above, pp 96 f

[493] Art 85(1) TFEU calls for the adoption of regulations which will inter alia determine 'arrangements for involving the European Parliament and national parliaments in the evaluation of Eurojust's activities'.

[494] Art 88(1) TFEU calls for the adoption of regulations which will inter alia lay down 'the procedures for scrutiny of Europol's activities by the European Parliament, together with national parliaments'. See also Art 12(c) TEU on the role of national parliaments in scrutinising Europol and Eurojust.

[495] The entry into force of the Lisbon Treaty may also bring about changes in the data protection supervision of third pillar bodies—for details see ch 5.

which may include inter alia 'the coordination, organisation *and implementation of investigative and operational action* carried out jointly with the Member States' competent authorities or in the context of joint investigative teams, *where appropriate in liaison with Eurojust*'(emphasis added).[496] This wording leaves open the possibility for Europol to be granted 'operational' powers in the future, a prospect that is reinforced by the wording of Article 88(3) of TFEU which states that '*any operational action by Europol* must be carried out in liaison and in agreement with the authorities of the Member State or States whose territory is concerned', but adding that 'the application of *coercive measures*' (emphasis added) will be the exclusive responsibility of the competent national authorities.[497]

Similarly, a specific provision on Eurojust states that its mission will be to support and strengthen co-ordination and co-operation between national investigating and prosecuting authorities in relation to serious cross-border crime or crime 'requiring a prosecution on common bases', on the basis of operations and information provided by Member States and Europol.[498] As with Europol, future legislation will determine the structure and tasks of Eurojust, which may include '*the initiation of criminal investigations*, as well as proposing the initiation of prosecutions conducted by competent national authorities'(emphasis added),[499] as well as 'the strengthening of judicial cooperation, *including by resolution of conflicts of jurisdiction*'(emphasis added).[500] As with the provision on Europol, this Article may provide the *impetus* for new legislation (with the involvement of the European Parliament) redrawing the boundaries between Union and Member States' powers in criminal justice, with Europol and Eurojust operating under a wider mandate and with increased, 'operational' powers with binding force over Member States. While these development will not happen overnight, the Lisbon Treaty may contribute towards a more fundamental reconfiguration of the relationship between Member States and the Union, but also the relationship between EU bodies themselves: the Treaty provides a legal basis for the establishment of a European Public Prosecutor's Office 'from Eurojust'.[501]

E. The Transformation of EU Bodies in the Light of the European Public Prosecutor (EPP)

The establishment of a European Public Prosecutor (EPP) has been perhaps the most contested issue in the development of EU criminal law in recent years. The

---

[496] Art 88(2)(b).

[497] It has been argued that the wording would not prevent the granting to Europol of the power to instruct national authorities to apply coercive measures—Ladenburger, n 481 above, p 39.

[498] Art 85(1) TFEU.

[499] Art 85(1)(a).Note the clarification in Art 85(3) TFEU that in the prosecutions referred to in the first para, and without prejudice to the provision on the European Public Prosecutor, formal acts of judicial procedure will be carried out by the competent national officials.

[500] Art 85(1)(c).

[501] Art 86(1) TFEU.

establishment of an EPP was proposed in the *Corpus Juris* an academic study funded by the European Commission which resulted in a mini-criminal code for the protection of the Community's financial interests. [502] The *Corpus Juris* would cover offences of fraud, market-rigging, money laundering, conspiracy, corruption, misappropriation of funds, abuse of office and disclosure of secrets pertaining to one's office (Articles 1–8). It then included provisions on criminal law principles and sanctions, as well as prosecution. In this context, it called for the establishment of a European Public Prosecutor, defined as follows:

> The EPP is an authority of the European Community, responsible for investigation, prosecution, committal to trial, presenting the prosecution case at trial and the execution of sentences concerning the offences defined above (Articles 1–8). It is independent as regards both national authorities and Community institutions.[503]

According to the *Corpus Juris*, for the purposes of the investigation, prosecution, trial and execution of sentences concerning the offences mentioned therein, 'the territory of the Member States of the Union constitutes a single legal area'.[504] It contained a number of detailed provisions on the European Public Prosecutor, including provisions on the opening of proceedings,[505] powers of investigation (including inter alia powers to conduct investigations and powers of questioning, collecting documents and search and seizure),[506] the termination of the investigation[507] and the bringing and termination of a prosecution, stating that 'the EPP prosecutes at the court of trial, according to the laws of the Member State'.[508] The EPP would also have a role in the execution of sentences.[509]

The proposal to create a Union prosecutorial body with coercive powers in the territory of Member States, and the treatment of the Union as a single legal area, was met with strong opposition by a number of Member States, objecting to what seemed as a loss of sovereignty over criminal justice.[510] Member States' reactions led to the *Corpus Juris* not becoming EU law, and, as mentioned earlier in this chapter, to proposals for the establishment of Eurojust as a counter-weight of the centralising EPP proposals. The Commission reiterated—in a watered down version—proposals to establish the EPP in 2001,[511] but these proposals were not taken up by the Council (which was in the process of agreeing the Eurojust

---

[502] On the *Corpus Juris*, see also ch.2. For the text and further details regarding its potential implementation, see M Delmas-Marty and J A E Vervaele (eds), *The Implementation of the Corpus Juris in the Member States*, vol 1, Antwerp, Oxford, Intersentia, 2000.

[503] Art 18(2) of the *Corpus Juris*.

[504] Art 18(1).

[505] Art 19.

[506] Art 20(2).

[507] Art 21.

[508] Art 22(1).

[509] Art 23.

[510] For an early overview of the debate, see House of Lords European Union Committee, *Prosecuting Fraud on the Communities' Finances—the Corpus Juris*, 9th Report, 1998–99, HL paper 62.

[511] See the Commission, 'Criminal-law protection of the financial interests of the Community and the establishment of a European Public Prosecutor' (Green Paper) COM (2001) 715 final, Brussels, 11 December 2001.

Decision at the time).[512] The debate continued in the deliberations of the Justice and Home Affairs Working Group at the Convention on the Future of Europe, with the Group finally unable to reach a conclusion and its Report noting that 'the discussion in the Group showed that members were divided on the issue'.[513] This disagreement led to a compromise provision on the establishment of the EPP in the Constitutional Treaty, reiterated in the Lisbon Treaty. Article 86 TFEU states inter alia that:

1. In order to combat crimes affecting the financial interests of the Union, the Council . . . may establish a European Public Prosecutor's Office from Eurojust. The Council shall act unanimously after obtaining the consent of the European Parliament.

. . .

2. The European Public Prosecutor's Office shall be responsible for investigating, prosecuting and bringing to judgment, when appropriate in liaison with Europol, the perpetrators of, and accomplices in, offences against the Union's financial interests . . . It shall exercise the functions of prosecutor in the competent courts of the Member States in relation to such offences.

The Treaty thus contains an express legal basis for the establishment of a European Public Prosecutor, but only if there is unanimous agreement by Member States and the European Parliament consents.[514] The EPP, who will exercise prosecutorial functions, will—at least initially—be competent to act only to combat crimes affecting the financial interests of the Union.[515] Legislation establishing the EPP will contain specific rules on the functioning of the EPP—including rules on the admissibility of evidence and judicial review.[516] In the light of these rather general provisions, the precise role, powers and functions of the EPP are far from clear—and the degree to which such a body will impact on State sovereignty in criminal justice is hard to determine. However, Article 86 TFEU provides some important insights with regard to the future and relationship of EU criminal justice bodies. It confirms that Eurojust is currently well-established (with the EPP coming 'from Eurojust'), but it is not clear what form it will take if an EPP is established from it. The wording seems to confirm Europol's role as a partner of the EPP (in furtherance of its current partnership role with Eurojust)—rather than establishing a mechanism subordinating Europol to the judicial control of the EPP. The biggest question mark concerns the future of OLAF. OLAF already overlaps with Eurojust, and such overlap will be even greater should a specialised EU body mandated to fight fraud is established. The prospect of OLAF being separated from the Commission and absorbed by the EPP is not unrealistic, with legislation

---

[512] See also House of Lords European Union Committee, *Strengthening OLAF*, n 392, paras 91–92.
[513] ibid, p 20.
[514] Art 86(1) TFEU continues in providing the possibility of an emergency brake if a group of at least 9 Member States refer the proposal to the European Council—in case of disagreement within the set deadlines, enhanced co-operation can take place.
[515] But this scope may be extended under the procedure set out in Art 86(4) TFEU.
[516] Art 86(3) TFEU.

establishing the EPP being an opportunity to provide greater accountability and judicial protection safeguards than those currently in place.[517] In any event, it is likely that the Lisbon Treaty, if it enters into force, and future proposals on an EPP, will trigger an extensive existential debate with regard to the future of EU bodies in criminal law.

IX. CONCLUSION: EXTENDING THE FIELD OF ENFORCEMENT IN THE EU?

A number of attempts have been made to provide neat categories or typologies of agencies in the first pillar.[518] This is far from an easy task given the ever increasing number of Community agencies and their diverse mandate. While it is difficult to come up with precise categories of agencies, some key functions emerge—most notably functions of information, persuasion and co-ordination, placed within the more general framework of market regulation in the Community.[519] For the purposes of this chapter, and in any attempt to categorise 'criminal law' bodies (existing primarily in the third pillar), the question arises whether the criminal law bodies bear similarities with Community agencies. Some of the functions described above can be found in criminal law bodies in one form or another—in particular information and strategy (see especially Europol and its organised crime and terrorism situation reports), persuasion (most notably Eurojust and OLAF, in asking national authorities to investigate and prosecute), and co-ordination (in particular Europol and Eurojust in the context of joint investigation teams and Eurojust in concurrent jurisdiction cases). However, one cannot help noticing a major difference between Community agencies and bodies dealing with criminal matters: the fact that the latter's acts (which can increasingly be deemed 'operational') have a significant impact on the position of the individual in the criminal justice process, the protection of his/her fundamental rights and his/her relationship with the State more generally. Acts of criminal law bodies may have consequences such as the deprivation of liberty, and their impact calls for a high level of accountability and judicial control. As with mutual recognition, transposing the features of Community agencies to criminal law may not reflect the reality of action in criminal matters. Market considerations cannot be equated with criminal justice considerations.

---

[517] For various scenarios regarding the fate of OLAF, Eurojust and Europol post-EPP, see House of Lords, *Strengthening OLAF*, n 392 above and *Judicial Cooperation in the EU*, above n 206; Ladenburger, n 481 above.

[518] For attempts at categorisation, see inter alia E. Chiti, 'The Emergence of a Community Administration: The Case of European Agencies', *Common Market Law Review*, vol 37, 2000, pp 309–343; and A Kreher, 'Agencies in the European Community—A Step towards Administrative Integration in Europe', *Journal of European Public Policy*, vol 4, no 2, 1997, pp 225–245. See also the overview by E Vos, 'Reforming the European Commission: What Role to Play for EU Agencies?', *Common Market Law Review*, vol 37, 2000, pp 1113–1134.

[519] See in particular G Majone, 'The New European Agencies: Regulation by Information', *Journal of European Public Policy*, vol 4, no 2, 1997, pp 262–273; see also M Shapiro, 'The Problems of Independent Agencies in the United States and the European Union', *Journal of European Public Policy*, vol 4, no 2, 1997, pp 276–291

The recognition of the 'special nature' of criminal law does come into play in Member States' choices regarding the establishment, powers and accountability of EU criminal law bodies. As has been noted in the context of the Community agency entrusted with the public function of border management (FRONTEX), delegation in this context is from the Council to the agency and not from the Commission.[520] This certainly applies to criminal law EU bodies (with the exception of OLAF). What is also noteworthy is the avoidance of calling these bodies 'agencies', even in the current proposals amending Europol and Eurojust law. This may be significant in recognising the more 'intergovernmental' nature of these bodies, but also in shielding these bodies to the extent possible from accountability mechanisms which they so need. In this context of the battle between State and EU interests in the criminal justice field, two interesting parallel phenomena arise. On the one hand the steady proliferation of EU bodies in the field of criminal law. This proliferation and further development of criminal law bodies may be explained by a number of factors, such as the integrationist vision of certain Member States (see in particular Europol), the need for the Council to 'tone down' Commission proposals deemed over-ambitious (see the establishment of Eurojust as a response to the European Public Prosecutor), and the need to be seen to respond to high profile phenomena such as corruption within the Commission (OLAF) or terrorism (Europol, Eurojust, SitCen, the Counter-terrorism Coordinator). The establishment of these bodies has contributed significantly to the development of EU criminal law. On the other hand, and notwithstanding attempts to develop the mandate of these bodies, their powers remain contested and to some extent unclear. This lack of clarity is even more visible in these bodies such as SitCen which have not been established under a clear legal basis. Lack of clarity and certainty in the sensitive criminal law sphere is exacerbated by limits to the accountability and judicial control of these bodies—both bodies established by secondary EU legislation such as Europol and Eurojust, but also—perhaps more importantly—bodies with no legal basis. The increased emphasis on informality and operational co-operation between bodies and under central committees presents further challenges for transparency, accountability and legal certainty.[521]

This lack of clarity and transparency—and the definition of the mandate of EU criminal law bodies and the terms of their relationship with national authorities in broad terms—may lead to a significant expansion of the enforcement field in the EU. Rather than *replacing* national authorities, EU criminal law bodies work *with* and *in addition to* national authorities. This may lead to situations of investigative or prosecutorial 'forum shopping', especially in the light of the shielding of EU

---

[520] See D. Curtin, 'Holding (Quasi-)Autonomous EU Administrative Actors to Public Account', *European Law Journal*, vol 13, no 4, 2007, pp 523–541 at pp 528–529.

[521] Highlighting perhaps the point about differences between regulatory market approaches and the criminal law, it is noteworthy that, in the context of the internal market, Community agencies have been perceived as legitimacy providers, contributing to the improvement of transparency in the regulatory process—see R Dehousse, 'Regulation by Networks in the European Community: the Role of European Agencies', *Journal of European Public Policy*, vol 4, no 2, 1997, pp 246–261 at p 257.

bodies from any responsibility for their decisions and choices. Two prime examples of this trend are the assertion by the ECJ that the OLAF activities in the *Tillack* case did not have an impact on the legal position of the applicant; and the exercises by Eurojust to allocate jurisdiction in cases of concurrent jurisdiction on the basis of vague, largely unchalleangable criteria and at informal meetings.[522] This extension of the enforcement field is also the outcome of the lack of clarity and overlap between the mandate of the various EU bodies, with a prime example being that Europol and Eurojust are both involved in 'investigations'—although the first is supposed to be a police and the second a judicial/prosecutorial body. This may be the outcome of the differences in national criminal justice systems on the stages of criminal investigations and prosecutions, but at EU level they are translated in the expansion of the field of action of EU bodies.

If it enters into force, the Lisbon Treaty will bring about significant developments, in boosting to some extent the judicial control and accountability of a number of EU criminal law bodies, but also—in the case of Europol and Eurojust—launching again a debate (this time under co-decision) over their role, powers and accountability and their relationship with the national level. This may provide an opportunity to have a detailed look at the implications of the work of these bodies for the individual, for enforcement in the EU, but also for the shaping and legitimacy of EU criminal law and policy. This is in particular the case in the light of the increasing powers and action of these bodies on the operational level, but also on the strategic level with a number of EU bodies called to inform the development of EU criminal law strategy (see for instance Europol with its Situation Reports and the Counter-terrorism Coordinator with his implementation and issues Reports). The promotion of fundamental criminal justice choices by bodies with limited accountability and transparency may lead to the increased depoliticisation of EU criminal law, with highly political decisions obtaining the guise of 'technical' choices.[523] This may not bode well for achieving the increased legitimacy that further EU action in criminal matters requires.

---

[522] See also ch 3.

[523] On this point in relation to agencies in general, see Shapiro above. On depoliticisation in the context of the European Border Agency (FRONTEX), see Mitsilegas, 'Border Security', n 468 above.

5

Databases

Reconfiguring the Relationship between Security and Privacy

I. INTRODUCTION

A KEY ELEMENT OF the development of EU criminal law in recent years has been the establishment of legal and technical mechanisms aiming to facilitate the collection, exchange and analysis of personal data, in particular in the context of counter-terrorism. Steps in this direction have taken the form of initiatives aiming both at eliminating obstacles to the exchange of personal data between *national* authorities, and at creating EU-wide structures and databases, which interact between themselves and with national authorities. Information collection and exchange has also been boosted by the involvement of the private sector, increasingly being called to co-operate with the State in the fight against crime. This chapter will examine what happens to personal data in the development of EU criminal law by following this threefold structure: the first section will focus on the development of EU databases and attempts to maximise access to databases and make them 'interoperable'; the second section will examine attempts to boost co-operation between national law enforcement authorities; and the third section will examine the privatisation of the collection, analysis and transfer of personal data. A fourth section will examine these developments in the context of the EU legal framework on data protection and privacy, in particular in the light of the Lisbon Treaty. The chapter will conclude by assessing the significance of the establishment of mechanisms enabling the growing collection and use of personal data for the individual and the State in the European Union.

II. EU DATABASES

A central method of collection, analysis and exchange of personal data in the European Union has been the establishment of EU-wide databases for a wide range of different purposes. Some of these databases, such as the Europol

Information System, are linked with a specific EU law enforcement body.[1] Others, such as the Schengen Information System, are more stand-alone centralised EU databases.[2] All these databases have a strong element of interaction with national authorities. in this context the question of which authorities have access to these databases becomes of primary importance. The question of access has also become relevant with regard to EU databases seemingly unrelated to criminal law, such as the Visa Information System—with increased pressure to allow national police authorities access to these databases also. Widening access, along with efforts to extend the categories and type of data included in the databases, may lead to a significant increase in the exchange of personal data across the EU. This is also the case in the light of sustained efforts to render the various EU databases 'interoperable'. It is in the context of attempts to maximise collection and access of personal data that this part will examine the major EU databases in criminal matters.

A. The Europol Information System and Beyond

The legal framework underpinning Europol and its operations, including the relevant provisions on the Europol data collection and analysis and its databases have been examined in detail in chapter four. For the purposes of this chapter, it is important to reiterate that the collection, analysis and exchange of information are central to Europol's work, and that in terms of the collection of personal data, the key is the Europol Information System and the Analysis Work Files that can be opened by Europol for specific cases. The Europol Information System contains information on a wide range of individuals—including persons who have been convicted for one of the offences which fall within Europol's mandate;[3] persons who are suspected of having committed or having taken part in one of these offences; and persons for whom there are serious grounds under national law for believing that they will commit such offences.[4] This broad list may become even more extended in cases where Europol opens Analysis Work Files (AWF): the latter may also include a wide range of information on witnesses (actual or potential), victims, contacts and associates and informers.[5] This wide range of personal data collected and analysed by Europol may be further extended via its co-operation with third countries and EU and third bodies—with a prime example of co-operation with third countries being the Agreement on the exchange of personal data concluded between the Director of Europol and the USA.[6] The broad

---

[1] Personal data is also processed by Eurojust: see ch 4.

[2] The Schengen Information System is currently maintained by the participating Member States: see in particular Art 92 of the Schengen Implementing Convention—OJ L239, 22 September 2000, p 19.

[3] On the offences falling within the mandate of Europol, see Art 2 of the Convention and annex attached therein, as well as the Protocols amending the Convention.

[4] Art 8(1) of the Europol Convention.

[5] Art 10 of Europol Convention and Europol rules on analysis files—for details see ch 4.

[6] For details, of the Europol–USA Agreement, see V Mitsilegas, 'The New EU–US Co-operation on Extradition, Mutual Legal Assistance and the Exchange of Police Data', *European Foreign Affairs Review*, vol 8, 2003, pp 515–536; see also ch 6.

categories of collected personal data and their potential use for analysis and exchange purposes pose prominently the question of whether Europol's work is covered by adequate standards for the protection of personal data and privacy. The Europol Convention itself contains a number of provisions on data protection, and also provides the legal basis for the establishment of a Joint Supervisory Body (JSB) for data protection.[7] However, the powers of the JSB are limited.[8]

Current proposals to amend the Europol Convention by a Decision will lead to an increase in the personal data collected and analysed by Europol. In particular the new proposals allow for: the possibility of establishing a further information system—alongside the Europol Information System (EIS)—including data contained in Analysis Work Files (AWFs) (with the categories of AWF personal data being much more extensive than EIS data); the insertion of wide categories of data including DNA data into the EIS; the extension of access to Europol's databases beyond the national units in Member States; the involvement of associated experts in Europol's AWFs; the launch of Europol co-operation with the private sector; and the intensification of Europol co-operation with EU and third bodies and third States. At the same time, no major changes (with the exception of the establishment of a Data Protection Officer post) have been introduced with regard to data protection in the Europol Decision.[9] It is thus evident that the potential challenges of Europol's work to privacy could proliferate given the expansion of its databases and mandate.

B. The Schengen Information System

Another important EU database in the area of Justice and Home Affairs is the Schengen Information System (SIS).[10] Established by the Schengen Implementing Convention, which was incorporated in EC/EU law by the Amsterdam Treaty, the Schengen Information System contains data categorised in the form of various 'alerts': these alerts concern both immigration data (alerts on third country nationals who should be denied entry into the Schengen territory), and data related to police and judicial co-operation in criminal matters (alerts on persons wanted for extradition to a Schengen State, on missing persons, on persons wanted as witnesses or for the purposes of prosecution or the enforcement of sentences, on persons or vehicles to be placed under surveillance or subjected to specific

---

[7] Art 24.

[8] This is in particular the case when Europol concludes agreements with third States or bodies—the Joint Supervisory Body has the mandate to give an Opinion on the adequacy of data protection in the third State/organisation involved, but does not have the power to block the agreement from going ahead.

[9] See ch 4.

[10] This section (and the sections on interoperability and Prüm) updates and expands sections in V Mitsilegas, 'Databases in the Area of Freedom, Security and Justice' in C Stefanou and H Xanthaki (eds), *Towards a European Criminal Record*, Cambridge, Cambridge University Press, 2008, pp 311–335.

checks, and on objects sought for the purpose of seizure or use in criminal proceedings).[11] The System works on a hit/no hit basis, and Member States determine which of its law enforcement or immigration authorities have access to the respective part of the Schengen Information System.[12] The System, whose content has been increasing steadily,[13] became operational in 1995, for an initial group of seven Member States—by 2001 it applied fully to 13 out of the 15 'old' Member States (excluding the UK and Ireland).[14] Meeting the SIS requirements by candidate countries was a central requirement of the EU in accession negotiations for the 2004 and 2007 enlargements[15]—with the majority of the countries which joined the EU in 2004 now being full Schengen members.[16]

The challenge of adaptation of candidate countries to SIS standards (and their participation to the System after their accession to the EU) was particularly complex in the light of efforts by the Schengen Members to develop further the Schengen Information System, in order for the latter to respond to both events such as terrorist attacks and to technological advances. Particular aims of proposals to develop SIS have been to extend the data included in the database and to broaden the categories of national authorities having access to Schengen data. A significant step towards the achievement of the latter goal has been made on the basis of counter-terrorism considerations: in 2004, the Council adopted a first pillar Regulation and a third pillar Decision concerning the introduction 'of some new functions for the Schengen Information System, including in the fight against terrorism.'[17] The Regulation extended access to SIS data to national judicial authorities and access to immigration data specifically to authorities responsible for issuing visas and residence permits and examining visa applications. The Decision extended access to certain categories of 'criminal law' SIS data to Europol and Eurojust.

---

[11] Arts 95–100 of the Schengen Implementing Convention, OJ L19, 22 September 2000, pp 42–45. For further details, see House of Lords European Union Committee, *Schengen Information System II (SIS II)*, 9th Report, session 2006–07, HL Paper 49; for overviews see also S Peers, *EU Justice and Home Affairs Law*, 2nd edn, Oxford, OUP, 2006, pp 547–549; and C. Stefanou, 'Organised Crime and the Use of EU-wide Databases', in I Bantekas and G Keramidas (eds), *International and European Financial Law*, London, Butterworths, 2006, pp 215–243 at pp 224–225.

[12] For further details see House of Lords European Union Committee, *SIS II*, n 11 above.

[13] For details of the development of the Schengen Information System, see E Brouwer, 'Data Surveillance and Border Control in the EU: Balancing Efficiency and Legal Protection', in T Balzacq and S Carrera (eds), *Security versus Freedom? A Challenge for Europe's Future*, Aldershot, Ashgate, 2006, pp 137–154.

[14] House of Lords European Union Committee, *SIS II*, n 11 above.

[15] See V Mitsilegas, J Monar and W Rees, *The European Union and Internal Security* (Basingstoke, Palgrave Macmillan, 2003) ch 5; see also J Monar, *Enlargement-related Diversity in EU Justice and Home Affairs: Challenges, Dimensions and Management Instruments*, WRR (Netherlands Scientific Council for Government Policy) Working Document 112, The Hague, December 2000.

[16] With the exception of Cyprus, all other 2004 entrants are now full Schengen members, with controls on land and sea borders lifted on 21 December 2007 and controls on air borders lifted on 30 March 2008: see Justice and Home Affairs Council Conclusions of 6–7 December 2007, p 31 (Council doc 15966/07, Presse 275).

[17] Reg 871/2004, [2004] OJ L162, 30 April 2004, p 29; Dec 2005/211/JHA, [2005] OJ L68, 15 March 2005, p 44.

A broader debate on the nature and development of the Schengen Information System has been taking place in the context of discussions on the establishment of a so-called 'second generation' System, or SIS II. In May 2005, the Commission tabled three draft legislative proposals (two first pillar Regulations and one third pillar Decision—reflecting the fact that SIS covers both immigration and criminal law data), which would constitute the legal basis for the establishment of SIS II.[18] This resulted in the formal adoption of the Regulations in 2006,[19] and the adoption of the third pillar Decision some months later.[20] However, in the light of delays in the operational development of the second generation Schengen Information System, it was decided that Member States will at the first stage be integrated in a developed version of the original Schengen Information System (SIS1+), a proposal called 'SISone 4all'.[21] At the time of writing, migration from SIS 1+ to SIS II was planned for September 2009.[22]

The provisions of the general SIS II Regulation are largely mirrored in the third pillar Decision. Both instruments replace the current provisions on the first generation Schengen Information System. The Decision states (as does the Regulation) that SIS II will be composed by a central EU system (Central SIS II) and a national system (N. SIS II).[23] After lengthy negotiations, the management of SIS II was not given to the Commission, but after a transitional period to a 'Management Authority'.[24] The Commission will have according to the SIS II legislation the interim operational management of the system,[25] but in reality the Commission will delegate the management to France and Austria, where the back up of the system will be located.[26] According to Article 20(1) of the Decision, the police part of SIS II will include personal data on alerts in respect of persons

---

[18] 'Proposal for a Council Decision on the establishment, operation and use of the second generation Schengen Information System' COM (2005) 230 final; 'Proposal for a Regulation on the establishment, operation and use of the second generation Schengen Information System' COM (2005) 236 final; and 'Proposal for a Regulation regarding the access to SIS II by the services of Member States responsible for issuing vehicle registration certificates' COM (2005) 237 final.

[19] Regulation 1987/2006 on the establishment, operation and use of the second generation Schengen Information System (SIS II), OJ L381, 28 December 2006, p 4; Regulation 1986/2006 regarding access to the second generation Schengen Information System (SIS II) by the services in the Member States responsible for issuing vehicle registration certificates, OJ L381, 28 December 2006, p 1.

[20] Council Decision 2007/533/JHA of 12 June 2007 on the establishment, operation and use of the second generation Schengen Information System (SIS II), OJ L205, 7 August 2007, p 63.

[21] See the Conclusions of the Justice and Home Affairs Council of 4–5 December 2006, doc. 15801/06 (Presse 341), pp 20–22. For further details, see S. Peers, 'Key Legislative Developments on Migration in the European Union: SIS II', *European Journal of Migration and Law*, vol.10, 2008, pp 77–104 at pp 79–81.

[22] Justice and Home Affairs Council Conclusions of 5–6 June 2008, Council doc. 9956/08 (Presse 146), p 8. See also the detailed Conclusions on Schengen developments, Justice and Home Affairs Council of 28 February 2008, Council doc 6796/08 (Presse 48), p 8. In this context, see also the proposal for a Council Decision on the tests of the SIS II, tabled by the Commission in December 2007 (COM (2007) 837 final, Brussels, 20 December 2007).

[23] Art 4(1) of the Regulation and the Decision.

[24] Art 15 of the Regulation and the Decision.

[25] Art 15(3) of the Regulation and the Decision.

[26] Peers, 'Key Legislative Developments', n 21 above, p 86. See Peers also for details on the negotiations.

wanted for arrest, surrender or extradition,[27] in respect of missing persons,[28] persons sought to assist with a judicial procedure (including witnesses)[29] and alerts on persons for discreet checks.[30] A number of data on objects will also be included in the system.[31] Alerts on persons entered in SIS II must be kept only for the time required to achieve the purpose for which they were entered.[32] The need to keep an alert in the system must be reviewed by the Member State issuing the alert within three years of its entry into SIS II.[33] Member States may decide to keep the alert longer, following a 'comprehensive individual assessment'[34]—they may also decide to have shorter review periods.[35] If data are no longer needed, alerts will automatically be erased after the expiry of the review period.[36]

A major change involves the nature and use of personal data included in the System. Both the Regulation and the Decision provide the legal basis for the inclusion of biometrics, in the form of photographs and fingerprints, in SIS.[37] The provisions on the use of biometrics—whose use is gradually being generalised in both EU and national databases—are extremely significant in this context.[38] In the first stage, biometrics will be used only for 'one-to-one' searches—seeking to confirm someone's identity by comparing the biometric identifiers of the person only with those existing in SIS under this person's name; however, in the future (following the presentation by the Commission of a Report on the availability and readiness of the required technology), biometrics will also be used for 'one-to-many' searches, where biometric data of one person will be compared with the whole SIS database.[39] This development may have substantial implications for privacy, but also for the nature of the Schengen Information System, which is increasingly developing from a hit/no hit database to a general intelligence database. The fact that such an important decision to instigate one-to-many searches is essentially deemed as a technical issue and will be taken with little debate (the European Parliament being merely consulted), raises serious concerns of transparency and democratic scrutiny.

---

[27] See Arts 26–31 for specific rules.

[28] Arts 32–33.

[29] Arts 34–35.

[30] Arts 36–37.

[31] See objects required for discreet checks (Arts 36–37) and objects for seizure or use as evidence in criminal proceedings (Arts 38–39).

[32] Art 44(1).

[33] Art 44(2)—the period is one year for alerts issued for the purposes of discreet checks.

[34] Art 44(4).

[35] Art 44(3).

[36] Art 44(5).

[37] Art 20(3)(e) and (f) of the Regulation and the Decision. See also their Preamble (recitals 14 in both the Regulation and the Decision).

[38] On the use of biometrics in EU databases, with emphasis on the immigration databases, see A Baldaccini, 'Counter-terrorism and the EU Strategy for Border Security: Framing Suspects with Biometric Documents and Databases', *European Journal of Migration and Law*, vol 10, 2008, pp 31–49; see also E Brouwer, 'The Use of Biometrics in EU Databases and Identity Documents', in J Lodge (ed), *Are You Who You Say You Are? The EU and Biometric Borders*, Nijmegen, Wolf Legal Publishers, 2007, pp 45–66.

[39] Art 22 of Regulation and Decision. For further explanation of these searches, see House of Lords European Union Committee, *SIS II*, n 11 above, paras 57–60.

Another sign of the development of SIS into a general intelligence/investigative database is the provision, in both the Regulation and the Decision, allowing the interlinking of alerts.[40] Such interlinking is allowed only if there is a 'clear operational need',[41] but is subject to the national law of the Member State which decides to use this option[42]—thus rendering possible the creation of significantly different systems across the EU. Interlinking of alerts is a major departure from the limited hit/no hit character of the current SIS and its potential for profiling is significant. As the European Data Protection Supervisor has noted in his Opinion on the SIS II proposals, 'the person is no longer "assessed" on the basis of data relating only to him/her, but on the basis of his/her possible association with other persons', which may lead to their treatment with greater suspicion if they are deemed to be associated with criminals or wanted persons—moreover, the Supervisor notes, interlinking extends investigative powers because it makes possible the registration of alleged gangs or networks (eg data of illegal immigrants and data on traffickers).[43] The Supervisor noted that authorities with no right of access to certain categories of data should not even be aware of the existence of these links.[44] The Regulation and draft Decision seem to have taken this view on board to some extent, by stating that authorities with no right of access to certain categories of alert will no be able to *see* the link to an alert to which they do not have access.[45] However, this may not necessarily mean that these authorities will be unaware of the *existence* of a link.

A further extension to SIS I standards is the provision—in the third pillar Decision only and with regard to the criminal law part of the System—that processing of such data may take place for other purposes than those expressly mentioned in the draft Decision—for this to be allowed processing must be linked with a specific case and justified by the need 'to prevent an imminent serious threat to public policy and public security, on serious grounds of national security or for the purposes of preventing a serious criminal offence'.[46] This provision (which does not exist in the Schengen Implementing Convention)[47] challenges the purpose limitation principle and may lead to a considerable extension of the use of Schengen data. On the other hand, in a departure from the Commission's original proposals, the rules on access to SIS data have not changed drastically.[48] Some changes have been introduced in the context of access to SIS II data by Eurojust—

---

[40] Art 37 of Regulation and 52 the Decision (see also Preamble, recitals 17 in both instruments).

[41] Art 37(4) of the Regulation and Art 52(4) of the Decision.

[42] Art 37(5) of the Regulation and Art 52(5) of the Decision.

[43] European Data Protection Supervisor, Opinion of 19 October 2005, OJ C91, 19 April 2006, p 38. Also available at www.edps.eu.int.

[44] ibid.

[45] Art 37(3) of the Regulation and Art 52(3) of the Decision.

[46] Art 46(5) of draft Decision.

[47] See Arts 101 and 102 of the Schengen Implementing Convention—House of Lords European Union Committee, *SIS II*, n 11 above, para 92.

[48] See House of Lords European Union Committee, *SIS II*, n 11 above. In particular, see the express prohibition of transferring or making available SIS II data to third countries or international organisations (Art 39 of Regulation and 54 of draft Decision).

along with access to extradition and missing persons data, Eurojust will also have access to alerts concerning wanted persons and objects.[49] However, the more general question has been raised of what happens to SIS data which are accessed by other EU bodies and whether the limits to access of such data set out by the SIS legislation can be circumvented by the relevant rules governing these bodies. The question has been raised in particular with regard to whether Europol can treat SIS data as its own data (considered as Member States contribution to Europol).[50] If SIS data become Europol data in this process, the express prohibition in the SIS II legislation of transferring such data to third countries[51] may be circumvented.[52]

The SIS II Decision contains a specific chapter on data protection.[53] The standard of protection is the 1981 Council of Europe Convention on data protection;[54] processing of sensitive data is prohibited.[55] The Decision also includes provisions establishing rights of access, correction of inaccurate data and deletion of unlawfully stored data,[56] as well as a provision on remedies: actions may be brought before courts *or* the authority competent under the law of any Member State by any person to access, correct, delete, or obtain information or to obtain compensation in connection with an alert relating to them.[57] The data protection chapter also contains provisions on supervision, with the main change from the first generation SIS being that supervision of the activities of the Schengen Management Authority (the 'EU' part of Schengen) will now be undertaken by the European Data Protection Supervisor (EDPS), and no longer by the existing Schengen Joint Supervisory Authority (JSA).[58] In the light of the difficulty to distinguish the 'immigration' and the 'police' parts of the Schengen Information System, granting the supervisory function of the police part of SIS II to the EDPS (who is also, under the SIS II Regulation, responsible for the supervision of the immigration part[59]) certainly makes sense from an operational point of view. However, this choice may have important legal repercussions should SIS II become operational while the current Treaty pillar structure remains in force: the EDPS has currently powers of supervision in the first, but not in the third pillar, and the first pillar data

---

[49] Art 42; see also House of Lords European Union Committee, *SIS II*, n 11 above, para 45. This extension reflects related calls by Eurojust: see Eurojust's contribution to the discussion on the SIS II, Council doc 11102/06, Brussels 30 June 2006.

[50] Art 41 regulates access to SIS II data by Europol. The latter will have access to alerts related to arrest for surrender, discreet checks and seizure or use as evidence in criminal proceedings.

[51] See Art 54 of the SIS II Decision. However, there is a derogation with regard to the exchange of data on lost and stolen passports with Interpol (Art 55).

[52] House of Lords European Union Committee, *SIS II*, n 11 above, para 108.

[53] Ch XII, Arts 56–63.

[54] Art 57.

[55] Art 56.

[56] Art 58.

[57] Art 59(1).

[58] Art 61. On the JSA, see Art 115 of the Schengen Implementing Convention. Supervision of the 'national' part of SIS II will continue to be provided by an independent national supervisory authority—Art 60 of the SIS II Decision.

[59] See Art 45 of the Regulation.

protection legislation—underpinning the functions of the EDPS[60]—does not apply to third pillar activities, bodies and systems.

C. The Customs Information System

The Customs Information System (CIS) was established by a 1995 third pillar Convention.[61] In 1997, a first pillar Regulation also established the CIS for the purposes of mutual assistance in respect of customs and agricultural matters.[62] The Convention has since been supplemented by a series of Protocols on the jurisdiction of the ECJ to give preliminary rulings on the Convention,[63] the definition of money laundering for the purposes of the Convention,[64] and the creation of a customs identification database.[65] The Convention has now been ratified by all EU Member States.[66] The Customs Information System itself was launched in March 2003.[67] After a very slow start, when it was stated that the CIS had been underused and the system held only a limited amount of data,[68] it seems that now the system is used somewhat more extensively, although a number of issues regarding its operation still remain.[69]

According to the CIS Convention, the aim of the Customs Information System is 'to assist in preventing, investigating and prosecuting serious contraventions of national laws by increasing, through the rapid dissemination of information, the effectiveness of the co-operation and control purposes of the customs administrations of Member States'.[70] It is managed by the Commission[71] and a Committee consisting of representatives from the Customs Administrations of the Member States.[72] It consists of a central database accessible via terminals in each Member

---

[60] See also Art 61(1) of the SIS II Decision which states that the duties and powers referred to in Arts 46 and 47 of Regulation (EC) No 45/2001will apply accordingly (Regulation (EC) No 45/2001 of 18 December 2000 on the protection of individuals with regard to the processing of personal data by the Community institutions and bodies and on the free movement of such data, OJ L8, 12 January 2001, p 1).

[61] Convention drawn up on the basis of Art K.3 of the Treaty on European Union, on the use of information technology for customs purposes, OJ C316, 27 November 1995, p 34.

[62] Council Regulation (EC) No 515/97, OJ L82, 22 March 1997, p 1.

[63] OJ C151, 20 May 1997, p 15.

[64] OJ C91, 31 March 1999, p 1.

[65] OJ C139, 13 June 2003, p 1.

[66] See Council doc 16245/07, Brussels, 7 December 2007.

[67] Council doc 5160/04, Brussels, 9 January 2004.

[68] The CIS Joint Supervisory Authority, Supervising the Customs Information System, Council doc 7106/05, Brussels, 4 March 2005.

[69] Art 16 Committee, Proposal for a Report concerning the period of 1 January 2007 to 2 November 2007, Council doc 16245/07, Brussels, 7 December 2007. At the time of writing, the document was only partially accessible with key findings remaining classified.

[70] Art 2(2). In this context, the Council also adopted a Convention on mutual assistance and cooperation between customs administrations (the 'Naples II' Convention), OJ C24, 23 January 1998, p 1.

[71] Which is involved in the technical management of the system—Art 3(2).

[72] Responsible inter alia for the proper functioning of the CIS and for reporting annually to the Council—see Art 16.

State and contains a number of data, including personal data.[73] The Convention enumerates exhaustively the categories of personal data which may be included in the system.[74] Personal data will only be included in the CIS for the purposes of sighting and reporting, discreet surveillance and specific checks, as well as if there are real indications that the person concerned has committed, is in the act of committing, or will commit serious contraventions of national laws.[75] Direct access to CIS data is reserved exclusively for national authorities whose designation is left to Member States—it is noteworthy that these may include authorities other than customs administrations.[76]

The Convention contains a purpose limitation clause regarding the use of CIS data by Member States (use only for the Convention purposes); however, this clause is effectively undermined by a provision allowing Member States to use CIS data 'for administrative or other purposes with the prior authorisation of and subject to any conditions imposed by the Member State which included it in the system'.[77] Moreover, data obtained from the CIS may under certain conditions imposed by the inputting Member State be communicated for use not only by national authorities other than those designated but also to non-Member States and international organisations.[78] Regarding data retention, in a provision structured similarly to the SIS Implementing Convention[79] data is kept 'only for the time necessary to achieve the purpose for which it was included'.[80] The Convention includes a number of provisions on data protection, containing provisions on the application of the 1981 Council of Europe Convention,[81] purpose limitation[82] and access,[83] as well as data protection supervision. Again in a formulation similar to the SIS provisions, supervision is conducted by national supervisory authorities designated by Member States,[84] and a Joint Supervisory Authority supervising the operation of the CIS.[85]

---

[73] Art 3(1).
[74] Art 4. These include inter alia names, date and place of birth, nationality, sex, 'any particular objective and permanent physical characteristics', and a warning code indicating any history of beig armed, violent or escaping.
[75] Art 5.
[76] Art 7(1).
[77] Art 8(1).
[78] Art 8(4).
[79] See Art 112(1). According to this provision a review will take place no later than three years after the entry of data into the system (one year on Art 99 data).
[80] Art 12(1).
[81] Art 13(1). But note also that according to Art 18(2), the CIS Joint Supervisory Authority will take into account not only the 1981 Convention, but also Council of Europe Recommendation R (87) 15 on personal data in the police sector in the performance of its tasks.
[82] Art 14—but note also the provisions in Art 8.
[83] Art 15—but note also the provisions in Art 7.
[84] Art 17.
[85] Art 18. For other similarities between the CIS and the SIS see Peers, *EU Justice*, n 11, pp 550–551.

D. Interoperability and Access to Immigration Databases

In efforts to enhance the exchange of personal data, great emphasis has been placed in the recent past on enabling the flow of data between the various EU databases and/or EU agencies and bodies. Examples of developing legal bases to enable access by EU bodies to databases for the purposes of police co-operation and judicial co-operation in criminal matters have been examined above in the context of access by Europol and Eurojust to the Schengen Information System. These efforts have been coupled by initiatives such as agreements enabling the exchange of personal data between EU bodies, with the agreement between Europol and Eurojust being a prime example.[86] However, largely justified on the basis of the 'war on terror', efforts for greater synergies in data sharing have been proliferating in the recent past under the guise of two main initiatives: to enhance the 'interoperability' between EU databases;[87] and to allow access by law enforcement authorities to immigration databases, in spite of the undoubtedly different purposes of managing migration and fighting crime—the justification put forward being that access by police authorities to immigration data is necessary for security reasons.[88] These trends were clearly visible already in 2004, when the European Council, in the Declaration on combating terrorism issued shortly after the Madrid bombings, linked the monitoring of the movement of people with the 'war on terror' by stressing that 'improved border controls and document security play an important role in combating terrorism'.[89] The European Council also stressed the need to enhance the interoperability between EU databases and the creation of 'synergies' between existing and future information systems (such as SIS II, VIS and Eurodac) 'in order to exploit their added value within their respective legal and technical frameworks in the prevention and fight against terrorism'.[90]

Justifying the observation that immigration and security are increasingly linked in EU JHA discourse and policy-making, thus creating an (in)security continuum,[91] the Hague Programme—adopted by the European Council later in 2004—articulated more clearly the perceived link between movement, migration and terrorism, stating that

> the management of migration flows, including the fight against illegal immigration should be strengthened by establishing *a continuum of security measures* that effectively

---

[86] For more details on these agreements, see ch 4.

[87] For a discussion of interoperability in the context of police databases, see P de Hert and S Gutwirth, 'Interoperability of Police Databases within the EU: An Accountable Political Choice?' *International Review of Law, Computers and Technology*, vol 20, nos 1–2, 2006, pp 21–35.

[88] See V Mitsilegas, 'Contrôle des étrangers, des passagers, des citoyens: Surveillance et anti-terrorisme', *Cultures et conflits*, vol 58, 2005, pp 155–182.

[89] Pt 6, p 7.

[90] *ibid.* pt 5, p 7. Text to be found at www.consilium.europa.eu under 'European Council Conclusions'.

[91] See in this context the seminal work of Didier Bigo, in particular *Polices en réseaux: l'éxperience européenne*, Paris, Presses Sciences Po, 1996.

links visa application procedures and entry and exit procedures at external border cross-ings. Such measures are also of importance for the prevention and control of crime, in particular terrorism. In order to achieve this, a coherent approach and harmonised solu-tions in the EU on biometric identifiers and data are necessary. (emphasis added)[92]

The Hague Programme also mentions interoperability both in the context of strengthening security (calling for interoperability of *national* databases or direct online access including for Europol to existing central EU databases)[93], and in the context of migration management—where the European Council called on the Council to examine 'how to maximise the effectiveness and interoperability of EU information systems' and invited the Commission to present a Communication on the interoperability between the Schengen Information System, the Visa Information System (VIS), and Eurodac.[94] The Commission presented its Communication a year later, in November 2005.[95] The purpose of the Communication was to highlight how, beyond their present purposes, databases 'can more effectively support the policies linked to the free movement of persons and serve the objective of combating terrorism and serious crime'.[96] On the basis of this approach, the Commission argued strongly in favour of access of authori-ties responsible for internal security to immigration databases such as SIS, VIS and Eurodac.[97] The Communication provided a definition of 'interoperability', which is the 'ability of IT systems and of the business processes they support to exchange data and to enable the sharing of information and knowledge'.[98]

According to the Commission, interoperability is a technical rather than a legal/political concept.[99] The attempt to treat interoperability as a merely techni-cal concept, while at the same time using the concept to enable maximum access to databases containing a wide range of personal data (which become even more sensitive with the sustained emphasis on biometrics) is striking.[100] It can be seen as an attempt to depoliticise an issue which may have major repercussions for the

[92] Para 1.7.2.
[93] Para 2.1. It is important to note in this context that the European Council expressly states that new centralised European databases should only be created on the basis of studies that have shown their added value.
[94] Para 1.7.2.
[95] 'Communication on improved effectiveness, enhanced interoperability and synergies among european databases in the area of justice and home affairs' COM (2005) 597 final, Brussels, 24 November 2005.
[96] ibid, p 2.
[97] ibid, p 8. The Commission also took the opportunity to float proposals for longer-term devel-opments, including the creation of a European Criminal Automated Fingerprints Identification System, the creation of an entry-exit system and introduction of a border crossing facilitation scheme for frequent border crossers, and European registers for travel documents and identity cards (pp 8–9).
[98] ibid, p 3.
[99] ibid.
[100] See also the criticism by the European Data Protection Supervisor in his Opinion on the Communication (10 March 2006), www.edps.eu.int . The Supervisor highlighted the potential over-reach of those having access to databases under interoperability, noting that the latter 'should never lead to a situation where an authority, not entitled to access or use certain data, can obtain this access via another information system'.

protection of fundamental rights and civil liberties, and which has the potential to shield far-reaching developments (including the blurring of the boundaries between databases established for different purposes and containing different categories of data for the benefit of law enforcement agencies) from effective scrutiny and democratic control.[101] The emphasis on interoperability may lead to the justification of the development of important initiatives in this context at the operational level, with the adoption of negotiated legislative standards underpinning the evolving databases (or their capacities) potentially deemed unnecessary.[102]

While the Commission's far-reaching proposals for access by internal security agencies to the second generation Schengen Information System have not been accepted, the situation has not proven to be the same with regard to the Visa Information System (VIS).[103] The development of the VIS is a clear example of the trend to blur the boundary between immigration and police databases. The Justice and Home Affairs Council adopted detailed conclusions on the development of VIS in February 2004, stating clearly that one of the purposes of the system would be to 'contribute towards improving the administration of the common visa policy and towards internal security and combating terrorism'.[104] It also called for access to VIS to be granted to border guards and 'other national authorities to be authorised by each Member State such as police departments, immigration departments and services responsible for internal security'.[105] In June 2004, the Council adopted a Decision forming the legal basis for the establishment of VIS[106] and negotiations began to define its purpose and functions and formulate rules on access and exchange of data. The Commission subsequently tabled a draft Regulation aiming to take VIS further by defining its aims and rules on data access and exchange.[107] The Justice and Home Affairs Council of 24 February 2005 called for access to VIS to be given to national authorities responsible for 'internal security', when exercising their powers in investigating, preventing and detecting criminal offences, including terrorist acts or threats and invited the Commission to

---

[101] For a similar argument, see also de Hert and Gutwirth, n 87 above, pp 31–32. On the broader trend towards de-politicisation in the context of border security in the EU, see V Mitsilegas, 'Border Security in the European Union. Towards Centralised Controls and Maximum Surveillance' in E Guild, H Toner and A Baldaccini, *EU Immigration and Asylum Law and Policy*, Oxford, Hart Publishing, 2007, pp 359–394.

[102] A similar trend can also be discerned in the negotiation of legislative instruments on databases, where a number of issues perceived as 'technical' are left to be decided by comitology. See for example the development of 'technical rules for linking alerts' in the SIS II Regulation—Art 37(2).

[103] The Visa Information System would contain data (including biometrics) on visa applicants, but also a series of data on the visa application, including details of sponsors (see Arts 3 and 6 of the draft VIS Regulation). For further details, see Peers, *EU Justice*, n 11 above, pp 165–167.

[104] Doc 5831/04 (Presse 37). The Council called for the inclusion in VIS of biometric data on visa applicants.

[105] ibid.

[106] Council Decision of 8 June 2004 establishing the Visa Information System (VIS), [2004] OJ L213/5, 15 June 2004.

[107] Proposal for a Regulation of the European Parliament and of the Council concerning the VIS and the exchange of data between Member States on short-stay visas, COM (2004) 835 final, 28 December 2004.

present a separate, third pillar proposal to this end.[108] The Commission tabled such a proposal in November 2005.[109]

The two texts were linked and thus negotiated in parallel (co-decision was required formally for the first pillar Regulation, while for the third pillar Decision the European Parliament had a consultation role).[110] Agreement on both proposals was confirmed at the Justice and Home Affairs (JHA) Council of 12–13 June 2007 [111] and they were published in the Official Journal with considerable delay, in August 2008.[112]

Reflecting the logic of the Conclusions of the 2005 JHA Council, the VIS Regulation expressly states that one of the purposes of the Visa Information System is to contribute to the prevention of threats to internal security of the Member States.[113] The Regulation also contains a bridging clause to the third pillar Decision allowing access to VIS by Europol within the limits of its mandate and when necessary for the performance of its tasks, and by the relevant national authorities 'if there are reasonable grounds to consider that consultation of VIS data will substantially contribute' to the prevention, detection or investigation of terrorist offences and of other serious criminal offences.[114] The wording of this clause has been subject to extensive debate, with the view being put forward that a higher threshold is necessary for allowing access, requiring also the existence of factual indications as the basis for the reasonable grounds mentioned above.[115]

The terms of access of internal security authorities and Europol to the VIS are set out in detail in the third pillar Decision.[116] The national authorities with access to the VIS are 'authorities which are responsible for the prevention, detection or investigation of terrorist offences or of other serious criminal offences' which are designated by each Member State.[117] Member States must also designate central access points—it is through these access points that consultation of the VIS will take place.[118] Access to the VIS is thus potentially extended to a wide range of national authorities with diverse tasks.[119] It is up to the Member States to

---

[108] Doc 6228.05 (Presse 28), pp 15–16.

[109] COM (2005) 600 final, 24 November 2005.

[110] For details see V Mitsilegas, 'Human Rights, Terrorism and the Quest for Border Security', in M Pedrazzi (ed), *Individual Guarantees in the European Judicial Area in Criminal Matters*, Brussels, Bruylant, forthcoming.

[111] Council doc 10267/07 (Presse 125).

[112] Regulation (EC) No 767/2008, OJ L218, 13 August 2008, p 60; Decision 2008/633/JHA, OJ L218, 13 August 2008, p 129.

[113] The Regulation also enables the recording of biometric data into VIS—see Art 5(1).

[114] Art3(1).

[115] See Council doc 5456/1/07 REV 1, Brussels, 20 February 2007.

[116] In particular Arts 5–7.

[117] Art 2(1)(e).

[118] Art 3(3) of the Decision and Art 3(2) of the Regulation. Similarly, according to Art 7(3) of the Decision, Europol must designate a specialised unit with Europol officials acting as the central access point to the VIS. Access to the VIS only via central units seems to be a safeguard advocated by the European Parliament—see Council doc 8540/07, Brussels, 18 April 2007

[119] Note also the possibility to transfer VIS data to third countries—for further details, see Mitsilegas, 'Human Rights, Terrorism', n 110 above.

designate such authorities, and the only specification regarding their mandate is the remit of the prevention, investigation or detection of terrorism and serious crime. A wide range of agencies may be responsible for the prevention of terrorism at national level across the EU, not excluding intelligence agencies. The Decision does include further limits when specifying the conditions of access (including the requirement that access for consultation must be necessary in a specific case),[120] but the potential for access to VIS by a wide range of national agencies remains considerable.

E. EU Databases: Maximising the Collection of and Access to Personal Data

These developments confirm the blurring of the boundaries between databases established for different purposes and containing information on different categories of individuals. Databases established for immigration purposes (especially VIS and Eurodac) contain data on individuals engaging in legitimate activity, such as applying for a visa or for asylum, or sponsoring a visa applicant. Yet as seen above access to these databases is increasingly allowed to law enforcement authorities—this is the case with the VIS and a similar move is planned for Eurodac.[121] In EU law terms, these developments run counter to the data protection principle of purpose limitation as well as to the principle of proportionality; in broader terms, they signify the elimination of the distinction between innocent and suspect activity under a maximum securitisation approach, whereby the quest for security justifies the maximum collection and exchange of personal data, regardless of their nature. Further challenges are posed by the move towards 'interoperability' of databases: if viewed as a 'technical' issue, we may be led to a situation where databases containing different categories of data, accessed by different types of authorities, and operating with different methods (eg hit/no hit basis or broader analysis databases) will be linked *de facto* with no or little legislative intervention or parliamentary scrutiny. In this context, it is noteworthy that the European Council has recently invited the Commission 'to present possible solutions for the long-term management of large-scale IT systems in the area of Freedom, Security and Justice'.[122]

---

[120] See Art 5 of the Decision, in particular Art 5(1)(b).

[121] The German Presidency Programme on Police and Judicial Co-operation (Council doc. 17102/06, Brussels 22 December 2006) included such a proposal, but this did not go very far. However, the Justice and Home Affairs Council meeting of 12/13 June 2007, asked the Commission to present "as soon as possible" an amendment to the Council Regulation 2725/2000 on the establishment of Eurodac to allow for police access to the database' (Council doc 10267/07, Presse 125). The Commission will present such a proposal in 2009: see Commission Communication on a Policy Plan on Asylum. An Integrated Approach to Protection Across the EU, COM (2008) 360 final, Brussels, 17 June 2008.

[122] Conclusions of European Council of 19–20 June 2008, Council doc 11018/08, Brussels, 20 June 2008, para 15.

III. EXCHANGE OF DATA BETWEEN NATIONAL AUTHORITIES

Along with the proliferation and development of European Union databases and attempts to enhance their synergies and interoperability, another central element to the development of law enforcement co-operation in the EU has been the promotion of co-operation between *national* authorities. Such efforts have surfaced most prominently in the field of police co-operation (with the principle of availability appearing as a motor for integration in the field), with mutual legal assistance and judicial co-operation being pushed primarily via specialised proposals such as the exchange of national criminal records. Attempts to establish a framework facilitating the exchange of personal data between national authorities, in particular police authorities, represent formidable challenges of legality and fundamental rights. This is the case in particular with regard to the differences in the regulation of police authorities between Member States, differences which are closely related to the position of the police in the criminal justice system and the domestic constitutional framework. This section will examine these challenges when looking at mechanisms of boosting the exchange of personal data between national authorities in criminal matters.

A. Criminal Records

Efforts to boost the exchange of personal data in the context of mutual legal assistance in criminal matters in the EU have focused in recent years in facilitating the exchange of criminal records between national authorities.[123] A first, modest step in this context has been a 2005 third pillar Decision 'on the exchange of information extracted from the criminal record'.[124] This Decision called upon Member States to designate a central authority,[125] which will inform without delay the central authorities of the other Member States of criminal convictions and subsequent measures in respect of their nationals,[126] answer to requests by central authorities of other Member States,[127] and request criminal record data from these authorities on behalf of requesting individuals in its Member State.[128] Exchange of information takes place on the basis of a form annexed to the Decision. As a second step, the Commission tabled in 2005 a further proposal, this time for a Framework Decision on the organisation and content of the exchange of information extracted

---

[123] See also the more general provisions (including data protection provisions) in the EU Mutual Legal Assistance Convention—OJ C197, 12 July 2000, p 1.
[124] Council Decision 2005/876/JHA, OJ L322, 9 December 2005, p 33. See also in this context the recently adopted Framework Decision on taking into account of convictions in the Member States of the European Union in the course of new criminal proceedings, OJ L220, 15 August 2008, p 32.
[125] Art 1.
[126] Art 2.
[127] Art 3(1) first indent.
[128] Art 3(1) second indent.

from criminal records between Member States which would repeal the 2005 Decision.[129] The Council reached a 'general approach' on the proposal in 2007,[130] with the agreed (but not yet formally adopted at the time of writing) text[131] containing more detailed provisions on the exchange of information on criminal records between national authorities.[132]

These developments have not stopped the Commission from pushing for further centralisation and the establishment of an EU-wide criminal records database.[133] Based on Article 11 of the new instrument on criminal records, which contains a general statement to the effect that the format and other ways of exchanging criminal records will be set up by the Council at a future date,[134] the Commission has tabled a Decision establishing a European Criminal Records Information System (ECRIS)[135], which would consist of national criminal records databases, a 'common communication infrastructure that provides an encrypted network' and interconnection software allowing the exchange of information between various criminal records databases.[136] In the light of the fact that the parent Framework Decision has not been formally adopted yet, this proposal appears premature especially in the light of the variety of institutional issues and human rights raised by the exchange of criminal records.[137] These concerns are exacerbated by the diversity in what constitutes a 'criminal conviction' and what is included in a 'criminal record' in national systems, as well as the lack of clarity as to the categories of information which would be exchanged, the purpose of the exchange and the use of such information in the receiving State.[138] While this is a very specialised area of EU criminal law covering specific and relatively limited categories of information, it may provide an example where boosting the exchange of personal data between national authorities may gradually result in a centralised EU database.

---

[129] COM (2004) 664 final, Brussels, 13 October 2004.

[130] Justice and Home Affairs Council of 12–13 June 2007, Council doc 10267/07 (Presse 125), p 30.

[131] Council doc 5968/08, Brussels, 31 January 2008.

[132] For background and analysis, see J B Jacobs and D Blitsa, 'Major "Minor" Progress Under the Third Pillar: EU Institution Building in the Sharing of Criminal Record Information', *Chicago-Kent Journal of International and Comparative Law*, vol 8, 2008, pp 111–165, downloaded from www.kentlaw.edu/jicl/Arts/spring2008/jacobs_major_progress_2008.pdf . The Commission has also tabled a proposal for a Framework Decision on taking account of convictions in the EU Member States in the course of new criminal proceedings—COM (2005) 91 final, Brussels, 17 March 2005, and latest Council doc 9675/07, Brussels, 2 July 2007.

[133] For a discussion of the development of a centralised, EU criminal records database, see C Stefanou and H Xanthaki (eds), *Towards a European Criminal Record*, Cambridge, Cambridge University Press, 2008.

[134] Which would coincide with the deadline for the implementation of the Framework Decision: Art 11(3).

[135] COM (2008) 332 final, Brussels, 27 May 2008.

[136] Art 3.

[137] On these issues, see contributions in Stefanou and Xanthaki, n 133 above.

[138] There is ongoing debate in particular regarding the exchange of data on convictions on administrative offences (along with criminal offences), and whether data on disqualifications (which may not constitute criminal convictions) should be exchanged. Moreover, it is noteworthy that the new Framework Decision on criminal records requires also the exchange of fingerprints. See Mitsilegas, 'Databases', n 10 above.

B. Exchange of Information Between Police Authorities—The Swedish Initiative

It is in the field of police co-operation that major initiatives to boost the exchange of personal data between national authorities have occurred in recent years. The first such major initiative was tabled by Sweden[139] following political impetus by the European Council in its Declaration on combating terrorism after the Madrid bombings.[140] According to the Swedish government, the point of departure for the proposal was

> that a national competence to detect, prevent or investigate a crime or a criminal activity attributed to a national authority by national law should be recognised by other Member States and constitute a right to request and obtain information and intelligence available in other Member States without any other formal requirements than those laid down in the Framework Decision.[141]

Negotiations resulted in the adoption, in 2006, of a Framework Decision on simplifying the exchange of information and intelligence between law enforcement authorities of Member States.[142] The Framework Decision is a Schengen-building measure, in that it replaces Articles 39(1)–(3) and 46 of the Schengen Implementing Convention in so far as they relate to the exchange of information and intelligence.[143] The purpose of the instrument is 'to establish the rules under which Member States' law enforcement authorities may exchange *existing information and intelligence* effectively and expeditiously for the purpose of conducting criminal investigations or criminal intelligence operations' (emphasis added).[144]

In the light of this broad objective, one of the major tasks has been to define with clarity the scope of the instrument, in particular: what is meant by law enforcement authorities; what is included under information and intelligence; and what constitutes criminal investigations and proceedings for the purposes of the Framework Decision.[145] The Framework Decision does contain a specific provision on definitions.[146] A competent law enforcement authority is an authority designated as such by Member States and is 'a national police, customs *or other authority* that is authorised by national law to detect, *prevent* and investigate offences or criminal activities and to exercise authority and take coercive measures in the context of such activities' (emphasis added).[147] It is clear (in particular by

---

[139] Council doc 10215/04, Brussels, 4 June 2004.
[140] www.consilium.europa.eu/ueDocs/cms_Data/docs/presiData/en/ec/79637.pdf.
[141] Explanatory Memorandum, Council doc 10215/04 ADD 1, Brussels, 16 June 2004.
[142] Council Framework Decision 2006/960/JHA, OJ L 386, 29 December 2006, p 89.
[143] Art 12(1). See also Preamble, recitals 13 and 14.
[144] Art 1(1).
[145] For a discussion of the treatment of some of these issues in the negotiations of the Framework Decision, see the correspondence between the House of Lords European Union Committee and the Home Office, reproduced in House of Lords, European Union Committee, *Correspondence with Ministers. March 2005 to January 2006*, 45th Report, session 2005–06, HL Paper 243, pp 512–520.
[146] Art 2.
[147] Art 2(a).

the potential extension to 'other' authorities and the reference to prevention) that the definition is broad, and may lead both to the inclusion of a wide range of authorities within the scope of the instrument and to considerable diversity in the implementation of the instrument among Member States.[148] Moreover, information will also be exchanged with Europol and Eurojust.[149] However, the Framework Decision also contains a limitation in the categories of 'competent authorities': it states that agencies or units dealing *especially with national security issues* are not covered by the concept of competent law enforcement authority.[150] While the wording is not entirely clear, the provision is designed to exclude intelligence agencies from the scope of the Framework Decision.[151]

Intelligence does fall within the scope of the Framework Decision from the point of view of the information exchanged—'information and/or intelligence' is defined very broadly, including 'any type of information or data which is held by law enforcement authorities', and even 'any type of information or data which is held by public authorities or by private entities and which is available to law enforcement authorities without the taking or coercive measures'.[152] The scope of the Framework Decision with regard to the information to be exchanged is thus extremely broad. This is particularly the case in the light of the fact that the scope of the Framework Decision is defined—in a departure from the original Swedish proposal[153]—in general terms and applies to *any* offence, as no provisions defining its scope on the basis of specific offences—or serious crime in general—have been included in the text.[154]

The Framework Decision also contains definitions of a criminal investigation and a criminal intelligence operation. Criminal investigation is defined as

> a procedural stage within which measures are taken by competent law enforcement *or judicial authorities, including public prosecutors*, with a view to establishing and identifying

[148] On this point, see also the study by Geyer, who has provided an overview of the implementation of the Framework Decision with regard to the competent authorities in Member States: F Geyer, *Taking Stock: Databases and Systems of Information Exchange in the Area of Freedom, Security and Justice*, CEPS Research Paper No 9, May 2008, www.ceps.be . Geyer notes more generally that efforts to limit the number of competent authorities having access to EU databases and involved in the exchange of data might be fruitless due to the discretion left to Member States to designate competent authorities (p 6).

[149] Art 6(2).

[150] Art 2(a) Emphasis added.

[151] The Commission has also tried unsuccessfully to expressly include intelligence services within the EU legal framework of information exchange—see the 'Proposal for a draft Decision on the transmission of information resulting from the activities of security and intelligence services with respect to terrorist offences' COM (2005) 695 final, Brussels, 22 December 2005.

[152] Art 2(d).

[153] This defined the scope on the basis of various categories of persons data on whom could be exchanged by national authorities—see Art 6 of original proposal.

[154] But note that national authorities may refuse a request in cases where the latter pertains to an offence punishable by a term of imprisonment of one year or less in the requested Member State—Art 10(2). In a sense this reverses the approach of the original Swedish proposal, which stated that all offences punishable by a maximum sentence of 12 months or more would be included in its scope—Art 3. Member States thus agreed to in principle extend the scope of the Framework Decision beyond the 12 month minimum maximum custodial sentence threshold (with refusal to execute a request if an offence falls below this threshold being only discretionary).

facts, suspects and circumstances regarding one or several identified concrete criminal acts. (emphasis added)[155]

Criminal intelligence operation is defined as

a procedural stage, *not yet having reached the stage of a criminal investigation,* within which a competent law enforcement authority is entitled by national law to collect, process and analyse information about crime or criminal activities with a view to establishing whether concrete criminal acts have been committed or may be committed in the future. (emphasis added)[156]

Three points are noteworthy here: the wide range of information that can be exchanged for the purposes of criminal intelligence operations; the wide range of competent authorities included in the definition of a criminal investigation, which include judges—the definition reflects diversity in national criminal justice systems as to which authorities are involved in the various stages of the criminal justice process; and last, but not least, the fact that—although definitions depend largely on national law—this is one of the marked instances where an EU instrument provides definitions of what constitutes a criminal investigation or a criminal intelligence operation.

In the light of the potentially broad scope of the instrument, the Framework Decision also contains a series of caveats and limitations. It is a rare example of an instrument beginning with clarification of what is not covered and what is not required by EU law. The opening article clarifies that the Framework Decision does not impose any obligation on Member States to: gather and store information and intelligence for the purpose of providing it to the competent law enforcement authorities of other Member States;[157] obtain information or intelligence by means of coercive measures;[158] and provide information and intelligence to be used as evidence before a judicial authority.[159] It is also clarified that the Framework Decision does not give any right to use such information or intelligence for that purpose.[160] This is one of the major limitations of the scope of the proposal and may lead to further proposals aiming to address the thorny issue of the use of exchanged police information as evidence in courts. Overall, these provisions can be seen as an attempt to safeguard national autonomy in not requiring national authorities to be proactive in obtaining information or intelligence on behalf of their counterparts in other Member States.

Subject to these definitions and limitations, the Framework Decision aims to boost and speed up the exchange of information and intelligence. Requests for information are made—in a manner reminiscent of the operation of the mutual recognition instruments—on the basis of a minimum standard set out in a form

[155] Art 2(b).
[156] Art 2(c).
[157] Art 1(3).
[158] Art 1(5). However, information or intelligence previously obtained by coercive measures may provided when permitted by the law of the sending State—Art 1(6).
[159] Art 1(4).
[160] ibid.

annexed to the Framework Decision, which aims at standardisation and a degree of automaticity in the process. However, the Framework Decision itself also sets out a number of conditions governing such requests—these require the requesting authority to substantiate in detail the request.[161] Member States are under obligation to ensure that information is provided to the competent authorities of other Member States conducting a criminal investigation or a criminal intelligence operation.[162] They must ensure that conditions *are not stricter than those applicable at national level* for providing and requesting information to these authorities[163]—introducing thus one facet of the principle of equivalence in the exchange of information.[164] Requests may be refused only if one of the following exhaustively enumerated in Article 10 grounds apply: the provision of information or intelligence will harm essential national security interests of the requested State, or jeopardise the success of a current investigation/intelligence operation or the safety of individuals, or clearly be disproportionate or irrelevant;[165] the request pertains to an offence punishable by a term of imprisonment of one year or less in the requested Member State; and a judicial authority in the requested Member State has not authorised the access and exchange of information.[166]

The Framework Decision also introduces speed: Member States must respond to requests within at most eight hours for urgent requests regarding the offences included in Article 2(2) of the European Arrest Warrant Framework Decision[167] when the information is held in a database directly accessible by a police authority[168]; for non-urgent cases of this nature, the deadline is one week,[169] and for all other cases it is two weeks.[170] This is a significant change from Articles 39 and 46 of the Schengen Implementing Convention which did not contain specific rules on time limits. The Framework Decision also allows the spontaneous exchange of

---

[161] See Art 5 of the Framework Decision. Art 5(1) states that the request must set out factual reasons to believe that relevant information and intelligence is available in another Member State and explain the purpose for which the information and intelligence is sought and the connection between the purpose and the person who is the subject of the information and intelligence. Moreover, Art 5(2) states that the requesting authority must refrain from requesting more information or intelligence or setting narrower timeframes than necessary for the purpose of the request.

[162] Art 3(1) and (2).

[163] Art 3(3).

[164] However, it has been argued that equivalence is not being achieved, as the Framework Decision no longer includes expressly the caveat of Art 39 of the Schengen Implementing Convention that mutual assistance between police authorities must take place in compliance with national law. It was thought that the Framework Decision would give the authorities of requesting Member States more privileged access than the authorities in the requested Member State—see letter of Chairman of the House of Lords European Union Committee to Hazel Blears MP, then Minister of State for Policing, Security and Community Safety, Home Office, 26 May 2005, reproduced in House of Lords European Union Committee, *Correspondence March 05–January 06*, n 145 above, p 512.

[165] The first two grounds are similar to those in Art 4(5) of the Europol Convention.

[166] Art 10(1)-(3).

[167] This is the list of 32 offences for which dual criminality has been abolished for the purposes of the European Arrest Warrant.

[168] Art 4(1). If the requested authority is unable to respond within the deadline it must provide reasons—Art 4(2).

[169] Art 4(3).

[170] Art 4(4).

information or intelligence—that is without a prior request—on the basis of the law of the sending Member State in cases involving offences referred to in Article 2(2) of the European Arrest Warrant Framework Decision. A provision on data protection is included, aimed at regulating the exchange of information. Applicable data protection rules include the rules governing existing channels of international law enforcement co-operation should Member States wish to apply these channels to transfers under the Framework Decision.[171] Moreover, it is note-worthy that the use of data which has been exchanged is governed by the law of the *receiving* State.[172] Council of Europe initiatives (such as the 1981 Convention and the 1987 Recommendation) are the legal standard for data protection.[173]

The Framework Decision has the potential to boost the exchange of a wide range of personal data between national authorities. In doing so, it raises a num-ber of questions concerning the legality and human rights implications of such exchanges, as the answer to the question of what happens to the personal data once it has been transmitted to another authority (and thus another jurisdiction) remains open.[174] A central question in this context is whether the requesting authority will be able to obtain information from authorities in other Member States which it would not be able to obtain by their equivalent authorities in their own Member State (as there are discrepancies in the national authorities desig-nated as competent authorities by Member States). Moreover, there is the danger that national authorities would circumvent limitations in their domestic law (eg regarding the use of investigative techniques or coercive measures) by obtaining information by authorities in other Member States where the law does not provide for equivalent safeguards (a kind of information and intelligence forum shop-ping). Similar concerns arise with regard to data protection, with the Framework Decision adopting the standards of the receiving (and not the sending) State as regards the use of transferred data. The Framework Decision addresses some of these concerns by including caveats with regard to the use of coercive measures and the need for judicial authorisation. It also includes a general clause on the respect of fundamental rights.[175] However, the issue of the consequences of treat-ing foreign police authorities (subject to the law of another Member State) as equivalent to authorities of one's own Member State remains. These issues will become more marked should police co-operation proceed further in the European Union on the basis of the principle of availability.

[171] Art 8(1) and 6.

[172] Art 8(2).

[173] ibid. See also the provision on purpose limitation in Art 8(3) and the possibility for the sending authority to impose conditions on the use of information in Art 8(4).

[174] A similar debate has arisen in relation to the operation of the European Evidence Warrant: see ch 3.

[175] Art 1(7)—very similar to the general clause introduced in the European Arrest Warrant Framework Decision.

C. The Principle of Availability

The principle of availability has assumed a dominant position in EU policy discourse as a method of further enhancing the exchange of personal data between national authorities. According to the Hague Programme, exchange of information under the principle of availability means that

> throughout the Union, a law enforcement officer in one Member State who needs information in order to perform his duties can obtain this from another Member State and that the law enforcement agency in the other Member State which holds this information will make it available for the stated purpose, taking into account the requirement for ongoing investigations in that State.[176]

The Commission tabled in 2005 a proposal for a third pillar legal instrument in the field.[177] The general principle of availability is established in Article 6 of the draft, according to which Member States must ensure that 'information shall be provided to *equivalent* competent authorities of other Member States and Europol ... *in so far as these authorities need* this information to fulfil their lawful tasks for the prevention, detection or investigation of criminal offences' (emphasis added).

The principle of availability, as outlined in the Commission proposal, is based on a maximal version of mutual recognition and may have far-reaching implications for both the protection of human rights but also for the legitimacy of EU action in the police field.[178] It calls for the provision of information to 'equivalent' authorities of other Member States almost exclusively on a 'need to know basis', with exchange of information taking place on the basis of standard, pro-forma documents, and with very few grounds for refusal available to the requested authorities.[179] Information exchange becomes thus almost automatic. This form of co-operation may have substantial implications for the protection of fundamental rights, in particular the right to privacy. As conceived by the Commission, the principle would apply without any harmonisation in Member States' systems. Competent authorities potentially covered by the principle would be national authorities responsible for police and judicial co-operation in criminal matters,

---

[176] Point 2.1, p 27. The Hague Programme calls for the principle of availability to be applied from 1 January 2008.

[177] 'Proposal for a Council Framework Decision on the exchange of information under the principle of availability' COM (2005) 490 final, 12 October 2005. The same month also saw the publication of a Report on availability by a 'Friends of the Presidency' Group made up of national and Commission experts, and representatives of Europol and Eurojust—see Report by the Friends of the Presidency on the technical modalities to implement the principle of availability, Council doc 13558/05, Brussels, 24 October 2005. See also the follow-up document 5595/06, Brussels, 25 January 2006. Both documents remain only partially accessible.

[178] See V Mitsilegas, written evidence for House of Commons Home Affairs Committee, Inquiry on EU Justice and Home Affairs: reproduced in Report on *Justice and Home Affairs Issues at European Union Level*, 3rd Report, session 2006–07, HC 76-II, Ev 146.

[179] See Art 14 of the Commission draft. It must be noted however that, unlike the Framework Decision on the European Arrest Warrant, the draft Framework Decision would allow for refusal on human rights grounds.

but also Europol.[180] However, there are differences between the powers and mandate of national police and judicial authorities across the EU. The Commission proposal does require a level of equivalence between such authorities, but equivalence is to be defined by a comitology procedure, thus evading full parliamentary scrutiny.[181] National authorities (and Europol) are to be given inter alia online access to databases of their counterparts in other Member States,[182] and are obliged to provide information to their counterparts for the very broad purpose of preventing, detecting or investigating criminal offences.[183]

This framework enables a very extensive access to national data, by establishing a far-reaching legal obligation to provide information to authorities of other Member States. As it has been noted, if applied the principle 'will reconfigure the sociological norms regulating the practices among law enforcement authorities'.[184] However, along with human rights concerns, such co-operation raises important constitutional questions regarding the extent of the legal obligation to provide information: can a national authority obtain, under the principle of availability, information that it would not be allowed to obtain under its national law?[185] Can the requested authority be obliged to collect or transfer information on behalf of the requesting authority, even by using coercive measures?[186] These questions are similar to those raised by the Swedish initiative, but answers may be more complex in the light of the differences between the two approaches both in terms of caveats and safeguards, and in terms of the degree of the obligations imposed: under the 'Swedish' Framework Decision, the requesting authority must justify and substantiate the request; under availability, the requested authority must provide information merely because it is available. A number of questions arise also from the application of the principle to Europol, which seems to be treated in the same way as a national police authority.

[180] Art 3(b) of draft Framework Decision, which refers to authorities covered by the first hyphen of Art 29 TEU.

[181] Art 5. Moreover, measures adopted under this procedure will be classified as 'confidential'.

[182] See Art 9—access will be given to databases to which the corresponding competent authorities have online access.

[183] The proposal also contains a provision on purpose limitation (Art 7)—information can be used for the prevention, detection or investigation of the criminal offence for which the information is provided.

[184] D Bigo, 'The Principle of Availability of Information', Briefing Note for European Parliament Civil Liberties Committee, reproduced in D Bigo and A Tsoukala (eds), *Controlling Security*, Paris, L'Harmattan and Centre d'études sur les conflits, 2008, pp 21–36 at p 27.

[185] Similar questions have arisen in the context of mutual recognition in judicial co-operation in criminal matters with regard to the European Evidence Warrant.

[186] According to Art 2(2) of the proposal, requesting police authorities and Europol cannot ask for information to be obtained –with or without coercive measures—by the requested authority solely for the purposes of co-operation—but information already lawfully collected by the requested authority by coercive measures may be provided (even though these measures may not be lawful in the requesting State—something that would potentially infringe national constitutional provisions through the 'back door').

D. Prüm

The Commission legislative proposal introducing the principle of availability gave a flavour of the direction of police co-operation in the EU but although tabled in 2005, negotiations have not proceeded very far. The reason for this has been the parallel emphasis of a number of EU Member States on enhancing police co-operation between them outside the EU framework. This has led to the signing, in May 2005, by seven EU Member States[187], of a Convention on the 'stepping up of cross-border co-operation, particularly in combating terrorism, cross-border crime and illegal immigration'—the Prüm Convention.[188] Like Schengen, the Prüm Convention was named after the town where it was signed. Like Schengen, it is a pioneering document, where a number of EU Member States decide to push ahead on an intergovernmental basis and forge closer co-operation in home affairs matters—presumably in an effort to address obstacles in co-operation resulting from the lack of trust in a Europe of 25 and legislative paralysis in the light of the 'frozen' Constitution.[189] The Convention contains far-reaching proposals which may have significant consequences for the protection of civil liberties and fundamental rights. In the context of exchange of information, these include the establishment of national DNA analysis files and the automated search and comparison of DNA profiles and fingerprinting data.[190]

From the very outset, Prüm members stated that participation in their group is open to all EU members, and that a proposal would be tabled in three years from the entry into force of the Convention leading to its incorporation into the legal framework of the EU.[191] Such initiative happened in fact much earlier, due to the fact that the incorporation of the Treaty of Prüm into the EC/EU legal order has been one of the top priorities of the 2007 German EU Presidency.[192] In February 2007, the Justice and Home Affairs Council agreed to integrate into the EU legal framework the majority of the parts of the Prüm Treaty relating to police and judicial co-operation in criminal matters.[193] Evoking the perceived operational success of automatic information exchange brought about by the Prüm Treaty in the context of DNA data exchange between Germany and Austria, the Council noted that:

---

[187] Belgium, Germany, Spain, France, Luxembourg, the Netherlands and Austria.

[188] Council document 10900/05, Brussels, 7 July 2005.

[189] See V Mitsilegas, 'What are the Main Obstacles to Police Co-Operation in the EU?', Briefing Paper for European Parliament LIBE Committee, IP/C/LIBE/FWC/2005–24, 14 February 2006, reproduced in Bigo and Tsoukala, n 184 above, pp 7–20.

[190] For an early analysis, see T Balzacq, D Bigo, S Carrera and E Guild, *Security and the Two-Level Game: The Treaty of Prum, the EU and the Management of Threats*, CEPS Working Document no 234, January 2006, www.ceps.be.

[191] Mitsilegas, 'Main Obstacles to Police Co-Operation?', n 189 above.

[192] See also D Kietz and V Perthes (eds), *The Potential of the Council Presidency. An Analysis of Germany's Chairmanship of the EU, 2007*, SWP Research Paper 1, January 2008, Berlin, www.swp-berlin.org.

[193] Justice and Home Affairs Council of 15 February 2007, doc 5922/07 (Presse 16), p 7.

the special value of the Treaty lies in the substantially improved and efficiently organised procedures for the exchange of information. The states involved may now give one another automatic access to specific national databases. This amounts to a quantum leap in the cross-border sharing of information.[194]

No less than fifteen Member States tabled a proposal for a third pillar Decision incorporating the police co-operation aspects of Prüm into the EU legal framework.[195] This was finally published—along with an accompanying Decision on Prüm implementing measures—in August 2008.[196] The Preamble of the Decision makes express reference to the principle of availability and refers to the need to introduce procedures for promoting fast, efficient and inexpensive means of data exchange.[197] The text of the proposal effectively mirrors the provisions of the Prüm Treaty.[198] On data gathering and exchange, the proposal effectively obliges Member States to establish national DNA analysis files for the investigation of criminal offences.[199] Member States must ensure the availability of DNA data from their national DNA files,[200] and allow automated searches by comparing DNA profiles in these databases conducted by other Member States' national contact points.[201] Cellular material may also be collected and become available.[202] Moreover, Member States must ensure 'the availability of reference data from the file for the national automated fingerprint identification systems established for the prevention and investigation of criminal offences'.[203] It is not clear whether this wording assumes that such databases have already been established in all Member States. Similarly to the DNA databases, automated searching and comparison of fingerprint data is allowed.[204] Automated searching of vehicle registration data is also allowed.[205]

[194] Justice and Home Affairs Council of 15 February 2007, doc 5922/07 (Presse 16), p 8.

[195] Initiative of the Kingdom of Belgium, the Republic of Bulgaria, the Federal Republic of Germany, the Kingdom of Spain, the French Republic, the Grand Duchy of Luxembourg, the Kingdom of the Netherlands, the Republic of Austria, the Republic of Slovenia, the Slovak Republic, the Italian Republic, the Republic of Finland, the Portuguese Republic, Romania and the Kingdom of Sweden, with a view to adopting a Council Decision on the stepping up of cross-border cooperation, particularly in combating terrorism and cross-border crime, Council doc. 7273/1/07 REV 1, Brussels 17 April 2007.

[196] Decision 2008/615/JHA on the stepping up of cross-border cooperation, particularly in combating terrorism and cross-border crime, OJ L210, 6 August 2008, p 1; Decision 2008/616/JHA on the implementation of Decision 2008/615/JHA, OJ L210, 6 August 2008, p 12.

[197] Recitals 4 and 8 respectively.

[198] For an overview, see House of Lords European Union Committee, *Prüm: An Effective Weapon Against Terrorism and Crime?*, 18th Report, session 2006–07, HL Paper 90; see also T Balzacq, D Bigo, S Carrera and E Guild, 'The Treaty of Prüm and EC Treaty: Two Competing Models for EU Internal Security', in T Balzacq and S Carrera (eds), *Security versus Freedom? A Challenge for Europe's Future*, Aldershot, Ashgate, 2006, pp 115–136.

[199] Art 2(1).

[200] Art 2(2).

[201] Art 3(1)—the latter can thus compare DNA profiles. Comparisons of unidentified DNA profiles with all DNA profiles are also allowed—see Art 4.

[202] Art 7.

[203] Art 8.

[204] Art 9.

[205] Art 12.

The potential impact of the 'Prüm' Decision on privacy and the relationship between the individual and the State is significant. The Decision effectively obliges Member States to establish DNA databases in the first place—which means that, due to the way in which the Prüm standards are being inserted into EU law, in a number of Member States, DNA databases will be introduced effectively by the back door, with virtually no domestic debate or scrutiny.[206] Moreover, the Decision calls for availability of sensitive data if a hit is found and automated searches of national databases containing sensitive data by authorities of other Member States. DNA and fingerprint searches in this context will be conducted in compliance of the law of the *requesting* Member State[207]—something that again may bring significant changes to the legal framework governing these sensitive matters in the requested Member State without debate or scrutiny. On the other hand, the Decision does contain a separate chapter with data protection provisions;[208] but beyond this, the mechanism of co-operation it would introduce would operate in an environment with rules that are far from clear and based largely on national legislation. The proposal does not specify what kind of data could be included in DNA or fingerprint databases. This may lead to substantial discrepancies in national approaches, with some Member States including data only of persons convicted of serious crimes, and others including data on a wide range of individuals, including suspects or persons subject to disqualifications.[209] There may also be substantial differences on the reasons for collecting DNA data or fingerprints between national systems.[210]

A number of questions arise in this context, including whether this will lead to Member States extending the collection of personal sensitive data,[211] and whether

---

[206] On this point, see also R Bellanova, 'The "Prüm Process:" The Way Forward for EU Police Cooperation and Data Exchange?', in E Guild and F Geyer (eds), *Security versus Justice? Police and Judicial Cooperation in the European Union*, Aldershot, Ashgate, 2008, pp 201–221 at p 212.

[207] Art 3(1) and 9(1) respectively.

[208] Ch 6, Arts 24–32.

[209] See also the Opinion of the European Data Protection Supervisor, para 37.

[210] See in this context the debate in the House of Lords on the Report by the European Union Committee on the Prüm Treaty—Lords Hansard for 6 December 2007, cols 1854 f Lord Jopling, at the time of writing Chairman of the Home Affairs Sub-Committee of the EU Committee, noted in the debate that 'it other states use the UK evidence, they are in danger of assuming that the people on the database could have been involved in serious crime; they have different national standards'—col 1901. For a brief overview of the UK DNA gathering system, see G Crossman, 'Nothing to Hide, Nothing to Fear?', *International Review of Law Computers and Technology*, vol 22, nos 1–2, 2008, pp 115–118. For recent critical Reports on the UK DNA databases, see The Ethics Group: National DNA Database, *1st Annual Report*, April 2008; and Citizens' Report, *A Citizens' Inquiry into the Forensic Use of DNA and the National DNA Database*, July 2008. Both reports cautioned against the widespread and unqualified storage, use and access to DNA data and were critical as to the generalised or forcible inclusion of DNA data from innocent members of the public in national databases.

[211] The European Data Protection Supervisor reads the proposal as requiring from the Member States to collect and store information, even if it is not available yet in the national jurisdiction: see para 4 of his *Opinion* on www.edps.europa.eu In an attempt to alleviate concerns in this context Jonathan Faull, Director, Commission Directorate for Freedom, Security and Justice, stated in his evidence in the House of Lords EU Committee in their inquiry on the Prüm Convention: 'We are not obliging Member States to build up DNA databases of innocent people just in case one day somebody else in another Member State might be interested in knowing about them'—House of Lords EU Committee, n 198, above Q98.

co-operation on that basis would lead to the requesting Member State gathering sensitive data from databases in other countries which it would not be allowed to gather under its national law.[212] Notwithstanding these very important issues, and the changes that the Decision is bound to bring about, scrutiny and debate on the issues concerned remains extremely limited.[213] In the first place, the Prüm Convention was negotiated largely in secret as an international Treaty prior to its submission to national parliaments for ratification. Thereafter, it has been presented as essentially a *fait accompli* to European Union Member States, and is being negotiated under the third pillar (with a limited role for the European Parliament) and, in a manner reminiscent of the adoption of the European Arrest Warrant, under very tight deadlines[214] and in a rush that has not been justified.[215]

E. Boosting the Exchange of Personal Data Between National Authorities—Automaticity at What Cost?

From the Swedish proposal to the incorporation of Prüm into Union law, via the principle of availability, it is evident that the trend in police co-operation in the EU has been to gradually overcome obstacles arising from differences in national laws on police powers and boost the exchange of a wide range of personal data between national police authorities, with a high degree of automaticity and with few questions asked. This approach has led to a number of questions with regard to both the legality of information exchange (in the light of the potential legal gaps that may arise during the interaction of different legal systems in the exchange of information) and fundamental rights, in particular privacy. In the latter context it is striking that the push for information exchange has effectively led to the call—with little domestic debate or scrutiny—to a number of Member States to establish databases for sensitive personal data, in particular DNA data. It remains to be seen whether the implementation of these instruments will justify the legality and fundamental rights concerns raised, and whether it will increase the flow of police data and trust between national police authorities. These questions will resurface again in the light of the renewed emphasis on the principle of availability: although the Commission availability proposal has taken a step back in the light of the integration of the Prüm Treaty into the Union legal order, the European Council of June 2008 stressed

---

[212] Arts 3(1), 9(1) and 12(1) of the draft Decision contain a safeguard by stipulating that automated searches may be conducted only in individual cases and in compliance with the requesting Member States' national law.

[213] See also the criticism in the House of Lords debate on the Report, in particular by the then Chairman of the Home Affairs Sub-Committee, Lord Wright of Richmond (Lords Hansard above n 210, col 1895).

[214] With Germany aiming to achieve agreement on the proposal within its Presidency—see Kietz and Perthes, n 192 above.

[215] The transfer of the Treaty to the EU framework seems to weaken national parliaments of Member States, which would have to ratify the Convention if it remained outside the EU framework and their Member States wished to accede to it.

the need for a coordinated and coherent approach to the implementation of the principle of availability, aiming for effective use of information technology and information networks. Agreement has been reached on the integration of the provisions on exchange of information in the Prüm Treaty into the Union's legal framework, but further initiatives to enhance the exchange of information should be examined, taking due account of the protection of personal data.[216]

IV. DATA COLLECTION AND THE PRIVATE SECTOR

Another level of boosting the collection, analysis and exchange of personal data for criminal law purposes in the EU has been via the involvement of the private sector. This aspect of privatisation of law enforcement consists of calling on private companies or professions to co-operate with state authorities in the fight against crime. This co-operation can take a variety of forms: the collection of information and reporting of such information if suspicious to the authorities (as in the case of money laundering counter-measures); the retention of data already collected by the private sector for business purposes (as in the case of the retention of traffic data by telecommunications companies); and the extension of the collection of data already collected for business purposes and their retention (as in the case of passenger records retained by airlines). All these mechanisms reconfigure the relationship between the private and the public and lead to the collection of a wide range of personal data which can then be used by the State.

A. Anti-Money-Laundering: Suspicious Transactions and the Financial Intelligence Units (FIUs)

A major move to involve the private sector in co-operating with the State in the fight against crime has occurred in the field of anti-money-laundering law. Since its inception in the late 1980s/early 1990s, global anti-money-laundering initiatives have placed the private sector at the heart of their proposed legal and regulatory framework. Highlighting money laundering as an evil sustaining security threats such as drug trafficking, organised crime, and lately terrorism, the public policy and legislative discourse has sought to demonise the private sector (banks in particular—at least initially) for their potential involvement in the phenomenon, and translated the perceived moral obligation not to be associated with this evil with a legal obligation to positively and proactively assist the State in the fight against money laundering. This discourse has led globally, but also at EU level, to legislation imposing on banks, the financial sector, and a wide range of professions—including lawyers—of a wide range of duties, such as customer identification and record keeping duties, but perhaps more importantly, duties to report to the authorities transactions they suspect are related to money laundering and

---

[216] Council doc 11018/08, Brussels, 20 June 2008, para 14.

lately also terrorist finance. This has led to the proactive participation of the private sector in gathering information from every day, largely ordinary transactions and passing them on to State authorities—with considerable implications for privacy but also, in the case of the involvement of lawyers, for the right to a fair trial and for the administration of justice and the rule of law.[217]

However, EU legislation did not initially contain details of the authorities which would receive suspicious transaction reports from the private sector. This has resulted in the development of different systems of suspicious transaction reporting in Member States, which reflect differences in the focus of the domestic anti-money-laundering framework, but also differences in the view of the relationship between the private sector and the State. National systems can be broadly categorised into three models: the police model, where suspicions are transmitted to a police/intelligence agency (such as SOCA in the UK); the judicial model, where responsibility lies with the Public Prosecutor's office; and the independent/administrative model, where financial institutions report suspicions to an independent unit or a unit based within a Government Department (such as the Ministry of Finance).[218] Following the establishment of national reporting system, it became increasingly obvious that this diversity in national models had the potential to result in obstacles to co-operation in the light of the different nature and legal regulation of these units. In order to address this situation, Member States adopted a third pillar Decision in 2000 on co-operation between financial intelligence units (FIUs).[219] The Decision called on each Member State to set up a 'financial intelligence unit', which is defined in accordance with the definition adopted in 1996 by an ad hoc group of countries and international organisations called 'the Egmont Group'.[220] The Decision aimed at boosting information exchange between national FIUs regardless of their nature and states that their performance must not be affected by their internal status, 'regardless of whether they are administrative, law enforcement or judicial authorities'.[221]

---

[217] For details of the development of the EU anti-money-laundering framework in this context, see V Mitsilegas, *Money Laundering Counter-Measures in the European Union: A New Paradigm of Security Governance versus Fundamental Legal Principles*, London, Kluwer Law International, 2003.

[218] For an analysis of these models with national examples of such units see V Mitsilegas, 'New Forms of Transnational Policing: the Emergence of Financial Intelligence Units in the European Union and the Challenges for Human Rights—Part I', *Journal of Money Laundering Control*, vol 3, no 2, 1999, pp 147–160. See also J F Thony, 'Processing financial information in money laundering matters: the financial intelligence units', *European Journal of Crime, Criminal Law and Criminal Justice*, no 3, 1996, pp 257–282.

[219] OJ L271, 24 October 2000, p 4. See also the Commission, 'Report on the implementation of the Decision' COM (2007) 827 final, Brussels, 20 December 2007.

[220] According to this definition, a financial intelligence unit (FIU) is

a central, national unit which, in order to combat money laundering, is responsible for receiving (and to the extent permitted, requesting), analysing and disseminating to the competent authorities, disclosures of financial information which concern suspected proceeds of crime or are required by national legislation or regulation.

See Art 2 of the 2000 Decision. On the Egmont Group, see W Gilmore, *Dirty Money. The Evolution of Money Laundering Countermeasures*, 3rd edn, Council of Europe Publishing, 2004, pp 79–88 and Mitsilegas, 'New Forms', n 218 above, pp 155–156.

[221] Art 3. On the Decision, see Mitsilegas, *Money laundering counter-measures in the EU*, n 217 above, pp 176–179.

Further developments with regard to financial intelligence units in the EU emerged with the adoption of the so-called third money laundering Directive in November 2005.[222] The (first pillar) Directive includes express provisions covering financial intelligence units. Member States are asked to establish FIUs with specific tasks, and the units are given maximum powers of access to national databases—Member States must ensure that FIUs have access, directly or indirectly, on a timely basis, to the financial, administrative and law enforcement information that they require to properly fulfil their tasks .[223] Moreover, suspicious transaction reporting is now viewed within the specific context of FIUs, as the institutions and persons involved must now send suspicions not to the 'competent authorities' in general, but to the FIU specifically.[224] This applies also to the case of legal professionals, notwithstanding the fact that the second money laundering Directive of 2001 (repealed and replaced—as the first money laundering Directive of 1991 by the third Directive) allowed Member States to make provisions for suspicious transactions to be transmitted to self-regulatory bodies (eg bar associations) instead of the 'competent authorities'. The 2005 Directive continues to allow for this option, but these designated bodies must in such cases 'forward the information to the FIU promptly and unfiltered'.[225] The impact of this provision to the independence of lawyers remains to be seen.[226]

The challenges of the suspicious transaction reporting systems under EU anti-money-laundering legislation for private life are evident. A wide range of everyday information is transmitted by an increasing range of private sector companies and professionals (including lawyers) to national units whose powers and nature are different across the EU—maximising thus the surveillance of everyday financial activity.[227] Safeguards that are introduced in national systems (such as the transmission of suspicions not to the police but to an independent filtering authority, recognising that the information provided may reflect innocent everyday behaviour and not be linked to crime) are undermined by legislation aiming at boosting FIU co-operation *regardless of the nature of national FIUs*. This may lead to an independent FIU effectively transmitting data to a police authority in another Member State. Moreover, the third money laundering Directive greatly extends the powers of FIUs, potentially transforming them from filtering bodies to intelligence/investigative bodies, with EU law providing little with regard to the data protection provisions governing access of FIUs to national databases. The

---

[222] Directive 2005/60/EC of the European Parliament and of the Council of 26 October 2005 on the prevention of the use of the financial system for the purpose of money laundering and terrorist financing, OJ L309, 25 November 2005, p 15.

[223] Art 21(3),

[224] Art 22.

[225] Art 23(1).

[226] For details, see V Mitsilegas and B Gilmore, 'The EU Legislative Framework Against Money Laundering and Terrorist Finance: A Critical Analysis in the Light of Evolving Global Standards', *International and Comparative Law Quarterly*, vol 56, 2007, pp 119–141 at p 129.

[227] Note also the recent global and EU initiatives to monitor wire transfers and control the movement of cash: see Mitsilegas and Gilmore, n 226 above.

multiplicity of EU provisions raises not only human rights, but also legality concerns. As it has been noted,

> the FIU provisions in the 2005 Directive co-exist with the 2000 third pillar Decision on FIUs, which has not been repealed. The relationship between these two instruments is unclear. *Prima facie* it could be argued that the Directive regulates the relationship between the institutions and persons covered by the Directive, while the Decision covers the relationship between FIUs of the different Member States and their co-operation. However, there are provisions which overlap, such as the definition of an FIU (which is broader in the Directive as its work also covers terrorist finance). Moreover, the existence of Community competence to require, via a first pillar instrument, Member States to ensure that FIUs have access to *inter alia*, police data is questionable.[228]

The duplication of instruments regulating FIUs across pillars raises similar questions with regard to the applicable law regarding data protection. The FIU third pillar Decision contains a rather general data protection provision referring to the Council of Europe 1981 Convention and 1987 Recommendation and to the national law of the requesting FIU.[229] Being a first pillar measure, the implementation of the 2005 Directive could be subject to the provisions of the 1995 data protection Directive. However, again in this context the question arises whether the exchange of information between FIUs under the Directive falls within the criminal law exception rendering the data protection Directive inapplicable. On the one hand, viewing all FIU activities as related to criminal law may disregard efforts in a number of EU Member States to leave FIUs as far as possible outside the criminal justice system—for instance by establishing independent authorities as FIUs. On the other, the criminal law purpose of FIU data exchange seems hard to deny and is strengthened by the approach of both EU instruments to facilitate the exchange of information between FIUs regardless of their nature and status. The issue is inextricably related to the legality of the adoption of criminal law anti-money-laundering standards under the first pillar.[230]

B. Data Retention

Another instance where the private sector has been summoned to assist the State in the fight against crime via the collection and retention of information concerns the retention of telecommunications data. The relevant first pillar measure—a 2002 Directive which applied data protection provisions to the telecommunications sector[231]—provided for the erasure of communications data.[232] However, at

---

[228] Mitsilegas and Gilmore, n 226 above, pp 128–129.

[229] Art 5(5).

[230] On the debate with regard to the money laundering offences, see ch 2.

[231] Directive 2002/58/EC, OJ L201, 2002, p 37. The provisions of the Directive 'particularise and complement' the provisions of the 1995 data protection Directive (Art 2(2)).

[232] According to Art 6(1) of the Directive traffic data must be erased or made anonymous when it is no longer needed for the purpose of the transmission of a communication.

the same time calls were made to use such data in the investigation and prosecution of organised crime, ensured by the retention of electronic communications data for a limited time by the private sector.[233] These calls intensified following the Madrid bombings in 2004: the subsequent Declaration on Combating Terrorism, issued by the European Council on 25 March 2004, instructed the Council to examine proposals for establishing rules on the retention of communications traffic data by service providers.[234] Shortly afterwards, a third pillar Framework Decision on data retention was tabled by France, Ireland, Sweden and the United Kingdom.[235] This resulted in difficult and slow negotiations, leading to the Justice and Home Affairs Council—this time responding to the London bombings in July 2005—stating that it would agree the Framework Decision on data retention by October 2005.[236] Negotiations were subsequently prioritised and speeded up by the then UK Presidency of the EU (second half of 2005). Perhaps to address the difficulty in reaching agreement by unanimity in the third pillar, the proposal was relaunched as a first pillar Directive by the Commission in September 2005.[237] The majority voting required in the Council under the first pillar may have facilitated agreement on the Directive which was formally adopted, under an Article 95 EC (internal market) legal basis, in early 2006.[238]

The Directive aims to harmonise Member States' data retention provisions, 'in order to ensure that the data are available for the purpose of the investigation, detection and prosecution of serious crime, as defined by each Member State in its national law'.[239] It is noteworthy that the scope is broader than terrorism or organised crime. On the other hand, the Directive applies to traffic and location data on both legal entities and natural persons, but not to the content of electronic communications.[240] Telecommunications providers are placed under an obligation to retain data, by derogation from Directive 2002/58/EC.[241] This includes the obligation to retain data relating to unsuccessful call attempts.[242] Data must be retained for periods 'no less than six months and not more than two years from

---

[233] See the Conclusions of the Justice and Home Affairs Council of 19 December 2002 on Information Technologies and the Investigation and Prosecution of Organised Crime, (doc 15691/02, Presse 404). The Council called in particular for the approximation of data retention rules (para 7).

[234] www.consilium.europa.eu/ueDocs/cms_Data/docs/presiData/en/ec/79637.pdf at p 4.

[235] Council doc. 8958/04, Brussels, 28 April 2004.

[236] Extraordinary Justice and Home Affairs Council meeting of 13 July 2005, Council Declaration on the EU Response to the London Bombings, para 4 (Council doc 11116/05, Presse 187).

[237] COM (2005) 438 final, 21 September 2005.

[238] Directive 2006/24/EC of the European Parliament and of the Council of 15 March 2006 on the retention of data generated or processed in connection with the provision of publicly available electronic communications services of public communications networks and amending Directive 2002/58/EC, OJ L105, 13 April 2006, p 54. On the negotiations and content of the Directive see F Bignami, 'Protecting Privacy against the Police in the European Union: The Data Retention Directive', Duke Law School Science, Technology and Innovation Research Paper Series, Research Paper no 13, January 2007, downloaded from www.ssrn.com/abstract=955261.

[239] Art 1(1).

[240] Art 1(2). On controversies as to what constitutes content, see Bignami, n 238 above.

[241] Art 3(1).

[242] Art 3(2). On specific categories of data to be retained see Art 5.

the date of the communication'.[243] This provision may reflect disagreements in the negotiation process and is far from providing a harmonised EU standard.[244] Moreover, the retention period may be extended by Member States 'facing particular circumstances that warrant an extension'.[245] Access to retained data is limited 'only to the competent national authorities in specific cases and in accordance with national law'—[246] however, what constitutes a competent authority is not defined further, and leaving the designation to the Member States may result in a wide range of authorities with access, as well as a lack of harmonisation across the EU. Access is to be governed again by national law, in accordance with necessity and proportionality and subject to EU and international law, in particular the ECHR.[247] Specific provisions on data protection[248] (including a provision on the designation of supervisory authorities by Member States[249]) and remedies[250] are also included in the Directive.

The Directive will result in the retention by the private sector of a wide range of everyday personal data and in the access to this data by potentially a wide range of national authorities—raising thus the question of the compatibility of the Directive with fundamental rights, in particular the right to privacy.[251] It is noteworthy in this context that the Directive contains very limited provisions on data protection and remedies, and leaves the detail to be determined largely by national law. The Directive further raises the question of the extent of the co-operation between the private sector and the State in criminal matters, including issues of responsibility, liability and cost. From an EU constitutional law point of view, the choice of a Directive raises further a serious legality issue. This is a measure which has been adopted under an internal market legal basis (Article 95 EC), to amend EC data protection legislation adopted under a similar legal basis. However, as is evident from the Preamble of the Directive[252] and the text itself, the purpose and content of the measure are primarily—if not exclusively—geared to combat crime. On these grounds, it is submitted that the measure should have been

---

[243] Art 6.

[244] See also in this context Letter from the Chairman of the House of Lords European Union Committee to Caroline Flint MP, then Parliamentary Under Secretary of State, Home Office, 21 July 2004, in House of Lords European Union Committee, *Correspondence with Ministers. June 2004 to February 2005*, 4th Report, session 2005–06, HL Paper 16, pp 330–331.

[245] Art 12(1).

[246] Art 4.

[247] ibid.

[248] Arts 7–9.

[249] Art 9.

[250] Art 13. According to Art 13(1) these are left to Member States to designate and include judicial remedies.

[251] On the compatibility of blanket data retention with privacy, but also freedom of expression and property rights, see P Breyer, 'Telecommunications Data Retention and Human Rights: The Compatibility of Blanket Traffic Data Retention with the ECHR', *European Law Journal*, vol 11, no 43, 2005, pp 365–375. The author demonstrates forcefully the negative impact that blanket data retention may have on private life. For a contrary view, arguing that the data retention Directive in particular is proportionate, see Bignami, n 238 above.

[252] In particular indents 8 and 9.

adopted under a third (and not a first) pillar legal basis. This conclusion is strengthened by the Court's judgment in the PNR case, which also involved the storage of personal data by the private sector and involved the annulment of a first pillar agreement justified as such by its data protection content.[253] The Court will have the opportunity to rule on the legality of the data retention Directive following a challenge on legality grounds by Ireland.[254]

C. PNR

Another instance where the private sector was called to actively co-operate with State authorities in the fight against crime involved the transfer by airlines of passenger name record (PNR) data. Requirements on airlines to transfer such data—which is wide ranging and includes information such as credit card details, dietary requirements, seating, no show etc—to the US Department of Homeland Security for all flights to or via the US were introduced post-9/11 by US law. The requirement for EU-based airlines to comply with US law (notwithstanding the potential conflict with EU and national data protection and constitutional law) has led to the negotiation and conclusion of a series of agreements between the EC initially and then the EU on the one hand and the US on the other, allowing the transfer of PNR data to the US and stipulating that the US offer an adequate level of data protection. All these agreements were met with concerns and strong criticism by the European Parliament, specialist EU data protection bodies and civil society, on the grounds that, by collecting and transmitting to State authorities of a wide range of everyday information—which may lead to profiling of individuals—they fall foul of EU data protection and privacy standards.[255]

Notwithstanding this criticism, the Commission has recently tabled a proposal for a Framework Decision similar system of transmission of PNR data by carriers flying into the EU.[256] The Commission justified the proposal as a result of the 'policy-learning' from the existing PNR Agreements with the US and Canada, as well as the development of pilot projects in the UK. Both these developments (involving countries, in particular the US and the UK, which as seen above have pushed forward a specific concept of 'border security' linked with technology and the fight against terrorism) have demonstrated, according to the Commission, the potential of PNR data for law enforcement purposes.[257] However, it must be noted in this context that the EU already has established a system requiring airlines to transmit passenger data—via a Title IV 2004 Directive on the transfer of Advanced

---

[253] For details on the case, see ch 6.

[254] See Action brought on 6 July 2006, *Ireland v Council of the European Union, European Parliament*, OJ C237, 30 September 2006, p 5. Ireland argues that the measure should have been adopted under the third pillar. The case is pending at the time of writing.

[255] For further details, see ch 6.

[256] Proposal for a Council Framework Decision on the use of Passenger Name Record (PNR) for Law Enforcement Purposes, COM (2007) 654 final, Brussels, 6 November 2007.

[257] p 2.

Passenger Information (API) from airlines to Member States' border authorities.[258] In the light of the API Directive (which required the transfer of limited categories of data mostly found in one's travel documents), one could question the necessity and added value of an essentially similar system in the third pillar. Mindful of this criticism, the Commission attempts in the Explanatory Memorandum to the PNR proposal to distinguish between the two initiatives. The Commission notes that:

> For the purposes of the fight against terrorism and organised crime, the information contained in the API data would be sufficient only for identifying known terrorists and criminals by using alert systems. API data are official data, as they stem from passports, and sufficiently accurate as to the identity of a person. On the other hand, PNR data contain more data elements and are available in advance of API data. Such data elements are a very important tool for carrying out risk assessments of the persons, for obtaining intelligence and for making associations between known and unknown people.[259]

From this passage, it is clear that the Commission has adopted an intelligence-led model of border controls very similar to the 'border security' models in the US and the UK.[260] The emphasis is on risk assessment and profiling, on the basis of the collection of a wide range of personal data at the earliest possible stage in time. From the limited categories of passport data to be transmitted prior to departure under the API Directive, we are now moving to the transfer of a wide range of information related to air passengers at a considerably earlier stage. The transfer of PNR data is viewed as necessary not only for border controls/immigration, but also for broader counter-terrorism and security purposes.[261]

This model of 'border security' legislation is confirmed when one looks at the content of the Commission proposal. It is instructive to start with the annex, containing the categories of PNR data to be transferred. These are strikingly similar to the list of PNR data contained in the latest EU–US PNR Agreement and includes a wide range of data such as all forms of payment information, seat information and 'general remarks'. The text of the proposal contains similarly broad provisions. It envisages a retention period of a maximum of no less than 13 years—5 initially and a further 8 when data can be accessed in exceptional circumstances.[262] Transfer of PNR data to third countries is allowed, subject to a number of conditions pre-

---

[258] Council Directive 2004/82/ECof 29 April 2004 on the obligation of carriers to communicate passenger data, OJ L261, 6 August 2004, p.24. On the API Directive, see V Mitsilegas, 'Contrôle des étrangers, des passagers, des citoyens: surveillance et anti-terrorisme' *Cultures et conflits*, no 58, 2005, pp 155–182; see also House of Lords, European Union Committee, *Fighting Illegal Immigration: Should Carriers Carry the Burden?*, 5th Report, session 2003–04, HL Paper 29.

[259] p 3.

[260] On the UK border security model and a comparison with recent EU initiatives, see Mitsilegas, 'Human Rights, Terrorism 'Human Rights, Terrorism', n 110 above.

[261] In this context, see also the Explanatory Memorandum submitted by the Home Office with regard to the Commission PNR proposal, where it is stated that 'we need to allow the processing and exchange of PNR data for wider border security and crime-fighting purposes'. The UK Government further advocated a wider scope to the proposal than the one envisaged by the Commission—see House of Commons European Scrutiny Committee, 7th Report, session 2007–08.

[262] Art 9.

scribed in the proposal but also more fundamentally in the Framework Decision on data protection[263]—however, the latter text has not been formally adopted yet. Air carriers are required to send data to Passenger Information Units (PIUs) to be established under the Framework Decision[264] 24 hours before departure and immediately after flight closure—but the PIUs may require transmission prior to 24 hours from departure responding to specific threats of terrorism and organised crime.[265] Data will be transferred to 'competent authorities', which may be many and wide ranging, as their designation is again left to Member States—with the caveat that they will only include authorities responsible for the prevention or combating of terrorist offences and organised crime.[266] As with the EU money laundering legislation, the establishment of PIUs is left to Member States and no detailed rules with regard to their nature, status and powers exist.[267] Passenger data may be processed by the PIUs and the competent authorities receiving data from PIUs in Member States (these are authorities responsible for the prevention of terrorism and organised crime)[268] in order to identify persons who are or *may be* involved in terrorism and organised crime offences and their associates, to *create and update risk indicators* for the assessment of such persons, to *provide intelligence on travel patterns* and other trends relating to terrorist offences and organised crime, and to use data in criminal investigations and prosecutions.[269] The emphasis on profiling of suspect populations, regardless of their actual involvement in criminal offences, is evident in this context.

The trend towards maximising the benefits for security purposes is visible in the negotiations of the proposal thus far.[270] Member States have indicated that they wish to: be allowed to go beyond the limitation of the scope of the Directive to air travel and extend in the future PNR systems to other modes of transport; go beyond the limited scope of the proposal to terrorism and organised crime, and extending the scope one way or another to other forms of crime as well; include sensitive data in the scope of the instrument; and (at least in the case of some of them) extend the scope of the instrument to intra-EU flights as well.[271] The latter proposal seems strikingly at odds with free movement, especially in the Schengen area, but confirms the desire of some Member States—especially those like the UK

---

[263] Art 8. Further references to data protection standards in accordance with this Framework Decision can be found in Art 11 of the Commission proposal.

[264] Art 3.

[265] Art 5(3).

[266] Art 4(2). However, this limitation may not in practice be extensive, as the term 'prevention' may lead to the inclusion of a wide range of authorities.

[267] This point was also raised by the European Data Protection Supervisor in his evidence to the House of Lords European Union Committee: see European Union Committee, *The Passenger Name Record (PNR) Framework Decision*, 15th Report, session 2007–08, HL Paper 106, Q194.

[268] Art 4(2).

[269] Art 3(5).

[270] Negotiations are ongoing, with a number of complex issues—including issues of legality, scope and privacy—remaining unresolved. See Justice and Home Affairs Council of 24–25 July 2008, doc 11653/08 (Presse 205), pp 16–17. See also the French Presidency document 11281/08, Brussels, 1 July 2008.

[271] Council doc. 9514/1/08 REV 1, Brussels, 29 May 2008.

which may wish to promote their domestic counter-terrorism/border security model[272]—to achieve maximum surveillance of movement.[273] In the light of efforts to expand the scope of the proposal, the existing data protection safeguards appear extremely limited: as it has been noted, the latest drafts of the Framework Decision on data protection (which forms under the Commission proposal the data protection framework for PNR transfers) will only apply to cross-border data transfers and thus not apply to the PNR instrument (which involves transfers from airlines to domestic authorities).[274] The solution may be to draft specific data protection rules for inclusion in the PNR Framework Decision.[275]

D. Privatisation, Everyday Information and Profiling

It is thus clear that the private sector has been increasingly obliged to gather and store a wide range of personal data from customers. All the forms of private sector involvement analysed in this section have one distinguishing common feature: they all involve the collection, storage and transfer to state authorities of *vast categories of personal data linked with ordinary, everyday and mostly legitimate activity*. The exchange of personal data in this context is thus qualitatively different from data already included in police databases, with the emphasis here being on prevention and suspicion and the potential for profiling of individuals being evident. In this context, it is not always clear how to determine where responsibility lies—with the private sector or with the State? This question is inextricably linked with the question of the reach of the criminal law sphere: by collecting information for law enforcement purposes on their customers, do banks, telecommunications companies, or airlines operate within the criminal law/justice system? The answer to this question will determine not only responsibility, but also safeguards for both companies and customers. At the EU level, the situation becomes more complex in the light of cross-pillarisation, and the different legal frameworks applicable in the first and third pillars.

V. PRIVACY AND DATA PROTECTION IN THE LIGHT OF LISBON

The proliferation of mechanisms for the collection, exchange and analysis of personal data in the EU has not been accompanied by a coherent framework for the protection of personal data and privacy. There is currently no horizontal EU legal

[272] On the UK model, see Mitsilegas, 'Human Rights, Terrorism', n 110 above.

[273] Indeed, the UK Government has stated that they wish at least not to be precluded from broadening the scope of the instrument to include intra-EU journeys and to extend PNR requirements to sea and rail travel: see letter of Meg Hillier MP, Parliamentary Under Secretary of State to (then) Vice President Franco Frattini, European Commission, 18 March 2008, reproduced in House of Lords, European Union Committee, *PNR Report,* n 267 above, evidence pp 8–10.

[274] House of Lords European Union Committee, *PNR Report,* n 267 above, para 27.

[275] This is a live option with Member States: see Council doc 9514/1/08.

instrument in force governing data protection or privacy in the third pillar. The 1995 Data Protection Directive, the horizontal instrument which governs first pillar activities, explicitly excludes its application to activities falling within the third pillar.[276] This has led to the fragmentation of data protection arrangements in the third pillar. From the analysis in this chapter, it transpires that different legal instruments establishing EU bodies (such as the Europol Convention and its amending Decision), databases (such as the SIS Implementing Convention and the SIS II Decision), or co-operation mechanisms in the public (such as the Swedish Framework Decision and Prüm) and the private sector (in particular the draft PNR Framework Decision), each contain its own, sector-specific data protection rules. In terms of substantive data protection, these instruments contain in general specific provisions on data protection principles (such as purpose limitation) and rules on matters such as access, retention period and data security. They also contain references to international law, in particular the 1981 Council of Europe Data Protection Convention, which acts as a data protection benchmark in EU law. In terms of supervision, different databases have different supervisory arrangements in the form of system-specific Joint Supervisory Bodies or Authorities.[277]

In order to address the lack of a horizontal third pillar data protection instrument, the Commission tabled in 2005 a proposal for a Framework Decision on the protection of personal data processed in the framework of police and judicial co-operation in criminal matters.[278] Negotiations proved lengthy and controversial, with a number of attempts to water down the text and a number of amended proposals being tabled.[279] At the time of writing, nearly three years since the Commission's original proposal, the Framework Decision had not formally been agreed yet[280] although a text has been more or less finalised.[281] The text contains a number of provisions on matters such as data protection principles,[282] data quality,[283] data retention,[284] data processing,[285] transmission to third States or bodies[286] and to private parties,[287] rights of access,[288] rectification[289] and

---

[276] Directive 95/46/EC on the protection of individuals with regard to the processing of personal data and on the free movement of such data, OJ L281, 23 November 1995, p 31 Art 3(2).

[277] Some of these bodies are serviced by a joint secretariat—see Council Decision of 17 October 2000 establishing a secretariat for the joint supervisory data protection bodies set up by the Europol, CIS and SIS Implementing Conventions, OJ L271, 24 October 2000, p 1.

[278] COM (2005) 475 final, Brussels, 4 October 2005.

[279] For the negotiations history, see M McGinley and R Parkes, *Data Protection in the EU's Internal Security Cooperation. Fundamental Rights vs. Effective Cooperation?*, SWP Research Paper 5, May 2007, Berlin, www.swp-berlin.org

[280] The Mixed Committee agreed on a 'general approach' at the end of 2007: see Justice and Home Affairs Council of 8–9 November 2007, Council doc 14617/07 (Presse 253), p 9.

[281] The latest text at the time of writing: Council doc 9260/08, Brussels, 24 June 2008.

[282] See Art 3 on the principles of lawfulness, proportionality and purpose.

[283] Art 8.

[284] Art 9. See also Art 5 on the erasure of data.

[285] Arts 11 and 12.

[286] Art 13.

[287] Art 14.

[288] Art 17.

[289] Art 18, also on rectification and blocking.

compensation,[290] judicial remedies,[291] and supervision[292]. However, negotiations have led to a substantial limitation of the scope of the Framework Decision. It now applies only to cross-border transfers between Member States and to transfers between national authorities and third pillar information systems.[293] The Framework Decision will not, however, affect the data protection provisions in specific sectoral third pillar instruments, 'in particular those governing the functioning of Europol, Eurojust, the Schengen Information System (SIS) and the Customs Information System (CIS), as well as those introducing direct access for the authorities of Member States to certain data systems of other Member States'.[294] Neither will the Framework Decision affect the provisions in the Decision incorporating Prüm into EU law.[295] It thus transpires that the scope of the data protection Framework Decision is very limited, and the aim of reaching a coherent data protection legal framework for the exchange of information in criminal matters is far from being achieved.[296]

The impact of the Lisbon Treaty, should it come into force, on the existing data protection framework for the third pillar remains to be seen. In terms of substantive data protection law, the abolition of the third pillar will not signify the applicability of the 1995 Data Protection Directive to criminal law, given that it explicitly excludes its application 'in any case to processing operations concerning public security . . . and the activities of the State in the areas of criminal law'.[297] The data protection Framework Decision and the plethora of the sectoral measures on databases and police co-operation will thus continue to provide the relevant data protection framework, at least in the short term. The Lisbon Treaty creates a momentum for new data protection legislation, both by the general transitional provisions which may lead to Commission proposals to replace existing third pillar legislation with new instruments[298] and by the insertion, in the part on the Treaty on the European Union, of a specific provision on a right to data protection:[299] according to this provision, the European Parliament and the Council will

> lay down the rules relating to the protection of individuals with regard to the processing of personal data by Union institutions, bodies, offices or agencies, and by the Member States when carrying out activities which fall within the scope of Union law, and the rules relating to the free movement of such data

[290] Art 19.
[291] Art 20.
[292] Arts 23 and 25.
[293] Art 1(2).
[294] Preamble, recital 39.
[295] ibid.
[296] See also Art 26 of the draft Framework Decision, according to which the—already limited—protection standards with regard to transfers of data to third States included therein will be without prejudice to any obligations and commitments incumbent upon Member States or upon the Union by virtue of bilateral and/or multilateral agreements with third States existing at the time of its adoption. This means in practice that the Framework Decision will have no impact on the low standards agreed in instruments such as the EU–US PNR Agreement (for more see ch 6).
[297] Art 3(2).
[298] See ch.1.
[299] Art 16(1) TFEU.

adding that compliance with these rules will be subject to the control of independent authorities.[300]

In terms of supervision, the position of the European Data Protection Supervisor remains unclear. The 2001 Data protection Regulation which establishes the EDPS office, defines its mandate as 'ensuring that the fundamental rights and freedoms, of natural persons, and in particular their right to privacy, are respected by the Community institutions and bodies'.[301] It is not clear whether the abolition of the third pillar by Lisbon would mean that bodies such as Europol and Eurojust would fall under the supervision of the EDPS if and when the Treaty enters into force. The legal basis of the 2001 Regulation is Article 286 TEC (replaced in Lisbon by Article 16 TFEU), according to which Community data protection law applies to institutions and bodies set up by the EC Treaty.[302] The abolition of the pillars and the succession of the Community by the Union would lead to the streamlining of the data protection provisions[303] could be read as enabling to interpret Regulation 45/2001 as being applicable by analogy to Union bodies post-Lisbon—leading thus to them being placed under EDPS supervision. However, two main arguments seem to indicate that this is not the case and that the drafting of the Treaty implies that specific legislation is required post-Lisbon to regulate data protection and supervision in particular. The first argument stems from Article 16 TFEU itself. The provision—which replaces Article 286 TEC—does not contain a specific reference to the EDPS (it refers in general to 'the control of independent authorities') and calls for the adoption of *future* data protection legislation after the entry into force of the Lisbon Treaty. The second arguments stems from the specificity of the subject matter of EU action in criminal matters. Current first pillar data protection legislation which applies to EC institutions and bodies under Article 286 TEC (in particular the 1995 Data Protection Directive) has been adopted under an 'internal market' legal basis. The automatic application of such legislation—which, as in the case of the 1995 Directive, does not currently apply to action in criminal matters—to EU action in criminal matters post-Lisbon is not self-evident and would disregard the specificity—and heightened need for privacy—of action in the criminal law field. This specificity is confirmed by a Declaration annexed to the Lisbon Treaty acknowledging that specific rules on the protection of personal data and the free movement of such data in the fields of judicial co-operation in criminal matters and police co-operation based on Article 16 TFEU may prove necessary because of the

---

[300] Art 16(2).

[301] Regulation (EC) No 45/2001 of 18 December 2000 on the protection of individuals with regard to the processing of personal data by the Community institutions and bodies and on the free movement of such data, OJ L8, 12 January 2001, p 1 Art 41(2).

[302] Art 286(1) TEC. Art 286(2) calls for the establishment of an independent supervisory body responsible for monitoring the application of Community data protection law to Community institutions and bodies.

[303] Note also in this context that Art 39 TEU introduces a derogation from the right to data protection as stated in Art 16(1) TEU with regard to CFSP matters. However, the Art does call for the adoption of specific data protection legislation, including supervision for CFSP matters.

specific nature of these fields.[304] In the light of the fragmentation of data protection legislation and supervision in matters currently falling under the third pillar, involvement of the EDPS would contribute towards achieving coherence in data protection, especially in the light of the proliferation and increasing interconnection and interoperability of EU databases. It remains to be seen whether legislation to be adopted under Article 16(2) of the EU Treaty under Lisbon will confer specific supervision powers to the EDPS and, if yes, what will be the fate of the various sectoral joint supervisory authorities.

Another significant development under Lisbon is the incorporation of the Charter of Fundamental Rights into Union law.[305] The Charter contains two distinct rights: one on the respect for private and family life,[306] and one on personal data protection.[307] The distinction between privacy and data protection is noteworthy and significant.[308] As has been noted, data protection differs from privacy as it does not aim to create zones of non-interference by the State, but rather operate on a presumption that public authorities *can* process personal data.[309] It follows that 'the sheer wordings of the data protection principles ... already suggest heavy reliance on notions of procedural justice rather than normative (or substantive) justice', with data protection law creating 'a legal framework based upon the assumption that the processing of personal data is in principle allowed and legal'.[310] However, it has been argued that the two concepts should be combined, as data protection may cover a wide range of data processing, and may extend the scope of protection as the complex question 'is this a privacy issue?' Is replaced by a more neutral and objective question 'are personal data processed?'.[311]

This analysis is highly instructive in approaching the combination of privacy and data protection provisions in the Lisbon Treaty. In looking at their potential impact, it is submitted that one must take into account a further, fundamental distinction between the two concepts: while data protection is centred on *the various categories of personal data,* with the specific information collected and processed being the reference point, privacy focuses on *the person* in terms of identity and the Self, providing thus a more holistic framework for protection. In an era where the

---

[304] Declaration No 21 on the protection of personal data in the fields of judicial cooperation in criminal matters and police cooperation. Note also the amending legislation for Europol and Eurojust which continues to provide a role for sectoral Joint Supervisory Authorities—see ch 4.

[305] See ch 1. For the text of the Charter see OJ C364, 18 December 2000, p 7. See also the texta s proclaimed by the European Parliament, the Council and the Commission, OJ C303, 14 December 2007, p 1.

[306] Art 7.

[307] Art 8. This contains provisions on purpose limitation, fair processing and rights of access and rectification. It also states that compliance with data protection rules must be subject to control by an independent authority. See also Art 16 TEU mentioned above.

[308] For an excellent analysis of the distinction between privacy and data protection, see P de Hert and S Gutwirth, 'Privacy, Data Protection and Law Enforcement. Opacity of the Individual and Transparency of Power', in E Claes, A Duff and S Gutwirth (eds), *Privacy and the Criminal Law,* Antwerp/Oxford, Intersentia, 2006, pp 61–104.

[309] ibid, p 77.

[310] ibid, p 78.

[311] ibid, p 94.

erosion of purpose limitation and State boundaries (with the safeguards they entail) and vast categories of everyday data processed via the privatisation of information exchange, it is essential that the law addresses the new challenges arising from the extension of everyday surveillance and its profiling potential. While data protection is undoubtedly a useful layer of protection, it is submitted that privacy—linked with freedom, autonomy and dignity and having the Self as a reference point—may provide a more appropriate, flexible framework to address the rapid changes in the collection, processing and exchange of personal data.

VI. CONCLUSION: WHAT FUTURE FOR PRIVACY IN AN ERA OF SECURITY?

The above analysis has demonstrated that the collection, analysis and exchange of personal data has become increasingly central in the development of EU criminal law. Recent years witnessed the proliferation of databases at EU and national level and the intensification of the collection of personal data by both widening the categories of data collected and deepening the reach of authorities to sensitive personal data such as biometrics and DNA information. Information is collected and analysed at three levels: at the level of the development of centralised, EU databases, which interact with national authorities/databases; at the level of co-operation and information exchange between national public authorities, in particular the police; and at the level of the involvement of the private sector, and the co-operation between the latter and the State. This proliferation of mechanisms of information gathering and exchange has been accompanied by increasing calls to link databases, make them interoperable, as well as extending access to a wide range of databases (including those established for non-criminal law purposes, such as immigration databases), to a number of national law enforcement authorities, as well as Europol. These steps betray the aim of a maximum collection and exchange of personal data across the EU under the banner of a general 'security' justification. It is no coincidence that the majority of the new instances of information collection and exchange at EU level have been justified as responses to terrorism. However, their reach extends much further. From the Hague Programme—which focused largely on information exchange—onwards, it is clear that the collection of personal data and its management form—and will continue to form—a central part of EU policy on criminal law and security.[312]

This considerable extension of the reach of the State has occurred following very limited debate and scrutiny. As regards the development of EU databases, the

---

[312] In this context, see the Report by the Future Group (consisting mainly of Ministers of Interior of a number of Member States), published in June 2008 and aiming to contribute to the formulation of the next 5-year plan on EU Justice and Home Affairs, to succeed the Hague Programme. The centrality of information exchange in the Report is evident, with two of the four cross-cutting points identified by the Future Group being relevant: balancing mobility, security and privacy; and ensuring the best possible flow of data within Europe-wide information networks (Conclusions of Justice and Home Affairs Council of 24–25 July 2008, Council doc 11653/08 (Presse 205), p 18). For further details on the Future Group see ch 1.

European Parliament is currently merely consulted on the development of third pillar bodies such as Europol—with Member States speeding up negotiations to replace the Europol Convention with a Decision before the entry into force of the Lisbon treaty which would render the Parliament a co-legislator in the field. The Parliament did have a greater say with some success in the development of SIS II, as negotiations on the third pillar part were inextricably linked with the first pillar part of SIS II—although it did not manage to prevent access by police authorities to the VIS in negotiations of similar nature. However, even should the Lisbon Treaty enter into force, considerable challenges to transparency and democratic scrutiny are posed by the growing emphasis on the interoperability of databases, and the treatment of interoperability as a technical and not a legal issue—such an approach may lead to a depoliticisation of the proliferation of databases and information exchange, and the de facto extension of access to a wide range of databases via the development of 'technical solutions' and without the adoption of legislation prescribing the conditions of interoperability and access. Similar concerns are raised by the incorporation of the Prüm standards into EU law. Not only was Prüm presented to the EU as a fait accompli—with standards agreed behind closed doors outside the EU effectively imposed on the EU legal order—but moreover the Prüm EU legislation leaves a number of key implementing measures—such as measures concerning DNA databases—to comitology.

Prüm, and the principle of availability in particular, raise a further challenge related to the *method* of integration envisaged for the exchange of personal data between national authorities. Largely reminiscent of mutual recognition, this method aims at achieving maximum co-operation via automaticity and speed, and with very few questions asked. A requested police authority in a Member State is under a duty to provide information available to it to a requesting authority in another Member State with very few questions asked—in the case of Prüm, obligations as far reaching as providing DNA data will lead to a number of Member States establishing DNA databases in the first place. This form of co-operation implies mutual trust and aims to circumvent legal provisions which are perceived as hurdles in the achievement of operational efficiency. However, these 'legal hurdles' reflect constitutional and human rights traditions in Member States and are linked with the internal coherence of domestic criminal justice systems, including the place and role of the police in these systems. Availability in extremis may lead to circumventing the law in both the requesting and requested State, with the relationship between the various legal orders and their interaction far from being clarified in the various adopted and proposed instruments. Moreover, it may have significant legitimacy consequences: by agreeing on Prüm or availability, EU institutions (currently essentially the Member States in the Council) agree not on Union standards of police co-operation, but to in essence recognise the validity of the various national systems and to accept information produced by them and its movement across the EU without many preconditions. As with mutual recognition, this choice effectively shields the development of EU action on police co-operation from meaningful democratic scrutiny and debate.

This lack of scrutiny and transparency is particularly problematic in the light of the significant consequences that the development of mechanisms of collection, analysis and exchange of personal data may have for fundamental rights, in particular privacy. As mentioned above, a wide range of data is being collected and retained, in various databases which—notwithstanding their different purposes—become increasingly accessible to a wide range of police authorities. Access to immigration databases in particular, as well as the collection of information by the private sector, be it phone records, bank transactions or passenger data, lead increasingly to the collection and use by the State of *everyday personal data* related to largely legitimate transactions and innocent behaviour. Use of such information by the State is linked with a growing focus on prevention and suspicion, and is highly likely to be translated in real terms into the profiling of individuals. This is particularly the case with the growing collection of pieces of everyday personal data (such as PNR, phone records, bank records) over time, and pieces of biometrics in different databases which may be cross-checked for the purposes of identification in various points over time. The combination of these pieces of information may be used to create profiles by the State and challenges traditional concepts of privacy and the Self.

In the light of these challenges, the existing EU legal framework on data protection and privacy is limited to say the least. There is currently fragmentation with regard to data protection standards, with each EU database and each EU legal instrument establishing co-operation between national authorities having its own, separate data protection provisions both on substance and supervision. At the time of writing, no horizontal data protection legislation for the third pillar had been formally adopted—and in any case, it seems that this text will not put a stop to the current fragmentation of data protection. This situation will probably continue post-Lisbon, unless EU institutions decide to revisit the current instruments within the framework of developing the so-called EU Information Strategy. Lisbon, however, is significant for the collection and exchange of personal data, by incorporating the Charter on Fundamental Rights into EU law. The Charter contains provisions on both data protection and the protection of private life. The incorporation of the Charter into EU law may prove to be extremely significant in allowing European judges to develop privacy standards to be taken into account in both the implementation of existing legislation and the formulation of subsequent laws. The right to data protection may prove to be extremely useful in this context, especially in the light of the emphasis of data protection principles on purpose limitation. However, it is privacy which may provide a more appropriate, flexible framework to address the rapid changes in the collection, processing and exchange of personal data mentioned above and place limits on practices of profiling. The development of a right to privacy—linked to autonomy, freedom, dignity and personhood—has the potential to raise standards by placing the individual and the Self at the heart of protection.

6

The External Dimension

I. INTRODUCTION

T
HE RAPID DEVELOPMENT of internal European Union action in criminal matters in recent years has been accompanied by a strong emphasis on external action in the field. Criminal law and police and judicial co-operation in criminal matters (including counter-terrorism measures) have been prominent in the development of EU external action in a number of ways. Implementation of the EU *acquis* in the field has been required in the context of accession negotiations and has been an important (if not thorny) issue in both the 2004 and the 2007 enlargements; and co-operation in criminal matters is regularly requested by the neighbours of the Union. Moreover, recent years saw the European Union launching itself as an international actor in criminal matters by negotiating and concluding a series of—heavily contested—international agreements with third countries (primarily with the United States) in the field. Less visible, but perhaps equally far-reaching, has been the Union's involvement in the development and application of international criminal law standards via its participation in international treaties and organisations, and its acceptance in the Union legal order of standards forged in international organisations and bodies. This chapter will examine the many facets of EU external action in criminal matters, focusing in particular on enlargement and the EU's relations with its neighbours, international agreements and the role of the Union in international organisations. Taking into account the development of internal Union action in criminal law, developments in the external field will be viewed in the light of the challenges that the emerging Union external action in criminal matters poses on internal EU standards and values, while at the same time looking at the institutional factors influencing the conduct and content of EU external action in the field.

II. ENLARGEMENT

One of the most influential areas of EU external action is the process of accession of new Member States in the Union. The road of third countries towards their accession to the Union is marked by a very strong role for the EU as a 'rule generator', exporting Union law to third countries.[1] The latter are obliged to adopt and implement the Union *acquis* as an indispensable condition for them joining the Union, with accession thus being dependent on conditionality in those terms.[2] Conditionality is central to the enlargement process in ensuring that the new Member States are able to absorb the—at times heavy—demands of the Union *acquis* and ultimately fully assume their membership obligations. From the point of view of 'old' Member States, conditionality is crucial in creating trust towards the newcomers, thus contributing to mutual trust within the Union post-accession.[3]

The link between conditionality and trust appeared very prominently in the process leading to the eastward enlargements of the Union. In this context, the Union had to face a situation whereby countries in transition, with a very different economic, social and political background, were aiming at being further integrated with the EU. To address this complexity, the Union adopted a gradual approach, much broader than simply requiring candidates to adopt the Union *acquis*. The European Council adopted in 1993 the so-called Copenhagen criteria—these included inter alia institutional stability guaranteeing democracy, the rule of law, human rights and minority protection, and the existence of a functioning market economy.[4] These criteria in effect co-existed with the specific requirements to implement the specific Union *acquis* in criminal matters in the accession process, and continue to be of relevance in the assessment of candidates' (but also new Member States') progress in meeting EU standards. Moreover, compliance with aspects of Union criminal law such as anti-money-laundering measures was also prompted—much earlier than the adoption of specific negotiating Justice and Home Affairs chapters—by the need to achieve internal market integration.[5]

The issue of trust to the candidate countries of Central and Eastern Europe was central in the field of integration in criminal matters. The transitional state of these countries in the early 1990s raised fears that political, societal and economic instability would lead to the development of criminogenic factors which would 'export' criminality to the Union. The East was thus increasingly viewed as a source of insecurity, threatening the 'safe' inside of the European Union—with mistrust regarding the potential capacity of the relevant candidate countries to provide security in

---

[1] On the concept of the Union as 'rule generator', see M. Cremona, 'The Union as a Global Actor: Roles, Models and Identity', *Common Market Law Review*, vol 41, 2004, pp 555–573 at pp 557–558.

[2] On conditionality and enlargement, see K E Smith, 'The Evolution and Application of EU Membership Conditionality', in M Cremona (ed), *The Enlargement of the European Union*, Oxford, OUP, 2003, pp 105–140; see also F Schimmelfennig and U Sedelmeier, 'Governance by Conditionality: EU Rule Transfer to the Candidate Countries of Central and Eastern Europe', *Journal of European Public Policy*, vol 11, 2004, pp 661–679.

[3] On the link between conditionality and trust see M Cremona, 'Introduction', in Cremona, *Enlargement*, n 2 above, pp 1–8 at pp 5–6.

[4] For an overview, see C Hillion, 'The Copenhagen Criteria and their Progeny', in Hillion (ed), *EU Enlargement. A Legal Approach*, Oxford, Hart Publishing, 2004, pp 1–22.

[5] See European Commission, White Paper—Preparation of the Associated Countries of Central and Eastern Europe for integration into the internal market of the Union, COM (95) 163 final. For further details, see V Mitsilegas, *Money Laundering Counter-Measures in the European Union*, The Hague and London, Kluwer Law International, 2003, pp 79–80.

home affairs being prevalent.[6] Linked to the background of the candidate countries, exiting from a Communist past,[7] a related source of mistrust involved the ability of these countries to actually implement the EU criminal law standards in the light of the weakening of their internal control structures (an ability which would mean –along with the implementation of specific EU measures—a remodelling of institutions and mentality/culture in the criminal law sphere).[8]

It is this lack of trust in implementation capacity that was to some extent behind the recommendation by the European Council[9] and the subsequent adoption by the Justice and Home Affairs Council of a 'Pre-Accession Pact' on Organised Crime between the Member States of the European Union and the applicant countries of Central and Eastern Europe (and Cyprus).[10] The Pact, which called inter alia for intensified police and judicial co-operation in criminal matters and action to combat corruption and money laundering, was soon followed by the establishment, via a Joint Action, of a mechanism for collective evaluation of the Justice and Home Affairs *acquis* by candidate countries.[11] This evaluation mechanism (conducted by experts from Member States and the Commission) was 'without prejudice' to the accession negotiations[12] but the Commission was invited to take account of the collective evaluations produced in the context of the pre-accessions strategy and evaluations would be taken into account 'in the context of future discussions on enlargement'.[13] This move is another example of the emphasis placed by the existing EU Member States on addressing the lack of trust and the perceived limited capacity of candidate countries to effectively implement Union measures in criminal matters.

In this climate of mistrust and with negotiations on the Justice and Home Affairs chapter beginning at the end of the 1990s, the candidate countries had to face considerable challenges prior to their eventual accession in the European Union.[14] A central challenge has been the 'moving target' character of the EU *acquis* in criminal matters—with EU criminal legislation proliferating following the entry into force of the Amsterdam Treaty and events such as 9/11, which rendered EU action in criminal matters a top priority for Member States. Candidate

---

[6] See V Mitsilegas, J Monar and W Rees, *The European Union and Internal Security,* Basingstoke, Palgrave Macmillan, 2003, pp 126–127.

[7] For an overview of crime control features under Communism, see A. Fijakowski, 'The Paradoxical Nature of Crime Control in Post-Communist Europe', *European Journal of Crime, Criminal Law and Criminal Justice,* 2007, pp 155–172.

[8] On the implementation challenges, see K Henderson, 'Perceptions of Internal Security Issues in the New Member States', in Henderson (ed), *The Area of Freedom, Security and Justice in the Enlarged European Union,* Basingstoke, Palgrave Macmillan, 2004, p 15.

[9] In its 1997 Action Plan on Organised Crime—OJ C251, 15 August 1997, p 1 (Recommendation 3).

[10] OJ C220, 15 July 1998, p 1.

[11] OJ L191, 7 July 1998, p 8.

[12] See Art 1 of the Joint Action.

[13] Art 4(2).

[14] For a detailed overview of the various stages in the accession negotiations, see W de Lobkowitz, 'La sécurité intérieure de l'Union Européenne élargie', in G de Kerchove and A Weyembergh (eds), *Sécurité et justice: Enjeu de la politique extérieure de l'Union Européenne,* Brussels, Éditions de l'Université de Bruxelles, 2003, pp 31–65.

countries were thus asked to implement a constantly growing *acquis,* the novelty of which posed significant challenges to the 'old' Member States.[15] Along with this quantitative change, the EU *acquis* in criminal matters presented a qualitative change as well: the integration of the Schengen *acquis* in the EC/EU legal framework in Amsterdam (and the related proclaimed Union objective of developing into an 'area' of freedom, security and justice) on the one hand, and the furthering of integration in criminal matters primarily on the basis of mutual recognition (with the European Arrest Warrant Framework Decision being a prime example[16]) on the other, a key requirement for integration in criminal matters within the European Union has been the existence of mutual trust between the authorities (and arguably the citizens) of Member States.[17] With the internal Union *acquis* in criminal matters requiring an enhanced degree of trust for the 'area of freedom, security and justice' to function, the benchmark has been set even higher for the candidate countries.

The lack of trust and the considerable challenges that the candidate countries faced in trying to align themselves with the EU criminal law *acquis* and related EU standards were not eventually an obstacle to the accession of 10 new member states (8 of which from Central and Eastern Europe) in the EU in 2004. However, elements of mistrust remained in and post-accession. Accession to the European Union did not mean automatic Schengen membership for the newcomers— although the latter had to implement the Schengen *acquis* pre-accession, the old, 'intergovernmental' mechanism of granting full Schengen membership remains, with the existing Schengen members required to agree unanimously on the readiness of candidate countries to be members.[18] Moreover, the Act of Accession included a so-called 'safeguard clause' to cover potential shortcomings in the implementation by newcomers of EU instruments relating to mutual recognition in criminal (and civil) matters. In case of serious shortcomings or imminent risks thereof in the field, the Commission may adopt, after consulting the Member States, safeguard measures including the temporary suspension of the provisions on judicial co-operation in criminal matters.[19]

The safeguard clause could be invoked for three years after accession. This period has passed without the clause having being invoked. The implementation

[15] For a detailed overview of the *acquis* see Mitsilegas, Monar and Rees, n.6 above.

[16] OJ L190, 18 July 2002, p 1.

[17] On the issue of trust in the context of mutual recognition in criminal matters, see V Mitsilegas, 'Trust-building Measures in the European Judicial Area in Criminal Matters: Issues of Competence, Legitimacy and Inter-institutional Balance', in S Carrera and T Balzacq, *Security versus Freedom? A Challenge for Europe's Future,* Aldershot, Ashgate, 2006, pp 279–289.

[18] On the sensitivity of Schengen membership for newcomers see Mitsilegas, Monar and Rees, n 6 above; and J Monar, *Enlargement-Related Diversity in EU Justice and Home Affairs: Challenges, Dimensions and Management Instruments,* Dutch Scientific Council for Government Policy, Working Document W112, The Hague, 2000.

[19] Art 39 of the Accession Act. For an overview, see C Hillion, 'The European Union is Dead. Long Live the European Union: A Commentary on the Treaty of Accession 2003', *European Law Review,* vol 29, 2004, pp 583–612 at pp 605–607. Hillion notes the role of the Commission in this context, notwithstanding the fact that mutual recognition in criminal matters is a third—and not a first pillar issue.

and practical application of the European Arrest Warrant by Member States are currently being evaluated across the Union. If the attitude of the judiciary is a reliable indication, it is striking that the highest courts of new Member States, faced with potential conflict between the domestic Constitution and the European Arrest Warrant implementation requirements, attempted to some extent to accommodate EU law requirements in their domestic legal order, taking into account both the security rationale of the Warrant and Luxembourg case-law on the third pillar.[20] This stance may be viewed as an attempt to address the general climate of mistrust towards the newcomers—and the existence of safeguard clauses specifically, attempting to demonstrate that every effort should be made to fully implement EU criminal law domestically.[21]

Concerns regarding the implementation of the EU criminal law *acquis* by new Member States persisted in the context of the sixth EU enlargement which saw Bulgaria and Romania joining the Union in 2007. Compliance of these two countries with the EU *acquis* on Justice and Home Affairs has been perceived over a period of time to be problematic.[22] In its pre-accession monitoring Reports, the Commission has been consistently critical of progress in the field—with gaps in institutional capacity raising broader questions regarding the feasibility of the 2007 accession date for both countries.[23] Getting closer to the accession date, the Commission published a critical monitoring Report, where it pointed out remaining gaps regarding progress in the two countries' justice systems and the fight against corruption, with Bulgaria also being singled out for gaps in the field of measures against organised crime and money laundering.[24] The Commission recommended—along with the introduction of a safeguard clause allowing the unilateral suspension of Member States obligations with regard to judicial co-operation in civil and criminal matters vis-a-vis Bulgaria and Romania—the introduction, additionally, of a mechanism verifying progress by the newcomers *after* accession. The Commission's recommendations were taken up by Member States, with the Act of Accession including a safeguard clause in criminal matters similar to the one used in 2004[25], and the Commission adopting—using as legal basis the Accession Treaty and the safeguard clauses in the Accession Act—two Decisions establishing 'a mechanism for co-operation and verification of progress'

---

[20] For details, see ch 3.

[21] It has been argued that the safeguard clause has had an impact on the outcome of the Polish Constitutional Tribunal judgment—see A Lazowski, 'Constitutional Tribunal on the Surrender of Polish Citizens under the European Arrest Warrant. Decision of 27 April 2005', *European Constitutional Law Review*, vol 1, 2005, pp 569–581 at p 580.

[22] For an analysis of Bulgaria's efforts to implement the EU *acquis* see D Bozhilova, 'Measuring Success and Failure of EU: Europeanization in the Eastern Enlargement: Judicial Reform in Bulgaria', *European Journal of Law Reform*, vol 9, 2007, pp 285–319.

[23] For a background, see A Lazowski, 'And Then They Were Twenty-Seven: A Legal Appraisal of the Sixth Accession Treaty', *Common Market Law Review*, vol 44, 2007, pp 401–430.

[24] European Commission, Monitoring Report on the state of preparedness for EU membership of Bulgaria and Romania, COM (2006) 549 final, Brussels 26 September 2006, pp 4–5.

[25] Arts 37 and 38. For an overview, see Lazowski, 'And Then They Were Twenty-Seven', above n 23.

to address specific benchmarks in the areas of judicial reform and the fight against corruption (Romania) and these areas plus organised crime (Bulgaria).[26]

The benchmarks themselves are attached as annexes to the Commission Decisions and are indicative of the concerns regarding the preparedness of Bulgaria and Romania to take up fully their EU obligations in the criminal law field. Romania is asked to ensure a 'more transparent and efficient judicial process', and to combat corruption by establishing an integrity agency, conducting 'professional, non-partisan investigations' into allegations of high-level corruption, and taking 'further measures' to prevent and fight corruption in particular within the local government. The latter benchmark (including also corruption at the borders) applies also to Bulgaria, as does the benchmark on corruption investigations and the one regarding ensuring a more transparent and efficient judicial process. However, the benchmark list for Bulgaria is somewhat more extensive: it also includes two further benchmarks dealing with the independence of the judiciary (adopting constitutional amendments 'removing any ambiguity' regarding the independence and accountability of the judicial system; and continue the reform of the judiciary) and an additional, separate benchmark urging Bulgaria to implement a strategy to fight organised crime, focusing on serious crime, money laundering and confiscation. It is thus evident that the benchmarks essentially are targeted towards broader institutional changes and not so much on the implementation of specific legislation forming part of the EU criminal law *acquis*. Even the benchmarks involving specific areas of EU action in criminal matters (such as corruption) refer to broader measures aiming to change the culture and practices of the administration and judiciary.

Bulgaria and Romania are required to report once a year to the Commission on progress made in addressing each of these benchmarks.[27] The Commission may gather and exchange information on the benchmarks and organise expert missions for that purpose.[28] The benchmarks may be adjusted in the future by amending the two Decisions.[29] If Bulgaria and Romania fail to address the benchmarks adequately the Commission may apply safeguard measures based on Articles 37 and 38 of the Accession Act, including the suspension of Member States' obligation to recognise and execute, under the conditions laid down in Community law, judicial decisions from the two countries 'such as European arrest warrants'.[30] However, the progress verification Decisions do not preclude the adoption of safeguard measures at any time, if the conditions for such measures are fulfilled.[31] Thus far the Commission has been publishing regular reports, with the latest reports being extremely critical with regard to the progress of the two countries under the agreed benchmarks, in particular with regard to efforts to tackle

[26] OJ L354, 14 December 2006, p 56 and p 58 respectively.
[27] Art 1 first indent of both Decisions.
[28] Art 1 second indent of both Decisions.
[29] Preamble, recital 9 in both Decisions.
[30] Preamble, recital 7 in both Decisions.
[31] Preamble, recital 8 in both Decisions.

corruption, and especially in the case of Bulgaria.[32] The Commission stopped short from recommending the suspension of the relevant criminal law *acquis*, but linked—in the case of Bulgaria—compliance with the stated benchmarks with the issue of administration of EU funds and decided to suspend certain EU funds until the Bulgarian authorities are able to demonstrate that sound financial management structures are in place and operating effectively[33]

The design of the progress verification process is noteworthy. This is an ex post monitoring mechanism, operating after the entry of the new Member States in the European Union. This means that, for the time being, Bulgaria and Romania are subject to further, more detailed, evaluation and monitoring in the criminal law sphere than the other 25 EU Member States. The role of the Commission in this context is significant. Notwithstanding the fact that the object of the monitoring exercise (and the ambit of the safeguard clause) falls primarily within the third pillar, the Commission has an extensive monitoring role by setting benchmarks, gathering information, organising expert missions and ultimately evaluating progress. This role for the Commission—which can be viewed as a continuum of its role *before* accession, where it was involved actively in negotiations on the Justice and Home Affairs chapter, in spite of its third pillar reach—is again at odds with its current limited role in the third pillar with regard to the other 25 Member States. One could speak thus of 'double standards' with regard to the two newcomers. However, on the other hand one cannot help but notice the *content* of the benchmarks—which, beyond looking at the implementation of specific EU criminal law standards, take us back to the fulfilment of the very fundamental Copenhagen criteria (namely institutional stability which guarantees the rule of law) and examine the institutional and justice system of the assessed States as a whole. It appears that the perceived lack of preparedness to fulfil the fundamental Copenhagen criteria—at least in the context of the functioning of criminal law in the 'are of freedom, security and justice'—was not deemed sufficient to change the political decision to admit Bulgaria and Romania in the Union in 2007. In the light of the serious shortcomings revealed in the assessment of progress of the 2007 newcomers, this choice might not be repeated in future EU enlargements. Moreover, the effect of such a choice on the development of *internal* EU criminal law remains to be seen, in particular the extent to which a borderless area in criminal matters requiring mutual trust will function smoothly when the mistrust towards the judicial system of some of its members is not only perceived, but declared officially via safeguard clauses and verification mechanisms.

---

[32] See 'Report on Progress in Romania under the Co-operation and Verification Mechanism' COM (2008) 494 final, Brussels, 23 July 2008 and SEC (2008) 2349/2; and 'Report on Progress in Bulgaria under the Co-operation and Verification Mechanism' COM (2008) 495 final, Brussels, 23 July 2008 and SEC (2008) 2350/2.

[33] See in this context the additional Commission Report 'On the Management of EU Funds in Bulgaria' COM (2008) 496 final, Brussels, 23 July 2008.

III. THE UNION AND ITS NEIGHBOURS

The eastward enlargement of the Union in 2004 focused the minds within the EU on how to deal with its new neighbours in the East (with developments regarding the relationship of the Union with its southern neighbours being ongoing). In 2003, the Commission launched a Communication on the 'Wider Europe'—aiming at a 'new framework' for relations with the Union's eastern and southern neighbours.[34] Central to the Commission's vision was reform in the Union's neighbours, based on a 'differentiated, progressive and benchmarked approach'.[35] The ideas were taken forward by the Commission in 2004, when the term 'European Neighbourhood Policy' (ENP) was put forward.[36] In its Strategy Paper, the Commission put forward underlying principles for the ENP, including a coherent framework, joint ownership (based on shared values and common interests), differentiation with regard to the various neighbours, and added value to the existing forms of EU co-operation with these countries. These principles were reaffirmed recently by the General Affairs Council, which also reiterated that the ENP 'remains distinct from the question of EU membership and does not prejudge any possible future developments of partner countries' relationship with the EU'.[37] On the basis of these stated principles a number of country Action Plans were adopted setting out priorities and targets for action on a wide range of issues within the framework of the ENP.[38]

As it has been noted, the ENP is a cross-pillar policy, aimed essentially at security.[39] Security is viewed as a fundamental, underpinning dimension of the ENP as a whole, and as implying 'security within the neighbouring states, security within the region, security at the external borders of the EU, and security within the EU itself'.[40] In this quest for security, which is also visible in the European Security Strategy,[41] action in criminal matters has a central role, in particular as regards action against terrorism, organised crime and money laundering. This emphasis is

---

[34] COM (2003) 104 final, Brussels, 11 March 2003.

[35] ibid, p 15 f.

[36] 'Communication from the Commission, European Neighbourhood Policy. Strategy Paper' COM (2004) 373 final, Brussels 12 May 2004. For the latest assessment, see Communication from the Commission, 'A Strong European Neighbourhood Policy' COM (2007) 774 final, Brussels, 5 December 2007.

[37] Council doc 11016/07, Brussels, 19 June 2007, endorsed in the GAERC Council of 18 June 2007, doc 10657/07 Presse 138.

[38] On the various Action Plans for each of the ENP countries, see www.ec.europa.eu/world/enp/documents_en.htm.

[39] M Cremona and C Hillion, *L'Union fait la force? Potential and Limitations of the European Neighbourhood Policy as an Integrated EU Foreign and Security Policy*, EUI Working Paper LAW No 2006/39.

[40] ibid, p 5.

[41] A Secure Europe in a Better World, Brussels, 12 December 2003. The Strategy includes a separate section on 'building security in our neighbourhood'.

discerned both at Commission and Council proclamations[42] and at the various ENP Action Plans, which include generally sections on Justice and Home Affairs and references to counter-terrorism. Consistent with the principle of differentiation, the emphasis is not the same within the various Action Plans (for instance, some Action Plans such as the ones on Jordan and Morocco emphasise anti-money-laundering action, while others emphasise aspects such as trafficking in human beings (Ukraine)), especially in relation to other JHA policies such as borders and immigration. Justice and Home Affairs co-operation (including action against organised crime and terrorism) is particularly flagged up with regard to Ukraine, with the EU having adopted in 2001 a specific Action Plan on Justice and Home Affairs in Ukraine.[43] Along with specific provisions on criminal matters, this Action Plan (but also the general ENP Action Plans) also contain references to institutional reform ensuring the application of the rule of law.

Like the enlargement process, the ENP is based on benchmarking mechanisms and targets. However, the effectiveness of benchmarking in the ENP context is questionable, given the lack of an express promise of EU membership to ENP partners. As it has been noted, if it works the ENP will create EU candidates, but the absence of EU membership as an ultimate goal may lessen the incentive for meeting the various Action Plan targets.[44] This lack of incentives is very relevant in the context of reform in criminal matters, where effective action against terrorism organised crime and money laundering is arguably also linked with reform in the institutions guaranteeing judicial independence, the rule of law and respect for fundamental rights. Given the absence of the enlargement prospect, it is less likely that the Union will insist on institutional and legislative reform in the criminal law sphere if this would jeopardise other political objectives—which could include other Justice and Home Affairs objectives such as immigration control.[45] Terrorism is key in this context. Rather than viewing institutional reform (including respect for the rule of law) as a continuum with legislative reform, a distinction could be made between targets for reform on specific fields (eg the adoption of anti-money-laundering legislation) and the general evaluation of a neighbour as respecting fundamental rights—thus justifying (in the Union's eyes) the expulsion and interrogation of terrorist suspects in the neighbours. It is in counter-terrorism co-operation where the assertions about 'partnership' between the Union and its neighbours based on 'shared values' may be tested in practice.

---

[42] See COM (2004) 373 and GAERC Council of 13–14 December 2004, doc 15461/04 (Presse 344), pp 9–10.

[43] OJ C77, 29 March 2003, p 1. A revised Action Plan was endorsed by the EU-Ukraine Co-operation Council on 18 June 2007—see Council doc 11003/07 (Presse 142).

[44] Cremona and Hillion, n 39 above, p 17.

[45] Another factor that may hinder reform is the non-legally binding character of the ENP Action Plans. However, at least as regards Ukraine, the Council is in the process of negotiating a new, 'enhanced agreement', which would be legally binding. For details see C Hillion, 'Mapping-Out the New Contractual Relations between the European Union and Its Neighbours: Learning from the EU-Ukraine 'Enhanced Agreement'', *European Foreign Affairs Review*, vol 12, 2007, pp 169–182.

Similar challenges may surround the co-operation between the European Union and Russia. The latter is consciously not part of the European Neighbourhood Policy, insisting on distancing itself from the 'neighbours' and projecting an image of an equal partner with the Union.[46] EU–Russia relations are based on a 1997 Agreement on Partnership and Co-operation (PCA) and a series of subsequent initiatives and documents. All emphasise the mutual partnership between Russia and the Union. Co-operation in criminal matters is central in this context. In 2000, the Council adopted an EU Action Plan on Common Action for the Russian Federation on combating organised crime.[47] This aims at closer judicial and police co-operation in criminal matters, including the ratification of a series of Council of Europe Conventions. In 2003, the EU and Russia agreed to enhance co-operation by creating four 'common spaces' in the framework of the PCA based on 'common values and shared interests'.[48] Along with an economic, external security and research and education space, parties agreed to a common space of freedom, security and justice. Following the adoption of a Roadmap for implementation in 2005, detailed priorities have been set out in an Action-oriented paper on the implementation of such space.[49] While the issues of visa facilitation and readmission are dominant (similarly with the EU's relations with the eastern neighbours in the context of the ENP), the Plan includes targets for detailed action on police and judicial co-operation in criminal matters, as well as action against forms of criminality including organised crime, money laundering and human trafficking. Once more, the 'genuine strategic partnership' between the EU and Russia is emphasised, as is the fact that such partnership is founded on 'common interests and shared values'.[50]

Another dimension of the Union's relations with its neighbours regarding external action in criminal matters comes into play in the context of the Union's strategy in the Western Balkans.[51] Given the fact that the area is largely a post-conflict zone the central role of the Union is one of a 'stabilizer'.[52] In 1999, the Union launched a Stabilization and Association Process (SAP) for the Western Balkan countries.[53] Subsequently, the 2000 Feira European Council stated that all

---

[46] For the Russian stance see L Delcour, 'Does the European Neighbourhood Policy Make a Difference? Policy Patterns and Reception in Ukraine and Russia', *European Political Economy Review*, no 7, 2007, pp 118–155; see also Cremona and Hillion, n 39 above.

[47] OJ C106, 13 April 2000, p 5.

[48] *EU–Russia Relations*, May 2007, in www.europa.eu.

[49] Council doc. 15534/1/06 REV 1, Brussels, 28 November 2006.

[50] ibid, p 3.

[51] For an assessment, see E T Fakiolas and N Tzifakis, 'Transformation or Accession? Reflecting on the EU's Strategy Towards the Western Balkans', *European Foreign Affairs Review*, vol 13, 2008, pp 377–398.

[52] See Cremona, 'The Union as Global Actor', n 1 above.

[53] The same year saw also the launch of the Stability Pact for Southern Europe. The Pact is an OSCE (rather than an EU) instrument but the EU has played an important part in its development. The issues of democratisation and human rights and security (including justice and home affairs) constitute two of its three specific themes (the other being economic reconstruction and development). See F Trauner, *EU Justice and Home Affairs Strategy in the Western Balkans*, CEPS Working Document No 259, www.ceps.eu.

Western Balkan countries were potential candidates for EU membership (since then two of these countries, Croatia and the FYR of Macedonia have obtained formal candidate status).[54] Conditionality, benchmarking and monitoring are central here too, with the Commission publishing annual country progress reports since 2002.[55] Progress in Justice and Home Affairs (JHA) issues is central in this process, with the Union focusing largely on institutional reform. Moreover, 2006 saw the adoption of a detailed Action oriented paper 'on improving co-operation on organised crime, corruption, illegal immigration and counter-terrorism between the EU, Western Balkans and relevant ENP countries'.[56] The Action Oriented Paper was envisaged by the 2005 EU Strategy on the JHA External Dimension and invited the Commission and the Council Secretariat to report every 18 months to the JHA and GAERC Councils.[57] The title and content of the Paper demonstrate the importance for the EU of action against organised crime, corruption and counter-terrorism in an area that is largely viewed as criminogenic and a source of instability in the region and beyond. The accession target available to the Western Balkan countries may prove to be a catalyst for reform in criminal matters (both more broadly on the institutions and substantive criminal law), but concerns arising from the 2007 enlargement may mean that the benchmarks will be raised higher prior to approval of EU accession.

IV. INTERNATIONAL AGREEMENTS

Another form of EU external action in criminal matters is international agreements between the Union and third countries or organisations. Given that criminal law falls primarily within the third pillar, a considerable level of complexity is added to the emergence of the Union as an international actor in the field given the absence of (at least express) conferral of legal personality to the Union (as opposed to the Community) in the Treaties. The issue of Union legal personality has been central in theory and in practice in the context of the negotiation and conclusion of international agreements in criminal matters.

A. The Legal Personality of the Union and International Agreements

The Treaties do not confer expressly legal personality upon the Union. This absence of express conferral has led to a lively academic debate on whether, nevertheless, the

---

[54] For a background see Trauner, previous n.
[55] ibid.
[56] Council doc 9272/06, Brussels, 12 May 2006.
[57] The first Report was submitted at the end of 2006—see Council doc 15736/06, Brussels, 24 November 2006. For a recent assessment on progress, see the Commission Communication, 'Western Balkans: Enhancing the European Perspective' COM (2008) 127, Brussels, 5 March 2008.

Union has in some form or another legal personality.[58] Notwithstanding the lack of clarity in the Treaty wording, it has been pointed out that a distinction should be made between the legal *personality* and the legal *capacity* of the Union: even if the Union does not have legal personality, one must examine whether, and on which terms, the EU Treaty has attributed to the Union the capacity to negotiate and conclude international agreements.[59] Article 24 TEU (in combination with Article 38 TEU for the third pillar, which states that 'agreements referred to in Article 24 may cover matters falling under this Title'), allow for the negotiation and conclusion of international agreements. The question is whether these agreements are negotiated and concluded on behalf of the Union, or merely on behalf of Member States.

The ambiguous Treaty wording does not help towards reaching clear conclusions on the matter. Arguments supporting the conclusion of international agreements solely on behalf of Member States collectively are based primarily on Article 24(5) TEU, which states that no agreement will be binding on a Member State whose representative in the Council states that it has to comply with the requirements of its own constitutional principles.[60] Moreover, Declaration no. 4 to the Final Act to the Amsterdam Treaty states that Article 24 shall not imply any transfer of competence from the Member States to the EU; and Article 12 TEU does not list agreements as CFSP instruments, suggesting that these are not to be considered external relations instruments of the Union as such.[61] Counter-arguments, supporting the negotiation and conclusion of international agreements on behalf of the Union, are primarily based on amendments introduced by the Nice Treaty. Article 24(6) TEU, inserted by Nice, states that Article 24 agreements shall be binding on the Union institutions while Article 24(2) has been revised to require

---

[58] For views in favour of some sort of legal personality of the Union see inter alia A Dashwood, 'External Relations Provisions of the Amsterdam Treaty', in D O'Keeffe and P Twomey (eds), *Legal Issues of the Amsterdam Treaty*, Oxford, Hart Publishing, 1999, pp 219–220; and P Eeckhout, *External Relations of the European Union. Legal and Constitutional Foundations*, Oxford, OUP, 2004, in particular p 155. For the contrary view, see E Denza, *The Intergovernmental Pillars of the European Union*, Oxford, OUP, 2002, pp 174–176. For an analysis of the relevant Treaty provisions, see further R A Wessel, 'Revisiting the International Legal Status of the EU', *European Foreign Affairs Review*, vol 5, 2000, pp 507–537; and N Neuwahl, 'Legal Personality of the European Union—International and Institutional Aspects' in V Kronenberger (ed), *The European Union and the International Legal Order: Discord or Harmony?*, The Hague, Asser Press, 2001, pp 3–22.

[59] See in particular Neuwahl above. See also T Georgopoulos, 'What Kind of Treaty-Making Power for the EU? Constitutional Problems related to the Conclusion of the EU–US Agreements on Extradition and Mutual Legal Assistance', *European Law Review*, vol 30, 2005, pp 190–208 at pp 191–192.

[60] However, the same provision continues, the other members of the Council may agree that the agreement will nevertheless apply provisionally. In a change from the earlier version of the Treaty, the Article no longer states with regard to the other Council members that the agreement will apply provisionally 'to them'. This has been interpreted as being intended to counteract the impression that Art 24 agreements are not binding on the Union as such. See the editorial comments in the *Common Market Law Review*, vol 38, 2001, pp 826–827.

[61] The same could be argued with regard to the third pillar, where the main legal instruments cited in Art 34 TEU are common positions, framework decisions, conventions and decisions. However, this argument is not very convincing as even if one looks in the first pillar (where the Community's legal personality and capacity are well established), international agreements are not mentioned in Art 249 TEC but in a separate part of the Treaty.

unanimity in the Council only in cases where the agreement covers issues for which unanimity is required for the adoption of internal decisions. In the specific context of the third pillar, it has also been argued that the objectives defined in that pillar (for which the conclusion of an international agreement under Articles 24 and 38 is necessary) are Union objectives (and not objectives of the Member States acting collectively).[62] These views have been tested in the negotiation and conclusion of third pillar international agreements on the basis of Articles 24 and 38,.[63] in particular agreements prompted or justified by the so-called 'war on terror'.[64]

B. The EU–US Agreements on Extradition and Mutual Legal Assistance

9/11 became the catalyst for the adoption of a series of internal Union criminal law measures, justified as necessary to fight terrorism. These included long-negotiated and contested proposals whose adoption was speeded up (such as the Decision establishing Eurojust and the second Money Laundering Directive) as well as new measures such as the Framework Decisions on Terrorism and on the European Arrest Warrant. All these measures were negotiated as a matter of urgency post-9/11—with a speed that did not give much leeway for parliamentary scrutiny and open debate—and had been agreed in one form or the other by the close of the EU Belgian Presidency in December 2001. Although justified as necessary in the 'war on terror' the majority of these measures were not limited to terrorism but covered a wide range of criminal matters.[65] In parallel with these internal developments, the European Union demonstrated a clear willingness to strengthen channels of co-operation with the United States on counter-terrorism. Shortly after 9/11, on 20 September 2001, the EU and the US issued a joint statement demonstrating their willingness to work in partnership on counter-terrorism and vigorously pursue co-operation in the fields of police and judicial co-operation in criminal matters. The Justice and Home Affairs Council on the same day proposed

---

[62] See J. Monar, 'The EU as an International Actor in the Domain of Justice and Home Affairs', *European Foreign Affairs Review*, vol 9, 2003, pp 395–415 at pp 400–403. See also S Marquardt, 'La capacité de l'Union européenne de conclure des accords internationaux dans le domaine de la coopération policiere et judiciaire en matiere pénale', in de Kerchove and Weyembergh, n 14 above, pp 179–194 at pp 185–187. Marquardt notes in support of the Union's role that the Presidency, which negotiates Art 24 agreements, shall, according to Art 18(1) TEU, represent the Union in CFSP matters. However, it is not clear whether this provision could also be applied to the third pillar, action under which (in terms of form, instruments and institutions) arguably falls much closer to the first (rather than the second) pillar.

[63] Note that a number of Agreements have also been concluded between the Union and European states which are associated with Schengen (including Switzerland, Norway and Iceland). See recently the Agreement between the Union and Iceland and Norway on a surrender procedure between the parties (OJ L292, 21 October 2006, p 1). This may include cross-pillar agreements (see Switzerland). For an analysis, see N Wichmann, 'The Participation of the Schengen Associates: Inside or Outside?', *European Foreign Affairs Review*, vol 11, 2006, pp 87–107.

[64] Note that counter-terrorism clauses are also inserted in Community agreements with different objectives, such as the Cotonou Agreement.

[65] See Mitsilegas, Monar and Rees, n 6 above.

a series of initiatives designed to improve co-operation with the US. The Council proposed inter alia the negotiation, on the basis of Article 38 TEU, of an Agreement between the EU and the US on criminal law co-operation on terrorism and an Agreement between Europol and the United States. Following a series of discussions to define the precise mandate of negotiations with the US on judicial co-operation, such mandate was eventually adopted—for the negotiation of EU–US Agreements on extradition and mutual legal assistance—in April 2002.[66] The initiation of such negotiations—though uncharted territory—was a significant step for the European Union. The EU–US Agreements on extradition and mutual legal assistance would be the first ever third pillar international agreements to be concluded. The conclusion of such agreements would cement EU action in the field, boost its image as an international security actor and establish a firm precedent regarding the conclusion of third pillar international agreements (it must not be forgotten in this context that the legal basis of such agreements, Article 38 TEU, seems like an 'aftermath' addition to the main international agreements provisions—especially Article 24 TEU—of the second, foreign policy, pillar). The Agreements were negotiated for most of 2002 and the first months of 2003. A predominant feature of these negotiations was their secrecy and lack of transparency. The situation can partly be explained by the relevant EU constitutional framework: Articles 24 and 38 TEU do not provide for a role in the negotiations for the European Parliament. However, the European Parliament intervened on a number of occasions putting forward their views on the need for transparency and the desired content of the EU–US extradition and mutual legal assistance agreements.[67] Moreover, national parliaments—in their role as scrutineers of proposals for EU law—were left with very little space and time to meaningfully examine the agreements. These were declassified only at the last minute, and usually when dates for signature had already been arranged—presenting thus national parliamentarians with a fait accompli.[68]

The final texts were signed in June 2003 and involved co-operation for a wide range of criminal offences.[69] Although they could be seen (and could constitute in the future) a benchmark for EU external action in the respective fields and represent (as regards the extradition and mutual legal assistance Agreements) a level of

---

[66] For details, see V Mitsilegas, 'The New EU–USA Cooperation on Extradition, Mutual Legal Assistance and the Exchange of Police Data', *European Foreign Affairs Review*, vol 8, 2003, pp 515–536.

[67] See in particular the European Parliament Recommendation B5-0540/2002, where the European Parliament requested the Council to inform it as well as national parliaments on the progress of negotiations. Moreover, by its earlier Resolution of 13 December 2001 (B5-0813/2001) the European Parliament insisted on safeguards such as not allowing extradition if the defendant could be sentenced to death in the US.

[68] See Mitsilegas, 'The New EU–USA Cooperation', n 66 above. See also House of Lords European Union Committee, *EU–US Agreements on Extradition and Mutual Legal Assistance*, 38th Report, session 2002–03, HL Paper 135.

[69] Agreement on extradition between the European Union and the United States of America, OJ L181, 19 July 2003, p 27; Agreement on mutual legal assistance between the European Union and the United States of America, OJ L181, 19 July 2003, p 34. See also the Council Decision, on the basis of Arts 24 and 38 TEU, concerning the signature of these agreements: OJ L181, 19 July 2003, p 25.

standards which could not be lowered in the bilateral dealings of individual EU Member States with the United States, the Agreements presented a number of significant challenges on EU law and fundamental rights. Unsurprisingly, a major sticking point in the negotiations of the extradition agreement has been the issue of extradition to the US to face the death penalty. In order to accommodate the rigidity of US State law, the final agreement—in a change to the initial negotiating mandate which prohibited extradition if the death penalty would be imposed— allows extradition on the condition that the death penalty if imposed will not be carried out.[70] Further concerns include the absence of an express specialty provision and express human rights bars to extradition, an issue which became particularly acute in the Guantanamo Bay era.[71] These concerns are exacerbated by the fact that the remedy in cases where extradition poses constitutional concerns for the parties is only 'consultations' between the parties.[72]

Less publicised, but equally valid concerns related to the mutual legal assistance agreement, and concerned the challenges that its provisions pose on privacy and data protection. The Agreement calls for the exchange of a wide range of every day information about financial transactions but does not contain extensive data protection provisions.[73] Major concerns—which, as will be seen below, were also prominent in the context of the Europol–US Agreement, and in the EU–US PNR Agreement—involve the lack of an extensive and specific data protection framework in the US which would provide, if not equivalent to the EU, at least an adequate level of protection of personal data in the light of its maximum exchange envisaged by these agreements. In this context, it is noteworthy that the mutual legal assistance agreement expressly states that 'generic restrictions with respect to the legal standards of the requesting State for processing personal data may not be

---

[70] The Justice and Home Affairs Council of 26 April 2002, which adopted the negotiating mandate, expressly stated that 'the Union will make any agreement on extradition conditional on the provision of guarantees on the *non-imposition* of capital punishment sentences, and the securing of existing levels of constitutional guarantees with regard to life sentences' (Council document 7991/02, p 13, emphasis added).

[71] Although a reference to both parties 'having due regard for rights of the individuals and the rule of law' can be found to the Preamble of both Agreements (recital 3). The Preambles also provide that the parties are 'mindful of the guarantees *under their respective legal systems* which provide for the right to a fair trial to an extradited person, including the right to adjudication by an impartial tribunal established pursuant to law' (recital 4, emphasis added). The legal force of these preambular provisions is however unclear.

[72] Art 17(2) of the extradition Agreement provides for 'consultations' between the parties 'where the constitutional principles of, or final judicial decisions binding upon, the requested State may pose an impediment to fulfilment of its obligation to extradite'. The reference to 'final binding judicial decisions' was added at the very last stages of negotiations and may be read as covering decisions by the Luxembourg and Strasbourg Courts—see the address by Mr Petsalnikos, then Minister of Justice of Greece, the holder of the EU Presidency a the time of the signature of the agreements, to the European Parliament Civil Liberties Committee, 10 June 2003, www.eu2003.gr/en/Arts/2003/6/11/3037/. This mechanism for dispute solving has been criticised in that 'the most fundamental norms of domestic law are rendered negotiable between states'—Georgopoulos, n 59 above, p 195.

[73] Art 4(1)(b) of the Agreement provides for mutual legal assistance for the purpose of identifying information regarding natural or legal persons convicted 'or otherwise involved in a criminal offence', information in the possession of 'non-bank financial institutions' or 'financial transactions unrelated to accounts'.

imposed by the requested State as a condition . . . to providing evidence or information'.[74]

The Agreements on extradition and mutual legal assistance were hailed as a great success by those involved in their negotiation and conclusion from the EU side. They are deemed to be significant in showing the ability of the European Union to emerge as an international actor in the field and speak with 'one voice' in sensitive issues of international security. The Agreements constitute a precedent of third pillar action in the field and their very conclusion may be used to argue that—notwithstanding the lack of legal personality of the European Union in the current Treaties—the Union has a de facto legal personality in counter-terrorism and criminal matters by virtue of the very conclusion of international agreements in the third pillar. This precedent may explain the willingness of the relevant EU institutions to negotiate and conclude the Agreements and may challenge the generally accepted view that EU action in the field was merely a response to US pressure (especially in the light of the fact that the US had already concluded bilateral agreements on extradition with all and on mutual legal assistance with most Member States and could presumably exercise greater pressure on the bilateral level).

In the light of the considerable criticism that the Agreements have attracted on human rights grounds however, the issue of the legitimacy and 'added value' of these Union third pillar agreements becomes increasingly contested. Is it acceptable for the Union to emerge as an external actor—by agreeing standards which could violate not only its internal legislation, but also the very values and principles that it proclaims to be based upon? Are such 'double standards' to some extent justified in order to accommodate the diversity of the EU interlocutors at the international scene and achieve the objective of the EU speaking with 'one voice', a voice stronger than the individual Member States?[75] Or is the conclusion of international agreements in criminal matters by the Union an end in itself for pro-integrationist institutions aiming at expanding EU powers and competence? The EU–US Agreements provide fertile ground for these questions to be tested. On a number of instances, the Agreements certainly introduce standards which are lower than those on the internal EU level—thus casting doubt on the extent to which the Union can 'assert itself on the international scene' while fully upholding its own internal standards and very foundational principles such as the protection of fundamental rights and raising fears about the potential erosion of these internal standards by the Union's external action. This criticism is exacerbated by the lack of transparency and virtually non-existence of ex ante parliamentary scrutiny and public debate on the content of the agreements. On the other hand,

---

[74] Art 9(2)(b)—see also the detailed Explanatory Note attached to the Agreement. Note also the leeway that the Agreement leaves for assistance to the US executive—Art 8 allows for assistance to be provided to a wide range of US authorities, beyond the national level. On these and other points of concern, see Mitsilegas, 'The New EU–USA Cooperation', n 66 above

[75] For a defence of the agreements, see G Stessens, 'The EU–US Agreements on Extradition and Mutual Legal Assistance: How to Bridge Different Approaches' in de Kerchove and Weyembergh, n 14 above, pp 263–274.

a more optimistic view may be centered on the fact that the agreements, with all their flaws, constitute a benchmark for future action in the field, in particular as regards bilateral agreements between Member States and the US. Both Agreements contain a 'benchmark' clause stating that they do not preclude the conclusion of such bilateral agreements which are 'consistent' with the EU–US agreements.[76] A minimum EU standard—at least as regards the extradition agreement—appears thus to have been set below which Member States are not allowed to go in their future relations with the US.[77]

The two agreements cast some light on issues related to the legal personality of the Union and the relationship between the Union and Member States in external action. As regards the question of competence, the Agreements are clear: the conclusion of future bilateral agreements on the matter between Member States and the US is not precluded if these are consistent with the Union agreements.[78] On the question of whether the agreements have been effectively concluded by the Union or by the Member States acting collectively, the situation is much more nuanced. It is true that both agreements envisage a certain co-ordinating role for the Union: the Union will co-ordinate Member State actions regarding their exchange of written instruments with the US setting out the application of their relevant bilateral agreements;[79] it will ensure that the provisions of the EU agreements are applied to bilateral extradition Treaties between Member States and the US;[80] and it will be engaged in consultation and review processes with the US regarding the content of the agreements.[81] However, to the co-ordinating role of the Union one can contrast the stark emphasis on the maintenance and regulation of bilateral relationships between Member States and the US. As it is clear from both Agreements, these do not replace, but supplement existing bilateral agreements.[82] In case of the extradition agreement posing constitutional challenges, consultations will take place between 'the requested and requesting Member States' (and not the Union or one of its institutions).[83] The entry into force of the agreements follows the exchange of instruments by the parties indicating that they have completed their internal procedures for this purpose[84]—a provision that triggers Article 24(5) TEU which allows Member States to indicate that they need to follow internal constitutional

---

[76] Art 18 of the Extradition Agreement and Art 14 of the Mutual Legal Assistance Agreement.

[77] Note that Art 3(4) of the EU–US mutual legal assistance agreement states that
nothing in this Agreement may be interpreted in a manner that would prejudice or restrict the provisions of any Mutual Legal Assistance Treaty, working law enforcement relationship or any other arrangement for the exchange of information between the USA and any EU Member States.

[78] Art 18 of the extradition agreement and Art 14 of the mutual legal assistance agreement.

[79] Decision concerning the signature of the agreements, Art 2(2).

[80] Art 3(1) of both Agreements.

[81] Art 15 and 21 of the Extradition agreement and 11 and 17 of the Mutual Legal Assistance Agreement. Moreover, note that it is the Council on behalf of the EU which will decide on the extension of the territorial scope of the agreement (Art 3 of the Decision concerning the signature of the agreements).

[82] Art 3 of both Agreements.

[83] Art 17.

[84] Art 22(1) of the Extradition Agreement and Art 18(1) of the MLA Agreement.

procedures.[85] Last, but not least, both Agreements require the exchange of written instruments between Member States and the US which acknowledge the application of their bilateral Agreements in the light of the provisions of the EU–US Agreements.[86] It has been noted that this clause was inserted at the insistence of the United States as a means of establishing a legal link with the Member States as far as the Agreements are concerned—stemming from the acknowledgement that, even if Member States are bound by the Agreements internally, this link does not have a direct legal effect vis-a-vis the United States.[87] This clause, along with the insistence of the US to demand the simultaneous entry into force of the EU–US Agreements and the bilateral instruments, may serve to demonstrate that in the eyes of the United States Union action is not sufficient per se to produce comprehensive legally binding effects.

C. The EU–US PNR Agreements

i. Background and the EC–US PNR Agreement

Along with the EU–US Agreements on extradition and mutual legal assistance—which resulted from the political will in both the EU and the United States for further co-operation on counter-terrorism and in criminal matters more generally—further forms of EU–US co-operation emerged from the need for the EU to respond to the adoption of domestic US law post 9/11. In a response to the nature of the 9/11 attacks, US legislation adopted in November 2001 required all air carriers operating flights to, from or through the United States to provide US Customs with electronic access to data contained in their automatic reservation and departure control systems.[88] Such legislation involved a wide range of passenger data and inevitably was also addressed to EU carriers flying to or via the US. In case of non-compliance, carriers were faced with heavy financial sanctions, including the loss of landing rights at US airports. However, compliance by EU carriers with US law could mean that they were in breach of domestic and EU data protection legislation, as US standards required the transmission of a wide range of

---

[85] According to Council document 5916/1/07 REV 1, Brussels, 20 February 2007, no less than 22 of the Member States after the 2004 enlargement made use of this possibility (with Austria, France and Greece the only ones which did not use this). Bulgaria has since indicated that it will also make use of 24(5)—Council doc. 7987/07, Brussels, 2 April 2007. Document 5916/1/07 indicates that, as far as the US are concerned, the bilateral instruments negotiated with Member States contain a provision which stipulates that the bilateral instruments will only enter into force at the same time as the EU–US Agreements—implying that all ratification procedures with regard to the bilateral instruments will need to have taken place before the exchange of ratification instruments for the EU–US Agreements can take place. For the latest publicly available information on the Council website with regard to the state of play of ratification, see doc.5462/08, Brussels, 22 January 2008.

[86] Art 3(2)(a) of both Agreements.

[87] Marquardt, n 52 above, p 193.

[88] On the US response regarding border security see A Ceyhan, 'Sécurité, frontières et surveillance aux États Unis apres le 11 Septembre 2001' in *Cultures et conflits*, vol 53, 2003, downloaded from www.conflits.org.

(including sensitive) personal data. Airlines approached domestic data protection authorities in Member States and eventually the Commission, which started negotiations with the US in order to reach a mutually acceptable arrangement. In the meantime, the US decided to suspend the application of their domestic law vis-a-vis EU airlines until March 2003 pending an agreement. Negotiations sought to reconcile US demands with the EU data protection regime.[89]

Negotiations proved to be protracted and lasted well beyond March 2003, when US law formally entered into force vis-a-vis EU airlines. In the course of negotiations, the European Parliament adopted a series of Resolutions urging the Commission to ensure that these standards are fully respected.[90] The US requirements were also scrutinised by the 'Article 29 Working Party' on data protection,[91] which was highly critical of US demands.[92] Eventually an agreement was reached between the Commission and the US authorities in December 2003. Following a series of undertakings by the US authorities, the Commission accepted that US data protection standards in the context of PNR transfers were adequate and noted that the way forward was to establish a legal framework for existing PNR transfers to the US. This would consist of an 'adequacy' Decision by the Commission, certifying that the US data protection standards were adequate, followed by a 'light' bilateral international agreement between the Community and the US. It is important to note that in accepting the US standards, the Commission emphasised the importance of the international role of the European Union in this field (by calling for the adoption of a global approach on the issue) and more than hinted at the presence of the EU negotiators as agents of influence vis-a-vis the US—embracing the logic described in the previous section that some sort of an agreement is preferable to no agreement at all. As the Commission noted in a Communication issued on 16 December 2003,

> the option of insisting on the enforcement of the law on the EU side would have been politically justified, but . . . would have undermined the influence of more moderate and co-operative counsels in Washington and substituted a trial of strength for the genuine leverage we have as co-operative partners.[93]

In spite of the Commission's statements, the adequacy of the US data protection was seriously questioned by expert bodies in the EU. A draft adequacy Decision

---

[89] For details, see V Mitsilegas, 'Contrôle des étrangers, des passagers, des citoyens: Surveillance et anti-terrorisme', *Cultures et conflits*, vol 58, 2005, pp 155–182.

[90] See Resolutions P5_TA(2003)0097 and P5_TA(2003)0429.

[91] The Working Party was established under the 1995 EC Data Protection Directive (Art 29) and consists of Member States' Information Commissioners. Its role is advisory.

[92] Opinion 4/2003 on the level of protection ensured in the US for the transfer of passengers' data, 11070/03/EN, WP 78. The Working Party urged the Commission to ensure inter alia that the purposes of data transfer and the bodies having access to such data should be specified and that proportionality should be ensured not only in relation to these aspects but also regarding the categories of data to be transferred (including sensitive data) and data retention.

[93] Communication from the Commission to the Council and the Parliament, 'Transfer of Air Passenger Name Record (PNR) Data: A Global EU Approach' COM (2003) 826 final, Brussels, 16.12.2003, p 5.

was examined by the Article 29 Working Party on Data Protection.[94] In an Opinion published in January 2004, the Working Party expressly stated that 'the progress made does not allow a favourable adequacy finding to be achieved'.[95] Their view (shared largely by the European Parliament and national parliamentary committees such as the House of Lords European Union Committee) was that US requirements were disproportionate and contrary to fundamental data protection principles (such as the collection and use of data for specified purposes and limited access only by specified authorities) and could lead to data mining and generalised surveillance.[96]

These concerns led to the adoption by the European Parliament in March 2004 of a Resolution calling on the Commission to withdraw the draft adequacy Decision.[97] The European Parliament drew attention to many of the data protection points made above, and, on the issue of legality, noted that there was no legal basis in the EU permitting the use of PNR commercial data for public security purposes—there was a need, according to the Parliament, for a specific legal basis covering these cases. The draft adequacy Decision might well be a lowering of the data protection standards in the 1995 Directive. The European Parliament also took the step of requesting an Opinion from the European Court of Justice on the compatibility of the draft PNR international agreement, which would be concluded after the adoption of the adequacy Decision, with the EC Treaty.[98] However, the European Parliament had limited say—namely a consultative role— in the agreed negotiating procedure for the agreement. This involved as seen above a comitology 'adequacy' decision—required by the 1995 Data Protection Directive[99]—plus a first pillar international agreement whereby the role of the European Parliament is merely consultative. With time pressure piling up and the conclusion of the agreement deemed a matter of urgency, the Commission eventually adopted the adequacy Decision and the Council the Decision allowing for the conclusion of the agreement in May 2004.[100] The European Parliament— which had called on the Commission to withdraw its adequacy assessment— declined to give an opinion under its consultative role within the timeframe given by the Council pending the Court's Opinion.

[94] The Working Party has a mandate to do so under Art 30(1)(b) of the Data Protection Directive.
[95] Opinion 2/2004 on the adequate protection of personal data contained in the PNR of air passengers to be transferred to the United States' Bureau of Customs and Border Protection (US CBP), adopted on 29 January 2004, doc. 10019/04/EN, WP 87.
[96] See Mitsilegas, 'Contrôle des étrangers', n 89 above.
[97] P5_TA-PROV (2004) 0245
[98] See Mitsilegas, 'Contrôle des étrangers', n 89 above.
[99] Art 25(6) of the 1995 Data Protection Directive (OJ L281, 23 November 1995 p 31).
[100] Commission Decision on the adequate protection of personal data contained in the Passenger Name Record of air passengers transferred to the United States' Bureau of Customs and Border Protection, OJ L235, 6 July 2004, p 11 (including an Annex with the relevant US Undertakings); and Council Decision on the conclusion of an Agreement between the European Community and the United States of America on the processing and transfer of PNR data by Air Carriers to the US Department of Homeland Security, Bureau of Customs and Border Protection, OJ L183, 20 May 2004, p 83 (the Agreement is annexed to the Decision).

This did not stop the conclusion—on the basis of Articles 95 and 300(2) TEC—of the (first pillar) EC–US PNR Agreement. Its terms had not changed from the draft that was so heavily criticised by the data protection authorities and the European Parliament. The combination of the adequacy Decision and the agreement itself meant that: a wide range of personal data—which could lead to extensive profiling of passengers—would be transferred to the US authorities;[101] the US authorities would 'pull' data from airline databases; PNR data would be used for purposes of preventing and combating, terrorism and related crimes, but also for 'other serious crimes that are transnational in nature'; storage of PNR data (excluding data linked with a law enforcement record) would take place for three to five years.—data which have been accessed would be kept for a further eight years; CBP could provide data to other government authorities, including foreign government authorities. All these features led to significant concerns regarding the compatibility of the Community external commitments with internal EU data protection and privacy standards. The concerns were not alleviated by the fact that, as expressly stated, the US protection Undertakings did not create or confer any right or benefit on any person or party.[102]

ii. The ECJ Judgment

The Council thus prevailed and concluded an agreement in the face of strong human rights concerns in the name of co-operation in the 'war on terror'. The conclusion of the agreement meant that it was inevitable that the European Parliament withdrew its ex ante request for the Court to issue an Opinion on the agreement. However, linking its human rights and institutional grievances, the European Parliament (supported by the European Data Protection Supervisor[103]) made a further challenge in the Court of Justice, asking for the annulment of the Decision authorising the Conclusion of the EC/US Agreement, on the grounds of the latter breaching fundamental rights and the principle of proportionality, breaching the fundamental principles of the data protection Directive, but also on legality grounds.

The Court of Justice addressed some of these questions in a judgment delivered in May 2006.[104] Unlike Advocate General Léger (who largely upheld the content of the agreement[105]), the Court did not examine the compatibility of the PNR agreement with fundamental rights. The Court focused exclusively on the legality

---

[101] No less than 34 categories including name, address and billing address, email address, all forms of payment information, travel itinerary, frequent flyer information, travel status of passenger, no show information, one-way tickets, all historical changes to the PNR and 'general remarks'.

[102] For further details see Mitsilegas, 'Contrôle des étrangers', n 89 above.

[103] It is noteworthy that the Court accepted the intervention of the European Data Protection Supervisor, in spite of the fact that the latter is not an EU institution founded directly by the Treaty but a body created by the Council on the basis of Art 286 TEC—see V Michel, Case note, *Revue trimestrielle du droit européen*, vol 42, 2006, pp 549–559 at pp 550–551.

[104] Joined cases C-317/04 and C-318/04, *European Parliament v Council*, [2006] ECR I-4721.

[105] Opinion delivered on 22 November 2005.

point and found that both the adequacy decision and the agreement were adopted under the wrong legal basis and should be annulled. According to the Court, the transfer of PNR data constitutes processing operations concerning public security and the activities of the State in areas of criminal law—and these operations would not be covered by the first pillar legal bases that were used in the adequacy Decision and Agreement.[106] In reaching this conclusion, the Court made a distinction between the initial *collection* of passenger data by airlines—which takes place in the course of an activity falling within Community law—and the subsequent *processing* of PNR data, which is different in nature as it is necessary for safeguarding public security and for law-enforcement purposes.[107] According to the Court, the fact that data is being transferred by private operators does not suffice to bring the activity within the first pillar—the transfer falls 'within a framework established by the public authorities that relates to public security'.[108]

The judgment is of great constitutional significance, in delimiting competence between the first and the third pillar at a time when the academic, policy and judicial debate over the relationship between the two pillars has taken centre-stage.[109] In contrast with the judgment in the environmental crime case, the Court here found a way to ascertain (correctly, in this author's view) that action related to public security and law enforcement does not fall within the first pillar, notwithstanding the fact that the challenge by the European Parliament was not necessarily aimed at such a conclusion.[110] It is noteworthy that, in doing so, the Court focused primarily on the adequacy Decision, in particular its Preamble which emphasised that the measures in question concerned counter-terrorism and the fight against crime—focusing largely on the objective and not the effect of the examined measures.[111] The Court thus rejected the argument, raised by the Commission and quoted in the AG Opinion, that the measures had a dual objective: counter-terrorism as far as the US were concerned, and data protection as far as the Community was concerned.[112] The Court also seems to have departed in this context from the AG approach, which seemed to accept that the instruments had a dual objective of counter-terrorism and data protection.[113] In doing so, the

---

[106] See in particular paras 56, 59, 67 and 68.

[107] Para 57.

[108] Para 58.

[109] For details, see V Mitsilegas, 'Constitutional Principles of the European Community and European Criminal Law', *European Journal of Law Reform*, vol 8, 2006, pp 301–324.

[110] By excluding any first pillar application on the matter, the Court departed somewhat from the AG approach. The AG examined the possibility of a first pillar incidence, and took the view that the first pillar objective of preventing distortions of competition, 'to the extent that it is actually pursued by the Council' is incidental in character to the two main objectives of combating terrorism and other serious crimes and protecting passengers' personal data (para 147). For a discussion of possibilities of bringing security-based legislation under the first pillar under this or other constructions, see the Case Note by G Gilmore and J Rijpma, *Common Market Law Review*, vol 44, 2007, pp 1092–1096.

[111] This has been criticised by Cremona—M Cremona, *External Relations of the EU and the Member States: Competence, Mixed Agreements, International Responsibility, and Effects of International Law*, EUI Working Paper LAW No 2006/22.

[112] AG Opinion, para 123.

[113] AG Opinion, in particular para 139.

Court chose not to look at the prospect of cross-pillar mixity and the possibility of having an agreement based on both the first and third pillars.[114] It also chose not to accept the possibility that the purpose of measures such as the transfer of personal passenger data to public authorities can be—along with its public security function—the protection of personal data.[115]

The Court's approach towards the position of a measure involving the transfer of passenger data to public authorities of third countries within the EU constitutional framework (but also the earlier approach of the Council and the Commission) diverges somewhat from the position regarding the legal basis of *internal* Community measures in the same field. In 2004, the Council adopted a Directive obliging carriers to transfer of passenger data to public authorities.[116] The categories of the data transferred were much more limited to PNR and were named differently (API—for Advance Passenger Information)—however, the essence of the exercise is the same—the transfer of personal passenger data to the authorities. Yet, the internal Community measure was justified, and ultimately adopted, under Articles 62(2)(a) and 63(3)(b) of the EC Treaty. These serve as the legal basis for the adoption of measures relative to external border controls and illegal immigration respectively. It can be argued that the difference in approach is justified by the fact that, while the API transfer is necessary for immigration control purposes, PNR transfers are necessary for counter-terrorism purposes.[117] However, although the text of the Directive has the stated aim of combating illegal immigration, there have been attempts to frame it also as a national security and counter-terrorism matter.[118] Following such pressure, the finally agreed text of the Directive allows Member States to also use personal passenger data for law enforcement purposes.[119] A degree of inconsistency can also be discerned at the external level: a similar international agreement on passenger data between the

---

[114] On this point, see S. Adam, 'Quelques réflexions sur les relations entre les procédures *a priori* et *a posteriori* d'examen de compatibilité des accords communautaires suite á l'affaire dite de l'accord PNR', *Cahiers de droit européen*, vol 42, 2006, pp 659–696 at p 669. By excluding any first pillar incidence, the Court excluded both the co-existence of a counter-terrorism and a data protection objective, but also the co-existence of a counter-terrorism and internal market objective.

[115] See Michel, n 103 above, in particular pp 556–557. She examines the possibility of the 1995 data protection Directive forming the legal basis for an implied external EC competence in this context.

[116] Council Dir 2004/82/EC of 29 April 2004 on the obligation of carriers to communicate passenger data, OJ L261, 6 August 2004, p 24. See also ch 5.

[117] Art 1 of the API Directive states that the Directive 'aims at improving border controls and combating illegal immigration by the transmission of advance passenger data by carriers to the competent national authorities'.

[118] In particular by the UK Government—see V Mitsilegas, 'Border Security in the European Union. Towards Centralised Controls and Maximum Surveillance' in E Guild, H Toner and A Baldaccini (eds), *Whose Freedom, Security and Justice? EU Immigration and Asylum Law and Policy*, Oxford, Hart Publishing, 2007, pp 359–394. The UK position—that passenger data transfer by the private sector can be both a first pillar and a security matter is also reflected in its intervention in support of the Council in the PNR case (see in particular the AG Opinion, para 80).

[119] See Mitsilegas, 'Border Security', n 118 above. See also House of Lords Select Committee on the European Communities, *Fighting Illegal Immigration: Should Carriers Carry the Burden?* 5th Report, Session 2003–04, HL Paper 29.

Community and Canada refers to the processing of both API and PNR data.[120] This Agreement has not been challenged in Luxembourg as no significant privacy concerns were raised.[121] However, given the fact that it is also a counter-terrorism measure, its legality is dubious in the light of the PNR judgment.[122] While the PNR litigation started from a dispute concerning both the EU inter-institutional balance and the adequacy of data protection by a third country, the Court ultimately judged on legality and competence.

The Court's annulment of the adequacy decision and the agreement meant that they would have to be replaced by measures outside the first pillar if a common EU approach was still the aim—and led ultimately to the conclusion of agreements on the basis of Articles 24 and 38 TEU. In terms of its institutional prerogatives, the European Parliament's challenge thus spectacularly backfired, as its role in (second and) third pillar international agreements is as mentioned above virtually non-existent, and in any case less than its (admittedly limited) consultation role in the first pillar. The third pillar framework would also—at least on paper—limit the role of other Community institutions and organs. The Commission would no longer be involved via the adoption of an adequacy Decision or in the negotiations of the agreement. And the European Data Protection Supervisor covers only first pillar matters, with the third pillar at present not having a horizontal data protection instrument in place (a data protection Framework Decision has been long negotiated but not yet adopted). The impact of this change will be examined below.

iii. The EU–US PNR Agreements

a. The First Agreement

The Court's annulment of the Agreement and Adequacy decision led to the denunciation of the Agreement by the Council[123] and the opening of negotiations

---

[120] Council Decision on the conclusion of an Agreement between the European Community and the Government of Canada on the processing of API/PNR data, OJ L82, 21 March 2006, p 14 (the Agreement is annexed to the Decision). Note however that the recent PNR Agreement with Australia was signed on behalf of the Union (and not the Community)—OJ L213, 8 August 2008, p 47.

[121] See also Adam, n 114 above, who notes that the status of this agreement is uncertain—p 697. See also House of Lords European Union Committee, *The EU–US Passenger Name Record (PNR) Agreement*, 21st Report, session 2006–07, HL Paper 108 (*PNR Report*).

[122] Similar inconsistencies, in the light of the PNR judgment, can be discerned with regard to two further measures: as regards the use of information, a Directive on Data Retention has been adopted under the first pillar, although in the author's view its main objective is counter-terrorism (OJ 2006, L105, 13 April 2006 p 54). The legality of the adoption of the Directive is currently subject to a challenge which is pending before the ECJ (Case C-301/06, *Ireland v Council and Parliament*). With regard to border management (and external relations), note also the successful action for annulment brought by the European Parliament against a Commission Decision approving a Philippine Border Management Project (Case C-403/05, *Parliament v Commission* ECR [2007] I-9045). The Court annulled the first pillar Decision adopted on the basis of Regulation No 443/93 which deals with financial and technical assistance and economic co-operation issues, on the grounds that the Decision pursued an objective concerning the fight against terrorism and international crime falling outside the framework of (first pillar) development co-operation policy pursued by the parent Regulation.

[123] OJ C219, 12 September 2006, p 1.

for a new—albeit interim—Agreement to address the legal vacuum resulting from the Court's ruling.[124] Such an Agreement was concluded on the basis of a Decision under Articles 24 and 38 TEU in October 2006.[125] Notwithstanding the fact that the first pillar legal framework was no longer applicable, the Commission was actively involved in negotiations[126] and both the Decision and the Agreement referred to the earlier US Undertakings and confirmed 'adequacy', ie that the Undertakings could be considered as ensuring an adequate level of data protection.[127] It is unclear what the benchmark under which 'adequacy' would be evaluated is in the absence of horizontal third pillar data protection legislation.[128] Moreover, as mentioned above, the Undertakings are not legally binding. On top of that, the US attempted to 'reinterpret' their Undertakings by a letter to the Council and the Commission.[129] In essence the US advise the EU that a number of Undertakings restricting the sharing of information may impede the implementation of the so-called 'Information Sharing Environment' established by US law after the conclusion of the EC–US PNR Agreement and must be interpreted as not to impede this scheme—with access and use of PNR stemming from the EU de facto extended. The letter also adds that PNR data will be used for the added objective of addressing infectious diseases.[130] By a form of a letter therefore—which has been acknowledged by the EU[131]—the US appear to attempt unilaterally to change the terms of the PNR Agreements.[132]

[124] Mindful of such legal vacuum, the Court maintained the validity of the first pillar instruments until 30 September 2006.

[125] Council Decision 2006/729/CFSP/JHA on the signing, on behalf of the European Union, of an Agreement between the European Union and the USA on the processing and transfer of PNR data by air carriers to the US Department of Homeland Security (L298, 27 October 2006, p 27—the text of the Agreement is annexed to this Decision). It is noteworthy that the Decision has been classified as both a CFSP and JHA Decision. It is unclear whether this classification is there to reflect the dual legal basis only (Art 38 TEU must be used by reference to Art 24 TEU, but the Agreement is essentially a third pillar measure) or whether the Agreement is both a second and third pillar instrument. It must be noted in this context that, as will be seen below, counter-terrorism is viewed by the EU institutions as an objective also linked to the second pillar.

[126] House of Lords, *PNR Report*, n 121 above.

[127] Decision Preamble, recital 2; Agreement, ss 1 and 6.

[128] Given the fact that privacy is a fundamental right upon which the Union is based (Art 6 TEU), standards could stem from the common constitutional traditions of Member States and the ECHR (and to the extent that it serves as an interpretative tool, the Charter).

[129] OJ C259, 27 October 2006, p 1.

[130] The letter also hints at changes to data retention and the addition of new data elements in addition to the original 34.

[131] See the reply by the Council Presidency and the Commission, OJ C259, 27 October 2006, p 4. According to the reply, The EU institutions 'took note' of the US letter, adding that 'the commitments of DHS to continue to implement the Undertakings allow the EU to deem that, for purposes of the implementation of the Agreement, it ensures an adequate level of protection'.

[132] See also the House of Lords PNR Report. According to the Director of the JHA DG in the Commission, 'things have changed in Washington in the last couple of years'—para 60.

b. The Second Agreement[133]

The interim EU–US PNR Agreement expired in July 2007 and was replaced by a new third pillar Agreement signed on behalf of the EU on 23 July and on behalf of the US on 26 July.[134] Like the earlier texts, the agreement includes an adequacy assessment—the US is deemed to ensure an adequate level of PNR data protection for PNR data transferred from the European Union—an assessment which is linked with the issue of transmission of 'EU' PNR data to third countries: the adequacy assessment means that the EU 'will not interfere with relationships between the US and third countries for the exchange of passenger information on data protection grounds'.[135] Moreover, in a statement reminiscent of the one in the EU–US Mutual Legal Assistance Agreement, the parties recognise that 'US and European privacy law and policy share a common basis and that any differences in the implementation of these principles should not present an obstacle to cooperation between the US and the EU'.[136] The preservation of the US standards is further ensured also by a provision making clear that the Agreement is not intended to derogate from or amend existing US (and EU) law, and expressly stating (as in earlier texts) that the Agreement 'does not create or confer any right or benefit on any other person or entity, private or public'.[137] Interestingly, the Agreement also seems to be creating, on the basis of reciprocity, a link between the level of data protection in the two parties: as is stated, the DHS 'expects that it is not being asked to undertake data protection measures in its PNR system that are more stringent than those applied by European authorities for their domestic PNR systems' and vice-versa.[138]

However, the text of the Agreement—which is in the process of being ratified[139]—does not include details of the PNR data transfer per se. These are set out in a separate 'US letter to the EU', signed by Homeland Security Secretary Michael Chertoff, which accompanies the Agreement.[140] The letter enumerates 19 types of

---

[133] See also the relevant section in V Mitsilegas, 'Human Rights, Terrorism and the Quest for Border Security', in M Pedrazzi (ed), *Individual Guarantees in the European Judicial Area in Criminal Matters*, Brussels, Bruylant, forthcoming, upon which this sub-section is based.

[134] Agreement between the European Union and the United States of America on the processing and transfer of Passenger Name Record (PNR) data by air carriers to the United States Department of Homeland Security (DHS) (2007 PNR Agreement), OJ L204, 4 August 2007, p 18. See also Council Decision approving the signing of the Agreement on the basis of Arts 24 and 38 TEU, at p 16.

[135] Para 6.

[136] Preamble, recital 5.

[137] Penultimate paragraph.

[138] Para 5. See also point IX of the 'US letter to the EU' accompanying the Agreement—see below.

[139] The ratification process from the EU side is similar to the one for the EU–US extradition and mutual legal assistance agreements, with a number of EU Member States having indicated that they would have to comply with their domestic constitutional procedures in accordance with Art 24(5) TEU—for the latest state of play, see Council doc 11163/08, Brussels, 26 June 2008.

[140] OJ L204, 4 August 2007, p 21. This is in turn followed by an 'EU letter to the US' confirming that, on the basis of the assurances provided in the US letter, the EU deems that the US ensure an adequate level of data protection and that, based on this finding, 'the EU will take all the necessary steps to discourage international organisations or third countries from interfering with any transfers of EU PNR data to the United States'—p 25

PNR data covered by the Agreement (these are more or less similar to the broad categories in the earlier agreements and include data such as payment information, seat information and 'general remarks').[141] These can be accessed by US government authorities with law enforcement, public security or counterterrorism functions and can also be transferred to government authorities in third countries.[142] The Agreement also contains provisions regulating the move, under certain conditions, from a 'pull' to a 'push' system for PNR data transfer[143] and provisions defining its purposes as fighting terrorism and other serious crimes, but leaves the option of the unilateral broadening of the scope by the US open.[144] The letter also extends the retention period of PNR data essentially to a minimum of 15 years—7 years in an 'active analytical database' and a further 8 years in dormant status.[145] This provision has met with the critical reaction of the European Parliament, which raised its concern that such databases lead to 'a significant risk of massive profiling and data mining'.[146] The European Data Protection Supervisor has also raised concerns,[147] as has the Article 29 Working Party on Data Protection.[148]

It appears that—like the two previous agreements—the third EU–US PNR Agreement will also cause considerable concerns regarding the ability of the Union to uphold and promote its internal legal and constitutional standards (related to the protection of fundamental rights such as the protection of private life) in its external action.[149] The PNR agreements have justifiably been the object of severe and sustained criticism by the European Parliament, national parliaments, expert data protection bodies and civil society—yet these criticisms were not addressed in any of the three agreements—with standards seemingly being lowered, instead of rising, in the latest agreement. The inaction on the part of the EU to address these widespread concerns presents a serious blow to the legitimacy of EU external action in the field, and demonstrates the counter-productive effects that the limited role of the European Parliament in examining the content of legislation with such far-reaching effects. Concerns are exacerbated by the apparent push by EU institutions—evident in the latest draft Agreement, in particular in the provisions on reciprocity—for the establishment of an internal EU PNR system.[150] Union external action is thus used to import into the Union legal order a policy

---

[141] Point III of the letter.

[142] Point II.

[143] PointVIII.

[144] By stating that 'DHS will advise the EU regarding the passage of any US legislation which materially affects the statements made in this letter'—point I.

[145] Point VII.

[146] European Parliament Resolution of 12 July 2007 on the PNR agreement with the USA, P6_TA-PROV (2007)0347, point 20.

[147] Letter of 27 June 2007 to Wolfgang Schäuble, at www.statewatch.org.

[148] See comments of 27 September 2007.

[149] Similar concerns have been raised in the context of US demands for personal data from private sector companies located in the EU (the 'SWIFT' saga): for details, see G. González Fuster, P de Hert and S Gutwirth, 'SWIFT and the Vulnerability of Transatlantic Data Transfers', *International Review of Law, Computers and Technology*, vol 22, 2008, pp 191–202.

[150] The Commission has already tabled a proposal for an EU PNR system—for details, see ch 5.

option and a system which has been much criticised and whose necessity and compatibility with fundamental rights is far from proven.

D. Agreements by EU Bodies

A further aspect of EU external action in criminal matters involves the conclusion of international agreements in the field not by the EU as such, but by EU third pillar bodies such as Eurojust and Europol. Unlike the EU itself, these bodies have been endowed with legal personality by their founding secondary law instruments.[151] These instruments also provide with procedures for exchange of information with third countries for Europol[152] and Eurojust.[153] This legal framework has enabled the conclusion of international agreements between these bodies and third countries. Unlike the EU third pillar agreements, an assessment of adequacy of data protection when agreements involve the exchange of personal data is provided for.[154] The majority of the existing agreements involve former or current candidate countries and Schengen associates. Third countries not falling into these categories include Canada (for Europol) and the United States (for both Europol and Eurojust).[155] It is again in the context of co-operation with the United States that concerns regarding the consistency of EU external action with internal standards have been raised, most notably regarding co-operation involving the exchange of personal data, in particular as regards Europol.

[151] Europol Convention, Art 26(1) (OJ C316, 27 November 1995); Eurojust Decision, Art 1 (OJ L63, 6 March 2002, 1).

[152] Art 18 of the Europol Convention allows Europol to communicate personal data to third states and bodies if it is necessary for preventing and combating criminal offences falling within Europol's remit and the third State or body offers an adequate level of data protection. On the basis of Art 18(2), the Council adopted in 1999 an Act setting out the rules governing the transmission of personal data to third States and bodies. This provides a procedure for the negotiation and conclusion of agreements between Europol and third countries. The agreements are negotiated by the Director of Europol and conclusion is not permitted prior to the Europol Joint Supervisory Body on data protection giving a non-binding Opinion. The Act was amended in 2002 (OJ C76, 27 March 2002, p 1).

[153] Art 27 of the Eurojust Decision provides for a similar mechanism. Its rules were supplemented by the Eurojust Rules of Procedure on the processing and protection of personal data (OJ C68, 19 March 2005, p 1). Art 28(1) of the Rules states that Eurojust 'shall endeavour to put in place co-operation agreements containing suitable provisions regarding exchange of personal data with all partners with whom exchanges of data take place on a regular basis'. Art 28(2) adds that Eurojust shall only transfer personal data to a third country if it is subject to the 1981 Council of Europe data protection Convention or when an adequate level of protection is ensur(ed) According to Art 28(3), the decision concerning transfers to non-parties to the 1981 Convention will be taken by the national members involved, on the basis of an adequacy assessment by the Eurojust Data Protection Officer. In case of difficulties, the Officer must consult the JSB before making an assessment on a specific transfer. However, it is not clear that the Data Protection Officer's assessment is binding to the national member. See V Mitsilegas, 'Judicial Co-operation in Criminal Matters between the EU and third states: International Agreements', in M Leaf (ed), *Cross-border Crime*, London, JUSTICE, 2006, pp 79–92.

[154] Agreements by Europol can be distinguished between those involving the exchange of personal data and those involving the exchange of strategic information.

[155] Note that Europol has also concluded an agreement on the exchange of personal data with Interpol. For details and texts of Agreements concluded by Europol and Eurojust see www.europol.europa.eu/index.asp?page=agreements and www.eurojust.europa.eu/official_documents/eju_ agreements.htm respectively.

Calls for an agreement between Europol and the US were made immediately after 9/11, by the JHA Council of 20 September 2001. Authorisation to enter into negotiations with the US was given to the Director of Europol at the December 2001 JHA Council, with the Agreement eventually signed at the end of 2002.[156] Unsurprisingly, the central difficulty in the negotiations was to ascertain the adequacy of data protection in the US, which was compounded by the reportedly rigid stance of US negotiators.[157] Negotiations went on with minimum transparency, with the text unveiled for scrutiny for national parliaments only shortly before the designated signature date which was presented as a matter of urgency. The European Parliament has no scrutiny role in such agreements. The Europol Joint Supervisory Body, which initially had reservations regarding the level of data protection in the US, eventually lifted these reservations. The ensuing Agreement[158] allows for the exchange of data for a wide range of offences and beyond[159] and for the transfer of Europol data to a wide range of US authorities (including at the local level), but also to third states. Significant concerns therefore arise regarding the compliance of such an agreement with internal EU privacy standards, but also regarding the creation of 'double standards translated into more favourable standards for US authorities in comparison with their counterparts in EU Member States.[160] These concerns remain valid in the light of reports highlighting a number of problems arising from the practical implementation of the Agreement (and questioning its added value)[161] and will be tested in the context of current negotiations for agreements between Europol and other third countries, including Russia.[162]

[156] For details, see Mitsilegas, 'The New EU–USA Cooperation', n 66 above.

[157] ibid. It has been argued that this was due to the fact that the US already had bilateral agreements with all Member States thus the added value of the particular agreement was for them limited.

[158] The Agreement was accompanied by an exchange of letters between the parties and has not been published in the Official Journal (the text can be found on the Europol website).

[159] Including, according to the Exchange of Letters, information pertaining to immigration investigations and proceedings, and to those relating to *in rem* or *in personam* seizure or restraint and confiscation of assets that finance terrorism or form the instrumentalities or proceeds of crime, even where such seizure, restraint or confiscation is not based on a criminal conviction.

[160] At present, Europol data are communicated directly to a limited number of national contact points—however, according to the Europol/USA Agreement a wide range of US authorities may have access to such data.

[161] See Council doc. 11502/05, Brussels, 27 July 2005, on the mutual evaluation of the co-operation agreements between Europol and the US. The report notes the fundamentally different structural approaches to the work of the law enforcement authorities concerned. It is noteworthy that Europol makes a significantly higher number of requests to the US than it receives and that any added value that Europol can provide is either not perceived by the US authorities or is deemed outweighed by the benefits of direct bilateral co-operation with Member States—for the US, relations with Europol were never intended to replace bilateral relations with the Member States. It is also noted that US authorities anticipated that Europol would not make requests on behalf of Member States, but rather provide analysis—whereas Europol believes that it can represent Member States without liaison officers in the US and provide co-ordination.

[162] Along with these formal avenues of co-operation, it should be reminded that both Europol and Eurojust have established a number of informal channels of co-operation, evidenced mainly by the posting of officers of third countries (in particular the US) in these bodies' headquarters in The Hague, and by the move to open Europol's Analysis Work Files to third country analysts—see ch 4.

V. THE UNION AND INTERNATIONAL ORGANISATIONS

Another form of Union external action with implications for criminal law involves the relationship of the Union with international organisations. This can take the form of common positions in the negotiations and becoming party (to the extent that there is Community competence) to international (in particular multilateral) Conventions in criminal matters—with UN and Council of Europe Conventions being prime examples in this context. At the same time, standards adopted in international instruments and bodies can have an influence in internal Community and Union law—both by being copied or followed in internal legislation, and by influencing the interpretation of internal law by the Court of Justice.[163] The cross-pillar character of external action in criminal matters can be discerned in all these instances.

A. The Union and Multilateral Treaties on Criminal Matters

A major instrument in this context has been the United Nations Convention on Transnational Organised Crime, signed at Palermo in 2000, and its Protocols.[164] The Council adopted in 1999 (on the basis of the Maastricht third pillar Article K.3 TEU) a Joint Position aiming at co-ordinating as far as practicable Member States' positions in the Convention negotiations and ensuring that the Convention is consistent with pre-existing Community and Union law standards—in particular with regard to the criminalisation of organised crime, anti-money laundering and confiscation standards .[165] Parts of the Convention dealt with first pillar, Community law issues (such as anti-money laundering standards), while others belonged to the third pillar. For that reason, the Community decided to conclude the Convention, by declaring exactly which areas of the latter the Community has competence upon.[166] The Declaration of competence takes into account the potential future development of Community law to cover matters originally not included therein.[167] Such developments have already taken place via the third Money Laundering Directive, which introduced in the first pillar provisions such

[163] Both the Union's contribution to the adoption of international standards and the implementation at Union level of international commitments are central elements of the EU Action Plan on combating terrorism—for the revised plan see Council doc 7233/1/07 REV 1, Brussels, 29 March 2007.

[164] For an analysis, see D McClean, *Transnational Organized Crime: A Commentary on the UN Convention and its Protocols*, Oxford, Oxford University Press, 2007.

[165] OJ L87, 31 March 1999, p 1. According to the Joint Position, the Commission would be 'fully associated' with such co-ordination efforts (notwithstanding the fact that a number of issues fall within the third pillar). See also C Rijken and V Kronenberger, 'The United Nations Convention against Transnational Organised Crime and the European Union', in Kronenberger, n 58 above, pp 481–517.

[166] Council Decision on the conclusion, on behalf of the European Community, of the United Nations Convention against Transnational Organised Crime, OJ L261, 6 August 2004, p 69. For the Declaration of competence, see p 115.

[167] The Declaration will be completed or amended if necessary to take account of developments.

as the regulation of financial intelligence units, and by further Community legislation covering the monitoring of funds transfer.[168] Similar Declaration of competence followed the conclusion by the Community of the Convention Protocols.[169] In the light of the recent debate regarding the extent of Community competence in criminal matters, the content of such Declarations in the external field obtains additional significance and may not be devoid of controversy.[170]

Of greater intensity has been the co-operation between the Union and the Council of Europe in criminal matters. For reasons of overlapping membership of the organisations (and in the light of the Union's enlargement and neighbourhood objectives) adoption of Council of Europe standards in criminal matters—combined with co-operation in the areas of evaluation and monitoring—have been central to the Union's strategy (in particular regarding the candidate countries). Moreover, standards adopted in Council of Europe Conventions (such as the 1990 Money Laundering Convention) have been incorporated in internal Community law (such as legislation on confiscation and money laundering) and have provided a reference point by which Member States have to comply thus extending the ambit of the prohibition of money laundering and the reach of confiscation provisions.[171] In this manner, Council of Europe benchmarks have proven to be very influential in the development and implementation of Union internal criminal law.[172]

Notwithstanding this close co-operation, relations between the Council of Europe and the European Union in criminal matters have been under some strain recently. The reason has been the insistence of the Union on inserting so-called disconnection clauses in a series of recent Council of Europe Conventions in criminal matters.[173] These clauses state essentially that parties to the Conventions

---

[168] On such developments, see V Mitsilegas and B Gilmore, 'The EU Legislative Framework Against Money Laundering and Terrorist Finance: A Critical Analysis in the Light of Evolving Global Standards', *International and Comparative Law Quarterly*, vol 56, 2007, pp 119–141. The Declaration referred specifically to FIUs and cash movements.

[169] See for instance the two Decisions on the conclusion of the smuggling Protocol—two separate Decisions were adopted to take into account the different legal bases in TEC with respect to different areas of competence (179 and 181a TEC—OJ L262, 22 September 2006, p 24; and Title IV TEC—OJ L262, 22 September 2006, p 34).

[170] See for instance the debate over the content of the Declaration of Community competence regarding the smuggling Protocol—see Council document 5535/2/06, Brussels 16 February 2006, showing Member States' objections.

[171] See Mitsilegas and Gilmore, n 168 above.

[172] It is indicative in this context that the Report by the EU Counter-terrorism Co-ordinator on the implementation of the EU counter-terrorism Action Plan includes a scoreboard indicating the state of play with regard to the Union implementation of Council of Europe (and UN) agreements—see doc 9416/08 ADD 1 REV 1, Brussels, 26 May 2008.

[173] These include the 2005 Conventions on terrorism, money laundering and human trafficking and the very recent 2007 Convention on the sexual exploitation of children. For details, see M. Smrkolj, 'The Use of the "Disconnection Clause" in International Treaties: What does it Tell us about the EC/EU as an Actor in the Sphere of Public International Law?', downloaded from the Social Science Research Network site, www.ssrn.com/abstract=1133002; for a background on disconnection clauses in Council of Europe Conventions, see J Polakiewicz, *Treaty-Making in the Council of Europe*, Council of Europe Publishing, 1999, pp 68–70; on the use of disconnection clauses by the EU in general, see J Klabbers, 'Safeguarding the Organizational *Acquis*: The EU's External Practice', *International Organizations Law Review*, 2007, pp 57–89 at pp 70–71.

which are Union members will apply in their mutual relations Community and Union rules on the matter covered by the Convention.[174] Disconnection clauses are justified by the Community as necessary to take into account the Union's institutional structure and mean that Member States cannot invoke and apply the rights and obligations of the Conventions directly among themselves.[175] However, they have provoked reactions by other Council of Europe members, who fear that they could lead to the Union falling short of the standards accepted at Council of Europe level[176] and have led to calls by the Council of Europe for them to be replaced by 'modulation clauses' making it clear that the EU Member States are to abide by Council of Europe Conventions.[177]

The debate over disconnection clauses may reflect a broader scepticism on behalf of the Council of Europe regarding the expanding size and role of the Union in traditional areas of Council of Europe action such as criminal law. The very insertion of disconnection clauses however, raises important issues regarding external action competence for the Community. As the Court of Justice noted in its Opinion on the Lugano Convention[178] disconnection clauses—which are designed to ensure compliance with Community law and avoid conflicts between different legal orders—may not necessarily guarantee that internal Community rules are not affected—but on the contrary, they may provide an indication that these rules are affected.[179] This may hint at the assertion of possible exclusive competence for the Community in the area which is potentially affected.[180]

B. The Union and International Bodies Generating Criminal Law—The Example of the Financial Action Task Force (FATF)

The past two decades witnessed a plethora of legislative and regulatory instruments aimed at countering a newly perceived global threat—that of money laundering. An unprecedented normative production of global standards took place, largely the outcome of a broad political consensus and synergies between the global, regional and national level. The motor in the development of global standards has been the Financial Action Task Force, an ad hoc, sui generis body based at (but not forming part of) the OECD. FATF membership consists mainly of rich, industrialised countries. It adopts global anti-money-laundering standards which

[174] See for instance Art 52(4) of the 2005 Money Laundering Convention.
[175] See for instance the Declaration by the Community and Member States annexed to the 2005 Money Laundering Convention.
[176] See the Report by J -C Juncker, Council of Europe–European Union: 'A Sole Ambition for the European Continent', Strasbourg 11 April 2006.
[177] Council of Europe Parliamentary Assembly, Recommendation 1743 (2006).
[178] Opinion 1/03, ECR [2006] I-1145.
[179] Para 130 of the Opinion. See the analysis in Cremona, *External Relations*, n 111 above.
[180] However, as Cremona rightly notes, the Lugano Opinion 'should not be regarded as opening the door to a new wider reading of the scope of exclusivity'. As she notes, the field covered by the Lugano Convention is very specific and governed by an extensive Community legal regime. The situation may be different with Community law touching upon criminal law.

are revised regularly—with the centrepiece being the 40 FATF Recommendations on money laundering, first published in 1990 and subsequently revised. These have been complemented by specific Recommendations on terrorist finance. FATF members are called to implement the Recommendations—which are the outcome of policy and technical discussion largely shielded from public debate or democratic scrutiny—and the FATF reaches beyond its members, by spreading standards primarily via regional. FATF-style bodies. Compliance is achieved by rigorous monitoring and evaluation.[181]

The European Union is represented in this highly influential organisation by the European Commission and 15 Member States which are members.[182] FATF action, in particular the 40 Recommendations, have been the basis upon which Community and Union anti-money laundering activity has evolved. Thus far the Community has adopted 3 Directives on money laundering (and a series of other measures including on confiscation and cash movements) which have been justified on the basis of the need to comply with FATF requirements and incorporate FATF produced standards in Community law.[183] This has happened as early as 1991 (pre Maastricht) with the first Money Laundering Directive, parts of which were adopted notwithstanding the debate over the existence and extent of a Community law competence in criminal matters.[184] The Community has similarly taken forward FATF anti-money-laundering standards in the face of constitutional objections recently in the third Money Laundering Directive (which includes provisions on the largely police-style financial intelligence units) and a Regulation on the monitoring of cash movements.[185] Moreover, the Community adopted a highly controversial FATF imperative in domestic Community law, namely the imposition of obligations on lawyers under certain conditions to report suspicions of their clients to the relevant authorities—something that arguably poses a significant challenge to the right of fair trial but also to the administration of justice more broadly.[186] The uncritical introduction in the Union legal order of standards challenging fundamental rights produced by an elite body with little transparency in its work (under the justification of the need to comply with such standards which is taken for granted) raises important issues of legitimacy and rule of law. As will be seen below, a similar pattern can be discerned with

---

[181] On the FATF, see B Gilmore, *Dirty Money*, 3rd edn, Council of Europe Publishing, 2004; see also V Mitsilegas, 'International Regulation of Money Laundering and Terrorist Finance' in I Bantekas and G Keramidas (eds), *International and European Financial Criminal Law*, London, Butterworths, 2006, pp 41–64.

[182] This raises issues of double standards with regard to the EU Member States which are not FATF members.

[183] For the most recent examples, see Mitsilegas and Gilmore, n 168 above.

[184] See Mitsilegas, *Money Laundering Counter-measures*, n 5 above. As far as the prohibition of money laundering was concerned, the Directive also incorporated the approach taken by the 1988 United Nations Convention on drug trafficking.

[185] On the legality issues raised by these developments, see Mitsilegas and Gilmore, n 168 above.

[186] See Mitsilegas, *Money Laundering Counter-measures*, n 5 above; see also the recent ECJ judgment on the matter, Case C-305/05, *Ordre des Barreaux Francophones et Germanophone and Others v Council*, ECR [2007] I-5305.

regard to the work of other international organs addressing the fight against terrorism.

C. International Standards in the Union Legal Order—The Security Council Resolutions

The UN Security Council has increasingly assumed a central role in promulgating counter-terrorism standards, most notably by establishing a Sanctions Committee.[187] A number of Security Council Resolutions were adopted aimed at ensuring the freezing of assets of individuals and entities designated by the Committee as being associated with Osama bin Laden.[188] The European Union implemented these Resolutions by CFSP Common Positions and EC Regulations (regularly updated to take into account developments in the UN Sanctions Committee designations).[189] Given the significant invasive effect of such measures on individuals, it is not surprising that the relevant Community/Union law has been challenged repeatedly before the Union courts. The first set of challenges resulted in the set of Court of First Instance judgments on *Yusuf*[190] and *Kadi.*[191] In these judgments the Court had to examine the legality of the adoption of Regulation 881/2002 which included the names of the applicants; and the compatibility of the Regulation with fundamental rights protection under Community law.[192] The Court found that the Regulation was adopted under the correct legal basis.[193] It also found that the only leeway for the Court to examine the compatibility of the Regulation with fundamental rights was to check indirectly the lawfulness not of the Regulation itself, but of the Security Council Resolutions in question with regard to *jus cogens*.[194] Since the Community institutions did not

[187] See R Foot, 'The United Nations, Counter Terrorism, and Human Rights: Institutional Adaptation and Embedded Ideas', *Human Rights Quarterly*, vol 29, 2007, pp 489–514; and E J Flynn, 'The Security Council's Counter-Terrorism Committee and Human Rights', *Human Rights Law Review*, vol 7, 2007, pp 371–384.

[188] See initial Resolutions 1267 (1999) and 1333 (2000) and their subsequent amending Resolutions.

[189] For a concise and clear background, see J Helikoski, Case-note on *Ayadi, Common Market Law Review*, vol 44, 2007, pp 1143–1157 at pp 1145–1147.

[190] Case T-306/01, *Yusuf and Al Barakaat International Foundation v Council and Commission* [2005] ECR II-3533.

[191] Case T-315/01, *Kadi v Council and Commission* [2005] ECR II-3649. Both cases are currently on appeal to the Court of Justice.

[192] For details see inter alia: P Eeckhout, 'Community Terrorism Listings, Fundamental Rights, and UN Security Council Resolutions. In Search of the Right Fit', *European Constitutional Law Review*, vol 3, 2007, pp 183–206; case note by Tomuschat, *Common Market Law Review*, vol 43, 2006, pp 537–551; N Lavranos, 'Judicial Review of UN Sanctions by the Court of First Instance', *European Foreign Affairs Review*, vol 11, 2006, pp 471–490; C Eckes, 'Judicial Review of European Anti-Terrorism Measures—The *Yusuf* and *Kadi* Judgments of the Court of First Instance', *European Law Journal*, vol 14, no 1, 2008, pp 74–92; and P Stangos and G Gryllos, 'Le droit communautaire à l'épreuve des réalités du droit international: lecons tirées de la jurisprudence communautaire récente relevant de la lutte contre le terrorisme international', in *Cahiers du droit européen*, 2006, pp 429–481.

[193] Arts 60, 301 and 308 TEC.

[194] Para 277, *Yusuf*; para 226, *Kadi*.

have any autonomous discretion in implementing such Resolutions, the Court could not review the Community Regulation on the basis of the general principles of Community law relating to the protection of fundamental rights. This would amount to a review of the Security Council resolutions per se and would be incompatible with international and Community law.

The Court of First Instance adopted the same stance regarding the intensity of the review in the subsequent cases of *Ayadi*[195] and *Hasan*.[196] The Court there went slightly further than the earlier cases by stating that the individuals concerned had a right to address the Sanctions Committee through their national authorities in order either to be removed from the list of persons affected by the sanctions or to obtain exemption from the freezing of funds—and such right is also guaranteed by the Community legal order.[197] However, the Court of First Instance adopted a more protective stance regarding judicial protection in the recent judgment of *O.M.P.I.*[198] The Court annulled a Council Decision implementing UN and EC restrictive measure requirements on the grounds of breach of the applicant's right to a fair hearing, absence of an adequate statement of reasons in the Decision, and infringement of the right to a legal protection. The decisive factor differentiating this case to the earlier ones is that here the Union institutions had a higher degree of discretion as to the content of the EC measure in question.[199]

The implementation of the UN Resolutions in the Union legal order presented a number of dilemmas regarding both the extent of Community and Union competence to accommodate such international standards internally,[200] and the extent to which the Community/Union could diverge from the content of the UN requirements in order to protect fundamental rights by upholding the internal Union standards of human rights protection.[201] The approach of the Court in *Kadi* and *Ayadi* can be criticised in disregarding not only the level of fundamental rights protection in the Union legal order, but also the autonomy and special features of this legal order.[202] By adopting external legal standards without any extensive (and arguably meaningful—since the *jus cogens* standard is very high) review on the basis of fundamental EU legal principles, the internal EU legal order may be 'contaminated' by externally imposed standards which offer a lower level of protection and contradict the internal standards. The Court may have tried to appear taking

---

[195] Case T-253/02, *Chafiq Ayadi v Council*, ECR [2006] II-2139.
[196] Case T-49/04, *Faraj Hassan v Council and Commission*, ECR [2006] II-0052.
[197] See the analysis of Helikoski, n 189 above, pp 1151–1152.
[198] Case T-228/02, *O.M.P.I. v Council*, ECR [2006] II-4665.
[199] Paras 100–102 of the judgment. For an analysis, and a comparison with *Kadi* and *Ayadi* see Helikoski, n 189 above, pp 1155–1157.
[200] On the CFI legality choice, see in particular the comments by Cremona, *External Relations*, n 111 above,
[201] See in this context J Almqvist, 'A Human Rights Critique of European Judicial Review: Counter-Terrorism Sanctions', *International and Comparative Law Quarterly*, vol 57, 2008, pp 303–331.
[202] For critical views, see also: Eeckhout, n 192 above; Helikoski, n 189 above; Cremona, *External Relations*, n 111 above; Lavranos, n 192 above; and 'UN Sanctions and Judicial Review', *Nordic Journal of International Law*, vol 76, 2007, pp 1–17. For a contrary view, see Tomuschat, n 192 above.

seriously its own—and the Union's—international security responsibilities[203], but its rulings leave much to be desired in terms of protection of fundamental rights and features of the Union legal order.

VI. THE FUTURE IN THE LIGHT OF LISBON

The Lisbon Treaty addresses some of the concerns arising from the lack of transparency and democratic control in the negotiation of international agreements falling currently under the third pillar. It leaves a number of outstanding issues: for instance, procedures for external action of EU bodies such as Europol and Eurojust are not in principle changed (although some extra layers of scrutiny of these bodies in general are provided for); issues like counter-terrorism may remain 'cross-pillar' (with foreign policy having its own distinct provisions); and the impact of a potential UK 'opt-out' from criminal matters on EU external action in the field remains to be seen. However, the Lisbon Treaty also brings about significant simplification and transparency. With the Union having legal personality[204] and the third pillar in principle abolished,[205] the process of negotiating and adopting international agreements becomes largely 'communitarised': in criminal matters, in principle the Commission will negotiate on the basis of a mandate given by the Council, which will adopt the decision after obtaining the consent of the European Parliament.[206] However, limits have been introduced to EU criminal law competence in the context of external action: the attribution of legal personality 'will not in any way authorise the Union to legislate or to act beyond the competences conferred upon it by the Member States in the Treaties';[207] and Member States may still continue to negotiate and conclude agreements with third countries in criminal matters in so far as such agreements comply with Union law.[208]

But perhaps the greatest impact that the Lisbon Treaty may have on the Union's external action in criminal matters is its emphasis on the Union's values. These include respect for human dignity, freedom, and the rule of law and fundamental rights[209]; and the promotion of such values is one of the primary

---

[203] See in this context M. Nettesheim, 'U.N. Sanctions against Individuals—A Challenge to the Architecture of European Union Governance', *Common Market Law Review*, vol 44, 2007, pp 567–600 at p 584.

[204] Art 47 TEU.

[205] See ch 1.

[206] Art 218 TFEU. According to Art 218(6)(a)(v), the consent of the European Parliament is required for agreements covering fields to which the ordinary legislative procedure applies—this is the case post-Lisbon with EU criminal law measures, in particular measures on mutual recognition and judicial co-operation in criminal matters and harmonisation of substantive criminal law and criminal procedure—for details, see ch 1.

[207] Declaration 24 concerning the legal personality of the Union.

[208] Declaration 36 on Art 218 TFEU concerning the negotiation and conclusion of international agreements by Member States relating to the area of freedom, security and justice.

[209] Art 2 TEU.

Union objectives.[210] Moreover, the values of the Union are the foundation of the relationship of the Union with its neighbours[211] and respect for the Union values and a commitment to promoting them is a prerequisite for application for EU membership.[212] The emphasis on values is reiterated in the specific chapter on external action—where it is stated that the Union's external action will be guided 'by the principles which have inspired its own creation, development and enlargement, and which it seeks to advance in the wider world'—including to a great extent the values included in Article 2 of the Treaty (but also the principles of the UN Charter and international law)[213]—with the Union aiming at safeguarding its values in external action.[214] The transformational potential of these provisions—which emphasise the proactive role of the Union to safeguard and promote its values in the international scene—for all aspects of the Union's external action in criminal matters is significant.[215] Such potential will depend, of course, on the direction and content of internal Union criminal law, which is bound to expand both via legislation and via judicial interpretation.

VII. CONCLUSION: THE QUEST FOR COHERENCE IN EU EXTERNAL ACTION

European Union external action in criminal matters has been developing rapidly and on a number of levels. In the light of this rapid development, a key challenge for the Union is the achievement of coherence. Coherence in this context can be viewed from two perspectives: coherence between the different aspects of EU external action, and coherence between EU internal and external action in criminal matters. With regard to the first aspect (coherence between the different areas of EU external action in criminal matters), the Union institutions have been attempting to place these multifaceted areas as far as possible within a single policy framework. For that purpose, in 2005 the Commission proposed[216] and the Justice and Home Affairs Council adopted a so-called 'strategy for the external dimension of Justice and Home Affairs'.[217] The Council confirmed areas and mechanisms of strategic focus in the field (including enlargement, European Neighbourhood Policy, co-operation with the US and Russia and work with

---

[210] Art 3(1) TEU.

[211] Art 8(1) TEU states that the Union will develop 'a special relationship with neighbouring countries, aiming to establish an area of prosperity and good neighbourliness, founded on the values of the Union and characterised by close and peaceful relations based on cooperation'.

[212] Art 49 TEU.

[213] Art 21 (1) TEU.

[214] Art 21(2)(a) TEU.

[215] This is in particular the case in the light of the emphasis of Lisbon on the protection of fundamental rights by recognising the EU Charter of Fundamental Rights as legally binding (Art 6(1) TEU) but also, in a significant development for EU external action in the field, by providing an express legal basis for the accession of the Union to the ECHR (Art 6(2) TEU).

[216] COM (2005) 491 final, Brussels, 12 October 2005.

[217] Council doc 15446/05, Brussels, 6 December 2005.

regional groupings and international organisations).[218] It also developed a series of 'underlying principles' of EU external action in Justice and Home Affairs, which include partnership with third countries, but also a differentiated and flexible approach to individual third countries and regions.[219] However, these attempts at external coherence may disregard the differences in the nature and characteristics of the various levels of EU external action in the field. They also sit at odds with the significant institutional fragmentation in internal EU criminal law action produced by the persistence of the pillars, which as has been demonstrated in this chapter trigger a number of constitutional dilemmas for the Union. These cross-pillarisation dilemmas are ongoing,[220] and are likely to persist even if the Lisbon Treaty enters into force.[221]

The question of coherence between internal Union values, objectives and standards and external action arises on a number of occasions: in instances when the Union is exporting its own standards; when it co-operates on a perceived equal footing with third States; and when it is called to incorporate, in its internal legal order, standards agreed in international organisations. Coherence is important for two main reasons: one is the content of the projected identity of the Union in the international scene; and the other is the potential effect of standards agreed externally on internal Union law. In the field of criminal law (and given the rapid development of the internal Union *acquis* in the field), in both instances, the impact that external action can have on the protection of fundamental rights and the upholding of the rule of law both outside and inside the Union cannot be stressed enough. In this context, the Union can be criticised in compromising to some extent its internal standards on the protection of fundamental rights and criminal law in order to achieve broader political objectives such as enlargement or good relations with its neighbours. It can also be criticised for uncritically imposing standards agreed on the international level (sometimes by procedures marked by a lack of transparency, such as in the FATF or the UN Security Council) on the Union legal order, without sufficient regard for fundamental principles of such legal order. Moreover, concerns are raised by instances where the Union has allowed internal Union standards to be compromised in order to reach agreement

---

[218] The Report on the implementation of the Justice and Home Affairs external strategy further refers to the development of geographical (but also thematic) priorities for external action (Council document 15001/06, Brussels, 20 November 2006). These are also reflected in the recently adopted second progress Report, Council doc. 9391/08, Brussels, 21 May 2008.

[219] For further details, see V Mitsilegas, 'The External Dimension of EU Action in Criminal Matters', *European Foreign Affairs Review*, vol 12, 2007, pp 457–497.

[220] These issues continue to arise in cross-pillar policy areas such as border security, which led to the ECJ ruling in the PNR case. A similar case may arise in the context of the current visa waiver negotiations between the EU and the US. A 'twin-track' approach was agreed between the EU and the US regarding discussions, with the Commission discussing with the US matters under EU responsibility, and Member States discussing issues under their responsibility (Justice and Home Affairs Council of 18 April 2008), or matters concerning the movement of EU citizens to a third country (with Title IV TEC currently covering EU measures regarding *the EU external border*).

[221] This is the case in particular with regard to the EU Counter-terrorism Coordinator, a post located largely within the framework of the second pillar (which largely retains its intergovernmental elements post-Lisbon)—for details on the Coordinator, see ch 4.

with third States (such as the US), even at instances where the added value of international co-operation in the agreed form is not self-evident—with agreement on the side of the Union at times looking largely like an end in itself.[222] These criticisms are exacerbated by the current lack of transparency and the extremely limited democratic scrutiny and debate on Union external action, in particular the conclusion of international agreements. Agreements such as the EU–US extradition and mutual legal assistance and PNR have been reached in the face of staunch opposition by the European Parliament and national parliament as well as civil society. It remains to be seen whether this will change if the Treaty of Lisbon enters into force.

[222] These concerns are reinforced by recent attempts to import much criticised standards negotiated in external action into the EU legal order (with the PNR example being characteristic in this context).

Conclusion

Is Criminal Law a Special Case in the
EU Legal Order?

NUMBER OF RECURRING themes emerge in the discussion of the development and content of EU criminal law. The first such theme, permeating all aspects of the evolution of criminal law at Union level, is *sovereignty*. Criminal law is deemed by EU Member States to be linked to a lesser or greater extent with their sovereignty and capacity to impose power. At the same time, and because of the impact of criminalisation and punishment on the individual and society as a whole, criminal law is the outcome of negotiated solutions at national level, circumscribing the parameters of the relationship between the individual and the State. The acceptance by citizens of the democratically negotiated powers of the State in criminal matters grants *legitimacy* to State power, which in turn reinforces sovereignty translated into the capacity of the State to impose power.[1] It comes thus as no surprise that the prospect of the transfer of power in the criminal law field from the State to the Union level has been met with consistent and considerable resistance by Member States, with sovereignty concerns being at the heart of every single attempted step to bring criminal law within the realm of the European Union. The most commonly discussed aspect of such resistance is the limits to the powers of EU institutions, as reflected in the provisions of the especially created third pillar, which have led to considerable shortcomings in terms of the democratic scrutiny and judicial control of EU criminal law. However, as has been demonstrated throughout this book and will be further highlighted in this conclusion, resistance to the transfer of power from the national to the Union level as regards criminal law—in particular the adoption of uniform or highly harmonised criminal law—has taken the form of a number of other measures transcending the traditional third pillar institutional limits.

One such aspect of resistance to the transfer of powers from the national to the Union level has been the reluctance of Member States towards criminal law harmonisation. Member States have gone for the route of mutual recognition instead, both in the field of judicial co-operation in criminal matters, but also more recently in the field of police co-operation in particular via measures premised

---

[1] See also in this context my earlier analysis in V Mitsilegas, *Money Laundering Counter-measures in the European Union. A New Paradigm of Security Governance versus Fundamental Legal Principles*, The Hague, Kluwer Law International, 2003, in particular pp 58–59.

upon the principle of availability. At first sight, mutual recognition seems less threatening to State sovereignty than harmonisation: governments do not have to negotiate (and explain to their citizens) commonly negotiated EU standards, and ultimately do not have to change their substantive criminal law to implement Union law. However, as has been repeatedly highlighted in this book, mutual recognition may have far-reaching consequences for both the internal coherence of domestic criminal justice an constitutional systems, and for the protection of the rights of the individual. In this context, mutual recognition brings into the fore the second major theme of EU criminal law, *territoriality*. It is *national* criminal justice systems which have to interact under umbrella Union instruments, on the basis of mutual trust and maximum automaticity. This push towards co-operation on these terms is reinforced by the reconfiguration of territoriality in the European Union, in particular the Schengen area. The concept of a borderless 'area' of freedom, security and justice is key in this context. This has led to significant steps towards developing principles of EU criminal law by the Court of Justice, as reflected in particular in its mutual recognition and *ne bis in idem* case law. A certain paradox can be discerned here: the Court did not feel constrained from developing EU criminal law principles by the fact that there has not been prior harmonisation of criminal law across the EU; but such harmonisation was exactly to be avoided by Member States' choice of mutual recognition as a form of action. Key concepts of criminal law and justice are thus being redefined by judges and not legislation in a Union with no borders but still consisting of States.

It is in the absence of legislative intervention that the link between mutual recognition and the third common theme in the development of EU criminal law, namely *democracy, transparency* and *legitimacy* appears most prominently. As mentioned above, mutual recognition does not entail a discussion on harmonised standards of criminal law or a change in domestic substantive criminal law that can be seen as the outcome of top–down EU harmonisation. Rather, an authority in one Member State must respond positively to a request from a similar authority by another Member State with a minimum of formality. This leads, however, to what I have called a 'journey into the unknown', both by the requested authority and, it is submitted, for the citizens in the executing Member State: they have to accept a request stemming from the criminal justice and constitutional system of another Member State, the standards of which are not clear and have not been debated in the executing Member State. This export of territoriality raises thus serious issues of democracy, transparency and legitimacy of EU criminal law, in particular in the light of the reconfiguration of the relationship between the citizen and the State as criminal law provide they entail. Similar issues, along with the more accentuated theme of *accountability*, arise in the context of the development of European integration in criminal matters by EU bodies and databases. Similarly to mutual recognition, EU action in the field reflects the twin desire of Member States to on the one hand boost their enforcement capacity via enhanced EU action, while on the other maintaining as far as possible their sovereignty in criminal matters. This has led to a situation whereby EU bodies and databases with a far-reaching enforcement potential have been established, but their functions and powers (in particular in the case of EU bodies) are constantly contested. Moreover, these powers are not matched by adequate mechanisms of scrutiny and accountability, hampered to a great extent by the wish of Member States to shield EU bodies and databases from the control of EU institutions. In this context, the very choice of boosting integration in criminal matters via specific EU bodies and databases can be seen as signifying an increasing trend towards the depoliticisation of EU action in criminal matters, and the avoidance of transparency and debate with regard to the proliferation of enforcement mechanisms at EU level.

The emphasis on EU criminal law as an enforcement tool inevitably leads to the fourth major theme, which is of course related to *security* and the *protection of fundamental rights*. Even a cursory examination of the content of the EU legislative production in criminal matters thus far would lead to the following conclusions: that EU criminal law focuses predominantly on enforcement, with limited space for the protection of fundamental rights; and that a great part of EU criminal law is 'emergency law', its adoption speeded up and justified as a response to terrorism. In the 'area of freedom, security and justice, security is prominent and confirmed as Member States' priority in both the activist role of the European Council and the measures eventually adopted—with the two flagship protective measures tabled by the Commission (on defence rights and data protection) proven extremely difficult to adopt. 'Emergency law' has further led to boosting enforcement action across the board, by justifying as counter-terrorism measures instruments applying to a wide range of crimes (such as the European Arrest Warrant and the Eurojust Decision, as well as a wide range of police measures mounting a massive challenge to the protection of the individual in particular with regard to privacy). This emphasis on the rhetoric of counter-terrorism and security has also led to a boost in the Union's external action in criminal matters, exemplified by the conclusion of a series of enforcement agreements with the USA. EU external action in criminal matters not only raises a series of fundamental rights concerns, but also brings to the fore the broader, existential question of European *identity* and *values* as the compatibility of the Union's external action with the—already highly securitised—internal action in criminal matters is questionable.

The emphasis on security, along with the centrality of sovereignty in the development of EU criminal law brings us to the question that permeates a great part of this book: is criminal law a special case in the EU legal order? Answers to this question seem to depend on the actors involved. In examining issues of competence, and in the face of fierce opposition by a great number of Member States, the Court of Justice has answered the question in the negative: criminal law is just another field of law which can be deployed to achieve Community objectives. The Court has also repeatedly subordinated criminal law to Community/Union law, and did not hesitate to transfer Community law principles to the third pillar. The Court's stance leads to the fifth major theme in EU criminal law, namely *the transformation of criminal law* in an 'area' of freedom, security and justice. This transformation may come as quite a shock to both governments concerned about their loss of sovereignty as well as scholars used to viewing criminal law from a purely domestic perspective. In a rapidly growing field, this transformation is ongoing and the full impact on domestic and Union criminal law is not yet crystallised. Important insights for the future can again be discerned from the Luxembourg case law, with for instance criminal law and related fundamental rights principles (such as the principle of legality and *ne bis in idem*) being transformed into *Community/Union* law principles in the context of EU criminal law. The entry into force of the Lisbon Treaty promises to intensify the debate on the future of EU criminal law, with new legislation likely to be adopted, the role of the EU institutions changing and at the same the emphasis on the national level in the scrutiny of EU criminal law boosted. In this context, the enhanced debate, scrutiny and examination required to assess the future transformation of EU criminal law and the fundamental constitutional issues it entails may prove to be a significant step towards another transformation, that of the EU from a market to a *demos*.

Bibliography

Adam, S, 'Quelques réflexions sur les relations entre les procédures *a priori* et *a posteriori* d'examen de compatibilité des accords communautaires suite á l'affaire dite de l'accord PNR', *Cahiers de droit européen*, vol 42, 2006, pp 659–96.

Albors-Llorens, A, 'Changes in the Jurisdiction of the European Court of Justice under the Treaty of Amsterdam', *Common Market Law Review*, vol 35, 1998, pp 1273–94.

Albrecht, P-A and S Braum, 'Deficiencies in the Development of European Criminal Law', *European Law Journal*, vol 5, 1999, pp 293–310.

Alegre, S and M Leaf, 'Mutual Recognition in European Judicial Co-operation: A Step Too Far Too Soon? Case Study—The European Arrest Warrant', *European Law Journal*, vol 10, no 2, 2004, pp 200–17.

Alldridge, P, *Money Laundering Law*, Oxford, Hart Publishing, 2003.

Almqvist, J, 'A Human Rights Critique of European Judicial Review: Counter-Terrorism Sanctions', *International and Comparative Law Quarterly*, vol 57, 2008, pp 303–31.

Alston, P and O de Schutter (eds), *Monitoring Fundamental Rights in the EU: The Contribution of the Fundamental Rights Agency*, Oxford, Hart Publishing, 2005.

Anderson, M, M den Boer, P Cullen, W Gilmore, C Raab and N Walker, *Policing the European Union*, Oxford, Clarendon Press, 1995.

Armstrong, K, 'Mutual Recognition', in C Barnard and J Scott, *The Law of the Single European Market: Unpacking the Premises*, Oxford, Hart Publishing, 2002, pp 225–67.

Arnull, A, *The European Union and its Court of Justice*, 2nd edn, Oxford, OUP, 2006.

——, 'Taming the Beast? The Treaty of Amsterdam and the Court of Justice', in D O'Keeffe and P Twomey (eds), *Legal Issues of the Amsterdam Treaty*, Oxford, Hart Publishing, 1999, pp 109–22.

Assemblée Nationale, *Rapport d'information sur les consequences de l'arret de la Cour de Justice du 13 Septembre 2005*, 25 January 2006, Rapport No 2829.

Baldaccini, A, 'Counter-terrorism and the EU Strategy for Border Security: Framing Suspects with Biometric Documents and Databases', *European Journal of Migration and Law*, vol 10, 2008, pp 31–49.

Balzacq, T and S Carrera, 'The Hague Programme: The Long Road to Freedom, Security and Justice', in S Carrera and T Balzacq, *Security versus Freedom? A Challenge for Europe's Future*, Aldershot, Ashgate, 2006, pp 1–34.

Balzacq, T, D Bigo, S Carrera and E Guild, *Security and the Two-Level Game: The Treaty of Prum, the EU and the Management of Threats*, CEPS Working Document no 234, January 2006, www.ceps.be.

——, ——, ——, ——, 'The Treaty of Prüm and EC Treaty: Two Competing Models for EU Internal Security', in T Balzacq and S Carrera (eds), *Security versus Freedom? A Challenge for Europe's Future*, Aldershot, Ashgate, 2006, pp 115–36.

Barnard, C, *The Substantive Law of the EU. The Four Freedoms*, Oxford, OUP, 2004.

Barrett, G, 'Cooperation in Justice and Home Affairs in the European Union—An Overview and a Critique', in G Barrett (ed), *Justice Cooperation in the European Union*, Dublin, Institute of European Affairs, 1997, pp 3–48.

'Belgian Police Drop Case Against EU Journalist' euobserver.com (30 January 2008) at www.euobserver.com/9/25567/?print=1.

Bell, M, *Race, Equality and the European Union*, Oxford, OUP, forthcoming.

Bellanova, R, 'The "Prüm Process:" The Way Forward for EU Police Cooperation and Data Exchange?', in E Guild and F Geyer (eds), *Security versus Justice? Police and Judicial Cooperation in the European Union*, Aldershot, Ashgate, 2008, pp 201–21.

Benyon, J, 'The Politics of Police Co-operation in the European Union', *International Journal of the Sociology of Law*, vol 24, 1996, pp 353–379.

Bignami, F, 'Protecting Privacy against the Police in the European Union: The Data Retention Directive', Duke Law School Science, Technology and Innovation Research Paper Series, Research Paper no 13, January 2007, downloaded from www.ssrn.com/abstract=955261.

Bigo, D, 'Liberty, whose Liberty? The Hague Programme and the Conception of Freedom', in S Carrera and T Balzacq, *Security versus Freedom? A Challenge for Europe's Future*, Aldershot, Ashgate, 2006, pp 35–44.

——, *Polices en réseaux: l'experiénce européenne*, Paris, Presses de Sciences Po, 1996.

——, 'The Principle of Availability of Information', Briefing Note for European Parliament Civil Liberties Committee, reproduced in D Bigo and A Tsoukala (eds), *Controlling Security*, Paris, L'Harmattan and Centre d'études sur les conflits, 2008, pp 21–36.

Bigo, D and E Guild (eds), *Controlling Frontiers. Free Movement Into and Within Europe*, Aldershot, Ashgate, 2005.

Bigo, D *et al*, *The Field of the EU Internal Security Agencies*, Paris, L'Harmatan/Centre d'études sur les conflits, 2007.

Biolley, S de, 'Liberté et sécurité dans la constitution de l'espace européen de justice pénale: cristallisation de la tension sous présidence belge', in G de Kerchove and A Weyembergh (eds), *L'espace pénal européen: enjeux et perspectives*, Brussels, Éditions de l'Université de Bruxelles, 2002, pp 169–98.

Biolley, S de and A Weyembergh, 'L'espace pénal européen et les droits des victimes', *Revue de la Faculté de droit université libre de Bruxelles*, vol 31, 2005, pp 93–122.

Biondi, A and R Mastroianni, 'Case Note', *Common Market Law Review*, vol 43, 2006, pp 553–69.

Bitzilekis, N, M Kaiafa-Gbandi and E Symeonidou-Kastanidou, 'Theory of the Genuine European Legal Interests', in B Schünemann (ed), *A Programme for European Criminal Justice*, Cologne, Berlin, Munich, Carl Heymanns Verlag, 2006, pp 467–76.

Blekxtoon, R, 'Commentary on an Art by Art Basis', in R Blekxtoon (ed), *Handbook on the European Arrest Warrant*, The Hague, TMC Asser Press, 2005.

Boer, M den, 'An Area of Freedom, Security and Justice: Bogged Down by Compromise', in D O'Keeffe and P Twomey (eds), *Legal Issues of the Amsterdam Treaty*, Oxford, Hart Publishing, 1999, pp 303–22.

——, 'Europe and the Art of International Police Co-operation: Free Fall or Measured Scenario?', in D O'Keeffe and P Twomey (eds), *Legal Issues of the Maastricht Treaty*, London, Wiley Chancery, 1994, pp 279–94.

——, 'The Incorporation of Schengen into the TEU: A Bridge Too Far?' in J Monar and W Wessels (eds), *The European Union After the Treaty of Amsterdam*, London and New York, Continuum, 2001, pp 296–320.

——, 'New Dimensions in EU Police Co-operation: the Hague Milestones for What They Are Worth', in J de Zwaan and FANJ Goudappel (eds), *Freedom, Security and Justice in the European Union*, The Hague, TCM Asser Press, 2006, pp 221–32.

Bibliography

Boer, M den and W Brüggeman, 'Shifting Gear: Europol in the Contemporary Policing Era', *Politique européenne,* no 23, 2007, pp 77–91.

Boer, M den, C Hillebrand and A Noelke, 'Legitimacy under Pressure: The European Web of Counter-Terrorism Networks', *Journal of Common Market Studies,* vol 46, no 1, pp 101–24.

Böse, M, 'Die Zustaendigkeit der Europäischen Gemeinschaft fuer das Strafrecht Zugleich Besprechung von EuGH, Urteil vom 13.9.2005', *Goldtammer's Archiv,* 2006, pp 211–24.

Bossong, R, 'The Action Plan on Combating Terrorism: A Flawed Instrument of EU Security Governance', *Journal of Common Market Studies,* vol 46, no 1, 2008, pp 27–48.

Bozhilova, D, 'Measuring Success and Failure of EU: Europeanization in the Eastern Enlargement: Judicial Reform in Bulgaria', *European Journal of Law Reform,* vol 9, 2007, pp 285–319.

Bradley, R, 'The Joint Initiative of the UK, France and Sweden for the Adoption of a Council Framework Decision on the Application of the Principle of Mutual Recognition to Financial Penalties', in Gde Kerchove and AWeyembergh, *La reconnaissance mutuelle des décisions judiciaires pénales dans l'Union européenne,* Brussels, Éditions de l'Université de Bruxelles, 2001, pp 125–32.

Brammertz, S, 'Eurojust: Parquet Européen de la Première Génération?', in G de Kerchove and A Weyembergh (eds), *Vers un espace judiciaire pénal européen = Towards a European Judicial Criminal Area,* Brussels, Éditions de l'Université de Bruxelles, 2000, pp 105–118.

Braum, S, 'Das Prinzip der gegenseitigen Anerkennung', *Goldtammer's Archiv für Strafrecht,* 2005, pp 688–692.

Breyer, P, 'Telecommunications Data Retention and Human Rights: The Compatibility of Blanket Traffic Data Retention with the ECHR', *European Law Journal,* vol 11, no 43, 2005, pp 365–75.

Bridge, JW, 'The European Communities and the Criminal Law', *Criminal Law Review,* 1976, pp 88–97.

Brouwer, E, 'Data Surveillance and Border Control in the EU: Balancing Efficiency and Legal Protection', in T Balzacq and S Carrera (eds), *Security versus Freedom? A Challenge for Europe's Future,* Aldershot, Ashgate, 2006, pp 137–54.

——,'The Use of Biometrics in EU Databases and Identity Documents', in J Lodge (ed), *Are You Who You Say You Are? The EU and Biometric Borders,* Nijmegen, Wolf Legal Publishers, 2007, pp 45–66.

Brunsden, J, 'France Seeks Quick Deal to Penalise Employment of Illegal Immigrants', *European Voice* (17 July 2008).

——, 'Member States Split over Commission Powers', *European Voice* (28 February 2008).

Buck, B de, 'Joint Investigation Teams: The Participation of Europol Officials', *ERA Forum* vol 8, 2007, pp 253–264.

Buzan, B, 'New Patterns of Global Security in the Twenty-First Century', *International Affairs,* vol 67, no 3, 1999, pp 431–451.

——, *People, States and Fear. An Agenda for International Security Studies in the Post-Cold War Era,* Brighton, Harvester Wheatsheaf, 1991.

Buzan, B, O Waever and J de Wilde, *Security. A New Framework for Analysis,* Boulder and London, Lynne Rienner, 1998.

Carrera, S, and E Guild, *An EU Framework on Sanctions against Employers of Irregular Immigrants,* CEPS Policy Brief No 140, Brussels, CEPS, August 2007.

Cesoni, ML, 'Droit pénal européen: une harmonisation périlleuse' in G de Kerchove and A Weyembergh (eds), *L'espace pénal européen: enjeux et perspectives,* Brussels, Éditions de l'Université de Bruxelles, 2002, pp 153–68.

Ceyhan, A, 'Securité, frontières et surveillance aux États Unis après le 11 Septembre 2001' in *Cultures et conflits*, vol 53, 2003, downloaded from www.conflits.org.

Chiti, E, 'The Emergence of a Community Administration: The Case of European Agencies', *Common Market Law Review*, vol 37, 2000, pp 309–43.

Citizens' Report, *A Citizens' Inquiry into the Forensic Use of DNA and the National DNA Database*, July 2008.

Cooper, I, 'The Watchdogs of Subsidiarity: National Parliaments and the Logic of Arguing in the EU', *Journal of Common Market Studies*, vol 44, no2, 2006, pp 281–304.

Corstens, GJM, 'Criminal Law in the First Pillar?', *European Journal of Crime, Criminal Law and Criminal Justice*, vol 11, 2003, pp 131–44.

Craig, P , *EU Administrative Law*, Oxford, OUP, 2006.

——, 'The Fall and Renewal of the Commission: Accountability, Contract and Administrative Organisation', *European Law Journal*, vol 6, no 2, 2000, pp 98–116.

——, 'The Treaty of Lisbon: Process, Architecture and Substance', *European Law Review*, vol 33, 2008, pp 137–166.

Craig, P and G de Búrca, *EU Law. Text, Cases and Materials*, 4th edn, Oxford, OUP, 2008.

Cremona, M, *External Relations of the EU and the Member States: Competence, Mixed Agreements, International Responsibility, and Effects of International Law*, EUI Working Paper LAW No 2006/22.

——, 'The Union as a Global Actor: Roles, Models and Identity', *Common Market Law Review*, vol 41, 2004, pp 555–73.

Cremona, M and C Hillion, *L'Union fait la force? Potential and Limitations of the European Neighbourhood Policy as an Integrated EU Foreign and Security Policy*, EUI Working Paper LAW No 2006/39.

Crossman, G, 'Nothing to Hide, Nothing to Fear?', *International Review of Law Computers and Technology*, vol 22, nos 1–2, 2008, pp 115–18.

Cuesta, JL de la, 'Concurrent National and International Jurisdiction and the Principle "*ne bis in idem*"—General Report', *International Review of Penal Law*, vol 73, 2004.

Curtin, D, 'The Constitutional Structure of the Union: A Europe of Bits and Pieces', *Common Market Law Review*, vol 30, 1993, pp 17–69.

——, Curtin, 'Delegation to EU Non-majoritarian Agencies and Emerging Practices of Public Accountability', in D Geradin, R Munoz and N Petit, *Regulation through Agencies in the EU. A New Paradigm of European Governance*, Cheltenham, Edward Elgar, 2005, pp 88–119.

——, 'Holding (Quasi-) Autonomous EU Administrative Actors to Public Account', *European Law Journal*, vol13, no 4, 2007, pp 523–41.

Curtin, D and A Nollkaemper, 'Conceptualizing Accountability in International and European Law', *Netherlands Yearbook of International Law*, 2005, pp 3–20.

Daman, M, 'Cross-Border Hot Pursuit in the EU', *European Journal of Crime, Criminal Law and Criminal Justice*, vol 6, 2008, pp 171–207.

Dashwood, A, 'External Relations Provisions of the Amsterdam Treaty', in D O'Keeffe and P Twomey (eds), *Legal Issues of the Amsterdam Treaty*, Oxford, Hart Publishing, 1999, pp 219–20.

——, 'Issues of Decision-making in the European Union after Nice', in A Arnull and D Wincott (eds), *Accountability and Legitimacy in the European Union*, Oxford, OUP, 2002, pp 13–40.

Deen-Racsmány, Z, 'The European Arrest Warrant and the Surrender of Nationals Revisited: The Lessons of Constitutional Challenges', *European Journal of Crime, Criminal Law and Criminal Justice*, vol 14, no 3, 2006, pp 271–306.

Dehousse, R, 'From Community to Union', in R Dehousse (ed), *Europe After Maastricht. An Ever Closer Union?*, Law Books in Europe, Munich, Law Books in Europe, 1994, pp 5–15.

——, 'Regulation by Networks in the European Community: The Role of European Agencies', *Journal of European Public Policy*, vol 4, no 2, 1997, pp 246–61 at p 257.

Delcour, L , 'Does the European Neighbourhood Policy Make a Difference? Policy Patterns and Reception in Ukraine and Russia', *European Political Economy Review*, no 7, 2007, pp 118–55.

Delmas-Marty, M , 'The European Union and Penal Law', *European Law Journal* vol 4/1, 1998, 87–115.

——, 'Guest Editorial: Combating Fraud—Necessity, Legitimacy and Feasibility of the *Corpus Juris*', *Common Market Law Review*, vol 37, 2000, pp 247–256.

——, 'Towards an Integrated European Criminal Law', *Cambridge Yearbook of European Legal Studies*, vol 7, 2004–05, pp 17–31

Delmas-Marty, M and J Vervaele (eds), *The Implementation of the Corpus Juris in the Member States*, vol 1, Antwerp, Intersentia, 2000.

Denza, E , 'The 2000 Convention on Mutual Legal Assistance in Criminal Matters', *Common Market Law Review*, vol 40, 2003, pp 1047–74.

——, *The Intergovernmental Pillars of the European Union*, Oxford, OUP, 2002.

Dine, J, 'European Community Criminal Law?', *Criminal Law Review*, 1993, pp 246–54.

Dougan, M , 'The Treaty of Lisbon 2007: Winning Minds, Not Hearts', *Common Market Law Review*, vol 45, 2008, pp 617–703.

Douglas-Scott, S , 'The Rule of Law in the European Union—Putting the Security into the 'Area of Freedom, Security and Justice', *European Law Review*, vol 29, 2004, pp 219–42.

Eckes, C, Case-note, *Common Market Law Review*, vol 44, 2007, pp 1117–29.

——, 'Judicial Review of European Anti-Terrorism Measures—The *Yusuf* and *Kadi* Judgments of the Court of First Instance', *European Law Journal*, vol 14, no 1, 2008, pp 74–92.

Eeckhout, P , 'Community Terrorism Listings, Fundamental Rights, and UN Security Council Resolutions. In Search of the Right Fit', *European Constitutional Law Review*, vol 3, 2007, pp 183–206.

——, *External Relations of the European Union. Legal and Constitutional Foundations*, Oxford, OUP, 2004.

The Ethics Group: National DNA Database, *1st Annual Report*, April 2008

'EU Plan to Fight Terror in Tatters', *Financial Times* (23–24 September 2006).

'EU States Muscle in on Bloc's Judicial Body', euobserver (6 May 2008), www.euobserver. com/9/26082/?print=1.

'Eurodefensor' in B Schünemann (ed), *A Programme for European Criminal Justice*, Cologne, Berlin, Munich,Carl Heymanns Verlag, 2006.

European Law Review, editorial, 'The Court of Justice and the third pillar', *European Law Review*, vol 30, 2005, 773–74.

Fakiolas, ET and N Tzifakis, 'Transformation or Accession? Reflecting on the EU's Strategy Towards the Western Balkans', *European Foreign Affairs Review*, vol 13, 2008, pp 377–98.

Fennelly, N , 'The Area of "Freedom, Security and Justice" and the European Court of Justice—A Personal View', *International and Comparative Law Quarterly*, vol 49, 2000, pp 10–14.

Fijakowski, A , 'The Paradoxical Nature of Crime Control in Post-Communist Europe' *European Journal of Crime, Criminal Law and Criminal Justice*, 2007, pp 155–72.

Fijnaut, C , 'Police Co-operation and the Area of Freedom, Security and Justice', in N Walker (ed), *Europe's Area of Freedom, Security and Justice*, Oxford, Oxford University Press, 2004, pp 241–82.

——, 'The Schengen Treaties and European Police Co-operation', *European Journal of Crime, Criminal Law and Criminal Justice*, vol 1, 1993, pp 37–56.

Fijnaut, C, and L Paoli (eds), *Organised Crime in Europe. Concepts, Patterns and Control Policies in the European Union and Beyond*, Dordrecht, Springer, 2004.

Fletcher, M, 'Extending "Indirect Effect" to The Third Pillar: the Significance of *Pupino*?', *European Law Review*, vol 30, 2005, 862–77.

——, 'Some Developments to the *ne bis in idem* Principle in the European Union: *Criminal Proceedings against Huseyn Gözütok and Klaus Brügge*', *Modern Law Review*, vol 66, 2003, pp 769–80.

Flore, D and S de Biolley, 'Des organes jurisdictionnels en matière pénale pour l'Union européenne', *Cahiers de droit européen*, 2003, pp 597–637.

Flynn, EJ, 'The Security Council's Counter-Terrorism Committee and Human Rights', *Human Rights Law Review*, vol 7, 2007, pp 371–84.

Foot, R, 'The United Nations, Counter Terrorism, and Human Rights: Institutional Adaptation and Embedded Ideas', *Human Rights Quarterly*, vol 29, 2007, pp 489–514.

Foreign and Commonwealth Office, *Government Response to the European Union Select Committee on The Treaty of Lisbon: An Impact Assessment*, Cm7389, June 2008.

Garlick, P, 'The European Arrest Warrant and the ECHR', in R Blekxtoon (ed), *Handbook on the European Arrest Warrant*, The Hague, TMC Asser Press, 2005, pp 167–82.

Genson, R, 'Observations Personelles à propos des initiatives récentes relatives aux sanctions pécuniaires', in G de Kerchove and A.Weyembergh, *La reconnaissance mutuelle des décisions judiciaires pénales dans l'Union européenne*, Brussels, Éditions de l'Université de Bruxelles, 2001, pp 141–46.

Genson, R and Wvan de Rijt, 'L'évaluation de Schengen dans le cadre de l'élargissement', in A Weyembergh and S de Biolley (eds), *Comment évaluer le droit pénal européen?*, Brussels, Institut d'études européennes, 2006, pp 219–234.

Genson, R and P Zanders, 'Le développement de la coopération policiere dans l'Union européenne. Quel avenir pour Europol?', *Revue du Marché Commun et de l'Union européenne*, 2007, pp 5–13.

Georgakakis, D, 'La démission de la Commission européenne: Scandale et tournant institutionnel (octobre 1998—mars 1999)', *Cultures et conflits*, nos 38–39, 2000, at www.conflits.org.

Georgopoulos, T, 'What Kind of Treaty-Making Power for the EU? Constitutional Problems related to the Conclusion of the EU–US Agreements on Extradition and Mutual Legal Assistance', *European Law Review*, vol 30, 2005, pp 190–208.

Geyer, F, 'Case Note: European Arrest Warrant. Court of Justice of the European Communities', *European Constitutional Law Review*, vol 4, 2008, pp 149–61.

——, 'The European Arrest Warrant in Germany. Constitutional Mistrust towards the Concept of Mutual Trust', in E Guild (ed) *Constitutional Challenges to the European Arrest Warrant*, Nijmegen, Wolf Legal Publishers, 2006, pp 101–124.

——, *Taking Stock: Databases and Systems of Information Exchange in the Area of Freedom, Security and Justice*, CEPS Research Paper No 9, May 2008, www.ceps.

Gilmore, B , *Dirty Money, The Evolution of Money Laundering Countermeasures*, 3rd edn, Council of Europe Publishing , 2004.

——, *The Twin Towers and the Third Pillar: Some Security Agenda Developments*, EUI Working Paper LAW no 2003/7, Florence, European University Institute, 2003.

Gilmore, G and J Rijpma, Case Note, *Common Market Law Review*, vol 44, 2007, pp 1092–96.

Gilmore, W, C, 'The EU Action Plan to Combat Organised Crime: The Scope and Implementation of Legal Instruments', in E Bort and R Keat (eds), *The Boundaries of Understanding. Essays in Honour of Malcolm Anderson*, Edinburgh, The University of Edinburgh Social Sciences Institute, 1999, pp 97–106.

Giudicelli-Delage, G and S Manacorda (eds), *L'intégration pénale indirecte*, Paris, Société de législation comparée, 2005.

Gless, S , 'Mutual Recognition, Judicial Inquiries, Due Process and Fundamental Rights', in JAE Vervaele (ed), *European Evidence Warrant. Transnational Judicial Inquiries in the EU*, Antwerp/Oxford, Intersentia, 2005, pp 121–30.

Gless, S and HE Zeitler, 'Fair Trial Rights and the European Community's Fight Against Fraud', *European Law Journal*, vol 7, 2001, pp 219–37.

Goldirova, R, 'EU States Clash over Penalties for Hiring Illegal Immigrants', www.euobserver.com, 24 July 2008.

González Fuster, G, P de Hert and S Gutwirth, 'SWIFT and the Vulnerability of Transatlantic Data Transfers', *International Review of Law, Computers and Technology*, vol 22, 2008, pp 191–202.

González Fuster,G and P Paepe, 'Reflexive Governance and the EU Third Pillar: Analysis of Data Protection and Criminal Law Aspects', in E Guild and F Geyer (eds), *Security versus Justice? Police and Judicial Cooperation in the European Union*, Aldershot, Ashgate, 2008, pp 129–152.

Goodall, K, 'Incitement to Religious Hatred: All Talk and No Substance?', *Modern Law Review*, vol 70, 2007, pp 89–113.

Groenendijk, K, E Guild and P Minderhoud (eds), *In Search of Europe's Borders*, The Hague and London, Kluwer Law International, 2003.

Georgopoulos, T, 'What Kind of Treaty-Making Power for the EU? Constitutional Problems related to the Conclusion of the EU–US Agreements on Extradition and Mutual Legal Assistance', *European Law Review*, vol 30, 2005, pp 190–208.

Grünhage, J, 'The 1996/97 Intergovernmental Conference: A Survey of the Process', in J Monar and W Wessels (eds), *The European Union After the Treaty of Amsterdam*, London and New York, Continuum, 2001, pp 9–30.

Guild, E, 'Crime and the EU's Constitutional Future in an Area of Freedom, Security and Justice', *European Law Journal*, vol 10, no 2, 2004, pp 218–34.

——, *Moving the Borders of Europe*, Inaugural Lecture, University of Nijmegen, www.cmr.jur.ru.nl/cmr/docs/oratie.eg_pdf.

——, 'The Uses and Abuses of Counter-Terrorism Policies in Europe: The Case of the 'Terrorist Lists', *Journal of Common Market Studies*, vol 46, no 1, pp 173–93.

Guild, E and J Niessen, *The Developing Immigration and Asylum Policies in the EU*, The Hague and London, Martinus Nijhoff, 1996.

Haguenau-Moizard, C, 'Vers une harmonisation communautaire du droit pénal?', *Revue trimestrielle du droit européen*, vol 42, 2006, pp 377–89.

Harding, C, 'Exploring the Intersection of European Law and National Criminal Law' *European Law Review*, vol 25, 2000, pp 374–390.

——, 'The Offence of Belonging: Capturing Participation in Organised Crime', *Criminal Law Review*, 2005, pp 690–698.

Harlow, C, *Accountability in the European Union*, Oxford, OUP 2002.

Hassemer, W, 'Strafrecht in einem europäischen Verfassungsvertrag', *Zeitschrift für die gesamte Strafrechtswissenschaft*, vol 116, 2004, pp 304–19.

Hefendehl, R, 'European Criminal Law: How Far and No Further?', in B Schünemann (ed), *A Programme for European Criminal Justice*, Cologne, Berlin, Munich, Carl Heymanns Verlag, 2006, pp 450–66.

Helikoski, J, Case-note on *Ayadi, Common Market Law Review*, vol 44, 2007, pp 1143–57.

Henderson, K, 'Perceptions of Internal Security Issues in the New Member States', in Henderson (ed), *The Area of Freedom, Security and Justice in the Enlarged European Union*, Basingstoke, Palgrave Macmillan, 2004.

Herlin-Karnell, E, '*Commission v. Council*: Some Reflections on Criminal Law in the First Pillar', *European Public Law*, vol 13, 2007, pp 69–84.

——, 'In the Wake of *Pupino: Advocaten voor der Wereld* and *Dell'Orto*', *German Law Journal*, vol 8, 2007, pp 1147–60.

Hert, P de and S Gutwirth, 'Interoperability of Police Databases within the EU: An Accountable Political Choice?' *International Review of Law, Computers and Technology*, vol 20, nos 1–2, 2006, pp 21–35.

——, ——, 'Privacy, Data Protection and Law Enforcement. Opacity of the Individual and Transparency of Power', in E Claes, A Duff and S Gutwirth (eds), *Privacy and the Criminal Law*, Antwerp/Oxford, Intersentia, 2006, pp 61–104.

Hetzer, W, 'Fight Against Fraud and Protection of Fundamental Rights in the European Union', *European Journal of Crime, Criminal Law and Criminal Justice*, vol 14, no 1, 2006, pp 20–45

——, 'National Criminal Prosecution and European Tendering of Evidence. Perspectives of the European Anti-Fraud Office (OLAF)', *European Journal of Crime, Criminal Law and Criminal Justice*, vol 12, no 2, 2004, pp 166–83.

Hijmans, H, 'The European Data Protection Supervisor: The Institutions of the EC Controlled by an Independent Authority', *Common Market Law Review*, vol 43, 2006, pp 1313–42

Hillgruber, C, Anmerkung, *Juristenzeitung*, no 17, 2005, 841–44.

Hillion, C, 'The Copenhagen Criteria and their Progeny', in Hillion (ed), *EU Enlargement. A Legal Approach*, Oxford, Hart Publishing, 2004, pp 1–22.

——, 'The European Union is Dead. Long Live the European Union: A Commentary on the Treaty of Accession 2003', *European Law Review*, vol 29, 2004, pp 583–612.

——, 'Mapping-Out the New Contractual Relations between the European Union and Its Neighbours: Learning from the EU-Ukraine "Enhanced Agreement"', *European Foreign Affairs Review*, vol 12, 2007, pp 169–82.

Hinarejos, A, 'Recent Human Rights Developments in the EU Courts: The Charter of Fundamental Rights, the European Arrest Warrant and Terror Lists', *Human Rights Law Review*, vol 7, no 4, 2007, pp 793–811.

Hinarejos Parga, A, Case note, *Common Ma.rket Law Review*, vol 43, 2006, pp 583–95.

Home Office, 'One Step Ahead. A 21st Century Strategy to Defeat Organised Crime' (White Paper Cm 6167, 2004), pp 40–41.

House of Commons European Scrutiny Committee, 7th Report, session 2007–08.

——, *Democracy and Accountability in the EU and the Role of National Parliaments*, 33rd Report, session 2001–02, HC 152.

——, *Recognition and Enforcement of Judgments Given in Absentia*, 20th Report, session 2007–08.

House of Commons Home Affairs Committee, *Justice and Home Affairs Issues at European Union Level*, 3rd Report, session 2006–07, vol 1, HC 76-I.

——, *Justice and Home Affairs Issues at European Union Level*, 3rd Report, session 2006–07, vol 2, HC 76-II.

House of Lords Constitution Committee, *European Union (Amendment) Bill and the Lisbon Treaty: Implications for the UK Constitution*, 6th Report, session 2007–08, HL Paper 84.

House of Lords. European Union Committee/Select Committee on European Communities, *After Madrid: the EU's Response to Terrorism*, 5th Report, session 2004–05, HL Paper 53.

——, *Behind Closed Doors: The Meeting of the G6 Interior Ministers at Heiligendamm*, 40th Report, session 2005–06, HL Paper 221.

——, *Breaking the Deadlock: What Future for EU procedural Rights?*, 2nd Report, session 2006–07, HL Paper 20.

——, *Combating Racism and Xenophobia—Defining Criminal Offences in the EU*, 29th Report, session 2001–02, HL Paper 162.

——, *Correspondence with Ministers*, 18th Report, session 2001–02, HL Paper 99.

——, *Correspondence with Ministers, June 2004 to February 2005*, 4th Report, session 2005–06, HL Paper 16.

——, *Correspondence with Ministers, March 2005 to January 2006*, 45th Report, session 2005–06, HL Paper 243.

——, *Correspondence with Ministers, January 2006 to September 2006*, 40th Report, session 2006–07, HL Paper 187.

——, *The Criminal Law Competence of the European Community*, 42nd Report, session 2005–06, HL Paper 227.

——, *The Criminal Law Competence of the EC: Follow-up Report*, 11th Report, session 2006–07, HL Paper 63.

——, *The European Arrest Warrant*, 16th Report, session 2001–02, HL Paper 89.

——, *European Supervision Order*, 31st Report, session 2006–07, HL Paper 145.

——, *Europol's Role in Fighting Crime*, 5th Report, session 2002–03, HL Paper 43.

——, *Fighting Illegal Immigration: Should Carriers Carry the Burden?*, 5th Report, session 2003–04, HL Paper 29.

——, *The Future of Europe: National Parliaments and Subsidiarity—The Proposed Protocols*, 11th Report, session 2002–03, HL Paper 70.

——, *The Hague Programme: A Five Year Agenda for EU Justice and Home Affairs*, 10th Report, session 2004–05, HL Paper 84.

——, *Human Rights Protection in Europe: the Fundamental Rights Agency*, 29th Report, session 2005–06, HL Paper 155.

——, *Judicial Cooperation in the EU: The Role of Eurojust*, 23rd Report, session 2003–04, HL Paper 138.

——, *The Passenger Name Record (PNR) Framework Decision*, 15th Report, session 2007–08, HL Paper 106.

——, *Priorities of the European Union: Evidence from the Minister of Europe and the Ambassador of Slovenia*, 11th Report, session 2007–08, HL Paper 73, p 28.

——, *Procedural Rights in Criminal Proceedings*, 1st Report, session 2004–05.

House of Lords. European Union Committee/Select Committee on European Communities, *Prosecuting Fraud on the Communities' Finances—the Corpus Juris*, 9th Report, 1998–99, HL paper 62.

——, *Prüm: An Effective Weapon Against Terrorism and Crime?*, 18th Report, session 2006–07, HL Paper 90.

——, *Prospects for the Tampere Special European Council*, 19th Report, session 1998–99, HL Paper 101.

——, *Schengen Information System II (SIS II)*, 9th Report, session 2006–07, HL Paper 49.

——, *Strengthening National Parliamentary Scrutiny of the EU—The Constitution's Subsidiarity Early Warning Mechanism*, 14th Report, session 2004–05, HL Paper 101.

——, *Strengthening OLAF, the European Anti-Fraud Office*, 24th Report, session 2003–04, HL Paper 139.

——, *The Treaty of Lisbon: An Impact Assessment*, 10th Report, session 2007–08, HL Paper 62-I.

——, *The Treaty of Lisbon: An Impact Assessment*, Volume II: Evidence, 10th Report, session 2007–08, HL Paper 62-II.

Jacobs, F, 'The Role of the European Court of Justice in the Protection of the Environment', *Journal of Environmental Law*, vol 18, 2006, 185–205.

Johnston, A, 'The European Union, the Ongoing Search for Terrorists' Assets and a Satisfactory Legal Framework: Getting Warmer or Colder?', *Cambridge Law Journal*, 2007, pp 523–25.

Kaiafa-Gbandi, M, 'Das Corpus Juris und die Typiesierung des Strafphänomens im Bereich der Europäischen Union', *KritV*, vol 82, 1999, pp 162–80.

——, 'The Development towards Harmonization within Criminal Law in the European Union—A Citizen's Perspective', *European Journal of Crime, Criminal Law and Criminal Justice*, vol 9, 2001, pp 239–63

——, *To poiniko dikaio stin Europaiki Enossi [Criminal Law in the European Union]*, Athens-Thessaloniki, Sakkoulas, 2003.

——, 'The Treaty Establishing a Constitution for Europe and Challenges for Criminal Law at the Commencement of 21st Century', *European Journal of Crime, Criminal Law and Criminal Justice*, vol 13, no 4, 2005, pp 483–514.

Keijzer, N, 'The Double Criminality Requirement', in R Blekxtoon (ed), *Handbook on the European Arrest Warrant*, The Hague, TMC Asser Press, 2005, pp 137–63.

Keohane, D, 'The Absent Friend: EU Foreign Policy and Counter-terrorism', *Journal of Common Market Studies*, vol 46, no 1, pp 125–46.

Kerchove, G de and A Weyembergh (eds), *La reconnaissance mutuelle des décisions judiciaires pénales dans l'Union européenne*, Brussels, Éditions de l'Université de Bruxelles, 2001.

——, ——, *Vers un espace judiciaire pénal européen = Towards a European Judicial Criminal Area*, Brussels, Éditions de l'Université de Bruxelles, 2000.

Kietz, D and V Perthes (eds), *The Potential of the Council Presidency. An Analysis of Germany's Chairmanship of the EU, 2007*, SWP Research Paper 1, January 2008, Berlin, www.swp-berlin.org.

Klabbers, J, 'Safeguarding the Organizational *Acquis*: The EU's External Practice', *International Organizations Law Review*, 2007, pp 57–89

Klip, A, 'European Integration and Harmonisation and Criminal Law', in D Curtin et al, *European Integration and Law*, Antwerp and Oxford, Intersentia, 2006, 109–50.

Klip, A and H van der Wilt, *Harmonisation and Harmonising Measures in Criminal Law*, Amsterdam, Royal Netherlands Academy of Arts and Sciences, 2002.

Bibliography

Komarek, J, *European Constitutionalism and the European Arrest Warrant: Contrapunctual Principles in Democracy*, Jean Monnet Working Paper 10/05, New York, Jean Monnet Center, NYU School of Law, 2005, at www.jeanmonnetprogram.org.

Kostakopoulou, D, 'The Area of Freedom, Security and Justice and the European Union's Constitutional Dialogue', in C Barnard (ed), *The Fundamentals of EU Law Revisited. Assessing the Impact of the Constitutional Debate*, Oxford, OUP, 2007, pp 153–92.

——, 'Is There an Alternative to "Schengenland"?', *Political Studies*, vol 46, 1998, pp 886–902.

Koutrakos, P, editorial, 'Development and Foreign Policy: Where to Draw the Line between the Pillars', *European Law Review*, vol 33, no 3, pp 289–290.

Kowalik-Banczyk, K , 'Should We Polish It Up? The Polish Constitutional Tribunal and the Idea of Supremacy of EU Law', *German Law Journal*, vol 6, 2005, pp 1355–66, www.germanlawjournal.com.

Kreher, A, 'Agencies in the European Community—A Step towards Administrative Integration in Europe', *Journal of European Public Policy*, vol 4, no 2, 1997, pp 225–45.

Kuhne, H-H, Case note, *Juristenzeitung*, vol 20, 2006, pp 1018–21

Kuijper, PJ, 'The Evolution of the Third Pillar from Maastricht to the European Constitution: Institutional Aspects', *Common Market Law Review* vol 41, 2004, pp 609–26.

Kumm, M, 'The Jurisprudence of Constitutional Conflict: Constitutional Supremacy in Europe before and after the Constitutional Treaty', *European Law Journal*, vol 11, 2005, pp 262–307.

Labayle, H, 'Architecte ou spectatrice? La Cour de justice de l'Union dans l'espace de liberté, sécurité et justice', *Revue trimestrielle du droit européen*, vol 42, 2006, pp 1–46.

——, 'La coopération européenne en matière de justice et d'affairs intérieures et la Conférence intergouvernmentale', *Revue trimestrielle du droit européen*, vol 33, no 1, 1997, pp 1–35.

——, 'Un espace de liberté, de sécurité et de justice', *Revue trimestrielle du droit européen*, vol 34, 1998, pp 813–81.

——, 'L'ouverture de la jarre de Pandore: réflexions sur la compétence de la Communauté en matière pénale', *Cahiers de droit européen*, 2006, pp 382–428.

——, 'Three Principles of Reflection' in Notre Europe, *Protecting European Citizens against International Crime*, 2000, pp 12–22.

Ladenburger, C, 'Police and Criminal Law in the Treaty of Lisbon. A New Dimension for the Community Model', *European Constitutional Law Review*, vol 4, 2008, pp 20–40.

Lavenex, S, 'Mutual Recognition and the Monopoly of Force: Limits of the Single Market Analogy', *Journal of European Public Policy*, vol 14, no 5, 2007, pp 762–79.

Lavranos, N, 'Judicial Review of UN Sanctions by the Court of First Instance', *European Foreign Affairs Review*, vol 11, 2006, pp 471–90.

Lazowski, A, 'And Then They Were Twenty-Seven: A Legal Appraisal of the Sixth Accession Treaty', *Common Market Law Review*, vol 44, 2007, pp 401–30.

——, 'Constitutional Tribunal on the Surrender of Polish Citizens under the European Arrest warrant. Decision of 27 April 2005', *European Constitutional Law Review*, vol 1, 2005, pp 569–81.

Lebeck, C, 'National Constitutional Control and the Limits of European Integration—The European Arrest Warrant in the German Federal Constitutional Court', *Public Law*, 2007, pp 23–33.

Leczykiewicz, D, Case Note, *Common Market Law Review*, vol 43, 2006, 1181–1191.

Leczykiewicz, D, 'Constitutional Conflicts and the Third Pillar', *European Law Review*, vol 33, 2008, pp 230–42.

Lenaerts, K, 'The Rule of Law and the Coherence of the Judicial System of the European Union', *Common Market Law Review*, vol 44, 2007, pp 1625–59.

Lenaerts, K and T Corthaut, 'Of Birds and Hedges: The Role of Primacy in Invoking Norms of EU Law', *European Law Review*, vol 31, 2006, 287–315.

Lenaerts, K and M Desomer, 'New Models of Constitution-Making in Europe: The Quest for Legitimacy', *Common Market Law Review* vol 39, 2002, pp 1217–53.

Levi, M and B Gilmore, 'Terrorist Finance, Money Laundering and the Rise and Rise of Mutual Evaluation: A New Paradigm of Crime Control?', *European Journal of Law Reform*, vol 4, 2002, pp 341–68.

Lindahl, H, 'Finding a Place for Freedom, Security and Justice: The European Union's Claim to Territorial Unity', *European Law Review*, vol 29, 2004, pp 461–84.

Lobkowicz, W de, *L'Europe et la sécurité intérieure. Une élaboration par étapes*, Paris, La Documentation française, 2002.

——,'La sécurité intérieure de l'Union Européenne élargie', in G de Kerchove and A Weyembergh (eds), *Sécurité et justice: Enjeu de la politique extérieure de l'Union Européenne*, Brussels, Éditions de l'Université de Bruxelles, 2003, pp 31–65.

Majone, G, *Dilemmas of European Integration. The Ambiguities and Pitfalls of Integration by Stealth*, Oxford, OUP, 2005.

——, 'The New European Agencies: Regulation by Information', *Journal of European Public Policy*, vol 4, no 2, 1997, pp 262–73.

Manacorda, S, '*Judicial Activism* dans le cadre de l'espace de liberté, de justice et de sécurité de l'Union européenne', *Revue de science criminelle et du droit pénal comparé*, 2005.

Mangenot, M, 'Jeux européens et innovation institutionnelle: Les logiques de création d'Eurojust', *Cultures et conflits*, vol 62, 2006, pp 43–62.

Manoledakis, I, 'Das Corpus Juris als falsche Grundlage eines gesamteuropäischen Strafjustizsystems', *KritV*, vol 82, 1999, pp 181–90.

Marquardt, S, 'La capacité de l'Union européenne de conclure des accords internationaux dans le domaine de la coopération policiere et judiciaire en matiere pénale', in G de Kerchove and A Weyembergh (eds), *Sécurité et justice: Enjeu de la politique extérieure de l'Union Européenne*, Brussels, Éditions de l'Université de Bruxelles, 2003, pp 179–94.

McClean, D, *Transnational Organized Crime. A Commentary on the UN Convention and its Protocols*, Oxford, Oxford University Press, 2007.

McDonagh, B, *Original Sin in a Brave New World. An Account of the Negotiation of the Treaty of Amsterdam*, Dublin, Institute of European Affairs, 1998.

McGinley, M and R Parkes, *Data Protection in the EU's Internal Security Cooperation. Fundamental Rights vs. Effective Cooperation?*, SWP Research Paper 5, May 2007, Berlin, www.swp-berlin.org.

Mégie, A, 'L'institutionnalisation d'un pouvoir judiciaire européen incertain en quête de légitimité: l'unité de coopération Eurojust', *Politique européenne*, no 23, 2007, pp 57–75.

——, 'Mapping the Actors of European Judicial Cooperation' in D Bigo *et al*, *The Field of the EU Internal Security Agencies*, Paris, L'Harmatan/Centre d'études sur les conflits, 2007, pp 67–87.

Michel, V, Case note, *Revue trimestrielle du droit européen*, vol 42, 2006, pp 549–59.

Mitsilegas, V, 'Border Security in the European Union. Towards Centralised Controls and Maximum Surveillance', in E Guild, H, Toner and A Baldaccini (eds), *Whose Freedom, Security and Justice? EU Immigration and Asylum Law and Policy*, Oxford, Hart Publishing, 2007, pp 359–94.

——, 'The Competence Question: The European Community and Criminal Law', in E Guild and F Geyer (eds), Security versus Justice. Police and Judicial Co-operation in the European Union, Aldershot, Ashgate, 2008, pp 153–70.

——, 'The Constitutional Implications of Mutual Recognition in Criminal Matters in the EU', *Common Market Law Review*, vol 43, 2006, pp 1277–1311.

——, 'Constitutional Principles of the European Community and European Criminal Law', *European Journal of Law Reform*, vol 8, 2006, pp 301–24.

——, 'Contrôle des étrangers, des passagers, des citoyens: surveillance et anti-terrorisme', *Cultures et conflits*, vol 58, 2005, pp 155–82.

——, 'Countering the Chameleon Threat of Dirty Money: "Hard"and "Soft" Law in the Emergence of a Global Regime against Money Laundering and Terrorist Finance', in A Edwards and P Gill (eds), *Transnational Organised Crime: Perspectives on Global Security*, London, Routledge , 2003, pp 195–211.

——, 'Databases in the Area of Freedom, Security and Justice', in C Stefanou and H Xanthaki (eds), *Towards a European Criminal Record*, Cambridge, Cambridge University Press, 2008, pp 311–35.

——, 'Defining Organised Crime in the European Union: The Limits of European Criminal Law in an Area of Freedom, Security and Justice', *European Law Review*, vol 56, 2001, pp 565–81.

——, 'Drafting to Implement EU Law: the European Arrest Warrant in the United Kingdom', in H Xanthaki (ed), *Legislative Drafting: A Modern Approach. Essays in Honour of Sir William Dale*, Aldershot, Ashgate, forthcoming.

——, 'The External Dimension of EU Action in Criminal Matters', *European Foreign Affairs Review*, vol 12, 2007, pp 457–97.

——, 'From National to Global, from Empirical to Legal: The Ambivalent Concept of Transnational Organised Crime', in M Beare (ed), *Critical Reflections on Transnational Organized Crime, Money Laundering and Corruption*, University of Toronto Press, 2003, pp 55–87.

——, 'Human Rights, Terrorism and the Quest for Border Security', in M Pedrazzi (ed), *Individual Guarantees in the European Judicial Area in Criminal Matters*, Brussels, Bruylant, forthcoming.

——, 'International Regulation of Money Laundering and Terrorist Finance' in I Bantekas and G Keramidas (eds), *International and European Financial Criminal Law*, London, Butterworths, 2006, pp 41–64.

——, 'Judicial Co-operation in Criminal Matters between the EU and third states: International Agreements', in M Leaf (ed), *Cross-border Crime*, London, JUSTICE, 2006, pp 79–92.

——, 'Legitimacy, Accountability and Fundamental Rights in the Area of Freedom, Security and Justice', in M Martin (ed), *Crime, Rights and the EU. The Future of Police and Judicial Cooperation*, London, JUSTICE, 2008, pp 34–43.

——, *Money Laundering Counter-measures in the European Union. A New Paradigm of Security Governance versus Fundamental Legal Principles*, The Hague, London, Kluwer Law International, 2003.

——, 'The New EU–US Co-operation on Extradition, Mutual Legal Assistance and the Exchange of Police Data', *European Foreign Affairs Review*, vol 8, 2003, pp 515–36.

Mitsilegas, V, 'New Forms of Transnational Policing: the Emergence of Financial Intelligence Units in the European Union and the Challenges for Human Rights—Part I', *Journal of Money Laundering Control*, vol 3, no 2, 1999, pp 147–160.

——, 'Operational Co-operation and Counter-terrorism in the EU', in F Pastore (ed), *Supranational Counter-Terrorism. A Test under Duress for EU Principles and Institutions*, CeSPI Working Paper 22/2005, Rome, Centro Studi di Political Internazionale (CeSPI), pp 10–20, at www.cespi.it.

——, 'The Transformation of Criminal Law in the 'Area of Freedom, Security and Justice', *Yearbook of European Law 2007*, vol 26, pp 1–32.

——, 'Trust-building Measures in the European Judicial Area in Criminal Matters: Issues of Competence, Legitimacy and Inter-institutional Balance', in S Carrera and T Balzacq, *Security versus Freedom? A Challenge for Europe's Future*, Aldershot, Ashgate, 2006, pp 279–89.

——, 'What are the Main Obstacles to Police Co-Operation in the EU?', Briefing Paper for European Parliament LIBE Committee, IP/C/LIBE/FWC/2005–24, 14 February 2006, reproduced in D Bigo and A Tsoukala (eds), *Controlling Security*, Paris, L'Harmattan and Centre d'études sur les conflits, 2008.

Mitsilegas, V and B Gilmore, 'The EU Legislative Framework Against Money Laundering and Terrorist Finance: A Critical Analysis in the Light of Evolving Global Standards' *International and Comparative Law Quarterly*, vol 56, 2007, pp 119–41.

Mitsilegas, V, J Monar and W Rees, *The European Union and Internal Security*, Basingstoke, Palgrave Macmillan, 2003.

Mölders, S, 'European Arrest Warrant is Void—The Decision of the Federal Constitutional Court of 18 July 2005', *German Law Journal*, vol 7, 2005, pp 45–57.

Monaco, F.R, 'Europol: The Culmination of the European Union's International Police Cooperation Efforts', *Fordham International Law Journal*, vol 19, 1995–96, pp 247–308.

Monar, J, 'Common Threat and Common Response? The European Union's Counter-Terrorism Strategy and its Problems', *Government and Opposition*, vol 42, no 3, 2007, pp 292–313.

——, 'The Dynamics of Justice and Home Affairs: Laboratories, Driving Factors and Costs', *Journal of Common Market Studies*, vol 39, no 4, 2001, pp 747–64.

——, *Enlargement-related Diversity in EU Justice and Home Affairs: Challenges, Dimensions and Management Instruments*, WRR (Netherlands Scientific Council for Government Policy) Working Document 112, The Hague, December 2000.

——, 'The EU as an International Actor in the Domain of Justice and Home Affairs', *European Foreign Affairs Review*, vol 9, 2003, pp 395–415.

——, 'Justice and Home Affairs: Europeanization as a Government-Controlled Process', *Proceedings of the British Academy*, vol 119, 2003, pp 309–23.

——, 'Justice and Home Affairs in the EU Constitutional Treaty. What Added Value for the 'Area of Freedom, Security and Justice'?', *European Constitutional Law Review*, vol 1, 2005, pp 226–46

——, 'Justice and Home Affairs in the Treaty of Amsterdam: Reform at the Price of Fragmentation', *European Law Review*, vol 23, 1998, pp 320–35.

——, *Specific Factors, Typology and Development Trends of Modes of Governance in the EU Justice and Home Affairs Domain*, NEWGOV Deliverable 01/17, May 2006, at www.eu-newgov.org/database/DELIV/D01D17_Emergence_NMG_in_JHA.pdf. http://www.eu-newgov.org/database/DELIV/D01D17_Emergence_NMG_in_JHA.pdf

Monar, J and R Morgan (eds), *The Third Pillar of the European Union. Cooperation in the Fields of Justice and Home Affairs*, Brussels, European Interuniversity Press, 1994.

Morgan, C, 'Proposal for a Framework Decision on Procedural Safeguards for Suspects and Defendants in Criminal Proceedings throughout the European Union' , 4 *ERA-Forum* (2003).

Müller-Graff, P -C, 'The Legal Bases of the Third Pillar and Its Position in the Framework of the Union Treaty', *Common Market Law Review*, vol 31, 1994, pp 493–510.

Müller-Witte, B, 'The Effect of International Terrorism on EU Intelligence Co-operation', *Journal of Common Market Studies*, vol 46, no 1, 2008, pp 49–73.

——, *For our Eyes Only? Shaping an Intelligence Community within the EU*, European Union Institute for Security Studies, Occasional Paper no 50, January 2004, p 29, www.iss-eu.org.

Nettesheim, M, 'U.N. Sanctions against Individuals—A Challenge to the Architecture of European Union Governance', *Common Market Law Review*, vol 44, 2007, pp 567–600.

Neuwahl, N, 'Legal Personality of the European Union—International and Institutional Aspects' in V Kronenberger (ed), *The European Union and the International Legal Order: Discord or Harmony?*, The Hague, Asser Press, 2001, pp 3–22.

Nicolaidis, K, and G Shaffer,'Transnational Mutual Recognition Regimes: Governance without Global Government', *Law and Contemporary Problems*, vol 68, 2005, pp 263–317.

Niemeier, M, *La sécurité intérieure dans l'union européenne: après la présidence allemande et avant la présidence française*, Université Robert Schuman, Strasbourg, Collection Securint, Working Paper No 6, 2008.

Nieto-Garrido, E and I Martín Delgado, *European Administrative Law in the Constitutional Treaty*, Oxford, Hart Publishing, 2007.

Nilsson, H, *Decision-Making in EU Justice and Home Affairs: Current Shortcomings and Reform Possibilities*, Sussex European Institute Working Paper No 57, November 2002.

Nilsson, H, 'Eight Years of Experiences of Mutual Evaluation within the EU', in A Weyembergh and S de Biolley (eds), *Comment évaluer le droit pénal européen?*, Brussels, Institut d'études européennes, 2006, pp 115–24.

——, 'EUROJUST: The Beginning or the End of the European Public Prosecutor?', paper presented to the third EUROJUSTICE conference in Santander, Spain, 24–27 October 2000 (typescript with author).

——, 'Mutual Trust or Mutual Mistrust?', in G de Kerchove and A Weyembergh (eds), *La confiance mutuelle dans l'espace pénal européen=Mutual Trust in the European Criminal Area*, Brussels, Éditions de l'Université de Bruxelles, 2005, pp 29–33.

Nuotio, K, 'Harmonization of Criminal Sanctions in the European Union—Criminal Law Science Fiction' in J Husabo and A Strandbakken (eds), *Harmonisation of Criminal Law in Europe*, Antwerp, Oxford, Intersentia, 2005, pp 79–102.

Obokata, T, 'EU Council Framework Decision on Combating Trafficking in Human Beings: a Critical Appraisal' *Common Market Law Review*, vol 40, 2003, pp 917–36.

Occhipinti, J.D, *The Politics of EU Police Cooperation. Toward a European FBI?*, Boulder and London, Lynne Rienner, 2003.

O'Keeffe, D, 'Recasting the Third Pillar', *Common Market Law Review*, vol 32, 1995, pp 893–920.

Peers, S, '*Caveat Emptor?* Integrating the Schengen *Acquis* into the European Union Legal Order' *Cambridge Yearbook of European Legal Studies*, vol 2, 1999, pp 87–124.

——, *EU Justice and Home Affairs Law*, 2nd edn, Oxford, Oxford University Press, 2006.

Peers, S, 'The European Community's Criminal Law Competence: The Plot Thickens', *European Law Review*, vol 33, no 3, 2008, pp 399–410.

——, 'Governance and the Third Pillar: the Accountability of Europol', in D.M, Curtin and R.A, Wessel (eds), *Good Governance and the European Union. Reflections on Concepts, Institutions and Substance*, Oxford, Intersentia, 2005, pp 253–76.

——, 'Key Legislative Developments on Migration in the European Union: SIS II', *European Journal of Migration and Law*, vol 10, 2008, pp 77–104 at pp 79–81

——, 'Mutual Recognition and Criminal Law in the European Union: Has the Council Got it Wrong?', *Common Market Law Review*, vol 41, 2004, pp 5–36.

——, 'Salvation Outside the Church: Judicial Protection in the Third Pillar After the *Pupino* and *Segi* Judgments', *Common Market Law Review*, vol 44, 2007, pp 883–929.

Plachta, M and W van Ballegooij, 'The Framework Decision on the European Arrest Warrant and Surrender Procedures between Member States of the European Union' in R Blekxtoon (ed.), *Handbook on the European Arrest Warrant*, The Hague, TMC Asser Press, 2005, pp 32–36.

Poiares Maduro, M, 'So Close and Yet So Far: The Paradoxes of Mutual Recognition', *Journal of European Public Policy*, vol 14, no 5, 2007, pp 814–25.

Polakiewicz, J, *Treaty-Making in the Council of Europe*, Council of Europe Publishing, 1999, pp 68–70.

Prechal, S, 'Case note', *Common Market Law Review*, vol 42, 2005, 1445–63.

——, 'Direct Effect, Indirect Effect, Supremacy and the Evolving Constitution of the European Union', in C Barnard, (ed), *The Fundamentals of EU Law Revisited. Assessing the Impact of the Constitutional Debate*, Oxford, OUP, 2007, pp 35–70.

Pujas, V, 'Les difficultés de l'OLAF pour s' imposer en tant qu'acteur légitime de la protection des interets économiques et financiers européens', *Cultures et conflits*, no 62, 2006, pp 107–29.

——, 'The European Anti-Fraud Office (OLAF): A European Policy to Fight Against Economic and Financial Fraud?', *Journal of European Public Policy*, vol 10, no 5, 2003, pp 778–97.

Rijken, C, 'Joint Investigation Teams: Principles, Practice, and Problems. Lessons Learnt from the First Efforts to Establish a JIT', *Utrecht Law Review*, vol 2, issue 2, 2006, pp 99–118.

Rijken, C and V Kronenberger, 'The United Nations Convention against Transnational Organised Crime and the European Union', in V Kronenberger (ed), *The European Union and the International Legal Order: Discord or Harmony?*, The Hague, Asser Press, 2001, pp 481–517.

Rijken, C and G Vermeulen (eds), *Joint Investigation Teams in the European Union. From Theory to Practice*, The Hague, T.M.C. Asser Press, 2006.

Sadurski, W, 'Solange, Chapter 3: Constitutional Courts in Central Europe— Democracy—European Union', *European Law Journal*, vol 14, no 1, 2008, pp 1–35.

Sarmiento, D, 'European Union: The European Arrest Warrant and the Quest for Constitutional Coherence', *International Journal of Constitutional Law*, vol 6, no 1, 2008, pp 171–83

——, 'Un paso más en la constitucionalización del tercer pilar de la Union europea. La sentencia *Maria Pupino* y el efecto directo de las decisiones marco', *Revista electronica de estudios internacionales*, vol 10, 2005.

Satzger, H and T Pohl, 'The German Constitutional Court and the European Arrest Warrant. "Cryptic Signals" from Karlsruhe', *Journal of International Criminal Justice*, vol 4, 2006, pp 686–701.

Schalken, T and M Pronk, 'On Joint Investigation Teams, Europol and Supervision of Their Joint Actions', *European Journal of Crime, Criminal Law and Criminal Justice*, vol 10, no 1, 2002, pp 70–82.

Schimmelfennig, F and U Sedelmeier, 'Governance by Conditionality: EU Rule Transfer to the Candidate Countries of Central and Eastern Europe', *Journal of European Public Policy*, vol 11, 2004, pp 661–79.

Schünemann, B, 'Fortschritte und Fehltritte in der Strafrechtspflege der EU', in *Goldtammer's Archiv für Strafrecht*, 2004, pp 193–209.

Schutter, O de, 'The Role of Fundamental Rights Evaluation in the Establishment of the Area of Freedom, Security and Justice', in M Martin (ed), *Crime, Rights and the EU. The Future of Police and Judicial Cooperation*, London, JUSTICE, 2008, pp 44–88.

Sevenster H.G, 'Criminal Law and EC Law', *Common Market Law Review*, vol 29, 1992, 29–70.

Shapiro, M, 'The Problems of Independent Agencies in the United States and the European Union', *Journal of European Public Policy*, vol 4, no 2, 1997, pp 276–91.

Shaw, J, P Magnette, L Hoffmann and A Vergés Bausili, *The Convention on the Future of Europe. Working Towards an EU Constitution*, London The Federal Trust, 2003.

Sieber, U, 'Union européenne et droit pénal européen', *Revue de science criminelle et du droit pénal comparé*, 1993, 249–64.

Smith, K.E, 'The Evolution and Application of EU Membership Conditionality', in M Cremona (ed), *The Enlargement of the European Union*, Oxford, OUP, 2003, pp 105–40.

Smrkolj, M, 'The Use of the "Disconnection Clause" in International Treaties: What does it Tell us about the EC/EU as an Actor in the Sphere of Public International Law?, downloaded from the Social Science Research Network site, www.ssrn.com/abstract=113300.

Spencer, J.R, 'An Academic Critique of the EU Acquis in Relation to Trans-Border Evidence Gathering', *ERA-Forum*, 2005 (special issue on European Evidence in Criminal Proceedings), pp 28–40; and

——, 'Child Witnesses in the European Union', *Cambridge Law Journal*, 2005, 569–72.

——, 'The Corpus Juris Project and the Fight Against Budgetary Fraud', *Cambridge Yearbook of European Legal Studies*, vol 1, 1998, pp 77–106.

——, 'The Corpus Juris Project—Has it a Future?', *Cambridge Yearbook of European Legal Studies*, vol 2, 1999, pp 87–124.

——, 'The European Arrest Warrant', *Cambridge Yearbook of European Legal Studies*, 2003–04, pp 201–17.

Stangos, P and G Gryllos, 'Le droit communautaire à l'épreuve des réalités du droit international: leçons tirées de la jurisprudence communautaire récente relevant de la lutte contre le terrorisme international', in *Cahiers du droit européen*, 2006, pp 429–81.

Stefanou, C, 'Organised Crime and the Use of EU-wide Databases', in I Bantekas and G Keramidas (eds), *International and European Financial Law*, London, Butterworths, 2006, pp 215–43.

Stefanou, EA and A Kapardis, 'The First Two Years of Fiddling around with the Implementation of the European Arrest Warrant in Cyprus', in E Guild (ed) *Constitutional Challenges to the European Arrest Warrant*, Nijmegen, Wolf Legal Publishers, 2006, pp 101–24.

Stessens, G, 'The EU–US Agreements on Extradition and Mutual Legal Assistance: How to Bridge Different Approaches' in G de Kerchove and A Weyembergh (eds), *Sécurité et justice: Enjeu de la politique extérieure de l'Union Européenne*, Brussels, Éditions de l'Université de Bruxelles, 2003, pp 263–74.

Stessens, G, 'The Joint Initiative of France, Sweden and Belgium for the Adoption of a Council Framework Decision on the Execution in the European Union of Orders Freezing Assets and Evidence', in G de Kerchove and A Weyembergh (eds), *La reconnaissance mutuelle des décisions judiciaires pénales dans l'Union européenne*, Brussels, Éditions de l'Université de Bruxelles, 2001, pp 91–100.

Symeonidou-Kastanidou, E, 'Defining Terrorism', *European Journal of Crime, Criminal Law and Criminal Justice*, vol 12, 2004, pp 14–35

Tadic, F.M, 'How Harmonious Can Harmonisation Be? A Theoretical Approach towards Harmonisation of (Criminal) Law' in A Klip and H van der Wilt, *Harmonisation and Harmonising Measures in Criminal Law*, Amsterdam, Royal Netherlands Academy of Arts and Sciences, 2002.

'The Tampere Summit: The Ties that Bind *or* The Policemen's Ball', editorial, *Common Market Law Review*, vol 36, 1999, pp 1119–26.

Taylor, S, 'Brüner: Court Paralyses EU's Anti-Crime Efforts', *European Voice* (17–23 July 2008), p 1.

Thony, F, 'Processing financial information in money laundering matters: the financial intelligence units', *European Journal of Crime, Criminal Law and Criminal Justice*, no 3, 1996, pp 257–82.

Trauner, F, *EU Justice and Home Affairs Strategy in the Western Balkans*, CEPS Working Document No 259, www.ceps.eu.

Thwaites, N, 'Eurojust. autre brique dans l'édifice de la coopération judiciaire en matière pénale ou solide mortier?', *Revue des science criminelle et de droit pénal comparé*, 2003, pp 45–61.

——, 'Mutual Trust in Criminal Matters: The European Court of Justice Gives Its First Interpretation of a Provision of the Convention Implementing the Schengen Agreement', *German Law Journal*, vol 4, 2003, pp 253–62, www.germanlawjournal.com.

Thym, D, 'The Schengen Law: A Challenge for Legal Accountability in the European Union' *European Law Journal*, vol 8, no 2, 2002, pp 218–45.

Tobler, C, Case note, *Common Market Law Review*, vol 43, 2006, 835–54.

Toggenburg, G.N, 'The EU Fundamental Rights Agency: Satellite or Guiding Star?', SWP Comments 5, March 2007, www.swp-berlin.org.

——, 'The Role of the New EU Fundamental Rights Agency: Debating the "Sex of Angels" or Improving Europe's Human Rights Performance', *European Law Review*, vol 33, no 3, 2008, pp 385–98.

Tomkins, A, 'Responsibility and Resignation in the European Commission', *Modern Law Review*, vol 62, no 5, 1999, pp 744–65.

Tomuschat, C, Case note, *Common Market Law Review*, vol 43, 2006, pp 537–51.

——, 'Inconsistencies—The German Federal Constitutional Court on the European Arrest Warrant', *European Constitutional Law Review*, vol 2, 2006, pp 209–26.

Tridimas, T, *The General Principles of EU Law*, 2nd edn, Oxford, Oxford University Press, 2006.

Tsadiras, A, Case Note, *Common Market Law Review*, vol 44, 2007, pp 1515–28.

Tulkens, F, 'La reconnaissance mutuelle des décisions sentencielles. Enjeux et perspectives' in G de Kerchove and A Weyembergh (eds), *La reconnaissance mutuelle des décisions judiciaires pénales dans l'Union europeenne*, Brussels, Éditions de l'Université de Bruxelles, 2001

Twomey, P , 'Constructing a Secure Space: The Area of Freedom, Security and Justice', in D O'Keeffe and P Twomey (eds), *Legal Issues of the Amsterdam Treaty*, Oxford, Hart Publishing, 1999, pp 351–74.

Bibliography

Venemann, N, 'The European Arrest Warrant and its Human Rights Implications', *Zeitschrift für Ausländisches Öffentliches Recht und Völkerrecht*, vol 63, 2003, pp 103–21.

Vergés Bausili, A, *Rethinking the Methods of Dividing and Exercising Powers in the EU: Reforming Subsidiarity and National Parliaments*, Jean Monnet Working Paper 9/02, NYU School of Law, 2002.

Vermeulen, G, 'A European Judicial Network linked to Europol? In Search of a Model for Structuring Trans-national Criminal Investigations in the EU' *Maastricht Journal of European and Comparative Law*, vol 4, 1997, pp 346–72.

Vervaele, J, Case note, *Common Market Law Review*, vol 42, 2004, pp 795–812

——, 'The European Community and Harmonization of the Criminal Law Enforcement of Community Policy', *European Criminal Law Associations' Forum*, vols 3–4, 2006.

——, 'European Criminal Law and General Principles of Union Law', in Vervaele (ed), *European Evidence Warrant. Transnational Judicial Inquiries in the EU*, Antwerp, Oxford, Intersentia, 2005, pp 131–56.

——, 'The Transnational *ne bis in idem* Principle in the EU', *Utrecht Law Review*, vol 1, issue 2, 2005, pp 100–18

Vervaele, J.A.E, 'Towards an Independent European Agency to Fight Fraud and Corruption in the EU?', *European Journal of Crime, Criminal Law and Criminal Justice*, vol 7, no 3, 1999, pp 331–46.

Vogel, J, 'Europäischer Haftbefehl und deutsches Verfassungsrecht', *Juristenzeitung*, vol 60, 2005, pp 801–809.

Vos, E, 'Reforming the European Commission: What Role to Play for EU Agencies?', *Common Market Law Review*, vol 37, 2000, pp 1113–34.

Waever, O, 'Securitization and De-securitization' in R.D, Lipschutz (ed), *On Security*, New York, Columbia University Press, 1995, pp 46–86.

Wakefield, J, Case note, *Common Market Law Review*, vol 45, 2008, pp 199–221.

——, 'Good Governance and the European Anti-Fraud Office', *European Public Law*, vol 12, no 4, 2006, pp 549–75.

Walker, N, 'In Search of the Area of Freedom, Security and Justice: A Constitutional Odyssey', in N Walker (ed), *Europe's Area of Freedom, Security and Justice*, Oxford, OUP, 2004, pp 3–40.

Wall, S, *A Stranger in Europe. Britain and the EU from Thatcher to Blair*, Oxford, OUP, 2008.

Wasmeier, M and N Thwaites, 'The "Battle of the Pillars": Does the European Community have the Power to Approximate National Criminal Laws?', *European Law Review*, vol 29, 2004, 613–35.

——, ——, 'The Development of *ne bis in idem* into a Transnational Fundamental Right in EU Law: Comments on Recent Developments', *European Law Review*, vol 31, 2006, pp 565–78.

Weatherill, S, 'Harmonisation: How Much, How Little?', *European Business Law Review*, 2005, pp 533–45.

——, 'Why Harmonise?', in T Tridimas and P Nebbia (eds), *European Law for the Twenty-First Century. Rethinking the New Legal Order*, vol 2, Oxford, Hart Publishing, 2004, pp 11–32.

Weber-Panariello, P A, *The Integration of Matters of Justice and Home Affairs into Title VI of the Treaty on European Union. A Step Towards More Democracy?*, EUI Working Paper RSC No 95/32, Florence, European University Institute, 1995.

Wessel, RA, 'Revisiting the International Legal Status of the EU', *European Foreign Affairs Review*, vol 5, 2000, pp 507–37.

Wesseling, M, *Gijs de Vries: Vers la coordination des politiques antiterroristes européennes, efficacité ou symbolisme?*, Master Mémoire, Institut d'Etudes Politiques de Paris, 2005.

Weyembergh, A, 'Approximation of Criminal Laws, the Constitutional Treaty and the Hague Programme', *Common Market Law Review*, vol 42, 2005, pp 1567–97.

——,'The Functions of Approximation of Penal Legislation within the European Union', *Maastricht Journal of European and Comparative Law*, vol 12, 2005, pp 149–72.

——, *L'harmonisation des législations: condition de l'espace pénal européen et révélateur de ses tensions*, Brussels, Éditions de l'Université de Bruxelles, 2004.

——, 'Le principe *ne bis in idem*: pierre d'achoppement de l'espace pénal européen?', *Cahiers de droit européen*, 2004, pp 337–75

Weyembergh, A and S de Biolley (eds), *Comment évaluer le droit pénal européen?*, Brussels, Institut d'études européennes, 2006.

Weyembergh, A and S Khabipour, 'Quelle confiance mutuelle ailleurs?', in G de Kerchove and A Weyembergh (eds.), *La confiance mutuelle dans l'espace pénal européen=Mutual Trust in the European Criminal Area*, Brussels, Éditions de l'Université de Bruxelles, 2005, p 265

Weyembergh, A and V Santamaria, 'Le contrôle démocratique dans l'espace pénal européen', in M Doni and LS Rossi, *Démocratie, cohérence et transparence: vers une con-stitutionnalisation de l'Union européenne?*, Brussels, Institut d'Études européennes, 2008, pp 73–92.

——, 'Lutte contre le terrorisme et droits fondamentaux dans le cadre du troisième pilier. La décision-cadre du 13 juin 2002 relative à la lutte contre le terrorisme et le principe de la légalité', typescript with author.

White, S, 'Harmonisation of Criminal Law under the First Pillar', *European Law Review*, vol 31, 2006, 81–92.

——, *Protection of the Financial Interests of the European Communities: The Fight against Fraud and Corruption*, The Hague, London, Kluwer Law International, 1998.

Wichmann, N, 'The Participation of the Schengen Associates: Inside or Outside?', *European Foreign Affairs Review*, vol 11, 2006, pp 87–107.

Wils, W, 'The Principle of "*ne bis in idem*" in EC Antitrust Enforcement: A Legal and Economic Analysis', vol 26, no 2, 2003 *World Competition*, pp 131–48.

Wilt, H van der, 'Case Note', *European Constitutional Law Review*, vol 2, 2006, pp 303–309.

——, 'The European Arrest Warrant and the Principle *ne bis in idem*', in R Blekxtoon (ed), *Handbook on the European Arrest Warrant*, The Hague, TMC Asser Press, 2005, pp 99–118.

Wolf, S, 'Demokratische Legitimation in der EU aus Sicht des Bundesverfassungsgerichts nach dem Urteil zum Europäischen Haftbefehlsgesetz', *Kritische Justiz*, vol 38, 2005, pp 350–58.

Wouters, J and F Naert, 'Of Arrest Warrants, Terrorist Offences and Extradition Deals: An Appraisal of the EU's Main Criminal Law Measures against Terrorism after "11 September"', *Common Market Law Review*, vol 41, 2004, pp 911–26.

Wyngaert, C van den, 'Eurojust and the European Public Prosecutor in the *Corpus Juris* Model: Water and Fire?', in N Walker (ed), *Europe's Area of Freedom, Security and Justice*, Oxford, Oxford University Press, 2004, pp 201–40.

Wyngaert, C van den and G Stessens, 'The International *non bis in idem* Principle: Resolving Some of the Unanswered Questions', *International and Comparative Law Quarterly*, vol 48, 1999, pp 779–804.

Bibliography

Xanthaki, H, 'Eurojust: Fulfilled or Empty Promises in EU Criminal Law?', *European Journal of Law Reform*, vol 8, 2006, pp 175–98.

——, 'Fraud in the EU: Review of OLAF's Regulatory Framework' in I Bantekas and G Keramidas (eds), *International and European Financial Criminal Law*, Buttterworths, 2006, pp 120–53.

Zwaan, JW de and FANJ Goudappel (eds), *Freedom, Security and Justice in the European Union*, The Hague, TCM Asser Press, 2006

Index